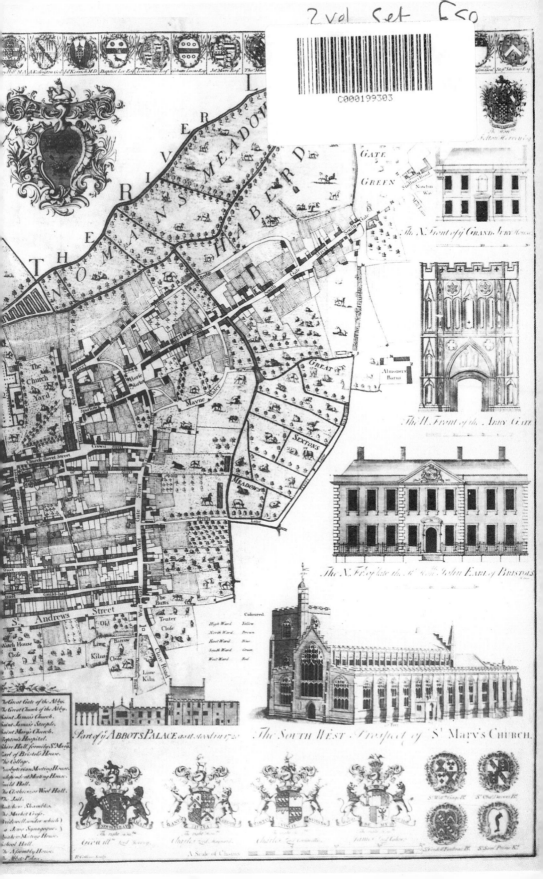

2 vol Set £50

C000199303

Elsie McEntolan.

THE OAKES DIARIES

BUSINESS, POLITICS AND THE FAMILY
IN BURY ST EDMUNDS
1778–1827

Volume I

Introduction

James Oakes' Diaries
1778–1800

SUFFOLK RECORDS SOCIETY

President
Sir Anthony Wagner, Clarenceux King of Arms

Vice-Presidents
Sir John Plumb, FBA
James Campbell, FBA

Chairman
Dr John Blatchly

General Editors
Norman Scarfe (post-medieval)
G. H. Martin (medieval)
Christopher Harper-Bill (Suffolk charters)

Secretary
Peter Northeast
c/o Suffolk Record Office,
County Hall, Ipswich, Suffolk IP4 2JS

1. James Oakes as a young man.

THE OAKES DIARIES

BUSINESS, POLITICS AND THE FAMILY
IN BURY ST EDMUNDS
1778–1827

Edited by
JANE FISKE

Volume I

Introduction
James Oakes' Diaries
1778–1800

The Boydell Press

Suffolk Records Society
VOLUME XXXII

Introduction and editorial matter © Jane Fiske 1990
The text of the Oakes Diaries © Suffolk Records Society 1990

All Rights Reserved. Except as permitted under current legislation
no part of this work may be photocopied, stored in a retrieval system,
published, performed in public, adapted, broadcast,
transmitted, recorded or reproduced in any form or by any means,
without the prior permission of the copyright owner

A Suffolk Records Society publication
First published 1990 by The Boydell Press
an imprint of Boydell & Brewer Ltd
PO Box 9, Woodbridge, Suffolk IP12 3DF
and of Boydell & Brewer Inc.
PO Box 41026, Rochester, NY 14604, USA

ISBN 0 85115 275 9

Issued to subscribing members
for the year 1989–90

British Library Cataloguing in Publication Data
Oakes, James *b. 1741*
   The Oakes diaries : business, politics and the family in
   Bury St Edmunds 1778–1827. – (Suffolk Records Society v.32)
   1. England. Social life, 1714–1820 – Biographies
   I. Title II. Fiske, Jane III. Series
   942.07092
   ISBN 0–85115–275–9

Endpaper map: Survey of the Borough of St Edmunds Bury
by Thomas Warren, 1776
(Moyses Hall Museum, Bury St Edmunds)

This publication is printed on acid-free paper

Printed in Great Britain by
St Edmundsbury Press, Bury St Edmunds, Suffolk

Contents

INTRODUCTION

Introduction; The Yarn Industry in Bury St Edmunds; Ray Oakes and Company; Wool Supply; Protection of the Wool Supply; Sorting and Scouring; Combing; Spinning; Yarn Marketing; Labour Relations; The Decline of the Suffolk Yarn Industry.

The Receivership: Introduction – James Oakes's Appointment – Preparation – Tax Collection – The Remittance and Investment of Tax Balances; The Search for Investment: Land and Utilities – Brewing – Banking; The Bury New Bank: Note Issue – The 1797 Cash Crisis and the Bury New Bank; The Bury and Suffolk Bank: The Grigby Case – The London Agent – The Bill Broker and Stock Brokers – Local Investments in Utilities – Agriculture, Business and Trade – Running Accounts – Branch Banking at Stowmarket – Clare – Mildenhall – Brandon – Thetford – Relations with other Banks – The Clerks – Post War Depression and the Financial Crisis 1825–26.

THE OAKES DIARIES, 1778–1800

Illustrations

Endpaper map: Survey of the Borough of St Edmunds Bury by Thomas Warren,
      1776 (Moyses Hall Museum, Bury St Edmunds)

Jacket painting: The Departure of Captain Poole from St Edmundsbury on
      15 October 1785 by J. Kendall.

Credits

Mrs Joyce Oakes for Plates 1, 2, 3, 4, 5, 6.
Robert Fiske for Plates 7, 8, 9, 10, 11, 16, 17, 23, 25, 26, 34, 35, 37, 38, and for
photographing plates 1, 2, 3, 4, 5, 6.
His Grace the Duke of Grafton and the Courtauld Institute of Art for Plate 12.
The National Trust for Plates 13, 14, 31, 32.
Suffolk Record Office for Plates 15, 18, 22, 29, 30, 33, 36.
Norfolk Museums Service for Plates 19, 20.
Norfolk County Council Library and Information Service for Plate 21.
Borough of St Edmundsbury for Plates 19, 24, 27, 28, book-jacket.

General Editor's Note

In December 1963, Martin Statham, West Suffolk's County Archivist, wrote to tell me that the Bury Borough Council was 'almost certainly going to buy the Oakes Diaries'. It did, and I soon went over to see them. A reader of this note turning forward immediately to look at the transcript of these diaries will probably share my slowness to respond to the text: it is laconic and business-like, requiring prodigious labours of background research to comprehend, let alone appreciate. This is why in publishing these invaluable diaries, we have encouraged their editor to supply a substantial part of her exemplary researches in her introduction, so that we come to the diary almost as well informed about his family and his affairs as James Oakes himself.

Jane Fiske not only acquaints us with the Oakes family – characteristically ramified – but she constructs round them, very fully, the local society of Bury and its broad neighbourhood, to which this family made such a contribution. In the process, she has written a brilliant chapter in the economic history of a distinct part of East Anglia, which is usually thought of as having supplied only improvements in farming practices to the English economy in those years of 'industrial revolution'.

The editor is perhaps above all successful in helping us to see, through Oakes's eyes, the way that, in Bury, politics, economics and society are as closely interwoven as the textiles themselves that had for over four centuries lain at the heart of local industry. More than all that, these ostensibly dull diary-entries are made to yield a sense of being present in the daily lives of the Oakeses – what they ate, how the children were brought up, what their family weddings and funerals were like; in short, how they enjoyed life in Bury and its neighbourhood from the years of the American War of Independence, through the great French Revolutionary and Napoleonic Wars, to the tail-end of Georgian England with the onset of political and municipal reform.

In the S.R.S.'s thirtieth volume, we saw the responses of young François de La Rochefoucauld to the experiences of a whole year in Bury – 1784, just after these diaries begin, and wondered what it was about England that saved us from the revolutionary convulsions he soon had to face at home. A specific and substantial part of the answer to that question may be here in this edition of *The Oakes Diaries*.

N.S.

Acknowledgements

My thanks are due to the Archivists of both Lloyd's and Barclay's Banks for permission to work on the documents in their care and for all their help and advice: to the late Col Orbell Oakes who kindly gave me access to his family papers; to his wife, Mrs Joyce Oakes, for allowing us to photograph portraits in her possession; and to Dr Stanley Chapman and the Passold Foundation Ltd for permission to use their transcriptions of the Sun Fire Insurance Policy Registers. I have had unfailing kindness and assistance from the staff of all the record offices and libraries in which I have worked but I hope it is not invidious to single out those at the Bury Branch of the Suffolk Record Office for particular mention because I have spent so much time there. The staff, both past and present, have been unstinting in their help and advice and have made working in Bury a delight. I should also like to thank Mrs Eileen Byers for her help with the Cullum Family Papers and the Bury Improvement Commission.

My very special thanks are due to Dr Richard Wilson of the University of East Anglia, whose comments and ideas were always stimulating and helpful; to Norman Scarfe, Esq., the editor, who is so generous with his vast knowledge of Suffolk history and whose patience appears to be inexhaustible; and finally to N. J. F. for his constant support and his patient forebearance with James Oakes.

J.F.

Abbreviations

Add. MSS.	Additional Manuscripts
BA	Barclays Bank Archive
Bailey	*Bailey's British Directory 1784*
BL	British Library
BNP	*Bury and Norwich Post*
BPP	British Parliamentary Papers.
CRO	Cambridge Record Office
Diary	SROB HA521/1–14, James Oakes's Diary, 1778–1827
IJ	*Ipswich Journal*
LA	Lloyds Bank Archive
NNRO	Norfolk and Norwich Record Office
N&Q	*Notes and Queries*
PRO	Public Record Office
SC	*Suffolk Chronicle*
SROB	Suffolk Record Office, Bury St Edmunds Branch
SROI	Suffolk Record Office, Ipswich Branch
UBD	*Universal British Directory*
VCH	*A History of Suffolk: The Victoria History of the Counties of England,* edited by William Page, 2 vols (1907–11)

THE OAKES FAMILY (I)

William Oakes m Elizabeth Beck

James 1701–59 m 1. Mary Godfrey 1697/8–1737
2. Susan Ray 1706–88

Esther m ——Edge
Richard m Ann Wood
Esther m James Greenway

Susan 1740–1822 m George Green 1734/5–1808

James 1741–1829 m Elizabeth Adamson 1738–1802

Mary 1744–1835 m James Bridge –1791

Elizabeth 1747–1814 m Rev. Richard Baker 1741–1818

Orbell Ray 1768–1837 m Elizabeth Plampin 1768–1811

James 1769–1861 m Elizabeth Tyrrell

Maria Susan 1765–1849 m William Gould 1759–1836

Charlotte 1770–98 m Hervey Aston Adamson 1803– Elizabeth Elwin

Sarah 1772–75

Orbell Ray 1767

Orbell Ray 1800–82 m Caroline Bryan

Charles Frederick Adamson 1802

Frederick Aston 1826

Henry James 1796–1875 m Maria Ann Porteus 1794–1876

Elizabeth Frances 1799–1831 m Robert Hustler

Orbell Plampin 1824–81 m Louisa Evans

Frances Marian

James Henry Porteus 1821–1901

THE OAKES FAMILY (II)

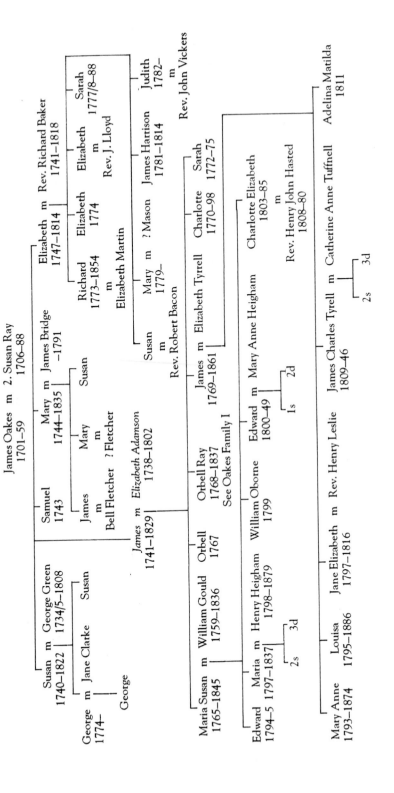

THE ADAMSON FAMILY OF WEREHAM

Thomas m 1. Frances Moreley
-1698   2. ——— ?

Thomas 1660–   Frances 1665–1719   Elizabeth 1667–1711 m Luke Shinn [?] curate   Thomas 1675

Thomas m 1. ——— ?
1660–   2. Cisley

Anne 1672–   Christopher 1673–1744 m Martha Clark 1674–1765

Christopher 1702–86 m Elizabeth Athill 1698/9–1778   Thomas 1703–   William 1706–36

John 1700–?1762

William 1707/8–81   Robert 1708   Benjamin m 1. Susanna Crutchfield 1715–42
1704–83   2. Alice Westley 1712–72

Mary 1711–1711/12   James 1713–16   Richard 1717–1800

Martha m John Heaton
1709/10–43   1696–1779

Richard m Sarah

Mary 1742–43

Robert –1817

Daughter m Rev. Horner

Mary 1731/2–62   Sarah 1740/1–91   James 1741–83

Elizabeth m James Oakes
1738–1802   1741–1829

THE RAY FAMILY (I)

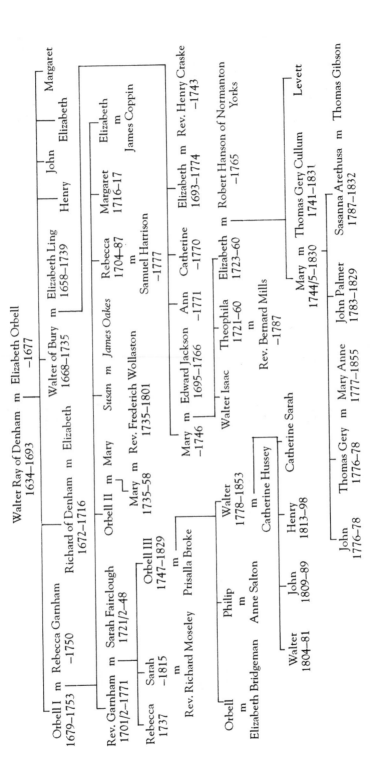

THE RAY FAMILY (II)

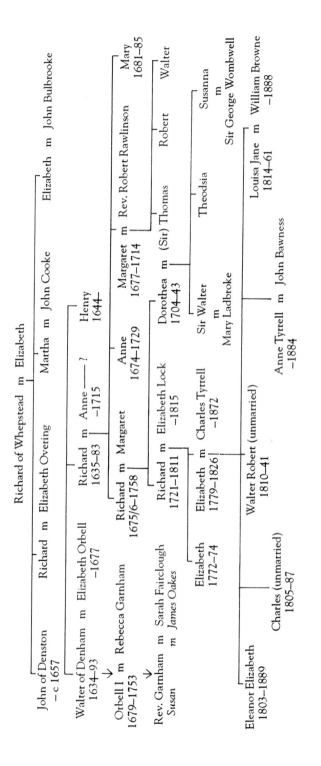

INTRODUCTION

CHAPTER I

Introduction

I

James Oakes's diaries span nearly 50 years in the life of a provincial businessman. They begin in November 1778 when Oakes was 36 years old and had been a yarn merchant for 16 years. He was already a man of consequence in Bury St Edmunds: a member of the Corporation, Alderman (the equivalent of mayor in Bury), and a trustee of the town's major charities. He had a wife and four children, whose ages ranged from eight to thirteen, and lived in a pleasant brick house in the centre of the town. By the time the diaries end in October 1827 he was nearly 86, arthritic and deaf.[1] Yarn making had long ceased to be his occupation and he had become a banker in partnership with his elder son, Orbell. He was the most senior member of the Corporation with an unparalleled knowledge of local affairs.

His diary has survived in its entirety[2] in 14 leather bound octavo volumes. The volumes vary in length, volumes I and II covering a period of just over 12 years while volume IX, by far the longest, covers only 1809 and 1810. All the rest contain three years each except the final volume which has entries for four and three quarter years. The early entries are scrappy but as the habit of diary writing gripped him they become increasingly detailed and informative.

Oakes's reasons for beginning a diary are never explained and it seems probable that it developed accidently from another record. He was a methodical and orderly man who liked to have books and files in which to make notes on almost every aspect of his life. He kept separate account books for all his business enterprises, stock books, letter books, cellar books, brewing books, estate books, journey books and numerous memorandum books and files, very few of which

[1] The diary ends abruptly on 14 October 1827 although Oakes clearly intended to write more because he had ruled out the following pages in readiness. There is no further mention of him in Bury public life apart from his attendance at the Alderman's election the following August, although he wrote sporadically in his Memorandum Book until November 1827. SROB Corporation Minutes D4/1/5; James Oakes's Memorandum Book HA535/1/4.

[2] Diary 31 December 1806 Oakes states that he began writing his journal in November 1778. The diary was discovered in the library of the Oakeses' family home, Nowton Court, and was sold to a dealer in 1955. In 1963 it was bought for the Suffolk Record Office, largely through the efforts of Martin Statham, the archivist.

have survived.[3] The early diaries were written in small, marbled-paper covered account books with red-ruled columns and recorded only the family's social life. They began with a list of families with whom the Oakeses exchanged visits and those who merited dinner invitations, and went on to detail where the family had dined and with whom on specific dates. They were written hastily, with much amendment, certainly not with an eye to posterity which their subsequent binding in leather suggests. Gradually other information was included until by 1782 they were written almost daily in books with plain pages. This change of use was reflected in a change of name and they were no longer referred to as 'account books' but as 'journal books'.

To a certain extent they retained their function as social and general memorandum books in that Oakes continued to use them to document dinner guests and other disparate information which either did not fit into any of his existing files, or that he wanted to record immediately so that it could be entered in the appropriate place later. As a result there are brief notes to remind him of journeys to be charged as a business expense, the weight of candles used in the house during the course of a week, the births, marriages and deaths of relations, friends and servants, distances travelled and money spent. By 1782 they provide a daily record of the family, business and social life of a prosperous merchant in a small Suffolk town.

II

Bury St Edmunds lies on relatively high ground in the middle of Suffolk where the good light lands of the west meet the boulder clays of High Suffolk.[4] It was the second largest town in the county, having a population of almost 8,000 in 1801. A period of more rapid growth between 1811 and 1821 increased it to nearly 10,000, and by 1831 there were 11,436 inhabitants.[5]

The town owed its existence to the abbey, the ruin of which lies to the east of Angel Hill and which, in the early Middle Ages, was one of the most powerful and wealthy Benedictine monasteries in Europe. After the Norman Conquest its privileges were confirmed and increased and it was rebuilt on a larger scale by Abbot Baldwin (1065–97). In addition to his ecclesiastical building programme

---

[3]   An early bank letter book was in existance in Lloyd's Bank Archive until the 1939–45 war after which it seems to have disappeared. A photocopy of notes made from this book by a director of the bank in the late nineteenth century may be found at SROB Acc 2191 and in Lloyd's Bank Archive. An early stocktaking account book of Ray and Oakes and Company, a memorandum book and one or two files concerning property have survived in papers recently deposited by the Oakes Family and catalogued under SROB HA535.
[4]   P. J. O. Trist, A Survey of the Agriculture of Suffolk (1971), p. 2.
[5]   Appendix to the First Report of the Commission Appointed to Enquire into the Municipal Corporations, part IV Eastern and North Western Circuit, 1835 (116) XXIII–XXVI.

Abbot Baldwin laid out a new town at the gates of the abbey on a grid pattern which can still be seen today at the heart of modern Bury.[6]

Administratively the town had inherited many of the privileges of the abbey. It had a closed Corporation whose 37 members alone held the Parliamentary franchise, and boasted numerous well endowed charities, the most important of which was the Guildhall Feoffment Trust. Although not the county town, it was the venue for the county assizes and quarter sessions as well as petty sessions and other borough courts.

Bury acted as a service centre for those attending the courts and for the rich agricultural hinterland that surrounded it. Industry within the town, apart from that which catered for local needs, was limited to brewing, malting and yarn making. Since the decline of the Suffolk woollen cloth industry in the early seventeenth century it had become the head-quarters of yarn manufacture in the county, chiefly supplying the Norwich worsted industry but also markets further afield. It was, as every visitor noted, a beautifully situated and prosperous town which had become thoroughly gentrified by the eighteenth century. Its fair, held annually in October, was widely famous for the splendid social entertainments that it provided.

III

James Oakes was born in Bury St Edmunds on 7 November 1741, the son of James Oakes senior and his second wife Susan Ray.[7] His father had come from Ardwick near Manchester at some time before 1726 when he opened a ware-house at the upper end of Cook Row (now Abbeygate street), dealing wholesale in Manchester goods.[8] Little is known of his background. His father was a Manchester bolster maker and other members of the family were cotton-goods and yarn merchants, fustian dressers and dyers. They continued to live in Ardwick and in King Street in the centre of Manchester, and were on friendly terms with many of the leading merchants of the city. Oakes senior may well have acted as a salesman for their products as a deed of 1729 described him as a chapman of Norwich.[9] In June of that year he married Mary Godfrey of St James's parish in Bury St Edmunds, the niece of an illiterate milliner John Woods.[10] She bore him three daughters, none of whom survived infancy,[11] and died in August 1737, leaving him property in the nearby villages of Depden and

6   See Nikolaus Pevsner, *The Buildings of England: Suffolk* (1961), pp. 117–37, for a good description of the town and its major buildings.
7   SROB 55.1 BUR *Saint James's Parish Registers.*
8   *Suffolk Mercury* 28 March 1726.
9   Oakes Family Papers catalogued SROB Tem 240/1 but still in the family's posession. See also SROB HA535 Box 5.
10 Woods signed his will with a mark. SROB HA535 Box 5.
11 SROB 55.1 BUR.

Wickhambrook inherited from her uncle.[12] Three and a half years later he married Susan Ray.[13]

Although James Oakes senior owned some of the most valuable commercial properties in Bury[14] and must, therefore, have been reasonably prosperous, his marriage to Susan Ray sealed his entry into the leading commercial, social and political families of the town. The Rays were substantial clothiers and yarn makers. Susan Ray's father and one of her brothers, Orbell Ray, were members of the Corporation; both had served in the office of Alderman and were trustees of the town's largest charities. In addition to the family's important position in the town they were related to many of the local gentry and clergy. Through his second marriage James Oakes senior gained admission to this charmed circle. He became a member of the Corporation, was Alderman twice and acquired further property. At his death in 1759 he was described as an 'eminent Tradesman'.[15]

James Oakes junior, the writer of the diary, was educated at King Edward VI School in Bury St Edmunds. At the age of 16 he left to begin a four year apprenticeship with his uncle, Orbell Ray, who was a yarn maker. Eleven years later, in 1768, Ray died leaving his share of the business to his fortunate young nephew.

Oakes had three sisters. The two eldest, Susan and Mary, married prosperous Liverpool merchants, George Green and James Bridge. Elizabeth, the youngest, married a Norfolk clergyman, the Reverend Richard Baker of Cawston. In December 1764 James Oakes himself married a Norfolk woman, Elizabeth Adamson 'an agreeable Lady with an handsome Fortune',[16] the daughter of an attorney from Wereham in the south west of the county. They had six children, four of whom survived into adulthood.[17] Their elder son, Orbell Ray, followed his father into the yarn trade while the younger, James, became a clergyman. Maria, their elder daughter, married William Gould a vicar's son from north Suffolk; Charlotte died unmarried at the age of 28.

James Oakes was one of the wealthiest merchants in Bury St Edmunds. Apart from the manufacture and marketing of yarn he dealt in coal and hops. He was the Duke of Grafton's political agent in the town and through his influence became Receiver General of the Land Tax for the Western Division of Suffolk in 1787. Ten years later, with the Duke's help, the office was transferred to his son Orbell. Receiverships were lucrative and influential offices which gave the holders tax balances to invest for a period before payment into the Exchequer. The extra capital that the receipt provided enabled Oakes to open a bank in 1794 although he had been carrying out many of the functions of a banker for some

---

[12] T. G. Milner Gibson Cullum, *Ray of Denston* (1903), p. 27.
[13] SROB Bradfield St George Parish Registers FL 533/4/4.
[14] SROB St Mary's Parish Rate Assessment N3/3/33.
[15] IJ 1 September 1759.
[16] IJ 15 December 1764.
[17] SROB St Mary's Parish Registers FL 545/4/4.

2. *William Oakes of Ardwick, James Oakes's paternal grandfather.*

years before. He was also treasurer to the Improvement Commission, to various turnpike trusts and enclosure commissions, was a proprietor of the Assembly Rooms and a trustee of the Suffolk Amicable Insurance Company.

In addition to his business activities Oakes played an important part in the administration of the town and county. He was a justice of the peace for the borough, a deputy lieutenant, a regular member of the Grand Jury, a member of Bury Corporation, Alderman five times, a trustee of the Guildhall Feoffment Trust, a governor of the Grammar School and an ex-officio guardian.

3. Obell Ray I, James Oakes's maternal grandfather.

4. *Rebecca Ray, née Garnham, James Oakes's maternal grandmother.*

5. Elizabeth Adamson, James Oakes's wife.

6. The Rev. James Adamson, vicar of West Dereham, Rector of Sloley and of Barton St Andrew, Norfolk, James Oakes's brother-in-law.

In many ways Oakes was a contradictory character. He had enormous drive and energy, capable when in his late seventies of rounding off a day spent working in the bank with an assembly lasting into the early hours of the following morning and working next day as usual. He was still occupied in the bank every day at the age of nearly 86 when the diary ends in October 1827. A highly organized man himself, he was easily irritated by inefficiency in others and one suspects did not suffer fools gladly. It annoyed him greatly when functions were badly run and when professional men failed to live up to his standards. Incompetent employees or tenants were not to be tolerated and those suspected of dishonesty firmly dealt with. He was zealous and intensely hard-working in both his business and political life and used his connection with the Duke of Grafton to further the fortunes of his family shrewdly and incisively.

Yet he was often pessimistic and indecisive about business prospects, and his confidence was easily shaken. In many ways he was quite unsuited to being a banker, particularly during the period of great economic uncertainty, from 1794 to 1827, that wholly coincided with his years in the profession. He disliked taking risks, seldom took the initiative in expanding the bank's activities, and acted in response to competition rather than setting its pace. Crises depressed him and provoked bouts of minor illness; he was always anxious about his health.

He does not appear to have been an especially imaginative or intelligent man although it is perhaps arrogant to make such judgements on the basis of a diary in which he rarely confided his thoughts or hopes. He was, however, a shrewd judge of character and achieved success in his own small world through sheer diligence. He rarely missed a Corporation, Militia or charity meeting or a court sitting. Charitable property was regularly inspected and kept in good order. Tenancies were awarded to the highest bidder and were not exploited for personal gain. He was also scrupulously honest in his business and personal life. Private travelling expenses were carefully separated from business ones and his diary shows him to have been an accurate reporter of events even when one might have expected special pleading or exaggeration. Yet, in his political management he displayed a certain toughness and was not above using bribery to gain support, or breaking his word when there was no political advantage in keeping it.

Although an exacting employer he was humane. One boy caught stealing was not indicted but sent to join the Navy after a conference with his mother and uncle;[18] and another young man, heavily in debt to the bank, was quietly slipped five guineas 'for present necessarys'.[19] He was paternalistic to an extraordinary degree towards his servants, tenants, and the poor of the town generally. Hours were spent investigating the best means of feeding the poor during food shortages, the advice of local doctors and bakers was sought as to the most suitable

---

[18] Diary 18 January 1796.
[19] SROB Bank Letter Book Acc 2191, April 1796.

types of bread flour to be used,[20] and Oakes himself helped in the distribution. The poor were given food and blankets at Christmas and the welfare of servants, yarn workers and bank clerks was a matter of personal concern. In 1800 he was the only guardian to vote against badging the inmates of the town workhouse.[21]

Unquestioning loyalty to the King and to the Church of England formed the bed-rock of his political beliefs. His love of good order and tradition meant that he was naturally conservative. Yet he supported the abolition of slavery and was the only Anglican to sign a non-conformist petition against the proposed Treasonable Practices and Seditious Meetings Acts in 1795.[22] Like so many of his countrymen events in France gradually provoked a shift in his outlook and he became increasingly inflexible, vigorously opposing political change and upholding the prerogatives of the Church of England. His support of the church was not merely a concomitant of his political beliefs. He was a devout Anglican with marked Evangelical leanings, who seldom failed to attend church twice on Sundays. He supervised Sunday Schools, sought out Sunday tipplers and was a founding member of the Society for the Propagation of the Gospel in Suffolk.

Oakes's religious convictions were not so strongly held as to exclude a hearty enjoyment of life. He was a gregarious man who was never happier than when sharing convivial dinners with his friends, accompanied by quantities of fortified wine, innumerable toasts and the rumbustuous singing of patriotic songs.[23] He loved company and was clearly miserable if no one dined with him on market days, there were no dinner parties in prospect,[24] or assemblies failed to live up to expectations. He enjoyed playing cards and gambling, was impressed by military displays, not to mention military rank, and took an almost child-like pleasure in illuminations, fire works and special celebrations.

Yet he was not simply an unsophisticated provincial. He visited London regularly and was interested in books, the theatre, pictures, country houses, and fine landscapes. New inventions and the opportunities offered by the rapidly expanding towns that he visited in Lancashire excited him. He was aware of national affairs yet was no chauvinist and viewed foreigners kindly.[25] Although many of his pleasures verged on the bucolic his favourite words of approbation were 'genteel', 'elegant', and 'orderly'. He talked and drank happily with men from all walks of life but was very aware of status. An affectionate and totally faithful husband, a dutiful son, and a doting father and grandfather, he nevertheless demanded life-long obedience from his children in the choice of their careers and in the disposal of their incomes.

Money seems to have brought out an obsessive side to his character possibly

20 e.g. Diary 11 July 1795, 15 July 1795.
21 SROB Guardians Court Book N5/1/3; diary 4 November 1800.
22 Diary 23 November 1795.
23 e.g. Diary 15 August 1803.
24 e.g. Diary 8–13 April 1782, 8 May 1782, 7 April 1789.
25 Oakes entertained the young La Rochefoucauld and his party, and his wife visited a group of Belgian nuns who lived in exile at Hengrave Hall during the war.

provoked by his inherent lack of business confidence and insecurity. He recorded every penny that he spent on housekeeping, clothes and journeys and, although a wealthy man, was much irritated when small personal debts to him remained unpaid. The Oakes family papers are full of scraps of paper on which the elderly James Oakes had made numerous calculations of his financial worth. They show his great disappointment that, as a result of falling land values, he would die worth only a massive £180,000 and not £200,000. He obviously expected to be judged on his financial worth, the public manifestation of his success.

Generally fair and honest, his advice was sought by family and friends alike. He was accessible to all from farm workmen to the Duke of Grafton. His portrait shows him to have had a kind, strong, pleasant face with slightly sandy hair and a ruddy complexion. He did indeed discharge 'with fidelity every civil, social, moral and religious obligation' that he undertook,[26] and do 'un grand bien dans le pays'.[27]

V

James Oakes's diary has no literary merit and was clearly written in haste, at the end of the day when the light was bad, in cramped scrawl quite unlike his usual bold and even script. Although his letters show that he wrote clearly and succinctly his diary consists of little more than rough notes or jottings in the early years. It seldom contains the delightful personal comments found in well known, published journals. Unlike Woodforde, Oakes rarely gives terse and vivid descriptions of people and places nor does he have the wit and capacity for self examination of Pepys. He did not move in high political circles like Fanny Burney, or have the descriptive power or waywardness of the Hon. John Byng. He was not able to report doings at Court, he did not make exciting tours abroad like his friend and neighbour Arthur Young

While the diaries of leisured ecclesiastics and influential aristocrats abound in the eighteenth century there were few written by men in Oakes's social and economic position. Urban merchants of the period were hardworking men usually far too involved in the cut and thrust of business life to indulge the luxury of diary keeping. There are, for example, those by William Stout of Lancashire,[28] Joseph Rogerson of Bramley,[29] John Izzard Pryor of Baldock[30] and Thomas Turner

[26] *Gentleman's Magazine*, 99, I (1829), p. 189.
[27] *A Frenchman's Year in Suffolk, 1784: François de La Rochefoucauld*, edited and translated by Norman Scarfe (Suffolk Records Society, 1988), XXX, p. 28 n.9.
[28] *The Autobiography of William Stout of Lancaster 1665–1752*, edited by J. D. Marshall (Manchester, 1967).
[29] W. W. Crump, *The Leeds Woollen Industry 1760–1820* (Thoresby Society, 1931).
[30] Gerald Curtis, *A Chronicle of Small Beer: The Early Victorian Diaries of a Hertfordshire Brewer* (1970).

of East Hoathly[31] together with early business biographies of Peter Stubbs of Warrington[32] and John Marshall of Leeds.[33] None of these men was quite in Oakes's position. Turner was a village shop keeper, Pryor did not begin writing his diary until he was 53 in 1827 and, while Stubbs and Rogerson prospered, they were in origin skilled tradesmen, whereas Oakes wrote his diary while actively engaged in business and was born into a family that had produced eminent merchants for generations.

More importantly the study of Rogerson, Stubbs, Stout, Marshall and others is a product of the enormous interest taken in the origins of the Industrial Revolution. Less attention has been paid to the situation in the economically declining areas of the country beyond a few local studies. It is in this area that Oakes's diary is of such value. Oakes was a yarn merchant at a time when the Suffolk industry was in decline due to competition from cheaper yarns produced in Ireland and in Yorkshire. His diary shows how the industry was organized, where the raw wool was purchased, combed and put out to be spun and where the finished product was sold. It suggests that there were in fact large and complex businesses at a period when the Suffolk industry was generally regarded as being almost defunct.

As the Suffolk yarn industry came under increasing pressure the diary describes Oakes's quest for an alternative form of investment. Investment opportunities in agricultural counties like Suffolk were few and Oakes turned to banking. Most manufacturers and merchants carried out many of the functions of bankers in the ordinary course of their business lives buying bills, providing credit and, in some cases, issuing their own notes so that it was a logical step for him to take. He had the added advantage of being Receiver which put large sums of money into his hands and helped to underpin the bank and enable it to survive the many financial crises of the period.

The diary supplies much useful information on the problems of businessmen working in declining industries at a time of intense economic change. It gives a picture of the day to day problems involved in starting up a country bank, its premises and staff. It also provides useful information on bank customers, note issue and investment policy although, in the complete absence of accounts, these are necessarily impressionistic. In addition it provides the type of information on these subjects not readily available from other sources: the difficulties involved in tax collection, for example, which were not important enough to come to the attention of the Tax Office and therefore do not appear in either the Taxation or King's Remembrancer documents.

Of course Oakes was not unique in turning his back on trade to become a banker. Merchants all over the country were following the same path. His diary is

[31] The Diary of Thomas Turner 1754–1765, edited by David Vaisey (Oxford, 1985).
[32] T. S. Ashton, The Eighteenth Century Industrialist: Peter Stubbs of Warrington 1756–1806 (Manchester, 1939, reprint 1961).
[33] W. G. Rimmer, Marshalls of Leeds Flax Spinners 1788–1886 (Cambridge, 1960).

important, not because he is atypical but because it gives information on the totality of his life which was probably not far removed from that of many other men like him in towns all over England but who left no personal record.

Because of his central position in the political and social life of Bury St Edmunds his diary affords a rare insight into the interaction of politics and society in provincial towns. Apart from showing Oakes's conscientious devotion to public service it demonstrates that he could never afford to relax. There were always others anxious to assume the political agent's mantle in order to reap the rewards that it offered. Oakes was forced to manage Corporation as well as general elections in order to protect his own interests quite as much as those of the Duke of Grafton. At a period when corporation minutes tend to be brief and uninformative his diary provides detail on political management in the borough unobtainable elsewhere and vividly illustrates the fact that life under the patronage system, even in a relatively small closed borough, could be fraught with tension and anxiety.

Diaries and letters have always been a major source for social historians and although Oakes's diary rarely provides detailed descriptions of houses, dress or food yet much useful information does emerge from it about eighteenth and early nineteenth century urban provincial middle-class family life. It is possible to deduce patterns of child care, education, attitudes to birth, health, marriage and death. It also describes social life in Bury St Edmunds, particularly the annual fair held in October, and demonstrates its importance in the continuing prosperity of the town after the decline of its only major industry.

As a banker and member of a long established family Oakes knew everyone of any importance in Suffolk so that his diary gives a unique glimpse of economic, political and social life centred on Bury St Edmunds at a period during which Britain was at war for over 20 years, when industrialization was altering the structure of the economy and demands for political reform were becoming increasingly strident. It was on such men as James Oakes that the stability and economic well-being of towns like Bury St Edmunds depended.

CHAPTER II

James Oakes and the Suffolk Yarn Industry: 1778–1795

INTRODUCTION

Although Suffolk had been an important textile manufacturing region since the Middle Ages by the eighteenth century very little cloth was produced in the county. Early in the seventeenth century, continental wars, which disrupted its foreign markets, together with competition from the new draperies, almost extinguished the Medieval broad cloth industry. Flemish refugees had introduced the manufacture of the new draperies to the old broad cloth-making centres in the Stour, Gipping, Brett and Box valleys. However, during the course of the century growing competition from both the Norwich and the Colchester weavers had virtually eliminated its production from Suffolk.[1]

By the first quarter of the eighteenth century there was still 'a great manufacture of says and perpetuanas' in Sudbury and Long Melford.[2] This was flourishing sixty years later, despite serious set-backs suffered during the American War.[3] Calimancoes were made in Lavenham, tammies in Stowmarket, and bays and says in Nayland. Apart from this, little cloth was produced in the county by the end of the century other than linen in the towns of the Waveney valley. Former cloth towns like Bildeston and Clare were described as 'dirty' places with 'mean' buildings, and the poverty of Needham Market had 'passed into proverb'.[4]

Elsewhere weaving had been superseded by wool combing and spinning yarn for the worsted manufacturers of Colchester and of Norwich. Wool combers and

---

[1] For further information on the Suffolk textile industry see: George Unwin, 'The History of the Cloth Industry in Suffolk', in *Studies in Economic History: the Collected Papers of George Unwin*, edited by R. H. Tawney (1958), pp. 262–301 (also found in VCH, II, pp. 254–71); J. E. Pilgrim, 'The Cloth Industry in Essex and Suffolk' (unpublished M.A. thesis, London School of Economics and Political Science, 1938); David Dymond and Alec Betterton, *Lavenham: 700 Years of Textile Making* (Woodbridge, 1982); Eric Kerridge, *Textile Manufacture in Early Modern England* (Manchester, 1985)

[2] Daniel Defoe, *A Tour Through the Whole Island of Great Britain*, 2 vols (Everyman Library, 1962), I, pp. 47–48.

[3] Arthur Young, *General View of the Agriculture of the County of Suffolk in 1804*, p. 231.

[4] *Universal Magazine* (1759), XXIV, pp. 57, 169–71.

yarn makers were to be found concentrated in the south of the county and in Bury St Edmunds and its neighbouring villages. There were very few in north east Suffolk beyond those serving the needs of local knitters.

THE YARN INDUSTRY IN BURY ST EDMUNDS

To read contemporary accounts one would not imagine that eighteenth century Bury St Edmunds was a manufacturing town. Most writers were more impressed by the town's healthy situation and plentiful supply of gentry than by its industry. Although Celia Fiennes discovered the countryside on her way from Norwich to be 'full of spinners and knitters' and described Bury as 'a thriving industrious town' she made no mention of yarn.[5] Defoe, usually such a keen observer of business and commercial life, was seduced by the social attractions of the town and could see 'no manufacturing except a very little spinning' to spoil its well-heeled charm or sully its health-giving air.[6]

In contrast early nineteenth century writers bemoaned the demise of industry in the town and remarked on the wool halls as reminders of former business activity. One writer, reminiscing on the later eighteenth century worsted industry, claimed that far from having no industry Bury St Edmunds together with Norwich was the headquarters of worsted yarn production for the Norwich weavers. He recalled the industry as being in the hands of 'men of property and intelligence' who presided over a 'vast spinning and combing system' extending throughout Norfolk, Suffolk, Essex, Cambridge and Bedfordshire. He described how combed wool was delivered throughout this region by travellers or packmen who left it with the spinners, collecting and paying for spun yarn at the same time. According to this author an 'incredible number of families rose to independence and affluence and respectability' through yarn manufacture.[7]

Later writers, while accepting that Bury St Edmunds was 'the head and heart of a combing and spinning region' a dozen miles across[8] have felt that the evidence did not support these memories of large scale yarn making companies and their complex 'domestic' spinning networks.[9] The early volumes of James Oakes's diary go some way towards resolving this contradiction and, although they often contain no more than brief notes at this period, it has been possible to piece together a picture, however inadequate, of the way in which the industry was organized.

5   The Journeys of Celia Fiennes, edited by Christopher Morris (1947), pp. 150–52.
6   Defoe, A Tour Through the Whole Island of Great Britain, p. 52.
7   East Anglian Daily Times, 14 February 1832.
8   E. Kerridge, Textile Manufacture in Early Modern England (Manchester, 1985), pp. 153–54.
9   J. K. Edwards, 'The Economic Development of Norwich 1750–1850 with special reference to the Worsted Cloth Industry' (unpublished Ph.D. thesis, University of Leeds, 1963), p. 171.

There were many large yarn-making concerns in Bury St Edmunds by the second half of the eighteenth century among them those of Messrs Cumberlands, Corsbie and Buck, Harmers, Maling, Umfreville, Rutter, Johnson and Branwhite Green. One of the largest was that of Ray Oakes and Company. The Rays had been wealthy and influential clothiers since the beginning of the century, dealing in wool and yarn, and owning extensive property in the town and neighbouring villages. Orbell Ray the younger inherited the business from his father in 1753. It operated from a red brick-fronted house in Guildhall Street, possibly renovated at some time between 1730 and 1742,[10] which had extensive outbuildings in the yard behind it and further buildings and land in St Andrew's Street.

James Oakes was apprenticed to his uncle, Orbell Ray, at the age of 16 and four years later became a partner in the company. His uncle was a shrewd businessman and the young Oakes was thought by family and friends 'likely to do very well in the Partnership'.[11] There seems to have been no question that he go into his father's business dealing in Manchester goods. It must have been felt that he would have better prospects with his wealthy and childless uncle.[12] His father died less than two years after he began his apprenticeship, leaving the bulk of his property to provide for his wife and three daughters and £1,000 to his only son.[13] Indeed in 1768 his father's predictions were proved correct when Orbell Ray died leaving the entire business to his nephew. Thus at the age of nearly 27 Oakes was at the head of one of Bury St Edmunds's most prosperous concerns aided by a manager, Peter Chambers, who had joined Ray six years before.

By the time the diary begins Ray Oakes and Company were primarily yarn merchants but also dealt in coal and hops. The company was unusual in that both Ray and Oakes were Anglicans while the majority of their fellow merchants in Bury, as in textile towns elsewhere,[14] were dissenters. All the other leading yarn makers, with the exception of Branwhite Green, were members of either the Whiting Street or the Churchgate Street Chapels. Although Oakes seems to have had a great amount of business contact with them sharing companionable evenings at the *Wool Pack* and visits to wool fairs, the only ones with whom he and his family mixed socially, and that to a limited degree, were the Corsbies.

---

[10] Sun Fire Office Policy Register vols 31 and 61 show that Orbell Ray's house was timber framed under a tile roof in October 1730 but by April 1742 was described as partly of brick.

[11] SROB Cullum Letters E2/25/1 fol. 33.

[12] Orbell Ray the younger had one daughter who died in 1753.

[13] PROB 11/849 fol. 335.

[14] Alfred P. Wadsworth and Julia de Lacy Mann, *The Cotton Trade and Industrial Lancashire 1600–1780* (Manchester, 1931).

Until the seventeenth century Suffolk worsted yarn was made from long-staple wool largely produced locally. By the eighteenth century the increasing practice among East Anglian farmers of folding sheep resulted in the production of animals with a heavier carcase and a shorter staple. Thus, by the 1760s the Suffolk industry was supplied with long-fleeced wool produced in Lincolnshire, Leicestershire, Northamptonshire and Kent. It was generally accepted that wool from Lincolnshire sheep combined superior length of fibre with strengh, fineness and whiteness.[15] Meanwhile the short-fleeced wool from Norfolk and Suffolk sheep was sent to Yorkshire to be carded and spun for use in the manufacture of woollen cloth.

The yarn makers of Bury St Edmunds bought long staple wool from wool halls in the town, from Stourbridge Fair and from London wool markets. An early nineteenth century guide book described Bury as 'anciently the greatest wool staple in the Eastern part of England'.[16] By the time that James Oakes began to write his diary it had two wool halls: one at the end of St Andrew's Street owned by John Green and one at the upper end of the market owned by the Corporation and leased to James Mathew.[17] Mathew also owned the *Wool Pack Inn*[18] which was conveniently placed between his wool hall and the hemp hall and was 'frequented by many respectable dealers and traders'.[19] Both wool halls were considered 'very small in comparison with the spacious warehouses where all the wool in the county was deposited.'[20] It was claimed that 'great quantities of wool' were brought to the wool halls by local producers as well as those from the Midlands.[21] Short fleeced wool was sold to agents appointed by the Yorkshire manufacturers[22] and the long-staple Lincolnshire wool was eagerly sought by local worsted yarn producers.

Lincolnshire wool arrived in Bury St Edmunds through various channels. Some undoubtedly came directly from Lincolnshire as there was a regular waggon service between the town and Stamford. Bury also had access to the Midlands via the Lark Navigation which connected it to the Ouse and thence to Kings Lynn. Toll books show that the proprietors of the wool halls and others

---

[15] Edwards, 'The Economic Development of Norwich', p. 171; Arthur Young, *A Farmer's Tour Through the East of England* (1771), p. 74.

[16] Edmund Gillingwater, *An Historical and Descriptive Account of the Ancient Town of Saint Edmunds Bury in the County of Suffolk* (1811).

[17] SROB Saint James's Parish Rate Assessment N3/6/1.

[18] The inn was renamed *Everards's Hotel*, after the proprietor of the brewery in Guildhall Street in the first half of the nineteenth century. It closed recently.

[19] IJ 5 July 1783.

[20] Gillingwater, *An Historical and Descriptive Account of the Ancient Town of Saint Edmunds Bury*, p. 264.

[21] G. Ashby, *A Description of the Ancient and Present State of the Town and Abbey of Bury Saint Edmunds in the County of Suffolk* (Bury, 1782), p. 75.

[22] BNP 23 July 1788.

were paying toll on considerable quantities of wool brought into the town by this route.[23] Some may also have come via the coast to Ipswich and from thence by waggon to Bury. Advertisements in the *Ipswich Journal* frequently advised customers of the arrival of the appropriately named ship, the *Bishop Blaze*, in Ipswich from Hull and Gainsborough.[24] The owner of the ship, Ralph Hare, had a wool warehouse in the town.[25] Much of the Lincolnshire wool combed in Norwich itself came by sea to Yarmouth and thence by river to the city. It is very likely that Bury combers also obtained supplies of raw wool from this source as Yarmouth and Bury are only 60 miles apart.[26] Sir Francis Hill wrote of Lincolnshire graziers who took their wool to market in Colchester, Norwich, Leeds and Halifax at great expense rather than sell it to chapmen because they feared their prices would be reduced by buyers' rings. It was a costly operation because it necessitated the employment of factors and the hiring of warehouses, and because buyers expected long credit.[27] It is probable that some of these Lincolnshire graziers sold directly to the yarn makers of Bury St Edmunds and to the wool merchants of Ipswich. In 1741 Bury Corporation threatened to prosecute those who were buying and selling Lincolnshire wool in the wool halls without paying toll and determined to advertise their decision in Stamford as well as on the market cross.[28]

A second source of Lincolnshire wool was through Stourbridge Fair to which graziers took it by packhorse or waggon.[29] Defoe described the fair as 'not only the greatest in the whole nation, but in the world'. It specialised in the sale of wool, particularly the Lincolnshire long-staple wool, and hops. According to Defoe the wool was sold mainly to 'the manufacturers of Norfolk and Suffolk and Essex, and it is a prodigious quantity they buy'. He estimated that from £50,000 to £60,000 worth was sold in one fair and 'some say a great deal more'.[30]

Oakes bought wool at both the Bury wool halls, although he seems to have had closer contact with Mathew than with Green. He only once mentions buying wool from a Mr Braughton at Mr Greens's hall, noting with pleasure a fall in price on that occasion of nine shillings a tod.[31] He twice mentions buying wool from Mr Mathew, in August 1793 and in April 1794, and regularly attended Stourbridge Fair with him. Both Mathew and Oakes were members of the

---

23 SROB Lark Navigation Toll Book 1780–1810, E2/17/7.
24 IJ 18 April 1778 for example.
25 BNP 11 September 1782 for example.
26 'Norwich's textile industry in 1784, observed by Maximilien de Lazowski', edited and translated by Norman Scarfe. Typescript in Mr Scarfe's possession. I am most grateful to Mr Scarfe for bringing this document to my attention. He hopes it will soon be published as an article in *Textile History*. And see *A Frenchman's Year*, p. 206.
27 Sir Francis Hill, *Georgian Lincoln* (Cambridge, 1966), p. 108.
28 SROB Corporation Minutes, D4/1/3A.
29 Hill, *Georgian Lincoln*, p. 101.
30 Defoe, *A Tour Through the Whole Island of Great Britain*, pp. 80, 82–84.
31 Diary 12 June 1793.

Corporation and entertained each other socially. Oakes had no social contact with the non-conformist John Green, although men from both the wool halls acted as bearers at his wife's funeral in 1802.[32]

Oakes went to Stourbridge every year on 25 September in the company of other yarn merchants from Suffolk as well as that of James Mathew, the wool factor. It was customary for them to share the cost of hiring a chaise and for 'the party from Bury' to breakfast, dine and drink tea together during the trip.[33] The fair was not confined to trade for, apart from the booths of manufacturers of every conceivable type of goods arranged in streets, there were 'coffee houses, taverns, brandy shops and eating houses innumerable, and all in tents and booths'[34] not to mention the Norwich Comedians performing at the theatre.[35] As they grew older Oakes took his children with him, guests who were staying with the family at the time, or interested local friends unconnected with the yarn trade. It was a great social occasion at which the members of the industry from all over the country could meet, exchange information and discuss problems. Oakes never actually mentions buying wool at the fair, although it would seem likely that he did so, either on his own account or in partnership with other merchants or wool factors. It was the practice for the larger West Riding and Colchester manufacturers to buy the bulk of their wool supplies through the major fairs and wool markets of the country.[36] Oakes probably began dealing in hops as a result of these regular trips to Stourbridge.

His diary shows that Oakes also purchased wool at the Bermondsey Wool Market but does not reveal how it was transported home.[37] It could have been sent to Bury by road. Wool bought in London by Colchester merchants was left for collection at the *Bull Inn*, Leadenhall Street,[38] an inn much frequented by Oakes on his London visits. Alternatively it could have been sent by sea to Ipswich to await collection. Oakes and his manager Peter Chambers made frequent visits to the county town, the purpose of which was not explained, but it is clear that Oakes's cart went there regularly.

On two occasions Oakes mentions buying Kent wool[39] having first sent an employee, John Waller, 'into Kent by coach to Mr Barker's at Ashford'.[40] A contemporary letter implies that Lincolnshire and Kent provided most of the

---

32   Diary 2 December 1802.
33   Diary 25 September 1793.
34   Defoe, A *Tour Through the Whole Island of Great Britain*, pp. 82–84.
35   BNP 25 September 1782.
36   Herbert Heaton, *The Yorkshire Woollen and Worsted Industries* (1965), p. 297; A. F. J. Brown, 'Colchester in the Eighteenth Century', in *East Anglian Studies*, edited by Lionel Munby (Cambridge, 1968), pp. 146–73, p. 148.
37   Diary 23 April 1793.
38   Brown, 'Colchester in the Eighteenth Century', p. 148.
39   Diary 4, 17 October 1789.
40   Diary 11 August 1789.

wool used in the Suffolk worsted yarn industry at this time[41] while another suggests that the 'well sorted, the finer parts' of Romney Marsh wools were always sent to Bury and to Norwich.[42]

It seems curious that Oakes should go to the trouble of sending a man into Kent to buy wool and to travel to the Stourbridge and London wool markets, yet never buy directly from Lincolnshire or the other Midland counties which provided the bulk of his supplies. The diary is very scrappy for these years and he could have failed to record journeys to the Midlands made either by himself or an employee, although this would be unlikely. The toll books show that two Suffolk yarn makers, William Buck and George Wilkinson, paid tolls on packs of wool in 1787, but there is no evidence that Oakes did the same and neither Buck nor Wilkinson appears to have repeated the exercise.[43] On the whole it was probably easier and cheaper to buy from a factor who would give long credit rather than having to pay for an employee to spend several nights away arranging purchases and transport. In the absence of letter and account books this must remain supposition.

The lack of business records also means that it is impossible to calculate the amount of wool that Ray Oakes and Company bought in the course of a year. Hardly surprisingly Oakes made no systematic record of wool purchases in his diary although he does mention it on a few occasions. He records buying 35,560 pounds of wool in 1789 and 71,988 pounds between April 1793 and April 1794, assuming that the wool bought in partnership with Mr Buck was shared equally.[44]

The wool bought between April 1793 and April 1794 represents an investment of well over £2,000 using the prices Oakes gives.[45] This may well be an underestimate of the company's expenditure as it is possible that other purchases

---

[41] *The Sheep and Wool Correspondence of Sir Joseph Banks 1781–1820* Library Council of New South Wales in association with the British Museum (Natural History) (1979), p. 65, letter dated 5 February 1782.

[42] BL Tracts B545, p. 349. An early Stocktaking Account Book makes it clear that Kent wool was bought by Ray Oakes and Company in 1765. SROB HA535 Box 10.

[43] SROB E2/17/7.

[44] In January 1789 he bought 1,250 tods of fleece wool and in October '80 clo' of Kent fleece wool. 24 April 1793 he bought 40 tods of Northants wool and 4 'clos' of 'super cast' with Mr Buck; in June 1793 1,000 tods of long fleece wool, in August 800 tods and in April 1794 700 tods of wool.

[45] Wool prices given by James Oakes for fleece wool per tod:

Date	Price in shillings
9 August 1792	26
8 March 1793	24–28
12 June 1793	19
23 August 1793	15
5 April 1794	15s.6d.–16s.6d.

SROB HA535 Box 10 shows that at stocktaking over 30 years earlier, in the years 1765–67 inclusive, the company had £6,032 11s. 9¼d., £7,477 8s. 4½d. and £5,972 0s. 10d. respectively, worth of wool in their warehouse or with spinners.

were not recorded. Oakes provides no information as to how the wool was paid for or what credit, if any, was given.

PROTECTION OF THE WOOL SUPPLY

Since the sixteenth century the prohibition of wool exports had been seen as vital to the prosperity of the British textile industry and any attempt to lift it was met with violent opposition from manufacturers. The question was raised again during a period of very sharply falling wool prices in 1780 by the Lincolnshire growers, whose aim was to free the export of wool and to allow the import of Irish yarn. By 1782 their attempt had fizzled out in the face of lobbying from the manufacturers who appeared to have been efficiently organized and to have had the support of many members of Parliament. Oakes claimed that there were 50 at their delegate conference in London early in 1782[46] and two months later it was resolved that both Suffolk county Members would oppose any proposals to free the export of wool placed before Parliament.[47]

The question surfaced once more in 1786 when manufacturers began to agitate for further stringent laws to prevent the export of wool and improve its quality. They had become alarmed at government proposals to free trade with France and with Ireland where a flourishing textile industry had developed during the American War. They also claimed that the existing law was being evaded and that large quantities of raw wool were being smuggled to France. Whereas the earlier campaign by the Lincolnshire wool growers provoked little reaction from their counterparts in Suffolk this later agitation produced a sharp clash between the landed and manufacturing interests of the county in which feelings ran very high. Once again Oakes took a leading part on behalf of the Suffolk yarn makers attending a delegate conference in London in May 1786[48] and chairing a general meeting of manufacturers three months later at Stowmarket.[49] It was decided to raise a subscription, to write to all the local Members of Parliament requesting support, and to place notices in both the Suffolk papers. Oakes together with William Buck and Thomas Barnard were elected to act as delegates 'to attend to the prosecution of the business'.[50]

Oakes makes no reference to opposition to the bill in Suffolk, although it was obviously noisy. The Suffolk growers were led, or more realistically, whipped into action by Arthur Young. The indefatigable Young saw the manufacturers' proposed bill as a means by which manufacturing and commercial interests sought to monopolize the home supply of raw materials in order to keep farm prices down

[46] Diary 7 February 1782.
[47] IJ 6 April 1782.
[48] Diary 26 May 1786.
[49] Diary 15 August 1786.
[50] IJ 19 August 1786.

and consequently wages and production costs. It was, in is opinion, nothing but 'a conspiracy of manufacturers against the landed interest'.[51] At Young's instigation meetings of wool growers were held throughout the county, a representative committee was elected, and resolutions passed deploring attempts to restrict exports and to control the washing, winding, marking and sale of wool. The resolutions, which bore the stamp of Young's redoubtable style, condemned the clauses aimed at quality control as 'impracticable to be carried into execution' and to have been formulated in 'total ignorance of the business and to have no other tendency than to place the grower at the mercy of the manufacturer . . . [and to] form monopolies of the most injurious kind'.[52] These clauses were published in detail to emphasize the difficulties which they would present to the farmer. It was felt that the whole scheme was entirely motivated by the 'private avarice' of the manufacturers and it was resolved to apply, through the Grand Jury, to the High Sheriff to call a county meeting should he get 'authentic' information that the bill was to be passed. A notice to this effect was signed by 26 members of the Grand Jury.[53] Further meetings were held, a committee formed to manage opposition to the bill and subscriptions raised to finance the campaign. It was also decided to leave petitions against the bill for signatures at various places throughout the county.[54]

At the same time Arthur Young waged a vigorous battle against the manufacturers in print focusing his indignation on the low wages paid to spinners. He claimed that it was the spinners' dependence on the Norwich industry which made them so vulnerable and that manufacturers were using the wool bill as an excuse to lower their wages still further.[55] To counteract their dependence he suggested that the spinning of hemp should be introduced on a wider scale in the county to provide an alternative employment, while one of his correspondents thought that stone picking would make a delightful change from spinning for women and children.[56] Others more sensibly suggested that the power of magistrates under the Elizabethan statute to settle wages should be effectively enforced.[57] Young and his correspondents saw the bill as 'injurious to commerce' and 'as incompatible with constitutional freedom', because the proposals to prevent smuggling were so complex that 'all idea of liberty and freedom are done away with'. The growers' interest was completely submerged by 'the inordinate desires of extravagant profit — the arithmetic of the counter — the policy of the shop — to buy wool cheap will add so much per cent on the manufacturers' capital'.[58]

51 BL Tracts B545, p. 95.
52 IJ 17, 24 February, 10, 31 March 1787.
53 IJ 7 April 1787.
54 IJ 17 November 1787.
55 BL Tracts B545, p. 266.
56 Ibid., p. 450.
57 Ibid., p. 352.
58 Arthur Young, Annals of Agriculture, VII, 37, pp. 37, 151, 156.

The manufacturers kept a low profile during this propaganda war although a letter from one calling himself *Candor* did attempt to defend their pay policy towards spinners.[59] A second subscription was opened by the yarn makers in November 1787[60] and amendments to the bill were discussed in an attempt to placate the growers. In the event the growers' committee did not feel 'sufficiently acquainted with [the] specific propositions' to discuss them and adjourned their December meeting to February 1788.[61]

This was a tactical mistake on their part as the bill was due to come before Parliament in March 1788. Meanwhile the diary shows that Oakes was busy on behalf of the manufacturers attending a five day delegate conference in February.[62] and lobbying the support of Sir Charles Davers, one of the Members of Parliament for Bury St Edmunds.[63] Oakes must have convinced Davers as both men rushed to London in response to a letter from the manufacturers' national chairman, Mr Anstie, to lobby all the Suffolk Members to support the bill when the evidence of wool smuggling given before a Commons committee was presented to the House.[64] Although the bill passed easily through the Commons, trouble was expected in the Lords and Oakes went to London again, this time to lobby the Duke of Grafton and Lord Chedworth.[65] The manufacturers were victorious and the bill received the royal assent in July.[66]

Oakes had played an important part in the progress of the Wool Bill. He had chaired the general meetings held in Suffolk and taken on himself all the delegate duties. He was also able to exert political pressure in a way which was not open to his fellow non-conformist yarn makers. He was the political manager for the Duke of Grafton in Bury and therefore had a particular influence which he used shrewdly and efficiently to gain support for the manufacturers' cause. Lady Banks, wife of Sir Joseph Banks PRS and leader of the Lincolnshire growers, wrote to her husband in June 1788 telling him that, despite Mr Pelham's frequent requests, the Duke of Grafton had refused to go to the House of Lords to speak against the bill claiming that he was ill and that anyway he had not been to the House for five years.[67]

The growers, although more numerous and of greater political and economic significance within the county, were probably a less cohesive group than the manufacturers and were therefore more difficult to mobilize. This was not only the case in Suffolk. The Earl of Sheffield complained that the landowners of Kent were supine, tame and void of energy. Others complained that country

59 IJ 12 January 1788.
60 Diary 15 November 1787.
61 IJ 15 December 1787.
62 Diary 13–18 February 1788.
63 Diary 21 February 1788.
64 Diary 9 March 1788.
65 Diary 9 May 1788.
66 28 Geo III c38.
67 Banks, *Sheep and Wool Correspondence*, p. 152, letter dated June 1788.

gentlemen never agreed about anything in contrast to the manufacturers who always agreed to man, while yet others felt that it needed 'a great proportion of Hunger to excite' them to any sort of activity otherwise they were too idle and dissipated to bother.[68] Many of Banks's correspondents regretted the growers' failure to manage their campaign well. No subscriptions were taken at the first Lincoln meeting although everyone expected it.[69] The growers failed to match the manufacturers in gathering information, preparing a well argued case and finding Members of Parliament willing to promote it in the House.[70] The only counties that showed any real interest in the cause were Suffolk and Lincolnshire where Arthur Young and Sir Joseph Banks goaded the growers into action. In Kent the subject had 'scarcely been a topic of Conversation'.[71]

Even in Suffolk the growers' organization appeared inefficient, always one step behind the manufacturers and never able to get their subscriptions paid in full and on time. They were taken by surprise by the manufacturers early in 1788 and petulently described them as 'ungenerous and uncanded' in keeping their moves secret to prevent opposition mustering.[72]

The episode highlighted tensions between the manufacturing and the landed interests. In Norfolk the Under Sheriff was anxious to avoid a county meeting on behalf of the growers because he feared that it would divide the county, the Norwich manufacturers having been intrumental in framing the proposed bill.[73]

Suffolk landowners thought that the manufacturers' exploitation of their spinners was the cause of rising poor rates, that they were, in effect, subsidizing the low wages paid by yarn makers. These tensions must have been emphasized for some landowners by their own negotiations with yarn makers over the price of spinning in their local parish and union workhouses.

Suffolk manufacturers, for their part, doubtless felt misunderstood by their opponents but were in a difficult position. Their dependence on the Norwich industry allowed them little flexibility over prices and quality on one hand, and on the other may have pushed them into support of a bill which they questioned. Although the *Ipswich Journal* had declared in 1782, during the Lincolnshire growers' attempt to free the export of wool, that the import of Irish yarn would be 'greatly beneficial to the trade and manufacturers' of the county[74] it was not in the best interests of the Suffolk industry which depended solely on yarn production. This may explain the apparent reluctance of Suffolk yarn makers to join the Norwich combers in promoting the bill at the outset.[75]

68 *Ibid.*, p. 88, letter dated 8 October 1786; p. 76, letter dated 12 August 1782; p. 62, letter dated 31 January 1782; pp. 46–47, letter dated 15 December 1781.
69 *Ibid.*, pp. 46–48.
70 *Ibid.*, p. 62, letter dated 31 January 1782.
71 *Ibid.*, p. 57.
72 IJ 5 April 1788.
73 Banks, *Sheep and Wool Correspondence*, p. 94, letter dated 26 November 1786.
74 IJ 21 March 1782.
75 Diary 10 April 1786.

After the Bill had passed, Arthur Young claimed that some Suffolk yarn manufacturers had hinted that if he would 'stir for a bill to allow an export of yarn they will not oppose' and might support him. Young thought that if he could 'bring them forth manfully' it would be a good moment to apply for such a bill 'for it will rarely happen that we can be backed by a manufacturing petition and even fro[m] men who supported the Wool Bill'.[76] The export of yarn would have benefitted the Suffolk industry greatly at a time when Young claimed manufacturers were heavily overstocked and demand for yarn was falling.[77] As users of raw wool they would not want to oppose the bill in its major aim but could not support the export of yarn without incurring the displeasure of the Norwich worsted manufacturers on whom they depended for the bulk of their market.

Throughout the campaign Oakes was in an uncomfortable situation, socially isolated from his fellow non-conformist yarn makers while, at the same time, economically and politically at odds with most of his family, friends and associates. The difficulty of his position is well illustrated by the fact that he was the only member of the Grand Jury who did not sign a notice requesting a county meeting on behalf of the growers in 1787.[78] When the Wool Bill became law in July 1788 there was great rejoicing in Suffolk. Bells rang in Sudbury for two days on end and fireworks were let off in the streets.[79] In Bury St Edmunds wool combers rode in procession with 'bells ringing, music playing, colours flying and every demonstration of Joy'.[80] However enthusiasm for the new Act was not universal among manufacturers in the county. Combers employed by James Oakes and by John Corsbie were forbidden by their masters to take part, ostensibly 'on acct of the melancholy and oppressed state of the trade at this time'.[81] Both men must have felt that wild celebrations would only exacerbate local feelings and that the Suffolk yarn industry would in time come to regret the unrestricted import of Irish yarn.

SORTING AND SCOURING

Once the wool had been purchased and brought to Bury St Edmunds it was stored in wool chambers behind the Guildhall Street house where it was sorted into different grades and blended by highly skilled sorters. Oakes employed between five and seven sorters together with three of four warehousemen and a couple of apprentices to help them. There is even a suggestion that he may have

[76] Banks, *Sheep and Wool Correspondence*, p. 168.
[77] *Ibid.*, p. 168, letter dated 3 November 1788.
[78] IJ 17 November 1787.
[79] BNP 2 July 1788.
[80] IJ 12 July 1788.
[81] Diary 19 July 1788.

employed women in these jobs as '2 women' were included in a list of sorters and warehousemen entertained in the house at Christmas 1786.

It had been customary for master combers to scour and to sort wool on their own premises but by the second half of the eighteenth century sorting was becoming a specialist occupation.[82] Plans of Oakes's property show extensive warehousing behind his Guildhall Street houses backing on to St Andrew's Street with one especially large warehouse approximately 75 feet by 20 feet.[83] The upper floor of this building with its long sides facing north and south would have been particularly suitable for wool sorting because it was important for sorters to have a good north light so that no shadows fell across their work.

Oakes does not mention the operation of scouring or washing the wool. In the West Country the job was done by woolstaplers.[84] In other areas it was sometimes carried out by the farmer himself before the wool was sold and many of the proposed provisions of the Wool Bill dealing with washing and winding suggest that this was the case. It is probable that Oakes organized the scouring as well as the sorting. Early accounts show that the company had bought considerable quantities of soap in 1765 and 1767 [85] while there were adequate drying grounds in St Andrew's Street and plenty of warehouse space. Dymond and Betterton found that the inventories of Lavenham manufacturers of the period included equipment for scouring[86] and a few insurance policies of the period show wash-houses among manufacturers' insured property.[87]

COMBING

Once the wool had been sorted and scoured it was ready to be combed, a process in which heated iron combs were used to draw out the fibres of the oiled wool so that it could be spun. An analysis of combers recorded in the Apprenticeship registers for the 15 years between 1750 and 1765, together with other sources, suggests that there was a much heavier concentration of combers in Bury St Edmunds and the surrounding villages than elsewhere in Suffolk.[88] Hadleigh was next in importance followed by the other old cloth-making centres of Kersey, Boxford, Lavenham, Glemsford, Nayland and Sudbury. There were also a few in

---

[82] Edwards, 'The Economic Development of Norwich', p. 168.
[83] SROB Acc 2581.
[84] Heaton, *The Yorkshire Woollen and Worsted Industries*, p. 328.
[85] SROB Copys of Inventory's HA 535 Box 10.
[86] John A. Iredale, 'Preparation of Wools', in *The Wool Textile Industry in Great Britain*, edited by J. Geraint Jenkins (1972), pp. 65–70 (p. 68); Dymond and Betterton, *Lavenham*.
[87] For example Thomas Addison a Sudbury clothier insured, among other things, his 'warehouse, woolchamber and wash-house and stable' for £60. Sun Fire Policy Register, vol.146/197225; SROB E5/11/2 Ledger of Thomas Ridley 1779–1800, shows that Cumberlands of Bury bought considerable quantities of soap.
[88] PRO Inland Revenue IR1/51.

the Gipping valley. The relative importance of these places as combing centres is confirmed by the representation on the Suffolk Yarn Committee, Bury St Edmunds having seven members while Sudbury, Lavenham, Needham Market, Bildeston and Hadleigh each had one.[89] There do not appear to have been many combers north or east of Ipswich although doubtless detailed local studies would reveal more probably combining the work with that of the village draper.

Wool combing was a highly skilled job almost always carried out by men. Oakes maintained that a comber delivered to his master approximately 33 pounds of combed wool and wastage a week and that this in turn 'provided full employ for 30 spinners including women and children' for the same period.[90] Allowing combers 45 weeks combing work during a year, the 2,571 tods of fleece wool that Oakes bought between April 1793 and April 1794 would have provided work for approximately 48 combers and 1,448 spinners.[91] This figure is probably too low because it is based on the assumption that Oakes only made the wool purchases mentioned in the diary. It is also likely that he was running his business down by this time and therefore buying less wool than in the past when yarn making was his main source of income. In June 1791 50 combers and 12 sorters and warehousemen were given a 'treat' in celebration of his eldest son's twenty third birthday and the end of his apprenticeship. The complete staff would have been entertained on such an occasion apart from those who were ill or away on business.

The combers worked in comb shops in St Andrew's Street behind Oakes's Guildhall Street house which were built at some time between 1745 and 1758 on land purchased by Orbell Ray for £52 0s. 10d. in 1745.[92] They were housed in a long narrow building, over twice the length of the Guildhall to judge from contemporary maps, with individual shops partitioned off within it. This is suggested by an entry in November 1791 which recorded that 'no 16 was broke into and robbed of 5 Dozen of Rough Wool'. Assuming that three or four men could work in one shop, the fact that Oakes had at least 16 shops at that time again suggests that he was employing between 48 and 64 wool combers. A later note in 1799 claimed that there were only 13 comb shops in the building.[93] Possibly some of them had been dismantled after Oakes opened his bank in 1794. By having all his combing done on his own premises Oakes would have saved the

[89] IJ 13 December 1783.

[90] Young, *Suffolk Agriculture*, p. 232. Oakes gave the information on the Suffolk yarn industry to Young in 1784.

[91] 2,570 tods of wool = 71,688lb. One comber produces 33lb. combed wool per week which equals 1,485lb. combed wool per year of 45 weeks. Therefore the number of combers needed to comb 71,988lb. of wool per year is 48.5.

[92] SROB Tem 141/7 Deeds deposited by Robert Boby Ltd. The land was described as being in three messuages and a tenement in 1745 and is shown as such on a map of that date. By 1758, the date of the earliest surviving rate books, the property was described as 'combing shops late Gray's Tenement' and was valued at £2 a year.

[93] Note book bound in volume IX of the diary between entries for the years 1809 and 1810.

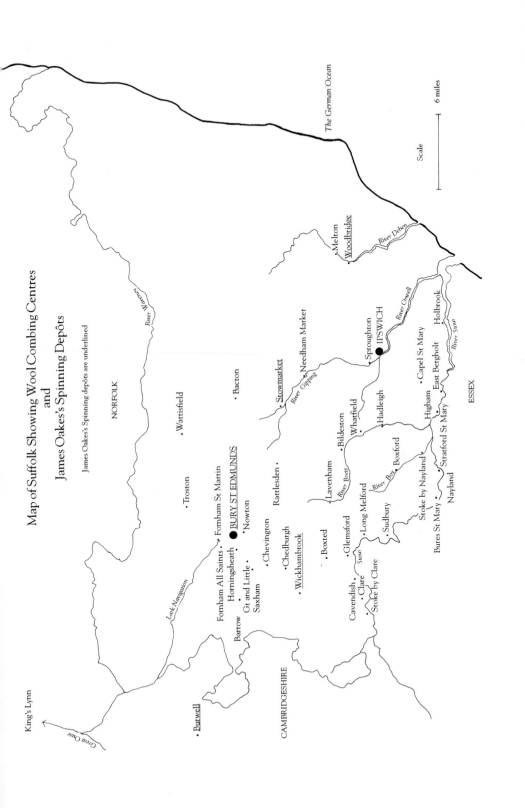

Map of Suffolk Showing Wool Combing Centres
and
James Oakes's Spinning Depôts

James Oakes's Spinning depôts are underlined

NORFOLK

CAMBRIDGESHIRE

ESSEX

King's Lynn

The German Ocean

Scale

6 miles

River Waveney

River Ouse

Great Ouse

Lark Navigation

River Gipping

River Orwell

River Deben

River Brett

River Box

River Stour

Stour

• Burwell

• Troston

• Wattisfield

• Bacton

Fornham All Saints • Fornham St Martin •
● BURY ST EDMUNDS
Horningsheath • • Nowton
Barrow • Gt and Little •
Saxham • Chevington

• Chedburgh
• Wickhambrook

• Boxted

Cavendish • • Glemsford
Clare • • Long Melford
Stoke by Clare • Sudbury

Ratlesden •

Lavenham •
• Bildeston
Wharfield • • Hadleigh

Stoke by Nayland •
Bures St Mary • Nayland •
Stratford St Mary •
East Bergholt •
Higham •

Holbrook •
• Capel St Mary

Sproughton •
IPSWICH ●

Stowmarket
• Needham Market

Melton •
Woodbridge •

cost of transporting raw wool to and from the master combers and would have avoided the risk of loss or damage inherent in the putting-out system. It would also have enabled him to supervise work, maintain good quality control and flexibilty of production.

Oakes's comb shops represent a considerable concentration of labour and capital for the pre-industrial period and they would appear to have been as unusual as were the large work shops of Spring of Lavenham and Paycocke of Coggeshall in the fifteenth and sixteenth centuries. Only one other Bury St Edmunds yarn maker, John Corsbie, had comb shops of comparable size and scope, and they were built at least 20 years later than those of Ray Oakes and Company. As far as one can tell from the evidence of insurance policies, rate books, newspaper advertisements and maps, no other Suffolk yarn maker had this elementary form of factory. Indeed it would seem to have been unusual in the country at large. In the West of England, for example, Fox of Wellington, while employing over 100 combers, put the wool out to be combed in the combers' own workshops, albeit supplying them with oil from a leaden cistern in the company's yard.[94] Although Heaton claimed that there were many preparing yarn on a large scale for the West Riding worsted industry he does not specifically say that large numbers of combers worked under one roof, but rather emphasizes the combers' relative power and independence at a period when other textile workers were increasingly submitting to factory discipline. For his part Eric Kerridge found it 'difficult to imagine how anyone in those times would have set about building a large shop to house a great number of comb pots each with its own flue and chimney'.[95]

The diary does not reveal on what basis the combers worked. Each shop could have been let to a group of three or four combers who combed wool provided by Oakes which would explain why the shops were separated from each other. In the Leicester hosiery industry there was a growing trend by the end of the eighteenth century for middlemen employers to assemble a large number of frames in one workshop and to charge the knitters rent for the frames, standing room in the shop, light, fuel and needles and then to buy the finished goods from them. Temple Patterson saw this as a transitional stage between the domestic and the factory system.[96] Regular inclusion of 'combers' debts' amounting to between £23 and £28 in the annual stocktaking statements suggests that Ray Oakes and Company's combers may have been employed on this basis by the mid 1760s.[97]

Oakes, in evidence to Arthur Young in 1784, claimed that a good comber

---

[94] Hubert Fox, *Quaker Homespun: The Life of Thomas Fox of Wellington Serge Maker and Banker* (1958), p. 14. SROB HA535 Box 10 shows payments of £111 6s. 9d. and £157 1s. 0d. in 1766 and 1767 respectively to John Nunn for tallow.

[95] Kerridge, *Textile Manufacture in Early Modern England*, p. 203.

[96] A. Temple Patterson, *Radical Leicester: The History of Leicester 1780–1850* (Leicester, 1954), p. 44.

[97] SROB HA535 Box 10.

7. *John Corsbie's, later William Buck's, house in Westgate Street.*

could earn ten shillings a week,[98] while Young himself, 13 years earlier, suggested an average comber's wage in Norwich was seven shillings.[99] This compares with 12 shillings for a full week's work which could be earned by Yorkshire combers at the end of the eighteenth century, although apparently they rarely bothered to work for a full week so that their actual wages were lower. Combers' wages varied according to the prosperity of the industry but were not subject to the same arbitrary cuts that were applied to those of spinners. When trade was bad combers, as highly skilled workers, had more industrial muscle than spinners and were able to protect their own interests. They failed to get a wage rise in 1792, just before the start of the war, but were given a rise in May 1795 in spite of the fact that the Suffolk yarn industry was far from healthy.[100]

Oakes makes no mention of the equipment used in combing. Craftsmen generally provided their own tools and so combers probably provided their own combs and the discs through which the sliver of wool was drawn off the comb. The comb pots were a different matter being small fixed stoves made of iron or brick on which the combs were heated prior to combing. They were fuelled either by charcoal or by coal and therefore needed a chimney. The combs were put to heat on an iron plate on top of the 'pot', while the fuel was put in through

---

[98] Young, *Suffolk Agriculture*, p. 232.
[99] Young, *A Farmer's Tour*, p. 75.
[100] Diary 1, 6 November 1792, 30 May, 1 June 1795.

a door at the base and the draught was controlled by an opening to the chimney on the opposite side. Up to four men could use one pot.[101]

Although Ray Oakes had clearly used charcoal to fuel their comb pots 30 years earlier[102] it seems likely that by the last quarter of the century coal was the preferred fuel. Bury St Edmunds was supplied with coal from the North Eastern coal fields via Kings Lynn and the Lark Navigation. The existing toll book, which starts in 1780, shows that Oakes imported regular quantities from at least 1781 and that other Bury firms later began to do the same: Messrs Cumberland and Corsbie in 1784 and Messrs Harmers in 1786.[103] An advertisement in the *Ipswich Journal* in 1769 placed by a John Beets, undertaking to build comb pots fired by sea coal, suggests that it was being used for combing in Bury St Edmunds by that date.[104]

Probably in order to make the most of bulk purchases Oakes began to combine his yarn business with that of coal dealer, appearing in a list of Bury St Edmunds coal merchants in 1788[105] and supplying the Cullum family with coal on a regular basis.[106] The diary and the toll book show that he continued to carry on this business long after he had left the yarn industry. Thomas Harmer, a Bury yarn maker, also became a coal merchant and it was not unknown for the Norwich manufacturers to diversify in this way.[107]

The import of coal via the Lark Navigation was not without problems. The Navigation was owned by the Palmer family and was in a poor state of repair. In 1797 the coal merchants of Bury actually thought of buying it from Palmer's widow but decided against this because the asking price was too high. They contented themselves with appointing a committee to visit Mrs Palmer to make clear to her 'the sad Condition of her Navigation & the absolute Necessity for an Engineer to be appointed to examine & advise what was to be done'.[108] There can have been little response to their representations as during a drought in November 1802 the Navigation was so short of water that no coal could be obtained from Kings Lynn except 'at the enormous prize from 18/– to 21/–' with the result that all the coal yards were empty.[109]

There were other problems with coal supplies. A scheme involving seven Bury coal merchants, including Oakes, to buy coal at Thetford was a failure and

[101] Hugo Lemon, 'The Evolution of Combing', in *The Wool Textile Industry of Great Britain*, edited by J. Geraint Jenkins (1972), pp. 85–100 (pp. 87–88).
[102] SROB HA535 Box 10 shows a payment in 1765 to John Stedman for £7 9s. 0d. for charcoal.
[103] SROB E2/17/7.
[104] IJ 11 March 1769.
[105] BNP 11 June 1788.
[106] SROB E2/29/5.
[107] Edwards, 'The Economic Development of Norwich', p. 47.
[108] Diary 3 February 1797.
[109] Diary 20 November 1802.

ended up with the participants loosing £3 12s. 0d. each on the deal.[110] Coals were not always of good quality when they arrived and Ray Oakes had on occasion 'much complaint of . . . coals running so very small'.[111] Oakes gives no information on how he obtained coal from Kings Lynn. His wife's family lived at Wereham and while visiting them he often went to meet the Everards who were merchants of importance in Lynn. Perhaps he obtained his supplies through them.

SPINNING

The difficulties encountered in the management of wool and coal supplies paled into insignificance beside the problem of organizing spinning networks. While combing was concentrated in the old centres of cloth production, spinning was carried on throughout the county by women and girls as a by-industry with agriculture. Combed wool was distributed by packmen employed by the yarn maker to putters-out in the villages who gave it to the spinners in parcels of nine and eleven pounds each.[112] The spinners returned the spun yarn to the putters-out from whom it was collected and returned to the merchant. Collection and payment were undertaken by the packmen.

Given Oakes's own estimate of one comber providing full employment for 30 spinners, he must have employed at least 1,500 spinners.[113] There were probably three or four firms of comparable size in Bury St Edmunds and possibly one or two elsewhere in the county. This, together with the marked concentration of yarn makers and master combers in Bury and the surrounding villages, would have been enough to force the town's yarn makers to look further afield for spinners. It is therefore not entirely surprising to find that the spinning networks of the larger Bury firms, including Ray Oakes and Company, were widespread. Both Wadsworth and Mann and Heaton describe how expansion forced Lancashire cotton and linen manufacturers and West Riding wool and worsted manufacturers to put their spinning out over an ever widening area as competition for spinners grew.[114] Some of the largest West Riding worsted clothiers put spinning out over 40 miles away: one Otley clothier in Cheshire and North Derbyshire and a Halifax manufacturer in the Craven District, North Riding and Lancashire.[115] The diary and other evidence suggest that Oakes's spinning network stretched from Burwell in Cambridgeshire to the West and to the coast to the

---

[110] Diary 3 February 1797.
[111] SROB Acc 2191, Notes made from a letter book of the Bury New Bank.
[112] Edwards, 'The Economic Development of Norwich', pp. 29, 36.
[113] Young, Suffolk Agriculture, p. 232.
[114] Wadsworth and Mann, The Cotton Trade and Industrial Lancashire, p. 415; Heaton, The Yorkshire Woollen and Worsted Industries, p. 297.
[115] Heaton, The Yorkshire Woollen and Worsted Industries, p. 335.

East, a distance of about 60 miles, and from North West Essex to the South and the parishes of High Suffolk to the North.

Oakes and three other Bury St Edmunds yarn makers had what can only be described as branch offices or depots in Woodbridge. Oakes owned property in New Street, Messrs Cumberlands in the Market Place and Messrs Harmers in Well Street, later moving to Pound Street in 1788.[116] It is not possible to discover when this arrangement began from the existing rate books but stocktaking accounts show that Ambrose Taylor, Oakes's Woodbridge agent, was being paid wages, rent and town charges as early as 1765[117] while a notice in the *Ipswich Journal* suggests that Cumberlands were operating in the area three years later.[118] At some time before 1780 Oakes expanded his Woodbridge business and began to supply the Melton House of Industry with combed wool. Messrs Harmers were still operating in the area in 1793 when the death of their agent was reported in the *Bury and Norwich Post*.[119]

Early accounts show that one other man besides Taylor was paid rent, town charges and wages in 1765 and 2 others in 1766 and 1767 which suggests that there were branches elsewhere.[120] Oakes owned property in Stowmarket, although no rate books survive to show when it was acquired or where it was.[121] This property could have been used in the same way as that at Woodbridge, to service the spinners in the Union workhouses at Onehouse near Stowmarket and at Barham between Stowmarket and Ipswich. Spinning worsted yarn for the Norwich industry was carried out in both these houses but the existing records fail to show how it was organized or by whom. He was also taxed on the ownership of horses, waggons and carts in three places besides Bury and Woodbridge: Burwell, Bacton and Wickhambrook.[122] If Woodbridge was at the centre of the East Suffolk operation, Bacton, almost exactly in the middle of Suffolk, would have been well placed to control the parishes of High Suffolk. Wickhambrook could have been used to control South West Suffolk and North West Essex, if competition with Stour Valley combers and weavers permitted, while West Cambridge and North West Suffolk could be organized from Burwell. Oakes owned a farm at Wickhambrook inherited from his mother. It is not possible from the available evidence to tell whether he owned property in either Burwell or Bacton. The diary also gives the impression that one of the carts went

[116] SROI Woodbridge Church Rate 1784–1790 FC25/F2/1.
[117] SROB HA535 Box 10.
[118] IJ 12 March 1768. The notice announced that a bag and a letter addressed to Messrs Cumberlands had been lost out of the wool cart between Bury and Woodbridge and asked the finder to contact Messrs Cumberland and Carlisle at Bury or their agent in Woodbridge Stephen Haywood. The letter was addressed to a Bedford firm of wool merchants.
[119] BNP 12 June 1793.
[120] SROB HA535 Box 10.
[121] Diary 16 October 1798.
[122] SROB Window Taxes 1778–1801 D17/1/1.

regularly to the county town, suggesting that Ipswich was a collecting point for yarn spun in that area.

Oakes ran his spinning network with the assistance of his manager Peter Chambers and with local agents. When the diary begins Ambrose Taylor was still operating from Woodbridge; followed, in 1787, by Thomas Scott.[123] J. Hills was the Burwell agent.[124] At most Christmas and stock-taking parties, besides the sorters and warehousemen, there were usually four or five other men referred to by name including Scott and Taylor the Woodbridge agents and various members of the Hill family. It is highly likely that these men were in charge of Oakes's other spinning divisions. One of them, Isaac Smith, was robbed of gold and silver 'entrusted' to him by Oakes in May 1789, probably the money with which to pay the spinners and putters-out in his division. One of Oakes's combers was later charged with the offence.[125]

Oakes never specifically mentions his pack-men. His warehousemen and sorters may have undertaken to deliver wool and to collect yarn in Bury and the neighbouring villages as this seems to have been common practice. An advertisement in the *Ipswich Journal* required a man both to sort wool and to ride to the spinners for a Norwich yarn maker,[126] while the packman employed by the Melton House of Industry organized the whole spinning operation within the House as well as distributing combed wool to the out-poor in the Wilford Union parishes.[127] Putters-out were usually local shopkeepers or publicans.

The organization required to put wool out to be spun over such a wide area was complex and fraught with frustration. Apart from the risk of agents being robbed, the quality of yarn spun was variable, much wool and yarn was embezzled by workers or stolen in transit and competition for spinners was keen. Maintaining the quality of yarn and preventing frauds among spinners had long been a major problem for yarn makers. Indeed some writers have felt that it was crucial in preventing the full exploitation of available markets in the years between the American and the French wars. Losses through false and short reeling exacerbated the existing shortage of spun yarn, and formed a 'powerful reason for the rapid acceptance of spinning machinery' which not only reduced basic production costs but also elimated much of the loss suffered through crime.[128]

Oakes never mentioned having any difficulties in maintaining adequate quality-control over his yarn spinning. Once again this could be a reflection of the scrappy nature of the diary at this period or could show that the problem was taken for granted as part of the 'anxious and laborious occupation' of an eight-

---

[123] Diary 24 October 1783 and 17 December 1787 for example.
[124] Diary 21 September 1793.
[125] Diary 2 July 1789.
[126] IJ 15 November 1741.
[127] SROI Draft Quarterly Minute Book 1776–85 ADA11/AB2/4.
[128] Edwards, 'The Economic Development of Norwich', pp. 131–32.

eenth century yarn maker.[129] It would seem improbable that Oakes was unaffected and he played an active part in trying to improve the quality of Suffolk yarn and in seeking an act of Parliament to that end.

The quality of yarn had been a constant bone of contention between the Norwich manufacturers and the Suffolk yarn producers since the seventeenth century. An order in Council giving the Norwich weavers the power of search and forfeiture was regranted in 1662. This aggravated the situation and led to further disputes because the Norwich weavers were seen to be acting as both judge and jury in their own cause by the Suffolk producers. The Suffolk wool combers asked to be incorporated but no action was taken other than to condemn malpractices on the part of the weavers.[130] Attempts were made to improve quality control under the existing Acts of Parliament, nearly always in response to threats from the Norwich manufacturers. Following a notice from them in July 1768 stating that no false or short-reeled yarn would be accepted in Norwich after 29 September 1768, yarn makers held meetings in Hadleigh, Bildeston, Bury and in Essex afterwards placing notices in the newspapers warning recalcitrant spinners that they would be prosecuted 'to the utmost Extent of the Law'. Takers-in were ordered to insert the spinner's name in every pound of yarn that they spun so that they could be traced and held accountable for any faults.[131] In practice there were few prosecutions because the yarn makers were 'unwilling to expose themselves singly to the Loss attending the Resentment of the Spinners and work People by prosecuting them'.[132] Matters did not improve and in October 1779 the Norwich manufacturers declared that from 1 January 1780 they would accept 'warrented yarn' only and that deficient yarn would be cut up and returned to the seller.[133] This threat had more effect than previous ones and 12 Bury and district yarn makers, headed by Ray Oakes and Company, appointed John Merrills to inspect yarn made 'at our several and respective spinning houses in Cambridgeshire and that part of Suffolk adjoining'.[134]

In spite of Merrills's appointment there was little improvement, probably because of the yarn makers' unwillingness to prosecute wayward spinners and risk individual unpopularity. The Norwich manufacturers therefore took further action. They held a general meeting in November 1783 at which it was resolved that statutory force must be given to attempts to improve the quality of Suffolk yarn. They suggested that a bill before Parliament to prevent abuses in the industry in the Midlands should be extended to include Suffolk.[135] A general meeting of Suffolk yarn makers, under the chairmanship of James Oakes, was

---

[129] John James, *The History of the Worsted Manufacture in England* (1968), p. 311, quoting Henry Hall a Leeds manufacturer.
[130] Unwin, VCH, II, p. 268.
[131] IJ 13 August 1768.
[132] 24 Geo III c3.
[133] IJ 14 August 1779.
[134] IJ 17 November 1779.
[135] IJ 20 December 1783.

held at Stowmarket on 9 December 1783 with between 50 and 60 men present, at which it was resolved to petition Parliament for an act modelled on the 1776 Act governing the Yorkshire, Lancashire and Cheshire industries.[136] A representative committee was set up, composed of seven yarn makers from Bury St Edmunds: Oakes, John Cumberland, William Buck, Thomas Harmer, Thomas Rutter, Thomas Umfreville and William Johnson and one each from Sudbury, Lavenham, Needham Market, Bildeston and Hadleigh.

Oakes took an active part in promoting the legislation attending committee meetings in Bury and rushing to London with William Buck to help draft the bill and appear before committees of both Houses.[137] Unfortunately, neither the Lords nor the Commons Journals give more than a brief mention of the bill's progress. It passed early in July and its main clauses were published in the Ipswich and Bury papers. The Act stipulated that a general meeting of yarn makers was to elect a chairman and a committee which would meet quarterly and was to recommend 'such Inspectors for such Districts in the County of Suffolk as the said Committee . . . shall think proper' to be appointed by magistrates at the next Quarter Sessions.[138] Details of reels to be used and lengths to be reeled plus penalties for default were also explained. The cost of prosecution was to be met by a drawback of four pence in the shilling on the duty on soap used in the wool trade. The Act gave inspectors and masters the power to enter the homes, shops or outhouses of employees solely on suspicion of a crime having been committed. Wadsworth and Mann pointed out that had it been possible to enforce the provisions of the Act fully it 'would have imposed a discipline not far removed from that of the factory' on domestic out-workers.[139]

The first quarterly yarn committee met on 28 July 1784 at the *Wool Pack* under the chairmanship of Simon Maw with William Plumb, a Bury wool comber, as clerk. Seven of the 13 who attended this meeting were Bury yarn makers: Oakes, Buck, Barnard, Maling, Humm and Umfreville.[140] The general meeting was held at Stowmarket with William Buck in the chair and Mr Collett, the Clerk of the Peace, in attendance.[141] Oakes was elected a member of the county committee and attended the first meeting on 23 September when 14 out of the 15 members were present. Prospective inspectors were interviewed, the members of the committee looking for men of honesty, sobriety, industry and a thorough knowledge of the industry. Thomas Rand, William Prentice, Benjamin Downs and William Towler were chosen.[142]

Oakes makes no mention of the working of the Act beyond recording regular yarn committee meetings, some lasting the better part of a day. On 15 November

[136] IJ 20 December 1783; diary 9 December 1783.
[137] Diary 16 December 1783, 17, 28 June 1784.
[138] Diary 28 June 1784; Geo III c3.
[139] Wadsworth and Mann, *The Cotton Trade and Industrial Lancashire*, p. 395.
[140] IJ 29 July 1784.
[141] Diary 9 August 1784.
[142] IJ 21 August 1784.

1784 he 'passd the whole Day at [the] *Wool Pack* attending [the] Yarn Committee. Both din'd and supp'd there —— did not get Home till one o'clock ys morning' and in December the nine men present did not finish their business until midnight. How much this was the result of pressure of work and how much the hospitality offered by the *Wool Pack* is not clear. Alleged offenders against the Act were summarily tried and lists of prosecutions were published in the local papers as a deterrent. They show that the Act was severely enforced at first. Over 500 cases were reported between October 1784 and the end of 1785. There were three times as many in East Suffolk as in West, possibly as a result of the difficulties in providing adequate supervision so far away from Bury. After the first year the number of cases reported declined rapidly as the yarn makers' enthusiasm waned.

The diary gives no evidence of the spinners' reaction to the 1784 Act. Two fires were reported on woolcombers' premises in December. One was in a warehouse in Glemsford belonging to Mr Watson, which was thought to have been started deliberately, various 'combustibles' having been found on the site. The other, in the workshop of Mr Galbraith, in the parish of St Mary Elms in Ipswich, was potentially more dangerous because '19 casks of cartridges with ball' were stored above the workshop by the East Suffolk Militia. Luckily the fire was quickly contained and little damage done. The cartridges were removed to Landguard Fort.[143] Although there is no evidence to link these fires directly with the implementation of the 1784 Act it is a coincidence that the first two reports of fires on wool combers' premises noted in the *Ipswich Journal* during the period should appear so soon after it was put into effect.

Apart from the problems of short and false reeling there were other difficulties associated with the management of such a widespread spinning network. In 1793 Oakes's Burwell manager was either incompetent or deliberately defrauding him. Chambers discovered that over £53 had been 'chargd to Putters-out beyond what they really stand – bad indeed' when he went to check on the Burwell operation in September.[144] Some of the other problems that could beset an eighteenth century yarn maker are well illustrated by Oakes's experiences with his Woodbridge division.

Oakes supplied the Melton House of Industry to the north of Woodbridge with combed wool which was spun in the House and collected and paid for by his agent. During the severe depression of 1780 the directors and guardians of the Melton House decided that profits from spinning were so low that they would dispense with Oakes's services and run their own operation employing the out poor in the Union parishes as well as the inmates of the House. A wool comber was engaged as packman to run the business, combed wool was to be bought from a Nayland factor and the spun yarn delivered to Norwich by the Melton carrier,

---

[143] IJ 4, 24 December 1784; diary 8 January 1785.
[144] Diary 21 September 1793.

where it was to be sold on commission by a Norwich factor. The scheme was a disaster and abandoned after two years.[145]

In spite of the fact that Oakes had what must have been a considerable part of his Woodbridge spinning network disrupted by the directors' and guardians' action, and despite the fact that the governor was discovered to have been embezzling wool supplied by Oakes two years before and selling it through an Ipswich merchant,[146] Oakes, together with two other Bury firms, tendered to supply the House with combed wool as before.[147] Indeed Oakes seemed so anxious to secure the contract that he wrote immediately pressing his claim and entertained Mr Revett, one of the directors, to dinner at the Stowmarket *White Horse*.[148] His efforts were all in vain and the contract went to Messrs Cumberlands of Bury with Messrs Harmers coming second in the ballot and Ray Oakes and Company a poor third.[149] Perhaps Oakes's proposals drove too hard a bargain, or possibly the directors and guardians felt that their previous association had not been entirely successful.

The failure of the directors and guardians of the Melton House with their captive labour force demonstrates that great skill and knowlege were needed to make a success of yarn manufacture. The episode also illustrates some of the problems with which a manufacturer had to contend in his business life. Through the guardians' decision Oakes lost not only the spinners in the House itself but those living in the Wilford and Loes Union parishes receiving out-relief. Secondly the episode highlights the difficulties involved in supervising such a widespread organization and preventing frauds and abuses. Thirdly it underlines the dominance of Bury merchants over the Suffolk industry and demonstrates the resultant competition between them for adequate supplies of spinners which forced them to have extensive spinning networks. No Ipswich merchants operated in Woodbridge or tendered for the Melton House spinning although they would have been so much nearer and incurred lower transport costs. The only Ipswich merchant mentioned in the minutes of the Melton House was Mr Maw and it is significant that he is supposed to have bought the stocks of combed wool from the governor, suggesting that he had little to do with putting out in the area. Had he been involved it would have been a risk to sell him stolen wool or to claim that he had bought it.

Oakes's energetic efforts to recover the Melton House contract has parallels in some other union workhouses in Suffolk. For example, there was vigorous competition among Norwich combers to supply the Wangford and Blything Houses in the north of the county[150] Workhouses provided a form of elementary factory

145 SROI ADA11/AB2/4.
146 Ibid.
147 Ibid.
148 Diary 21 July 1783.
149 SROI ADA11/AB2/4.
150 SROI Wangford Weekly Minutes, ADA9/AB1/1; Blything Minutes, ADA1/AB3/1.

organization where, as Wadsworth and Mann bracingly expressed it, 'the idea of labour discipline within the shop' was fully grasped.[151] Greater supervision was possible than under the domestic system and costs were lower. There would also have been increased flexibility of production in that spinners could be quickly and easily organized to spin different qualities of yarn as the market demanded. A large proportion of the inmates of the Melton House at this time were children, who would have been cheaper to employ and easier to discipline and to train than adults. Contemporary writers were constantly concerned about poor standards of spinning, the need for good teaching and the importance of workhouses and industrial schools in providing this.[152]

There were no incorporated union workhouses in west Suffolk or in Cambridgeshire but Oakes used village poor houses and had a monopoly of the spinning done in the charity school in Bury where spinning was undertaken by boys under the supervision of a spinning master, as well as by girls.[153] Although the inmates of the Bury St Edmunds workhouse had been employed in yarn spinning since its its inception in 1748 no details of the terms under which they worked survive until 1787. In that year the guardians invited the yarn makers of the town to tender for the spinning in the House, pointing out that they could provide large quantities of high quality yarn which would also be very cheap to collect. After six months 'by Reason of a Combination of the Yarnmakers no individual offer' had been received and the guardians decided to manage their own spinning business under the supervision of a comber. This lasted eight years until 1794 when a local yarn maker finally took over.[154] Bury yarn makers must have felt that they would all forego the spinning in the Bury House rather than lose all the cost advantage by out-bidding each other for such a convenient supplier.

Certainly Wadsworth and Mann saw workhouses as 'a tentative approach' towards industrial capitalism and gave an example of early spinning machines being invented specifically for use in Lancashire workhouses while Heaton found the adoption of machinery more general in West Riding workhouses than elsewhere.[155] In 1782 Mr Herring, a Norwich comber, suggested that the Wangford House use his spinning machine which, he claimed, had been accepted by the directors and guardians of the Heckingham House in Norfolk[156] while, in 1766, the first governor of the Blything House was advanced £10 towards making a machine to employ 20 people 'according to his own design'.[157] No more is heard

[151] Wadsworth and Mann, The Cotton Trade and Industrial Lancashire, p. 108; see also Heaton, p. 355.
[152] Wadsworth and Mann, p. 415; Heaton, p. 297.
[153] BL B545, pp. 448–49; SROB St Mary's Parish Charity School Records FL545/12/3.
[154] SROB N5/1/2.
[155] Wadsworth and Mann, The Cotton Trade and Industrial Lancashire, pp. 108, 414; Heaton, The Yorkshire Woollen and Worsted Industries, p. 356, n.1.
[156] SROI Wangford Union Minutes ADA9/AB1/11.
[157] SROI Blything Union Minutes ADA/AB3/1.

of either plan and it would appear from the available evidence that the bulk of spinning done in both union and parish workhouses was done on wheels rather than with distaff and spindle. Spinning jennies were not introduced into Suffolk until the early nineteenth century.

Spinners were paid on a piece-work basis according to the fineness of yarn produced. Oakes stated in 1784 that spinners earned on average about three pence a day for 11 months a year with one month off to help with the harvest.[158] Others maintained that a good spinner could earn five pence a day and children and moderate spinners not more than one or two pennies.[159] According to the Reverend Mr White of Chevington, Oakes paid one penny less per shilling reel than other combers in the district although White did concede that 'he has no more profit than others because his tops cost him more; neither do his spinners earn less than others because his tops of the same denomination are of better quality.'[160]

Spinners' rates of pay were subject to fluctuations according to the prosperity of the trade. Putters-out arbitrarily docked money from their wages in times of slack demand. 'Considerable' reductions were made in spinners' wages in January 1793 and again in March of that year in response to the violent contraction of trade caused by the onset of the French Wars.[161] When criticized for exploiting spinners the yarn makers and combers claimed that spinning rates were raised in times of good trade and were kept up as a result of keen competition among masters for spinners.[162] Indeed evidence from the Wangford Union House of Industry shows that John Herring, the Norwich comber, raised as well lowered the rates which he paid for the spinning done in for him in the House according to the state of the market.[163]

However it would appear that Suffolk spinners' rates of pay were decided once a year at a meeting of yarn makers at Mr Mathew's wool hall so that the manufacturers' claim that free competition among them for spinners kept wages up was less than the truth. The only time that Oakes recorded raising spinners' wages was in response to competition for spinners from Norfolk combers in High Suffolk.[164]

Considerable amounts of capital and organizing ability must have been needed to support Ray Oakes and Company's wide-spread spinning network and to finance such large-scale wool purchases. The high cost of management limited the spinning networks of Essex manufacturers to between 20 and 30 miles

[158] Young, *Suffolk Agriculture*, p. 232.
[159] BL B545, p. 289.
[160] *Ibid.*, pp. 448–49.
[161] Diary 16 January 1793; 13 March 1793.
[162] IJ 12 January 1788.
[163] SROI ADA9/AB1/10, 11, wages were raised 8 January 1783 and 14 December 1791, for example, and were lowered on 9 January 1792 and 12 December 1792.
[164] Diary 15 November 1792.

diameter[165] and a Lancashire linen draper, employing 2,400 spinners, used high management costs as an excuse to reduce spinners' wages in the 1740s.[166] The spinning network of Ray Oakes and Company was larger than those of the Essex manufacturers covering an area about 60 miles across.

The firm must have been large before Oakes joined it in 1757. His grandfather, Orbell Ray senior, had insured his household goods and stock in trade for £500 in 1730 while in 1742 his uncle, Orbell Ray junior, insured his trade premises and stock for £600 and his house for £400.[167] These were sizeable valuations to find in a provincial town in the early eighteenth century particularly when one considers that property was usually grossly undervalued for insurance purposes at this period.[168] Unfortunately no policy has survived for Ray Oakes and Company. The only accounts in existence are copies of the annual stocktaking statements for the years 1764 to 1767.[169] These show that the company had a total capital value of between twenty and twenty one thousand pounds and made an annual net profit of over £1,650. Apart from the money invested in wool and in unsold yarn it had between two and three hundred pounds invested in 'Utensils, Fixtures & Appurtances' and between £768 and £1,103 in cash in Scotchmer's Bank. Orbell Ray's share of the capital value varied over the period from between £16,000 in 1764, £19,600 in 1765 and £16,800 in 1767. At the same time James Oakes was building up his stake in the business. His share of the capital had risen from £3,000 in 1764 to £4,200 by 1767. In addition he was paying four per cent interest on over £6,000 which Orbell Ray 'has advanc'd for ye present Capitol more than the said James Oakes'. Other members of the family had money in the firm. Garnham Ray, Orbell Ray's brother, lent £500 at four per cent and Susan Oakes, James Oakes's mother, £800 at four per cent in 1767. Both Orbell Ray and James Oakes took out an annual income of between £400 and £575, a considerable sum for the mid eighteenth century, although not quite the profits estimated by Arthur Young.[170] The remaining profits were ploughed back into the company.

Some of the other leading Bury yarn makers were similarly wealthy men. In 1738 Samuel Cumberland had insured property, held jointly with his partner, of £1,500.[171] Over fifty years later in 1809 his nephew, Simon Cumberland, in

[165] K. H. Burley, 'The Economic Development of Essex in the Later Seventeenth and early Eighteenth Centuries', (unpublished Ph.D. thesis, University of London, 1957), p. 112.

[166] Wadsworth and Mann, The Cotton Trade and Industrial Lancashire, p. 274.

[167] Sun Fire, vols 31, 61.

[168] Stanley D. Chapman, 'Fixed Capital Formation in the British Cotton Industry 1770–1815', Economic History Review, 2nd series, 23 (1970), 235–66 (p. 238).

[169] SROB HA535 Box 10.

[170] In 1788 Arthur Young estimated that a yarn maker could make a return on capital of 40% but that profit could be increased in proportion to the credit given to customers. See BL 545. Sennex remembered yarn makers earning between £500 and £2,000 a year. See East Anglian 7 February 1832.

[171] Sun Fire, vol. 50, 4 January 1738.

partnership with his brother John in a yarn company, died leaving the enormous sum of £200,000.[172] William Johnson, variously described as a wool stapler and comber of Risbygate Street, was able to spend £9,500 on a farm at the end of the eighteenth century[173] while advertisements suggest that a medium size yarn business required at least £1,000 working capital in addition to the purchase price.[174]

Oakes calculated that there were 120 yarn makers of 'all degrees' in Suffolk employing 1,200 journeymen wool-combers and 36,000 spinners.[175] That is 17.4 per cent of the total population of Suffolk.[176] This means that Oakes was employing roughly five times the average number of combers and spinners and about four per cent of the total labour force involved in the Suffolk industry. His organization seems to have had more in common with the larger manufacturers of the West Country and Lancashire. Indeed it is not without interest that Oakes's cousins were manufacturers and dyers in Manchester and that his sisters were married to well-to-do Liverpool merchants so that opportunities to study and to discuss Lancashire business techniques would have been plentiful during frequent visits. William Buck, a partner in the only other Bury firm to have large comb shops, came from the West Riding so that he would have been keenly aware of developments in the fast-growing Yorkshire industry.

The evidence suggests that in Suffolk as elsewhere[177] many of the smaller master wool-combers were being pushed out as larger amounts of capital were required to finance ever widening spinning networks in the face of fierce competition for spinners. Norfolk combers controlled the spinning in the north east corner of the county beyond the Blyth and were encroaching upon Suffolk territory still further.[178] In 1792 Suffolk combers were forced to raise spinners' wages in East Suffolk in the face of competition from Norfolk combers in High Suffolk[179] and in 1794 Oakes actually sold his Woodbridge operation to a Norwich comber.[180] Indeed in 1759 a Norwich comber was even dealing as far south as Nacton to the south east of Ipswich.[181] A correspondent, writing to the *Ipswich Journal* in 1788, spoke of the 'unceasing competition of so many rivals in the same business' keeping spinning wages up in Suffolk.[182] Perhaps this regional competition would have squeezed Suffolk yarn makers out altogether, as it had

[172] Diary 16 February 1809; Alfred Harwood, *The Harwood Family* (published privately, 1933). Cumberland Street in Woodbridge is named after him. See W. G. Arnott, *The Place Names of the Deben Valley Parishes* (Ipswich, 1946), p. 24.
[173] SROB Cullum Commonplace Book, 317/1; BBD 1784.
[174] BNP 31 August 1796.
[175] Young, *Suffolk Agriculture*, p. 232.
[176] The population of Suffolk was estimated at 214,404 in 1801.
[177] Stanley D. Chapman, 'The Textile Factory Before Arkwright: A Typology of Factory Development', *Business History Review*, 48 (1974), 451–78 (p. 457).
[178] SROI ADA9/AB1/1; ADA1/AB3/1.
[179] Diary 15 November 1792.
[180] Diary 14–17 September 1794.
[181] SROI Colneis and Carlford Union Accounts 1758–64, ADA10/AC1/1.
[182] IJ 12 January 1788.

done most of the Suffolk weavers in the seventeenth century, had not other problems killed the Suffolk industry first.

Competition for spinners was seen as a problem by contemporaries and caused control of the industry to become concentrated in fewer hands with a consequent rise in the number of dependent journeymen combers. This trend may have been stimulated by the expansion of trade in the 1750s and 1760s, during what Arthur Young described as Norwich's 'famous aera'. It was during this period that Ray Oakes built their comb shops and the first evidence of yarn makers from Bury extending their spinning networks to the eastern edge of the county are found. At the same time the title *yarn maker* or *yarn merchant* began to appear rather than that of *wool comber* or *clothier* denoting the emergence of larger and more specialized undertakings.

YARN MARKETING

The Norwich worsted industry was the main outlet for Suffolk yarn. Oakes estimated that 3,397 packs were sent there annually, produced by just under 50% of those involved in the Suffolk industry.[183] Meanwhile the records of those union workhouses in which yarn was made show that their total output was used by Norwich manufacturers.

The bulk of the yarn produced by Ray Oakes was sent to Norwich. The firm specialized in making very fine yarn for use in the manufacture of camlets which were exported by the East India Company. This was a market which the Norwich trade had begun to develop in the 1780s and the diary contains many anxious notes commenting on whether or not the East India orders had arrived so that yarn sales would begin.[184] Oakes and his manager Peter Chambers were in charge of yarn marketing and both visited Norwich at least once a month, often twice, to sell directly to the City's leading manufacturers. The fact that Oakes was a close personal friend of so many of them, the Pattesons, Harveys, Herrings, Hudsons, Days and Partridges must have facilitated their sales enormously.

Existing Gurney ledgers show that between June 1781 and February 1783, a very slack period for trade, Ray Oakes sold yarn to the value of £1,372 4s. 0d. to Addey and Herring, over £350 worth to Richard and Starling Day and over £300 to Patteson and Iselin, a total of just over £2,043.[185] The same ledgers reveal that Cumberlands of Bury sold £1,150 worth of yarn in Norwich, Harmers over £1,130, Umfreville £1,231, Rutters £120 10s. 0d., Buck over £47 worth and Maling £25 over the same period. These figures are likely to represent a fraction of yarn sold by Bury companies in Norwich because they include only those

[183] Young, *Suffolk Agriculture*, pp. 232–33.
[184] *East Anglian* 6 March 1832. *Sennex* gives a good description of precisely how the East India orders were priced and organized by the Norwich manufacturers.
[185] Gurney Ledger I, kept at Barclay's Bank, Bank Plain, Norwich. I am much indebted to the Directors of Barclay's Bank for allowing me to use these ledgers.

8. *Peter Chambers' house in Guildhall Street, Bury.*

manufacturers who had accounts with Gurney's Bank. Had the records of the other Norwich banks survived a more complete picture would have emerged.

Yarn surplus to the requirements of the Norwich industry was sold to the Spittlefields weavers, to the tammie producers of Coventry, to the moreen, damask and bombazine producers of Kidderminster, and to manufacturers in the West Riding and in Lancashire. Oakes visited Spittlefields on his regular visits to London and Peter Chambers, sometimes accompanied by Bailey the clerk and later by Orbell Oakes, made three-week excursions to the Midlands and to the North West once or twice a year. The yarn was sold by sample as Oakes makes no mention of packhorses in his accounts of travelling expenses. Buying by sample

45

direct from the manufacturer was a growing trend in the West Riding at this period.[186]

The diary gives no information which throws light on how yarn was transported to the company's more distant customers. It could have been sent by road, using one of Bury's many carriers, or possibly by the Lark Navigation through to the Ouse, or by coast from Ipswich. Burley noticed that although no yarn was sent from Ipswich in the later seventeenth century, by the early eighteenth century considerable quantities were being handled which he thought suggested either the development of a large spinning industry in the town or that it was becoming a collection centre for yarn spun in East Suffolk. The evidence does not support the presence of a large Ipswich industry. Oakes's grandfather had exported wool and yarn from Ipswich in 1729[187] and Peter Chambers made regular visits to the town, so that it possible that Ray Oakes and Company sent yarn from there. Unfortunately the relevant Port Books have not survived.

LABOUR RELATIONS

Oakes directly employed between five and seven wool sorters with three or four warehousemen to help them and about 50 wool combers. These trades were highly skilled and required long apprenticeships. Ray Oakes's apprentices came in the main from the Charity Schools in the town. Between 1773 and 1786 the company took 17 boys from the school, four times as many as any of the other Bury yarn makers. Possibly Oakes position as a governor and a benefactor of the school and one of the few Anglican yarn makers placed an obligation on him to take his apprentices from this source. He charged a premium of four pounds and the apprenticeship lasted for seven years. Some of the boys were apprenticed to 'learn to comb' while others were probably trainee sorters and warehousemen as their names appear later in lists of workers entertained at stock-taking hawkeys and at Christmas.[188]

There were two levels of apprenticeship in the yarn industry. Those which presaged entry to the trade as journeymen woolsorters or combers for which a fairly small premium was asked and a period of seven years apprenticeship required, and those which provided management training for which premiums of between £50 and £80 or more were sought. These latter apprenticeships varied in time from four to seven years.[189] Orbell Oakes, James Oakes's eldest son, was

[186] Heaton, *The Yorkshire Woollen and Worsted Industries*, p. 299.
[187] PRO KRE190/636/2. Norman Scarfe has kindly sent me his transcription of Maximilien de Lazowski's letters describing the Norwich industry in 1784 in which he says that the spun yarn was imported through Yarmouth 'chiefly from Suffolk'. This would also suggest that yarn was being shipped from Ipswich.
[188] SROB FL545/12/3.
[189] PRO IR1/51, 54, 55.

apprenticed to his father at 16 for seven years while Oakes himself only served four.[190] Edward Brand, who was still serving his apprenticeship when Oakes gave up yarn manufacture in 1795, could have been taken on to replace Peter Chambers when he retired. He was not a Charity School boy and is not mentioned in lists of sorters and warehousemen. He left to continue his apprenticeship with his father.[191]

There is no evidence which throws light on the terms and conditions of apprenticeship and none of Oakes's workers lived on the premises except during the annual stocktaking in September when the warehousemen and sorters stayed in his house.[192]

Some early manufacturers had difficulty in pursuading workers to leave the 'fragile freedom' of their villages and their own workshops and to come and work in their factories and used apprenticeship to build up a homogeneous labour force.[193] Others helped with moving expenses, while yet others built company housing. In 1778 Oakes built 12 cottages next to the comb shops to house workers and their families and 12 years later bought another five tenements in Risbygate Street which joined Saint Andrew's Street to the North of his other property. The offer of a newly built cottage may have enticed reluctant workers into the comb shops and warehouses and made it easier to enforce discipline.[194] The rate books show that at least three of the early occupants came from villages outside Bury. Settlement certificates had to be obtained for William Wright from Woolpit in 1784 and for Charles Baker from Wattisfield while Robert Grist had gained the right of settlement through apprenticeship in St James's parish.[195]

In 1784 Oakes bought the *Green Dragon* in Guildhall Street.[196] This may have been a shrewd investment as it joined his existing property or, given combers' legendary capacity for drink, perhaps he was simply trying to make sure that a proportion of their wages found its way back into his pocket rather than into that of another publican. However it is tempting to see the *Green Dragon* in the light of a sports and social club which would also act to reinforce company loyalty. There is no evidence that any part of combers' wages was paid in tokens to be

---

[190] SROB E2/16/2; diary 11 June 1791. Abraham Maling, a Bury yarn maker, was apprenticed to Valentine Beldame, a woolcomber of Royston, for seven years at a premium of £63 in 1764. Samuel Rutter of Bury apprenticed John Smith Brown of Norwich for six years at a premium of £80 in 1766. The largest premium recorded in the Apprenticeship Registers for a Suffolk yarnmaker was £105. This was paid by Thomas Humm to be apprenticed to Daniel Humm, woolman and yarnmaker of Bury, for seven years in 1766. PRO IR1/54, 56. The Oakes do not appear to have paid the tax on any of their apprentices.
[191] Diary 11 September 1795, 7 November 1795.
[192] Diary 2 September 1781.
[193] Wadsworth and Mann, *The Cotton Trade and Industrial Lancashire*, pp. 291–92.
[194] SROB N3/2/4. When the property was sold by the Oakes family in 1877 it was described as consisting of 17 cottages. SROB N3/2/3.
[195] SROB N3/2/3.
[196] *Ibid.*

exchanged at the *Green Dragon* but it was certainly used to treat them when celebrating the completion of his son's apprenticeship.[197]

Combing was very skilled, hard, unhealthy work and was the highest paid in the textile industry. As far as manufacturers were concerned combers were an insufferably independent group whose 'vices and Intemperance are a Source of infinite Loss and Trouble'.[198] They had what Thompson described as an 'exceptional trade union organization' which originated as far back as the 1740s[199] and provided a national network of associations giving sickness and unemployment benefit and what were, in effect, union cards so that unemployed combers could find work in other parts of the country.[200] As a result 'of this combination, they counteract all the Interests and Pursuits of their Employers' so that when an employer had a disagreement with his workers he would be unable to replace them because no other combers would work for him until the difference was settled. It was also claimed that the combers took 'Advantage of the state of their Employers' Trade to raise their wages ad libitem, and frequently leave their Employer in the most unwarrantable manner [and] by their Combination put a stop to their whole Operations'.[201]

Although no East Anglian yarn makers had been among the petitioners relaying this tale of woe to the House of Commons in 1794, relations between combers and manufacturers in the region were uneasy. In 1752 there had been a famous strike by Norwich combers in pursuit of higher wages and against the employment of black-leg labour.[202] Again in 1778 Norwich combers were able to 'insist' on a wage rise and the manufacturers were forced to comply. However, the following year a drop in trade and consequent drop in yarn production enabled masters 'in revenge' to reduce wages 'even below the price of last year's' which resulted in about 400 combers leaving the City altogether. William Herring, in a letter to his friend John Patteson, feared that should trade improve the 'bad effects' of the dispute would be widely felt.[203] Arthur Young and many other contemporary writers on the trade all commented on combers' aggressive independence and the fact that they seldom worked for more than four days at a time and devoted the rest of the week to drink, even when work was plentiful.

Ray Oakes and Company may have been seeking to control this insubordinate behaviour and to ensure regular supplies of combed wool at all times by building their comb shops and tied cottages. Their combers did ask for a rise in

---

[197] Diary 11 June 1791.

[198] *Journal of the House of Commons* (1794), 49, p. 546.

[199] E. P. Thompson, *The Making of the English Working Class* (1968), p. 315.

[200] Heaton, *The Yorkshire Woollen and Worsted Industries*, p. 315.

[201] *Journal of the House of Commons*, (1794), p. 546.

[202] P. J. Corfield, 'The Social and Economic History of Norwich 1650–1850: A Study in Urban Growth' (unpublished Ph.D. thesis, University of London, 1976), p. 315; Edwards, 'The Economic Development of Norwich', p. 32.

[203] NNRO Patteson Papers, Q 171B Box 3, letter dated 15 October 1778.

1792 but after meeting with Oakes 'express'd themselves as perfectly well satisfied with the old wages'[204] which was hardly the action of a formidable body of workmen. Oakes was forced to grant a wage rise in 1795, but then only for the finest work.[205] War time price rises were probably pushing men into wage claims. Two days after the combers' award the bricklayers and their labourers in Bury St Edmunds 'all turnd out' demanding a rise of four pence a day. In 1788 Bury combers organized a procession to celebrate the passing of the Wool Bill. These celebrations were often the start of binges of such magnitude that the combers did not return to work again for days. It is interesting that Oakes and John Corsbie, the only Bury yarn makers with large comb shops, exercised such control over their combers that they were able to forbid them to take part in the procession. Dr Stanley Chapman, using the evidence of insurance policies, found that some of the wealthier Devon manufacturers were so anxious 'to exercise closer supervision over all the manufacturing processes when their financial resources made it possible' they built houses for their workers in squares or courts. Chapman viewed this development, together with aggregation of capital in the hands of a few leading families, as the two most dynamic elements in the Devon industry in the eighteenth century.[206]

Oakes was a good employer by the standards of the day if length of service and the numbers of men from the same family following each other into the business is anything to go by. Peter Chambers joined the firm in 1762 and remained closely associated with Oakes for the next 56 years until his death in September 1818. Ambrose Taylor was already in charge of the Woodbridge area in 1765 and Isaac Smith had nearly 30 years' service having come at some time before 1768.[207] He and his wife were still associated with family in 1802 when they were given a scarf, hatband and gloves for Mrs Oakes's funeral. There were several fathers and sons employed: James Hill senior and junior, William Hill senior and junior and Thomas Scott senior and junior, together with two members of the Hagon family, three of the Waller family, two Cricks, two Allens and two Langhams.

Workers rarely seem to have left Ray Oakes and Company. In April 1783 Oakes recorded that '3 of my Sorters quitted my works'. No explanation is offered although it is possible that two of them could have been about to set up in a small combing business on their own account. The rate books show that in 1783 a Robert Waller and a Henry Hagon rented a property together in St Andrew's Street described the following year as a comb shop and warehouse. It was let that

[204] Diary 1 November 1792.
[205] Diary 30 May, 1 June 1795.
[206] Stanley D. Chapman, 'The Textile Factory Before Arkwright; A Typology of Factory Development', Business History Review, 48, (1974), pp. 451–78 (456–57).
[207] SROB HA535 Box 10; Tem 240/16.

year to Jacob Reach senior. Perhaps the venture, if venture there was, had not been a success. Waller and Hagon are common Bury names.[208]

Oakes's attitude to his employees was basically paternalistic and like the Norwich merchants described by *Sennex* 'he exercised much kindness towards those beneath him'. 'Hawkys' or 'frolics' were held in mid September each year for sorters, warehousemen and domestic servants after they had finished stock-taking and Christmas dinners were given to employees and their families.[209] Those who were not well enough to join in the festivities had their meals sent out to them and Christmas boxes were given to all.[210] There is a suggestion that some past employees or their widows were given annuities and others allowances for drink on their retirement while an entry in the ledgers of Gurney's Bank in Norwich shows that Peter Chambers received a golden handshake of 100 guineas when he retired from the yarn trade in 1794.[211]

Oakes felt personal concern and responsibility for his workers taking the trouble to visit Ambrose Taylor in Woodbridge when he was ill, for example.[212] The deaths of old employees were recorded and their widows were entertained at Christmas, although it seems likely that when they were living in Oakes's property they had to move out. After the death of her husband from small pox Ann Scoulding left her Pump Court cottage to be replaced by Charles Baker, another employee.[213] In 1810 both Martha Beedham and Elizabeth Abbott took over their husbands' tenancies as by that time the yarn busiess had been given up and there was no longer the same need to provide houses for workers.[214] This close personal interest and care was not extended to his combers apart from treating them at the end of his son's apprenticeship. Whilst it was possible for Oakes to have a benign, paternalistic attitude towards the 20 or so men who were his warehousemen, sorters, apprentices and agents, together with their families, it was difficult to give the same degree of personal attention to over 50 combers. Oakes's attitude to them would seem to illustrate a decline in paternalism at this transitional stage between the domestic and factory systems.

THE DECLINE OF THE SUFFOLK YARN INDUSTRY

The Suffolk yarn industry faced increasing difficulties in the last quarter of the eighteenth century. In June 1785 and in August 1786 trade in Norwich was 'exceedingly bad', in July 1788 Oakes wrote of the 'melancholy and oppressed

[208] SROB N3/6/1.
[209] Diary 25 December 1779, 22 September 1787 for example.
[210] Diary 25 December 1793.
[211] Diary 4 February 1801 for example; Gurney Ledger M shows a payment to Peter Chambers of £105 on 7 October 1794. He retired at Michaelmas that year.
[212] Diary 24 October 1783.
[213] SROB St Mary's Parish Register, FL545/4/4; N3/2/3.
[214] SROB N3/2/4.

state of the trade at this time' and in September found that there was 'No possibility of doing ay Business at Norwich'.[215] Later the same year Arthur Young reported that Suffolk yarn makers had considerable stocks in hand which they were unable to sell and that spinners' wages had been reduced as a consequence.[216] Trade may have improved during the next four years, if only because Oakes makes no comment on it, but by June 1792 it was poor and manufacturers 'were not inclind to buy yarns'.[217]

In spite of the fact that the Norwich industry had been in a state of stagnation since the onset of the American War there remained a sizeable textile industry in the city until the mid nineteenth century. It was rather that it had ceased to grow relative to other areas of the economy.[218] In contrast the Suffolk yarn industry had dwindled to almost nothing by 1800. Suffolk manufacturers were unable to compete with the uniform quality and low price of the West Riding machine spun yarns used in the production of coarser materials.[219] This was not as important as it might have been because Norwich manufacturers concentrated on the production of high quality materials for export in the face of West Riding competition in the home market for cheaper goods. However these high quality goods were made from silk, wool, cotton and linen and wool mixtures which lessened their dependence on local worsted yarn supplies still further.

Contemporaries saw increasing imports of Irish yarn as a major reason for the decline of the Suffolk industry[220] and indeed large amounts were imported through Yarmouth[221] and overland from Bristol.[222] It was estimated that by the 1770s Irish yarn supplied one sixth of all yarn used in the Norwich industry and it was claimed in 1798 that imports had to be increased because local yarn supply was not adequate to meet demand.[223] Suffolk manufacturers were unable to compete in price because of the lower cost of wool and provisions in Ireland while the Irish labour supply, unlike that of Suffolk, was easily expanded so that production could be stepped up in boom times without violent price fluctuations.[224] In contrast competition for spinners forced Suffolk manufacturers to operate large and expensive spinning networks.

There is evidence to suggest that Suffolk yarn makers attempted to respond to this state of affairs by increasing the amount of very fine yarn that they manufac-

[215] Diary 8 June 1785, 1 August 1786, 19 July 1788, 3 September 1788.
[216] Banks, *The Sheep and Wool Correspondence*, p. 168.
[217] Diary 20 June 1792.
[218] Corfield, 'The Social and Economic History of Norwich', pp. 317–19.
[219] James, *The History of the Worsted Manufacture in England*, p. 360.
[220] BL B545, p. 322; James, *The History of the Worsted Manufacture in England*, pp. 252, 308.
[221] Corfield, 'The Social and Economic History of Norwich', p. 322.
[222] NNRO Q171B Box 3. Letter dated 21 July 1778, William Herring to John Patteson.
[223] James, *The History of Worsted Manufacture in England*, p. 303.
[224] NNRO Q171B Box 3, letters dated 15 October 1778, 21 July 1778; Arthur Young, *Annals of Agriculture* IV (1795), p. 27; Edwards, 'The Economic Development of Norwich', pp. 172–73.

tured. Oakes bought only top quality wool for its production,[225] while the success of the spinning enterprise at the Blythburgh House of Industry was attributed to the fineness of the yarn spun there.[226] Even the luckless guardians and directors of the Melton House of Industry attempted to institute the spinning of extra fine yarn in a last desperate attempt to right the Houses's faltering finances, although this project also ended in failure.[227]

The introduction of machinery was not a practical alternative at this period. It was not possible to spin fine worsted yarn by machine until the early nineteenth century[228] and the majority of worsted yarn spun in the West Riding in the 1790s was produced on wheels. Technical problems ensured that the worsted industry was the last to make use of spinning machines while wool combing was not successfully undertaken by machine until the 1840s.

Oakes must also have met with stiff competition in the Northern and Midland markets that he supplied. The damask and moreen trade was declining fast in the face of changing fashions for wall paper rather than wall hangings.

The final blow to the Suffolk industry came in 1793 with the onset of the French Wars. In March of that year Oakes found trade in Norwich 'in the most distress'd state I ever remember to have seen it' with what little yarn that he did manage to sell going at 'considerably under prime cost'. Disease among sheep he thought, pessimistically, likely to keep wool prices high and cause the 'turning out of most of the hands generally employed. I could not sell a skein of yarn except best soft Bom[ba]zeen'.[229] In February of the same year yarn makers from Bury St Edmunds had discussed the idea of a joint petition against the war with the Norwich manufacturers 'it being so particularly injurious to the manufacturing and trading interests of the kingdom'.[230] Nothing more is heard of the idea, although in 1795 Bury Corporation included anti-war sentiments in a petition to the King and the Norwich manufacturers petitioned specifically against the war.[231] By mid March spinners' wages had been cut twice[232] and in June Oakes wrote that he had 'never met with a more depressed Market never sold one Bundle of Yarn not withstanding every possible Endeavor. This is the 4th month of attending at Norwich without being able to make any sales – the manufacturers can get no Remittances owing to the Difference of Exchange and have nothing to do except a few East India orders wch came in yesterday'.[233] Although trade improved slightly in 1794 stock-taking that September showed that, taking

225 BL B545, pp. 448–49.
226 SROI ADA9/AB1/1.
227 SROI HB50/20/21.2(5).
228 Heaton, *The Yorkshire Woollen and Worsted Industries*, p. 336.
229 Diary 8 March 1793.
230 Diary 21 February 1793.
231 Corfield, 'The Social and Economic History of Norwich', p. 325; see also Chapter IV, section II.
232 Diary 16 January, 13 March 1793.
233 Diary 6 June 1793.

1793 and 1794 together, Oakes had lost between £1,600 and £1,700 and there was 'no prospect of much better Times'.[234] This would seem to corroborate the view that the French War caused an immediate disruption to the Norwich trade largely because manufacturers had overstocked at the prospect of war which caused a complete stop in 1793.[235] Demand picked up again in 1794 once old stocks had been used.[236]

In April 1794 Chambers had told Oakes that he wanted to retire at Michaelmas. He had been with the company for 32 years and the loss of his expertise would have been a severe blow at a difficult time. Perhaps his departure finally convinced Oakes that there was no future in yarn manufacture. The Woodbridge spinning division was sold early in September 1794 and on Michaelmas Day, the first day of the fair, Oakes officially opened his bank. Ray Oakes and Company continued to function for another year until the following September when Oakes resigned from the yarn committee, sent his apprentice, Edward Brand, to complete his training with his father, and paid for the last consignment of yarn spun in the charity schools.[237] In 1798 he sold his Stowmarket property[238] and in 1799 the comb shops were sold to John Clark, a brewer, for £900.[239]

The war had a similar effect on other Bury yarn makers. William Buck became a brewer, Thomas Harmer a malster and woolfactor, one farmed the management of the workhouse and others bought country properties and retired from business life altogether. Another, less fortunate, had debts if £300 and was reduced to selling tea and 'some little Grocery for the Country places round Bury'.[240] In 1793 24 men involved in the yarn industry were listed in the *Universal British Directory*. By 1823 the number had fallen to three and by 1830 there was only one wool stapler in the town.[241] On Mathew's death in 1806 his wool hall was leased to an earthenware man and finally pulled down in 1828 to make way for a road connecting the Market Place with St Andrew's Street.[242] John Green, the other wool factor, continued in business until 1823 when bankruptcy forced the sale of his property.[243]

Attempts were made by the guardians to revive yarn spinning in 1825 and by the Guildhall Feoffment Trust in 1833.[244] Both schemes were without success. By 1818 the town was said to have no manufactures and very few work shops and by

[234] Diary 20 September 1794.
[235] Corfield, 'The Social and Economic History of Norwich', p. 325.
[236] Edwards, 'The Economic Development of Norwich', p. 136.
[237] SROB FL545/12/3; diary 24 September 1795.
[238] Diary 18 October 1798.
[239] Tem 141/9.
[240] SROB James Oakes's Memorandum Book HA535/1/4.
[241] *Pigot's London Directory* (1823–24), *Pigot's General Directory* (1830).
[242] SROB Minutes of Assembly 1805–35 D4/1/5; SROB Minutes of the Paving Commissioners, L3/2/4.
[243] BNP 26 February 1823.
[244] SROB N5/1/2; SROB H2/8/4.1.

1821 almost all the wool combers were discharged 'and some of the combing shops entirely shut up'.[245] Seven years later men spoke of the 'total destruction of the spinning trade' and by 1841 Suffolk was described as 'entirely without manufactures' those at Sudbury and Lavenham being 'too trifling to deserve mention'.[246] Apart from brewing and malting there was no industry in Bury St Edmunds until the mid nineteenth century when Robert Boby bought Ray Oakes and Company's old comb shops, pulled them down and built a factory on the site which acquired an international reputation for the manufacture of agricultural machinery. How appropriate that this new industry should rise form the ashes of the old leaving only their elegant Georgian-fronted houses as reminders of those 'men of property and intelligence' who had risen to independence, affluence and respectibility through yarn making in Bury St Edmunds.[247]

[245] SROB L3/2/4; BNP 2 May 1821.
[246] BPP 1828(515), VIII, p. 97, evidence of Mr Worledge of Ingham; William and Hugh Raynbird, *The Agriculture of Suffolk* (1849), p. 281.
[247] *East Anglian* 14 February 1832.

CHAPTER III

The Receivership and Banking

THE RECEIVERSHIP

James Oakes was appointed Receiver General of the Land Tax for the Western Division of Suffolk in 1787. Although only a small commission was paid and the job involved a good deal of hard work and expense, receiverships were highly prized. They were of considerable financial value because they put large sums of money into the receiver's hands which could be invested for quite long periods before being paid into the Treasury. Equally they were of value politically in that the receiver had money which he could lend to supporters or withhold from opponents.

Officially the Treasury was responsible for appointing receivers but, by the eighteenth century, appointments had become part of the system of aristocratic patronage and by 1750 nomination by magnates was the rule. Many noblemen and gentry were given office as a reward for political services leaving the day to day duties to a deputy while they reaped the profit.[1] These deputies were either merchants and bankers who found the receipt a useful way of extending the circulation of their notes in the division, or manufacturers who found it an invaluable source of cash in periods of acute currency shortage. Indeed many manufacturers had private arrangements with receivers or tax collectors whereby they were supplied with cash in return for drafts on London.[2]

JAMES OAKES'S APPOINTMENT

The Receivership of the Western Division Suffolk was held by Thomas Fenn, a somewhat disreputable bay and say manufacturer and banker in Sudbury. He had obtained the appointment in 1753 through the influence of Thomas Fonnereau who sat as Member of Parliament for the borough. Despite frequent attempts to oust him , the Duke of Grafton's continuing support enabled him to hang on to the office for the next 34 years.[3]

---

1   W. R. Ward, *The English Land Tax in the Eighteenth Century* (1953), p. 110.
2   e.g. Hubert Fox, *Quaker Homespun: The Life of Thomas Fox of Wellington Serge Maker and Banker* (1958), pp. 74–75. Fox made approaches to the Taunton tax collector for cash with which to pay wages in 1797.
3   Ward, *The English Land Tax*, pp. 164, 170–71.

James Oakes was the Duke of Grafton's political manager in Bury St Edmunds, an arrangement which had begun before 1778. He made it his business to ensure that only those well disposed to the Grafton interest were elected to the closed Corporation, which returned the town's two Members of Parliament, and kept the Duke informed as to the political tenor of the Borough. It is clear from the diary that Oakes had had his eye on the receivership for some time and had exacted some kind of undertaking from the Duke. As a manufacturer Oakes would have found the receiver's cash balances of enormous value while, as political manager, the receivership would provide numerous ways in which to exert influence and to encourage support for the Graftons throughout the Division. In addition, the profitable investment of tax balances would bolster his income at a period of increasingly difficult trading conditions for the Suffolk yarn industry.

Fenn became ill in January 1787[4] and died two and a half weeks later.[5] Fenn's death came at a propitious time for Oakes because he had just organized the return of the Duke's candidate at a by-election held on 5 February 1787.[6] On hearing the news of Fenn's death he rode immediately to Euston to request the job for himself.[7] The appointment was confirmed in a letter from Pitt and announced in the local paper a week later.[8]

PREPARATION

In all his doings James Oakes was a cautious and methodical man and seldom undertook a new enterprise without careful consideration and consultation with knowledgeable friends. In the week following his appointment he visited several influential men in London, among them Monkhouse Davison and Abraham Newman, wealthy partners in Davison, Newman and Company, grocers and tea dealers in Fenchurch Street; to Newman's son-in-law George Caswall, and to Richard Heaton, a London merchant and and his wife's second cousin.[9] The following week he visited his old friend John Patteson, a leading Norwich merchant and manufacturer, and Richard Gurney, a partner in the Magdalen Street firm of Gurney and Bland, yarn merchants and bankers.[10] He was fortunate to have men of such wide business experience to advise him about the land tax and the profitable uses he might make of its balances.

Oakes acted as one of his own sureties together with Dr Symonds, the recorder of Bury and Professor of Modern History at Cambridge, Richard Adamson, a retired Stockholm merchant who was Mrs Oakes's uncle, and Sir

4   Diary 18 January 1787.
5   Diary 7 February 1787.
6   See Chapter IV section iv for an account of the election.
7   Diary 7 February 1787.
8   Diary 16 February 1787.
9   Diary 26 February 1787.
10 Diary 7 March 1787.

Charles Davers Member of Parliament for Bury and brother-in-law of the fourth Earl of Bristol. Between them they stood surety for a total of £21,000. Peter Chambers, Oakes's business manager, and George Chinery his attorney, undertook to see that the bonds were executed should the need arise.[11] That Oakes could contemplate taking on the receivership and act as one of his own sureties demonstrates that he had accumulated a substantial fortune by inheritance and through yarn manufacture. On 12 March 1787 a new clerk, Mr Bailey, arrived and after a final consultation with Fenn's partner, Addison, Oakes was ready for his first quarterly receipt in April.[12]

TAX COLLECTION

The receivership was a strenuous job requiring the receiver or his deputy to make quarterly tours throughout his division to receive tax money from the local collectors. In the interest of safety the collectors were not supposed to travel more than 10 miles to deliver their charge which meant that the receiver himself had to cover great distances.[13] Once all the taxes for the quarter had been received they were remitted to London by bill or in cash. Both methods involved expense, often exceeding the poundage allowed, and risk because there was no allowance for loss.[14] The money was then invested by the receiver before eventual payment into the Exchequer.[15] The receiver's accounts were audited annually by the Auditor of Inland Revenue and, when cleared, the sureties' bonds were returned.

Oakes's receivership coincided with a period of growing dissatisfaction with the tax system. The decline in the social status and influence of local tax commissioners had resulted in much tax avoidance, especially by the rich and powerful.[16] In some places commissioners met rarely or meetings were poorly attended. Failure to supervise collectors properly meant that many falsified their accounts and that tax collections were infrequent.[17] Most receivers seemed powerless to improve their collectors' performance,[18] and often the receiver general himself was not without fault.[19]

Oakes recorded almost every receipt from April 1787 until May 1827. At first

---

[11] PRO T22/8, p. 232.
[12] Diary 20 March, 16 April 1787.
[13] Ward, *The English Land Tax*, pp. 10–11.
[14] *Ibid*, p. 47.
[15] See section v.
[16] Ward, *The English Land Tax*, pp. 87–88.
[17] *Ibid*, p. 90.
[18] *Ibid*, pp. 140–41. William Fisher, one of the receivers for Norfolk, was out of pocket on each receipt because the collectors' accounts were so poor but was forced to accept the situation in order to get in any taxes at all.
[19] *Ibid*, pp. 130, 139. The Cambridge Receiver General, Mortlock, used his position to remove opponents from the Commission. The Tiverton receivers allowed tax arrears to accumulate in order to extend their influence in the town.

he followed Fenn's routine and made quarterly collections at inns in Sudbury, Clare, Eye, Stowmarket, Mildenhall and Bury St Edmunds, but soon moved the Clare collection to Wickhambrook so that he could combine it with an inspection of his property there.[20] His usual companions were his coachman and his clerk, Bailey, although visitors and grandchildren were often taken to view the proceedings. Later, once a routine had been established, his son Orbell sometimes went in his place, and later still clerks, usually accompanied by the coachman, would deal with some of the smaller collections. Travelling expenses were noted regularly, whether a hired horse or one belonging to the family had been used, or a post chaise taken because the weather was bad.[21] Other expenses were incurred during tax collections. A tetchy note in April 1796 complained that 'Mr Haycroft's charge for my dinner [at Sudbury was] very extr[vagan]t considering what we had',[22] while remitting money to London and dealing with business at the Tax Office in person involved not only the time and expense of travelling but also the cost of staying in London.

The Collection of the receipt could be a dangerous occupation. Large sums of money, sometimes amounting to several thousands of pounds, had to be conveyed from outlying collection points back to Bury in saddle bags or under the chaise seat at a period when highway robbery was common. On one occasion a footman 'on a hir'd Horse wh Pistols' rode with Oakes on the Sudbury receipt.[23]

In a country division collection was particularly hard work involving him and his employees in long hours of travel immediately followed by time spent balancing accounts. The increasingly heavy burden of taxation during the 1780s and the 1790s and the introduction of Treble Assessed Tax in 1798 expanded their work enormously.[24] The Treble Assessed Tax caused extra collections in June and August 1798, when it was first introduced, although it was later incorporated into the normal quarterly Land Tax collections in January, April, July and October.[25] Income Tax was introduced in 1799,[26] repealed in 1802, and re-introduced as the Property Tax in 1803.[27] The result of this was that balancing accounts often went on until between ten o'clock and midnight.[28] In October 1797, although the receipt was in Bury, there was so much work to do that they all 'had but time to get a Scrambling sort of Dinner & could spare only ¼ of an hour — shut the Door soon after 6 & quite finished balancing by 9 o'clock'.[29]

---

[20] Diary 20 January 1788.
[21] e.g. Diary 3 July 1797, 10 October 1796.
[22] Diary 18 April 1796.
[23] Diary 20 October 1801. Oakes's daughter, Maria, was robbed on Bagshot Heath. See diary 20 August 1794.
[24] e.g. 18 Geo III c26, 38 Geo III c16.
[25] e.g. Diary 11–20 June 1798, 13–22 August 1798.
[26] 39 Geo III c13.
[27] 43 Geo III c122.
[28] e.g. Diary 20 April 1796.
[29] Diary 25 October 1797.

Even the marriage of his daughter did not prevent Oakes attending the Sudbury receipt 'soon after 9 0'clock on Horseback as soon as the wedding was over'.[30]

The receiver's work load was also increased as a result of provisions under which receivers were to advance pay to officers and men on embodiment.[31] The diaries show that Militia business took up a great deal of Oakes's time, some of it in his capacity as a Justice of the Peace and Deputy Lieutenant, but also as part of his receivership duties. 'Marching guineas' were paid to the Supplementary Militia, volunteers' families were relieved and caps and helmets bought for Lord Brome's Fourth Troop of Yeomanry Cavalry in 1796 and 1798.[32] Letters to the Tax Office show that additional weekly advances of over £2,376 were made to the families of men serving in the Provisional Cavalry in Ireland in 1799 and 1800 and in 1810 the West Suffolk Receiver was requested to make available allowances for the repair of the arms of the Bury Voluntary Infantry.[33]

Although Oakes was a capable organizer there are signs that he faced difficulties with inefficient subordinates in most parts of the Division. There were frequent arrears at Wickhambrook. Several times he complained that only 10 or 11 parishes paid,[34] while in July 1797 only eight paid so that it was hardly 'worth going this Quarter'.[35] In April 1798 between £1,600 and £1,700 was in arrears[36] and the number of parishes paying had fallen to six by July.[37] There were arrears in other collecting centres; by far the worst being Mildenhall, where it was rare for more than half the parishes to deliver, and usually much less. On one occasion the number was down to three. The problem was caused by an inefficient clerk. In January 1790 the receipt had to be put off in Mildenhall because of his mistake[38] and in April 1796 there were 'great misunderstandings between the Grand Duplicate & Collectors' acct owing to the total neglect of the Clerk (Mr J. Isaacson Jnr) in makg the first ½ year copy'.[39] Things were no better the following year when the local commissioners held their first meeting to appoint collectors on the very day of the Mildenhall receipt 'so that no one of them came prepared to pay their 1st Qr land. There ever was & am afraid will continue to be great inequality in this Hundred whilst the prest Clerk, Mr Isaacson, is continued & there being only 3 acting Commissioners is against it'.[40] There is no evidence that the Tax Office made any attempt to improve the Mildenhall commission or

---

30 Diary 21 October 1793.
31 2 Geo III c35, 20 Geo III c14, 21 Geo III c21; L. S. Pressnell, Country Banking in the Industrial Revolution (Oxford, 1956), p. 58.
32 SROB Bank Letter Book Acc 2191, letters dated 9 June 1796, 23, 28 July 1798.
33 PRO T22/12, p. 180.
34 e.g. Diary 13 October 1796, 5 January, 13 April 1797.
35 Diary 6 July 1797.
36 Diary 19 April 1798.
37 Diary 4 July 1798.
38 Diary 8 January 1790.
39 Diary 15 April 1796
40 Diary 7 July 1797.

that Oakes complained of it to them. Indeed the collectors persisted in alleging that the shortage of money made tax collection nearly impossible. Oakes was still writing wearily in February 1821 that there was 'great complaint among the Collectors' and he supposed, pessimistically, that these problems could only increase.[41]

The receiver's job was also hampered by the acute currency shortage of the period. In a letter to his London bankers in October 1797, before the quarterly receipt, Oakes wrote that he felt 'at a loss' as to whether he was obliged to accept dollars in tax payment and if so how forgeries could be detected. He was anxious to know if the Bank of England would accept those that 'have been fild or cut to prove them [because] there is not a person who comes to our Bank will take one of them — as such we are not disposed to take any ourselves provided we can legally refuse them'.[42]

Matters came to a head again just before the recoinage in February 1817. Over 70 pounds of silver was taken at the Sudbury receipt in January but it caused 'a great deal of Trouble & took up much time' and Oakes was forced to reject a good deal of it because it was 'foreign Money and base'. The public was obviously trying to get rid of base silver before the official recoinage began the following week with the result that the quarter's receipt was greatly reduced.[43]

That a man as business-like as James Oakes was powerless to improve the tax collectors' performance in many parts of his Division suggests that Pitt's reforms in this area can only have met with very moderate success throughout the country as a whole, for large numbers of receivers had little or no business experience and many were openly corrupt.

THE REMITTANCE AND INVESTMENT OF TAX BALANCES

The abolition of receivers' allowances in 1732–33 and the subsequent reduction in the poundage allowed together with the difficulty of obtaining bills, the shortage of specie and high cost of rural tax collection and remittance gave receivers every incentive to speculate with their balances. Large sums of money were lost to the Treasury and many receivers were bankrupted through unwise dealings.[44] The failure in 1797 of the largest bank in Bury St Edmunds, Messrs Spink and Carss, was partly attributed to the fact that the late proprietor, who had been Receiver General for the Eastern Division of Suffolk, had died three years before heavily indebted to the Treasury.[45]

After the fall of Walpole very little was done to remedy this state of affairs

---

[41] Diary 6 February 1821.
[42] SROB Acc 2191, entry dated 11 October 1797.
[43] Diary 28, 29 January 1817.
[44] Ward, *The English Land Tax*, pp. 107–110.
[45] Diary 17 March 1797

until the last quarter of the eighteenth century when war-time needs stimulated interest in financial reform. In 1780 Commissioners on the Public Accounts were appointed to report on the Land and Assessed Taxes and to examine receivers' balances and their reports were debated in Parliament. It was estimated that £113,000 had been lost through the bankruptcy of recievers during the last 25 years.[46] Accounts of tax arrears were called for in Parliament and it was decided that no receiver was to be re-appointed unless his balances were fully paid. By 1788 it was rare for a receiver to be appointed without conditions being imposed upon him.[47] These reforms produced little improvement in the amount of tax paid but did reduce the size of balances retained by receivers despite the fact that assessed taxes had increased by over two thirds between 1780 and 1799.[48]

Although Ray Oakes and Company had an account with Messrs Gurneys, the Norwich bankers, Oakes does not appear to have used it once he became Receiver General.[49] There is no evidence in the diary to show how or where he remitted tax monies and invested them until October 1788, when he recorded going to London with the Michaelmas receipt accompanied by his nephew George Green from Liverpool. In later years it was common for friends who were going to London either to accompany Oakes or to take the receipt money up on his behalf. His ageing retired manager, Peter Chambers, was often pressed into service for this purpose.

A note written by Oakes in extreme old age states that he used Messrs Ladbroke and Company of Lombard Street for the remittance of his tax balances from 1787 until Lady Day 1789.[50] Oakes had direct links with Sir Robert Ladbroke's partner and son-in-law, Sir Walter Rawlinson. Rawlinson was related to his mother, Susan Ray, and had a house at Stowlangtoft near Bury St Edmunds.[51] However, Oakes continued to have some dealings with Ladbrokes until the end of November 1793 when he recorded balancing his account with them. There is no further mention of the bank in the diary but an entry in the letter book on 24 March 1797 suggests that they parted on bad terms. The letter complains that Ladbrokes had refused to pay a 10 guinea note issued by James Oakes and Son with the result that rumours were started locally that Oakes and Son were about to stop payment. The letter asked that the clerks responsible be reproved and in

---

46 Ward, *The English Land Tax*, p. 147.
47 *Ibid*, pp. 127–29, 145.
48 *Ibid*, p. 150.
49 Gurneys' Ledger I 1784–90 in the possession of Barclay's Bank, Bank Plain, Norwich, shows Ray Oakes's account between April 1785 and February 1788.
50 SROB HA535/1/18
51 Sir Walter Rawlinson (1735–1805) of Devonshire Place, London, and Stowlangtoft Hall, was the son of Sir Thomas Rawlinson and his wife Dorothea, sister of Richard Ray of Haughley. He was a partner in the London bank of Ladbroke and Company and in 1769 married Mary the daughter of Sir Robert Ladbroke.

future inform customers that all Oakes's notes were to be taken to Barclay Bevan and Company.[52]

In March 1789 James Oakes opened an account with Messrs Gurneys of Norwich[53] although there is no evidence that tax monies were remitted to them until July 1791.[54] Indeed in June of that year he recorded remitting money to Sir James Sanderson's bank in Southwark. Sanderson's was probably a discount bank with other London banking services provided by the associated City firm of Harrison and Company and had close connections with the hop and leather trades.[55] Oakes may have felt that he could get better discounts with Sandersons than through Gurneys. He may also have been attracted to it as a result of his own participation in the hop trade and the bank's closeness to the Bermondsey Street wool market.[56] Nevertheless there were obvious advantages to using Gurneys in that remittance of tax money could be combined with yarn selling trips to Norwich and would not involve the same expense in time and money as travelling to London. Ray Oakes and Company, together with several other leading Bury manufacturers, already had an account with Gurneys although it was never very active and does not appear to have been used at all after February 1788.[57] It is difficult to see why Oakes did not use such conveniently placed and familiar bankers in the first place. Perhaps he was pursuaded by his London friends that he would get better terms and investment advice in the City, but subsequent experience changed his mind.

The diary gives little information on the size of balances retained by Oakes, the length of time that he held on to them or how they were invested. A note in April 1790 that he had 'Bot into the Stocks' is surrounded by stars which suggests that this was a new departure.[58] For the next few months the state of the market was anxiously perused and the effect upon it of the Spanish possession of Nootka Sound and subsequent peace carefully recorded. It is also clear from the diary that by this time Oakes had acquired a stock broker, Messrs Lambert and Cotton of 25, Cornhill, London, which further suggests that he intended to invest regularly a proportion of his balances in this way. There is no information as to the type of stock in which the receipt was invested until May 1810 when he noted on visiting his brokers, that it was 'a remarkably busy Day on act of the Delivery of the Receipt for the Funding of the Ex[chequer] Bills'.[59] Exchequer Bills were a common form of investment for country bankers and receivers because they were relatively liquid and could be sold easily for cash when the

---

52 SROB Acc 2191, letter dated 24 March 1797.
53 SROB HA535/1/18.
54 Diary 15 July 1791.
55 Pressnell, *Country Banking in the Industrial Revolution*, p. 83.
56 *Ibid*, p. 84. Pressnell shows that many country bankers with particular trading interests preferred a London agent with trade connections to a City banker.
57 Gurney Ledger I.
58 Diary 27 April 1790.
59 Diary 6 May 1813.

time for tax payments came due.[60] Later entries in both the diary and James Oakes's banking memorandum book make it plain that they were a major form of investment for his bank.

There is no evidence in either the Tax Office or Exchequer documents that Oakes kept unusually large balances. There are no irate letters from the Commissioners asking for explanations or exhorting him to greater efficiency. This is probably in part because by the time that Oakes became receiver the Tax Office was exercising a much tighter control over the speed at which tax money was paid in and over the size of permanent balances retained by receivers. It would have been out of character for Oakes to exploit the office ostentatiously although doubtless he would not have been averse to getting the most out of it within the prescribed limits. He was extremely angry in 1810 when, as the result of misunderstanding new legislation, he began the receipt two or three weeks later than usual and furiously complained that two or three weeks' interest would be lost on the £30,000 produced by that quarter's collection.[61] Both the diary and the tax records give the impression that money was paid into the Exchequer regularly and that his receiver's accounts and other tax documentation were attended to efficiently. A visit from the Inspector General in September 1793 did not seem to cause any undue alarm or comment.[62] Notes in his memorandum book suggest that by the early 1820s tax monies were held for about seven weeks before payment into the Exchequer[63] but that payment was within two weeks by 1825.[64]

Gurney's ledgers for the period 1791–96 corroborate this. Although the diary refers to receipt-money being taken to Norwich on only five occasions during Oakes's association with them, the accounts show that his balance rose markedly in January, April, July and October reaching a peak of over £30,000 in April 1792. The ledgers contain only two large payments made directly to the Exchequer during this period: on 26 November 1792 for £16,000 13s. 6d., and on 6 May 1796 for £8,000. Presumably other tax payments were made through Gurney's London agents, Messrs Barclay Bevan and Company, or even through Sandersons. The accounts show that large payments were made to Barclays regularly in May and November while the letter book shows a payment to the Exchequer in May 1798 through Oakes's then London agents, Aytons. This suggests that Oakes held on to a proportion of his tax balances for at least three months, but the evidence in too flimsy to be certain.

Gurneys paid interest on the account which amounted to over £370 in the first full year of their association but dropped to between £225 and £235 in the

---

60 Pressnell, *Country Banking in the Industrial Revolution*, p. 66.
61 Diary 30 April 1810.
62 Diary 29 September 1793.
63 SROB James Oakes Memorandum Book HA535/1/4 fol. 38; see also diary 30 January 1821 to 9 February 1821.
64 SROB HA535/1/4 fol. 60; see also diary 8 May 1825 to 25 May 1825.

following two years. These were considerable sums to earn in bank interest in the early 1790s and would have been of immense use to Oakes in terms of liquidity for all his yarn and other business transactions. His search for long-term investment opportunities after becoming receiver general also suggests that he was accumulating a substantial amount of capital as a result of the appointment. Not only did he have the bank interest on balances left with Gurneys but also the profit of short-term investment in Exchequer bills and other stock. In spite of the hard work, expense, problems associated with implementing new legislation, the additional responsibilities heaped onto receivers, the frustration of dealing with inefficient local commissioners and collectors and the shortage of specie, the receivership remained highly desirable. The profits to be made from it and the influence exerted as a result of it made all the effort worthwhile.

In order to ensure that the Oakes family continued to enjoy these advantages for as long as possible Oakes took steps to secure the office for his son. This course of action was increasingly common and both Pressnell and Ward have shown that in some cases it was becoming almost hereditary.[65] Once again the Duke of Grafton's influence was brought to bear and Orbell Oakes was appointed in succession to his father in 1797.[66] In spite of the change of name James Oakes continued to play an active part in the collection of taxes in Suffolk: he last mentioned going to the receipt at Stowmarket in November 1826 at the age of 85.

The continued importance of the receivership to the Oakeses emerges in letters that James Oakes wrote to his son concerning proposed reforms in the system of tax collection. An inquiry into the land tax in 1821 had shown that many receivers still held on to large balances, often in order to try to compensate for the reduction of tax money passing through their hands as a result of the repeal of the property tax in 1816 and post war depression.[67] Legislation was proposed to reduce the cost of tax collection by abolishing the poundage and balance system of remuneration and paying receivers general a maximum salary of £600 a year plus mileage and maintenance allowances. The Commissioners of Taxes were to supervise remittance arrangements. Where there were two receiverships in a county one was to give the office up and the other to take over the collection for the whole area.[68]

Oakes's letters suggest that the proposed salary would not match the profit to be made by receivers under the old system writing that the 'Expenses, Risk & Attendance will far surpass any Emolument you are likely to receive' and that Orbell Oakes was 'certainly right' to refuse to accept 'any less than 21 Days date and 3 days Grace as Receiver'. Even this, in his opinion, would not make the

[65] Pressnell, *Country Banking in the Industrial Revolution*, p. 68.
[66] PRO T22/9, p. 359; diary 18, 19 April 1797, 6 May 1797. James Oakes was appointed County Treasurer to the Western Division of Suffolk in place of the bankrupted Carss.
[67] *Commission . . . on the . . . Receivers General of the Land Tax 1821*.
[68] Pressnell, *Country Banking in the Industrial Revolution*, pp. 548–50.

Receivership of the Eastern Division of the county worthwhile. Yet Oakes felt that despite reduced profits, as bankers, they could not afford to loose the Receivership of the Western Division 'however lessened the Emolument . . . situated as you are I would not have it go into other Hands on any Acct'. A note added to his letter next day reinforced this advice saying that 'as Bankers it [the Western Division Receivership] cannot fail being serviceable' and repeating that he 'should not at all like to see it get into any other Hands'.[69] Pressnell quoted Hume as saying that any banker was happy to remit taxes to London without charge because he gained benefit from the mere transition of public money through his hands.[70] Apart from this the collection of taxes at the bank's main office in Bury St Edmunds and its branches in the county would have attracted customers, stimulated the circulation of the bank's note issue and given the bank official recognition.

Orbell Oakes played an active part in discussions on the proposed reforms. He attended meetings of receivers at the Thatched House Tavern in London in October 1821 although he was disappointed to see so few of his fellow receivers there '& not anything determined except appointing another meeting'. He also took the precaution of seeking the Duke of Grafton's support to further his interests with the Tax Office. In 1822 he was appointed Receiver General for the Eastern Division of Suffolk in addition to that of the West.

The joint Receivership must have proved profitable judging by Orbell Oakes's rage when receivers general were finally abolished in 1831.[71] His anger was exacerbated by the refusal of the Tax Office to grant his claims for compensation and the fact that he had kept on his clerk, Haddock, solely 'under the expectation of being continued Receiver General'. Haddock was paid £200 a year 'a very handsome Allowance as [he] had not an hours employment in the day' but was made to understand that this 'Liberality' could not continue in the future.[72]

THE SEARCH FOR INVESTMENT

LAND AND UTILITIES

It is clear that as a result of the receivership Oakes had surplus funds to invest. The amount of accumulated capital that could be put back into his yarn business in plant or machinery was limited and it would have been almost impossible to have managed a larger spinning network. This was a common problem for manufacturers of the period. Manchester fustian dealers and Rochdale woollen merchants, for example, were forced to seek a variety of alternatives including

---

69 SROB Tem 240/21, letter dated 3 September 1821, James Oakes to Orbell Oakes.
70 Pressnell, *Country Banking in the Industrial Revolution*, pp. 62–63.
71 1 and 2 Will IV c18.
72 Orbell Oakes's Private Memorandum Book.

land, canals, turnpikes and stock until their sons withdrew from industry altogether to take a 'genteel interest' in commerce as bankers.[73]

Investment opportunities in late eighteenth-century Bury St Edmunds were few. Oakes approached the problem with his usual caution, concentrating to begin with on property. Six months before his appointment as Receiver General he had bought a small farm at Wickhambrook[74] and three years later four houses in Risby Gate Street.[75] In 1787 he purchased the ecclesiastical living of Harkstead for £2,000 which he sold the following year.[76] Apart from this he invested very little in land on his own account but during the course of the 1790s set up both his sons on estates after their marriages and bought his youngest son James the living at Tostock. The diary suggests that these purchases were made with money produced from the sale of property in Wereham left to his sons by their maternal grandfather, and that Oakes lent them the balance which was to be repaid with interest.[77]

It is probable that Oakes also invested in turnpikes at this period as he mentions atttending a meeting to promote a turnpke between Bury and Brandon in 1787 and meetings of the Thetford Turnpike trustees in 1792.[78] No turnpike records for the area have survived so it is impossible to be certain. He also seems to have given serious consideration to investment in local canal projects.

The period 1791 to 1794 marked the height of the national mania for canal investment. Eighty-one acts were passed and shares in existing canals were at a premium. The boom in shares of the more successful companies reached a peak in 1793. There were various local proposals in which Oakes took a cautious interest. In 1790 it was proposed to link the Lark Navigation at Bury and the Stour at Mistley with a canal 31 miles long.[79] Oakes was appointed treasurer and many leading Suffolk men undertook to subscribe an initial sum of £5,000. In May and June John Rennie, the engineer, made a survey which showed that a tunnel of 2,420 yards, to overcome the hill between Lavenham and Bury, plus 315 feet of lockage would be needed at an estimated total cost of £75,000. On seeing the plans Oakes doubted the wisdom of the project and resigned as treasurer. John Spink, the banker, was appointed in his place. Oakes also 'declind subscribing till Mr Spink should declare what sum he would put down but, to the disappointment of many, Mr Spink declin'd to subscribe'.[80] A prospectus was prepared and a public meeting held in January 1791 at which a committee,

[73] Alfred P. Wadsworth and Julia de Lacy Mann, *The Cotton Trade and Industrial Lancashire 1600–1780* (Manchester, 1931), pp. 33, 47, 279.
[74] SROB HA535/1/4 fol. 24.
[75] SROB St James's Rate Assessment N3/6/1.
[76] Diary 30 July 1787, 29 November 1788, 10 January 1789.
[77] See Chapter V.
[78] Diary 6 August 1787, 7 July, 6 August 1792.
[79] SROB Cullum Common Place Book 317/1, pp. 61–62; John Boyes and Ronald Russell, *The Canals of Eastern England* (1977), p. 180.
[80] SROB 317/1, p. 62.

surprisingly including Oakes, was chosen. It was proposed to raise £35,000 to bring the canal as far as Lavenham. In the event only £5,000 was raised, the project failed and nothing more was heard of it until 1817 when the idea was revived as a scheme to provide work for the poor of the parishes along the route.[81]

It is doubtful whether such a project could have been made to pay, given the poor returns of many rural canals projected during the early 1790s and Oakes's natural caution was totally justified. It is less easy to explain his failure to invest in the Stowmarket Navigation. In 1789 it was proposed to build a canal to link the port of Ipswich with Stowmarket by making the river Gipping navigable from Hanford Bridge to Stowupland Bridge.[82] A survey was made, and an act passed in 1790 which empowered the six trustees to borrow £14,000 and to raise £6,000 on mortgage if necessary.[83] A law suit delayed the work and a second act was needed three years later enabling the trustees to raise a further £15,000.[84] The project was a success and for many years the shares were quoted at a premium until the arrival of the railway in 1847.[85] At no time does James Oakes appear to have bought shares although it was promoted by men well known to him like Joshua Grigby of Drinkstone and Robert Walpole of Beyton and supported by friends including the Pattesons and the Herrings from Norwich and his cousins the Reverend Orbell Ray of Tostock and the Reverend Richard Moseley of Drinkstone.[86] The Navigation brought a brief prosperity to Stowmarket, stimulating the building of new maltings and the growth of fresh industries.

Oakes and other businessmen had wanted the Navigation extended as far as Bury St Edmunds and within a week of the first meeting held to promote it he had accompanied Sir Charles Davers, one of the Members of Parliament for the town, to a meeting at Stowmarket. But the promoters refused to consider it and the party from Bury dined alone before returning home.[87]

Possibly Oakes and his fellow businessmen felt that the project would bring prosperity to Stowmarket at the expense of Bury St Edmunds and for this reason refused to be involved in it after their overtures had been so brusquely rejected. It is noticeable that no prominent Bury merchants or manufacturers were either trustees or shareholders other than Robert Walpole, and he had retired to his farm at Beyton and was no longer actively engaged in business in the town.

[81] IJ 23 August 1817; SC 14 May 1817.
[82] Diary 3 July 1792; see also J. Boyes and R. Russell, The Canals of Eastern England, pp. 90–94; The Rev. A. G. Hollingsworth, The History of Stowmarket (1844); A. G. E. Jones, 'The Stowmarket Navigation' (1954), typescript in SROI S. 386.
[83] 30 Geo III c57.
[84] 33 Geo III c20.
[85] Jones, 'The Stowmarket Navigation'.
[86] NNRO Stowmarket Navigation Cash Account 1789–1802, EAW/11.
[87] Diary 24 September 1789.

By the end of the eighteenth century brewing was becoming an increasingly important industry in East Anglia. The rise of the common brewer, at the expense of the home and publican brewer, had been slower in Suffolk than elsewhere in the region because there were few large centres of population to provide a readily accessible urban market for such a bulky, low value product. In addition most farmers and country gentlemen brewed their own beer. However the production of malting barley in the dry Eastern Counties had enabled East Anglian brewers to combine malting with brewing, this profitable combination allowing them to expand their businesses.[88] Brewing was, therefore, a potentially lucrative enterprise in which to invest for those with funds to spare; and one that clearly held a certain attraction for Oakes, although he hesitated for years before finally taking the plunge. Again caution and consultation were his watchwords. In the summer of 1792 he had discussions with John Patteson and under the guidance of Mr Greaves, Patteson's partner in the Pockthorpe Brewery in Norwich, they inspected Buckley and Garnish's newly opened brewery in St Andrew's Street and Matthias Wright's Westgate Brewery, both in Bury.[89]

Oakes's faith in brewing as a safe investment was then severely shaken because Buckley and Garnish were bankrupted only four and half months after their much publicized opening at the end of 1791.[90] The brewery and two inns were auctioned in December 1792 and were sold for a total of £3,420 which was 'supposd full £500 under its real value' to a Mr Wright for his nephew Mr Clarke.[91] Although, by his own admission, it was cheap, Oakes made no attempt to buy it.

The following year Greaves wanted to sell his share of the Pockthorpe Brewery and Oakes inspected it when he was on an abortive yarn selling trip to Norwich. Discussions were held with Patteson and Greaves and proposals 'partly agreed to' before Oakes left Norwich next day.[92] The yarn trade was very severely hit by the onset of war and by this time Oakes may have been looking for an alternative occupation as well as for a safe investment. In spite of this caution prevailed once more and after a further visit to Pockthorpe in June he 'declind having any Connection in the Pockthorpe Concern with Mr G'.[93] Patteson bought Greave's share in 1793 and also acquired Postle and Beevor's brewery to form the nucleus of an enlarged Pockthorpe Brewery.[94]

---

[88] R. G. Wilson, Greene King: A Business and Family History (1982), pp. 12–15.
[89] Diary 16 August 1792.
[90] BNP 18 April 1792; UBD (1793), III, p.145. The 'populace were treated with 50 barrels of porter while many 'respectable' inhabitants were lavishly entertained to a 'cold collation'.
[91] IJ 1 December 1792; diary 19 December 1792.
[92] Diary 7, 8 March 1793.
[93] Diary 6 June 1793.
[94] Basil Cozens-Hardy and Ernest Kent, The Mayors of Norwich 1403–1835 (Norwich, 1938), pp. 140–42.

9. *James Oakes's house in Guildhall Street showing the wings designed by John Soane.*

Eventually James Oakes invested in the Yarmouth Brewery in order to provide a suitable income and occupation for his son-in-law, William Gould who had married his eldest daughter Maria in 1793. Gould was the son of the Reverend William Gould of Hoxne and was a first lieutenant of Marines. He was on half pay from 1793, attached to the North Gloucester Militia.

John Patteson bought the Yarmouth Brewery in 1796 together with a Mr Thompson who had been a partner with the previous owners, Fisher brothers. Once again Oakes went into the matter thoroughly before committing himself, travelling to Yarmouth 'to get some Information respecting Mr Patteson's Brewery there', discussing the project with Patteson's partner, Iselin, and making enquiries of local friends. The results of his enqiries must have been satisfactory because by the end of the month it had been agreed that Gould and Patteson were to be equal partners beginning on 1 October 1798.[95]

The diary is unclear as to the price and terms on which the partnership was to be set up. It would appear that the total cost of the brewery was £20,000 and that this was to be shared equally between Patteson and Gould. Oakes advanced £10,000 to Gould for his share and Patteson sent Oakes a draft for £336 12s. 4d. 'to balance' when the sale of a half share to Gould was finalized in February 1799.[96] Oakes's account with Messrs Alexander, the Ipswich and Needham

95 Diary 13,17 September, 1 October 1798.
96 Diary undated entry at the end of February and the beginning of March 1799.

Market bankers, shows that Oakes had already paid Patteson £2,060 2s. 6d. in October 1798 when the partnership began.[97]

By late 1801 it was clear that things were not going well. Patteson had assured Oakes that he could expect a 12% return on his capital, although Oakes had said that he would be happy with ten. In fact only nine per cent was produced in 1799, and in 1801 it was estimated that an average of seven per cent would be produced for the first three or four years as a whole.[98] The period between 1800 and 1810 was a particularly difficult one for brewers because high war time prices for raw materials were combined with unprecedented increases in malt and beer duties. Brewers found it difficult to raise their prices to compensate after a long period of stability at the end of the eighteenth century, especially since the working classes, hard hit by steep advances in bread prices during the 1790s, were buying less beer. In addition the profitable combination of malting with brewing, practiced extensively by East Anglian brewers, was undermined because of the sharp decline in malt exports to Holland as a result of the war.

On 1 February 1804 the partnership was dissolved and the brewery sold to Messrs Paget, Dawson Turner and Adcock for what appears, from the diary, to have been a total price of £25,500.[99] The profit made by the Yarmouth Brewery was reasonable for the period. Oakes's withdrawal at such an early stage may have been as a result of the timidity and fear of taking unnecessary risks which seems to have been part of his nature. It may also have been something to do with the business acumen of William Gould. Gould was still only an impecunious half-pay first lieutenant of Marines at the age of 39, who seems to have lied to the Oakes family about his age. His lack of achievement in the Marines, even in war time, may have forced Oakes to find him an alternative occupation. It is possible that he was either inattentive or ill equipped to run a brewery and that Oakes thought it better to cut his losses before too much damage was done. At all events, before the partnership with Patteson was dissolved, Gould was appointed Yarmouth's barrack master on the recommendation of the Duke of Grafton, a job in which his known talents could be safely utilized.[100]

Oakes's withdrawal may have been shrewd rather than timid for both he and Patteson had each made £2,500 on their original investment of £10,000, although Oakes missed the large profits subsequently made from brewing once malt and hop duties were relaxed. He also had some difficulty in getting Patteson to pay back money lent him at the beginning of the partnership.[101]

[97] BA Ledger of Alexander and Company 1797–99, p.329.
[98] Diary 10 November 1801.
[99] Diary 30 January to 1 February 1804.
[100] Diary 8 August 1803.
[101] Note numbered 'No 85 Particulars of New file of Memorandums' in the note book bound in volume IX between entries for 1809 and 1810.

Although there is little direct evidence in the diary for this period, it is clear that Oakes drifted into banking during the course of the seven years that followed his appointment as Receiver General. Cautious as ever, he wavered, performing some of the functions of a banker until the collapse of the Suffolk yarn industry at the beginning of the war finally forced him to commit himself.

Just over a year after his appointment as Receiver, having consulted with knowledgeable friends and aquaintances including John Spink, the most substantial banker in Bury, he embarked on extensive alterations to his house to provide a purpose-built banking office and a new family dining room.[102] These were designed by John Soane whom Oakes had probably met through the ever-obliging John Patteson.[103] Between November 1788 and April 1790 the diary records the visits of Soane and his clerk, Sanders, to inspect the existing house, to make plans and to supervise the building work.[104]

The new additions demonstrated Oakes's affluence for all to see. Soane designed handsome two-storied pedimented wings on either side of the existing five-bay redbrick house, joining them to the house by a narrower section containing a door. A tall screen wall with shallow pilasters and blank panels ran from each wing to the adjoining property. The southern wing contained the family dining room, which had a shallow arch and columns at one end and a fine white marble chimney piece.[105] The northern wing, next to the *Green Dragon*, was built specifically as a 'banking office'. It occupied the whole width of the wing and had shutters at the windows front and back, a Ketton-stone chimney-piece and a strong-room with a door. Above the banking room there was another dining room, reached by a curved staircase, which was to be used by Oakes to entertain customers on market days. The wings both had wide tripartite windows with wooden jambs supporting lintels on which were composition panels each containing nine-leaf pateras.[106]

Although Oakes possessed such splendid new premises and referred to them as his 'banking office' there is little evidence in his diary to suggest that he saw

---

[102] Diary 29 November 1788.

[103] Patteson and Soane had met in Italy when Soane was on a travelling studentship and Patteson was making a tour with other young men, including a future Governor of the Bank of England. Later, in 1780, Soane met the Earl of Bristol, a building fanatic, who persuaded him to give up his studentship in order to design houses for him at Ickworth and Downhill in Ireland. When the project failed and Soane was left without his scholarship his friends rallied round by giving him commissions during the years before he was appointed Architect and Surveyor to the Bank of England. Both Oakes and Patteson subscribed to his book *Plans, Elevations and Sections of Buildings* (1788), and Patteson commissioned him to work on his Surrey Street house in Norwich. Dorothy Stroud, *The Architecture of Sir John Soane* (1961); Arthur T. Bolton, *The Portrait of Sir John Soane* (1927).

[104] e.g. Diary 29 November 1788, 6–7 December 1788, 28 April 1789.

[105] There is a sketch of the cornice designed for this room in the Soane Museum.

[106] Soane's Account Book in the Soane Museum; D. Stroud, Typescript of notes in Lloyd's Bank, Bury St Edmunds.

himself as a banker. Yarn making was his chief occupation and he continued to receive taxes at the *Wool Pack*, the inn used by the Bury merchants for all their meetings. The receipt was not moved to Guildhall Street until October 1791, 18 months after the completion of the new building. The only possible references to banking in the diary at this period occur in May 1791 when Oakes had a conversation in London 'respecting Our Banking Business' and in March 1792 when his son was dispatched to Diss for cash.[107] The fact that Oakes acted as treasurer of the proposed Mistley Navigation in 1790 suggests that he may have been performing some of the functions of a banker. In that year also it was claimed that in spite of the fact that Oakes 'still continues the Bus[iness] of Yarnmaker in the year 1789 . . . he opened a Banking House in Bury under the Firm of himself and his sd son as Partners'.[108] Oakes confirmed this in a note written in extreme old age in which he recorded opening an account with Messrs Gurney of Norwich to coincide with the start of his new company.[109]

However, according to his diary, Oakes did not commit himself to banking until September 1794. Earlier in the summer he had discussed the project with John Spink and had informed the Yarn Committee that he intended to resign.[110] On Michaelmas Day, the first day of Bury Fair when the town was at its busiest, he took tea with friends and spent the evening at the *Angel* with the Corporation. Almost as an after-thought, squashed down one side of the page and nearly lost in the margin, but surrounded by the stars that he always used to mark entries of importance, a note reads 'Opend my Bank'.[111] No advertisement appeared in the local paper and it is apparent from both the diary and the letter book that he continued to manufacture yarn and to deal in coal and hops. Messrs Gurneys sent their chief clerk Mr Martin 'to assist us in a proper method of book-keeping . . . and make no doubt should through his Instructions be enabled to set out with most correctness'.[112] Perhaps Gurneys hoped that the Bury New Bank of James Oakes and Son would become an affiliated branch rather as their bank in Yarmouth had evolved.[113]

By June 1796 Oakes wrote that he was 'now pretty considerably with my son in the Banking line' and that the Bury New Bank was able to 'transact any business . . . in Norfolk or Suffolk with out puttg ourselves to any Inconvenience'.[114] By July they had 'declin'd the wool trade' and were 'entirely confin'd to Banking'.[115]

---

[107] Diary 27 May 1791; 15 March 1792.
[108] SROB 317/1.
[109] SROB HA535/1/18.
[110] Diary 8, 12 July 1794.
[111] Diary 29 September 1794.
[112] SROB Acc 2191, letter dated 19 November 1796.
[113] W. H. Bidwell, *Annals of an East Anglian Bank* (Norwich, 1900), p. 293.
[114] SROB Acc 2191, letter dated 13 June 1796.
[115] *Ibid*, letter dated 29 July 1796.

Oakes's slow and cautious steps towards banking were typical of country bankers elsewhere. It was nearly always difficult to pin-point the moment at which a man became a banker because many manufacturers discounted bills, gave credit to their customers and suppliers and took deposits at interest from local people. Others, because of currency shortages, issued their own notes in order to make wage payments. Many like the Foxes at Wellington continued to run both businesses side by side treating each with equal attention, while for some, like the Gurneys of Norwich, banking soon became dominent and their other business activities gradually dwindled.[116] J. R. Pease, the Hull banker, still earned only a quarter of his income from banking after over 40 years in the profession.[117] All the bankers in Bury St Edmunds at the time continued to combine banking with business. Messrs Spink and Carss and Robert Walpole were both drapers and Messrs Corks were leather cutters and tea dealers.

In addition to the opportunities presented to the manufacturer or merchant to indulge in banking activities, the Oakeses had the enormous advantage of being Receivers of the Land and Assessed Taxes. The method of collection and re-muneration provided opportunities to the aspiring banker at every stage. Remit-tance of tax money to London required the discount of bills and in retaining tax balances for a period for investment receivers were 'indulging in a species of deposit banking'. The receipt gave both prestige and deposits to a would-be banker and, in a period of severe currency shortage combined with increasingly heavy taxation, stimulated the circulation of their local note issue.[118] As a result, growing numbers of receivers were bankers by the end of the eighteenth century and many bankers acted as receivers' deputies, particularly after 1816 when they were no longer to be appointed receivers.[119] Spink and his predecessor Scotch-mer were both Receivers for the Eastern Division of Suffolk, while Oakes's predecessor as Receiver for the Western Division was a partner in the Sudbury bank of Messrs Fenn, Addison.

Oakes, like the Foxes and the Peases, may have hoped to keep banking as a lucrative side-line to yarn making. In the event the Suffolk yarn industry, already under pressure from Irish and West Riding competition and from encroachment by Norwich wool combers on its spinnning networks, suffered a blow from which it never recoverd with the onset of war in 1793. Meanwhile Peter Chambers, Ray Oakes's manager since 1762, had decided to retire at Michaelmas.[120] These factors must have propelled Oakes over the brink into the potentially profitable but highly risky business of banking. In many ways it was an odd choice given his

116 Pressnell, Country Banking in the Industrial Revolution, p. 52; Fox, Quaker Homespun, p. 23.
117 Gordon Jackson, Hull in the Eighteenth Century: A Study in Economic and Social History (1972), pp. 228–29.
118 Pressnell, Country Banking in the Industrial Revolution, pp. 56, 61.
119 Ward, The English Land Tax, p. 64; Pressnell, Country Banking in the Industrial Revolution, p. 60.
120 Diary 5–26 April 1794.

caution in financial matters and he must have suffered agonies during the various crises ahead. But the collapse of the yarn industry left him little choice. Alternative local industrial and investment opportunities were very limited as his long flirtation with canal schemes and brewing enterprises demonstrates. However his interest in the receivership and superb network of connections throughout Suffolk, the product of over 35 years in business in the county, gave him great advantages over his rivals and eventually pushed the cautious Oakes into becoming a full time banker.

THE BURY NEW BANK

NOTE ISSUE

Within two weeks of opening the Bury New Bank, James Oakes was issuing his own notes. The chronic shortage of cash in the eighteenth century meant that in most parts of the country, except Lancashire,[121] farmers and tradesmen were forced to rely on notes issued by country bankers for currency. As a result the widespread use of country bank notes continued well into the nineteenth century in the face of much controversy. There were two reasons for this. First, it was dangerous and expensive to get Bank of England notes and gold from London to towns many miles away. Secondly, and more important, note issue could be one of the most lucrative areas of country banking because it increased the country banker's ability to supply credit. Country bankers therefore sought any means at their disposal to push the circulation of their notes.

In a period of severe currency shortage there were various ways in which this could be done. Country bankers could urge local land-owing customers to give preference to them when receiving their rents and, if they were tax collectors, they could stipulate which notes they would accept in tax payments. Oakes was fortunate to act as banker to many of the local land-owning families living near Bury St Edmunds and to receive their rents,[122] but it was the receivership which gave the Bury New Bank a particular advantage. One of the major reasons that country bankers were anxious to be involved in tax collection was the boost that it gave to the circulation of their notes.

The manufacture of bank notes was expensive, involving the engraving of plates for each denomination of note, the use of high quality, water-marked paper, careful printing on both sides of the note, and numbering to prevent forgeries. At first the plates for the Bury New Bank notes were engraved by a Mr Gray and later by another London firm called Thorowgoods.[123] The account with

---

[121] See T. S. Ashton, 'The Bill of Exchange and Private Banks in Lancashire 1790–1830' in *Papers in English Monetary History* edited by T. S. Ashton and R. S. Sayer (Oxford, 1953), pp. 37–49.

[122] e.g. Diary 2 January 1807.

[123] SROB Acc 2191 letters dated 23 August 1797, 9 February 1797. A note in the note

74

Thorowgoods was closed and the business given to a Mr Row in 1820.[124] The notes were printed on paper with the Oakes's own watermark by Messrs Cobb and Company manufacturers of webbing and horse girths, who began banking in Banbury in 1784. Neither Pressnell nor Taylor mentions Cobbs as having printing interests and it is unlikely that there were two firms of the same name in Banbury.[125]

Despite precautions, the Bury New Bank's notes were forged or altered on several occasions. In 1798 a note was altered from one pound to two, in 1800 about 24 five guinea notes were changed to ten and in 1818 Hine, one of the clerks, had to spend a week in London dealing with a forged five guinea note presented for payment at their London Bankers.[126] On one occasion, in his late seventies, Oakes foiled an attempt to push forged notes onto his clerks at Stowmarket and dealt forcefully with the culprit.[127] There is no evidence that Oakes went to the same lengths as Messrs Fox of Wellington who, on discovering counterfeit versions of their notes were in circulation, ordered new watermarked paper with deliberate mistakes in the engraving to make the detection of forgeries easier.[128]

The only specific mention that Oakes made to the cost of producing cash notes was in 1798, when he estimated that to buy paper and to print the newly permitted one pound notes cost one pound per thousand notes.[129] By 1800, following a threatened run on the bank, he had decided not to issue any more because the expense involved was too high. Stamp duty had been doubled from two pence to four pence and they were not officially payable in London 'tho' always paid by our Bankers if presented to them'. With the extra stamp duty and 'with Paper Printing & uncommon wear they could not be made to answer'.[130] This view of their value to the country banker was echoed by John Smith, the Nottingham banker, over 20 years later when refuting the claim that one pound notes constituted 99% of all provincial circulation. He felt that they were the least profitable and most troublesome note that a country banker could issue.[131]

There is no evidence as to the value of Oakes's notes in circulation until 1801 when it was raised from £50,000 to £60,000 against which Oakes agreed to leave

---

book bound in volume IX between the entries for 1809 and 1810 reads 'Henry Cooper Engraver wth Specimen of Plates'.

124 Diary 3 November 1810, 3 July 1821.
125 SROB Acc 2191, entry dated 23 June 1798; Pressnell, Country Banking in the Industrial Revolution, p. 8; Audrey M. Taylor, Gilletts, Bankers at Banbury and Oxford: A Study in Local Economic History (Oxford, 1964).
126 SROB Acc 2191, entry dated 22 March 1798; diary 7 June 1800, 16 August 1815, 9 August 1818.
127 Diary 24 December 1818.
128 Fox, Quaker Homespun, pp. 75–76.
129 SROB Acc 2191, entry dated 23 March 1798.
130 Diary 19 November 1800
131 Pressnell, Country Banking in the Industrial Revolution, p. 147.

£6,000 on deposit without interest with his London bankers.[132] In 1820 this sum was raised to £8,000 because the value of notes in circulation had probably risen to £80,000. These figures are much in line with the evidence concerning the note issue of other country banks.[133]

The total issue for the Oakeses' bank and its branches in Sudbury, Stowmarket, Mildenhall and Thetford was £82,362 by 1844 with a further £10,657 issued by the associated banks in Diss and East Harling. This was after the bank's amalgamation with Messrs Crowe, Sparrow and Browne of Bury St Edmunds and after the 'great days of the private note' were over.[134] In fact the Oakeses had one of the largest note issues in East Anglia in 1844. In comparison, the note issue of the Norwich Crown Bank was £45,120; the Ipswich bank of Bacon, Cobbold, Rodwell and Cobbold only £21,901, and Messrs Alexander of Ipswich £80,699. Even Messrs Gurney of Norwich, the largest East Anglian bankers, had a smaller note issue in 1844 of £75,372.

In 1810 Tritton estimated that an average country bank's circulation was about £30,000[135] and it is surprising to find the cautious Oakes having a note issue two to two-and-a-half times higher. Bankers like the Peases in Hull made money from foreign exchange deals, from financing foreign and domestic trade, from underwriting and from investment in industry.[136] None of these opportunities was readily available to Oakes because of the 'very limited situation of Business' in an area where there was 'no discounting & no way of makg Immediate use of our monies without risk & loss of time'.[137] Indeed when Messrs Alexander of Needham Market and Ipswich appear to have suggested that Oakes stop issuing notes altogether during the 1797 cash crisis he replied that the 'Banking business of this town & neighbourhood is written so small a compass that without them [notes] it would hardly have been worth keeping open shop'.[138] The central place of note issue in their banking business might also help to explain the eagerness with which the Oakeses held on to the receipt after 1821 despite the fact that receivers were to be paid a fixed salary and were no longer able to benefit from the prolonged investment of tax balances.

Although Messrs Oakes' note issue was relatively large, James Oakes followed a prudent course with regard to it and varied his cash ratios according to the economic climate. He wrote to a customer in March 1798 that 'The times are so very perilous that we are by no means anxious to increase the Circulation of our Cash Notes more than is really necessary for their use & service in this part of

[132] Diary 19 May 1820; note book bound in vol IX.
[133] e.g. Jackson, Hull in the Eighteenth Century, p. 219; Bidwell, Annals of an East Anglian Bank, p. 317.
[134] Pressnell, Country Banking in the Industrial Revolution, p. 144; Bankers' Magazine (1844), I.
[135] Pressnell, Country Banking in the Industrial Revolution, p. 146.
[136] Jackson, Hull in the Eighteenth Century, p. 101.
[137] Diary 17 June 1801.
[138] SROB Acc 2191, entry dated 23 August 1797.

the Country . . . we shall always think it necessary to be prepared to the full amount of what we have in circulation and as such don't wish to extend beyond a certain degree at least until we can see the times settled'.[139] This was written in the aftermath of the cash crisis; later in 1800, when rumour threatened to cause a run on his bank, he wrote, with a degree of righteous indignation, that it had always been and 'most assuredly ever would be a maxim of this House never to issue more Notes than we are prepared to turn into Cash in 24 hours'.[140]

The evidence does not permit speculation on the cash ratios maintained in better times. It would seem that, in addition to the interest-free deposit held by his London agents, Oakes had large sums in readily convertible assets. He wrote to his brokers in May 1797 asking them whether 'in case of the worst . . . India Bonds be as readily turn'd into cash or made sale of as anything'.[141] Perhaps, like Rodwell of Ipswich, he tried to keep 100% cover in times of financial crisis while at others he was happy with a ratio of 50% or more. Leighton Boyce has shown that Smith's demand liabilities were covered by only 45% liquid assets, excluding promissory notes made by customers.[142] Pressnell cites the case of Praeds of Truro reducing their bank's debts and advances to cover the total amount of their notes in circulation when recession threatened in 1813 and, when the economic outlook improved, reducing the ratio of liabilities to assets to two thirds.[143] Above all Oakes was a prudent man and one cannot imagine him taking unnecessary risks.

THE 1797 CASH CRISIS AND THE BURY NEW BANK
This prudent approach to cash ratios and the limitation of note issue during times of economic stringency enabled Oakes to survive the 1797 cash crisis, although it occurred when the bank was newly established and vulnerable. In fact the crisis left Messrs Oakes one of the leading bankers in Suffolk. The events provide an interesting illustration of the way in which country bankers helped each other during crises in order to retain public confidence, and also of the stamina, courage and foresight needed by them to survive in such uncertain times.

The first three years of the Bury New Bank's existence was one of the most difficult periods for country bankers, coinciding with the start of the war with France, a severe commercial crisis and poor harvests. Payments to foreign allies, heavy grain imports and the French return to a completely metallic standard all

[139] SROB Acc 2191, entry dated 27 March 1798.
[140] Diary 19 November 1800.
[141] SROB Acc 2191, entry dated 31 May 1797.
[142] Pressnell, Country Banking in the Industrial Revolution, pp. 206–07 states that Gurneys kept the whole of their assets in convertible securities and that Stuckey kept enough assets in London in Stock Exchange Bills and other convertible securities to pay their notes. See also J. A. S. L. Leighton Boyce, London National Provincial Bank Ltd (1958), p. 24.
[143] Pressnell, Country Banking in the Industrial Revolution, pp. 206–07.

10. *Spink and Carss's Bank, Buttermarket, Bury St Edmunds.*

combined to cause a drain of gold abroad. As trade improved and prices began to rise again there was an increasing demand for money which was met by the issue of both Bank of England and country bank notes, the latter often backed by grossly inedaquate reserves. Early in 1797 invasion scares led many customers to demand cash from their banks which, in turn, sought payment in London. On 24 February 1797 news of Col Tate's raid on Fishguard leaked before the official government announcement, with the result that there was a stampede to withdraw money from the Bank of England. The government was forced to act and, two days later, issued an Order in Council empowering the Bank of England to refuse cash payments. This was confirmed by Parliament on 3 May 1797 in the Bank Restriction Act. Although intended to be temporary, the act remained in force for the next 24 years.

On the surface, 1796 was a promising year for the Bury New Bank. Oakes finally gave up the yarn trade, became a full-time banker and reorganized his accounting methods. However, 1797 opened with the Bury receipt 15 parishes short and the bankuptcy of Dennis Chandler, a corn and coal merchant with extensive property in Stowmarket and Ipswich.[144] Consols, which Oakes had bought at 56 in November 1796, were sold in February 1797 at 54¾ and news arrived of the total defeat of the Austrians by the French in Italy.[145]

---

[144] Diary 18, 25 January 1797.
[145] SROB Acc 2191, entries dated 7 November 1796, 4 February 1797; diary 4 February 1797.

11. Fanlight over a doorway in Spink and Carss's Bank.

In spite of these events there is no hint of alarm at the economic situation in either the letter book or the diary. Indeed Oakes's mood must have been relatively optimistic in the first half of February for he decided to build a new study for himself as an extension to the bank premises.[146] Eleven days later Messrs Watson and Wilcocks, the Norwich merchants, stopped payment, owing Oakes £494 9s. 6d..[147] The following night Oakes, always vulnerable to stress, returned home early from dinner at the *Angel* because of 'an indiff cold & cough' which was followed by a 'bad night'. Yet there were still no real signs of alarm: the weather was bright and clear and work was begun on the new study on 24 February. The next day, for the first time, Oakes remarked on the shortage of specie and his increasing anxiety about the future. Two days later he recorded the Order in Council suspending cash payments.[148]

The effect was immediate. On Tuesday the five Norwich banks suspended business until the legal situation was made clear in Parliament, and they were followed by the three Bury banks: Messrs Spink and Carss, Messrs Cork and Messrs James Oakes and Son.[149] A public meeting was held in the Guildhall under the chairmanship of the Alderman, Peter Chambers, Oakes's old yarn manager, and an agreement was signed by over 100 men who undertook to accept Bank of England notes and resident bankers' notes as usual. Three days

[146] Diary 11 February 1797.
[147] Diary 22 February 1797.
[148] Diary 25, 27 February 1797.
[149] Diary 28 February, 1 March 1797.

after the Suspension, Oakes and Son and the other Bury bankers began to pay their own notes with Bank of England notes and 'for the fractional parts only in specie drawing at 1 month on London for the provincial Bank notes whn payment for them was required & transacting all other business as usual'.[150] Specie was so short that 'not a Guinea could be procured from Town'. There was, however, encouraging news of Admiral Jervis's defeat of the Spanish Fleet which was 'at this critical juncture perhaps the most providential & happiest Event that could have happened to this Kingdom.'[151]

Orbell Oakes was dispatched to London to bring home the new one and two pound Bank notes and 'also if possible some specie & Dollars' on 5 March 1797. The following day some of Messrs Cork's notes were returned from London unpaid. Oakes's cough and cold returned. The uncertainty surrounding Cork's affairs caused 'A great number of applications for cash' to the Bury New Bank which were met satisfactorily. Although they ran out of one and two pound notes they ended the day with an increased amount of specie and 'the Day passd off upon the whole very pleasantly every Body seemd disposd to make the best shift possible'. Oakes hoped that 'a few weeks might remedy the prest Inconveniecys' but 'continued very unwell'.[152]

Orbell Oakes returned from London having been unable to get one and two pound bank notes 'of any consequence'. The Oakeses' London business was done with Barclay Tritton and Company through Gurneys of Norwich. It appears that Barclays did not regard Oakes and Son as being on their list of customers and had refused to give them small bank notes. Their need of small notes was very great and had it not been for the generosity of Messrs Eaton Hammond of Newmarket they might not have survived. Eaton Hammonds' London bankers had procured £100 of one and two pound bank notes for them half of which they readily gave to Oakes.[153] This experience caused him to consider issuing his own small notes.[154]

On Monday Messrs Cork stopped payment and the following Wednesday the leading Bury bank of Messrs Spink and Carss also stopped, causing 'Consternation & confusion' throughout the town'.[155] Within an hour of hearing the news Orbell Oakes rushed to Norwich to seek help from the Gurneys and, although the town 'continud in much confusion' there were 'several applications from the most respectable people' to become customers now that the Bury New Bank was the only bank in the town.[156]

For the next few days Oakes's 'concerns continu[ed] to go on very smoothly'. A new clerk was engaged, few notes were brought in for payment, and he

[150] SROB Acc 2191, entry dated 4 March 1797.
[151] Diary 4 March 1797.
[152] Diary 7 March 1797.
[153] SROB Acc 2191, entry dated 11 March 1797.
[154] Diary 8 March 1797.
[155] Diary 15 March 1797.
[156] Diary 16 March 1797.

restrained his cash notes from going out as far as possible, although small notes were still much in demand.[157] Threats of local bankruptcy continued as a result of Spink and Carss's failure but Oakes expected none of 'material consequence'. Indeed his confidence at being the only banker in Bury and hopes for increased business and influence was reflected in the decision to change the name of the bank from the Bury New Bank to the more impressive Bury and Suffolk Bank. The note engraver was instructed to alter the name on the new one pound notes accordingly.

Meanwhile the Oakeses' monopoly of banking in Bury was threatened by Edmund Squire, a liquor merchant, and his cousin William Dalton, an attorney, who planned to open a bank in Squire's premises and had begun touting for custom among local farmers. The idea seems to have come to nothing at this stage although Squire was to open a bank in Bury sometime later.[158] Tension in the town continued at such a pitch that a run on the Bury and Suffolk Bank was threatened because their old agents, Ladbrokes, had refused to pay one of their notes when it was presented in London.[159]

Oakes faced the day bravely 'determin'd to carry it thro' with Spirit' and confident that his business was on so sound a footing that he had nothing to fear. In the event few notes were presented and Orbell Oakes returned from London 'very amply supplyed'.[160] Indeed business flourished and the bank 'was resorted to from Morng till Night by the most respectable merchts Farmers &ca &ca. It is Impossible the prospect can be more flattering to us'.[161] The prospect was so flattering that Oakes estimated that nearly enough Bank of England notes had been brought in to pay all his cash notes in circulation at that time.[162] Fresh customers continued to arrive and the Bury and Suffolk Bank's new one pound notes were issued but were not to be exchanged for drafts with time on them except for a discount of nine shillings in £100.[163]

At the beginning of April, Oakes decided to give up the bank's agency with Messrs Barclay and Company through Gurneys and to have a London agent of their own.[164] Barclay's refusal to supply them with Bank of England notes and specie at the beginning of the crisis and trouble with Barclay's notes during the previous year must have influenced this decision. Oakes had complained that Barclay's notes were often defaced and torn and that letters and figures looked as though they had been written either 'with a very broad nibbed pen or, as it were, with a skewer' deliberately to make them illegible. They were so bad that many

157 SROB Acc 2191, entries dated 16,18 March 1797.
158 Diary 20 March 1797.
159 SROB Acc 2191, entry dated 24 March 1797.
160 Diary 21, 22 March 1797.
161 Diary 22 March 1797.
162 Diary 22 March 1797.
163 Diary 29 March 1797.
164 Diary 2 April 1797.

people refused to accept them.[165] On another occasion Oakes remarked that if Barclays were punctual in their attention to business then he would continue to be a customer which suggests that he was not totally satisfied with their service.[166]

Tactful letters were written to Barclays explaining that the business of the Bury and Suffolk Bank had so increased that they could not expect Barclays, with numerous Gurney branches on their books, to give them the attention that they required now that they were 'on their own bottom'.[167] One thousand pounds was left with Barclays while notes drawn on them were still in circulation and on 25 July 1797 the Bury and Suffolk Bank stopped issuing cash notes drawn on Barclays and began to do so on Aytons and Company.[168] By August their balance with Aytons was £5,561.[169]

The Bury and Suffolk Bank enjoyed a monopoly of banking in Bury for the next four years. Oakes's cautious policy with regard to cash ratios, his careful investment of funds, together with the support of influential local men and the help of neighbouring banks, had all combined to enable the firm to survive the crisis of 1797. However, the next four years were not easy, despite the absence of rivals.

THE BURY AND SUFFOLK BANK

THE GRIGBY CASE
The suspension of cash payments had unexpected and unpleasant repercussions for Oakes involving him in the only case in which an attempt was made to force payment in specie. The Bank Restriction Act only applied to the Bank of England guaranteeing the use of Bank notes in all government business. Bankers had voluntarily agreed to accept them leaving other creditors free to refuse payments in notes and to insist on legal tender coins. Country bankers could therefore pay Bank of England notes to the government, to merchants and to other bankers, but were legally liable to pay specie to those who refused to accept them.[170]

At the end of April 1798 Joshua Grigby, an ardent radical from Drinkstone, visited the Bury and Suffolk Bank on two occasions and refused Bank of England paper in payment of an Oakes note, insisting on specie.[171] No more is heard of the matter until January 1801 when Grigby repeated his demand. At first he

---

[165] SROB Acc 2191, entry dated 1 February 1796.
[166] *Ibid*, entry dated 31 March 1796.
[167] *Ibid*, entry dated 9 April 1797.
[168] *Ibid*, entry dated 25 July 1797; see also SROB HA535/1/18.
[169] *Ibid*, entry dated 8 August 1797.
[170] E. Coppieters, *English Bank Note Circulation* (The Louvain Institute of Economic and Social Research, 1955), pp. 36–37.
[171] Diary 30 April, 12 May 1798.

tendered 50 guineas in notes for which he eventually accepted Bank paper and some change. He then gave his man-servant a Bury and Suffolk Bank one pound note for which he received cash and then a five guinea note for which he also received cash. The clerk apparently gave him cash because the man was a servant. The luckless man was told by his master to present another five guinea note for which the clerk gave him five pounds in Bank paper and five shillings in specie. Grigby refused to accept this and left the bank vowing to bring an action against James and Orbell Oakes.[172] Both men were away at the time but their clerks made full notes of what had occurred. A writ was served on them on 9 February 1801 and two days later Grigby visited three times to demand specie. The following Wednesday he brought in £100 in Bury and Suffolk Bank notes and accepted Bank paper for most of it 'apparently very Gentlemanly'.[173] This was repeated on the next Wednesday. Oakes must have been becoming quite paranoid by this stage: he had a small window put in the bank room so that he could see who came into the bank from his inner study.[174]

The case was heard before Baron Hotham at the end of July. In his summing up the Judge had harsh things to say about Grigby's action describing it as 'the most wanton, busy, officious, unprecedented, and malignant attack that I have ever known in a court of justice', which would disrupt the trade of the country. The jury twice wanted to return a verdict for the defendants but the Judge said that although 'he admired their Feelings . . . the matter to be decided was a point of Law wch was not for their Determination & therefore their verdict must be special for the plaintiff subject to the Court of Common Pleas'.[175]

The case confirmed that Bank of England notes were not legal tender although the Bank Restriction Act permitted debtors to avoid arrest by offering them and any proceedings brought by creditors to secure cash payment were held in abeyance as long as the Act was in force.

Oakes was particularly upset by Grigby's action. They were friends of long-standing and Grigby had stated that he would 'rather hold Messers O cash Notes than the Bank of England' therefore, as Oakes said, 'Why bring an action against his friend and neighbour' when if he wanted to make a point he could 'go to his Lon[do]n Banker or make use of some Banking House out of the County'.[176]

Grigby also felt that he had been misrepresented and in an open letter to the *Bury Post* the following week defended his action. It would appear that in May 1798, when he had first demanded cash, it was was a matter of principle. He was refused payment initially but had eventually agreed that 'if he got in exchange for his Notes at the rate of 5 Gs per week' he would not ask for more specie

---

[172] Diary 31 January 1801.
[173] Diary 11, 18 February 1801.
[174] Diary 7 March 1801.
[175] Diary 24 July 1801; see also Grigby v Oakes 126 *English Reports* 1420; John Bernard Bosanquet and Christopher Puller, *Reports of Cases Argued and Determined . . .* (ud) II, p. 526; BNP 29 July 1801. Oakes's account of the case tallies with all these almost exactly.
[176] Diary 24 July 1801.

payments during wartime. However, in December 1800, he had deposited £1,300 with the Bury and Suffolk Bank, over £100 of which was in specie. Therefore he felt that he was entitled to payment in specie having already deposited it with the bank.[177]

The radical Grigby maintained that it was the right of every free-born Englishman to have gold in payment of his notes because he was concerned about the future purchasing power of paper currency if this were not the case. In his opinion Oakes, unlike the Bank of England, need 'not elude the payment of any just demand under the shelter of an Act of Parliament — His notes are not forged — It is in his power to supply specie sufficient for the details of Country business — and he may be obliged to do so'.[178]

LONDON INVESTMENTS: THE LONDON AGENT

Country bankers had an agent to pay their notes for them in London, to accept their drafts and to pay them, to buy stock and to do any other London business that they required. After consulting several London houses Oakes began his banking career by drawing indirectly on Barclays through Gurneys of Norwich until 1797 when he began to draw directly on Ayton, Brassey and Company. Aytons remained the London agents of the Bury and Suffolk Bank until its amalgamation with Messrs Sparrow Browne and Company of Bury St Edmunds in 1829.

There were regular contacts between the Bury and Suffolk Bank and their London agents to collect notes payable in London and accumulated by Aytons, to bring home specie and discounted bills and to take up the cash notes of bankers from other parts of the country, bills for discount and other money surplus to local requirements. The diary shows that at least once a month someone from the bank went to London with considerable sums of money, particularly after the receipt. In October 1800 a clerk took up 'full 23,000' in Bank cash notes and bills while in 1822 Oakes 'carried up abt £32,000 in Specie & cash besides Other matters'.[179] Equally large sums were brought back from London. In 1803, for example, Oakes took between eight and nine thousand pounds and returned with 1,350 guineas in specie and £17,000 in Notes. On another occasion he brought back nearly £15,000 in 'our Notes'.[180]

The movement of such large sums of money and notes presented a serious security problem. Highway robbery was not uncommon. Oakes's own daughter, Maria, had been robbed on Bagshot Heath when on her way to join he husband in Devonshire, while one of Messrs Alexander's clerks was robbed of a parcel

---

[177] BNP 5 August 1801.
[178] Roy Workman, 'The Joshua Grigbys' (1983), typescript in the possession of Mr Workman. I am much indebted to Mr Workman for allowing me to use it.
[179] Diary 25 October 1800, 13 May 1822.
[180] Diary 10 September 1805.

containing £31,199 in notes which he was bringing back to Ipswich from their London agents.[181] Various precautions were taken to avoid theft. In February 1798 Aytons were requested to address a parcel of notes to Ray Oakes and Company, the name under which the Oakeses dealt in yarn, coal and hops, and to put something in the package to make it heavier.[182] Friends and relations were pressed into service to transport notes and cash. The timing of London visits was varied deliberately from month to month so that a known routine was not established and clerks carrying notes were armed with pistols. There was particular anxiety as to the danger presented by the 14 miles of open road between Newmarket and Bury. Many people had been robbed on this stretch, and Oakes played an active part in the agitation to get an armed guard put on the mail coach.[183]

Most country bankers had a proportion of their liquid assets on deposit with their London agents. The Bury and Suffolk Bank had to leave an interest-free deposit to the value of 10% of their note issue there is no evidence as to the amount of money that they left on deposit at interest with Messrs Aytons. It was probably high immediately after the receipt until the money could be channelled into more lucrative fields of investment. A note between the volumes for the years 1809 and 1810 claims that Aytons allowed the Bury and Suffolk Bank four per cent on all deposits after the £6,000 interest-free deposit demanded to cover the payment of their notes in London. In April 1821 £16,000 was left with Messrs Ayton and Lees after other investments had been made and in May 1825 between twenty and thirty thousand pounds.[184]

LONDON INVESTMENTS: THE BILL BROKER AND STOCK BROKERS

The Bury and Suffolk Bank had a London bill broker and stock broker to manage their other London investments. Their bill brokers were Messrs Richardson and Company. Thomas Richardson had been a clerk with the Gurney's bill broker, Samuel Smith. In about 1801 he had left Smith following a disagreement over the commission charged on bills presented for discount and founded his own firm. He received so much help and encouragement in the venture from the Gurneys that Smith claimed that they had induced Richardson to leave him in the first place. The quarrel was resolved but by the summer of 1809 all the Gurneys' bills discounted through a London broker were handled by Richardson. He was joined by Overend in 1805 and the firm became the foremost bill broking agent for country bankers, receiving bills from industrial Lancashire in particular and sending them for discount to agricultural counties, like Norfolk and Suffolk,

[181] Bidwell, *Annals of an East Anglian Bank*, pp. 376–79; IJ 5 October 1822; diary 20 August 1794.
[182] SROB Acc 2191, entry dated 7 February 1798.
[183] *Ibid*, entry dated 26 October 1795; SROB 317/1, p. 37; diary 12, 14, 23 February 1796, 31 March 1796, 11 August 1797, 10 November 1797. The problem remained unresolved.
[184] SROB HA535/1/4.

which had accumulated funds for investment through war-time agricultural prosperity.[185]

During the Suspension period, bills were an increasingly popular form of short-term investment, especially for tax money, and were much in demand in agricultural counties as the level of taxation rose. They offered a higher rate of interest than would have been obtained by the country banker leaving the money on deposit with his London banker or investing it in government securities.[186] Certainly most of the diary references to Richardsons coincide with the end of a quarter's receipt. The specific amount sent to Richrdson for investment is mentioned only once, in 1810, when Oakes noted leaving for London with the receipt money 'clearing Ourselves of all Cash things Bills due &ca &ca abt 4,000 to Lea and Co & 11,000 to Richardson & co'.[187] On that occasion bills would seem to have been a more popular investment than deposit with his London bankers.

The importance of bills as a form of investment for tax monies is further demonstrated by the fact that immediately before embarking on the East Suffolk receipt for the first time Oakes went to London to discuss the matter with Richardsons.[188] Oakes gives the firm impression that he always dealt directly with Richardsons himself, possibly having been introduced to them by the Gurneys.[189] They are first mentioned in 1809, although from the tone of the entry this was not their initial contact, when Peter Chambers took 'large Remittances to Richardson & co' and to their London bankers following the quarter's receipt.[190] The next reference was in July 1810 when Oakes, anxious to see what effect the bankruptcy of Messrs Brickwood, Rainer, Morgan, Starkey and Company had had on the City, took the receipt to London himself. In spite of the general alarm he was relieved to find that his 'Bill Concern wh Richardson & co' was satisfactory and no losses were expected.[191] In January 1811, Oakes had to send a clerk to London because of the 'miscarriage of Richardson & co letters'.[192]

It is not possible to speculate on the level of business that Messers Oakes maintained with Richardsons. They are not mentioned in the diary as often as his bankers and stock brokers although the term *brokers* may have been used collectively to apply to both bill and stock brokers at times when names were not

---

[185] W. T. C. King, *The History of the London Discount Market* (1936), pp. 10,18–22; Bidwell, *Annals of an East Anglian Bank*, p. 77–81.
[186] King, *The History of the London Discount Market*, pp. 27–28; Pressnell, *Country Banking in the Industrial Revolution*, p. 100.
[187] Diary 1 November 1810.
[188] Diary 14 November 1822.
[189] Pressnell, *Country Banking in the Industrial Revolution*, p. 100 maintains that until well after 1815 the bill broking business of country bankers was conducted through their London agents.
[190] Diary 14 July 1809.
[191] Diary 20 July 1810.
[192] Diary 11 January 1811.

specified. Pressnell found no evidence that country bankers kept large balances at their bill brokers on a regular basis until about 1820, the size of balances varying inversely with the rate of discount.[193] From the inadequate evidence available in the diary it is impossible to draw conclusions beyond the observation that there appeared to have been regular contact between the bank and Richardsons from 1809 at least, especially after the quarterly receipt, and that large sums were involved. In a letter, probably written in the later 1820s, Richardsons thank Messrs Oakes 'for the steady & valuable connection which we have enjoyed so long with your firm' and begged that Messrs Oakes 'may not any time feel difficulty in sending here any extra sum you may have to dispose of'.[194] This suggests that not only did a long standing relationship exist between the two companies but also that the Oakeses, in common with other investors, made less use of the discount market once interest rates had fallen after the war, and that by this time the bank was lending money to the bill market rather than actually buying bills on their own account.[195]

The Oakeses had employed a stock broker since at least 1790 to advise on the investment of the receipt, using the firm of Lambert and Cotton of 25 Cornhill. They dealt directly with them as they did with their bill brokers, leaving them wide discretion to purchase stock on the bank's behalf.[196] In 1808, Lambert committed suicide leaving behind 'alarming Deficiencys in his Affairs'.[197] It was discovered that 'he had been acting most wickedly making away with the property of his clients' so much so that Oakes feared that when it became known there would be a run on the bank.[198] Cotton was made bankrupt and Oakes took his business to Messrs Dawes and Company of Threadneedle Street. After the death of William Dawes in 1812 the firm continued under the name of Talbot and Francis.

The Bury and Suffolk Bank was in regular contact with their brokers taking money up directly after each receipt. It is not surprising to find that most of the investments made through them by Oakes and noted by him in his diary were in short dated stock, in India Bonds, Exchequer Bills, Navy and Victualling Bills and the Omnium, together with some long-dated government stock. Probably, like other country bankers, having built up an adequate balance with his London agent, investment in the Funds presented an opportunity to extend his London reserves and to gain greater profit from his money than could be produced by

[193] Pressnell, Country Banking in the Industrial Revolution, pp. 438–40.
[194] Orbell Oakes's Private Memorandum Book.
[195] R. S. Sayer, Lloyds Bank in the History of English Banking (Oxford, 1957), p. 177. Sayer suggests that the first evidence of brokers becoming dealers and holding bills on their own account was in 1812.
[196] Sayer, Lloyds Bank, pp. 128–29 suggests that country bankers used their stock brokers indirectly through the agency of their London bankers until late in the nineteenth century.
[197] Diary 5 April 1808.
[198] Diary 13 April 1808

leaving it on deposit. His concentration on short-dated stock would also have minimized the loss of liquidity involved in employing his money.

Holdings in government stock were seen as a normal part of the reserves of country bankers until about the third decade of the nineteenth century. They were considered the 'third liquidity line' after cash and balances held by the London agent.[199] The letter book gives the impression of a preference for three per cent stock in the early days although four per cent seems to dominate later. Entries between March and May 1797 recorded the buying and selling of three per cent consoles, Oakes writing to Lamberts on the importance of 'frequently buying & selling upon our own account and little risks must be hazarded so long as the principal is safe. Our gains or Losses upon Interest acct must be averaged'.[200]

By far the most popular investments were East India Bonds and Exchequer Bills. In a gloomy letter written during the Suspension Crisis in May 1797, Oakes enquired of Lamberts whether in 'case of the worst . . . India Bonds be as readily turnd into cash or made sale of as anything'.[201] In 1805 Orbell Oakes is reported taking £25,000 of East India Bonds to London,[202] while in 1821 Oakes visited Dawes and Company with 'the first halves of 37,000 Exchequer Bills'.[203] Having received the interest due the first halves were left in his London bankers' hands while the other halves remained at Dawe's offices. In 1823 Oakes delivered over 50,000 Exchequer Bills to his brokers and in March 1824 Orbell Oakes took India Bonds up to London.[204]

Oakes's estimation of his losses through Lambert's fraud and Cotton's subsequent bankruptcy give further information about his investments. In them he stated that he had £36,401 9s. 10d. in Exchequer bills including interest of £1,101 13s. 1½d. plus a balance of £28 17s. 7d. up to 31 March 1808, making a total of £36,430 7s. 5d.. On the 'stocks Acct' there was £14,904 made up of 18,000 4% stocks standing at 81 on 4 April, plus the half yearly dividend of £360, 'less £36 property tax'.[205] It says much for the stability of the Bury and Suffolk Bank that it was able to withstand such losses less than 14 years after its foundation. In true style, Oakes was later demanding a reduction in his property tax to take account of the loss.

It is not possible to see to what extent Oakes varied his investment strategy according to market conditions beyond the occasional note. For example in March 1814 he recorded deciding not to sell stock because news from the war

[199] Pressnell, *Country Banking in the Industrial Revolution*, pp. 417–18; Sayer, *Lloyds Bank*, p. 126
[200] SROB Acc 2191, entry dated 25 May 1797.
[201] *Ibid*, entry dated 31 May 1797.
[202] Diary 28 November 1805.
[203] Diary 25 April 1821.
[204] Diary 20 June 1823, 19 March 1824; SROB HA535/1/4 also makes it clear that Exchequer Bills and India Bonds were the Bank's chief form of investment.
[205] Diary 18 May 1808.

front was more favourable than had been expected, while he invested in short term bills during the Suspension period when they offered a particularly good return.

India Bonds were a popular form of investment in the eighteenth century because they were easily converted into cash. By the 1780s their popularity was thought to be in decline in the face of competition from Exchequer Bills and Inland Bills of Exchange.[206] This would perhaps explain Oakes's pessimistic suggestion that they were a good investment because of their high liquidity rather than their profitability 'in case of the worst' and 'some internal convulsion' occurring.[207] India Bonds were mentioned on three other occasions but it is impossible to tell whether they were used to hold sums that had been set aside for a particular purpose at a later date.[208] A note in the back of the memorandum book states that in May 1805 the bank held £34,000 in India Bonds.[209]

The only Navy and Victualling Bills referred to were those held on behalf of Army customers who had been sent to Jersey.[210] By far the most popular form of investment, apart from three or four per cent consols, were Exchequer Bills. Their supply increased enormously between 1792 and 1814 from £11,000,000 to £59,000,000. They were less liquid than India Bonds and many commercial bills having a term of about a year, but they bore a high rate of interest which varied to reflect changes in the market. Between 1797 and 1815 interest on them was equivalent to an annual rate of 5.3%. They were therefore a profitable form of investment if they were held until maturity because it was not usurious to buy and sell a fixed interest security at a price giving more than five per cent. Pressnell quotes examples of country bankers holding large numbers of Exchequer Bills which matured at different periods to overcome liquidity problems and of others who used them as occasional rather than regular outlets for their surplus funds.[211] The diary shows that Exchequer Bills formed a regular part of Oakes's investment of the receipt and that they continued to do so even after the end of the war when yields had fallen and curbed enthusiasm for the discount market.[212] There is one entry in the diary that suggests that Oakes bought Exchequer Bills to mature monthly, but it is very unsafe to draw conclusions from a single example. In June 1823 Orbell Oakes is recorded as preparing to go to London to 'Exchange Excr Bills for prest month'. These were worth over £50,000 on that occasion.[213]

It is noticeable that in all the bank's London investment dealings it is James Oakes who played the dominant role in making decisions until he was well over

206 Pressnell, Country Banking in the Industrial Revolution, pp. 240,260.
207 SROB Acc 2191, entry dated 31 May 1797.
208 Diary 28 November, 2 December 1805, 19 March 1824.
209 SROB HA535/1/4.
210 SROB Acc 2191, entry dated 21 April 1796.
211 Pressnell, Country Bankinng in the Industrial Revolution, pp. 421–22.
212 Ibid, p. 423.
213 Diary 17, 20 June 1823.

80. This impression could be caused by the obvious bias of a diary which will naturally put the writer at the centre of affairs, or could be the result of saint-like tact on the part of his family in letting him think that he was. It is, however, corroborated in a letter from one of the trustees of Mrs Bevan, wife of a partner in the rival bank of Sparrow Browne, in which the writer claims that Orbell Oakes had little taste for business and that his son, Henry, was also inexperienced.[214]

As well as dealing with the investment of their own assets the Bury and Suffolk Bank handled the investments of its customers. What little evidence there is suggests that stock was bought and sold on their behalf. In January 1816, for example, Oakes went to London 'principally for transferring Stock to Duke of Norfolk and Revd T. G. Cullum'.[215]

LOCAL INVESTMENTS: UTILITIES

It is impossible from the limited evidence available to distinguish between James Oakes's personal speculations and investment undertaken on behalf of the Bury and Suffolk Bank. Either as individuals or as bankers, the Oakeses were involved in turnpikes and the Bury St Edmunds Improvement Commission besides other projects. Utilities were a popular form of investment for country bankers because they brought the banker into contact with potential customers and increased the amount of money passing through his hands. James Oakes was both a Commissioner and treasurer of the Thetford Turnpike, the Sudbury Turnpike and, from 1816, the Newmarket Turnpike, although at least two of these schemes were not particularly profitable.[216] Unfortunately no records have survived and Oakes gives little further information about them in his diary, although brief notes in his memorandum book suggest that by the 1820s their accounts were in deficit.[217]

The Bury and Suffolk Bank acted as bankers to the Bury Guardians and lent them money against the security of the rates. Existing accounts show that the debt stood at £600 between August 1799 and August 1800[218] and had risen to £800 by November 1800.[219] A rumour that a seven shilling rate was to be levied to pay their notes nearly provoked a run on the bank. At the time Oakes claimed that they charged no interest on the loan although later, in May 1822, the Guardians acknowledged that the Bury and Suffolk Bank had lent them £1,460 3s. 10½d. and were entitled to charge interest.[220] In addition to interest charges the bank must have benefitted from having rate monies passing through their

---

[214] LA 5030 undated letter postmarked 7 September 1829.
[215] Diary 31 January 1816.
[216] Diary entry following 21 July 1805 headed 'Thetford Turnpike road to Bury'; 4 June 1816.
[217] SROB HA535/1/4, fols 48,75.
[218] SROB 1557/8.
[219] Diary 19 November 1800.
[220] SROB Guardians' Court Book N5/1/3.

hands, especially during the early 1830s when the amount levied was over £2,000 in most quarters.[221]

On the bankruptcy of Spink and Carss, during the Cash Crisis of 1797, the Oakeses became bankers to the Corporation and took over a loan of £2,350 made by Spink to the Alderman and Burgesses at some time before 1778. Although the debt was steadily reduced between 1798 and 1819 by 1831 it had risen again and stood at £2,350.[222]

Both James and Orbell Oakes were Improvement Commissioners in Bury St Edmunds under the Act passed in 1811, and James Oakes was appointed treasurer. Each Commissioner was required to lend £1,000 at interest on the security of the rates and Oakes, as treasurer, to give security of £4,000. Between 1812 and 1816 the bank lent the Commission a total of £2,600 at interest and Oakes was influential in prompting a further Act in 1820 which gave the Commission powers to borrow up to £10,000 but never more that £8,000 at any one time.[223] This Oakes rightly predicted, would prove inadequate 'to complete the Paving & repair that which wants & to light next winter'.[224]

The Bury and Suffolk Bank also helped to fund other improvements to the amenities of the town. In 1798 James Oakes bought the church yard for £330 on behalf of the Corporation on his own initiative. A committee was set up to manage it and seven £50 bonds were issued 'to pay the same allowg 20£ for Expences'.[225] Three years later he was the instigator of a scheme to buy the Assembly Rooms and the adjoining house, paying £40 down, the remaining £1,710 to be paid at Michaelmas '(as per agreement between Mr Blachley & Self)'.[226] Twelve men, including James and Orbell Oakes contributed £500 each to improve the Rooms in order to provide a ball room, supper, coffee, billiard and card rooms. The Rooms were to be administered by a committee of five, including Oakes, with a separate committee to manage the billiard room. The subscription and entrance tickets for balls were raised and 150 subscribers enrolled. The Rooms (now the Atheneum) were opened in time for the fair in October 1803[227] and were felt by many 'scarcely to be parallelled in any part of this kingdom',[228] an 'Edifice worthy of the justly admired Town of Bury and replete with every

[221] Ibid.
[222] SROB Corporation Receiver's Accounts 1778–1832 D6/5/3.
[223] SROB Minutes of the Paving Commission L3/2/4.
[224] SROB HA535/1/4, fol. 38.
[225] Diary 16 June 1798. The loan was not paid off until 1830, SROB D6/5/3.
[226] Diary 7 August 1801; SROB D7/6/46.
[227] All the Bury guide books claim that the improvements were completed in 1804. Oakes's diary makes it clear that it was opened for the first time in October 1803. Gillingwater, St Edmunds Bury (1804), p. 265, says it 'is now, 1804, nearly finished in all its parts and in a style superior taste and convenience'.
[228] Guide to Bury Saint Edmunds (Bury, 1833), p. 86.

Convenience and comfort'.[229] The Rooms were conveyed to the subscribers in 1806.

In the early days of country banking many bankers were closely associated with insurance companies and often combined the two businesses.[230] The Oakeses were involved in insurance as early as 1795 although 'No more than £200 on one bottom' was to be expended at that time.[231] In 1802 the Suffolk and General County Fire Office was set up. It was proposed to raise £10,000 through the issue of 1,000 shares and both James Oakes and his son each made an initial investment of ten shares.[232] James Oakes was appointed a trustee and director and Orbell Oakes was made a director in 1806 but the Bury and Suffolk Bank was not appointed treasurer.[233] This office was filled by Messrs Alexanders of Ipswich for East Suffolk and Messrs Crowe, Sparrow, Browne of Bury for the West. Several other local bankers invested in the company including George Round of Colchester and John Spooner of Ipswich. The Oakeses' investment was fairly modest at first in comparison with that of Messrs Crowe, Sparrow, Browne who had 65 shares between their four partners, although similar to that of Messrs Alexander whose four partners acquired a total of 44 shares. The company was profitable and in 1804 Oakes began to buy up shares.[234]

LOCAL INVESTMENTS: AGRICULTURE, BUSINESS AND TRADE

Loans by country bankers to landowners to finance enclosures were thought to have been extensive during the agriculturally prosperous war years although they contracted after 1815.[235] There is little evidence to show to what extent the Bury and Suffolk Bank financed local agriculture generally and enclosure in particular. Oakes took a close interest in farming affairs and had many farmer customers who were entertained to dinner on market days, in the dining room above the bank, and who were invited to his aldermanic dinner in 1802.[236] The Bury and Suffolk Bank were appointed bankers to the Bardwell enclosure in 1829[237] and Oakes's memorandum book shows that they were involved in the Rougham, Chevington, Fornham, Hepworth and Nowton enclosures.[238] In 1816 the Guildhall Feoffment Trust was lent £1,300 to help to defray the cost of the Bury

[229] BNP 6 October 1802.
[230] Pressnell, Country Banking in the Industrial Revolution, pp. 55–56; Bidwell, Annals of an East Anglian Bank, p36 Bartlett Gurney invested in marine insurance in Yarmouth, Lynn and London.
[231] SROB Acc 2191, entry dated 5 September 1795.
[232] SROB Insurance Indenture HH500/1/1; Minute Book HH500/2/1.
[233] SROB HH500/2/1, p. 57.
[234] Ibid, pp. 30,61.
[235] Pressnell, Country Banking in the Industrial Revolution, pp. 344–55.
[236] Diary 30 September 1802.
[237] SROB Bardwell Enclosure Minutes and Papers 1028/4.
[238] SROB HA535/1/4 fols 5, 12, 23, 25, 48; HA535/1/18.

enclosure. The loan was to be repaid in instalments of not less than £300 a year plus interest.[239]

Messrs Oakes received the rents of many customers including the Tyrrells of Gipping, the Cocksedges of Rattlesden and Woolpit, Lord Bristol, the Reverend Richard Moseley of Drinkstone and the Marquess Cornwallis's Culford estates. Money was advanced on the security of the rents. Thomas Cocksedge was lent £200 'for a month or two'[240] and advances were made to the Earl Bishop and to his son to finance various building and agricultural projects. A letter written in 1797 warned that 'before his Lordship issues any further drafts it will be adviseable we should be satisfied that assets are in readiness'.[241] A further letter in May 1798 shows that the bank was advancing money to finance the building of the Earl's extraordinary house at Ickworth. Writing to the agent in Lincolnshire, Oakes asked when they might expect to receive the long-awaited rents from those estates and made it clear that the bank had made 'Considerable advances on his Lordship's acct that the works at Ickworth might be kept going', ending, a little ominously, that they wished 'to guard against any interruption which they conceive would very much hurt his Lordship'.[242] As a result Oakes was somewhat proprietorial towards the Earl's house and took friends to see the architect's model and to view the work in progress.[243] There is a suggestion in the diary that he helped to finance agricultural improvements on the Ickworth estate when in October 1815 Lord Bristol toured the estate with him pointing out intended projects.[244]

The Herveys must have been satisfied with the service that they were getting. Their Suffolk agent was a frequent visitor to the bank on market days, and in 1816 the then Marquess of Bristol asked that the Bury and Suffolk Bank 'carry the Balances of several Acct' for him.[245] It was common for landowning families to keep their estate accounts with a local bank and to have their other accounts with one of the West End banks in London.[246] Oakes's memorandum book shows the Marquess and his son regularly borrowing between £2,000 and £4,000 on a short term basis between 1819 and 1825.[247] The Duke of Grafton's steward was also a frequent visitor to the bank, but there is no evidence as to the business

---

239 SROB Guildhall Feoffment Papers H2/6/2.2 1777–1821, dated 3 December 1816.
240 Diary 13 January 1811.
241 SROB Acc 2191, entry dated 28 September 1797.
242 *Ibid*, entry dated 23 May 1798.
243 e.g. Diary 7 October 1798.
244 Diary 9 October 1815.
245 Diary 21 October 1816.
246 Leighton Boyce, *London National Bank Provincial Ltd*, p. 36. Smiths of Nottingham dealt with estate finance and the remittance of surplus funds to London for their landed customers who kept their main accounts in the capital.
247 SROB HA535/1/4.

transacted until 1820 when he was found to be in debt to the tune of £5,000, owing the Duke £2,200 and the Bury and Suffolk Bank £860, among others.[248]

After the collapse of farm prices in 1813 many farming customers were in trouble. At 6.30 one Saturday morning in July 1823 James Oakes set off in his chaise to discuss a farmer's balances, which had 'extended to 1,500'.[249] Three years later Mr Rayner junior was found to be in debt in excess of £15,000 although it is not clear how much of this was owed directly to the Bury and Suffolk Bank. Oakes promptly demanded 'the most positive Proof that the writings of the whole Property were at Home & should not be parted with to any other person. . . and our Debt should be Considerably shortened this year'. In September the unhappy man signed an agreement to this effect.[250] He had only managed to reduce the debt to £13,000 by April the following year. Another who owed nearly £2,000 and had been successfully avoiding the Oakeses was 'accosted' by James Oakes on the market and made to promise that the money would be repaid 'to a 6d.' within four months.[251]

It is always difficult to separate a country banker's private investments from those undertaken on behalf of his bank. In 1775 J. Pease of Hull lent £18,000 independently of his bank.[252] In 1817, Oakes's customary caution seems to have left him, and he lent £25,000 to the Duke of Norfolk on the security of his settled estates to finance the marriage of his son,[253] and £14,673 to Charles Tyrrell of Gipping and Plashwood, Haughley.[254] The Duke's debt remained unpaid at Oakes's death and was left in equal shares to his son, the Reverend James Oakes, and his daughter, Maria Gould,[255] while the Tyrrells still owed £10,673 in 1823.[256]

Bankers were usually reluctant to lock money up in mortgages which was thought, and often found to be, a risky business. Whatever he felt about loans from his personal fortune Oakes was clearly loath to allow private customers to be over-drawn to any great extent although not always able to prevent it. In the early days of the bank advances were repeatedly refused on the grounds that their London bankers allowed them none, and on several occasions Orbell Oakes declined to make a decision on loans in his father's absence.[257] In addition to their personal debt to James Oakes Charles Tyrrell owed the bank £4,630 at the end of 1820, a debt which had been growing over the previous two to three years. They were urged to borrow the money elsewhere because it 'was not the policy of

---

[248] Diary 24 February 1820; see also SROB535/1/4 fol. 26.
[249] Diary 19 July 1823.
[250] Diary 5 July, 27 September 1826.
[251] SROB HA535/1/4.
[252] Jackson, Hull in the Eighteenth Century, p. 228.
[253] Diary 21 March 1817.
[254] SROB HA535/1/4 fols 33, 47, 52.
[255] PROB 11/1753.
[256] SROB HA535/1/4 fol.52.
[257] SROB Acc 2191, entry dated April 1798.

the bank to lend large sums for a long period however good the security.[258] This message was made very clear to the head master of the Grammar School, Dr Malkin, who appears to have been in grave financial difficulties, owing the bank £2,100 by November 1818. In an ironic twist to the normal pattern of things with headmasters he was summoned to Oakes's study the following March to explain why he had allowed his debt, which had been reduced to £800, to leap up to £1,300 in the course of a week.[259] He was told that the bank could not 'find Standing capitals' but 'naturally expected a Balance frequently' in its favour. The payment of five per cent interest would not cover the 'wonderful Expence of book keeping. . .' Dr Malkin managed to reduce his over-draft to £416 by June the following year but it was £1,400 by May 1825 and in November 1826 'at the Doctrs Earnest Request' the bank paid tradesmens' bills for nearly £240 on his behalf. Poor Mrs Malkin was quietly lent £100, from James Oakes's private account, to tide her over temporarily in June 1820.[260] Although Oakes was cautious in granting loans to individuals those with enough backing were readily accommodated. Apart from Lord Bristol, Lord Calthorpe was 'immediately lent' £1,600 for six months in May 1827 (which does not appear to have been repaid within the stipulated period), and Sir John Shelley Bt was lent £2,000 for six months at five per cent on the security of a mortgage and a bond in 1823.[261]

This same reluctance to lend more than a limited amount of money for a relatively short length of time would seem to have applied to the bank's merchant and tradesmen customers also. For example Messrs Mower and Jannings, corn, coal and timber merchants, were told to reduce their debt of just over £5,150 by half in March 1820, Oakes firmly stating that 'it was quite out of the Question that we should find Capitals for our Friends — it behoves us at all times to hold ourselves prepard to answer every demand that might be made upon us'.[262] Since 1814 the Braddocks, brewers and malsters of Southgate Street, had borrowed between £1,500 and £2,500 from the Bury and Suffolk Bank. In February 1819 Oakes told them that he expected an 'early time for settlement' because 'if we locked up our monies in a few Hands we could not accommodate other our Friends & our wish was to keep ourselves prepard to supply temporarily many of our Friends'.[263] It would appear that the bank was quite prepared to lend businesses up to £2,000 but only for a limited time, generally not more than six months. However, all the evidence comes from the period of post-war depression. It is possible that Oakes would have taken greater risks with commercial customers before the slump.

---

[258] SROB HA535/1/4 fol.33. They still owed 2,000 in 1823.
[259] *Ibid* fol.21.
[260] *Ibid* fols 59, 65, 73.
[261] *Ibid* fols 53, 66, 76.
[262] *Ibid* fol. 27.
[263] *Ibid* fol. 20

Running accounts were a major source of loanable income for country bankers. Deposit accounts were few at this time and usually held relatively small sums of money for short periods of time. The total on deposit was negligible compared with that of note issue and current or running accounts. There is no evidence as to the size of running accounts kept with the Bury and Suffolk Bank. Farmers formed a large proportion of its customers and the bank must have benefitted from the deposits of those who had grown prosperous as a result of high war-time agricultural prices. It also included many of the gentry who came to live in the town among its clients.

The bank carried the accounts of the Corporation and of the Guildhall Feoffment Trust, with annual incomes of £600 and between £2,000 and £3,000 respectively, as well as that of the Guardians. James Oakes was County Treasurer so that all county rates levied in West Suffolk passed through his hands. In addition the bank acted as treasurer to a number of charities formed to raise money for specific purposes. For example, it was treasurer to the Infirmary and, at one time, held over £600 for the Committee of the Asylum for the Education of Deaf and Dumb Children of the Poor.[264]

There is little information in the diary on the Bury and Suffolk Bank's policy towards running accounts beyond passing references and a few notes in the letter book. From these it appears that no interest was given on accounts until 1801 when competition forced Oakes's hand. In the summer of that year Messrs Crowe, Sparrow, Browne bought Messrs Spink and Carss's banking house on the Cornhill, announced their intention of opening a bank and offered interest on running accounts as an inducement to customers. James Oakes was enraged at the prospect and had anxious discussions with Dykes and Samuel Alexander of Needham Market and Ipswich who 'allowd it to be a formidable opposition, but think if they were in our situation [they] could not think of allowing Int on running acct'.[265] Inspite of this advice Oakes decided that he had no alternative but 'to allow 3 p ct Int on all acct without Distinction' or lose customers. This course was against his better judgement because he felt that, whereas it was common practice for bankers in large industrial towns and in port towns and had 'been the practice of the Norfolk & Norwich Bankers for years back', it was not a viable proposition for him because of the limited investment opportunities available in Bury. As ever he decided to meet the challenge 'with becoming Spirit & with as little Ceremony as they have been pleasd to treat us' adding, hopefully, that he thought many account holders would refuse to accept interest when it was offered to them.[266] Alexanders continued to give no interest on running

---

[264] BNP 6 June 1810.
[265] Diary 13 June 1801.
[266] Diary 17 June 1801.

accounts although they feared that they would be forced into it if another bank were to open in Ipswich.[267]

In the summer of 1817, during a period of depression, business failure and deflation, Oakes decided to stop giving interest on running accounts although he was prepared to give promissory notes of hand to customers 'who were of [the] Opinion [that] their Ledgerments were too great to recompence us for the Business they did'. The promissory notes were to be given at 14 days after sight '17 Day Disc[oun]t at 3 p ct' but no interest to be given unless the money was in the bankers' hands for three 'whole' months.[268] In June 1818 Sir Thomas Cullum agreed to accept three per cent interest on his account above £1,000 and in June 1823 left £5,000 with the bank at four per cent.[269]

It is not possible to estimate how the Bury and Suffolk Bank's assets were apportioned. Leighton Boyce has shown that in 1752 Smiths of Nottingham kept over one third in liquid assets, cash, bills and their London balance, under a third in government securities and the same amount in advances.[270] The Bury and Suffolk Bank invested far more heavily in the London money market, particularly in government stock and bills, than in advances to local agricultural, commercial or industrial enterprises. In this they were typical of those country bankers with deposits to spare and acted as a channel through which country funds could be mobilized for investment in expanding areas of the economy.[271] In spite of the limited local investment opportunities the Oakeses, either as individuals or as bankers, played an important role in financing public utilities and private building projects in West Suffolk. Through their loans to landowners and their note issue, which facilitated local trade, they enabled farmers to expand and to benefit fully from war-time agricultural prosperity. They also helped to secure Bury's position as an important and much favoured social centre by financing grandiose improvements to the Assembly Rooms and by preserving the church yard with its lime-shaded promenade, for the town. But, above all, the Bury and Suffolk Bank's relatively large note issue, together with substantial investment in short-term London based securities, emphasizes the lack of alternative local investment opportunities and the importance of the receivership to both these areas of business. Without that it is doubtful if the bank would have expanded as it did.

BRANCH BANKING: STOWMARKET

The restricted openings for investment led to a concentration of branch banking in the agricultural counties of England during the early years of the nineteenth

---

[267] Diary 3 November 1806. There was one other bank in Ipswich at this time which had opened in 1786. This was the Ipswich Town and Country Bank of Bank Buildings, 13, Tavern Street.

[268] Diary 13 August 1817.

[269] SROB HA535/1/4 fols 15, 52.

[270] Leighton Boyce, *London National Provincial Bank Ltd*, p. 24.

[271] Sayer, *Lloyds bank*, p. 128.

century. People with accumulated savings were far more likely to leave them on deposit than to invest them in business.[272] Banking generally had been stimulated during the period by the issue of notes of values as low as one pound, permitted under the Bank Restriction Act, while the setting up of branches offered bankers a way of settling debts incurred in other places without paying commission.

James Oakes approached the problem of branch banking with his usual caution and never viewed the prospect with confidence. As a result of his attitude the Bury and Suffolk Bank's first branch was set up in Stowmarket in response to competition from Messrs Crowe, Sparrow, Browne, their rivals in Bury. Crowe, Sparrow, Browne had started a branch in Stowmarket at some time between 1801 and 1806 and by November of that year were carrying 'the whole Circulation of Notes & taking up all Checks drawn on [the Bury and Suffolk Bank] & payg their own Notes' in the town.[273] Browne could have invited Oakes to join him in the venture three years earlier as a cryptic entry in December 1803 stated that Oakes had 'calld upon Mr Brown & declind his offer'.[274]

Faced with unwanted competition Oakes asked the Ipswich bankers, Messrs Alexanders, to join him in a joint enterprise at Stowmarket. They rejected his suggestion because they claimed to expect fresh competition themselves in Ipswich and also did not want to be forced to give interest on running accounts in line with both the Bury banks. In spite of their reservations they 'very much encouraged' Oakes 'saying were they circumstanced as we were they should most certainly do it & that we might depend on their Friendship & any assistance in their power.'

The Stowmarket area was enjoying a period of relative affluence at this time. Farmers were prosperous as a result of high war-time agricultural prices and local merchants benefitted from the newly opened navigation linking them with the River Orwell at Ipswich. In spite of this Oakes had doubts about the profitability of the project and entered into it with misgivings, gloomily remarking that 'the Expence will be exceedingly heavy & much additional Trouble that is to be questioned if it answers'.[275] However, Browne's competition could not go unchallenged and the Bury and Suffolk Bank opened a branch in the shop of an ironmonger, Everett, in November 1806.[276] Alterations were made and a 'strong closet' installed on the premises. Everett was paid £200 a year, although he had hoped for more, claiming that Crowe, Sparrow, Browne's agent in the town received £300. The branch opened once a week, on Thursdays, market day in Stowmarket. For the first three Thursdays James Oakes and his clerk, Steel, attended 'to instruct' the Everetts in banking practice. After the opening Oakes

---

[272] Pressnell, *Country Banking in the Industrial Revolution*, pp. 126–28.
[273] Diary 26 November 1806.
[274] Diary 17 December 1803.
[275] Diary 26 November 1806.
[276] *Ibid.*

was careful to dine with local farmers and merchants in order to encourage custom. He was fortunate in that Charles Tyrrell of Gipping let it be known among his tenants that 'he gave preference to Oakes's Notes in Payment of his rents', and invited Oakes to his rent receipt dinner at the *White Hart* to meet them.[277]

The branch flourished for the next six years and Everett's salary was raised to £250.[278] Each week someone from the parent bank, often James Oakes himself, delivered specie and brought back surplus cash and notes. In 1807 an associated agency for the circulation of the Bury and Suffolk Bank's notes was opened in Debenham extending the bank's influence considerably.[279]

Although there is no evidence to suggest that the Everetts were unsatisfactory the branch was taken over in 1812 by another ironmonger, Mr Gross. The Everetts were not paid finally until February 1813 by which time they were still owed £312 10s. 0d. in salary dating back to 31 December 1810. They were paid interest on this but had to pay a half share of a loss incurred through a defaulting customer so that in the end they received only £106 4s. 6d. Gross ran the branch for the next seven years when, much to his displeasure, it was moved to the house of J.G.Hart, his brother-in-law. Hart had begun his working life as a clerk in the Bury and Suffolk Bank in Guildhall Street and was originally sent to Stowmarket to replace a clerk who had been caught stealing.[280]

The change of premises had been undertaken in response to increasing competition among bankers and the consequent pressure to improve services to the customer. The prospect of the resumption of cash payments in 1819, the withdrawal of country notes of less than five pounds in value and the resultant deflation, together with a trade depression and poor harvests, had all contributed to the reduction of banking business.[281] In June 1819 Oakes wrote that the Stowmarket corn market was 'thin & flat' with very little doing and that 'the Circulation of our Notes [is] every where diminishing'.[282] Meanwhile some people were dissatisfied with Gross's premises and had suggested that a private house would be 'more suitable for the Bank than going thr' a shop of general business'.[283] Apart from providing greater privacy the Oakeses felt that it would give Hart 'more Consequence in that Situation & of course prove more Serviceable' were he to have the bank in his house.[284] The need to have the branch run by a socially acceptable agent who had an entrée into Stowmarket society was clearly important. Indeed Hart became a man of consequence in the Town: post master, insurance

---

277 Diary 2 January 1807.
278 Diary 26 March, 4 April 1812.
279 Diary 26 March, 23 April 1807.
280 Diary 16 October 1805, 7 October 1813, 20 August 1819.
281 Pressnell, *Country Banking in the Industrial Revolution*, p. 474.
282 Diary 3 June 1819.
283 Diary 1 July 1819.
284 *Ibid.*

agent and Trustee of the Stowmarket Navigation. Ironically, after his death in 1861, it was discovered that he had been defrauding the bank for years.[285]

The move must also be seen as a step towards the professionalization of banking which was taken still further in 1825 when Hart bought a recently built house in the Market Square and converted it to accommodate the bank.[286] A later agreement gave the partners free access to the bank rooms 'at all Seasonable hours of the day' to inspect the books. In 1829 the branch was amalgamated with the Stowmarket branch of Messrs Crowe, Sparrow, Browne in Hart's premises.

BRANCH BANKING: CLARE

Oakes was pushed into opening a branch at Clare by the bankruptcy of Messrs Ray and Son (no relation) in December 1819. The Rays' London correspondents, Glyn Mills and Halifax, had refused to pay their notes in London, without informing them of the decision, with the result that they 'continued to pay as usual', on Monday, which was market day in the town. This caused much distress particularly among farmers who held a large proportion of their notes.[287] The Rays felt, not unreasonably, that 'they had been most unhandsomely treated' by their bankers and wanted nothing further to do with the business, although they undertook to support Oakes if he were to establish a branch in Clare.[288] Yet again Oakes sought the support of the Alexanders, suggesting a joint venture at Sudbury with an agency at Clare. This would have met competition from their rivals, Crowe Sparrow Browne, who had formed a partnership with Fenn, the Sudbury banker, earlier in the year as well as making the most of the opportunity presented by the Ray's collapse in Clare.[289] After two prolongued discussions the Alexanders must have rejected the offer because no more is heard of it.[290]

In the event Oakes decided to open an agency in Clare which would supply notes and cash, with the partners from Bury occasionally 'sendg over to shew' themselves. At the height of the post war agricultural recession the economic situation was far 'too precarious to engage in additional Concerns'.[291] From then on Orbell Oakes and a clerk visited the Clare bank every Monday. The decision to upgrade it to full branch status is not mentioned in the diary but must have taken place before 1823 because James Oakes and Company are named as bankers in Clare in a directory of that year.

---

[285] Hollingsworth, *History of Stowmarket*, p. 218n; Jones, 'Stowmarket Navigation'; SROB Acc 2191, Beckford Bevan's notes at the end of the letter book.
[286] Diary 28 April, 18 May 1826,
[287] Diary 8 December 1819.
[288] Diary 10, 11 December 1819.
[289] LA 4405, Sayer's Box Ig 3735.
[290] Diary 11, 14 December 1819.
[291] 15, 20 December 1819.

Oakes had made enquiries about starting an agency to issue their cash notes in Mildenhall in 1807 but 'it did not appear likely to answer' and nothing more is heard of the plan until 1822.[292] On 23 April 1822 he noted that Willetts, who were bankers in Thetford, Brandon, Bury and Mildenhall had stopped payment. Four days later, the 81-year-old Oakes set out to Mildenhall at 6.30 in the morning to discuss the matter with Mr Franx of Thetford and the following week had '½ an hours Close Conversation' with Sir Henry Bunbury and others while on the receipt at Mildenhall.[293] A decision was made quickly and Oakes went next day 'to establish an Agency for [the] Exchange of Notes & supply the Inhabitants wth what they might want of small change for prest Accommodation' with Mr Ward as agent.[294] Both Sparrow Browne and Company and the Bury and Suffolk Bank had full branches in Mildenhall by 1823.[295]

Willett's bankruptcy seems to have rekindled interest in an agency at Brandon. Between March 1807 and January 1808 Oakes recorded regular, sometimes weekly, dealings with an agent, Robert Smith. It is not clear when the arrangement began nor when it ended. Usually Oakes's coachman met Smith at Elvedon to exchange notes. Occasionally Oakes or his son, Orbell, went to Brandon themselves and once Smith sent a man to Bury.[296] The agency was not mentioned after 8 January 1808 until Willett's bankruptcy when Oakes recorded going with his solicitor, T. R. Holmes, to meet Mr Brewster to discuss the establishment of a Brandon agency. Brewster took £300 in Bury and Suffolk Bank notes '& promisd to turn his thoughts' to the problem.[297] It is difficult to tell how effective his thoughts were because the agency is only mentioned twice more.[298] This may reflect the fact that by this time Oakes was a very old man, playing a reduced role in the bank. The Brewsters were substantial Quaker merchants in Brandon and were related to the Ipswich bankers, Messrs Alexander. Indeed John Brewster senior was listed as a banker and merchant in 1784, although the family were described in all subsequent directories to 1844 as merchants. Despite the fact that contemporary directories are notoriously unreliable it would appear that the Bury and Suffolk Bank's presence in Brandon did not develope into a branch and may even have faded out in 1824 for a second time.

There had been an agent at Thetford since the early days of the Bury and Suffolk Bank. He was Noah Baker, a man of many parts described as an auction-

---

[292] Diary 22 May 1807.

[293] Diary 23, 27 April, 3 May 1822. Franx was probably the same man who was anxious to take the Bury and Suffolk Bank's one pound notes in November 1812. UBD (1793) III shows a Grey Franx, draper, ironmoger, builder, cabinet maker and upholsterer.

[294] Diary 4 April, 22 June 1822.

[295] Pigot (1823–24); LA 279 notes made by Beckford Bevan claimed that Willetts 'retired' from Mildenhall and was bought up by Oakes, Bevan and Company after 1829, which conflicts with directory evidence.

[296] e.g. Diary 24 April, 18 September 1807.

[297] Diary 25 June 1822.

[298] Diary 9 July 1822, 20 August 1824.

eer, brazier, shop-keeper and dealer in old and new furniture and corn inspector.[299] A letter written in May 1798 shows that Oakes was not entirely happy with his agency because he was using their notes against his own bills which they said that they would not do 'no not from 10 d[ay]s date' because it meant the loss of nearly ten shillings discount.[300] In 1812 Franx, the Thetford draper, wanted to take Bury and Suffolk Bank one pound notes because they would be useful to him in business.[301] There is no other information on the Thetford agency although both Franx and Baker are mentioned from time to time. In 1825 the only banks with agencies in Thetford were Harvey and Hudson of Norwich and Messrs Browne Bevan of Bury St Edmunds.[302] Low key agencies probably continued at Brandon and Thetford conducted by local shop-keepers but there was never enough business to justify a full-scale branch to the ever-cautious Oakes.

RELATIONS WITH OTHER BANKS

Because it was not possible to have agencies and branches throughout East Anglia to pay cash notes and drafts, exchange arrangements were made with other bankers in the area. Oakes continued to keep an exchange account with Messrs Gurney of Norwich after they had ceased to act as agents to the Bury and Suffolk Bank in 1796 and had a similar account with Messrs Alexander.[303] There are no references to exchange accounts with other banks although they must had existed. Between 1819 and 1823 the Tawneys of Banbury, for example, had exchange accounts with about 12 banks and received the notes of 270 more, while some country bankers acted as exchange agents for groups of fellow bankers. Notes from further afield were usually sent directly to London and presented by the receiving bank's agents to the issuer's agent. Notes of large denomination were also sent to London for clearance because it was thought that the boost given by London payment to local note issues was worth the expense.

In most places it was common for exchanges to be held weekly between local banks. Notes and drafts were exchanged and the balance settled by the transfer of London funds, the London agent having been notified by post that evening.[304] From 1804 exchanges took place between the Bury and Suffolk Bank and Messrs Crowe Sparrow Browne of Bury twice a week on Tuesday and Friday, which was the practice among the Norwich bankers.[305] They also took place with Messrs Alexander of Ipswich at the *King's Head* in Stowmarket and with Messrs Mills of

[299] UBD (1798) IV.
[300] SROB Acc 2191, entry dated 23 May 1798.
[301] Diary 13, 23 November 1812.
[302] BNP 21 December 1825.
[303] Gurneys' Ledgers; Alexanders' Ledgers.
[304] Pressnell, *Country Banking in the Industrial Revolution*, pp. 131–32.
[305] Diary 18 December 1804. See also the note book bound into vol IX entry headed 'New File of Memorandums No. 67'.

Hadleigh at Lavenham.[306] Notes and drafts from Messrs Eaton Hammond of Newmarket were either brought to Bury by one of their clerks or taken to Newmarket by James Oakes's coachman.[307]

It has already been seen that Oakes gave and received much help and advice from fellow bankers, especially during the bank's early years. He was on friendly terms with all the Norwich firms and usually called on them when he was in the city. Indeed he had close personal friendships with many of the leading banking families: the Hudsons, Harveys and Beevors. He was also on friendly terms with the Rounds of Colchester, who stayed at Guildhall Street for Bury Fair in 1820, and a frequent dinner guest of the Lacons and Turners when holidaying in Yarmouth. During the recoinage in February 1817 the Oakeses delivered a box of siver worth £6,000 to Messrs Eaton Hammond of Newmarket[308] and even their rivals, Sparrow Browne, warned them that Messrs Sparrow and Company were about to stop payment at Braintree so that they could take appropriate action.[309]

Oakes took part in national organizations of country bankers although he did not play the energetic role that he had played in the yarn committee. He was a relative new-comer to banking and no longer a young man. He wrote to the Secretary of the Country Bankers Association approving the new one pound notes in 1797.[310] When the Association reformed in the face of a proposal to increase the stamp duty on bank notes and bills of exchange in 1815 Oakes attended a 'numerous and respectable meeting of Bankers' which sent a deputation to the Chancellor of the Exchequer.[311]

THE CLERKS

The Bury and Suffolk Bank employed three clerks and a boy in 1797. The number had risen to four by 1798 and to five by 1804. This compares with the earliest known list of Messrs Gurney's employees which showed an initial total of nine clerks which had risen to 13 by 1822. Bidwell thought the estimate 'obviously incomplete' although it seems quite large when compared with that of other banks. Messrs Barclay Bevan and Company employed only three clerks at the end of the eighteenth century[312] and the Hull branch of Smith's Bank was established with one full time clerk plus help from Messrs Wilberforce and Smith's counting house staff when necessary. Smith's Bank in Lincoln employed

306 Diary 6 February 1800, 16 December 1800; SROB Acc 2191 entry dated 14 April 1798. Mills of Hadleigh were a branch of Messrs Twining and Mills, later Mills Bawtree and Company of Colchester.
307 SROB Acc 2191, entry dated 26 October 1795; diary 23 December 1816.
308 Diary 26 February 1817.
309 Diary 2 March 1826.
310 SROB Acc 2191, entry dated 18 March 1797.
311 Diary 1 June 1815.
312 Bidwell, Annals of an East Anglian Bank, p. 127; P. W. Matthews and Anthony W. Tuke, History of Barclays Bank Limited . . . (1926), p. 40.

one clerk and a manager in 1792 nearly 20 years after its establishment. Twenty five years later the number had grown to four clerks and a manager.[313] In comparison staffing levels in the Bury and Suffolk Bank appear to have been higher than average, probably in order to cope with the extra work created by tax collection.

The five clerks and two partners were joined by Henry Oakes, Orbell Oakes's eldest son in 1818. There was never any suggestion that other members of the family should become involved. Oakes's son-in-law, William Gould, helped to collect receipt money on occasions and to take it to London but his connection went no further.

The Bury and Suffolk Bank's staff had reasonably prosperous trading backgrounds. Richard Biggs came from a well known Mildenhall family and may have been recommended by the Gurneys. Two of his sisters were married to Bury merchants and shop-keepers, James Mathew and John Orbell. John Deck was the son of Philip Deck, post master, printer and stationer of Crown Street, Bury, and John Leese was the son of a school master of diarist Crabb Robinson. Several members of the same family became clerks in the Bury and Suffolk Bank. John Leese's brother joined the staff to help out during the 1797 crisis,[314] while another member of the family was employed in 1817. At least three and possibly four members of the Steel family were clerks at various times.

Oakes's diary gives no information on the education and training of his clerks and very little on the terms and conditions of their work. None lived on the premises, as was the case in some other country banks,[315] and their rates of pay appear low when compared with those of clerks working in banks in large industrial or port cities. Taylor Lloyd of Birmingham, for example, paid each of their two chief clerks £80 a year in 1779, raised it to £200 in 1791 and to £300 in 1807.[316] By 1791 Smith's Hull branch was paying its chief clerk £110 and when their Derby branch was opened in 1806 the manager received £325 and his clerk £90.[317] Richard Biggs and Thomas Hine, the Bury and Suffolk Bank's joint chief clerks, both earned £60 a year in 1797.[318] By 1832 John Haddock, the clerk in charge of the receipt, received £200 a year.[319] Gurney's junior clerks at their Yarmouth Bank were given between £50 and £60 a year compared with William Steel who earned £35 as under clerk at Stowmarket. Oakes offered a fully qualified clerk £50 in 1797.[320]

However, the Bury and Suffolk Bank's rates of pay were above average when

[313] Leighton Boyce, *London National Provincial Bank Ltd*, pp. 177, 197.
[314] Diary 18 March 1797, 3 December 1798.
[315] Sayer, *Lloyds Bank*, p. 68; Leighton Boyce, *London National Provincial Bank Ltd*, p. 143; Bidwell, *Annals of an East Anglian Bank*, p. 308.
[316] Sayer, *Lloyds Bank*, pp. 69–70.
[317] Leighton Boyce, *London National Provincial Bank Ltd*, pp. 143, 197, 246.
[318] Diary 3 April 1797.
[319] Orbell Oakes's Private Memorandum Book.
[320] Diary 27 March 1797.

compared with those given by other banks in rural areas. Sayer considered that a fully trained country clerk might expect between £30 and £40 a year and Hicks quotes a Devon clerk with a salary of £25 a year and unsecured overdraft of £800 in 1825.[321] The rates of pay were also generous when compared with those given in other professions in Bury. In 1809 the salary of the head master of the Grammar School was only £60 and that of the assistant master £30, although they could augment this by taking in boys as boarders.[322]

Sayer observed that most country bank clerks in the eighteenth and early nineteenth centuries were 'lifelong servants of the firm . . . firmly attached to the interest of the bank but having no prospect of eventual promotion to the parlour'.[323] Certainly this was the case for the majority of the Oakeses' clerks. None was made a partner and most remained with the bank for their entire working lives. Thomas Hine came in 1797 and was still with the bank in 1827, John Haddock, first mentioned in 1805, was still with Orbell Oakes in 1832, J. G. Hart, also first mentioned in 1805, remained in charge at Stowmarket until his death in 1861, and Samuel Steel was with the bank from 1798 until his death in 1817.

A few of the clerks left after a short time for various reasons. John Lease joined the bank in April 1794 and died in 1796 while Lease junior and William Steel were both discharged for stealing.[324] Richard Biggs left after five years to start his own grocery business in Abbeygate Street which must have prospered as he became a member of the Corporation in 1821 and was a subscriber to the Infirmary and to the Botanic Gardens.[325] John Deck, who came as an under clerk after Biggs left in 1801, resigned just over a year later and eventually took over his father's business in Crown Street. This practice was not unusual. Walter Ray, the third son of the Reverend Orbell Ray of Tostock, James Oakes's cousin, was a clerk with Messrs Spink and Carss for three years between 1792 and 1795.[326] Possibly a period as a clerk in a reputable bank was considered a sound business training for young men before setting up on their own account.

The Bury and Suffolk Bank opened six days a week, with the exception of Good Friday. The diaries give no information about the precise opening times. It was probably shut for an hour or two in the middle of the day but work often went on late into the night, especially after the receipt. The clerks worked hard although their hours appear tolerable when compared with contemporary London shop assistants, whose day regularly lasted from 8.00 am until 11.00 pm.[327]

---

[321] Sayer, Lloyds Bank, p. 70; C. E. Hicks, 'The Banking Crisis of 1825 in South West Devon' in Transactions of the Devon Association, LXXXI (1949) 287–96, (p. 295).
[322] R. W. Elliot, the Story of King Edward VI School (Bury St Edmunds, 1963), p. 91.
[323] Sayer, Lloyds Bank, pp. 62–63.
[324] Diary 14 April 1794, 28 April 1796, 18 March 1797, 3 December 1798, 7 October 1813; BNP 4 May 1796.
[325] Diary 26 December 1796; BNP 17 November 1834; SROB 1557/6.
[326] Diary 23 July 1792, 3 April 1795.
[327] A. F. Scott, Everyone a Witness: The Georgian Age (1970), p. 185.

Pressure of work forced Oakes to give up his membership of the Ixworth Book Club and was the cause of many missed dinner and theatre engagements.

There is no regular information on the subject, but it is clear that the clerks had holidays. Biggs had time off to visit his parents, Hart was reported 'going out for a few days' in June 1816 and Hine had two weeks holiday in August 1827. On several occasions the bank was shut for a week to be cleaned and decorated: the clerks must have been free for that time.[328]

The clerks specialized in different areas of work. Biggs, followed by Steel and Haddock, dealt with the receipt; while Orbell Oakes and the rest of the clerks, led by Hine, ran the bank. William Steel dealt with the Stowmarket branch business until he was dismissed, in 1813, and J. G. Hart took his place.

Country bankers had a paternalistic attitude towards their clerks. At their Hull bank the Smiths rented pews in the parish church for them , paid for physicians and apothecaries to attend them and for a maid to look after the resident clerk.[329] James Oakes usually dined with his clerks and any customers visiting Bury in the dining room built over the bank room. When work went on until late at night special suppers were prepared and both partners and clerks ate together.[330] The clerks were entertained by the Oakes family out of working hours. Mr and Mrs Hine were invited to Sunday dinner and tea in November 1801, all the clerks were given theatre tickets at various times, and one of the Steels was sent to London to consult doctors about his knee.[331] On one occasion, in 1827, a venerable quartet consisting of James Oakes and his three head clerks, Hine, Haddock and Steel, set out from Bury to dine with Orbell Oakes at his country house.[332]

Compared with most employment available in late eighteenth and early nineteenth century Bury St Edmunds, the life of a country bank clerk was varied, relatively well paid and not too strenuous although Oakes's standards were exacting and some new recruits failed to measure up to them. It also provided a useful training ground for aspiring young businessmen.

POST-WAR DEPRESSION AND THE FINANCIAL CRISIS OF 1825–26

The post war years were difficult ones for country bankers. The fall in government borrowing and the abolition of property tax in 1816 reduced the amount of money passing through their hands; at the same time, the end of high war time demand for agricultural produce resulted in distress among farmer customers. By 1819 a short-term boom was followed by a severe trade slump and further deflation caused by the prospect of the resumption of cash payments. Whatever may have been the case in the north west of the country, where the rapidly expanding

[328] e.g. Diary 16–22 July 1801.
[329] Leighton Boyce, *London National Provincial Bank Ltd*, p. 197.
[330] e.g. Diary 23 October 1799.
[331] Diary 7 June, 15 July 1800, 1 November 1801.
[332] Diary 25 May 1827.

urban market for food kept agricultural prices and production up, the situation in Suffolk was serious. The advanced state of Suffolk agriculture at the end of eighteenth century had enabled it to respond to war-time price rises quickly and effectively but had left it peculiarly vulnerable when prices began to fall in 1813 after a plentiful harvest. Wheat which was sold on Bury market for between 56/– and 63/– in 1812 had fallen to between 30/– and 42/– a comb by 1813, to 34/– by 1819 and to between 20/– and 28/– by 1823.[333] The price of wool and meat fell less quickly so that the effect of the fall in grain prices was cushioned for those farming on the lighter lands on which sheep could be folded to the west of Bury and on the coast to the east. Farmers on the clays were heavily committed to grain production and were unable to switch to other enterprises easily. Their land was unsuitable for good permanent grass because of the low East Anglian summer rainfall and poor drainage which made it water-logged in winter. This resulted in exceptional agricultural distress and what Thirsk and Imray have described as impoverishment on a scale unusual in other counties.[334]

In 1815 some farm workers, whose wages had been reduced or who had been layed off from work altogether, combined with ex-servicemen to riot against the threshing machines and mole ploughs, which they felt deprived them of the only possible winter work, while others directed their wrath against spinning jennies which they thought removed any possibility of alternative employment. Mobs at Ipswich and Gosbeck smashed machines and fired agricultural buildings, threatening letters were sent to farmers and the words 'bread or blood' were frequently seen daubed on walls in Ipswich. Some small farmers were so frightened of attack that they even contemplated working at night and sleeping in the day in order to avoid trouble.[335] At the beginning of 1816 the Reverend James Oakes wrote to Arthur Young that 'the County is in a very depressed state and I have reason to apprehend as bad as the present times are we are not got to the worst'.[336]

The violence reached Bury on 8 May 1816 when ominously large crowds gathered at the market and on 14 May Robert Gooday's barns in Southgate Street were burned to the ground by a mob. The following market day a large crowd demanding that Mr Wales, a hosier in Abbeygate Street, give up his spinning machines was disbanded by the magistrates, principal inhabitants and the Militia. Next day 200 special constables were sworn in, and it remained quiet

---

[333] e.g. Diary 9 September 1812, 6 October 1813, 15 October 1823.
[334] See E. L. Jones, *The Development of English Agriculture 1815–73* (1968) and Joan Thirsk and Jean Imray, *Suffolk Farming in the Nineteenth Century* (Suffolk Records Society, 1958), I.
[335] *East Anglian Daily Times* 23 March 1983 quoting a letter dated May 1815 from Robert Marriott of Thorney Hall, Stowupland, to the Rev. R. Marriott of Broadway, and a letter dated mid 1816 from Mary Carter of Stowupland to her sister in Barking, Essex.
[336] BL Add MS 35,133, f.179, letter dated 20 January 1816,

in Bury, although riots, threatening letters and the burning of ricks and farm buildings continued elsewhere in the county.[337]

Meanwhile farmers and landowners engaged in what Peacock described as a rowdy campaign to improve their situation, demanding the repeal of the income and malt taxes and a tight control on the import of cheap foreign grain. Country bankers were seen by many, on both sides, as one of the chief villains of the piece, whose unprincipled speculations were the cause of distress.

The effect of the slump on the country banks of Suffolk was immediate. Messrs Ray and Son of Clare were bankrupted in 1819 and Messrs Willetts, Bankers in Brandon, Thetford and Bury since 1806 stopped payment in 1822. The *Bury Post* was quick to point out that their demise was not the result of 'speculation, high living or imprudence' but was the result of the 'general depression of property' in agricultural areas. The paper felt sure that at any other period the landed gentlemen of the county would have 'stepped forward to prevent a Catastrophe so detrimental to the Agricultural Interest, but at the present moment, who so helpless as landed owners?'.[338]

On all sides landowners were forced to forgo large amounts of their rents and tythes. John Plampin wrote to his brother-in-law Orbell Oakes, in June 1821 that he had 'considerable arrears of Rent and Tythes still due without the smallest prospect of immediate payment — the failure of the Clare-Bank having render'd Useless a large portion even of what [he] had receiv'd'.[339] By the beginning of 1822 Oakes estimated that landlords had been forced to reduce their rents, and clergy their tithes, by between 10% and 25% and, in spite of this, little more than half of either had been paid.[340]

Land values had fallen appreciably by 1821. Oakes calculated that the value of Cobnall's Farm had dropped from £3,800 to £2,500 despite the fact that he had just spent £200 on the buildings.[341] Many landowners were forced to take land in hand because the existing tenants could not make a living and no one else would take them on. John Plampin had no alternative but to take back a farm at 'a most inconvenient season which of course cannot produce one sixpence from Mics 1820 to Mics 1821'.[342] James Oakes's tenant at Cobnall's Farm gave up in December 1822 and the property was still untenanted in 1826. Oakes would have sold it but could find no buyer.

The effect on the Bury and Suffolk Bank was so serious that Oakes thought, if action were not taken at once to help farmers, at least half of them would be

---

[337] Diary 8, 14–17 May 1816; see also A. J. Peacock, *Bread or Blood: A Study of the Agrarian Riots in East Anglia in 1816* (1965).
[338] BNP 1 May 1822.
[339] SROB Tem 240/21 letter dated 17 June 1821.
[340] Diary 9 January 1822. See also BNP 25 November 1822, 12 March 1823, 17 November 1824.
[341] Oakes's Papers.
[342] SROB Tem 240/21.

ruined.[343] His papers show solicitors' bills for work done to recover six debts between 1821 and 1826 and his diary a further seven bankruptcies among farmers and merchants between 1814 and 1824, three of them involving a total debt to the bank of £3,776 3s. 6d. Many country bankers supported farmers and merchants and enabled them to survive the economic crisis. Messers Gurney lent £20,000 to help traders in Norwich in 1825[344] and the Oakeses continued to make advances to customers who could provide adequate security. One had his credit extended in 1823[345] while another was lent 'one or two thousand more' in 1821.[346] This debt had grown to £15,000 by 1826 and the customer was asked to hand over the deeds of his property and to reduce his debt immediately.[347]

The sharp drop in rents and tithes severely lessened the amount of money passing through the Bury and Suffolk Bank. The Oakeses numbered many landowners and clerics among their customers as well as the Corporation and the Guildhall Feoffment Trust. Both these bodies had lowered rents on some of their agricultural property by as much as 25% between 1821 and 1823. In 1821 the Corporation had been forced to reduce tithes due to it by 10%, and by a further 10% in 1822.[348]

The receipt, the rock on which the bank had been founded, was much reduced as a result of the abolition of income tax in 1816 and tax payers' straightened circumstances. Oakes recorded that the first day's receipt in Bury in May 1821 was £700 less than it had been the year before and at the next Bury receipt in August only 20 parishes paid a total of £500. The extent of the reduction can be understood when compared with the first day of the October receipt in Bury in 1810 when 67 parishes paid £7,512 9s.7½d. and in 1812 when 58 paid £7,897 9s 8½d.[349]

Oakes's other money-making activities were also under pressure, and the general economic gloom naturally had a dampening effect on Bury's social life. In October 1822 the first fair ball was cancelled because only three ladies and seven gentlemen turned up compared with the 409 who had gone to the same event 10 years before. Takings for the three fair balls together were down by £200 on those of the previous year.[350]

Despite the economic misfortunes of the past nine years, the Bury and Suffolk Bank was able to withstand a run on it provoked six days after Messrs Willett stopped payment on 23 April 1822. Both Orbell and Henry Oakes were dispatched to London for Bank of England notes and specie and the emergency was

343 Diary 23 January 1822.
344 Bidwell, *Annals of an East Anglian Bank*, p. 343.
345 Diary 19 July 1823.
346 Oakes's Papers, letter dated 3 September 1821.
347 Diary 5 July 1826.
348 SROB H9/1/3 letters dated 2 January 1821, 27 November 1822; D4/1/5.
349 Diary 16 October 1810, 1 May, 8 August 1821.
350 Diary 9 October 1821, 9, 14 October 1822.

over in two days. The bank survived on this occasion because the run coincided with the April receipt which could be used to fund withdrawals temporarily.

Pressnell has described the four years, leading up to the financial crisis in December 1825, as decisive for country bankers.[351] The crisis took most of them by surprise. In spite of the fact that there were several country bank failures in agricultural areas in August, ominous stops in the Liverpool and Manchester cotton trade, and great distress among overseas merchants following the collapse of foreign trade in 1824, few were prepared. As late as September new companies were mooted and, although some circumspect country bankers had reduced their note issue, Pressnell has found little evidence that the profession as a whole had taken such a prudent step. Rumours of impending bankruptcies circulated provoking the collapse of Messrs Wentworth in Yorkshire on 8 December 1825 and on 13 December Messrs Pole and Company, a highly respected London bank, stopped payment causing runs on their country correspondents. During the next two days six more London banks failed bringing about a general loss of confidence and failures amongst their correspondents and where their influence was greatest. Thirteen country banks were bankrupt by the end of the week, a total of 33, excluding branches, during December and a grand total of 60 for the harvest year 1825–26.

By the end of 1825 James Oakes was 84 years old, deaf and suffering from a painful knee and shoulder. The diary shows that he often found writing difficult and at times the entries are quite confused. It would be unsafe to rely too heavily on it as evidence for the Bury and Suffolk Bank's perception of the crisis and reaction to it. However it does show plainly what a stimulating effect the emergency had on Oakes's failing health. His writing improved, his mind cleared, there was no further mention of arthritic joints because he was far too busy recording the latest financial developments. Bearing in mind these reservations, the diary certainly gives the impression that the crisis took the Bury and Suffolk Bank entirely by surprise. At the beginning of October Orbell Oakes brought home more favourable reports from London than expected and felt that 'all [was] likely to go on as well as we could wish it for the prest'.[352] Indeed there was no suspicion of trouble until 16 December when Oakes recorded the suspension of two or three London banks. This was a week after the collapse of Wentworths and the start of runs on country banks and four days after Pole and Company had stopped payment.

All three Bury banks survived the crisis, in large measure because none was involved in the failure of a London bank nor in any form of alliance with a weaker partner which could bring them down.[353] As in previous emergencies there was co-operation between local bankers. Orbell Oakes shared a chaise with

---

[351] The following account of the background to the 1825 financial crisis is based on Pressnell, Country Banking in the Industrial Revolution, pp. 477, 480–88.

[352] Diary 3 October 1825.

[353] Pressnell, Country Banking in the Industrial Revolution, pp. 493–96.

Edmund Squire and William Dalton in a hectic Sunday dash to London to secure enough gold and Bank of England notes to supply customers' requirements before their banks opened on Monday morning. They shared transport again when the stoppage of Sparrow and Company of Braintree threatened to provoke further runs on other East Anglian banks. Indeed Messrs Browne Bevan, who had links with the Braintree bank, warned Oakes of the impending stop so that there was enough time to take the necessary precautions.[354]

There were no country bank failures in Suffolk apart from one at Brandon where a branch of the Norwich bank, Day and Company, stopped payment in December 1825. The fact that it was possible to get to London and back again in less than two days gave East Anglian bankers an advantage over their more distant counterparts.[355]

As in so many other places, public meetings were held in Bury under the chairmanship of the Alderman to declare confidence in the local banks, while, at the instigation of the High Sheriff, the nobility and gentry of the neighbourhood 'signed a Paper expressive of their confidence of the Solidarity of the 3 several banks of this Town'. In Oakes's opinion this was quite 'the best method of putting a stop to any future proceedings of this Nature'. An editorial in the *Bury Post* claimed that it would be 'absolutely ridiculous' to question the credit of the Bury banks after all this support. The writer also pointed out that, even before these meetings took place, confidence in the local banks was such that no unusually heavy demands for cash had been made upon them.[356] This was born out by Oakes who recorded that no more than £2,000 was paid out on the first day of the crisis in Bury and that Orbell Oakes had probably brought about four times more gold and Bank notes from London than would be needed.[357] Again, following Sparrow's stop, the Bury and Suffolk Bank were 'amply supplyd with Cash & Bank and were much less troubled than expected' but took the precaution of sending gold to their Clare branch.[358]

This local confidence was, in part, a product of James Oakes's careful management of the bank since it was opened in 1794. He always erred on the side of caution, never went into a project without considering the implications fully and was never tempted to overstretch the bank's resources in pursuit of quick profit or self aggrandizement. Above all, the Oakes family had been wealthy businessmen in the town as long as anyone could remember. The very name of Oakes was

---

[354] Diary 18 December 1825, 2 March 1826.
[355] Maberly Philips, *History of Banks Bankers and Banking in Northumberland Durham and North Yorkshire* (1894), p. 55. The collapse of Richardson and Mowbray of Darlington in 1793 was blamed entirely on their distance from London which made it difficult to obtain specie quickly, particularly at times of general panic when a policy of first come first served was operated by London banks and the Bank of England. It took the Halifax banker, Stansfield Rawson, three days to bring specie from London in 1825.
[356] Diary 20 December 1825; BNP 21 December 1825.
[357] Diary 19, 20 December 1825.
[358] Diary 4 March 1826.

synonymous in most people's minds with wealth and prudence so that public confidence was never shaken. Equally, Oakes was very fortunate: throughout his career as a banker, his position was never seriously threatened by the collapse of his London correspondent or an associated bank. Few country bankers survived such a disaster, however well managed.

Orbell Oakes did not share this enthusiasm for business, but felt constrained to continue banking while his father was alive. Soon after James Oakes's death in 1829, he retired to Nowton where he pursed his interest in pictures and antiquities and in farming. The Bury and Suffolk Bank was amalgamated with Messrs Browne Bevan and Company at their Butter Market premises as Oakes Bevan and Company. Orbell Oakes's son, Henry, was senior partner and Robert Bevan and George Moor, Carss's old clerk, junior partners. Bevan saw the amalgamation with his 'opulent and respectable neighbours the Oakeses' as a means to make his business 'more safe as well as lucrative'. Hitherto he had seen banking as a highly insecure but profitable occupation.[359]

The Oakes family continued to be associated with the bank until 1899 when it was bought by the Capital and Counties Bank, eventually becoming the Bury branch of Lloyd's Bank in 1918. A plaque on the wall outside commorates the bank's origins. Inside, a pair of flintlock pistols and the night-watchman's blunderbuss are a more vivid reminder of the dramatic life of a country banker in the eighteenth and early nineteenth centuries.

---

[359] LA 5030, letter post marked 7 September 1829. A note written by James Oakes two months before he died suggests that the Bury and Suffolk Bank stopped payment in November 1825. There is no other evidence to support this: possibly Oakes was confused. See SROB HA535/1/4.4.

CHAPTER IV

James Oakes:
Bury Politics and Town Government

INTRODUCTION

James Oakes was born into one of the most prosperous and well established merchant families in Bury St Edmunds. His father had been a member of the Corporation, a justice of the peace and Alderman (the equivalent of mayor in Bury), while his mother's family had provided at least four leading citizens since the beginning of the century. James Oakes was thus assured, by right, of his place as a member of the Corporation by the time he was barely 22[1]; a justice of the peace at 28, and Alderman for the first time two years later.[2] During the course of his life he served as a justice for nearly 45 years and was Alderman five times. In addition he was a deputy lieutenant, a guardian of the poor, an Improvement Commissioner, a governor of the King Edward VI School, a trustee of the Guildhall Feoffment Trust, which encompasses most of the town's charities and the Duke of Grafton's political agent. He was, as the Webbs described the mayor of Penzance, the 'chief potentate' of the community 'uniting in his person practically all executive power.[3] There was no part of Bury's public and political life that did not concern him and that he did not seek to control. The fact that he was also a banker and had an intimate knowledge both of the town's trade and all his customers' affairs put him into a quite extraordinarily powerful and influential position in the community.

Apart from the view that it gives of Oakes's political attitudes and sympathies his diaries vividly illustrate the enormous amount of hard work that men like him devoted to public service. They also demonstrate the uncertain nature of life under the patronage system, even in a small closed borough where interests were settled. In spite of the fact that Oakes reaped great benefit from his association with the Duke of Grafton, his was a precarious position, and for most of his political career he was forced to spend much time and energy isolating those who would usurp him as the Duke's agent.

---

[1] SROB Corporation Minutes of Assembly D4/1/3a.
[2] SROB D4/1/4.
[3] Sidney and Beatrice Webb, *English Local Government from the Revolution to the Municipal Corporation Act* (1908), part II, p. 410.

Although Oakes wrote his diary as a record of events and rarely used it to reflect upon the wider political issues of the day it is possible to deduce from it some of his attitudes and sympathies. His outlook was neither rigid nor bigoted but was essentially pragmatic and conservative. Local rather than national issues were important to him and occupied most of his time. As his dealings with Joshua Grigby IV over the question of cash payments shows, he was quite unable to understand those who acted purely from political principle.[4]

At the root of Oakes's philosophy was an intense patriotism and devotion to the King, whose birthday he celebratd faithfully and whose bouts of madness he recorded with sympathy and understanding. No public dinner was concluded satisfactorily, in his eyes, without the lusty singing of patriotic songs. This loyalty to king and country was quite unaffected by personalities, and was given as readily to George IV as it had been to his father.

The early diary is too thin to record James Oakes's feelings about the American War of Independence and the nascent political radicalism of the period, but it clearly demonstrates the impact that the French Revolution and the subsequent war with France had upon his thinking and upon that of others of his class. He never expressed admiration for the Revolution as did some of his acquaintance[5] and he recorded the death of the French king with horror.[6] He had always been a devout member of the Church of England but the Revolution seems to have spurred him with a new found vigour in its defence. Thus, although previous rounds in the campaign to repeal the Test and Corporation Acts passed unnoticed, he attended a county meeting in February 1790 called 'to think [sic] the most effectual measures to preserve the Established religion in opposition to the meeting held some weeks since by the Dissenters'.[7] Oakes must have remained opposed to repeal all his life: in 1813 a petition from the clergy of the Sudbury Archdeaconary against further concessions to Catholics was left at his bank to be signed.[8]

Apart from reinforcing loyalties to the established church the Revolution had the effect of turning many previously liberal-minded men into loyalists who were prepared to condone the introduction of what, before 1789, they would have

---

4 See Chapter III, section IV i.

5 Capel Lofft was a founder member of the Society for Constitutional Information and supported Napoleon, counting him as one of his friends. Both Lofft and Joshua Grogby III were members of the Revolution Society which sent congratulations to the National Assembly in France in Novemember 1790, although neither was at the meeting which proposed the message. DNB (1889), XXVIV, p. 70; Roy Workman, 'The Joshua Grigbys' (1983), typescript in the possession of Mr Workman. I am much indebted to him for allowing me to use it.

6 Diary 21 January 1793.

7 Diary 23 February 1790.

8 BNP 6 January 1813.

considered repressive measures. The Revolution in France coincided with a period of severe food shortages and consequent widespread social unrest at home which fuelled the fears of the propertied classes that events were about to take a similar turn in England. Oakes noted the anniversary of the storming of the Bastille[9] and needed little persuasion that the naval mutinies in 1797 heralded 'the Commencement of a Revolution in this Kingdom'.[10] His responses to these events were tyical of propertied men throughout the country. He approved the King's proclamation against sedition in July 1792 and wrote approvingly of Reeve's Loyal Association but was away when a branch was founded in Bury,[11] largely through the efforts of Arthur Young. Young had been converted from a liberal to what he called 'an aristocrat' by the atrocities in France,[12] although the fear of disorder was such that the Association also had the support of many influential radicals including Capel Lofft, Joshua Grigby and the editor of the *Bury and Norwich Post*.[13] Oakes avidly read Young's proposals for the establishment of a yeomanry cavalry to be ready to quell local riots and to stem a French invasion, and was present at a meeting in April 1795 to raise a fencible corps.[14] In 1798 he was involved in 'forming a Civil Association for assisting the Magistrates of the Town'.[15]

Although party labels have little meaning in the late eighteenth century Oakes does seem to have shifted his position slightly from that of moderate liberal to moderate Tory albeit in a less dramatic and less easily defined conversion than that of Arthur Young. He supported the moderate Whig Sir Charles Bunbury at county elections but in 1802 found no difficulty in supporting Bunbury for Suffolk and two days later voting for the Tory Wodehouse in Norfolk.[16] By 1806 he was firmly in the Tory camp and rode to the hustings with Sir Thomas Gooch's party.[17] Thereafter he remained Tory in sympathy, becoming a vice president of the Pitt Club and regularly attending its meetings in Ipswich and Bury.[18]

Despite the fact that he had opposed the export of wool, once he had ceased manufacturing he supported the landed interest and, after 1815, was a keen advocate of the Corn Laws. His attitude to the poor remained paternalistic in the face of growing resentment among the town's smaller tradesmen and shop

9   Diary 14 July 1791.
10   Diary 9 May 1797.
11   Diary 10 December 1792.
12   SROB Hervey Papers 941/52/6, letter dated 19 August, Arthur Young to Lady Bristol.
13   BNP 19 December 1792.
14   Diary 3 April 1794.
15   Diary 26 April 1798.
16   Diary 15, 17 July 1802.
17   Diary 6 November 1806.
18   Diary 10 July 1821; BNP 6 June, 19 August 1821, 28 August 1822; BG 20 August 1823.

keepers at the unprecedented rises in poor rates.[19] He admired Lord Liverpool and saw his death as an irreparable loss to the nation.[20]

Yet Oakes's political attitudes were not entirely predictable. In signing a petition against slavery in 1788 he was acting in opposition to his fellow yarn manufacturers who opposed abolition and had petitioned against it on the grounds that it would 'bring great ruin to a great number of poor families'.[21] Neither was he swayed by the fact that his brother-in-law James Bridge, a Liverpool merchant, was involved in the trade. Possibly he was again influenced by Arthur Young who had seconded the motion in favour of a petition; while another old acquaintance, Joshua Grigby III, was one of the moving spirits behind it.[22] Oakes makes no mention of subsequent abolitionist meetings in February 1792.[23] By this time events in France had made him wary, as it had others, and later petitions against the African slave trade in 1814 and in 1823 received no support from him.[24]

Surprisingly Oakes never joined the Tory New Public Library founded in Bury soon after the outbreak of war, but remained a member of the Whiggish Suffolk Public Library.[25] Of greater interest is the fact that he signed a petition against the seditious meetings and the Treasonable Practices Bills in November 1795.[26] The petition, on Oakes's own admission, was 'Signd Principally by the dissenting party' and had been drawn up by the diarist Crabb Robinson with the help of the young barrister, Waller Wright, the only son of Mathias Wright a Bury brewer.[27] It was highly radical in tone both in its denunciation of the bills before Parliament and the continuance of the war.[28] However support for the petition was widespread, and Sir Charles Davers was asked to present it together with a petition from the Corporation which expressed anti-war sentiments. Robinson's petition was also adopted by a county meeting which requested that Fox and Sheridan present it because both County members had supported the bills in Parliament.[29]

---

[19] Diary 4 November 1800; SROB General Court Book of Guardians N5/1/2.

[20] Diary 8 August 1827.

[21] *Journal of the House of Commons* (1788–89), XLIV, p. 485; *Journal of the House of Commons* (1789–90), XLV, 27 January 1790.

[22] Grigby was a friend of Clarkson and had family connections with the Wilberforces. Together with John Kerrich of Harleston, Henry Bullen of Bury, the Rev. Richard Brome of Ipswich and Capel Lofft of Troston, Grigby had offered his services to the Committee for Abolition in 1787 and had promoted the petition in Bury. Workman, 'The Johsua Grigbys', pp. 88–89.

[23] BNP 22 February, 28 March 1792.

[24] Diary 25 June 1814; Diary 29 April 1823.

[25] See G.V.M.Heap, 'Subscription Libraries in Bury St Edmunds', typescript in SROB.

[26] Diary 23 November 1795.

[27] *The Diary of Henry Crabb Robinson*, selected and edited by Thomas Sadler, 3 vols (1869), I, p. 4.

[28] BNP 25 November 1795.

[29] *Crabb Robinson*, p. 33; BNP 2 December 1795.

It is difficult to see Oakes's action purely in economic terms. Had he been concerned merely with the effect of the war on the town's ailing yarn industry he could have supported the Corporation's petition without going to the lengths of adding his name to a petition so completely critical of the administration. Neither is it possible to see his action in terms of the influence of friends because he knew people in both camps. Grant Bage has suggested that, by 1795, the government was out of step with public opinion in the localities because the fear engendered by a period of revolution and war abroad coinciding with a period of acute food shortage and subsequent discontent at home had enabled ultra-loyalist opinion to predominate. Whereas many moderate men were prepared to support loyal associations, yeomanry cavalry and volunteers because they feared the French and were concerned with public order and social control, they were not necessarily prepared to see radicalism and disorder as synonymous. Thus when the government, dependent upon information supplied by loyalists in the counties, instituted repressive measures many felt that they had gone too far.[30] While in 1792 there had been almost universal support for government action, by 1795 this was no longer the case; with the result that the defendents in Treason Trials were discharged and there was considerable opposition to the two acts throughout the country, compared with the lukewarm support given to loyalist causes. Because Oakes rarely committed any of his thoughts to paper it is impossible to be certain of his motives, but his action in opposing the two acts suggests that he too felt that the government had overstepped the mark. His displeasure seems to have lasted into the following year because in April 1796 he stopped taking the ministerialist paper the *Sun*, and began to subscribe to the *Star*, described at that time as being 'a tepid opposition Paper'.[31]

Oakes made no unexpected political statements after that. For him local politics and public work in the town together with banking were all important and, except on rare occasions, influenced his political attitudes. Thus the only wider political issues that appear to have concerned him were the plight of agriculture and the need for protection together with government financial measures. His comments on the war were limited to recording victories and were never critical. The nearest he came to mentioning Parliamentary reform were brief references to Spa Fields in 1816 and to the imprisonment of Sir Francis Burdett. Whatever may have been his attitudes to radical politics in 1795 and 1796, by the end of the war he associated them with subversion, riot and disorder.

His apparently detached attitude to national politics may not have been

[30] I am much indebted to Grant Bage for allowing me to use his thesis while in preparation. See G. J. Bage, 'A provincial reaction to the French Revolution: radical politics, social unrest and the growth of loyal opinion in East Anglia at the end of the 18th century, with special reference to the county of Suffolk' (unpublished M.Litt. thesis, University of Cambridge, 1984).
[31] Diary 5 April 1796; SROB Acc 2171 entry dated March 1796; Lucyle Werhmeister, *The London Daily Press 1772–1792* (University of Nebraska Press, Lincoln, 1963), p. 377.

entirely due to lack of interest. In most towns it was common for banks to be seen in party terms. In Ipswich, the Whiggish, Quaker Alexanders were opposed by the Tory, Anglican Crickitt and Bacon. In Norwich, Messrs Harvey and Hudson's Bank was set up specifically as a Tory bank to counter existing Whiggish establishments, and in Lincoln customers at the city's two banks were divided on religious, social and political grounds.[32] Obviously in Bury, where the franchise was so restricted, this division was less likely to occur, but there is no evidence that other Bury banks became particularly associated with either the opposition in the Corporation or the reform party in the town while Oakes was alive. His attitude is summed up in a letter to his son Orbell who had asked whether they should subscribe to the *Bury Gazette* which was about to be launched in the town. Although the paper began as moderately Tory in character it soon became ultra loyalist and vociferously opposed religious freedom. In reply to his son Oakes wrote:

> As to the Bury Gazette I am very indifferent about it: In our Situation the less we intermeddle & the better, We cannot hold ourselves too impartial.[33]

As a result of this impartiality in political matters – except Catholic emancipation, opposition to which cut across party lines – the bank continued to have customers with a wide range of views from known Tories like Arthur Young to ardent supporters of reform and religious freedom including the Duke of Norfolk, the Duke of Grafton and Joshua Grigby as well as a large number of local shop keepers, clergy and farmers. The Oakeses were fortunate: two out of the three banks that could have attracted radical and Whiggish custom were bankrupted before the issue of Parliamentary reform sharpened party differences. Messrs Grigby and Cork, who collapsed in the cash crisis of 1797, were for a time the only provincial bank to which subscriptions in aid of the defendents in the Treason Trials could be sent.[34] There is also some evidence to suggest that George Willett of Willett's Bank, which went under in 1822, supported Whiggish causes.[35] George Browne, the managing partner of Messrs Crowe, Sparrow Browne, was probably a dissenter and moderately whiggish in outlook,[36] and his

---

[32] W.H.Bidwell, *Annals of an East Anglian Bank* (Norwich, 1900); Sir Francis Hill, *Georgian Lincoln* (Cambridge, 1966), p. 204; see also Chapter III.

[33] Oakes's Family Papers, letter dated Buxton 3 September 1821, James Oakes to Orbell Oakes.

[34] BNP 11 March 1795.

[35] George Willett signed a request for a meeting to prepare a petition congratulating Queen Caroline on her accession; diary 14 November 1820.

[36] George Brown(e) signed a declaration, with other leading Whigs, dissenting from the Suffolk magistrates' loyal address in February 1821, was involved in a long-running dispute over tythes and charities in Tostock where he had a house, and was involved in the reform movement in Bury before 1832. BNP 7 January, 23 April, 11 June 1817; SROB Town Clerk's Letters 1810–1853, D11/2/5, letter dated 23 April 1817 George Brown to T.R.Holmes.

partner, Robert Bevan was a Quaker.[37] That none of these companies appears to have established themselves as a Whig nonconformist bank in opposition to Messrs Oakes must be due to Oakes's determination to avoid overt support of any controversial political issue. For him national politics were nearly always peripheral. Local issues centering upon the Corporation and town charities were paramount.

POLITICS IN BURY ST EDMUNDS 1778–1827

Bury was first granted borough status under a royal charter of 1601. The privileges granted to it then were extended by two subsequent charters in 1608 and 1614 which gave it the right to elect two members to Parliament. A final charter in 1668 confirmed all the earlier rights, tightened the rules governing service on the Corporation and prohibited non tradesmen from carrying on their trades in the town.[38] In practice no attempt was made to consolidate a widely defined class of freemen although there were minor exceptions. Tradesmen were made free by the Corporation so that they could apprentice boys under the terms of various charities and all attornies practising in the borough were required by their licences to be freemen.

The Corporation was a self-selected body consisting of an Alderman or Mayor, 12 Capital Burgesses and 24 Common Councilmen. Burgesses of Common Council were nominated and elected for life by the 37 members of the Corporation from among the townsmen. Capital Burgesses were chosen from the Common Council again by the whole Corporation. In theory the most senior Common Councilman was elected to the upper house when a vacancy occurred but this convention was often broken in pursuit of party interest or because of refusal to take office.

The Alderman was elected annually from the Capital burgesses and the retiring Alderman automatically became Coroner for the following year. It was customary for the Capital Burgesses to take it in turns to be Alderman but again party feuding disrupted this pattern and many refused to act because they could spare neither the time nor the money to do so. The fact that Oakes himself was fined for refusal barely three years after first serving as Alderman suggests that it was becoming increasingly difficult to find men prepared to undertake the office.[39] In common with most boroughs the Alderman acted as Chief Magistrate and chose six Assistant Justices to serve with him in the Commission of the Peace although, theoretically, it was the right of the whole Corporation to elect them. Any townsmen was eligible to serve but there was a growing tendency to chose Capital Burgesses for this office. During the period 1767 to 1800 a total of

---

[37] I am indebted to John Jump Esq., for this information.
[38] See M. D. Lobel, *The Borough of Bury St Edmunds* (1935).
[39] SROB D4/1/7.

75 men outside the Corporation were chosen compared with 40 during the years between 1801 and 1834. For the last three years of the latter period the magistracy was totally confined to the Capital Burgesses. James Oakes was the only man chosen as Assistant Justice while still a member of the Common Council.[40] The Alderman and Capital Burgesses together elected one of their number to be Receiver or Treasurer and also elected the Town Clerk, while the whole Corporation elected the Recorder.

THE POLITICAL LEADERS OF BURY ST EDMUNDS

The political leaders of Bury St Edmunds included not only members of the Corporation and Assistant Justices but also those who acted as trustees of the various town charities including the Grammar School, those who were Improvement Commissioners and those who were Guardians of the Poor. It was a relatively homogeneous group bound together by ties of kinship and shared experience. Although the Test was applied to Corporation membership, dissenters acted as Guardians and as charity trustees and Improvement Commissioners.

These men were drawn from the most prosperous merchants and tradesmen, and from gentlemen living in the town on the profits of their investments or estates elsewhere. Many came from old Bury families whose members had provided office holders in the town for generations. Others had attained this status, as Oakes's father had done, by marrying into one of the established families. Apart from men destined by their wealth and family connections to be Capital Burgesses, the Common Council was made up of professional men: attornies, surgeons and apothecaries and less wealthy tradesmen. It was claimed that jealousy of Corporation rights and privileges prevented more than one representative of any trade from holding office at the same time.[41] Yet analysis of the occupational structure of the body shows that this was not entirely the case. There were always several representatives of the building trades whilst other trades: butchers and millers, for example, were not represented at all. Possibly this reflected the amount of patronage available to particular tradesmen from Bury's patrons, the Dukes of Grafton and the Earls of Bristol.

The homogeneity of the ruling group in Bury was further strengthened by the town clergy. The advowson of both churches was owned by the Corporation who invariably nominated their friends and relations to the livings. During the period of Oakes's diary all the clergy had some connection with Corporation members. The Rev. Bernard Mills, preacher of St Mary's Church until his death in 1787, was the son of a Bury cordwainer and Corporation member. The Rev. Henry Hasted, preacher of St Mary's for 40 years, was the son of a surgeon and apothe-

---

[40] Oakes was chosen as an Assistant Justice in 1769, 10 months before his election as a Capital Burgess. SROB D4/1/4.

[41] *Appendix to the First Report of the Commission Appointed to Inquire into the Municipal Corporations*, part IV (1835) (116), XXIII, XXVI, p. 2172.

12. *Augustus Henry, 3rd Duke of Grafton 1735–1811, by Hoppner.*

cary who had twice been Alderman; while Alderman Barwick's nephew, the Rev. John Barwick Sams, was reader of St Mary's Church for 50 years. Both these livings, the preachership and readership at St Mary's, ended in 1842, when the Corporation sold its right of nomination and the benefice became a 'perpetual curacy'. The clergy played no part in Corporation affairs but were active as charity trustees and school governors.

The majority of Corporation members were Anglican and Tory by persuasion, although in the late eighteenth century and the early years of the nineteenth century one or two belonged to non-conformist families; and some, not necessarily the same ones, did express views which differed from those of their peers. John Cooke was active in framing a petition calling for Parliamentary reform in 1783[42], and three members, Mathias Wright, Thomas Dickenson and Charles Blomfield, and two future members, John Creed and John Rackham, signed an abortive requisition for a county meeting in 1797 to draw up a petition highly critical of the administration.[43] But by 1825 the Corporation was described as being almost entirely Tory[44] even though it was claimed that men were never excluded from membership on the grounds of political belief.[45] Family was probably more important than party.

PATRONAGE IN BURY ST EDMUNDS

As a result of their membership of the Corporation, charitable trusts, Improvement Commission and Court of Guardians the ruling oligarchy of Bury St Edmunds had considerable patronage at their disposal in the form of salaried jobs, tenancies, licences, accommodation in almshouses, apprenticeships, grammar school scholarships, building contracts and provisions for Corporation, election and charity dinners, besides the rich harvest of places and benefices obtainable through their patrons the Duke of Grafton and the Earl of Bristol. Apart from the town clergy, the Town Clerk and the Recorder, the Corporation appointed the four serjeants at mace, who acted as law enforcement officers in the borough, and the two town criers. In addition the Guildhall Feoffment Trust, the school governors and other charities all had clerks and receivers who were usually attornies. The Corporation owned a moderate amount of property including the right to hold fairs and markets in the town,[46] a farm, the market cross and the wool hall which produced a rental of £389 7s. 0d. and tithes of £217 16s. 4½d. in 1797.[47] They were responsible for the upkeep of this property together with certain roads and bridges and the chancels of both parish churches and had difficulty in meeting all the demands made upon them. At the same time the Guildhall Feoffment Trust owned agricultural land in and around Bury together with the Guild Hall, Shire Hall, Angel Inn and the old gaol all of which produced a rental of nearly £3,000 by the early nineteenth century.

Under the 1614 charter the Burgesses of the town were given the right to elect two members to Parliament. Since then the right to election had narrowed until it rested with the 37 members of the Corporation alone. During the period

---

42 BNP 8 January 1783.
43 BNP 10 May 1797.
44 SROB Cullum Commonplace Book 317/1 p. 341, letter dated Bury 11 November 1824.
45 *Appendix to the First Report of the Commission Appointed to Inquire into the Municipal Corporations*, p. 2172.
46 The Alderman was clerk of the fairs and markets.
47 SROB D4/1/8.

13. *Frederick Augustus, 4th Earl of Bristol and Bishop of Derry (1730–1803), in 1790, by Vigée Le Brun.*

of Oakes's diaries the seat was controlled by three local families: the FitzRoys of Euston, the Herveys of Ickworth and the Davers of Rushbrook. All of them made liberal donations to town charities, patronized local tradesmen and found places for Corporation members and their friends in order to maintain their ascendency. In 1774 the Earl of Bristol gave £500 so that alterations and repairs could be made to the Theatre. Five days after the Corporation had returned Lord Frederick William Hervey in 1802 his nephew gave 400 blankets to the necessitous poor.[48] Even as late as 1840, the Marquess subscribed to the Eastgate Street improvements.[49] The Members could not afford to neglect such attentions. In 1782 General Conway, the Duke of Grafton's candidate, did not at first think it a good idea to raise a subscription to build a ship of the line but 'a hint from a Gentlemen at Bury' together with 'a direct application from Mr Middleton, the Sheriff' soon convinced him of the need and he subscribed £200.[50]

The newly elected Members of Parliament always paid for election dinners and balls for the better-off section of Bury society and gave beer and money to the 'populace'. In 1802 a dinner for 103 guests was followed by a ball for 500 'all of whom were provided with a handsome repast at the expence of the new members' who opened the dancing with the daughters of leading Capital Burgesses.[51]

In addition townsmen, particularly Corporation members, benefited financially from the 1802 election. Both of the town brewers provided six hogsheads of beer costing £24 6s. 0d. each; election 'favours' were obtained from both the drapers on the Corporation costing £30 each; the election chairs came from the furniture maker on the Corporation, the Town clerk and his clerk reaped fees between them of 12 guineas for drawing up the election indenture, and hosts of men performing various tasks, from chair carrier to morris dancers, all received payment and allowances for drink. The morrismens' drink allowances were taken at the *Green Dragon* in Guildhall Street belonging to James Oakes. In all over 160 men gained directly from the election that year excluding those employed by the brewers and innkeepers and those who received charity of some kind.

Corporation members and their families benefited from the Duke of Grafton's patronage in even more lucrative ways. Oakes himself was given the Receivership of the Western Division of the county within days of the successful election of the Duke's candidate in 1787.[52] Ten years later, with the Duke's help, the office was transferred to his son Orbell, while Oakes was made County Treasurer. His son-in-law William Gould was made Barrack Master at Great Yarmouth in 1803;[53] his nephew James Harrison Baker acquired a lieutenancy in the army;[54] his old friend and business partner Peter Chambers was appointed Central Commissary in 1798;[55] and his friend Thomas Haggitt was made clerk to the general subdivison meeting of militia in 1786.[56]

48   SROB N5/1/3.
49   SROB D11/3/5.
50   SROB Grafton Papers 423/140, letter dated 22 August 1782, H. S. Conway to the Duke of Grafton.
51   BNP 14 July 1802; diary 9 July 1802.
52   See Chapter III, section I, ii.
53   Diary 8 August 1803.
54   Diary 19 September 1797.
55   Diary 18, 20, 22 July 1798.
56   Diary 4 November 1786.

Oakes was not the only Corporation member in receipt of the Duke's largesse. George Pretyman was Receiver of Crown Rents, James Mathew was Deputy Commissary for government stores deposited at Bury,[57] while the Cullum family received places at Charterhouse which were in the Duke's gift[58] and the Rev. John Barwick Sams, during his 50 year's readership at St Mary's Church, acquired the living at Hunston.[59]

The Earl of Bristol had a richer patronage of livings than the Duke of Grafton. James Oakes's grandson, Edward Gould, was inducted to the Hervey living at Sproughton and the Rev. Henry Hasted, during his 40 year's preachership at St Mary's Church, was given that of Ickworth cum Chedburgh.

On a personal level Oakes was entertained once a year at Euston by the Duke of Grafton as a reward for his services, and more often by the Herveys at Ickworth. Regular gifts of venison from both estates appeared on his table and at public dinners. Much of Oakes's diary is concerned with his work as the Duke's political agent in Bury and vividly illustrates the amount of attention such a job demanded even in a small closed borough.

POLITICAL MANAGEMENT IN BURY ST EDMUNDS 1778-1802

Where an electorate was small and therefore possible to manage, aristocratic patrons usually installed an agent to look after their affairs in the constituency. It was the agent's job to keep his master informed as to the temper of the town, to report grievances, to see that patronage was distributed so as to produce maximum support and to undermine the opposition in any way that presented itself. In order to do this he had to ensure that friends to the interest filled as many positions of power in the town as possible. The Marquess of Exeter, for example, saw that his agent was elected Mayor of Stamford so that he could secure votes and distribute Corporation leases to the best advantage. Through his agent, loans were given to townsmen, places in almshouses and apprenticeships for poor children. Tenants were forbidden to use the shops or public houses of opponents and the sons of opponents were even removed from the grammar school.[60]

There is no evidence that James Oakes went to these lengths nor did he need to, with an electorate of 37. His chief concern was to see that the majority of Corporation members were favourable to the Grafton interest and to try to make certain that supporters were elected to fill Corporation vacanciees so that the Duke's candidate was always assured of a majority. This was of particular import-

---

[57] 'The Aldermen and Mayors of Bury St Edmunds', bound manuscript in SROB shelved at D42.2.

[58] *Alumni Carthusiani*, edited by Bower Marsh and Frederick Arthur Crisp (privately printed, 1913), pp. 121, 171.

[59] Diary 10 February 1807.

[60] J. M. Lee, 'Stamford and the Cecils: A Study in Political Control 1700–1835' (unpublished B.Litt. thesis, University of Oxford, 1957), p. 48.

ance before 1802 because neither the FitzRoys nor the Herveys controlled the seat.

Not all closed corporations were to be bought off by aristocratic patrons. Some showed a marked degree of pride and independence in supporting candidates of whom they thought highly but who had little largesse to distribute.[61] Although the FitzRoys had held one Bury seat for 30 years between 1754 and 1790, and the Herveys one seat for 17 years and both seats for four years,[62] Sir Charles Davers was the only candidate who could rely on the support of the Corporation in the last half of the eighteenth century.

The Daverses had come to Suffolk at the end of the seventeenth century. They had gained a speedy entrée into Suffolk politics and had acquired the Rushbrook estate, near Bury St Edmunds, through the marriage of the second baronet to the daughter of Sir Thomas Jermyn.[63] Sir Charles Davers, the 6th baronet was at Bury Grammar School with James Oakes and was his life-long friend, acting as one of Oakes's sureties when he first became Receiver General, giving him advice on founding his bank and even providing summer grazing for his horses in Rushbrook Park.[64] He represented Bury in Parliament for nearly 30 years from 1774 until his retirement in 1802. He was described as an independent country gentleman who, although against Pitt's ministry, was never formally associated with the Whigs. He voted for Shelburne's peace preliminaries, for Parliamentary reform in 1783 and in 1797, and supported Fox over the East India Bill.[65]

His sister was the wife of the Earl of Bristol but he cannot be seen as part of the Hervey interest. The Daverses and the Herveys had a long history of personal and political antagonism, the Herveys being Whigs and the Davers Tories in the late seventeenth and early eighteenth centuries. The fourth Earl and Elizabeth Davers had married in 1752 against the wishes of both families and, although happy at first, were no longer on speaking terms by 1782. By 1800 the Earl had also fallen out with Sir Charles over the terms of Lady Bristol's will.[66]

However it is difficult to see Davers as being in alliance with the Duke of Grafton to exclude the Herveys as has been suggested.[67] In the only two contested elections during the period of Oakes's diary, Davers's agent gave his second

[61] Lewis Namier and John Brooke, *The House of Commons 1754–1790*, 3 vols (HMSO, 1964), I, pp. 29–30.

[62] *Ibid.*, p. 378.

[63] *Rushbrook Parish Registers 1567–1850* (Woodbridge, 1903), pp. 349–53; R.G.Thorne, *The History of Parliament: the House of Commons 1790–1820*, 5 vols (1986), III, p. 572. The first baronet, Sir Robert Davers arrived in Suffolk in the 1680s and bought an estate at Rougham with the profits of his West Indian sugar plantations.

[64] Diary 4 June 1806.

[65] Namier and Brooke, II, p. 303; Thorne, III, p. 572.

[66] William Shakespeare Child-Pemberton, *The Earl Bishop: The Life of Frederick Hervey Bishop of Derry, Earl of Bristol*, 2 vols (1925) I, pp. 21–22, 26, II, pp. 612–14, 629–30.

[67] Thorne, I, pp. 35, 369, III, p. 572.

14. *Sir Charles Davers (1737–1806), by Reynolds, painted in 1773.*

vote to the Hervey candidate and all attempts to oust the Davers from the seat during the previous 30 years appeared to emanate from the FitzRoys. In 1760 the Duke had entered into an agreement with Sir Charles Davers's brother in which the Duke promised to make Davers his next nominee at Bury, or anywhere else that he should choose, provided that Col FitzRoy could have the seat at the 1767 election.[68] That they would have liked to have cut out Davers altogether is shown by a letter to the Duke of Grafton, written in March 1762, in which Lt General Ellison suggested that if the Graftons and the Bristols were to 'enter into an Offensive and Defensive Alliance I should think they might easily make Bury Their own'.[69]

In 1767 Sir Charles Davers agreed to give up the seat and to support Col FitzRoy at Bury. In return the Duke of Grafton undertook to find him an alternative seat elsewhere and to pay all his election expenses over £100. It was, however, 'still understood that each party with these dispositions is equally ambitious to keep up that separate interest in the Corporation of Bury with which they have hither to been honr'd'.[70]

Davers was returned for Bury at every subsequent election until 1802 and clearly commanded great personal support among the members of the Corporation. In 1789 only five out of 27 members failed to vote for him,[71] while in 1796 only two out of 29 did not support him, excluding two abstentions.[72] In addition voting lists show that those who voted for him were evenly divided in their loyalities between the other two candidates with their second votes. In 1780 13 supported the FitzRoy candidate and nine Lord Hervey. In 1796 the situation was reversed with Lord Hervey receiving 14 votes and Lord Charles FitzRoy nine votes from those who had also voted for Davers. It was generally accepted in Bury that Sir Charles stood in his own right and did not come 'recommended' as did other candidates.[73]

Thus it is not strictly accurate to claim, as Namier and Brooke have done, that the FitzRoys, Herveys and Daverses all contended for the constituency during the period.[74] All the contention from 1774 until 1802 was between the FitzRoys and the Herveys for the second seat. Before that date Sir Charles and his brother did not suffer electoral defeat in Bury but were bought off by the FitzRoys. Up to 1802, Oakes's task as the Duke's agent was to try to get his candidate elected for the second seat by defeating any Hervey challengers. In order to do this he had to make sure that FitzRoy supporters were elected to the Corporation and that a friend was chosen as Alderman because the Alderman had a casting vote in all elections other than Parliamentary ones.

In fact Oakes appears from the evidence of the diary to have made little overt effort to do this until after the defeat of the Duke's candidate in 1796. There was no urgency in filling vacancies: the Corporation was sometimes below strength by as much as eight or nine members. Apart from Oakes the membership in-

---

[68] SROB 423/835 letter dated 14 November 1760.
[69] SROB 423/729 letter dated 12 March 1762.
[70] SROB 423/836 letter dated 3 January 1767.
[71] SROB D4/1/7.
[72] SROB 719/1–4.
[73] BNP 5 February 1783.
[74] Namier and Brooke, I, p. 378.

cluded Sir Charles Davers's agent, James Ward, a Bury attorney, and there is some internal evidence to suggest that Roger Hasted, a surgeon and apothecary, and later his son the Rev. Henry Hasted, acted as agent for the Hervey family. There were no rigid groupings centred on these men and neither was the Corporation divided into parties on the basis of political belief. It was described in the last quarter of the eighteenth century as 'a fluctuating body . . . the allegiance of whose members changed over the years . . . from fresh connections starting up, and . . . new members joining it'.[75] The voting lists for the only contested elections during the period suggest that while most members suported Davers, some regularly supported either the FitzRoy or the Hervey candidate leaving the agents to battle for the votes of the uncommitted.

It is curious to find that Oakes apparently made so little effort to fill Corporation vacancies with the Duke's supporters, because the Herveys attempted a challenge at every election between 1780 and 1796, excluding the by election in 1787. Although Thorne maintains that after 1789 the Hervey family had no candidate ready, Oakes records that either Lord Hervey or his brother attempted to stand both in 1784 and in 1790.[76]

The Duke's relatively strong position in Bury at this time could have been the result of an election pact between the FitzRoys and the Daverses which Thorne suggests was cemented in 1774.[77] There is no evidence of one in 1780 or in 1784 but Oakes shows that Lord Charles FitzRoy and Sir Charles Davers canvassed the Corporation together in 1790.[78] However this hypothesis is belied by the fact that Sir Charles's agent, James Ward, voted for the Hervey/Davers combination in both 1780 and 1796 and that the Corporation were evenly divided in their second votes. It is also clear that General Conway, the Duke's candidate, was seen by the Herveys as their opponent in 1780.[79]

The Earl of Bristol blamed Lord Hervey's failure in 1780 on his long-suffering wife who was left at Ickworth to exert her influence with the Corporation while both her husband and her son were absent. Her highly principled missive, sent to each Corporation member, suggesting that the public good and not private profit should govern their choices in the election probably did little to prize votes from the more worldly of the uncommitted.[80] This lack of financial incentive to vote for Lord Hervey together with the fact that the Earl spent only two out of the following 12 years at Ickworth must have had an effect on his influence in the town. Possibly this led the Duke and his agent to become complacent about their

---

75 SROB Acc 1058 between pp. 276 and 282.
76 Thorne, II, p. 369; diary 2 April 1784, 12 June 1790.
77 Ibid.
78 Diary 12 June 1790.
79 Child-Pemberton, The Earl Bishop, I, p. 268.
80 Ibid, pp. 267–68.

support in the Corporation. However, during the period Oakes certainly kept the Duke of Grafton informed as to the tenor of the constituency.[81]

In April 1783 Shelburne's ministry fell and the coalition under the Duke of Portland took office: at the same time, a spirited reform movement led by Capel Lofft blossomed in Bury. For the next year the pages of the *Bury and Norwich Post* reverberated with arguments for and against reform, the provisions of the treaty of Versailles and the Coalition. Early in 1784 declamatory and histrionic letters signed *PRAESCIUS* set out 12 questions electors should ask of candidates before going to vote. Among them were some asking whether the candidate was 'the Creature of an aristocratic Junto' or of a 'peer or party', 'is he connected with the complicated business of India?', 'is he subject to the insinuations and threats of secret influence?'.[82] All of these questions could have been asked with point of the Duke's candidate, General Conway. He had joined the Coalition, voted with Fox on the India Bill, and the Duke of Grafton was his patron. A small paragraph in the *Bury and Norwich Post* just before the dissolution was severely critical of Fox and expressed sardonic surprise that neither the Bury not the Thetford Corporations had petitioned the King to change his ministers.[83]

In fact Bury Corporation was highly critical of Conway's membership of the Coalition and as a result he found that 'he was not likely to be well received' when he came to canvass their support. Oakes immediately left for Newmarket to inform his patron and to consult on an alternative candidate.[84] Yet, in spite of this upheaval, Lord Hervey made no headway and Captain George Ferdinand FitzRoy, the Duke's nephew, was elected with Sir Charles Davers.[85] FitzRoy resigned in 1787 and was replaced unopposed by Lord Charles FitzRoy, the Duke's second son.[86]

Although neither Lord Hervey nor his brother met with any support in the 1790 election[87] there is some evidence to suggest that the Herveys were attempting to undermine Oakes's position on the Corporation. Two months before the election Roger Hasted, the coroner, and others had forced Orbell Oakes to appear at the Borough Sessions 'to shew Cause why he refused the office of Constable' and offered a deputy in his stead.[88] The plan backfired when Counsel's opinion[89] demonstrated that the case had been brought on the flimsiest of grounds, while the Court Leet records show that substitutes were frequently used to undertake parish offices.

---

[81] e.g. Diary 12 September 1780.
[82] BNP 29 January 1784, undated letter.
[83] BNP 26 February 1784. Thetford was also a Grafton seat.
[84] Diary 24–26 March 1784.
[85] Diary 2 April 1784.
[86] Diary 4 February 1787.
[87] Diary 12 June 1790.
[88] SROB Court Leet Verdicts D8/2/5; diary 6 April 1790.
[89] SROB E2/16/2.

The reason for the Graftons' defeat in 1796 is unclear. The outcome was not entireley unexpected, Lord Euston having told the King 'that Bury had been for some time in a ticklish state'[90] and during the election feelings had run high. Oakes declared that they were so busy 'on the unpleasant contest for this Borough that we have scarce a minute to call our own'.[91]

The national political situation could have had an effect, but there is no evidence to support this. By mid 1796 the war was going increasingly badly for Britain and trade was under pressure. There was continuing trouble in Ireland and unrest at home because of high food prices following a disastrous harvest in 1795. As a result of the fears kindled by these events, radical opposition politics had little support. In Ipswich the radical William Middleton came bottom of the poll and Capel Lofft failed in his attempt to find a reform candidate to stand for the county.[92] It is possible that the electors of Bury were more easily dissuaded from their support of a Whiggish, pro-reform, Unitarian family at a time like this and may have disapproved of the Duke's solid opposition to Pitt and his constant attacks on the government's domestic and foreign policy. Yet Oakes himself and several of his colleagues on the Corporation were not uncritical of government policy. The Herveys were certainly more organized in their challenge than they had been in either 1784 or in 1790, canvassing nearly two months before the other candidates had entered the field.[93]

All three candidates canvassed separately, so an electoral pact is unlikely. However, the fact that the new Lord Hervey (his elder brother having died earlier in the year) was friendly to the government 'or nearly connected with parts of it' meant that there were limits to what Pitt could do to sway votes in the FitzRoy's favour as requested by Lord Euston.[94] Thorne claims that the Duke of Grafton had neglected the constituency, and the evidence of the diary seems to support this. At the same time the Earl of Bristol was probably exerting a more effective influence, having returned briefly to England in 1792 and having instigated the building of his extraordinary house at Ickworth in 1795. As a result he would have had greater inducements to offer Corporation members than the Duke of Grafton. Certainly John Hill, the foreman brick-layer employed on the house, switched his allegiance in 1796 and voted for Lord Hervey having voted for Conway in 1780.[95]

Until 1796 there is no evidence that Oakes made any attempt to sponsor candidates in order to build up a solid body of support within the Corporation. The fact that his old friend Sir Thomas Cullum and his manager Peter Chambers

90 Namier and Brooke, I, p. 37, quoting the King to Pitt.
91 SROB Acc 2191, letter dated 25 May 1796.
92 BNP 8 August 1796.
93 Diary 31 March 1796.
94 Thorne, II, p. 369. Lord Hervey's sister was married in 1795, to Robert Jenkinson, later Lord Liverpool, Prime Minister 1812–27.
95 SROB 317/1; 719/1–4.

could vote for different candidates on several occasions shows that it was personal, not party, loyalties that mattered.[96] Neither did there seem to be any urgency in filling Corporation vacancies. After the 1796 election all this changed and a greater professionalism marks his attitude to the job of political agent. The retirement or deaths of members were systematically noted in his diary. Vacancies were filled more speedily and private meetings of his supporters were held in order to plan election tactics. The events that followed the election in August 1796 are typical of election manoeuvres that occupied James Oakes and his opponents for the next 30 years.

By August 1796 there were eight vacancies on the Corporation: three Capital Burgesses and five Common Councilmen. The Hervey party boycotted the election meeting summonsed by the pro-FitzRoy Alderman, Joseph Maulkin, so that it was without a quorum, possibly fearing a FitzRoy plan to elect five sympathizers to the Common Council which would give them a majority when it came to the election of the Capital Burgesses, from whom the Alderman was chosen.[97] A meeting at the Angel in September to settle the matter and avoid a stalemate decided to nominate two Hervey supporters and one FitzRoy supporter to the Capital Burgesses[98] and nine men for the Common Council.[99] Five days later the three Capital Burgesses and four Common Councilmen, including Orbell Oakes, were elected unopposed and a contest for the fifth place resulted in a win for the Hervey candidate, John Gooday, by one vote. All the newly elected members had votes and were evenly divided in their loyalties. The pro-FitzRoy Alderman then refused to swear-in John Gooday because, although he had a majority of one among the Capital Burgesses, there had been a dead heat among the Common Council. There was also doubt about the validity of one of the votes cast for him, and it was claimed that he had not received the Sacrament within the last 12 months. Oakes made a note in his diary of the election figures and put crosses against five of those who had voted for Gooday who might be persuaded to defect, particularly as four of them had voted for Lord Charles at the general election.[100]

Meanwhile, a meeting at his house to discuss Corporation finances was used by Oakes to reach a compromise with the Hervey party. It was decided 'that Mr Pate should be given up and that Mr Gooday should be unanimously elected'. There were by now five vacancies among the Common Council and a list of candidates was prepared in order of their election. It was also agreed that when

---

[96] e.g. SROB D4/1/7 voting lists for Hustler v Fairfax, 15 August 1782.

[97] BNP 17 August 1796; diary 13, 16 August 1796.

[98] Diary 29 September 1796. The men chosen were Robert Carss, the banker, and John Cooke, a merchant, who had both voted for Lord Hervey, and Reuben Sturgeon, an apothecary who had voted for Lord Charles FitzRoy.

[99] There were nine vacancies because the election of Capital Burgesses reduced the number in the Common Council by another three.

[100] Diary 4 October 1796.

two further vacancies occurred Joshua Kitson, a plumber and glazier, should be elected for one of them and 'whoever We [the FitzRoy party] should wish to propose to nominate' to the other. Those present then 'pledgd to vote for Mr K as also for that Person Mr Maulkin or Mr Oakes should wish to nominate'.[101] A week later Gooday and the others were elected unanimously. Oakes concluded contentedly that 'There was not a single word of Dispute or anything unpleasant' and the day finished with a convivial evening at the Six Bells owned by Joseph Maulkin and run by his brother.[102]

The lessons of 1796 had been well learned and four years later, within weeks of Pitt's resignation in February 1801, Orbell Oakes, the current Alderman, gave a private dinner at his house to 14 members of the Corporation to plan their campaign.[103] As events turned out this proved to be unnecessary because at the end of the year Sir Charles Davers 'formally signifyd to the Alderman & Corporation his Intention of resigning any Thoughts of being a Candidate at the general Election'.[104] Davers had no legitimate heirs to stand in his place.

Meanwhile Oakes had begun to enhance his personal prestige and that of his patron by generous donations and judicious loans. In 1798 he bought the churchyard for the town hoping that the Corporation 'will be in a very few years Capable of repaying me the purchase money & all Expences'. The same year his bank took over a loan of £2,500 made to the Corporation by Spink and Carss whose bank had collapsed in the 1797 cash crisis.[105] Seven years later he presented a solid gold chain appropriately bearing the head of King James, who had given the town its first charter,[106] to be worn by the Alderman.[107] Loans were made to the Guardians[108] and to individual members of the Corporation[109] and the post of Central Commissary was obtained from the Duke of Grafton for Peter Chambers who had been Alderman in the year 1797.[110] Lavish aldermanic dinners were provided and a point was made 'of asking all those who bore office in the Town'.[111]

As a result Oakes's strength on the Corporation was such that by 1799 he was able to secure the election of his nephew, Richard Baker, to the Readership of St

---

[101] Diary 8 May 1797.
[102] Diary 15 May 1797.
[103] Diary 27 February 1801.
[104] Diary 9 July 1802.
[105] Diary 31 May, 16 June 1798; SROB Corporation Receiver's Account, D6/5/3. Oakes's loan to buy the churchyard was not paid until 1830.
[106] The chain is still worn by the Mayor of Bury St Edmunds although the centre medallion has been recast and now bears the head of William IV.
[107] Diary 3, 20 October 1805.
[108] SROB 1557/8; N5/1/2, 2 May 1799.
[109] The fact that James Oakes had a lien of Charles Peck's house in 1808 suggests that Peck was in debt to him. See diary 18 March 1808.
[110] Diary 18 July – 21 August 1798.
[111] Diary 6 October 1796.

James's Church with 19 votes more than his nearest rival, having failed to do the same for his brother-in-law 11 years earlier.[112] In mid August he was unanimously chosen to take the place of the Alderman John Cooke, who had died in office after a stroke,[113] and his son, Orbell, was elected to fill one of the two vacancies among the Capital Burgesses created by Cooke's death and the resignation of the bankrupt Robert Carss earlier in the month.[114] Never again were vacancies left unfilled for long periods. The following year Orbell Oakes was elected Alderman and Oakes's friend, Waller Rodwell Wright, was unopposed as Recorder on the resignation of Dr Symonds.[115]

POLITICAL MANAGEMENT IN BURY ST EDMUNDS 1802–27

The retirement of Sir Charles Davers enabled Oakes to use his pre-eminent position on the Corporation and the town charities to become the political agent of the Earl of Bristol as well as continuing to act for the Duke of Grafton. He was at Ickworth a month before the election in June 1802[116] and three days afterwards, in an entry surrounded by stars denoting its importance, he recorded that he 'had much Conversation with Lord H'.[117] From then on he made frequent visits to discuss Corporation affairs with the Herveys and often entertained both candidates at his house on election day. For the next 25 years the FitzRoys and the Herveys were returned unopposed regardless of the political questions that affected the outcome of elections elsewhere. Oakes took charge of the arrangements, carefully itemizing all election expenses and dividing them equally between the two candidates. By 1803 their election had become so routine that a committee was set up 'to order Tickets for the Dinner & Ball, Ribbands for Favors, Porters for carrying the Chairs, Beer for the Populace &ca'.[118]

The only problems that concerned Oakes as political agent at this time had to do with the smooth running of these events. In 1807 the FitzRoys had hoped that 'the Corporation of Bury will bring in the present members clear of all Expence, owing to this election so immediately following the last'.[119] However they were soon disabused of this idea and ended up paying slightly more than they had the year before.[120] The expense of an election ball was only avoided because the Alderman was too ill to be present. Oakes himself was dissatisfied with the dinner, feeling that there was '(much want of a proper Person as Nelson [the

---

[112] SROB D4/1/8; diary 16 May 1799. See also diary 4 August 1788.
[113] Diary 14, 19 August 1799.
[114] Diary 8, 22 August 1799.
[115] SROB D4/1/4; diary 1, 13 October 1801.
[116] Diary 5 June 1802.
[117] Diary 12 July 1802.
[118] e.g. Diary 11 August 1803, 28 October 1806.
[119] SROB 423/378, letter dated March 1807, Col Charles FitzRoy to Lord Euston.
[120] Diary 8 May 1807.

Admiral] to take & answer the Toasts from the Chair) and very great irregularity
. . . no order' in the seating of guests.[121] In 1812 the proprietors of the Assembly
Rooms refused to allow the election ball to be held there and, at Oakes's request,
the Duke of Grafton intervened with them in order to avoid 'very great disappointment' in the town. In the end, double the number that had bought tickets
attended and 'voraciously devoured all that was set before them'.[122] The only
hitch to be dealt with in the 1818 election occurred when Sir Thomas Cullum
proposed Lord Euston, and Reuben Sturgeon, the apothecary, objected because,
as senior Capital Burgess, he felt that he should have done it.[123]

Although the position of the FitzRoys and the Herveys in the borough was
unchallenged and Oakes's duties on their behalf appear to have been confined to
those of a master of ceremonies, this was a period of the most intense party
rivalry in the Corporation. The rivalry was not based on conflicting ideologies or
upon a desire to introduce another interest into the borough. Indeed those who
most fiercely opposed Oakes often proposed or seconded the candidates at Parliamentary elections. The battle was over who should control the rich store of
patronage available from their patrons. By 1802 Oakes was the sole channel of
this patronage and there were many who resented his privileged and controlling
position in the town and sought to destroy it by building up opposition to him on
the Corporation and on the Guildhall Feoffment Trust.

The only person who appears to have been a potential threat to James Oakes
on the Corporation at this time was Joseph Maulkin, a wealthy maltster who
lived in St Mary's Square. Between 1802 and 1808 Oakes set about isolating him
by trying to ensure that as many of his own supporters as possible were elected to
the Corporation and by instituting by-laws which would prevent one party from
gaining ascendency by having a large majority in the Common Council.[124] He
also set out to win over opponents by speeding up their election to Capital
Burgess. James Mathew junior was nominated by Oakes in June 1808 although
he was not the most senior Common Councilman.[125] In retaliation Reuben
Sturgeon nominated his fellow apothecary, George Hubbard, who had been a
member since 1782; but he failed to find a seconder. Mathew was elected and
there was 'much talk as usual by Mr Sturgeon but [to] no effect'.[126]

Maulkin tried to defeat these moves by protesting against the election of
Oakes's candidates on the grounds that they had either not taken the Sacrament

[121] *Ibid.*
[122] Diary 5 October 1812; BNP 14 October 1812.
[123] Diary 24 June 1818.
[124] SROB D4/1/4, D4/1/8 loose sheet dated 23 July 1803.
[125] SROB D4/1/8; diary 13 June 1808. Mathew had voted for Brown, the opposition
candidate in March 1805.
[126] Diary 13 June 1808.

in the last year or did not live in the town,[127] and by staying away from meetings with his supporters so that they did not have a quorum.[128]

By the middle of 1808, the fluid loyalties of Corporation members caused by the departure of Sir Charles Davers from active politics had hardened: the Corporation consisted of a large group loyal to Oakes commanding a regular majority in both houses, a small group of Capital Burgesses consisting of Joseph Maulkin, Reuben Sturgeon, Robert Maulkin and the yarn maker, Branwhite Green, who were antagonistic to Oakes, and a considerable number of uncommitted Common Councilmen who probably hoped to make their living from all sides and wanted to upset no one.

This happy state of affairs, from Oakes's point of view, might have gone on had it not been for the arrival in Bury of a man who was greedy for power and challenged his supremacy in all areas of town government. The battles that followed demonstrate how tough life under the patronage system could be even in a place where politics at the centre appeared moribund, with no contested elections, a small electorate and where the interests were seemingly settled. Oakes was forced to go to extraordinary lengths to protect his position.

THE TOWN CHARITIES AND PARTY STRIFE

The first challenge that Oakes faced was to his position on the Guildhall Feoffment and other charitable trusts in the town. Although, on the face of it, the challenge came from his old friends the Recorder, Dr John Symonds, and John Godbold, subsequent events make it clear that they were not the prime movers but were acting at the behest of a distant relation, John Benjafield, who had recently come to live in Bury.

By 1809 the charities in Bury produced an annual income of £3,000. Oakes could not afford to let such a rich store of patronage and power fall into other hands and still convince his noble patrons that he was the most influential man in the town. The Trust was administered by 36 feoffees, a clerk and a receiver. Although the clerk and receiver were annual appointments it was customary for the same men to be elected year after year. The Trust last had a full complement of Feoffees in 1771. By 1802 the number had fallen to a mere four: John Godbold, John Symonds, James Oakes and Dr Knowles, the lecturer of St Mary's Church.

The campaign against Oakes began when Godbold opposed the re-appointment of the receiver, John Fairfax, the proprietor of the Norwich Stage Waggons, at the annual meeting in January 1802, but was out voted three to one.[129] In October Dr Knowles died and the following year Dr Symonds, as senior Feoffee, issued a summons to elect replacements. Oakes, Symonds and Godbold all agreed

---

[127] SROB D4/1/5, p. 36; D4/1/8, loose sheet dated 23 July 1803; diary 3–20 July 1807.
[128] Diary 27 July 1803.
[129] Diary 14 January 1802.

that in future the number of Feoffees should be reduced to 18 whereupon 'Mr S then pull'd out of his pocket a List of Certain names as fit & proper Persons fixd upon by himself & Mr Godbold without' consulting Oakes. Oakes made various compromise suggestions 'that no exceptional Person to either of the Trustees should be brot on' but to no avail and he left the room obstinately refusing to hear Symond's list read out.[130] The next day Oakes submitted a list of seven names to the clerk with the promise that if they were accepted by Symonds and Godbold he would agree to the other 15.[131] This too was refused and Oakes began legal proceedings against the existing Feoffees in the name of his old friend Sir Charles Davers and, after Davers's death, in the name of Waller Wright the Recorder. Meanwhile all except one of the men on Symonds's list had accepted the invitation to become Feoffees and a trust deed was prepared by the clerk although nothing could be done without Oakes's co-operation.

During the next seven years Oakes was sorely tried with charity affairs. He was taunted at the annual dinner (to which friends were invited) with toasts to the 'new Trustees' from Dr Symonds[132] while Godbold continued to oppose John Fairfax as receiver. Fairfax died in February 1805 having had a fit at the annual meeting; brought on, according to Oakes, by Godbold's harassment.[133] Oakes's candidate to replace him, John Lawrence, was defeated by John Steel, supported by Godbold and Symonds.[134]

The Guildhall Feoffment case came before the Master of the Rolls in June 1809.[135] He upheld Oakes's claim to share in the nomination of new Feoffees and ruled that at least 24 men should be appointed to the Trust and that the costs of the action should be paid out of the Feoffment funds.[136] The matter was referred to one of the Masters of the Court to choose suitable men from lists supplied by Godbold and Oakes, Symonds having died in February 1807. The new Feoffees were finally installed in January 1811.[137]

Throughout the case, Oakes maintained that he had no objection to any of the individuals on Dr Symonds's list but that he objected to the arbitrary way in which he and Godbold had acted. He felt that their failure to elect Feoffees reflected badly on the running of the Trust and frequently tried to find a compromise solution. In the end, the lists submitted to the Master by Oakes and Godbold had seven out of 20 names in common. The final list contained five men nominated by Oakes who had appeared on Symonds's original list in 1803. A total of 14 of Godbold's submissions and 11 of Oakes's were chosen. Oakes's list was the least contentious containing nine Corporation members, three of

130 Diary 18 November 1803.
131 SROB H3/5/2.
132 Diary 12 January 1804.
133 Diary 10 January 1805, 12, 18, February 1805.
134 Diary 22 February 1805.
135 SROB H3/5/1; diary 26 June 1809.
136 SROB H3/5/3.1.
137 Diary 10 January 1811.

whom were regularly opposed to him, while Godbold's list included 12 Corporation members all of whom, by this time, were James Oakes's regular opponents. Both men included dissenters in their lists.[138]

Oakes claimed that Godbold and Symonds had previously organized the list between them[139] and that they 'Considered that mode of Election for the Sake of Patronage and power & for the purpose of Excludg . . .[Oakes] . . . from all Judgement or share in the said Election'.[140] Quite why two elderly men who had been Oakes's friends for years should suddenly challenge him is not immediately clear. Symonds had resigned as Recorder in October 1801 and although Godbold had been a county Justice of the Peace, a Deputy Lieutenant, school governor and a vice president with Oakes of the Dispensary, he had never shown any interest in the Corporation. He was 75 when the affair began and well over 80 by the time that it finished. Oakes always felt that Symonds had become involved against his will and that Godbold was the instigator of the challenge.[141] Certainly Symonds's embarrassment over the affair is evident in the diary and elsewhere, and the relationship between the two men was never severed as it was between Oakes and Godbold.

Godbold was a gentleman of independent means who had lived in Bury for most of his life. Since 1771 he had rented a house on the north side of the churchyard from John Spink, the banker.[142] In 1796 the house was sold by Spink's executors to John Benjafield and by some arrangement Godbold continued to live there. The families were connected: Mrs Godbold, who had died in 1789, was Benjafield's wife's great aunt and one of the Benjafield daughters, Rosa Delariviere, was named after her.[143]

Benjafield was also connected with Dr Symonds. He had married Symonds's niece, Mary Ann, in 1796, a year after his arrival in the town with the West Kent Militia.[144] Before coming to Bury he had had a curious career. In 1783 he was admitted to Lincoln's Inn and from 1784 until 1789 ran a London newspaper, the *Morning Post*. He had then served as an officer in the King's Yeoman of the Guard and later acquired a commission in the West Kent Militia through the influence of the Duke of Dorset.[145] It was probably also through Dorset's influence that he became Lord Whitworth's secretary when he was ambassador in Paris between

[138] SROB *Suffolk Tracts III* shelved at 01.4.
[139] *Ibid*, hand written paper between pp. 4 and 5 probably written by Sir Thomas Cullum.
[140] SROB H3/5/3.1.
[141] Diary 4 October 1806.
[142] SROB N2/3/1–2.
[143] *Horringer Parish Registers 1558–1850* (Woodbridge, 1900), p. 349. On her death Mrs Godbold left Mrs Benjafield £500 and in 1822 John Godbold left all his property to Benjafield's two daughters, Mary Ann and Rosa Delariviere. PROB 11/1619, fol. 210; SROB EL 159/12/16.
[144] Diary 29 December 1796.
[145] Wethmeister, *The London Daily Press*, p. 78; BNP 28 August 1811; SROB *The Bury Charities*, Cullum Collection shelved at B45.1.

September 1802 and March 1803.[146] At the outbreak of war later that year Benjafield returned to Bury and settled down to local affairs becoming captain of one of the units of the Bury Volunteer Infantry, a county magistrate, a property tax commissioner, a trustee of the Sudbury Turnpike and at various times a Governor of the Workhouse.

Early in their acquaintance there had been disagreements between Benjafield and the Oakeses which were suspended by a truce in July 1802.[147] The cause of dissension is not clear. In January 1802 a Corporation meeting called to discuss the possibility of leasing an additional piece of the churchyard to Benjafield, who had a house beside it, was without a quorum.[148] In the same month Oakes and his son were on the bench when three of Benjafield's servants were tried for stealing from their employer. The case against Benjafield's cook was dismissed, one maid was sentenced to seven year's transportation and the other to one year's solitary confinement.[149] A subsequent attempt by Benjafield to promote an Association for prosecuting Servants in Cases of Robbery in their Masters' Houses found little support from Oakes.

By March 1804 there was open rivalry between Benjafield and Orbell Oakes as captains fo their respective Volunteer Infantry Companies. Orbell Oakes, with his father's help, had succeeded in ousting Benjafield's company from guard duty at the Bury ordnance depot. This was a popular task because the men were on permanent pay while carrying it out.[150] Benjafield resigned as superintendent in charge of civil defence in St Mary's parish under James Oakes's command.[151]

In 1807, before the Guildhall Feoffment case had come to court, Benjafield with John Ranby, who had supported him in his Employers' Protection Society and who was James Oakes's tenant in Guildhall Street, thwarted the efforts of Sir Thomas Cullum and James Oakes to replace three trustees on Clopton's Hospital Charity.[152]

The fact that Godbold and Oakes had been on good terms until Benjafield's arrival in Bury, that there was a close connection between Godbold and Benjafield, that at least 50% of Godbold's list of possible Feoffees was composed of Oakes's opponents and that Benjafield had overtly challenged Oakes in other areas all combine to suggest that it was Benjafield rather than Godbold who was the true architect of the plan to undermine Oakes's influence on the Trust. When his attempts to gain access to patronage and power through the Trust were

---

146 BNP 10 August 1803. Charles, Earl Whitworth was appointed ambassador to France in September 1802 and took part in the famous scene with Napoleon in March 1803 which led to renewed war: Benjafield had been rather close to despotism at work. See DNB (1889), LXI, pp. 103–06.
147 Diary 22 July 1802.
148 Diary 22 January 1802.
149 Diary 22, 27 January 1802.
150 Diary 10, 17, 18 March 1804.
151 Diary 1 September 1804.
152 Diary 25 May 1807.

temporarily blocked by Oakes's legal action, Benjafield turned his attention to the Corporation and once more Oakes was forced to defend himself with all the means at his disposal.

PARTY STRIFE ON THE CORPORATION

Oakes saw Benjafield's attempt to join the Corporation as a threat from the start. That this was so is demonstrated by the fact that Benjafield allied himself to the small group of disaffected Capital Burgesses, led by Joseph Maulkin, who by now consistently opposed Oakes. In June 1808 Robert Maulkin nominated Benjafield to fill a vacancy in the Common council. He was opposed by Oakes's candidate, the cutler John Orbell,[153] and although Benjafield won by 17 votes to 15 various ploys by the Oakes's party prevented him from taking his seat for nearly three months. The bye laws of 1803 were used on three occasions to deny him the oaths of office on the grounds that he did not have the majority of the Capital Burgesses' votes.[154] At the same time an attempt was made to discredit him in the town by blackballing him from the Gentlemens' Club which met at the *Angel*.[155]

In August the Maulkin group unsuccessfully opposed Oakes's candidate Thomas Foster, as Alderman, in order to give Benjafield grounds on which to protest that he had been deprived of his vote in the election. That the contest was seen by all as one between Oakes and Benjafield was amply shown when, in an unprecedented move, Reuben Sturgeon proposed Robert Maulkin as an Assistant Justice 'against either of the Mr Oakes; but not standing the least Chance of more than three or four Votes, was given up'.[156]

Oakes's efforts were finally defeated the following month when Benjafield was sworn in as a Common Councilman,[157] his earlier application to the King's Bench for a mandamus to enforce his election having been granted. The court ruled that the bye laws were contrary to the Corporation's letters patent and held that it was sufficient for a candidate to have an overall majority in order to be elected.[158]

Benjafield had been elected in June 1808 because three of Oakes's regular supporters, Sir Thomas Cullum, his son Palmer and the surgeon John Smith were not at the meeting. Oakes was ruthless in his reaction. The Oakes family no longer exchanged visits with the Cullums and John Smith was removed from his position as surgeon to Oakes's daughter-in-law.[159] It is a measure of the seriousness with which Oakes viewed Benjafield's challenge that he was prepared to risk

---

[153] Orbell was not related to the Oakes family.
[154] SROB D4/1/4 24 June 1808; diary 24 June, 9 July, 18 August 1808.
[155] Diary 6 July 1808.
[156] Diary 18 August 1808.
[157] Diary 17 September 1808.
[158] SROB D4/1/8.
[159] BL Add MS. 35, 130, f. 214, Betsy Oakes to Arthur Young.

his life-long friendship with the Cullums and to upset his beloved Betsy in the process of defending his position.[160]

Oakes's judgement was at fault in dropping the Cullums because it opened the way for Benjafield to gain influential support. In October 1808 Benjafield nominated Sir Thomas's elder son, the Rev. Thomas Cullum, against Oakes's defeated candidate John Orbell for a vacancy in the Common Council.[161] With the Cullums in the Benjafield camp it was apparent that the vote would be very close and both sides used the well-tried tactic of protesting against the votes of the other.[162] The result was a tie and Orbell's election was decided only by the Alderman's casting vote.

With the parties so evenly balanced 'the necessity of having a Friend in the Chair . . . appeared Indispensible' to Oakes in order 'to frustrate the Artifices & unconstitutional Design of Mr B – and his Party'.[163] To that end private meetings were held before elections to choose candidates to stand as Alderman and Assistant Justices and to fill vacancies on the Corporation.[164] The Benjafield group seem to have been trying to confine the magistracy to the Corporation alone thus increasing the number of influential offices open to its members.[165]

At these meetings there was a marked reluctance, particularly among the Common Councilmen, to take office.[166] The cost and inconvenience of being Alderman, particularly at time when party feeling was running so high, was clearly making the position unattractive to all but the most dedicated or dependent, and few wanted to take the first step by becoming a Capital Burgess. All those considered had their livings to make and were anxious to avoid being too closely associated with one side or the other. After his salutory experience in 1808 the surgeon, John Smith, 'declard off attendg any Meetings'.[167] In 1810 the auctioneer and cabinet maker Laver Oliver and the surgeon John Creed 'declind meeting us for reasons best known to themselves',[168] and at least five men had to be approached in order to find a volunteer to fill the next vacancy.[169] Later that year Oakes was hurt and angry because no one rushed to his defence when Benjafield attacked him 'violently as havg been the Instigator & Mover of this Business & always his violent Opposer'.[170] Most rank and file members had

---

[160] Betsy Oakes must have sorted out the problem of John Smith fairly soon, as she had promised in her letter to Arthur Young, because Smith was attending her when she died in April 1811. See BL Add. MSS 35, 130 ff. 214, 35, 131 ff.81.

[161] Diary 22 October 1808.

[162] SROB D4/1/8 loose sheet dated 22 October 1808; diary 22 October 1808.

[163] Diary 13 July 1810.

[164] Diary 14 October 1809, 13 July 1810.

[165] e.g. Diary 18 October 1808, 17 August 1809.

[166] e.g. Diary 13 July 1810.

[167] Diary 14 August 1809.

[168] Diary 13 July 1810.

[169] *Ibid.*

[170] Diary 4 October 1810.

probably had enough of party battles which were time-consuming and damaging to their trades or professions. On that occasion a compromise was reached because the Common Council on both sides were unwilling to continue the fight.

In spite of his best endeavors, the election in 1810 was a fiasco and Oakes had begun to realize, possibly at Lord Charles FitzRoy's suggestion,[171] that he could not defeat Benjafield without coming to terms with Sir Thomas Cullum. His approaches[172] were successful and Sir Thomas came over to the Oakes's party 'very handsomely saying it was for 2 reasons: the one our old Friendship and Acquaintance & the other that he particularly wished to support the Interest of the Grafton Family'.[173] Formal calls were paid and the rift was healed.[174]

In order to frustrate Oakes's plans the Benjafield party absented themselves from the Aldermanic election on two occasions so that no business could be done.[175] This was not unexpected and the Oakes's party were careful to follow all the procedures correctly.[176] Counsel's opinion was sought as to whether action could be taken against members who deliberately stayed away from elections,[177] meetings were held at Oakes's house to lay plans,[178] and both patrons were consulted.[179]

It had been decided to proceed against Benjafield, Reuben Sturgeon and Charles Peck in the first instance[180] but, in spite of all the preparation, Oakes could not rely on his supporters to do the right thing. The first meeting had to be adjourned because a motion that it be held in private was passed and some of those who were to give evidence against Benjafield disapproved and refused to do so. Although Oakes opposed the motion it had been proposed by Sir Thomas Cullum and was carried because another of Oakes's supporters had become totally confused by the day's events and had voted the wrong way.[181]

Things went no better five days later. Reuben Sturgeon's summons was incorrectly worded and the principal witness against Peck was absent. For his part Benjafield spoke for an hour[182] and put 'a very ably written defence . . . [in which he] . . . then exhibited a pretty glowing picture of Corporation Intrigue, both from Internal and external influence' claiming that as it had been common practice for at least 200 years for Corporation members to absent themselves for

[171] Diary 6 August 1810.
[172] Diary 14 August 1810.
[173] Diary 23 August 1810.
[174] Diary 26 August 1810.
[175] Diary 23–24 August 1810.
[176] SROB D11/3/4, letter dated 21 August 1810, the Recorder to the Town Clerk.
[177] SROB D11/2/4(1); diary 24 August 1810.
[178] Diary 24, 28 September 1810.
[179] Diary 25, 27 September 1810.
[180] SROB D4/1/8, letter dated 19 October 1810.
[181] BNP 3 October 1810.
[182] Diary 4 October 1810.

party motives how could the present members remove him for an offence which they and their relations had committed 'at the will of the leader to whom they were subservient'.[183]

Oakes refuted Benjafield's claims and renewed a proposal that he must have made earlier that both he and Benjafield resign from the Corporation. Benjafield refused although he claimed that his side was ready 'to agree to any terms of reciprocal accommodation'. At this point Oakes suggested that each party should withdraw to find a compromise and that the Recorder should act as a mediator between them.[184] It is clear from the diary that Oakes's action was not quite as magnanimous as the editor of the *Bury and Norwich Post* made it appear. There had been other legal blunders in the preparation of the case and his rank and file members were so tired of the fight that he had been 'inducd to propose' the solution by them.[185]

The actions against Benjafield, Sturgeon and Peck were adjourned and before the next Corporation meeting Benjafield and Oakes came to an agreement over future appointments. Two days later Oakes was elected Alderman and chose men from both parties and one outsider as his Assistant Justices. The meeting finished with 'perfect Pleasantness' and the following day Lady Cullum gave a dinner party 'intended rather as a reconciliation Dinner' which brought the chief protagonists together socially for the first time for years.[186] Two months later in January 1811 the new Guildhall Feoffment Trustees met for the first time and Benjafield was elected unopposed as a Capital Burgess '& not a word said upon the subject'.[187]

Oakes's subsequent behaviour shows that he had no intention of abiding by his agreement with Benjafield, having been caught out by Benjafield before over the election of a clerk to the borough tax commissioners. It was customary for this office to be held by the Town Clerk but, on the death of Thomas Dickenson, Benjafield 'designedly Omitted Summonsing three of the Comm[o]n [Council] who had qualifyd after April'[188] in order to elect his candidate. In spite of protests against the votes of the Oakes's group Timothy Richard Holmes, the new Town Clerk, was elected and Oakes felt it unlikely that the matter would go further because 'they have not the slightest Ground to stand upon'.[189] He underestimated Benjafield who, the following year, succeeded in ousting Holmes by forcing an enquiry into the means of his fellow tax commissioners. It revealed that three of Oakes's supporters did not have sufficient income registered in the Land Tax Duplicate to qualify, and a fourth, Edmund Squire the liquor merchant,

---

183 BNP 10 October 1810.
184 BNP 10 October 1810; diary 4 October 1810.
185 Diary 4 October 1810.
186 Dairy 22, 23 November 1810.
187 19 January 1811.
188 Diary 12 November 1808.
189 *Ibid.*

preferred to withdraw rather than have his income investigated.[190] At the same time Benjafield had gained ground in the town charities. Having prevented the election of new trustees for Clopton's Hospital in 1807,[191] two years later his candidate defeated Oakes's for a place in the Hospital[192] and he was elected president of the charity.[193] In April 1810 he reinforced his position by becoming chairman of Dean Sudbury's Charity[194] while in January 1811 Oakes's influence was further diminished with the installation of the new Guildhall Feoffment Trustees.[195]

When Benjafield's supporter, Branwhite Green, died in April 1811 the Oakes party through careful pre-election planning organized that the vacancy in the Capital Burgesses and the subsequent vacancy in the Common Council should be filled by supporters.[196] This time the opposition were taken completely una-wares and many of them had not bothered to turn up assuming that their candidate would be elected automatically according to the agreement made in November 1810. Oakes recorded gleefully that they were 'most exceedingly chagrind & disappointed . . . [and] . . . repeatedly offer terms for accommodation but nothing could be accepted. We had already conceded greatly too much'.[197] The same plan was followed after the death of Oakes's supporter, Simon Buchanan, in May and, despite Benjafield's attempts to win over some of Oakes's supporters by nominating their relations, Oakes's candidate, the silversmith John Thompson, was elected without difficulty. Benjafield's pleas for a compromise were ignored and Oakes reaffirmed his intention to force the election of his own nominees as long as he could.[198]

Benjafield threatened to introduce a third interest into the borough if he were not elected Alderman, and made 'a long Harrangue' claiming that as senior Capital Burgess it was his right. It was to no avail and Oakes's candidate, Philip Case, was elected by 20 votes to 15 with two abstentions.[199] Much argument ensued and Reuben Sturgeon 'repeatedly attempted to speak, but not being attended to he soon gave up'. Case's Assistant Justices were chosen exclusively from the Oakes party.

Throughout Oakes's campaign against Benjafield he had frequently made use of his wealth to provide entertainment for his supporters. It was customary after

---

[190] Diary 27 March 1809. In order to qualify Land Tax Commissioners were required to have either £40 a year in real estate or £1,000 in property assessed in the Land Tax Duplicate.
[191] Diary 25 May 1807.
[192] Diary 31 January, 14 February 1809.
[193] Diary 16 November 1809.
[194] Diary 13 April 1810.
[195] See section III, vi.
[196] Diary 28 April 1811.
[197] Diary 3 May 1811.
[198] Diary 10 June 1811.
[199] SROB D4/1/4; diary 22 August 1811.

15. *Peter Gedge (1758–1818), editor of the Bury and Norwich Post.*

the Aldermanic election for the old Alderman to give a small private dinner to the Corporation. On this occasion Oakes gave dinner to about 150 men confined mainly 'to the Trading part of the Town' but including the Duke of Grafton, the Earl of Bristol and Lord Charles FitzRoy who had all been kept well informed of affairs in Bury by their agent.[200] The guests were showered with various wines, game and 'good Desert Pines, Mellan, Grapes & all other Fruits in season'.[201] The editor of the *Bury and Norwich Post* enthused that 'The polite attention of the Alderman (whose constant succession of patriotic and loyal toasts gave free circulation to the glass) . . . rendered the entertainment a scene of hilarity and cheerfulness throughout the evening'.[202] The whole affair smacked of a victory feast rather than the customary fairly discreet function, and was more than the

[200] Diary 27 June, 5 July, 2 August 1811.
[201] Diary 22 August 1811.
[202] BNP 28 August 1811.

opposing party could stomach. They had what must have been a rather dispiriting little dinner on their own at the *Six Bells*, and they boycotted Case's swearing in as Alderman and his Aldermanic dinner in October.[203]

BENJAFIELD'S DISGRACE

In the normal course of events Benjafield might have hoped to regain a bargaining position by clever strategies and deals had not news of a case in the Court of Chancery in August 1811 ruined his reputation in Suffolk. Although he continued to oppose Oakes he did so with little hope of success. The case concerned the trusteeship of Michael Peter Leheup of Hessett and Bury. The Leheups were a Huguenot family at the centre of Bury society. They were related to the Cullums, the Symonds, the Godbolds and Cocksedges and Michael William Leheup had served as an Assistant Justice in Bury until his death in 1809. The family was wealthy and owned extensive property in Suffolk, Norfolk, Hertfordshire and the Midlands.[204] When, after his death in 1809, his son, Michael Peter Leheup, went mad John Benjafield was appointed one of the trustees responsible for his property of £5,000 a year. Benjafield was distantly related to Leheup: Michael Peter's grandmother was Mrs Benjafield's great aunt. In 1811 Mary Wyche Leheup, Michael Peter's mother, petitioned the Court of Chancery against Benjafield's trusteeship making two very serious accusations against him to prove his unsuitability.

Firstly it was claimed that when editor, Benjafield had used the *Morning Post* to blackmail the Prince of Wales by threatening to publish damaging information concerning the Prince's marriage to Mrs Fitzherbert and that, as a result, he had continued to receive an annual tax free annuity of £350 indirectly from the Prince ever since.

The second accusation concerned a conversation that Thomas Clarkson, the great Abolitionist, who was living in Bury at the time, had had with Leheup before he became ill. Clarkson stated that Leheup had told him that Benjafield had tried to dupe him into selling him an estate in Hertfordshire for much less than it was worth.[205] Although Benjafield strenuously denied both accusations, the judge, Sir Samuel Romilly, decided not to confirm his trusteeship.

The *Bury and Norwich Post* carried a full report of the case in spite of Benjafield's threats to the Editor that he would prosecute him if he did not print his version of the facts. The Editor, Peter Gedge, refused 'to be intimidated from the performance of his duty to his readers', and claimed that Benjafield's version was so biased that it would be wrong to publish it without printing a full account

[203] Diary 3 October 1811.
[204] T. G. Milner Gibson Cullum, *The Cullum Family* (1928), pp. 314–15.
[205] BNP 28 August 1811.

16. *The Six Bells at the bottom of Churchgate Street, Bury, owned by Joseph Maulkin and run by his brother Solomon.*

of the proceedings gathered in an 'impartial manner' from various London papers.[206]

The effect on Benjafield must have been devastating. He was taunted at Peter Cases's Aldermanic dinner in October by toasts to Mr Clarkson 'the indefatigable abolitionist of the execrable Slave trade' and to Sir Samuel Romilly, 'reformer of penal laws'. This last toast was proposed by Capel Lofft who had defended Benjafield's servants in 1802.[207] In December the Recorder was told that if he invited Benjafield to the Borough Quarter Sessions dinner 'most of the Gentn would withdraw & not dine with him'.[208] In January his fellow county magistrates refused to sit with him after their chairman, Dr Ord, had received a letter from Lord Moira saying that Benjafield had deceived him.[209] In June the biannual dinner of the school governors did not take place because Benjafield was still in the chair and his fellow governors all pretended to have other more pressing engagements.[210] Meanwhile his supporters on the Guildhall Feoffment Trust turned against him when a further piece of sharp practice was brought to

---

[206] *Ibid.*
[207] BNP 9 October 1811.
[208] Diary 6 December 1811.
[209] Diary 20 January 1812; see also 'Benjafield's Statement' in *Bury Charities* SROB shelved at B45.1.
[210] Diary 1 June 1812; SROB Grammar School Minutes 1776–1836 E5/9/202.2.

light. It was discovered that he had forced one of the Trust's tenants to prevent anyone shooting or coursing on Trust land who did not have his permission to do so. The Feoffment indemnified the tenant from his bond to Benjafield and gave a vote of thanks to the member, William Dalton, who had brought the situation to light.[211]

The matter might have died down quickly had Benjafield not made his position worse by suing one of the papers which had carried reports of the Leheup case. The Lord Chief Justice summed up in Benjafield's favour because he felt that the facts of the case had not been proved, but the jury found against Benjafield and small damages were awarded to the defendents.[212] There were few who did not share the defence counsel's opinion 'that Benjafield had been in receipt of the Wages of his iniquity for over twenty years, and had had the effrontery to come before a jury to ask for damages for injuring that Character which he had long ago sold'.[213]

Broad sheets on the case circulated in Bury putting the case for and against Benjafield. Benjafield insinuated that the attacks on him were the result of the party struggle in the town 'it being perfectly consonant to the disposition and the feelings and particularly consistent with the interest of a certain party resident in this town' that he should be humiliated.[214] Although Oakes cannot have been anything but pleased at the turn of events there is no evidence in the diary or elsewhere that he engineered it. He was probably the Leheups' family banker and could have been a party to Mrs Leheup's action as he records attending a family meeting after Michael William Leheup's death in 1809.[215] Otherwise there is no mention of the court case and little of Benjafield's subsequent disgrace.

Having been found guilty of blackmail and sharp-practice of the most un-pleasant kind, Benjafield's reputation in Bury was in shreds. He continued to lead the opposition or 'out' party and on various occasions tried to get back 'in' without success.[216] As late as 1817 a mandamus had to be obtained in order to elect the Assistant Justices, two Capital Burgesses and one Common Council-man because Benjafield had kept the remnants of his party away from Corpora-tion meetings.In the end the Oakes's candidates won easily and Benjafield was forced to withdraw John Oliver, whom he had been trying to get onto the Corporation since 1809.[217] Although he must have known that it would do no good he continued to object to the election of the Assistant Justices.[218] Indeed he must have been obsessed with achieving office in the town and as late as

[211] SROB H2/6/1.16; diary 7, 17 20 December 1811.
[212] BNP 30 December 1812.
[213] Quoted by A. Aspinall, *Politics and the Press c1780–1850* (1949), p. 278.
[214] *Bury Charities.*
[215] Diary 3 November 1809.
[216] e.g. Diary 17, 20 August 1812, 18 August 1814; BNP 26 August 1812.
[217] SROB D4/1/5, 317/1; diary 5 December 1817.
[218] Diary 9, 30 December 1817.

February 1827 made the chemist Abraham Gall propose him as Recorder although Gall had made it clear that he was not going to vote for him. In the end Benjafield did not stand observing sardonically 'that he might as well expect to be appointed Emperor of the Turks, as Recorder of this Corporation'.[219] He was elected Governor of the Workhouse in 1819 and retained the office until February 1831 when he was forced to resign because of anomalies in the accounts.[220] At his death in 1832 his old enemy the *Bury and Norwich Post* kindly ignored the events of the last 30 years and described him as having been 'a most intelligent and valuable magistrate for this county'.[221]

Modern students of Press History have been less charitable and have concluded that Benjafield not only knowingly blackmailed the Prince of Wales but that he had deliberately set out to use the *Morning Post* as a vehicle for blackmail and in the process ruined it. Although it was common for newspapers in the eighteenth century to be used for the purposes of political intrigue, blackmail and the sale of puffs, Lucyle Werhmeister contends that Benjafield 'systematized and expanded these activities and turned them into the paper's chief source of income'.[222] As the *Bury and Norwich Post* put it, he used the *Morning Post* 'under the hedge of innuendo to shoot at the loftiest Characters of the Country, and with the safe ammunition of Stars and dashes, to keep himself out of reach and grasp of the Law'.[223] In addition he never denied Clarkson's accusations and the eagerness with which he sought to run the financial affairs of a wealthy, feeble-minded and distant relation of his wife's would have been enough to damn him in most people's eyes.

Benjafield must have been a persuasive and plausible man. The Prince of Wales went on paying him although Benjafield no longer had the power to hurt him. Dr Symonds's old age was marred by an argument which was not of his making, and Abraham Gall was forced to support Benjafield although he did not

[219] BNP 14 February 1827; SROB D4/1/5, p. 386.
[220] SROB N5/1/3, 26 August 1819.
[221] BNP 25 January 1832.
[222] Werhmeister, *The London Daily Press*, p. 90.
[223] BNP 30 December 1812. Benjafield had been persuaded to buy the *Morning Post* by George Rose, secretary to the Treasury, in 1784 because Rose wanted to build up support for the administration on the eve of the election. Benjafield received £200 from secret service funds to cover part of the cost plus £110 for expenses, so that any money that he subsequently made was clear profit. Thus his later claim that the annuity was for his share of the sale of the paper was untenable because it had cost him almost nothing. Under his management the paper's circulation dropped from 2,100 to 800 yet he had received more than £6,000 by the time the libel case came to court. Equally Benjafield's assertion that he did not know where the annuity came from was shown to be false. In 1790 and again in 1796 he took legal steps to ensure its continued payment and in 1810 complained that tax had been wrongly deducted from it and that unless this was put right he would have no option but to complain to 'that great personage on whose account the annuity was originally granted'. Whermeister, *The London Daily Press*, p. 79; Aspinall, *Politics and the Press*, pp. 275–78.

like him. Benjafield became Leheup's trustee in spite of the fact that both Mrs Leheup and her son disliked and distrusted him and that they had many closer relations who would have been more suitable. Guildhall Feoffment tenants did Benjafield's bidding and his staunch supporter on the Corporation, Branwhite Green, left him £1,000, rather more than he had left to his own grandchildren.[224] An opportunistic, unprincipled and charismatic man like Benjafield posed a very serious threat to Oakes. Such a man would never have been content with a share of patronage in Bury, and Oakes had no choice but to fight him or to be ousted from all positions of power and influence in the town.

In fact the outcome of their battle was clear before the Leheup case and subsequent libel action put an end to all Benjafield's hopes. Oakes was able to dominate because he had four major advantages over Benjafield. In 1802 he had become the sole channel of patronage from the FitzRoys and the Herveys to the town. He came from a family which had been firmly established as leaders of Bury society for generations. This, together with the fact that he was a respected banker meant that he was known and trusted by most people. He was also a wealthy man and used his money to provide lavish and prestigious entertainment for his supporters and to make generous donations to town charities.

Above all Oakes was extraordinarily conscientious and businesslike in his attitude to public work so that it would have been difficult to steal a march on him. During the course of the diary he rarely missed a Corporation or a charity meeting and tried to make sure that his supporters also attended when contests were expected. The fight with Benjafield provoked a growing professionalism in his attitude as a political agent. Parliamentary or Corporation elections were usually prefaced by a private meeting of his supporters to decide on candidates and to work out tactics. Careful note was made of those who were absent, and their excuses, so that party discipline could be maintained. James Oakes laid a strong foundation of effective political management in Bury. It enabled his son to ensure the election of the FitzRoy and the Hervey candidates when demands for political and religious reform provoked a widening gulf between the electorate and their patrons.

REFORM 1815–1827

Political management in Bury during this period presented Oakes with two major problems. Firstly the Corporation was under attack from reformers in the town and, secondly, there was a growing ideological split between the members and their patrons over the issues of reform and Catholic emancipation.

Agitation for Parliamentary reform had died down in Bury, as elsewhere, at the end of the eighteenth century and only re-emerged with force in the second decade of the nineteenth century although party feuding had stimulated some

[224] PROB 11/1523 fol. 286.

criticism of closed corporations at various times in the interim.[225] In common with many other towns the movement was led by influential non-conformist business and professional men like Charles Willett the banker, Charles Denton Leech, an attorney, the Robinsons, who were tanners and cousins of Crabb Robinson the radical diarist, the Braddocks who were brewers, and Thomas Harmer, a maltster whose father had been one of the wealthiest yarn merchants with James Oakes 20 years before.

Although he had no real hope of gaining power and influence Benjafield continued to boycott Corporation elections with the remnants of his party which gave fuel to reformers' fire. By 1817 letters began to appear in the *Bury and Norwich Post* demanding electoral reform.[226] The following year the editor proudly pointed to the fact that the paper's circulation was larger than at any time since its establishment in 1782 to show the degree to which reformist ideas had gained ground.[227] Yet, when in April 1819 Henry Braddock was nominated to fill a vacancy among the Common Council, only four men supported him.[228]

The FitzRoy/Hervey monopoly of the Bury seats was challenged for the first time since the retirement of Sir Charles Davers in 1802 at the general election of 1820. J. W. D. Merest, one of the leaders of the reform movement in the county, canvassed the Corporation and 'met with great success'.[229] However, despite the *Bury and Norwich Post's* optimistic prognostications, 'Lord John Fitzroy & Col Upton were elected unopposed'.[230] The growing divide between the Corporation and a large number of wealthy and influential townsmen was widened still further by the Queen Caroline affair which dragged on throughout 1820 and 1821. Reformers, including Braddock, John Ridley and George Willett signed requests for meetings to congratulate the Queen on her accession while the Corporation's own petition expressed loyalty to the King.[231]

The question of Parliamentary reform and Catholic emancipation together with the problem of agricultural depression, rising poor rates and the fear of a fresh tide of rural violence all combined to sharpen the political debate. Fox and Pitt Clubs were revived in 1821 with the leading reformers from the town joining the former and the wealthier members of the Corporation the latter. By March 1821 it was apparent that reform ideas were gaining more ground. A requisition for a reform meeting included not only the names of active supporters like Merest, the veteran reformer Joshua Grigby IV, the Robinsons and the Braddocks

---

[225] e.g. BNP 12 February 1817, 7 January 1818.
[226] e.g. BNP 12 February 1817.
[227] BNP 7 January 1818.
[228] SROB D4/1/5, pp. 237, 240, 242, 250; D11/3/4; diary 29 April 1819. Oakes is mistaken about Braddock's Christian name and the number of meetings called. Two of those who voted for Braddock were members of Oakes's party, one had supported Oakes since Benjafield's disgrace and one was a consistant opponent.
[229] BNP 28 February, 1 March 1820.
[230] SROB D4/1/5, p. 286.
[231] SROB 1157/5; diary 14 November 1820.

but also those of Timothy Richard Holmes, the Town Clerk, and James Mathew, a Capital Burgess.[232] It was estimated that one sixth of the county attended the subsequent meeting in April, including many farmers and tradesmen who had not hitherto been regarded as politically active. Speakers lambasted the government, in particular its handling of the Queen Caroline affair and Peterloo, and resolutions were drawn up expressing the view that high taxation feeding government extravagance and want of Parliamentary reform were the causes of the nation's problems. The petition was said to have been signed by 9,000 people.[233]

As support for reform spread and Benjafield continued his harrying tactics the need to keep Corporation membership in friendly hands was more important than ever. Meanwhile it was becoming increasingly difficult to find suitable men from the traditionally acceptable trades and professions to serve. In April 1821 Oakes was forced to pay the grocer John Lawrence £50 a year in return for his agreement to allow fellow grocers Richard Biggs, Oakes's old clerk, and John Oliver to become Common Councilmen.[234] Although his critics hailed him as 'Corruption's patriarch'[235] this was the only time in all his reports of pre-election planning that Oakes appears to have resorted to overt bribery.

At the same time as the Corporation was getting out of step with the political aspirations of the majority of people in Bury it was becoming ideologically isolated from its patrons, particularly from the Duke of Grafton. The majority of the Capital Burgesses and Common Councilmen were firmly opposed to both political and religious reform whereas the Duke and his family took a prominent part in the Parliamentary reform campaign in the county and supported Catholic emancipation. At the Aldermanic dinner in 1824 Lord John FitzRoy was forced to refrain from mentioning politics 'as he knew there was great discrepancy of opinion amongst them'.[236] The Marquess of Bristol did not share the Duke's reformist convictions, but he keenly supported Catholic emancipation.

By 1821 the issue had once more become one of the major importance throughout the country. The clergy of the Archdeaconry of Sudbury petitioned Parliament to protest against the Catholic Relief Bill, deliberately flouting their Archdeacon who had recommended its support.[237] Pro-reform letters in the *Bury and Norwich Post* answered anti-reform letters written to the moderately Tory *Ipswich Journal*.[238] Political feeling in Bury reached such a pitch that the need for a Tory paper to counter the *Bury and Norwich Post* was answered by the establishment of the *Bury Gazette or Ipswich and Norwich Advertiser* in September

[232] BNP 7 March 1821.
[233] BNP 18 April 1821.
[234] Diary 11 April 1821.
[235] SROB 406/7, an undated mock-heroic poem probably written between 1824 and 1829.
[236] BNP 6 October 1824.
[237] BG 9 June 1822.
[238] e.g. BNP 11 April 1821, letter dated 3 April 1821 from *Reformer* replying to one in IJ from *Anti-Reformer*.

1821. The paper soon became ultra Tory in outlook and made no pretence at unbiased reporting. While it opposed Parliamentary reform, its most purple prose was reserved for the defence of the established church against the threat of Catholic emancipation and Archdeacon Glover was singled out for particular vilification.[239] Two years later these loyalties were displayed pictorially at the head of the title page in a mitre and crown resting on a Bible, behind which were a crossed crosier and sceptre.

Catholic emancipation was one of the major issues at the general election in 1826 and, as a result of the Corporation's strongly held views, a national question affected the course, if not the outcome, of a Parliamentary election in Bury for the first time in over 40 years.[240] Abraham Gall, one of the three chemists elected in 1817, refused, on grounds of conscience, to vote for either the Earl of Euston or Lord Hervey because of their support for the Catholic cause. Eventually Sir Thomas Cullum declared the election complete, hoping that it would be recorded as a unanimous decision and one witty member could not resist the observation that Lords Euston and Hervey had been 'unanimously elected without GALL'.[241]

At the election dinner which followed, both candidates were anxious to distance themselves from the Corporation and to emphasize their roles as representatives of the whole town.[242] Toasts were drunk to the leaders of the reform movement in Suffolk, Joshua Grigby, J. W. D. Merest and J. H. Powell, and the election ball saw 'scenes of great disorder several Dozen of wine Glasses, Decanters broke &ca &ca, much confusion . . . all sorts of people broken in, more without than with Tickets, and were quite riotous'.[243]

By 1831 the vote at the general election came close to reflecting the true political sympathies of the Corporation with the FitzRoy candidate run very close for second place by the anti-reform candidate Philip Bennet of Rougham. It was generally accepted that the Tory Corporation had only been prepared to elect a Whig member at all through 'the influence of Mr Oakes [Orbell Oakes] who from his respectability, property and long-standing, had great influence'.[244] The old and by now inappropriate, association between the FitzRoys and the Oakeses was finally ended at the 1832 election when James Oakes's grandson, Henry James, chaired Lord Jermyn's election committee.

The extent to which the Corporation had become out of step with political feeling in the town is well illustrated in Henry's Oakes's comment that 'by far the greater majority of the voters are Reformers' who would never elect a Tory in the

[239] BG 9 June 1822.
[240] General Conway was forced to withdraw in 1784 because of his support of the Fox-North coalition. See La Rochefoucauld, op. cit. pp. 75–76.
[241] BNP 14 June 1826; BG 14 June 1826; SROB D4/1/5, p. 368 records the election as unanimous.
[242] BNP 14 June 1826.
[243] Diary 12 June 1826.
[244] BNP 13 November 1833.

event of there being only one vacancy.[245] That Orbell Oakes was able to maintain the status quo in these circumstances until 1832 must in great part have been due to the detailed practice of political management developed and laid down so methodically by his father, James Oakes.

By the time of the 1826 election James Oakes was nearly 85 and no longer took an active part in Bury political life although he continued to chair the election management committee.[246] His grasp on affairs was slipping. He forgot to dine with the candidates the night before the election,[247] failed to record the altercation with Abraham Gall, and failed to make his usual note of election expenses. General elections had become, for him, primarily social functions to be planned as carefully and run as efficiently and with as little waste as possible. He never thought to question the extraordinary fact that for the last 10 years at least, 37, mainly Tory, men had elected a pro-reforming Whig to Parliament and that his election was probably more satisfactory in political terms to the large body of unfranchised townsmen than to his electors.

In 1827 James Oakes failed to record the Aldermanic election for the first time in nearly 50, years and on 14 October 1827 the diary ends. Although he remained on the Corporation until his death in January 1829, Oakes attended only one other meeting: in August 1828.[248]

TOWN GOVERNMENT 1778–1827

Oakes's diary gives the impression that the government of the town was unaffected by the political gerrymandering and personal antagonisms that existed for the greater part of the period. It presents a picture of a town that was well and honestly governed by rulers who, for the most part, were competent, public spirited and embued with civic pride. One cannot but be impressed by the enormous amount of time and energy that Oakes himself devoted to local government at a period when many corporations and charity trustees were accused, at best, of apathy and, at worst, of blatant corruption.[249] This impression is corroborated by both the Feoffment and the Corporation records. They show that Corporation and charity property was well managed, in spite of the fact that the number of Guildhall Feoffment Trustees was so reduced for part of the time. Leases were always put out to tender and property let to the highest bidder.[250]

---

[245] SROB 941/3/2 letter dated 22 March 1833, Henry James Oakes to Lord Jermyn.
[246] Diary 6 June 1826.
[247] Diary 10 June 1826.
[248] SROB D4/1/5, p. 421.
[249] e.g. H.C.F.Lansbury, 'Politics and Government in St Albans 1685–1835' (unpublished Ph.D. thesis, University of London, 1964), pp. 55–56, 80; Lee, 'Stamford and the Cecils', pp. 52–53, 87; A.Temple Patterson, A History of Southampton 1700–1914, 2 vols (Southampton, 1966), I, Chapter IX.
[250] e.g. SROB H3/5/3 no.18; D11/3/4 and 5; D4/1/8; D4/1/4, pp. 245, 254.

Rents were fair in comparison with commercial rates and long or transferable leases were not encouraged.[251] Guildhall Feoffment property was inspected regularly, kept in good repair and where necessary alterations and improvements were made.[252] Special standing committees dealt with the upkeep and letting of specific Corporation property. The churchyard committee made and rigorously enforced regulations governing its use, laid down scales of fees and appointed nightwatchmen to forestall the activities of body snatchers.[253] Another committee reviewed the leases of the fairs and markets and regularly increased the rent.[254] Repairs and improvements were made to the stock-market,[255] while the cattle-market was rebuilt on a larger site in St Andrew's Street.[256] On the whole bridges and public buildings in the Corporation's care were also kept in good order,[257] repairs to ancient buildings were undertaken with sensitivity,[258] the advice of well known architects was sought,[259] and the old theatre was converted into a concert hall for the benefit of the town.

Inquiries into the management of the Guildhall Feoffment Trust and other charities, initiated by a radical activist Francis King Eagle after Oakes's death, found that the Trustees had carried out their tasks faithfully and had only failed to do so where the provisions of the trusts had become obsolete or funds were no longer adequate to meet them. No evidence of corruption or nepotism was uncovered, although it was suggested that rather less could have been spent on Feoffment dinners and rather more of Feoffment money on the two churches.[260]

Despite reporting on an antagonistic Tory corporation, the Whiggish Municipal Corporations Commissioners came to the same conclusion over the management of property and charities in the care of the Corporation.[261] It found no evidence of corruption in the granting of tenancies or in the apportionment of land following enclosure in 1814. Only one tenant was a Corporation member and he had been a tenant long before he was elected to the Common Council. In all cases land was let at its full value and property sold to redeem land tax was

[251] e.g. Diary 10 February, 17 March 1803.
[252] Not all were agreed that the alterations to the Guildhall were a success: 'Its ancient porch of flint, brick and stone seems silently to reprobate the modern alterations which the body has suffered'. G.Ashby, A Description of the Ancient and Present State of the Town and Abbey of Bury St Edmunds in the County of Suffolk (Bury, 1782), p. 74.
[253] SROB D4/1/5 22 August 1811.
[254] e.g. SROB D4/1/4, pp. 90, 296.
[255] SROB D4/1/4, p. 107; D4/1/5, p. 245; diary 19 April 1820.
[256] SROB D4/1/8; D4/1/5, pp. 359, 379, 382, 386, 390–92, 411.
[257] e.g. SROB D/4/1/4, pp. 91, 158; D4/1/5, pp. 173, 365.
[258] SROB D4/1/4, pp. 191. The repair of the roof of St Mary's Church was ordered, stipulating that care should be taken not to make any alteration 'in the internal Appearance of the Roof or Ceiling'.
[259] SROB D4/1/5. pp. 134–35.
[260] SROB J511, The Reports of the Commissioners to Enquire Concerning the Charities in England and Wales relating to the County of Suffolk 1819–37; BPP 1830 (139), vol.XII.
[261] Appendix to the First Report of the Commission Appointed to Inquire into the Municipal Corporations, p. 2178.

sold 'at a fair value and no part of it was purchased by any member of the Corporation'.[262]

The Commissioners found that the provision of justice in the town was equally satisfactory concluding that 'The conduct of the magistrates both at the general and petty sessions, appear to have been impartial, the juries fairly selected and the business properly conducted'.[263] Civil and criminal courts were held regularly, jury service at Quarter Sessions was open to all assessed to the poor rate at six pounds and over, and excluded those who already held public office in the town, while the cost of prosecution at Quarter Sessions was regulated by a table of fees approved by the judges.[264] Although no Recorder had been resident since the retirement of Dr Symonds in 1801, the Corporation appointed well qualified men of calibre and integrity who performed their duties efficiently and not, as so often happened elsewhere, local, influential men interested only in perks which the job could provide.

His diary shows that Oakes took his various judicial appointments seriously spending a great deal of time in his capacity as a justice and a deputy lieutenant on balloting and drawing up lists of men for militia service and swearing in those chosen; approving poor rates; and inspecting roads; apart from the usual court duties. Unlike some of his contemporaries he refused to go on serving into old age because he felt that his increasing deafness made him unfit to do so. As patron of both livings in the town the Corporation were responsible for appointing the clergy. The livings were regarded as 'very respectable and eligible pieces of Preferment'[265] and always attracted several candidates who eagerly lobbied members for support. Inevitably family and party loyalties played a part in their choice but candidates also had to audition for the job by taking a service, and those whose voices were considered inadequate or who had some other deficiency were discarded.[266] The Corporation's interest in the town's spiritual life did not end there. The Alderman and Capital Burgesses chose preachers to give the weekly lectures and clergy were asked to provide Communion on Good Friday.[267]

At the same time the Corporation zealously defended its rights from incursions from outside. Attempts by the Bishop of Norwich to claim the right of presentation to the town churches were forestalled,[268] plans to move the Assizes to Ipswich and an attempt by county magistrates to extend their jurisdiction

[262] *Ibid.*

[263] *Ibid.*

[264] *Ibid,* p. 2176.

[265] The Rev. R. Yates, 'History of Bury St Edmunds' (c1805), photocopy of a manuscript held at SROB Acc 1058. The original is in BL Egerton 2373–4.

[266] Diary 7, 28 April 1799, 29 July, 12 August 1810.

[267] Diary 22 January, 16 April 1802. *Cf.* La Rochefoucauld *op. cit.* p. 61.

[268] e.g. Diary 8, 16 April 1789. See also Yates's account pp. 275–82 and SROB D4/1/4, pp. 114, 116, 119, 124, 129, 131, 133, 138–39, 141, 144, 154–55; SROB D4/1/7, loose sheet dated 23 March 1778.

inside the Borough were both defeated.[269] The Corporation also insisted that the new gaol to serve both Bury and the county be built inside the Borough because by charter the Alderman was keeper of the gaol.[270] Other attempts by groups within the town to over-ride Corporation rights were also withstood. An injunction was served on the wardens of Saint James's church when they tried to erect a 'turet' on the steeple without permission.[271] Sir Charles Davers's claim that, as steward of the Liberty of Bury St Edmunds, he had the right to issue process out of his great court against inhabitants in order to recover small debts was challenged,[272] and an audacious tenant of the Theatre was made to undo an alteration that he had made without Corporation approval.[273] Claims were not, however, pursued regardless of cost. The battle to enforce the Corporation's right to small tithes on its land in the borough was eventually given up because it was felt that to proceed further would invite expensive litigation and cause great animosity.[274] Nine years later it was decided, in the interests of economy, that no legal suit of any kind was to be instigated unless first ordered by a full corporate assembly.[275]

In 1824 the *Bury and Norwich Post* had made a rather half-hearted criticism of the management of Corporation finances claiming that ordinary inhabitants had no means of knowing what was going on and suggesting that savings could be made in certain areas.[276] That this criticism was never repeated was probably because the Corporation's debts were not the result of financial mismanagement but rather because Corporation income was inadequate to meet the demands made upon it. The receiver's accounts were audited annually and discussions were held throughout the period to try to remedy the problem. Debts contracted since before the 1780s amounting to £2,800 were reduced by various forms of retrenchment, including limiting the amount of money to be spent on entertainment on public days, cutting out the music from Aldermanic dinners,[277] exchanging public dinners following Corporation meetings for 'an ordinary at the Angel',[278] by cutting the Alderman's allowance in times of crisis,[279] and by cutting 'tavern expences'.[280] All Corporation members were required on election to lend £25 and later £50 or a £100 on bond for seven years to liquidate the

---

[269] Diary 5, 8 March 1810, 17 April, 12 May, 8 December 1809; SROB D11/3/3; D4/1/5, p. 92.
[270] SROB D4/1/4, p. 171.
[271] SROB D4/1/5, pp. 132–33; diary 12,17 September, 3 October 1811.
[272] SROB D4/1/4, p. 107.
[273] SROB D4/1/4, 29 September 1786.
[274] SROB D4/1/4, p. 255.
[275] SROB D11/3/4.
[276] BNP 6 October 1824.
[277] SROB D4/1/4, p. 70.
[278] SROB *Suffolk Tracts*, vol. III, shelved at 01.4.
[279] *Ibid.*
[280] SROB D11/3/4.

debts.[281] Bonds were also issued to fund particular capital projects like buying the churchyard,[282] repairing the market cross,[283] and buying the land for the new beast market.[284]

As a result of these and other schemes the Corporation was in debt, by 1833, to the tune of £2,350. The Municipal Corporation Commissioners accepted that this was not the result of corruption or mismangement but questioned the Corporation's judgement in borrowing £950 to convert the old theatre into a concert hall on the grounds that it would generate little income.[285] They ignored the fact that Bury was largely dependent on its position as a social centre at this time and that a concert hall would have added to the attractions of the town.

Arguably, in the period of Oakes's diary Corporation finances were run reasonably efficiently, with members in effect subsidizing areas of town government with interest-free loans. It was also generally acknowledged that the Alderman's allowance came nowhere near covering the expenses of office, with the result that many members tried to avoid it.[286] Although the Oakes family lent money to the Corporation at various times, having bought the Churchyard and taken over the debt of £2,500 in 1798, the diary shows that Oakes was as keen as anyone to reduce it.[287] He bought Sir Thomas Cullum's Corporation bond and Orbell Oakes personally held bonds to the value of £550.[288]

Watching, paving, lighting, street cleaning, and the care of the poor had been in the hands of an Improvement Commission since an Act of 1811, which extended powers first granted by an Act of 1747. Under the 1811 Act James Oakes was appointed treasurer and Timothy Richard Holmes, the Town Clerk, as secretary.[289] The Commission enlisted surveyors, collectors, watchmen, lamplighters and street cleaners, and accepted tenders to drain, pave and light the centre of the town.[290] In 1812 the Commissioners published the Act to remind inhabitants of their duty to keep the areas of their houses clean and were zealous in their pursuit of 'nuisances'.

By 1820 the income from the rates was insufficient to meet the needs of the Commission and the lamps were not lighted in the winter. A new act was

[281] SROB D4/1/4, p. 72, D4/1/5, pp. 307, 419, 422.
[282] SROB D4/1/4, p. 199.
[283] SROB D4/1/4, p. 69.
[284] SROB D4/1/5, pp. 386–411.
[285] *Appendix to the First Report of the Commission Appointed to Inquire into the Municipal Corporations.*
[286] The aldermanic allowance was £60 in 1711. In 1781 it was reduced to £20, in 1805 raised to £30 and in 1814 to £100. The Municipal Corporations Commission estimated that it cost at least £300 a year to be Alderman by 1833 and Alderman Blomfield was reputed to have spent £500. See SROB D4/1/4, p. 70; D4/1/5, p. 11; BNP 13 November 1833; *Appendix to the First Report etc,* p. 2172.
[287] SROB Receiver's Accounts D6/5/3.
[288] SROB D11/3/4, list of bond holders 1830.
[289] SROB L3/2/4.
[290] *Ibid.*

obtained which allowed the Commission to raise more money through increased rates and by extending its power to borrow, widened the provisions of the 1811 Act to cover the whole borough, permitting the installation of gas lighting and increased the penalties for certain misdemeanors.[291] James MacAdam was appointed surveyor in what appears to have been a consultancy role, leaving the day-to-day supervision of road building and repairs to resident deputies. Gas lighting was not in fact installed for another 14 years.[292]

The commissioners were forced to apply for a further Act of Parliament because the church wardens of both parishes refused to co-operate in making an up-to-date rate assessment. The burden of rates had increased enormously since the start of the wars with France and the virtual demise of the town's staple industry. A record rate of seven shillings in the pound was set for the last quarter of 1800 and by 1807 James Oakes estimated that out of a total population of 7,500 there were nearly 4,500 paupers.[293] The coincidence of a period of rapid population growth between 1811 and 1821 with a disastrous agricultural slump from 1813, and the end of the war in 1815, made the situation worse. The high level of poor rates pressed particularly heavily on the smaller shopkeepers and artisans. The columns of both the town's newspapers were full of letters alleging that the wealthy had obtained exemptions for themselves and their servants or that paupers were working for Guardians at the public's expense.[294] Vestry meetings became so heated over the issue of rates that they had to be held in the Guildhall because it was felt that such discord was unsuitable in church.[295]

Consequently service as a Guardian was not popular and many were fined for neglecting their duties. In addition, rateable values were underestimated by 50% with the result that fewer men appeared eligible to serve than was in fact the case.[296] In 1818 it was decided that inhabitants with property assessed at four pounds could take office and those who had already acted were no longer to be excused future service.[297]

Throughout the period, the Guardians were caught between a paternalistic desire to provide for the poor and a more hawkish attitude aimed at reducing the rate burden. In their efforts to provide adequate care for the poor, out- relief was given, best coals from King's Lynn were supplied in the Workhouse and each pauper was allowed as much hot food as he could eat for dinner and plenty of time in which to eat it.[298] In order to reduce costs the House was farmed,

[291] SROB OB 41.2.
[292] SROB L3/2/4.
[293] Diary 8 May 1807.
[294] e.g. BNP 31 December 1817, 18 March 1818.
[295] SROB H9/1/3 No.60, undated letter from the clergy and churchwardens of both parishes to the Guildhall Feoffment Trust.
[296] SROB N5/1/3, 20 October 1818.
[297] SROB N5/1/3, 2 October. Under the Act those eligible to serve as Guardians had to be in possession of property with a rateable value of £8.
[298] SROB N5/1/2, 1 August 1799; N5/1/3, 6 January 1820.

although the Workhouse keeper was supervised and disciplined when he failed to maintain adequate standards.[299] Manufacturing projects, including wool and silk spinning, weaving and straw plaiting, were tried without a great deal of success and lists of those on relief were published to discourage applicants.[300] At various times bread was substituted for cash payments to the out-poor[301] while cows and a corn mill were purchased to make the workhouse more self-sufficient. Meanwhile a plan to subsidize the rents of the out-poor had to be abandoned in the face of public criticism because of the cost.[302] By 1822 the Guardians owed the Bury and Suffolk Bank £1,460 3s.10½d.[303]

At the same time private charity and ad hoc relief committees played a very important part in subsidizing poor relief during periods of particular crisis, as it did in many other towns.[304] Oakes's diary vividly illustrates the deep sense of obligation that he and others felt in this matter. Much time and trouble was spent in researching the most efficient methods of relief,[305] in measures to reduce wheat consumption among the better off,[306] and in the provision of subsidized coal and food.[307] The town charities also played their part and some increased allowances paid to objects in order to compensate for rising bread prices[308] while personal charity remained of great importance.[309]

Although the Alderman , Capital Burgesses and Assistant Justices were ex-officio Guardians they attended meetings only when important or controversial decisions were being taken. Given his paternalistic attitude it is hardly surprising to find that one of Oakes's few actions as a Guardian was to stand alone in opposing the badging of the poor in 1800.[310] After his death the Guardians were 'captured' by political activists, many of whom were radical dissenters, who used the Court as a base from which to attack the management of town charities and to try to discredit some of their predecessors.[311] The egregious John Benjafield, Governor of the Workhouse for 12 years, was forced to resign because it was claimed that he had failed to keep proper accounts.[312] The Guardians were less than efficient in this respect, but no evidence of corruption was found and, on

[299] e.g. SROB N5/1/3, 2 January, 2 March 1826.
[300] BNP 10 December.
[301] e.g. SROB N5/1/2, 7 February 1788, 24 October 1800.
[302] SROB N5/1/3, 1 April, 2 September 1819; SROB 1557/7.
[303] SROB N5/1/3, 30 May 1822.
[304] Roy A. Church, *Economic and Social Change in a Midland Town: Victorian Nottingham 1815–1900* (1966), p. 13; Hill, *Georgian Lincoln*, pp. 173–74.
[305] Diary 12, 13 January, 12 February, 11, 15 July 1795.
[306] e.g. Diary 14 December 1795.
[307] e.g. Diary 3 December 1798.
[308] Diary 19 January 1796.
[309] e.g. Diary 25 December 1796; BNP 9 February 1814.
[310] SROB N5/1/2, 8 November 1800; diary 4 November 1800.
[311] SROB N5/1/3 e.g. 4 January 1827.
[312] *Ibid.* entries from January to March 1831.

the whole, they appear to have done their best to make adequate provision for the poor in their care.

That the Corporation and the charities of Bury St Edmunds were efficiently and honestly administered in spite of the fierce party struggles that took place within them is the result of four main factors. First the town was small and was therefore never faced with type of problems that beset the rulers of some northern industrial towns like Leeds where there was a fourfold increase in population between 1780 and 1830.[313] In comparison the population of Bury rose by only 25% during the town's most rapid phase of growth between 1811 and 1821.

Secondly, the electorate was small so that widespread favours to win political support were unnecessary. For example in Stamford, a town very similar to Bury in size but which had an electorate of over 600 by the early nineteenth century, corruption was rife. The Cecil family totally dominated and controlled all aspects of town life, with the result that Stamford society became obsequious, close, arrogant, hostile to outsiders and incapable of independent action.[314] In contrast Bury Corporation displayed a marked degree of independence in electing Sir Charles Davers as one of the Borough Members of Parliament for nearly 30 years and Corporation and charitable funds were never perverted for political ends.

The relative lack of corruption in Bury may also have resulted from the fact that, like Hull,[315] the town had a distinctly religious atmosphere. The abolitionists Sir William Dolben and Thomas Clarkson had both married Bury women and lived in or near the town at various times, while Arthur Young who lived at Bradfield Combust was a much publicized convert to Evangelicanism after the death of his favourite daughter. Even William Wilberforce had local connections.[316] Although Arthur Young claims that the area round Bury was 'a region dead in iniquity and sins' and that in no other county was 'there such a set of clergy as in this neighbourhood. Dreadful',[317] religion strongly affected the behaviour of Oakes and most other members of the leading members of Bury society. No Assize assemblies or private dinner parties were permitted in Passion Week. At other times families returned from Saturday evening events before midnight in order to observe Sunday correctly. The Corporation banned the 'barbarous' practice of bull-baiting and supported a bill to out-law it in 1802. They took their duties as patrons seriously and, following Evangelical practice, requested that the clergy provide Holy Communion on both Good Friday and on

---

313 R. G. Wilson, Gentlemen Merchants: The Merchant Community in Leeds 1700–1830 (Manchester, 1971), Chapter 9.

314 Lee, 'Stamford and the Cecils', pp. 55,65.

315 Gordon Jackson, Hull in the Eighteenth Century: A Study in Economic and Social History (Oxford, 1972), p. 307.

316 Robert Wilberforce was married to Joshua Grigby III's sister-in-law.

317 The Autobiography of Arthur Young, edited by M. Bentham Edward (1898), pp. 423, 438.

Easter Day.[318] Shops were also shut on Good Friday.[319] Those living 'in sin' in charity property were energetically routed out by the Rev. Henry Hasted,[320] whose missionary zeal did not, however, prevent him from holding regular card parties. Frequent checks were made to stop tippling during Divine Service,[321] and, in an effort to curb drunkenness and violence, beer to celebrate George IV's coronation was no longer served to the populace in the traditional way, from waggons in the streets, but was given to each family in their own homes.[322]

Oakes himself attended church twice every Sunday, unless prevented by illness, and read improving religious works. He superintended the Sunday and Charity Schools, was treasurer of the Suffolk Society for the Education of the Poor in the Principles of the Established Church founded in Bury in 1819, and was interested in other philanthropic enterprises including schools for the blind and Lancastrian Schools.[323] He supported the Auxiliary Bible Society which had been established in Suffolk largely through the efforts of Arthur Young and his own son, the Rev. James Oakes, whose letters to Young had a distinctly Evangelical flavour.[324]

While religious belief helps to account for Oakes's highly paternalistic attitude towards his family, his employees, and the poor and for the lack of corruption in Bury public life, it also helps to explain the firmly anti-Catholic stand of many of the town's rulers in the first quarter of the nineteenth century. After 1789, Christianity had become synonymous in the minds of many Evangelicals with Protestantism. Papists were thought to have given way to revolutionary atheists in France and were therefore not to be trusted. Thus Catholic emancipation and radicalism were opposed on religious grounds as doctrines which threatened conventional religious belief. Enemies of the Constitution were also enemies of religion.[325]

At the same time Evangelicals were well-disposed to protestant nonconformists joining with them in such organizations as the Auxiliary Bible Society and Lancastrian Schools. Although the Test was applied to Corporation members, in Bury dissenters played an active part in most other areas of town government. They were members of the Guildhall Feoffment Trust, the Improvement Commission and, throughout the period of Oakes's diaries, served as

---

[318] Diary 12 November 1792, 22 January 1802.
[319] e.g. 20 April 1821.
[320] SROB H9/1/3 no.12.
[321] e.g. Diary 20 November 1821.
[322] Diary 19 July 1821.
[323] e.g. Diary 31 January 1813; note book bound in volume IX between entries for the years 1809 and 1810, nos 86, 90.
[324] BL Add. MS 35,131, f.267, letter dated 20 December 1811; 35,129, f. 106, letter dated 14 December 1803.
[325] See R.J.White, *The Age of George III* (1968), p. 203; Ian Bradley, *The Call to Seriousness: The Evangelical Impact on the Victorians* (1976), pp. 110–113.

Guardians, in various parish offices, and were invited to Aldermanic dinners. As a result, an often wealthy and important section of Bury society was not cut off from all positions of power in the town. This, together with the fact that the Corporation did not control all the charities and statutory bodies meant that a far larger number of people including dissenters were able to participate in local government than would have been the case, and this must help to explain why there were few demands for municipal reform before 1830.[326]

Finally Bury continued to be governed by men of relatively high social status whose wealth and occupations made them less susceptible to corruption. In many towns,[327] faction fighting, together with the heavy cost in time and money, made it increasingly difficult to find suitable men prepared to take office. Although during the height of Oakes's battles with Benjafield there was some reluctance among candidates, the social standing of the members of Bury Corporation was more than maintained. In the last quarter of the eighteenth century the professions – attorneys, doctors, surgeons and bankers – accounted for approximately 14% of the body. By the end of the first quarter of the nineteenth century their share of the membership had risen to just over 47%. The Webbs have shown that where corporations maintained social exclusiveness and had a good proportion of professional men among their members the administration of the towns in their care was carried out with integrity.[328]

Many of these men came from families with long traditions of public service behind them. Out of those on the Corporation in 1824 at least 12, including James Oakes, had fathers and, in some cases, grandfathers who had served before them. There was, as in Hull, 'a continuing unity of political and economic power in the hands of competant and public spirited men' which helps to account for good government in Bury.[329]

Complaints from 'such as Bakers, Builders, Ironmongers etc' that they were kept off the Corporation because 'all must for the present give way for the sons of Corporators'[330] were fully justified, but, as the Webbs have shown, more representative urban government was not necessarily synonymous with good government at this period. Closed corporations were often better managers of corporate property and providers of justice than municipal democracies with a wider franchise.[331] Oakes, like many of his contemporaries, was an honest, energetic, conscientious and public spirited man who was proud of his town and served it with honour. His struggle with Benjafield, although unedifying, was part of the price

[326] Lansbury, 'Politics and Government in St Albans', p. 263.
[327] See Sidney and Beatrice Webb, English Local Government: The Manor and the Borough (1908), Book III, part I, vol.II, p. 391.
[328] Ibid.
[329] Jackson, Hull in the Eighteenth Century, p. 307.
[330] SROB 317/1, p. 341; Suffolk Chronicle 11 November 1824.
[331] Sidney and Beatrice Webb, the Manor and the Borough, pp. 722–35.

17. James Oakes's front door, 81 Guildhall Street, Bury.

to be paid for life under the patronage system. Surprisingly, it did not affect the government of the town. Oakes died in January 1829 and Henry James Oakes was elected to fill his grandfather's place as a Capital Burgess and to carry the family tradition of public service on into the age of reform.

CHAPTER V

Family and Social Life

FAMILY LIFE

Although he rarely described characters or reported conversations, and never confided his personal hopes and anxieties, James Oakes's diary gives much clear and dependable information about provincial middle class family life at the end of the eighteenth century. When he began writing, Oakes was a relatively young man with a wife and four children, the youngest of whom was only just eight years old. It therefore throws light on his attitude to his family, to their education, choice of careers and marriages. As it began as a record of the family's social life it also described the Oakes's wide social circle: those with whom they exchanged calls and those who dined regularly with them at Guildhall Street.

THE HOUSE AND THE HOUSEHOLD
The Oakes family lived in a pleasant five bay red brick house in Guildhall Street, possibly built by Oakes's uncle Orbell Ray, which fronted an earlier timber framed building. It contained comfortable family sitting rooms, a dining room, a formal first floor drawing room, extensive kitchen and brewing facilities and a wine cellar. Early in 1790, John (later Sir John) Soane designed two new wings: the first to provide purpose-built banking rooms with a dining room above them and the second a family dining room with a drawing room above it. Throughout his life Oakes continued to make minor additions to the domestic offices of the house and to extend the bank premises as business expanded.

The house, like so many provincial merchant houses in the mid eighteenth century, functioned both as a family home and as a place of business. Before the arrival of the banking rooms, it had contained a counting house. In front, across the road, there were pleasure gardens next to the Guildhall, and there were wool warehouses and sorting rooms in the yard behind. The yard opened back into St Andrew's Street, on the opposite of which were Oakes's comb shops and workers' cottages. Next to these a meadow provided grazing for horses, an annual crop of hay, room to keep pigs and space on which to pitch a tent and enjoy family picnics on warm summer evenings. Oakes's household servants were as likely to be asked to cut hay, butcher a pig or to brew beer as if they had lived in the country.

When the Oakes children were young the house accommodated a governess and between six and ten household servants besides the family. There was a coachman, groom, two footmen, a housekeeper, a lady's maid for Mrs Oakes and her daughters, and two or three other maids. The coachman and groom did not live in but took their meals in the house. The women servants were all called by their Christian names and the men, like William Coachman, according to their job.

The eighteenth century is supposed to have marked a watershed in relations between masters and servants. Medieval ideas of rights and duties in which the servant was expected to be at his master's disposal at all times, to serve him with due deference and to identify with the interests of his employer's family, were giving way to a contractual basis of service in which work was exchanged for wages. This resulted in a period of potential conflict between masters and men. Servants seem increasingly to have been seen by their masters as recalcitrant, insubordinate, disloyal and dishonest and various suggestions were made in a bid to find practical and legal means to keep servants in their proper place.[1] In 1802 an abortive attempt was made in Bury St Edmunds to found an Association for Prosecuting Servants in Cases of Robbery in their Masters' Houses.[2] Servants were no longer cowed into submission by the fear of dismissal. The rapid increase of the middle classes in the eighteenth century had resulted in a correspondingly increased demand for domestic staff so that there were always jobs to be had, while generous gratuities from tradesmen and tips from guests might loosen their dependence on their masters' good will.

For the most part employers were kind and considerate towards their servants providing good food, clothes, religious instruction, education, medical care and help in time of trouble. Apart from the old ideas of duty, unhealthy, ill fed and ill clothed servants reflected badly on the good name of the family employing them. The plays of Sheridan are sound on all this. Good and bad masters tended to produce good and bad servants.

In spite of possible changes in the relationship between master and servant Oakes seems to have had little trouble with his staff. On one occasion his head footman, Mark Shepherd, left 'in a very disgraceful manner',[3] on another, over 20 years later, he replaced three women servants at once.[4] However, most of his servants appear to have stayed with him for a considerable part of their working lives. Melsome was his housekeeper for 22 years before she became ill.[5] George Farrow, his faithful groom and companion on many journeys, was with him for 18 years.[6] He was fond of his servants. They and their families were entertained in

[1] J. Jean Hecht, *The Domestic Servant Class in Eighteenth England* (1956); for a full discussion of the relationship between masters and servants, see there Chapter III.
[2] BNP 27 January 1802; diary 21 January 1802.
[3] Diary 24 December 1800.
[4] Diary 10 June 1822.
[5] Diary 8 April 1813.
[6] Diary 9 April 1803–3 August 1822 after which he is not heard of again.

the kitchen at Christmas and at stock-taking hawkeys. Retired family servants, his mother's old maid and Richard Adamson's Swedish footman and his wife, were included in these parties after their employers had died. Food was sent out to those too frail to leave their houses. Their illnesses and deaths were recorded and they were cared for when unwell. Melsome was nursed for two months at Guildhall Street after a stroke in February 1813 before she was taken back to Norfolk by her neice. When George Farrow's eye-sight began to fail in July 1821, the 79 year old Oakes took him to London to consult the father of modern eye surgery, Benjamin Travers, and found him a bed at St Thomas's Hospital.

Their welfare and working conditions were naturally considered. Christmas dinner was taken early so that they could get on with merry-making in the kitchen and the ageing James Oakes always dined out on Tuesday, 'washing day', to lessen the load on his maids and housekeeper. On the deaths of Charlotte Oakes and her mother their personal maids were given a year's wages and some old servants received weekly allowances for drink on retirement.

Although the work of many servants must have been hard and repetitive, others had an interesting and stimulating time. The ladies' maids accompanied Mrs Oakes and her daughters whenever they went to stay away from home, going with them to London, Bath, Yarmouth, Liverpool and Manchester, apart from more local visits. Likewise coachmen and grooms accompanied the family and also helped with tax collections and with the exchange of bank notes with representatives of other country bankers in the area.

It is no wonder that when James Oakes referred to his family, the term included his servants. They were present at family births, marriages and deaths and nursed those who were ill. Oakes gave them paternal care and in return expected filial duty.

FOOD AND DRINK

Catering for guests presented few practical problems when a household was as well endowed with servants as that of James Oakes. Oakes was gregarious, enjoyed entertaining and was never happier than when surrounded by family and friends. Relations made protracted visits to Guildhall Street and often stayed for six months or more which was common practice particularly among middle class women at this period. His children had friends to stay during school holidays and it was usual for the house to be full of guests for at least part of the fair held in October.

Dinner, tea, supper and card parties were held with great regularity. No attempt was made on these occasions to have an even number of men and women and there was no reluctance to seat an odd number at table, even thirteen.[7] As

---

[7] See Gerald Curtis, A Chronicle of Small Beer: The Early Victorian Diaries of a Hertford-shire brewer (1970), p. 61 which shows that the same practice was followed in a Hertfordshire brewer's house in the mid nineteenth century. The superstition that it is unlucky to seat 13 seems to be of mid nineteenth century origin.

has been observed elsewhere meal times changed during the period, breakfast getting earlier and dinner later. At the end of the eighteenth century the Oakeses dined between three and five, took tea at about eight and supper between ten and eleven in the evening in the winter, while in the summer dinner was between one and three, tea at six and supper at eight. By 1824 Oakes was dining between five and six in the winter and about four in the summer. These hours were also observed in the sophisticated households of the Duke of Grafton and Lord Bristol. Lunch was first mentioned as a mid-day meal in 1815[8] although it is clear that Oakes often bridged the long gap between breakfast and dinner with a 'snap' consisting of a chop or soup or a sandwich and wine.

A great deal of wine was drunk in eighteenth Bury St Edmunds. Oakes bought it in bulk, sometimes in conjunction with a friend or relation, and personally attended to its bottling and to laying it down. The wine was obtained either from merchants in London, who dispatched it by sea to Ipswich, or from Messrs Everards of King's Lynn to be transported via the Lark Navigation, or from local wine merchants. Red port and sherry comprised the bulk of his purchases until the French wars forced him to diversify by buying Lisbon, Tenerife and raisin wine and madeira to take the place of brandy and rum which could no longer be imported. None of these wines appears to have been bought after 1815 but one would need to see his 'Cellar Book' to be certain. Without this record it is also impossible to guess how much wine was drunk each year at the Guildhall Street house. In 1782 he recorded bottling 126 gallons of port and buying a further 126 gallons five months later.[9] It was his practice to keep port for nearly two years before bottling and another two years before drinking and to buy a replacement pipe as the previous pipe was bottled.[10]

Certainly most men of Oakes's class in Bury had well stocked cellars.[11] At his death Richard Adamson's (Mrs Oakes's uncle) cellar contained at least 1,476 bottles of hock and port, the port purchased in London and in Bury and the hock directly from Frankfurt.[12] It also held 819 gallons of table beer.

Oakes regularly brewed his own beer and built a new brewhouse for the purpose in April 1800. Again there is no record of how much and how often beer was brewed but cosiderable quantities must have been produced to provide for the household alone.

Little information is given about food apart from detailed descriptions of the servants' Christmas dinner and September hawkey. These followed an almost unvarying pattern. Large joints of meat weighing 18 pounds or more, usually roast or boiled beef, followed by apple pies were provided for the hawkey, while at Christmas there was a sirloin of beef and a leg of mutton, weighing between 40

---

8   Diary 23 October 1815.
9   Diary 8 March, 29 August 1782.
10   e.g. Diary 4 February, 17 May 1797.
11   SROB E2/29/6, Sir Thomas Cullum's Account Book contains plans of his cellars.
12   Diary 31 March 1800; 12 March 1826.

and 50 pounds in total, together with plum puddings and mince pies for dinner. Supper always consisted of the remains of the meat and apple pies. Sometimes the 'family in the kitchen' had 'Gravy soup, a large joint Rump of Beef & large Turkey 12 lb'.[13] Each servant would have had about a pound of meat during the course of the day. No vegetables were ever mentioned.

The family in the dining room had very similar food. At Christmas 1801 they were served pea soup, roast beef, plum pudding and boiled turkey and at Christmas 1812 the fare included a goose.

Food was a popular present. Local land-owners often presented Oakes with a haunch of venison or a fore-quarter of lamb which he then used as the basis of a dinner party. Although Bury was not very far from the sea, fish was scarce and expensive. Oakes usually brought it home from his holidays in Yarmouth to give to members of the family.[14] It cannot have been very fresh by the time that it arrived on the table. On one occasion a turbot from Yarmouth was not eaten until five days after its purchase.[15] Friends in London sent salmon-trout, lobsters and turbot and local friends gave fresh water fish from their fish ponds and lakes. The most exotic gift of all was a 112-pound turtle sent from Liverpool by James Bridge, Oakes's nephew, strapped to the roof of the coach. Oakes expressed mild surprise that in spite of its being 'sent out very lively' it had failed to survive the 270 miles in 'remarkably hot weather' and was dead on arrival in Bury.[16] He solved the problem of its disposal by graciously presenting it to the clergy for their annual dinner.

Pineapples, grapes and melons from the glass-houses of local magnates or from London were served at election and aldermanic dinners, while at parties, particularly those including children, there were jellies, cakes and sweet tarts.

Generous hospitality to guests was a matter of pride to Oakes and an outward sign of his prosperity, so that what must seem to modern taste to have been enormous amounts of food, particularly meat, were consumed at formal dinners. However, the family probably ate quite simply at other times.[17] Indeed, even when entertaining, food may not always have been so splendid. The diary shows the growing popularity of the 'sandwich supper' or 'sandwich party' from 1795 until about 1812 after which it was no longer mentioned. From 1795 until 1801 the sandwich supper was an occasion in its own right and after that date it followed most of the dinner parties held at Guildhall Street.[18] The sandwich was

13 Diary 25 December 1796.
14 Diary September 1802.
15 Diary 27 August 1797.
16 Diary 12 July 1803.
17 The same observation has been made about Parson Woodforde's eating habits. See R. L. Winstanley, 'Book Review', *Parson Woodforde Society Quarterly Journal*, XVIII, 3 (Autumn 1985), 39–44 (p. 44).
18 Sandwich parties seem to have been very popular in Nottingham at the same period. See *The Diary of Abigail Gawthern of Nottingham 1751–1810*, edited by Adrian Henstock (Thoroton Society, 1980).

also used as portable food to be taken on journeys so that there was no need to stop for meals, and was used as a mid-day snack. Breakfast consisted of tea, coffee, hot rolls and sausages and cold meat when it followed a wedding but, again, was probably a far simpler affair at other times.

CHILDHOOD

It has been suggested that, by the eighteenth century, the authoritarianism of the early modern period had given way to ideas of greater personal freedom and had resulted in the growth of warm, affective relationships within families. As infant and child mortality rates fell, parents placed greater emotional investment in their children and bonding between mother and child was reinforced by the growing popularity of prolonged breast feeding among upper-class women. Declining belief in original sin meant that children were seen increasingly as innocents to be nurtured carefully and as individuals whose feelings were to be considered. As a result of these changes it is claimed that families became more child-centred, less disciplinarian and less formal.[19]

Neither Oakes's daughter nor his daughter-in-law breast fed her children: presumably they were wet-nursed. Within two months of the birth of her first son, Betsy Oakes was at a dinner party lasting from mid-day until ten at night, less than three months after the birth of her daughter she spent the day at a race-meeting and just over a month after the birth of her second son went to London, without the baby, intending to stay several weeks. Maria, Oakes's elder daughter, came home to have her second child and after one month left her with her grandparents in Bury while she rejoined her husband in Winchester. The idea of prolonged breast feeding had either not filtered through to the provincial middle class or was less popular with them than with fashionable society on which the evidence in Lawrence Stone's book is largely based.[20]

Babies were often privately baptized within days of their births and publicly christened later when they were between eighteen months and two years old. Godparents were elderly by the standards of today and were more often than not relations. James Oakes was godfather to his grand-daughter Louisa Oakes and even to his great grandson Henry James Oakes. Maria Gould's godparents included her grandmother Gould and Henry Collett, the ageing Clerk of the Peace from Westerfield. It was customary for godparents to leave substantial tips of between two and five guineas for the child's nurse and maid servant. The ceremony took place in the morning and was followed by a sumptuous dinner party for godparents and other guests which generally lasted until late in the evening.[21]

[19] For a full discussion see Lawrence Stone, *Family, Sex and Marriage in England 1500–1800* (1977), particularly Chapter 6.
[20] SROB Cullum Letters E2/25/2, Mary Cullum to Elizabeth Hanson, letters dated 6 November 1776, 8 April 1778, show that Lady Cullum breast fed her children.
[21] Curtis, *A Chronicle of Small Beer*, p. 63 observed the same pattern in a mid nineteenth century Hertfordshire brewer's family.

Small children were not relegated to the nursery and only allowed to emerge, scrubbed and shining on special occasions, as were children in the later nineteenth and early twentieth centuries. Attitudes to young children were far more accommodating and relaxed. James Oakes and his wife constantly entertained Orbell's children to meals when their parents were away or unwell. Betsy Oakes first brought her sons to dine with their grandparents when they were two and her daughter when she was only eighteen months.[22] 'Dear little Maria' Gould stayed with them for two months at the age of one month while the family moved to Yarmouth.[23]

Children entered society at an early age. At family dinner parties it was the custom for very young children to be brought into the dining room after the cloth had been removed for dessert and tea.[24] In 1800 his grandparents took Henry Oakes out visiting with them when he was four and he was only nine when a guest at a tea, supper and card party given by his grandfather.[25] Six months later, with his cousin Louisa Oakes and his seven year old sister, he was among 23 guests at a full scale dinner party. Orbell Oakes was only 13 when first taken to dine with the Duke of Grafton by his father.

Oakes's children and grandchildren were regular visitors to the Theatre in Bury from the age of nine at least and both boys and girls had made their appearance at public balls by the time they were 15 and probably before.[26] La Rochefoucauld commented in 1784 that young people in Bury society went everywhere with their parents from an early age,[27] an observation that was equally true of other provincial towns. In Nottingham, for example, Abigail Gawthern's daughter went to the races for the first time at six, to her first concert at 10 accompanied by her eight year old brother, and to her first assembly at 12.[28]

Apart from joining in adult social life, childrens' parties and dances were held by many families living in and about Bury throughout the winter and a childrens' ball was included among the festivities of the fair.[29] Children had friends to stay and went to stay with them. They all rode and the boys hunted, shot, fished and coursed on Oakes's land at Depden, six miles south west of Bury, and with friends elsewhere.

Oakes himself was genuinely fond of children and liked to have them about him all his life. He noted their birthdays, recorded their childish ailments and innoculations anxiously and was much distressed when they were ill.[30] New

22 Diary 9 February, 5 June and 20 September 1800.
23 Diary 13 November 1798.
24 e.g. Diary 31 December 1825, 1 January 1826.
25 Diary 17 August 1800, 6 January 1806.
26 e.g. Dairy 26 October 1779, 20 March 1780.
27 François de La Rochefoucauld, A Frenchman's Year in Suffolk, 1784, edited and translated by Norman Scarfe (Suffolk Record Society, XXX, 1988), p. 27.
28 The Diary of Abigail Gawthern, pp. 52, 59, 66.
29 e.g. Diary 17 October 1783.
30 e.g. Diary 30, 31 December 1796, 1 January, 16 September 1797.

grandchildren and great grandchildren were visited within days of their births, older grandchildren were given a guinea and taken to Bury fair to have turns of side shows and to watch puppets and acrobats.[31] He went on giving parties for his grandchildren until well into old age, providing music for dancing and delicious cold 'collations' of cold turkey, pheasant, partridge, pyramids of jellies and sweet cakes.[32] He even allowed himself to be persuaded to join in the dancing. There can have been no nagging maternal fears about suitable bed-times as these parties, like the public assemblies, went on until two or three in the morning. The sons and grandsons of friends who were at school in Bury or up at Cambridge were invited to dine regularly, particularly on Sundays, and were taken for rides in the phaeton.[33] Even at the age of 84 Oakes asked 'some little young Ladys' to dine with his young great nieces who were staying in Bury.[34]

It has been suggested that the growth of such warm relationships within the 'nuclear family' promoted a corresponding decline in the influence of kin and of community on family affairs. This does not seem to have been the case with the Oakeses. James Oakes was devoted to his mother and to his wife's uncle both of whom lived in Bury. They took it in turns to dine at each others' houses on Sundays, apart from frequent meetings at social events during the week. Oakes looked to Richard Adamson for sound business advice and, as she grew old and frail, sat with his mother in the evenings.[35] Mrs Oakes's father and sister were visited regularly in Wereham and often stayed in Bury.

Grandparents and aunts played a very natural role within the family by having children to stay when their parents were ill, when away, or when a new baby was expected. Maria Oakes came home to have her first three children and her sister-in-law came to help her during the later stages of pregnancy. Oakes acted as a trustee for many family trusts and the wider family often looked to him for advice. After her husband's death Mary Bridge consulted him about her son James and sent him from Liverpool to his uncle when was in business difficulties, although Bridge did not always appear particularly amenable to Oakes's counsel.[36]

Relations from Liverpool, Manchester and London were visited and made welcome at Guildhall Street.[37] Nieces, nephews and even great nieces and great nephews brought their new wives, husbands and children to meet Oakes so that family ties remained strong over the generations and over a wide geographical distance. One of the things that stands out in his diary is the level of contact maintained between relations who lived so far apart.

[31] e.g. Diary 15 December 1795, 30 August 1803, 19 October 1804, 24 October 1805.
[32] e.g. Diary 1 January 1812.
[33] e.g. Diary 19 July 1807.
[34] Diary 27 February, 17 May 1826.
[35] e.g. Diary 22 July 1784, 23 October 1785.
[36] e.g. Diary 4–6 November 1804.
[37] e.g. Diary 12 April 1793– 30 October 1793 when Sister Bridge and her daughter Susan visited Bury from Liverpool.

Boys' careers were decided upon early in their lives by their parents and grandparents and they were educated accordingly.[38] It was intended that Orbell Oakes
should follow his father into the yarn trade and he was sent at 13 to Mr Shepherd's Academy, Clapton,[39] which presumably gave an education suited to the
needs of a business career. He left Clapton at 16 and was apprenticed to his father
in the yarn trade for seven years. His younger brother James who, like so many
younger sons, was destined for the church, followed his father to King Edward VI
School, widely known at this time for its excellent classical education. At 17 he
went up to Trinity College, Cambridge and was subsequently ordained priest.
Parental care and concern did not stop once the boys were away. They were
visited at school, their masters were invited to stay at Guildhall Street[40] and
Oakes took much trouble seeing James safely settled into his Cambridge lodgings
and keeping a very close eye on him during his three years there.[41]

Although it was planned that only Henry, among Orbell's three sons, should
join his father and grandfather in the bank, they were similarly educated. From
the age of eight they attended a private school in Wortham run by the Reverend
James Merest who had been the Reverend Henry Patteson's curate at Coney
Weston. By the time he was 12 Henry was at Charles Blomfield's private school
in Bury. He was probably sent there to give him a sound knowledge of subjects
that would be useful to him as a banker before acquiring a classical education at
the grammar school. In 1828 John Izzard Pryor, the Hertfordshire brewer, sent his
third son, Alfred, to the school to learn 'Mathematics, Mensuration, merchants'
accounts, Surveying and the use of globes' before sending him to Hamburg to be
trained as a merchant.[42] Similarly many Hull merchants in search of gentility
gave their sons a classical education but followed it up with vocational training.[43]
Orbell Oakes junior, destined ultimately for the Navy, left Wortham at 10 to go
to Bury Grammar School as a boarder for 18 months.

All three boys went on to Reading School when they were nearly 13: Aston,
the youngest, was dispatched straight from Wortham without an intermediate
period in Bury. Although Bury School had such a splendid reputation at this
time, Reading was probably chosen in preference because of Orbell Oakes's
friendship with Dr Valpy, the headmaster. Reading School was at a very low ebb

---

[38] This seems to have been common practice throughout the eighteenth and early nineteenth centuries. See Edward Hughes, *North Country Life in the Eighteenth Century: The
North East 1700–1750* (Oxford, 1952), Chapter VIII and Curtis, *A Chronicle of Small Beer*,
pp. 24–45.

[39] Diary 17 July 1781.

[40] e.g. Diary 8 July 1782, 13 July 1784.

[41] e.g. Diary 29 October 1787, 10 April 1788.

[42] Curtis, *A Chronicle of Small Beer*, p. 25. After leaving school Alfred Pryor spent five
years at home doing very little before going to Hamburgh. He eventually became a brewer
in Hatfield.

[43] Gordon Jackson, *Hull in the Eighteenth Century: A Study in Economic and Social History*
(Oxford, 1972), p. 276.

when he took it over, but improved under his stern direction to become one of the best in the country.[44]

While at Wortham, the boys had had regular visits from their parents and grandparents and must have found it difficult to adjust to life at Reading. It was common for boys at grammar and public schools of the period to be so unruly and debauched that many families sent their sons to private schools or had them educated at home to avoid contamination. In April 1784 boys at Bury School locked their master out of the school and 'afterwards left their master's House in Triumph'. Two boys were dismissed by the governors the next day.[45] The staff were often cruel and on one occasion the boys took retaliatory action with the result that the headmaster, Mr Laurents, was disciplined by the governors.[46]

Things were no better at Reading where Betsy Oakes feared that there was 'so bad a set of boys that it required no little resolution to preserve any tolerable conduct without being laughed out of it'.[47] Dr Valpy achieved results by energetic use of the cane and his regular Christmas visits to Orbell Oakes's house must have been viewed with mixed feelings by the younger members of the family. The difference between the gentle indulgence of home and the harsh regime at Reading must have come as an enormous shock to the Oakes boys. It is not surprising that Aston ran away and that none of them sent their own sons there.

Orbell Oakes junior only had to endure Reading for a year. He left at 13 to join his uncle, Admiral Plampin, on the *Oceana*, stationed in the Mediterranean, to begin life in the Navy. Both his brothers went up to Cambridge: Aston, destined for the church, to Jesus College and Henry, for the bank, to Emmanuel.

In spite of his time at Blomfield's Schoool and extra arithmetic lessons[48] Henry seems to have been ill prepared for a business career and not to have found the work easy. His mother had wished that 'he was quicker in learning' while he was at Reading.[49] Within three months of joining the bank in March 1818 his grandfather had reason to have 'a good deal of talk . . . respecting his application on his first coming to the Bank' which was followed by discussions with his father in May. By July his performance cannot have improved as Oakes had to speak to him again in front of his father.[50] There were no more grand-fatherly rebukes until May 1819.

Although the boys were treated kindly at home they had little, if any, say in their choice of career. James Oakes may have been an affectionate father and grandfather, and lenient in small matters, but expected total obedience where

---

[44] Edward Valpy (1764–1832) was usher at Bury Grammar School 1778–81, then head-master of Reading School from 1781 until 1830. See DNB, LVIII, pp. 84–85.
[45] Diary 28–29 April 1784; SROB Grammar School Minutes 1776–1836 E5/9/202.2, 29 April 1784 George Plampin and Thomas Barnard Sparrow were expelled.
[46] Diary 30 April, 2 May 1785; SROB E5/9/202.2, 2 May 1785.
[47] BL Add MS 35, 230 ff. 342, letter dated 5 January 1810.
[48] BL Add MS 35, 130 ff. 33, letter dated 19 December 1809.
[49] BL Add MS 35, 130 ff. 342, letter dated 5 January 1810.
[50] Diary 17 March, 17 May, 5 July 1817.

business was concerned. Orbell Oakes was in awe of his father and dared not retire from banking until after his death, although he disliked business and preferred country life at Nowton. He indulged his own sons with the result that Henry found adjustment to a working life difficult and his brother Orbell was hopelessly extravagant and ran up enormous debts which his father went on paying until the time of his death.[51]

Orbell Oakes was certainly more permissive than his father but whether this can be seen as part of a growing trend towards personal freedom and declining authoritarianism, or whether it was the natural reaction of a son to a strong father it is not possible to say. What is beyond question is that there was a great amount of affection shown towards children, attention paid to their needs and time spent with them, but in the earnest matter of careers total obedience was expected.

GIRLS' EDUCATION

During the eighteenth century there was a growing number of girls' schools and the curriculum expanded to include a wide range of subjects from mathematics and philosophy to such esoteric skills as making artificial flowers, filigree and hair work.[52] By the end of the century middle-class women no longer played an active part in their husband's business affairs or in the tasks involved in day-to-day housekeeping. This meant that they needed to be educated to fill empty hours with suitably lady-like occupations and to be satisfactory companions for their husbands. One Northumberland father frankly admitted that he had sent his daughters away to school in order 'to bring them home marriageable'.[53]

James Oakes's daughters and grand-daughters had governesses for their early schooling and at least one of these was of high calibre. Between 1780 and 1782 Maria and Charlotte, his daughters, were taught by Miss Routh who came from a family of educationalists. Her father, rector of two of the South Elmhams, was head master of the Fauconbridge School in Beccles, her eldest brother the president of Magdalen College, Oxford, another a fellow, while the eldest of the seven daughters, Mary, ran a successful school in partnership with two of her sisters from about 1784. The Oakes's governess was probably one of these women.[54]

In addition to Miss Routh's instruction Maria Oakes had French lessons from

[51] Orbell Oakes's Private Memorandum Book.
[52] T. S. Ashton, *The Eighteenth Industrialist: Peter Stubbs of Warrington 1756–1806* (Manchester, 1931, reprint 1961), p. 142.
[53] Hughes, *North Country Life*, p. 364. See also Stone, *Family, Sex and Marriage*, pp. 349–53.
[54] An advertisement, IJ 24 April 1784, suggests that they opened a school in Diss. By 1787 they were running one in Brooke, near Norwich. See R. D. Middleton, *Dr Routh* (Oxford, 1938), p. 29.

Dr Valpy, who came from Jersey and had been educated in France,[55] and both girls had dancing lessons. Despite La Rochefoucauld's opinion that in England both sexes danced 'equally badly, without the least grace, no steps and no rhythm. . . [the English making] no study of dancing' like the French[56] the Oakeses took the subject extremely seriously. Children's dancing displays were attended by the whole family and James Oakes even went to London to watch Charlotte perform at school.[57] In later years he was a proud spectator at similar displays given by his grand-daughters.[58] Miss Routh left when Maria was 17 and had completed her education. Charlotte, only 12, was sent to school in London until she was just over 16 in December 1786.

The diary gives some information on the education of two of Oakes's grand-daughters. Maria Gould was sent to Miss Ann Silke's Ladies Boarding School in Chapelfield Lane, Norwich, at the age of 11, and Orbell Oakes's only daughter went to Miss Davis's School in London at the age of 13.[59] Her mother had made it clear before she died that she felt it better to send her to school rather than to run the risk of unsatisfactory governesses.[60]

Once girls had left school they were treated fairly indulgently. Francois de La Rochefoucauld viewed their behaviour with approval, noting that they 'are part of the company and talk and amuse themselves with as much freedom as if they were married'.[61] Apart from visiting friends in Norfolk, Suffolk, Essex and London and having them to stay at Guildhall Street, the Oakes girls accompanied their parents on trips to local spa towns and to the theatre and public pleasure gardens in London. Indeed, were there not the relentless struggle for a husband to be attended to, the life of a young, prosperous provincial woman in the late eighteenth century must have been most pleasant, happily occupied with visits, balls, parties, riding, music, drawing, reading and entertaining friends at home.

Invariably they were treated with great affection and consideration. When Charlotte was mortally ill in 1797 it took the persuasion of several family friends, including William Gould's mother, and a family conference to coax her to have treatment in Norwich and later in Bristol.[62] At no time did Oakes try to impose a course of action on her and seemed prepared to go to any lengths to try to find a cure.

---

[55] Notes between 1809 and 1810 of volume IX of the diary.
[56] La Rochefoucauld, *op. cit.*, p. 43.
[57] e.g. Diary 23 August 1786.
[58] e.g. Diary 18 September 1804.
[59] There are two possible candidates for this school: Mrs Davis Ladies School, 47 John Street, Holland Street, Blackfriars Road; Mrs and Miss Davis, Boarding School for Young Ladies, 26, Pleasant Row, Pentonville. Oakes describes the school as being at the other end of Town from the City which makes the Pentonville school the most likely candidate. Holden (1805–07), I; diary 9 March 1814.
[60] BL Add MS 35,130, letter dated 19 October 1811, Margaret Metcalf to Arthur Young.
[61] La Rochefoucauld, *op. cit.*, p. 43.
[62] Diary 16, 23, 25 November 1797.

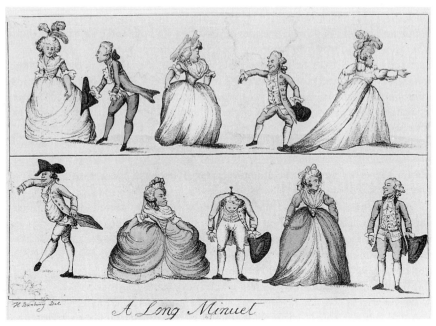

18. *A Long Minuet, by Henry Bunbury.*

There were some restrictions on the Oakes girls. They were not as liberated as Lucy Corsbie, grand-daughter of the non-conformist Bury yarn maker, who was supposed to have taken part in amateur theatricals in the Bury theatre, nor as serious minded as another grand-daughter, Catherine Buck and her friend Sarah Jane Maling, who liked nothing better than to discuss political philosophy with the young Crabb Robinson and Capel Lofft.[63] In the Oakes family only the boys took to the amateur stage or played in amateur concerts.[64] Girls were also accompanied wherever they went by a servant and, if going far by coach without their parents, were put into the care of a family friend who was making the same journey.

From the limited evidence available it would seem that girls' education was taken seriously, that the Oakes girls had the same type of education as most of their middle- and upper-class contemporaries, and that they enjoyed a large measure of personal freedom once they had left school.

---

[63] Alfred Harwood, *The Harwoods of Suffolk* (privately published, 1933), pp. 9–10, 28–29. See also *The Diaries of Crabb Robinson*, selected and edited by Thomas Sadler, 3 vols (1869), I; Edith J. Morley, *The Life and Times of Henry Crabb Robinson* (1935), p. 8.
[64] e.g. Diary 13 December 1783.

Family and social life provided ample opportunity for boys and girls to meet each other in a relaxed way from an early age. Apart from private family parties there were subscription balls at the Assembly Rooms in the winter and assemblies, theatres, concerts and parties during the annual fair in October for which friends and relations came to stay. The pool of marriageable men was broadened during the wars by the presence of militia officers who were billeted with their troops in Bury and added greatly to social life in the town. If Bury failed to provide a suitable husband for local girls, other opportunities existed. There were assemblies in nearby towns, and fresh fields could be explored by visiting friends and relations in other parts of the country during their social seasons, or by making trips to local spas and even to London or Bath.

Two of Oakes's sisters had married wealthy Liverpool merchants, of similar standing to himself, whom they must have met while staying with relations in Manchester. His youngest sister, Elizabeth, had married a Norfolk clergyman, the son of a Yarmouth merchant, and his own wife was the daughter of a Norfolk attorney whose brothers were either clergymen or prosperous London merchants.

The pursuit of a husband occupied much time. Maria Oakes was taken to Bath by her parents at the age of 15 to stay with her great uncle, Benjamin Adamson, who had a house there.[65] She made several trips with her family to Yarmouth, Norwich, Manchester, Liverpool and London during their social seasons, as well as the usual round of visits to friends. The Reverend James Oakes's family spent a great deal of time in London and Brighton when his daughters were about 15, ostensibly because of his wife's health; and all six of Oakes's grand-daughters 'ballotted' to take turns to go to Buxton, two at a time, with their grandfather. Many of Oakes's friends took London houses, including the Cullums, Tyrrells, Harveys, Pattesons and Arthur Young, besides friends who lived there permanently, so that there was never any shortage of places to stay or people to visit when in Town.

Thus opportunities for girls in the family to meet suitable young men from all over the country were legion. In spite of this Oakes's daughters and grand-daughters, with one possible exception, all married local men of the same social class, most of whose parents and grandparents were already known to them. Maria Oakes's husband was a lieutenant in the Royal Marines attached to a militia company stationed in Bury at the time of their meeting. He was a vicar's son from Hoxne in north Suffolk and did not appear to have known the Oakeses before coming to Bury with his regiment. Elizabeth, Orbell Oakes's only daughter, married Captain Robert Hustler, R. E., son of the Rev. James Hustler whose father and grandfather had been grocers in Bury and members of the Corporation.[66] Both Maria Gould's daughters were married to local men. Maria

---

[65] Diary 20 December 1780.
[66] Samuel Hustler (1722–87), son of Devereux Hustler of Barrow and his wife Elizabeth the daughter of Walter Ray of Denham. He was a grocer in Short Brackland. Thomas Hustler (1758/9–1800), was the younger son of Samuel Hustler and his wife Elizabeth

to Henry Heigham, son of the Rev. Henry Heigham, vicar and squire of Hunston and grandson of Pell Heigham, Town Clerk of Bury between 1761 and 1781; Charlotte to the Rev. Henry Hasted, son of the Rev. Henry Hasted preacher at the Oakes's parish church and grandson of Roger Hasted who was an apothecary and surgeon in Bury and also a Corporation member.

Jane Oakes, the youngest daughter of the Rev. James Oakes, was the only girl to marry into a more elevated social position although, again, she must have met her husband locally. He was the Hon. and Rev. Henry Leslie, rector of the neighbouring parish of Wetherden, the son of the Countess of Rothes and Sir Lucas Pepys, Bt.

The boys in the family followed much the same pattern. The Rev. James Oakes married the daughter of his father's life-long friend, the Rev. Charles Tyrrell, and Orbell Oakes married a childhood friend, Elizabeth Plampin. The Plampins had been apothecaries in Cook Row early in the eighteenth century but by the period of the diary had moved into a gracious country house, Chadacre Hall, and could afford to have their portraits painted by Thomas Gainsborough.[67] They also had a substantial house by the Churchyard in Bury St Edmunds. Certainly Elizabeth Plampin represented a step up the social ladder for the Oakeses since her mother was the daughter of the Hon. and Rev. Henry Hervey, fourth son of the first Earl of Bristol, but to suggest that it was through her that Orbell Oakes moved into the country gentry is a misjudgment.[68] Two of her brothers were clergymen, one of her sisters married a clergyman and another a surgeon. Another brother became an admiral and longed to crown this achievment with a knighthood. However, energetic pursuit of this goal was always thwarted, despite constant requests for honours in the appropriate quarters. Although the Herveys and the FitRroys ruled the roost in west Suffolk, and even distant family connection was made use of in the eighteenth century, Oakes, to his credit, never mentioned the Hervey connection. The relationship could have had a bearing on the Herveys' decision to patronize the Bury and Suffolk Bank and to appoint James Oakes as their political agent in 1802. While Oakes did not dwell on the distant Hervey relationship, he was much impressed by the admiral who was certainly used to further young Orbell Oakes's naval career.

James Oakes's eldest grandson, Henry James, continued the pattern of marrying girls from a similar background by marrying the daughter of an Essex clergyman who had a house in Bury and whose other daughter was already married to the Rev. George Haggitt, lecturer of St James's Church and grandson of Pell Heigham. Oakes's other grandsons married after his death. Edward Gould

---

daughter of Benjamin Barwick. He was a grocer in Abbeygate Street. His youngest son, Robert Samuel, married Elizabeth Frances Oakes.

[67] There is a delightful portrait of John Plampin, Elizabeth Plampin's father, by Gainsborough in the National Gallery.

[68] See John Gazley, *The Life of Arthur Young, 1741–1820* (American Philosophical Society, 1973), p. 481.

married Mary Ann Penelope Heigham, another of the prolific Pell Heigham's grandchildren, whose brother was already married to his sister Maria. James Charles Oakes married the daughter of an Essex clergyman. Thus the boys in the family also married local girls most of whom had been childhood friends. In spite of having every opportunity to meet potential spouses from a wide geographical area they nearly all married people whose families had been known to the Oakeses for generations and whose social standing was similar to their own. Only Oakes's sisters married men from other parts of the country highlighting the family's Manchester connections. Possibly this was also an age in which parents played a greater role in arranging their childrens' marriages than was the case by the later eighteenth and early nineteenth centuries.

As far as one can tell, during the period of the diaries the girls had a free choice of spouse. In Maria Oakes's case, the only one that is detailed in any way, the business part of the contract was settled between Oakes and the aspiring groom before she was 'acquainted' with the outcome by her father.[69] Orbell Oakes must have chosen Elizabeth Plampin freely. He was clearly so much in love with her that he could not bear to be parted from her during their courtship.[70] Orbell and his brother James were both engaged for over two years and their sister Maria for three and a half.

MARRIAGE SETTLEMENTS

The Oakeses were a prosperous family and this was reflected in the marriage portions given to their daughters. Although there was a large measure of freedom in the choice of spouse, the financial arrangements attached to marriage were all important. Elizabeth Adamson brought a dowry of just under £2,000 on her marriage to James Oakes, while his sisters had jointures of £3,000.[71] Oakes gave his own daughter Maria £5,000 on her marriage to William Gould together with an annual gift to her personally of about £125 which had risen to £400 by 1823.[72]

Gould was neither a wealthy nor an influential man so that Oakes had to provide him with an occupation[73] and further financial help by giving him the interest on £12,000 invested in 4% stock and by paying Edward Gould's fees at Cambridge.[74] As a result Oakes kept a very close eye on the family's accounts, itemizing their entire housekeeping costs from servants' wages, food, drink and house repairs to subscriptions, charitable donations and doctors' bills. He also provided the family with a house. After he had vetoed a plan that they should live in Norwich in 1808 on the grounds that the proposed property was unsuitable, they moved into Richard Adamson's old house on Angel Hill in October

[69] Diary 27 April 1791.
[70] e.g. Diary 22–26 December 1794.
[71] SROB Tem 240/17; PROB 11/1753.
[72] Oakes's Family papers and PROB 11/1753.
[73] See Chapter III.
[74] Oakes's Family Papers.

1809 after the tenant, the veteran Drury Lane actor William Smith, had been evicted. Gould owed his job as Barrack Master at Yarmouth, his home and most of his income to Oakes.

Orbell Oakes gave his daughter £3,000 on her marriage to Captain Hustler together with the interest from a further £3,000. In addition he continued the practice of making an annual gift to his daughter for her personal use. This gave them a generous annual income of £1,000. The money was remitted in quarterly instalments to Hustler's account with Messrs Greenwood Cox, army agents, saving him from the fatherly supervision that Gould had to endure. After Frances Oakes's death less than three years later her husband continued to receive an income from the marriage settlement. Orbell Oakes also felt that he had to give him an annual present which would be 'much better than naming any particular sum & leaves it open to give what I may think proper or I can best afford to spare out of my income'. He discontinued only the personal allowance that had been paid to his daughter.[75]

PROVISION FOR SONS

Oakes exercized as much control over the financial lives of his sons as he did over that of his daughter. Both had money derived from selling inherited land in Wereham (Norfolk), and on their marriages he used it to buy land in Suffolk. The difference in price was loaned at interest by their father. On his marriage, the Rev. James Oakes had an annual income of £600 and, with his father's help, bought the estate and living of Tostock and the living of Rattlesden.[76] It was his father who decided how much could be spent on additions and alterations to Tostock parsonage and who helped to supervise the work. An idea that the family should come to live in Bury in Richard Adamson's house on Angel Hill, after his death in 1800, was refused by Oakes with the firm direction that his son remain 'where he was on his Living'.[77] He was also expected to settle his accounts with his father once a year. His wife's ill health and subsequent need to spend long periods in Brighton and London must have provided a splendid excuse to escape James Oakes's authoritarian eye and the limited social life to be had in Tostock, which was an uncomfortable coach journey from Bury, only to be attempted on moon-lit nights.

Orbell Oakes was a partner with his father in the bank, and on his marriage in 1795 came to live in the substantial house that his father owned next to his own and for which he paid rent.[78] That year James Oakes spent £4,500 on some land in Nowton for his son. The proposed purchase of a further 150 acres in the parish

75 Orbell Oakes's Private Memorandum Book.
76 Oakes gives no information on the size of the estate. The Rev. James Oakes was presented to the living of Thurston by his father-in-law.
77 Diary 28 February 1800.
78 Papers in the Oakes Family's possession show that at his death Oakes was receiving rent from his son and grandson for their houses in Bury.

five years later fell through, although the following year he did buy 130 acres for £7,000.[79] Despite the fact that Orbell Oakes was a partner in the bank, his accounts did not escape his father's scrutiny. James Oakes had records of his son's property, income and expenditure together with 'particular remarks worthy of attention'.[80]

James Oakes was always extremely careful with money and kept accounts for everything in great detail which, unfortunately have not survived. He was determined that none of his children should fritter away in idle extravagance what he had worked so hard to accrue. Orbell Oakes seems to have failed to inculcate his own sons with such excellent habits. Between 1828 and 1831 he paid out over £2,500 to cover his son Orbell's debts and by 1831 was 'at a loss what to do or how to meet his unbridled extravagance'.[81] By the time of his marriage in 1832 his father had to give him £1,200 to pay off new debts and to leave some money over to cover his expenses for the next six months. Under the marriage settlement his future father-in-law put down £5,000 in trust while Orbell Oakes senior provided 6,000 in trust plus an annual sum of £128 13s. 2d. Three years later there were further requests for money and Orbell Oakes agreed to make his son's income up to £1,000 a year excluding his pay as a commander. After this Orbell Oakes junior used his wife Caroline to request funds of his father. Orbell Oakes senior was clearly less domineering than James Oakes. James Oakes had been able to exercise greater control over his own children because they banked with him and lived nearby. But the difference in attitude to family financial controls was largely one of temperament.

THE MARRIAGE CEREMONY

During the period covered by the diary there appears to have been a growing emphasis on the marriage ceremony itself and on the honeymoon. A Frenchman, writing of the English and their customs in 1719, described a typical English wedding as a rather secretive affair taking place early in the morning in front of the bride's parents, two bride maids and two bride men. The couple would then be 'married with a low voice and the doors shut, tip the minister a guinea and the clerk a crown, steal softly out . . . [have] a good dinner and return at night as quietly as lambs'.[82]

Maria Oakes was married to William Gould at eight thirty on a Monday morning, accompanied by her father, sister, aunt and cousin, but not by her mother or any of Gould's family. Immediately after the ceremony they returned home to breakfast which cannot have been elaborate because by 10 the newly

---

[79] Diary 24, 28 December 1795, 12 January 1796, 8 January, 19 March, 23 April 1800, 19 February 1802.
[80] Note between the years 1809 and 1810 in volume IX of the diary.
[81] SROB Tem 240/20; Orbell Oakes's Memorandum Book.
[82] A. F. Scott, *Everyone a Witness: the Georgian Age* (1970), pp. 55–56, quoting M. Misson, *Memoirs and Observations* (1719).

married couple were on their way to spend two days in Hoxne with the groom's mother and sisters. On coming back to Bury formal bride visits were exchanged before the couple left for Barnstable, where Gould was stationed at the head-quarters of the North Gloucestershire Militia.[83]

The Goulds' honeymoon was probably rushed because Gould, an active Marine, could not be spared for longer in war time. Maria's brother, the Rev. James Oakes, and his wife went to Lowestoft for two weeks after their wedding in 1792, although the ceremony was as brief and simple as that of the Goulds.[84] Two months before, in August 1792, Sir Patrick Blake had taken his newly married wife to Lowestoft,[85] while Orbell Oakes took his bride to London for over three weeks three years later, in 1795.[86] The marriage of James Oakes's grand-daughter, Jane Oakes, to the Hon. H. Leslie in 1816 took place at 10 in the morning and was attended by the groom's father and brother together with ten members of the bride's family, excluding her mother. Flowers were strewn about the church yard, and decorated the entrance gate to form a bower. The Rev. James Oakes married his daughter and her grandfather gave her away. After the service James Oakes gave the couple a note for £100 and the party repaired 'to a very splendid Breakfast' consisting of tea, coffee, hot rolls, hot sausages, cold tongue, cold chicken and more besides. At mid-day the bridal pair set off for Aldeburgh in the new carriage which Sir Lucas Pepys had given them as a wedding present. Oakes emphasized that they were by themselves, suggesting that their maid servant had travelled separately or gone ahead. Meanwhile, at Tostock Parsonage, the cel-ebrations continued with 'the near Relations' all being invited to 'a most sump-tuous Dinner' while 'handsome slices of Bride's Cake' were sent to more distant connections.[87]

Between the end of the eighteenth century and the early nineteenth century there seems to have been a trend in the Oakes family towards more elaborate weddings, held later in the day, with greater preparations made and larger num-bers of guests invited. However, guests were still restricted to close family and it was common for husbands or wives not to accompany their spouse to the mar-riage of the other's relation. This practice has been observed in mid-nineteenth-century Hertfordshire where weddings were still seen as a 'family event of a markedly private character' which was so heavily charged with emotion that the chief protagonists were expected to break down during the ceremony.[88] Perhaps this explains the absence of the bride's mother at Oakes family weddings.

The increasing emphasis on the wedding ceremony may reflect changing ideas of marriage. Greater stress on personal choice and companionship and less

---

[83] Diary 19 October 1793–5 November 1793.
[84] Diary 16 October 1792.
[85] Diary 12 August 1792.
[86] Diary 23 April–15 May 1795.
[87] Diary 15 February 1816.
[88] Curtis, A Chronicle of Small Beer, pp. 21–22.

on the economic and social benefits to be derived for the collective good of the family.[89] With flower-strewn churchyards the marriage ceremony had become a celebration of love and no longer simply a means of formalizing a legal contract between two families.

Marriage ceremonies did not always follow this pattern. Throughout the period Oakes records at least four elopements, three to Scotland and one to London, which appeared to have the parents' tacit, if not overt, agreement. In each case the couple returned home immediately to the customary round of post wedding visits. Ideas of romance and adventure provoked in young women by reading too many novels were not confined to Sheridan's heroines it seems.[90]

MARRIED WOMEN

Changes in marriage in the eighteenth century are supposed to have resulted in a greater overt affection between husbands and wives and a greater equality between the sexes than had previously prevailed.[91] Oakes always referred to his wife formally as 'Mrs Oakes' or 'Mrs E O'. In fact he used formal address to all friends and relations of his own or an older generation and called his daughter by her surname once she married. Indeed it was not until after his wife's death that he began to call his daughters-in-law by their Christian names. La Rochefoucauld claimed that three out of four English marriages were based on affection and that husbands and wives seemed happy and content in each others' company. 'Husband and wife are always together and are content with the same society. It is the rarest thing to see them one without the other'.[92] To a certain extent this was true of the Oakeses who went to dinner, card and supper parties, assemblies and balls regularly together. If Mrs Oakes were unwell and unable to go, Oakes would often come home early to be with her. On occasions they would go to different social functions separately or Mrs Oakes would go alone if her husband was working late. She also accompanied him to London and Norwich apart from visits to relations in other parts of the country.

Oakes was obviously very fond of his wife, and wedding anniversaries were usually recorded and often celebrated with a dinner party for close friends, a practice which was common among their acquaintances.[93] When she was ill, Oakes fetched the doctor himself rather than send a servant. At her death, it was the loss of someone with whom he had lived 'wh the truest Love and Affection for 38 years' that he mourned, not the thrifty housekeeper, the bearer of his

[89] See Stone, *Family, Sex and Marriage*, Chapter 8 for a discussion on the changing character of marriage in the eighteenth century.

[90] e.g. Diary 3 July, 15 October 1786, 22 January 1812, 22 August 1822. La Rochefoucauld found the matter of elopements to Scotland without the parents' consent was so interesting that he devotes section to it in his memoirs. See La Rochefoucauld, *loc. cit.*, pp. 37–38.

[91] Stone, *Family, Sex and Marriage*, Chapter 8.

[92] La Rochefoucauld, *op. cit.*, p. 36.

[93] e.g. Diary 5, 6 December 1793, 1 January 1795.

children and the source of land and money.[94] Orbell Oakes was made distraught by his wife's illness and spent as much time with her as he could when she was recuperating in the West Country. After her death he never remarried.

Just over a year after his wife's death, James Oakes may have considered remarriage. The diary entry recording a morning visit to Mrs White on Christmas Day 1803 is inexplicably surrounded by stars and a similar entry appears on 1 March 1805. Perhaps Mrs White refused his first offer and he tried again without success. Whatever the significance of these entries he continued to be on very friendly terms with her and often dropped in for tea on his way home from visiting his son at Nowton. He enjoyed female company. His grand-daughter, Maria Gould, regularly accompanied him to church and breakfasted with him on Sundays. In later life it was not unusual for him to have been the only man at supper and card parties surrounded by a group of attentive widows and spinsters.[95]

Both James and his son Orbell gave their daughters pin money for their own use after their marriages, ensuring them a small measure of economic independence.[96] There is no evidence that family size was deliberately limited, although none of them had particularly large families during the period of the diary. Pregnant women played a full part in social life until within a month of their confinements and were never prudishly removed from the scene once their condition became visible. Maria Oakes travelled to Bury from the West Country less than a month before the births of her first three children, and Betsy Oakes, Orbell's wife, dined with members of the family less than two weeks before the birth of her first two children.[97] Bastardy did not provoke censure. Frances Treice bore Sir Charles Davers eight children without being socially ostracized, Francis (Frank) Sandys's wife was illegitimate and there is even a suggestion that Oakes's own mother had a bastard child before her marriage.[98]

Women in Bury were freer than they had been. They were first admitted to the Grammar School speech day in August 1790. Women living on their own entertained and were entertained as much as anyone else, possibly because there was not the same anxiety about having an equal number of men and women at dinner parties, a practice which has consigned many later-nineteenth and twentieth century widows and spinsters to a dull social life.[99]

Yet society in Bury was still segregated in many ways. All Corporation dinners were men-only affairs and no provision was made for the entertainment of wives, unlike King's Lynn where a separate table was provided for married women and another for young unmarried men and women together.[100] Even the official

[94] Diary 25 November 1802.
[95] e.g. Diary 17 January 1804.
[96] See section I, viii.
[97] e.g. Diary 24 May –26 June 1797.
[98] Entry in Saint James's Parish Registers, 4 April 1733 'Robert a base child of Susan Ray'.
[99] *The Diary of Abigail Gawthern* shows that she had a busy social life as a widow at the same period.
[100] La Rochefoucauld, *op. cit.*, p. 186.

celebrations at the end of the war were segregated. In 1802 there was a cold meal for the gentlemen involved in the cavalcade, although it was followed by a 'Peace Ball'.[101] In June 1814 a splendid public dinner was held in the Market place to enable poor men to celebrate victory while poor women were relegated to taking tea and snuff in the afternoon and running races for tea kettles. Although both men and women attended the anniversary meeting of the British and Foreign Bible Society in 1812 the dinner afterwards at the Guildhall was for men only.[102] Book clubs and many of the sporting and social functions associated with the Assembly Rooms, except balls, assemblies and cards were confined to men. The women of the Oakes family could ride but they never hunted. The only form of sport in which women actively participated was archery and that did not become popular until the mid 1820s.[103]

There were also many private men-only dinners, often given in honour of visiting militia officers or to fix Corporation business. Men-only gambling or 'rookery' evenings were popular among the clergy quite as much as the laity. Even at mixed functions there was segregation: women withdrew from the room after dinner while the men sat on for two or three hours drinking heavily, proposing toasts and indulging their taste for racey stories which shocked the prudish young La Rochefoucauld. The fact that chamber-pots were ranged on the sideboard, so that nothing should interrupt the fun, was a further good reason for the exclusion of women.

At some mixed functions women actually ate separately. This happened at Miss Symond's ball in 1786 and at a subscription ball in 1809.[104] Men and women took tea in separate rooms before one of Oakes's childrens' balls in 1810[105] and in the Oakes family women rarely went to funerals or mothers to their childrens' weddings.

When men finally left the table to join the ladies they were often too drunk to be good company. La Rochefoucauld, writing of the 1784 election ball, claimed that 'Three quarters of the guests were very drunk, and everyone had drunk rather too much' at the preceding dinner. Indeed the Duke of Grafton's nephew was in such a poor state that he had to go to bed for a couple of hours in the middle of the ball in order to recover sufficiently to carry on.[106] Oakes records many dinners at which the company became very merry and times when there were few at winter balls or the men came in late. On one occasion members of the Yeomanry Cavalry, including his son, were so drunk after a public dinner to celebrate the King's birthday that the intended ball in the evening had to be

[101] Diary 7 May 1802.
[102] Diary 20 October 1812.
[103] e.g. Diary 21, 22 September 1826, 10 August 1827.
[104] Diary 16 February 1786, 21 November 1809.
[105] Diary 15 January 1810.
[106] La Rochefoucauld, *op. cit.*, p. 24.

cancelled because it was impossible to muster enough young men in a fit state to dance. The young women who had gathered for it had to go home.[107]

Although Oakes and his sons were very fond of their wives, considered their feelings and well-being, and spent much time with them and in the company of women generally, and although women were freer in some ways than they had been, one should not exaggerate the degree of social equality achieved by women at this period. Husbands and wives may often have been in each others' company, as La Rochefoucauld claimed, but some other continental visitors were surprised at the segregation of the sexes in England and remarked that there was little appearance of intimacy between them, particularly at assemblies, where women would cluster by the door leaving the body of the room and all the conversation to the men.[108] The fact that men and women went to the same functions together does not necessarily mean that there was a great deal of social contact between them. Most middle-class married women must have spent the major part of their time in the company of their children and other women, if not by themselves, and the range of their activities was severely limited.

ILLNESS AND DEATH

James Oakes took his health and that of others very seriously. He always recorded the progress of his own minor ailments faithfully and often sought medical advice. Taking the air, riding and walking were seen by him as important aids to health as much as a means of transport. When on holiday he made a point of riding his horse for a couple of hours every day and, at home, made most of his local visits on foot or on horseback from choice.[109] At the age of nearly 82, after a six-and-a-quarter-hour coach journey from London, he dined with his son at Nowton and then walked two miles home to Bury.[110] He was still taking daily rides, when the weather was suitable, at the age of 84 and after that went out in his chaise accompanied by his coachman.[111] He does not appear to have been remotely interested in any of the sports of the period: hunting, coursing and shooting, but only in riding and walking, to keep himself fit. Had jogging been invented he might have done it.

His own ailments, apart from deafness, rheumatism and a nasty attack of whooping cough in old age,[112] were minor. They were confined to feverish colds, infected teeth, gout and digestive problems which often followed particularly indulgent dinners, or were associated with periods of stress in his business life.

The family always tried to avoid infection and took precautions against it. Children were innoculated against small pox and great faith was put in the

[107] Diary 4 June 1795.
[108] Andre Parreaux, *Daily Life in England in the Reign of George III* (1969), p. 121.
[109] e.g. Diary 30 January 1784, 23 August 1791, 16 January 1795.
[110] Diary 15 August 1823.
[111] e.g. Diary 3 July 1827.
[112] Diary 9 December 1819–20 January 1820.

efficacy of sea bathing and spa waters both as a preventative measure and a cure for most complaints.[113] Indeed it is clear that holidays were taken primarily for medical reasons, not every year, but as the need arose, with assemblies, theatres and sight-seeing secondary considerations.[114] Oakes favoured Yarmouth until 1813, when, having consulted two eminent London doctors about a sprained knee, he transferred his allegiance to Buxton on their advice. He was so enchanted with the surrounding romantic countryside, the facilities, and the elegant company it offered, that he continued to go there each year for the next ten years leaving Bury after the Aldermanic election in August and arriving home in time for the fair at the end of September. By the age of 83 he no longer felt able to make the long journey and returned to Yarmouth and its hot baths, draughts and pills.

Children were taken to the sea-side for a change of air. Orbell Oakes, his wife and family went to Yarmouth, Aldeburgh, Cromer and Southwold at various times 'for bathing the Children'[115] and, after their mother's death, Henry Oakes accompanied his sister to the same resorts and to Leamington Spa.[116] The Rev. James Oakes's family spent long periods in London and Brighton for the sake of his wife's health, and the Goulds made do with Yarmouth and Aldeburgh to improve Maria's well-being.

No effort was spared to find cures for Charlotte and Betsy Oakes who both suffered from tuberculosis. Charlotte was rushed to Bristol for treatment as a last desperate measure, doctors in Bury, Norwich and Yarmouth having been tried and failed.[117] Betsy Oakes was ill for three years during which time she was exposed to cures in London, Cheltenham, Bath and Sidmouth, making her last months cruelly exhausting.[118]

After a death, James Oakes displayed an almost obsessional concern with the corpse and with detailed organization of the funeral. He kept the body of his daughter, Charlotte, at home for a week, first on her bed and then in an open coffin in her bedroom until 'an evident Change had taken place'. Only then was the wooden shell put into a lead coffin and sealed.[119] It was common for bodies to remain at home for a week, but that of Sir Thomas Gage was apparently kept above ground for a record 15 days before burial in April 1796. La Rochefoucauld thought this practice very strange, and assumed that it was a precaution against being buried alive.[120]

While the body was at home family and friends came to take their 'last

113 e.g. Diary 14 September 1779, 10 December 1798, 1 September 1808.
114 Diary 15 July 1791.
115 Diary 24 September 1805.
116 Diary 2 May 1823.
117 Diary 29 June–1 July 1797, 9 September, 5 December 1797.
118 Diary 14 October 1808, 9, 19 September 1809.
119 Diary 16–23 January 1798.
120 La Rochefoucauld, op. cit., p. 65; diary 5 April 1796.

farewell'[121] and the immediate family would not go to church until the funeral. In February 1800, after the death of Richard Adamson, 'Not any of the Family went to Church on acct of Mr Adamson laying by the Wall'.[122]

Enormous care and expense was taken over the design and manufacture of coffins, vaults and monuments. This is well illustrated by the detailed planning that went into the graves of Charlotte Oakes in January 1798, Betsy Oakes in May 1811 and Jane Leslie in December 1816. Public funerals in Bury were lavish affairs. They lasted longer and were more formal and widely attended than weddings, unless it was the wish of the deceased to be buried 'very privately'. Invitation cards were sent to friends and relations. Hat bands, scarves, gloves and mourning rings were bought for close relations, friends, servants and tenants and the clerks were given money to buy mourning clothes.

Funeral services took place at any time during daylight hours and lasted about an hour. When a member of the Corporation was buried the whole body processed to church dressed in their gowns, preceding the coffin in order of precedence, the most junior first, followed by the town clergy. The Alderman brought up the rear, with the mace covered in black crepe, accompanied by the beadles carrying staves.[123] The coffin was borne in a hearse pulled by black plumed horses followed by the carriages of near relations, servants and medical attendants.

Married women in the Oakes family almost never went to funerals and unmarried ones rarely although there were exceptions. In 1788 Mrs Susan Oakes's funeral was attended by her married daughter, Mary Baker, and by her granddaughter Charlotte Oakes,[124] Maria Gould was among the mourners at her aunt's funeral in 1791,[125] and in 1816 her mother, sisters and female cousins all attended the funeral of Jane Leslie.[126]

After the service, an unspecified period of mourning ensued during which the bereaved attended no social functions outside the family circle but received formal calls from friends offering their condolences. The length of time this lasted was a matter of inclination and was not fixed. Ten weeks mourning was observed for James Oakes's wife but none for his mother or for relations who lived far away.

James Oakes's attitude to death, particularly to the deaths of children, changed during the course of the diary. This is well illustrated by a comparison between the funeral of Maria Gould's first son in 1795, her second in 1799 and that of Orbell Oakes's third son in 1802. Edward Gould's death aged eight months is dealt with in a perfunctory manner by Oakes, who recorded briskly

---

[121] e.g. Diary 9 December 1803.
[122] Diary 16 February 1800.
[123] Diary 20 August 1799.
[124] Diary 10 October 1788.
[125] Diary 9 April 1791.
[126] Diary 19 December 1816.

that 'He was always a weekly Child & latterly rather warted. He was by other People not thought a living Child'.[127] The child was buried three days later at eight in the morning in the Garnham family vault in St James's Church with only his nurse and a maid servant in attendance. There was no mourning.[128]

There is less detail on the death of the Gould's second son in December 1799 as a result of innoculation, because he died while the Oakeses were on their way to visit the Goulds in Yarmouth. However Oakes's tone is quite different. He refers to 'our dear little Grandson' and describes their 'affecting meeting' with the parents and their efforts to comfort them. The child was buried in the chancel of Yarmouth Church at three in the afternoon and a period of mourning followed observed by the Oakeses even after their return to Bury.[129]

Charles Adamson Oakes died at the age of two months after almost continuous illness.[130] His parents were so upset that they could not face the funeral and went to stay with Betsy Oakes's sister leaving James Oakes to organize it.[131] The body was taken in the family carriage accompanied by Oakes and his nieces Elizabeth Baker and Susan Green and the child was buried in the family vault in St Mary's Church.[132] His name was later inscribed on the stone. Oakes was much upset by the child's illness and recorded its progress daily, while his parents were clearly anguished at watching their child 'dying by inches and suffering in the most dreadful manner'.[133]

The difference in reaction to these deaths is difficult to explain except in terms of a change of attitude. One would have expected similar, if not greater, sorrow at Edward Gould's death. He was the Gould's first child, the Oakes's first grandson, James Oakes's godson, and was born at Guildhall Street. Although not a strong child Oakes does not record that he was ill and one would have expected his death at the age of eight months to have been a sad shock. Possibly Oakes's sympathy was greater at his brother's death because it was the second child that the Goulds had lost. Charles Oakes was his parents' fourth child and third son. He was only two months old and had been so ill all his short life that his death was always expected. A post mortem subsequently showed that he would never have survived to adulthood.[134]

Charlotte Oakes's death in early 1798, coming between the deaths of Edward and William Gould, seems to have marked a watershed in Oakes's attitude to death and bereavement. Before that he treated death in a somewhat business-like way with no mention of sorrow or loss and no period of mourning. However,

[127] Diary 4 March 1795.
[128] Diary 7 March 1795.
[129] Diary 12 December 1799. James and Elizabeth Oakes did not dine out until 25 December 1799 and then with Richard Adamson.
[130] Diary 26 May 1802.
[131] Diary 27 May 1802.
[132] Diary 29 May 1802.
[133] BL Add MS 35, 128 ff.449, letter dated 8 May 1802, Orbell Oakes to Arthur Young.
[134] Diary 26 May 1802.

when Charlotte was dying both he and his wife did all in their power to find a cure for her, they both helped to care for her at the end. After her death, Oakes went to endless trouble to make new family burial arrangements in St Mary's Church, although there was room for three more coffins in the family vault in St James's Church.[135] Both parents grieved at the loss and did not go out, other than with immediate family, for ten weeks,[136] whereas within three days of his mother's funeral in October 1788 friends came to dinner and a party went on to the assembly. It is interesting to note that Arthur Young's favourite daughter, Bobbin, died almost exactly six months before Charlotte in July 1797.[137] Young was so affected by it that he nearly had a complete breakdown, and experienced a dramatic conversion to Evangelicanism as a result. Oakes knew Young well, and may have been influenced by his behaviour. It is impossible at this distance and with so little evidence to ascribe motive. All that can be said is that the late 1790s marked a change in Oakes's attitude to the dead and dying. There were greater expressions of remorse and sorrow, particularly over the deaths of children, and much time and energy was expended on arrangements for the disposal of the body. This could well have resulted from increased affection within the family and from a change in the psychological climate which made such attitudes acceptable.[138]

SOCIAL LIFE

THE TOWN

Long before the virtual extinction of the yarn trade at the beginning of the wars against France Bury had been an important social centre catering for a wide area. As early as the first quarter of the eighteenth century Defoe felt that it was 'a town of which other writers have talk'd very largely and perhaps a little too much' but allowed that of all the towns in the East of England it was the one in proportion to its size that 'most thronged with gentry, people of the best fashion, and the most polite conversation'.[139] The town was so enchanting and offered such opportunities for diversion that it attracted many aristocratic and gentle families to live there including the Earl of Bristol. According to Defoe the Earl had left 'a noble and pleasantly situated house in Lincolnshire for the most agreeable living on a spot so completely qualified for a life of delight as this of Bury'.[140]

[135] Diary 16–23 January 1798, 10 October 1788. James Oakes's father lived in St James's parish.
[136] Diary 23 January 1798.
[137] Diary 13 July 1797.
[138] See Stone, *Family, Sex and Marriage*, pp. 247–49.
[139] Daniel Defoe, *A Tour Through the Whole Island of Great Britain*, 2 vols (Every Man Library, Dent, 1962), I, pp. 49–50.
[140] *Ibid*, p. 51. His wife had brought him an estate at Aswarby near Sleaford, where the old Bristol Arms is now a shopping arcade.

Bury developed as a social centre for at least three main reasons. First, it had developed all through the Middle Ages as one of the great pilgrimage centres of Christendom. Second, the rights of Saint Edmund over the area, known later as West Suffolk, ensured that Bury lay at the heart of a network of local roads leading to all parts of the region. When the abbey was dissolved, the gentry who secured its great estates, took care preserve Bury as a centre of administration: holding the assizes and quarter sessions there. Thirdly, its broad neighbourhood lay within very convenient reach of Newmarket,the fashionable racing town. As a result Bury and its surrounding countryside was unusually well provided with houses of powerful and well-to-do gentry and successful tradespeople.

Although it was not a spa town its air, 'being somewhat piercing . . . was apt and fit for recovery of health' so that patients were often recommended by their doctors to live there.[141] Even the disenchanted Sylas Neville had to admit 'its high situation and the salubrity of its air'.[142] Apart from these natural advantages Bury could boast many good inns with regular chaise, coach and waggon services to London, Yarmouth, Norwich, Cambridge and Colchester, large numbers of coach and hack horses for hire,[143] and excellent public buildings. These included the 'two beautiful parish churches'[144] which stood in one well-kept churchyard, bisected by 'an alley of lofty lime trees' forming a 'pleasant promenade'[145] on which citizens could take the air, chat with friends and display their finery. The Assembly Rooms, renovated in the late 1780s and again in the early nineteenth century, comprised 'a more complete and tasteful assemblage of public rooms' which were 'scarcely to be paralleled in any part of this Kingdom'.[146] The Fair assemblies and four or five public subscription balls were held there, supported 'exclusively by the higher classes',[147] and a round of assize, election and charity balls permitted the admission of those slightly lower down the social scale.

There was a 'neat and beautiful Theatre' (1774–80), designed by Robert Adam in which the Norwich Company performed for three weeks each year during the fair. It was thought 'a great ornament to the spot on which it is erected . . . the two royal theatres in London are built more oeconomically'.[148] Such was the interest, that a new and larger theatre was built in 1818–19 in Westgate Street, designed by William Wilkin, which was 'equal to any in the Kingdom out

---

[141] Dr Yates, 'The History of the Monastic Abbey of Bury Saint Edmunds' (c1805), BL Egerton 2373, copy in SROB Acc 1409, p. 348.
[142] *The Diary of Sylas Neville 1767–1788*, edited by B. Cozens-Hardy (Oxford, 1950), p. 303.
[143] La Rochefoucauld, *op. cit.*, pp. 96–97.
[144] Defoe, *A Tour Through the Whole Island of Great Britain*, p. 51.
[145] *A Guide to the Town, Abbey and Antiquities of Bury Saint Edmunds* (1821), printed by R. Deck for J. Deck.
[146] *Ibid*, p. 86.
[147] *Ibid*, p. 105.
[148] G. Ashby, *A Description of the Ancient and Present State of the Town and Abbey of Bury Saint Edmunds in the County of Suffolk* (1782), p. 75. The building is now used as an art gallery.

of the Metropolis'.[149] The old theatre was used as a concert hall and ball room, and concerts were also held in the churches. There was a thriving body of amateur musicians who gave private concerts,[150] and no shortage of amateur theatricals. Cultural life was further enriched by the libraries,[151] book clubs, lectures and special weekly sermons organized by the Corporation and preached by guest clergy.

Bury provided an impressive range of services to people in the neighbouring countryside, and for those who came from further afield to the quarter sessions, assizes and annual fair. King Edward VI Grammar School had the highest reputation at this time, and attracted pupils from all over the country. There were many private schools, for both boys and girls, in the town. The best of these, owned by Charles Blomfield, was well known and respected throughout the region as providing a good education for those intended for a business career. Doctors, apothecaries and attorneys abounded while resident shop keepers supplied an increasingly wide range of goods and services. Once a year in October the range of goods on offer was expanded enormously during the fair, when the booths of traders, London hairdressers and showmen were set out on the Angel Hill.

Bury Fair had long since ceased to be of great importance commercially, but had remained one of the leading social events of the year in Suffolk, attended by the aristocracy and gentry of the area and beyond. As early as 1714 it was described as 'more a market for Ladies than merchandises',[152] while a mock heroic poem of 1721 described it as 'a kind of FEMALE Fair' resorted by 'promiscuous Crowds' where women in search of husbands outnumbered eligible men by a ratio of three to two.[153] Defoe saw it in 1724 as 'a fair for diversion more than trade' and implied that all the gentry of Suffolk, Norfolk and Cambridgeshire were to be found there.[154]

During the fair Bury's normally brisk social life turned to a frenzy. Apart from the fair-balls, theatre-performances, concerts and lectures, most leading families in the area had houseparties and gave dinners and suppers. During the day the men played billiards and cards at the Assembly Room Club or went into the country to course or to shoot. Children were taken to side-shows where 'the diversions of Sadler's-wells, rope-dancing both tight and slack' were demonstrated by 'Mr Richards and the celebrated Miss Andrews' together with 'lofty

---

[149] Deck, A *Guide etc*, p. 85. The Theatre is now owned by the National Trust and is in regular use for both professional and amateur productions.
[150] The Reverend James Oakes was part of a musical group which met once a month at the home of Frank Sandys in Saint Mary's Square.
[151] The Suffolk Public Library started in 1789 and the New Public Library in 1795. They were amalgamated in 1806 and survived until 1829. See G. V. M. Heap, 'Subscription Libraries at Bury St Edmunds', Typescript in SROB.
[152] Quoted by Peter Borsay, 'The English Urban Renaissance: the Development of Provincial Urban Culture c1680–c1760', *Social History* (May 1977), pp. 581–98.
[153] *Bury Fair a Poem Imposed as an Exercise at St Peter's College 1721*.
[154] Defoe, A *Tour Through the Whole Island of Great Britain*, pp. 51–52.

tumbling, and several other interludes with singing and dancing between the performances' ending with 'a variety of new pantomimical scenes of harlequin'.[155] Women were occupied with problems of dress, hairdressing, invitations and calls. By the early eighteenth century, Bury had become the focus of polite society, culture and communications for a large part of Suffolk, with its Fair attracting gentry from a far wider area and achieving almost national recognition as a marriage-market. The town had gained this relative eminence long before the decline of its major industry.

SOCIETY IN BURY ST EDMUNDS

Polite society in Bury — those who were members of the Assembly Rooms, the Gentlemens' Club, who attended balls and assemblies, concerts and the theatre and who regularly gave large dinner and supper parties — was on a broad scale. The town's role as an important social centre and its early gentrification ensured this. The possession of political power did not necessarily ensure inclusion. Most of the Capital Burgesses were men of substantial means: their wealth and their connections with established Bury families and with local parish gentry ensured their acceptability. Of the Common Council only those destined for the Upper House and those who belonged to the professions, but had no desire to become Capital Burgesses, were included. Men like Joshua Kitson, plumber and glazier, or John Hill, master brick-layer and plasterer, or John Lawrence, grocer,were not. Equally many gentry who lived permanently in Bury or who had town houses there, took little interest in local politics but played a full part in the social life of the town.

Many of Bury's richest businessmen were non-conformist, the Bucks, the Harmers, the Corsbies and the Cumberlands who were yarn makers; the Robinsons who were tanners; the Ridleys who were grocers and tea dealers; and Charles Leech, an attorney. As a result, they were barred from the Corporation membership although some were active on the Court of Guardians, on both vestries, on the Improvement Commission and the Guildhall Feoffment Trust. Religious scruples would have prevented most of these families from taking part in a social life of theatres, balls or dinner parties. Yet, according to a family history, Joseph Corsbie, son of the yarn maker, was an intimate of Arthur Young, the Duke of Grafton, Capel Lofft and the Bunburys and had a wife who was the belle of county balls in Bury.[156] The Oakeses and the Corsbies had been on friendly terms and exchanged visits when the families were both involved in yarn making, and James Oakes went to the funeral of Sarah Buck, John Corsbie's daughter, in 1804.[157] Their social contact seems to have dwindled after Oakes became a full-time banker, and there is no further evidence of the Corsbies, or

[155] IJ 9 October 1779.
[156] Harwood, The Harwoods of Suffolk, p. 28.
[157] Diary 15 July 1804.

194

any other Protestant dissenting family, taking part in Bury social life in the diary. The Oakeses were always on the friendliest terms with the Roman Catholic Gage family.

Society in Bury was led by those whose right to inclusion was unquestioned: the Duke of Grafton, the Earl of Bristol followed by men like Sir Charles Bunbury and Sir Charles Davers whose families had provided knights of the shire and MPs for the town for generations. The core of Bury society, which set the tone of social life in the town, was inextricably linked with that of the surrounding countryside. Apart from certain Corporation members it consisted of other professional men working in the town, clergy, retired naval and army officers, local gentry, their widows and elderly spinster daughters. Few Anglican merchants or tradesmen outside the Corporation had the necessary wealth or social standing.

In Bury, at this period, as in Stamford and in other places which functioned as centres of society,[158] large numbers of local landowners and clergy had houses in the town and preferred to live there for a considerable part of the year. Few wanted to live permanently in 'an obscure village, where the want of medical assistance would cause no small uneasiness to those who had been accustomed to it on all occasions at the shortest notice', and where 'the most common necessaries' of life were expensive and difficult to come by. Bury with all its amenities, not least an excellent education at the Grammar School, was infinitely preferable especially for those with large families.[159]

Entry into Bury society was through many channels. Some, like Sir Thomas Cullum of Hawstead Place and Northgate Street, and the Leheups of Hessett and Crown Street, belonged to long established Suffolk families. Others like Thomas Cocksedge entered through the accumulation of wealth gained locally in farming or trade. Cocksedge's father had been a farmer and the proprietor of the London Waggon Service in Bury, while he owned a substantial house in Northgate Street and became High Sheriff of Suffolk in 1803, the mark of arrival into landed society according to the Stones.[160]

Other members of Bury society had retired to Suffolk on the profits of trade and the professions in London. Thomas Mills of Saxham was a brandy merchant, Sir Walter Rawlinson of Stowlangtoft Place and Devonshire Square, was a banker, while the le Blancs of Cavenham were involved in the law and business in London; Robert Rushbrook, who bought Sir Charles Davers's estate in Rushbrook, was a barrister.

Entry through marriage or inheritance was also common. Charles Blachley

---

[158] J. M. Lee, 'Stamford and the Cecils: A Study in Political Control 1700–1835' (unpublished B.Litt. thesis, University of Oxford, 1957), pp. 76–81.
[159] See 'The Case of the Rev. Charles le Grice', pamphlet in Dr Yate's, 'The History of the Monastic Abbey of Bury St Edmunds', between pp. 276–82.
[160] Lawrence Stone and Jeanne Fawtier Stone, *An Open Elite? England 1540–1880* (Oxford, 1984), p. 52.

married one of the Town Clerk's daughters, John Benjafield one of Dr Symond's nieces, Philip Bennet had inherited the Rougham Estate of his father-in-law and John Vernon, Sir Thomas Cullum's nephew, his uncle, Lord Shipbrook's estates in Nacton, near Ipswich. Although not a wealthy man, William Gould had been assured of his place by marrying James Oakes's eldest daughter, Maria.

Bury society ranged from noble families to the wealthier tradesmen. During the course of the period, as the yarn industry and associated wool trade declined in the town, fewer merchants and tradesmen were wealthy and well connected enough to attain acceptance with the result that Bury Society became increasingly restricted to professional men living and working in the town, and to the local parish gentry. In becoming a banker James Oakes himself had moved from a trading background to a professional one.[161]

JAMES OAKES'S SOCIAL POSITION

James Oakes's seems to have been content with his social position and to have had no desire to alter it with the acquisition of a country house and estate. He owned land in Depden and Wickhambrook, inherited from his father's first wife, and added to it until he had a total of just under 400 acres including 16 acres of woodland. Although he was a conscientious landlord and kept the land and buildings in good order he had little emotional attachment to it, and he was prepared to sell at various times when either he wanted to realize capital or land no longer seemed a good investment.[162] At no time did he consider building a prestigious house on his land and living there, but continued to live in Guildhall Street with his wool warehouse behind, the bank in one wing and the garden on the other side of the road.

Oakes was obviously not interested in leading the life of a country gentleman. As far as one can tell he never hunted; he shot and coursed a little until 1782 and then gave it up. He went to no Newmarket race meetings after 1790. Unlike many of his contemporaries he was not interested in gardening or plant collecting, and barely mentioned his garden in his diary. His devotion to a life of business and public work left him little time for other interests apart from riding, reading and the theatre. His working day often went on until midnight if there were accounts to be finished. Dinner parties, theatres and concerts were often missed through pressure of work. Social life always came second to business and public affairs.

He made no attempt to marry his children to people of a markedly higher social standing nor to have educated them solely to be gentlemen. Their education was dictated by the professions that he had chosen for them. Unlike poor William Cotesworth of Gateshead, he felt no need to launch them into a 'more

[161] Stone and Stone, *An Open Elite?*, p. 52.
[162] Evidence from the diary and the Oakes family papers shows that he thought of selling in 1796 and in 1816.

Polite Way of Living'[163] than himself. He was unostentatious in his daily life, dressed simply, went everywhere that he could on horse-back or on foot. The family were unpretentious. His sister, Elizabeth Baker, cadged a lift from Cawston to Bury in the farm cart in order to pay her brother a visit.[164] Oakes himself would happily perform small errands for friends, buying smelts for his cousin Sarah Moseley, for example and dropping them off on his way to his bank in Stowmarket.

This concern with business and lack of pretention did not prevent him from having a remarkably wide circle of friends and acquaintances. Through his mother he was related to several of the local gentry including the Rev. Orbell Ray of Tostock, Richard Ray of Lincolns Inn and Plashwood, Haughley, Sir Walter Rawlinson, Sir George Wombwell and Sir Thomas Cullum. The relations on his father's side were equally prosperous cotton merchants and dyers whose sons became barristers in London. His sisters married well-to-do Liverpool merchants and on visits to both Liverpool and Manchester he mixed with leading merchants, bankers and local gentry. Elizabeth Oakes's father was an attorney whose brothers were clergymen and successful London merchants. One retired to an estate in Wiltshire and was High Sheriff of the county in 1764.[165]

Oakes's close friends included Abraham Newman, reputed to have been the richest man in London,[166] and many of the wealthiest Norwich merchants, bankers and barristers. At home his social circle comprised most of the clergy, professional men and gentlemen living in and around Bury and influential Corporation members belonging to his party. He was on friendly terms with Dr Symonds, Professor of Modern History at Cambridge and with Arthur Young. He dined with the Duke of Grafton once a year and with the Earl of Bristol and Marquess Cornwallis rather more often, although none of these great men ever did more than take tea with Oakes at Guildhall Street.

Oakes and other leading Bury citizens shared a similar cultural background with the local gentry. Many, like Sir Charles Davers, were educated with him at Bury School. Oakes was well travelled in England, if not abroad, loved the theatre and concerts, belonged to the same book club and libraries as they did. He used good architects, Soane and Hopper, when altering his houses; and reasonably well known painters to paint his portrait.[167] He was interested in agriculture and the latest inventions, liked to look at paintings and statuary in country houses. He entertained in the same way, with as much generosity, as local gentlemen and paid as much careful attention to his wine cellar as any of them. He attended the same balls, card and supper parties and assemblies.

---

[163] Joyce M.Ellis, A Study of the Business Fortunes of William Cotesworth c1668–1726 (New York1981), p. 213.
[164] Diary 3 August 1799.
[165] Benjamin Adamson (1704–83) of Oaksey Park, Wiltshire.
[166] He was reputed to have made £600,000 as a grocer by the time of his death in 1799.
[167] e.g. Charles Jagger, of Bath (1770–1827), who also painted the Cullums.

Apart from a similar family and cultural background Oakes was involved with the local aristocracy and gentry in the administration of the county as County Treasurer, a Deputy Lieutenant, Justice of the Peace, regular member of the Grand Jury and as Receiver General of the Land Tax. There were also business links through tax commissions, turnpike trusts, the Suffolk Commercial County Fire Office and the bank.

Clearly, as a banker, Oakes viewed these connections as important and to be encouraged. Yet there was little or no gap between the landed gentry and the prosperous urban merchant and banker in Suffolk. They knew and understood each others' worlds and there was none of the snobbery that later attached to those associated with trade. As Curtis has written of mid nineteenth century Hertfordshire 'there does not seem . . . ever to have been a divorce between trade and landed property'.[168] Jackson, writing of Hull at the end of the eighteenth century, observed that the merchant class of that city was self confident and that few sought county honours which amply illustrated 'the social acceptability of merchants to the leaders of British society'.[169] Oakes never felt the need to pretend to interests that he did not have nor to live in a country house in order to be accepted in county circles. It was not a matter of importance.

At the same time Oakes mixed freely with fellow yarn merchants of all degrees at the *Wool Pack* Tradesmens' Club. His tenants, bank clerks and farmer customers dined regularly with him at the bank, bottles of wine were shared with carpenters and bricklayers working for him. The deaf and dumb painter who was painting his portrait was invited to dine and 'made himself very companionable'[170] as was Mr Evans, the male harpist, who performed at the Assembly Rooms in June 1791.

Bury society was comparatively open. There was no discernible line between urban and country gentry, who were bound together by shared family ties, cultural, political and business experience and in which contact between men of vastly different social standing was common. In spite of this comparative openness, it was a finely graded society in which men were very conscious of status, even if the niceties of their grading is lost to us. Oakes always made a distinction between gentlemen, in which he included himself, and the middling or trading sort and the lower orders. He was very aware of his own standing in the Guildhall Feoffment Trust and the Corporation and carefully recorded his progress towards the most senior position as the older members died off. During the period of the diaries he stops referring to himself as 'gentleman' and changes to 'esquire'. He was agitated when rank was ignored at aldermanic dinners 'many Tradesmen of the Town <u>taking places</u> of the first Gentlemen'[171] and shocked that some election balls were so ill regulated that 'even footmen of the Town in Livery set down at

---

[168] Curtis, *A Chronicle of Small Beer*, p. 7.
[169] Jackson, *Hull in the Eighteenth Century*, p. 263.
[170] Diary 20 November 1814.
[171] Diary 1 October 1807.

Table',[172] although the fact that this could happen at all must be a measure of society's openness. At the other end of the scale the respectability of an affair was judged by the number of titled people involved: a Grand Jury was described as 'very respectable' because it contained five baronets,[173] an assembly attended by 'Two Dutchesses 1 marquis 7 or 8 Lords & as many Ladys . . . scarcely ever more brilliant'.[174] It was a matter of moment that the younger son of the Duke of Grafton should take precedence over the eldest son of the Earl of Bristol.[175]

In a society where everything was done in rank order from voting in the Corporation to the seating at dinner parties and the dancers' places in a minuet, a man's precise social position was displayed for all to see. It may have been pleasant to mix with those on a lower rung of the ladder and to act paternalistically towards ones' employees who would, one hoped, behave with respect. Equally when dining with those higher in the social scale one must have been made constantly aware of ones' relative inferiority in a number of ways, not least by one's place at table.

Oakes was nominated as Sheriff in 1805 but, to his deep disappointment, the office went to George Nassau, the younger son of an earl. Within months of the appointment Oakes and the other rejected candidate, Mr Berners of Woolverstone Hall, near Ipswich, were involved in a plan by which 'Gentlemen in the County liable to serve as Sheriff' contributed 10 guineas a year in order that those chosen would receive £300 to help to pay some of the expenses of office.[176] In effect this plan drew all those with any pretentions to office into a kind of club, which, without conferring the accolade of shrievalty suggested that a subscriber was worthy of it and could expect it in due course.

Failure to gain office may have undermined Oakes's confidence in his social position, and in May the following year arms were granted to him.[177] Later his attitude to land must also have changed because he left his estates entailed on his eldest son, having failed to sell them on several occasions. Yet the grant of arms cannot have been very important to him as he makes no mention of it in his diary. Perhaps he was urged to take the step by his son.

In contrast with his father, Orbell Oakes longed to lead the life of a country gentleman but was prevented from doing so by the force of Oakes's personality. Until his father's death Orbell Oakes divided his time between his house in Bury and his country retreat at Nowton where he spent the summer months. Nowton was only two miles from the bank so that he was able to commute. He enjoyed gardening, shooting, fishing and racing. From 1817 he accumulated land in and

---

172 Diary 27 May 1796.
173 Diary 24 July 1795.
174 Diary 14 October 1803.
175 Diary 9 July 1802.
176 Diary 4 August 1805.
177 Grant 26 May 1806. Sa. on a fesse engr. Or between six oak branches fructed Ppr, three oak leaves vert; Joan Corder, A Dictionary of Suffolk Arms, SRS, VII, p. 342.

around Nowton and between the death of his father in 1829 and his own death in 1836 he spent nearly £2,500 on further land purchases including the Manor of Nowton which he bought from the Marquess of Bristol.[178] He also started to build up a collection of Italian and Dutch paintings, and made a few additions to his house, although it remained essentially a country villa until much enlarged by his son Henry, and renamed Nowton Court, in the mid nineteenth century.

*   *   *

Oakes was very conscious of his precise position in the hierarchy and in acquiring a coat of arms may have had social pretentions but was too sensible to waste money in pursuit of such goals. Having failed to be made High Sheriff he knew where to stop. He was, as Sir John Plumb has said of Colonel Walpole, 'prudent, intelligent, but essentially homespun . . . with his ambition adjusted to those ends that were well within his reach'.[179] In Oakes's case the establishment of a country bank and the leadership of one of the most pleasant towns in England were proud limits.

[178] Orbell Oakes's Memorandum Book and Oakes's Family Papers.
[179] J. H. Plumb, 'The Walpoles; Father and Son', in *Studies in Social History: A Tribute to G. M. Trevelyan*, edited by J. H. Plumb (1955), p. 206.

THE OAKES DIARIES
1778–1800

Editorial Note

In order to reduce the diary to an assimilable form it has been necessary to cut it by about half. Attempts to show where this has been done were found to be cumbersome and to interfere with the flow of the text. However, by 1782 entries were written almost daily so that from that date it should be clear to the reader where they have been omitted. A list of those omitted from the years 1778 to 1781 will be found at the end of this note.

The original spelling and somewhat idiosyncratic use of capital letters have been kept throughout in order to retain some of the flavour of the diary. Where it is unclear whether lower case or capitals were intended I have used capitals for personal and surnames, place-names and for the beginning of sentences. Contractions have been left as they are where the meaning is clear and archaisms, *ye*, *per*, *pre* etc., have been modernized so that the entries will be more readily understood. A table of editorial conventions used in the text follows.

Where a note appears in the margin I have added it to the end of the entry, unless it appears to be an insertion in the body of the text, in which case I treat it as such.

To make the meaning clearer I have modernized the punctuation and used capital letters at the start of new sentences thus made. I have not stuck to Oakes's line lengths because the transcription would be of unmanageable size had I done so. Where page numbers appear in the manuscript they have been put on the right hand side of the page beside the appropriate entry in square brackets, to avoid confusion.

In order to reduce the number of footnotes an alphabetical list of biographical notes will be found at the end of volume II followed by alphabetically listed notes on London and country banks. A glossary and tables of weights and measures precedes the text.

DIARY ENTRIES OMITTED BETWEEN 1778 AND 1781

19 November 1778
14, 17, 21, 22, 25, 29, 31December 1778 (second entry for that date)
6, 8, 12, 14, 15,19, 20, 21 January 1779
4, 5, 9, 11, 12, 16, 22, 25, 26 February 1779
15, 16, 18 March 1779
7, 8, 9, 10, 11, 12, 13, 14, 21, 22, 23, 26, 28, 30 April 1779
4, 5, 11, 12, 13, 15, 21 May 1779

4 June 1779

15, 22, 23, 30 July 1779

2, 11, 13, 20, 24, 25, 28, 31 August 1779

2, 10, 11,15, 21, 22, 25, 26, 27, 30 September 1779

1, 8, 11, 12, 13, 14, 15, 16, 18, 19, 21, 22, 26, 27 October 1779

8, 16, 17, 22, 29, 30 November 1779

5, 6, 7, 9, 12, 14, 16, 20, 23 December 1779

6, 20, 21, 22, 28, 31 January 1780

2, 9, 11, 14, 16, 17, 22, 29 February 1780

4, 6, 8, 9, 14, 16, 17, 22, 30 March 1780

7, 12, 19, 24 April 1780

2, 3, 5, 11, 16, 19, 20, 24, 25, 26 27, 30 May 1780

5, 14, 15, 18, 21, 22, 24, 26 June 1780

7, 9, 12, 13, 28 July 1780

2, 3, 4, 5, 6, 7, 8, 9, 10, 11, 14, 16, 17, 18, 21, 30 August 1780

3, 4, 7, 8, 17, 18, 19, 22, 29 September 1780

1, 4, 5, 6, 7, 9, 10, 11, 13, 15, 18, 19, 20, 21,28 October 1780

3, 6, 9, 10, 15, 16, 17, 20, 26, 28, 30 November 1780

6, 14, 15, 16 December 1780

2, 5, 6, 7, 8, 11, 12, 13, 14, 16, 27 February 1781

12, 14, 16, 17, 29, 30 March 1781

3, 4, 8, 11, 15, 16, 18, 27, 28, 31 May 1781

3, 6, 7, 10, 17, 22, 27, 30 June 1781

1, 3, 4, 5, 6, 10, 23, 24, 25, 29, 30, 31 July 1781

2, 3, 4, 5, 13, 13, 14, 17, 19, 20, 22, 24, 27, 29 August 1781

1, 4, 7, 9, 10, 11, 14, 15, 16 September 1781

4, 6, 7, 8, 9, 10, 11, 12, 13, 16, 21, 23, 24, 25, 26, 27, 28, 29, 31 October 1781

1, 2, 3, 4, 5, 6, 7, 8, 9, 10, 15, 16, 17, 18, 19, 20, 21, 22, 23, 24, 25, 26, 27, 28, 30 November 1781

1, 3, 6, 7, 8, 9, 10, 11, 12, 13, 15, 20, 21, 22, 23, 24, 25, 27, 28, 29 December 1781

Symbols and Editorial Conventions

*****	Indicates a passage surrounded by crosses, stars or squiggles in the MS
(Oakes)	Indicates brackets used by the diarist
/ /	Indicates words which have been inserted
\<word illegible\>	Indicates deleted words that cannot be read
\<\<Oakes\>\>	Indicates deleted words that can be read
[word illegible]	Indicates words which cannot be read
[Blank]	Indicates a gap in the text of the MS
[?]	Indicates doubt about the transcription of a word
[the other]	Indicates missing words which have been supplied or the elucidation of doubtful words
[Specie?]	As above but there is doubt about the word
the Ald[erma]n	Indicates words or letters omitted in the text which have been supplied
[vol I, 1778]	Indicates the volume and year in which the entries on each page are to be found in the Ms
. . .	Indicates that part of the entry for that day has been omitted whether or not the omission ends a sentence

Glossary

Bait A refreshment taken on a journey or a mid-morning meal taken by a labourer. The word is still used in Suffolk

Bark Known variously as *Jesuit's Bark* or *Peruvian Bark* and as quinine today

Bombazine A twilled or corded material made from a mixture of silk and worsted and sometimes cotton and worsted. It was was often made in black for mourning clothes. James Oakes seems to have used the term to describe the yarn that was going to be used in the making of bombazine

Brush An evening party

Bushel A dry measure for grain containing eight gallons

Butt A large cask for wine, sherry or beer. A sherry and beer butt both contain one hundred and eight gallons and wine butt one hundred and twenty six

Camlets (Cambletts) A term originally used to describe a very expensive Eastern material made from camel hair and silk, then applied to light mixtures of silk and wool, wool and cotton or wool and linen

Casano A card game

Chaise A light open carriage for one or more people

Chaldron A measure of coal equivalent to thirty six heaped bushels or twenty five and a half hundred weight

Chariot A light four-wheeled carriage with back seats and a box

Cloth A measure of wool

Clove A measure of wool equivalent to seven pounds

Comb A measure of capacity equalling four bushels

Double horse Riding two on a horse, one behind the other

Erysypilas An inflammatory infection of the face

Filt Probably refers to wine that has been strained when the liquor was drawn off by dropping threads into the wine and letting them hang down below the bottom of the vessel so that the wine could drip into a container beneath

Firkin(furkin) The equivalent of fifty six pounds of butter

Graves Grapes

Guinea £1 1s. 0d. the equivalent of £1.05p

Hawkey Traditionally a harvest supper but in this case to celebrate the end of stock-taking

Haysel Hay-making

Higgler One who sells provisions by retail

Hogshead A hogshead of beer contains fifty four gallons and a hogshead of wine fifty two and a half gallons, although there can be local variations

Horstler Ostler

Keeping Parlour   The sitting room or parlour

Landau   A carriage with a folding top

Landaulette   A small landau coupe with a folding top first used in 1771

Leash   A set of three, usually applied to animals

Limner   A painter. Used particularly to describe portrait painters

Lisbon   A light coloured wine from Estremadura in Portugal but shipped from Lisbon

Livery   The type of wool that comes from the breach of a sheep

Locks   Used to describe coarse wool

Lowance(low)   An allowance usually given to a workman, over and above his wages, for drink

Lunch   During the early nineteenth century breakfast was taken increasingly early and dinner increasingly late so that lunch developed as a light meal taken in the middle of the day to bridge the gap between them

Lustres   Chandeliers

Madeira   A fortified wine from Portugal newly popular in the early nineteenth century when the French Wars upset imports of French wines

Mute   A funeral attendant

Negus   A drink said to have been originated in the early eighteenth century by Col Francis Negus consisting of wine, particularly port or sherry, mixed with hot water, spices, lemons and sugar

Noils   The coarse wool left over after the wool had been sorted for combing. It was used to make coarse baize cloth and heavy woollen 'Fearnoughts' and so gave rise to a separate industry

Opodeldoc   A proprietory liniment used to treat rheumatism, sprains and chilblains

Peck   A measure of capacity equal to one quarter of a bushel or two gallons of dry goods

Phaeton   An open, four-wheeled carriage drawn by one or two horses and usually driven by the owner. They were very light and fast, the equivalent of a sports car today

Pipe   A cask which contains two hogsheads, usually one hundred and five gallons but the amount varies according to the type of wine

Plumpers   Single votes given to one candidate. Freeholders in the county had two votes and were therefore entitled to vote for two candidates to fill the two positions as Knights of the Shire

Pollard   The coarsest flour or bran

Quadrille   A four-handed game played with forty cards

Quarten Loaf   A four pound loaf made with a quarter of a stone of flour

Rafty   A word used to describe a damp, muggy and raw day. By the mid nineteenth century Raynbird names it in a list of local words in use among the Suffolk labouring classes. It is still in use in Suffolk

Rookery   A gambling party

Rowings, Rowens or Roughings Used in Suffolk to describe after-grass, that is to say the second growth of a crop of grass or hay in a season

Round Gowds Plain gowns

Rout A large party or fashionable evening assembly

Score Twenty

Settee room A sitting room containing settees or large, long seats with backs

Shrub A drink made from orange juice, sugar and rum

Skout, scout To dismiss or reject with disdain

Smut A fungal disease of cereals

Snap A snack

Sorrel(l) horse A light chestnut horse

Sorts Probably wool that had been sorted and graded

Stroves Food for cattle

Super fine wool The finest wool used to produce top quality fine yarn

Tandem Vehicles with two horses harnessed singly, one in front of the other

Tilt A cover for a wagon

Tod A unit of weight of wool equal to twenty eight pounds

Variaged lamps Possibly variegated lamps: that is to say of different colours

Waites, Weights Muscians who played outside to welcome Christmas

Whiskey A light gig

Weights and Measures

i. AVOIRDUPOIS WEIGHT

27.3 grains (Gr)*	=	1 dram (Dr)
16 drams	=	1 ounce (oz)
16 ounces	=	1 pound (lb or ld)
14 pounds	=	1 stone (st)
28 pounds	=	1 quarter (qtr)
4 quarters	=	1 hundredweight (cwt)
20 hundredweights	=	1 ton, approximately equivalent to 1,016 kilograms

ii. WOOL WEIGHT

7 pounds	=	1 clove
2 cloves	=	1 stone
2 stone	=	1 tod
60 tods	=	1 wey
2 wey	=	1 sack
12 sacks	=	1 last
240 pounds	=	1 pack

iii. LIQUID MEASURE (ALE AND BEER MEASURE)

4 gills	=	1 pint (pt)
2 pints	=	1 quart (qt)
4 quarts	=	1 gallon (gal), approximately equal to 4.5 litres
9 gallons	=	1 firkin
2 firkins	=	1 kilderkin
2 kilderkins	=	1 barrel
1 1/2 barrels	=	1 hogshead
2 hogsheads	=	1 butt
1 butt	=	1 tun

iv. WINE MEASURE

10 gallons	=	1 anker
18 gallons	=	1 runlet
42 gallons	=	1 tierce
63 gallons	=	1 hogshead
84 gallons	=	1 puncheon
2 hogsheads	=	1 pipe

* Abbreviations used by James Oakes are shown in brackets

2 pipes	=	1 tun

v. DRY MEASURE

2 pints	=	1 quart
4 quarts	=	1 gallon
2 gallons	=	1 peck
4 pecks	=	1 bushel
4 bushels	=	1 comb
8 bushels	=	1 quarter
5 quarters	=	1 load
2 loads	=	1 last

vi. LONG MEASURE

12 inches (in)	=	1 foot (ft)
3 feet	=	1 yard (yd) approximately equal to 0.9 metre
5 1/2 yards	=	1 rod, pole or perch
4 rods	=	1 chain
10 chains	=	1 furlong
8 furlongs	=	1 mile
1 chain	=	100 links

vii. SQUARE MEASURE

144 square inches	=	1 square foot
9 square feet	=	1 square yard
301/4 square yards	=	1 square rod
40 square rods	=	1 rood
4 roods	=	1 acre approximately equal to 0.4 hectare
1 acre	=	10 square chains
		4,840 square yards

vi. MONEY

2 farthings (1/4d.)	=	1 halfpenny (1/2d.)
2 halfpennies	=	1 penny (1d.)
12 pennies	=	1 shilling (1/– or 1s.)
20 shillings	=	1 pound (or L)
21 shillings	=	1 guinea (1 gn)

19. *The Departure of Captain Poole from St Edmundsbury on 15 October 1785 by J. Kendall.*

[Vol. I]   [1778]

Familys We visit –

Lady Cullum   Mr Ord's
Mrs Vernon   Dr Norford's
Miss Cullum   Mr Adamson
Dr Mandeville's   Mrs Oakes
Dr Wollaston's   <<Mr Valpy>>
Mr Leheup's   Mr Waddington
Dr Knowles   <<Mr Stisted>>
Dr Mills   <<Mr>> Corsbie
Mr Heigham's   Dr & Mrs White
Mr Garnham's   Mrs Davers
<<Mrs Boehm>>   Mr & Mrs Craske
Mr Palmer   Dinner Company[1]
Mr Laurents   Sr Jno Cullum
Mr Brundish   Mr Rd Moseley
Mr Pretyman's   Mr Ray
Mr Hasted's   <<Mrs Hollingsworth>>
Mr Symons   Mr Stanniforth
Mr Cocksedge   Mr & Mrs Cocksedge
Mr Cullum   Mr & Mrs Prior
Mrs Johnson   Mrs Denton
Mrs Leman   Mr & Mrs Pateson, Weston
Mr Leathes   Mr & Mrs Pemberton
Mr Cowper   Mr & Mrs Tyrrell
Mr Moseley's
Mr Smith

Novr 11   1778 I dind at Aldn Hasted.

Dr, Miss & the Miss Knowles
Mr & Mrs Cullum
Mr Laurents
Mr Adamson   With Us a[t] Tea & Supper
Mr & Mrs Bridge   Nov 14 1778
Mrs Oakes
& Selves

---

[1]   The difference between 'Familys We visit' and those under this heading is unclear as many of the names appear in both categories. This is probably a list of families visited by the Oakeses and those with whom they had taken dinner recently.

March 1t Monday   Father Adamson, Bror Adamson, Mr W. Adamson came & spent the whole Week with Us at Bury.

Monday March 22 1779   I went to London & returnd Friday following.

Sun March 28 /to April 4/   Mr & Mrs Helsham brot their Son to Us for Change of Air. We were at Home this whole Week, Passion Week.

April 7   Mr & Mrs Helsham return'd Home & left their Son with Us. We have not eat a Meal out of our own House since I came from London.

Monday May 31   JO Dind at the Coffee House being the Militia meeting for swearing & Balloting.[2]

June 7 Monday   (Dind at Dr Norford's Christing & stood as proxies) & spent the Evening at Dr Mandeville's. Met Mrs Bowes, Mrs Jenny, Mrs, Miss Brooks, Mrs Green, Mrs Farrell & Mr Gage.

Monday Septr 6   Maria began to prepare for Innoculation.

Tuesday Septr 14   She was innoculated.

Octr 26 Tuesday   JO dind at Mr Adamson wh ½ Dozen Gentlemen.

Sat Novr 6   Mrs EO, Self & Maria & the Boys at the Play for the Benefit of an Acter in Gaol.[3]

Monday Novr 8 1779   Sessions Day for the Burgh. Din'd at the Angel.

Tuesday Nov 9 1779   JO din'd at Sr Charles Bunbury's. Met Mr Coldham & Mr Spink who I carried with Me in the Coach, also met Mr Macro of Barrow.

---

[2]   A brief note on the organization of the Militia may be useful as the subject occurs frequently in the diary. A General Militia Meeting was held once a year, theoretically on the last Tuesday in May and, after 1786, in October. At this meeting the Justices of the Peace and at least one Deputy Lieutenant received lists of men eligible to serve in the Militia from the Chief Constables of the hundreds. The county quota was then apportioned among the hundreds in proportion to the number of men liable to service in each. Subdivision meetings were held by the Justices of the Peace at which the High Constables produced their lists, complaints were heard and those wrongly included removed. The hundred quotas were apportioned among the parishes and a ballot was held to choose those men who were to serve for each. The Petty Constables were instructed to give the chosen men at least seven days notice at their homes of the next subdivision meeting in three weeks time, at which they were to appear. Substitutes, approved by the Deputy Lieutenants, could be paid for and some men took out insurance against being chosen. Funds were set up to provide substitutes for poor married men to prevent their families becoming a burden on the parish. For further information on the Militia and its organization see J. R. Western *The English Militia in the Eighteenth Century: The Story of a Political Issue 1660–1802* (1965).

[3]   At least one charity performance to benefit a good cause or one of the actors was held during the Theatre's season.

Xmas Day Decr 25 1779   Dinner

9 Plumb Puddings
A Surloin of Beef   37 1d
A legg of Mutton   10 1d ½
                          ————
                           47 ½

14 Bottles of Old Beer.

Mr Smith & Wife[4]	4/–	Jn Waller	1/6
Wm Hill Son & Daughter	4/–	Thos Waller	1/6
Thos Scot Junr & Wife	4/–	Rob Waller	1/6
Thos Scot Sr & Wife	4/–	Richd How	1/6
Mrs Allin	1/6	Henry Hagon	1/6
Mr Scoulding		Wm Hempstead	1/6
Mr T. Waller	1/6	Wm Burton	1/6
Boy Dent	2/6	Rd Hagon	1/6
	————	Jas Hill Jnr	1/6
	21/6		
	————		
	13/6		
	————		
	35/–		

Own Servants: 3 Maids, Wm Hill Jnr, James & Willm, Wm Scot Jnr & Mrs Hill not well, absent. About 26 in all.

Supper

6 own Servts
Mr Smith & Wife
Wm Hill & Daughter   1 Pint Brandy
Tho Scot Sr & Wife   1 D[itt]o Rum
Tho Scot Jnr   1 D[itt]o Shrub
Mrs Scoulding   4 Bottles Old Beer
Mrs Allin   Two hot Apple Pyes & Cold Meat
Boy Dent
  17

Friday Decr 31 1779   Tea & Supper Company at Home: Mr & Mrs Spink, Mr & Mrs Chambers, Dr Norford, Mr Mathew, Mr Jno Garnham (Mr Norman invited, not well enough) NB stay'd till the new year came in.

4   James Oakes's warehousemen, sorters and domestic servants.

[Vol. I]   [1780]

Monday Jany 10th 1780 My Wife, Self & our 4 Children all went to Wearham & spent the Week with Father Adamson, returng Home on the Saturday the 15th. Mr Adamson of Hockswold met us & staid the whole Time. Mr Helsham's Family once dind with /Us/&/we/ once with Them —— the only time we went out or had Company.

Wednesdy the 19th Janry 1780 Miss Routh came from Beccles as Teacher to our Daughter.

Febry 8 Tuesday Mr JO, Mrs EO, Maria & Miss Routh drank Tea & spent the Evening at Mr Spink's . . .

March 20 Monday Our Borough Sessions. I din'd at the Bell with the Justices. Judge Buller came into . . . Town this Evening to hold the /Assizes/.

March 21 Tuesday (Assizes) Mr & Mrs Plampins & Mr J.Plampin and the two younger Children din'd with Us. We all went to the Assembly that Evening which was a very good one. Lord Fielding came Home & suppd with Us. Miss Plampins lodgd at our House.

March 23 Thursday Miss Plampins returnd Home after Breakfast. [The] Judge left the Town.

March 26 Sunday We all drank Tea at my Mother's.

March 29 1780 Wednesday Tea & Supper Company at Home . . .

Wednesday June 7 1780 Mrs EO, Self, Maria & Servant Maid set off in the Bury Fly for London. At Sudbury, hearing of the Disturbances /in/ London, we determin'd to proceed no farther but took post Chaise & immediately return'd Home.[5]

Monday July 17 Mr JO, Mrs EO & 4 Children with Maid Servt went to Yarmouth to Mr Spurgeon's & spent 10 Days, returng the Thursday Sennight following, the 27h Inst.

	[£	s.	d.]
Own Horses to & from Scole Inn	6	06	—
4 Post Horses from Scole Inn to Yarmouth			
& from Yarmouth to Scole Inn			

[5] Riots were provoked when Protestant Association petitions for the repeal of the Catholic Relief Act (1778) presented by Lord George Gordon were considered in the House of Commons. A mob gathered round the House on 6 June 1780 and dragged Gordon in triumph in a carriage to Alderman Bull's house in the City where they burned Newgate, opened other prisons and destroyed the houses of Lord Mansfield and Sir John Fielding. On 7 June 1780 they destroyed the King's Bench Prison and the New Bridewell and threatened the Bank of England. The riot was quelled on 8 June by 20,000 troops, 300 were killed, 190 rioters were convicted and 125 were executed for high treason. Gordon was taken to the Tower on 9 June and tried for high treason in the Court of King's Bench. He was acquitted the following February because it could not be proved that he had encouraged the rioters.

Expences on the Road to & from	2	10	–
Hack Horses at Yarmouth	–	18	–
Servts & other Expences there	4	00	5
	13	14	5

[The following entries cover the Summer Assizes and two Assize assemblies, for which Miss Staniforth and Miss Quince came to stay with the Oakes Family. A present of a haunch of venison from the Earl of Bristol's estate provided a dinner party, Mrs Oakes's father, brother and sister came to stay for a week and Mr Cullum was elected the next Alderman.]

Wednesday Augt 30 JO went to Norwich & return'd on the Friday. JO went to Cawston[6] on the Thursday Evening & got to Norwich by breakfast the next Morng.

Tuesday Sept 12 The General Election. Three Candidates: Genl Conway 18 /votes/, Sr Chas Davers 22 and Lord Hervey 13 votes. The two former elected.[7] A Dinner provided at the Guild Hall at the Members' Expence for Corporation Gentlemen. Abt 60 in all din'd there. A very genteel Ball /& Supper/ in the Evening at the Assembly House for the Gentlemen, Ladys & principal Inhabitants. The whole conducted with a great deal of order & Regularity.

The 4 following Days Wednesday the 13, Thursday 14h, Friday /15h/ & Saturday /16h/, I was fully engag'd at Home in attending my Men to take stock &ca.

Wednesday Septr 20 JO went to the Nomination at Sto[wmarke]tt. Sr Charles Bunbury & Sr Jno Rous were named almost unanimously and no other Gentleman that Day put in Nomination.[8] Mrs EO, Self & Maria that Day din'd at Mr Rd Moseley's . . .

Thurs Septr 21 Mrs EO & Self Drank Tea & suppd at Mr Palmer's. Met Farmier & Mr Rd Adamson & Mr Jos /Grigby/.

Mond 25 Sept JO went to Sturbridge Fair & return'd the same Night. Mr Jno Cumberland & Mr Mathew accompanied Me in a post Chaise.

Tuesday Septr 26 Mrs EO & Self din'd & Drank Tea & spent the Evening at Mr Adamson's. Met Mr & Mrs Ord, Mr Craven Ord, Mr & Mrs Norman, Miss Moyle, Captn Jones.

Wednesday Sept 27 1780 JO breakfasted at Sr Charles Bunbury at Barton & accompanied Him from thence to the County Election at Ipswich which was determind without Opposition in Favor of Him & Sr Jno Rous. I dind with Sr Chas Party at the Golden Lyon & returnd the same Evening, drinking Tea at Mr Ray's at Tostock in my way.

6 James Oakes's brother-in-law, the Rev. Richard Baker, was Rector of Cawston, Norfolk.

7 Only members of the Corporation had the right to elect the two Members of Parliament for Bury. The electorate consisted of the Alderman, 12 Capital Burgesses and 24 Common Councilmen, a total of 37.

8 Nomination of candidates to stand for election as Knights of the Shire for Suffolk.

[Mr and Mrs Ray, Mr Patteson and Mr Jodrell came to stay for part of the Fair.]

Mon Oct 16   Mr Jodrell, Mr Patteson & Self went to Newmarkett, dind at Kennet upon our Return & got Home time enough to accompany the Ladys to the Assembly.

Tuesdy Oct 17   Mr Jodrell, Mr Patteson & the Ladys all went to the Play in the Evening with the Children. I did not.

Monday Oct 23   JO went to London & return'd the Friday followg. Lodg'd at Mr Houghton's Bull Inn, Leadenhall /Street/.[9]

Monday Oct 30   Mrs EO, Self, Miss Routh & Children all went to the Play being the Alderman's Bespoke Play – the Busy-Body.[10]

Mon Afternoon Nov 20   JO drank Tea at Mr Cullum's on Corporation Business. Met the Recorder, Mr Spink, Mr R.Rogers, Mr Norman & Mr Heigham. Return'd Home to supper.

Thursday Nov 23d   Tea & supper Company at Home . . .

Friday Novr 24   Tea & Supper Company at Home . . .

Monday Dec 18   Charlotte, Orbell & James went to their Grandpapa at Wearham & staid till Thursday the 18h January.

Wednesday Decr 20   Mr JO, Mrs EO, Maria & Maid Servt sett out for Bath. Staid with Mr Heaton in Town the Next Day. Went forward on Friday & arrived at Bath Saturday Evening at Mr B.Adamson's House, where we continued till Wednesday the 17h January. Got to Mr Heaton the next Day at 4 O'Clock Dinner. Remaind in Town till Tuesday following the 23rd & got well Home the Same Evening after 5 weeks Absence.

[Vol. I]   [1781]

Tuesday Febry 20   Mr O – Drank Tea at Mr Heigham's, ... Mr O returnd Home to supper, Mrs O not being well enough to go.

Tuesday April 13   Mrs EO, Self & Maria all went to Mrs Patteson's of Norwich to meet Mr & Miss Stanniforth & Mr Adamson & spent all that week with Mrs P – returning Home on Sunday.

Sunday May 13   . . . Mr Herring came from Norwich in the Eveng to spend 2 or 3 Days.

[9]   The coach from the Angel Inn, Bury, arrived at the Bull Inn every Monday, Wednesday and Friday.
[10]   Local people often chose plays on what were called 'bespoke nights' in return for buying a considerable number of tickets. *The Busy-Body* by Mrs Centilivre.

Monday May 14 1781 We all din'd at Mr Rd Adamson's. Met Mr & Miss Stanniforth, the 2 Mr Pattesons, Mr Iselin, Mr Herring & Ourselves. [They] spent the Evening with Us.

Monday May 21 JO went to Londn in a post Chaise with Mr Burch, log'd at Houghton's at the Bull Inn, return'd on Thursday Evening to Chelmsford & got Home on the Friday Evening.

Tuesday June 12 Mr & Mrs Moseley, Mr, Mrs Stanniforth, Miss Stanniforth, Mr Patteson, Mr H.Patteson, Mr Adamson & my Mother din'd with Us and drank Tea. Mess Wood & Dagvilles' Ball in the Eveng. We went to it at 8 & staid till 11.[11]

Wednesday June 13 Miss Stanniforth & Misses Pattesons call'd upon Us & partook of a Family Dinner.

Thursday June 14 *Mr Patteson and Miss Stanniforth were married.*

Saturday June 23 Miss Routh left Us for the Midsummer vacation.

Monday June 25 Mr & Mrs O – & 4 Children all went to Wearham carrying Home Sister A and there staid till Saturday, returning that Day to Dinner.

Sunday July 8h Mrs O –, Maria & Self went & drank Tea at Mr Ray's of Tostock to bring Home our Boys who had been for a week.

Tuesday July 17 1781 JO went to Londn with Orbell and deliver'd Him at Mr Sheperd's Accademy at Clapton, Hackney, on Sunday Eveng the 22d.

Monday Augst 6 Came to our House my Father Adamson, Bror & Sister D[itt]o and Mr Adamson from Hockwold and to Mr RA Mr Benj. Adamson & his Son. The whole Family dind with Us on a Haunch of Venison. We all spent the week together, din[in]g alternately at Mr RA & my House. Mr Humphrys met Them at mine on Wednesday & Friday and Dr Mills with Them all at my House on Friday upon a Haunch of Venison. Saturday Father A, Bror & Sister & Mr WA all returnd Hom[e].

Sat Aug 11 . . . Sister Green & her Daughter came to my Mother on Friday Evening Augt 10h by Post Coach from London.

Thursday Augt 23 Hall Day for electing [the] Alderman: Mr Jno Spink unanimously chosen.[12] We all din'd at the Angel for the first time.

Sept 4, 5, 6 & 7, Tuesday, Wednesday, Thursday & Friday I stock'd and the Sorters all liv'd in the House as usual.

---

[11] The ball given by the dancing masters at which their pupils demonstrated their proficiency.

[12] The Alderman was the equivalent of mayor and was elected annually in August from among the Capital Burgesses by the whole Corporation. He was also the Chairman of the Bench and chose his fellow Assistant Justices. The retiring Alderman became Coroner for the following year.

20. Elizabeth Patteson née Staniforth by Philip Reinagle.

Wednesday Sept 19 Mr & Mrs Patteson returnd out of Lancashire, drank tea with Us & went to Norton.[13]

Thursday Sept 20 Mr Chambers set off [on] his Journey into Yorkshire, Lancashire, Worcestershire &ca, Kidd[erminster], Coventr[y]. Returnd Friday Oct 12h

[13] Elizabeth Patteson's father, Robert Staniforth, came from Manchester. The Staniforths had inherited Little Haugh, Norton, through Mary Macro, only child of Cox Maccro DD of Bury and Little Haugh, who had married Robert Staniforth's brother, William.

21. John Patteson by Philip Reinagle.

followg, was absent 22 Days. Expences [£]9.9 – extra D[itt]o for Porters, Shoe[in]g &ca £1. 5 –.

Wednesday Sept 26 I din'd at Lord Bristol's carrying with Me in my Coach Dr Mills, Mr Humfrey & his Son. Spent that Evening at my Mother's.

Monday Oct 15 My Cousin Mr James Edge came to Us from Londn to Tea. We all went to the Assembly that Night being the last – abt 20 Couple of Dancers.

Wednesday Oct 17 at Home. Mr Edge & Mr Green Shooting.

Fridy Oct 19   We all went to the Races at Newmarkett with Mr Hunfrey. Din'd at the ramm & home in the Evening.

Saturday Oct 20 1781   At Home this Day. Mr Edge & Mr Green out shootg the whole Day. Mrs Schooley & her Daughter & Mr Ray drank Tea wh Us.

Monday Octr 22   I went Shooting wh Mr Edge in the morng. Mr Adamson, Mr & Mrs Cocksedge, Mr Humfrey, my Mother, Bror & Sister Green all din'd with Us.

Monday Nov 12h   I dind /& spent the Evening/ at Mr Symonds['s]. Met the Bishop of Peterborough & Mr Arthur Young; Mr Garnham & Mr Laurents came in the Evening.

Tuesdy Novr 13   Mr Pr[i]est calld upon Me, spent the Evening with Us.

Saturday Novr 29   Company At Home at Dinner: Mr & Mrs Patteson, Mr H. Patteson, Miss Plampins, Mr R. Plampin, Mr Adamson, my Mother &ca. At our second Subscription Ball in the Evening.

Monday Decr 2 [3rd]   I went to Norwich, Mr Humfrey accompanied me. We return'd on the Wednesday.

Sunday Decr 16   We all din'd at Mr Adamson's. Mr Thompson, [a] Candidate for the Usher-ship, spent the Evening with Us.[14]

Monday Decr 17   School meeting (12 Candidates) pres[en]t only Mr Pr[i]est & Mr Thompson. The former, Mr Pr[i]est, was elected. Mr Grigby, Mr Priest & Mr Thompson all returnd Home to dine with Me.
   Orbell return'd this Day from Hackney, Clapton, for [the] Xmas Vacation.

Wednesday Decr 26   We made a little dancing party at Home for our young Folks, 7 or 8 Couple. They had Tea & cakes and cold Tongue & Chicken for Supper.

Sunday Decr 30   I went to dine at Euston with the Duke of Grafton. Carr'd my son Orbell with Me. A very large Company /27/.

Monday Dec 31st   Met the Corporation to dispose of Badby's Gift,[15] afterwards adjournd with Them to the Angel to spend [the] Forfeites.[16]

[14] The usher was the equivalent of a junior master at the Grammar School.
[15] Under his will, dated 20 August 1651, Edward Badby left property, the income from which was to be used to provide two poor men and one poor woman from St James's parish with one pound each and ten shillings respectively and the same for two poor men and one poor woman from St Mary's parish. The charity was administered by the Capital Burgesses.
[16] Fines paid by those who did not attend the charity meeting or who refused office.

22. *Wereham Hall, Norfolk, the Adamson family home.*

[Vol. I]   [1782]

[January opened with the usual round of dinner, tea and supper parties, the Guildhall Feoffment dinner[17] and a brief business trip to Norwich made by James Oakes. At the end of the month the Oakes family, including Miss Routh, the governess, and a maid, went to stay with Mrs Oakes's cousin, Mr Heaton, in London. Orbell was returned to school and the family was joined by James Oakes's sister, brother-in-law and niece from Liverpool. Both families went to plays, the opera and dined with London friends, before returning to Bury.]

Thursday Febry 7 . . . My particular Business in London this Journey was to attend a Committee of Delegates from different parts of the Kingdom concernd in the woollen Manufactures to oppose an intended Petition to Parliament for Leave to export Long combing wool under certain Limitations and Restrictions.[18] Mr Ives of Norwich was our Chairman. We began our Meeting on Monday Janry 28th at the King's Arms, Palace yard. We went again on the Wednesday, the Day the Lincolnshire Gentlemen met at the St Albans Tavern. At that Day an united general Meeting was fix'd for the followg Saturday, Febry 2d, at the Thatch'd House in St James Street. There were 200 Gentlemen, Merchts & Manufacturers – abt 50 were members of Parliament. Lord Brownlow in the Chair. After many able Speaches, a Motion was propos'd in order to take the Opinion of the Company, "Viz" "That the Exportation of British raw wool would be prejudicial to the Landed & Commercial Interest of the Kingdom["], when Lord Brownlow <<quitted>> /left/ the Chair & together with between 30 & 40 Lincolnshire Gentlemen, quitted the room. Sr George Saville was unanimously voted in the Chair in his Lordship's room, when sd Motion was carried by 110 Gentlemen Nem. Con. We met again on the Wednesday when we appointed a Delegation of the Delegates to wait on Lord North – & the next Day I returnd Home.

/Saturday/ Febry 9 We all drank Tea & spent the Evening at my Mother, being Sister Bridge's Birth-Day.

Sunday Febry 25th Bror Bridge, Mr Humfrey & Self went out coursing. Mr Humfrey dind with Us, Bror Bridge drank Tea with Us.

Fridy March 8h I bottled off a pipe of Red Port & [a] Pipe of Old Beer. Sister Baker came to my Mother's this Day on a visit.

Fridy March 22 1782 . . . Sister Baker returnd Home.

---

[17] The Guildhall Feoffment Trust was a collection of Bury charities administered by trustees or Feoffees, of which James Oakes was one.

[18] The wool producing counties, led by Sir Joseph Banks and Arthur Young, mounted a campaign to obtain the repeal of longstanding legislation preventing the export of wool. This was strenuously opposed by the manufacturers who feared rising wool prices would result. See page 22.

Mondy March 25th includg Saturday March 30h Passion Week. At Home alone this whole week.

Mondy April 1st Miss Routh left Us, returng to Beccles by Yarmouth Coach. Bror & Sister Bridge with little Susan, set out at ½ past 8 O'Clock. My Coach carr'd them to Newmarkett and they proceeded on their way so far as Kettering that night. All at Home that Day.

Sunday April 21st 1782 My Mother & Mr Humfrey din'd with Us on a fine Pike, pres[en]t from Mr Humfrey . . .

Monday April 22 Mr Humfrey accompanied me to Newmarkett Races. We din'd together at the White Hart & return'd Home to Tea.

Sundy May 19 My Mother dind with Us. Charlotte, with Miss Green & Miss Scholey & master Spurgeon, Came Home for Whitsun Sunday, Monday & Tuesday. Mr Jno Spurgeon call'd & Supp'd with Us in his way to Yarmouth.

This Afternoon arriv'd the News of Admiral Rodney's Victory over Menr De Grass French Fleet.[19]

Friday May 24 I din'd at the Angel: Mr Jos Grigby & Mr Blachley's Treat being the Decision of their Wager. Met Mr Fitzroy, Mr Parker, Mr Grigby, Mr Metcalf, Mr Heigham, Mr Tyrrell & Mr Kedington. I returnd Home to Supper.

Mondy July 8 . . . Mr Shepherds, Orbell's master, came to spend a week with us.

Sundy July 28 I deliverd Orbell at Mr Sheperd's Academy.

Monday Augst 5 1782* I went to Stowmarket to the County Meeting call'd by the Sheriff to hear the Sentiments of the County respectg Building a ship of the Line or raising of Men. It was unanimously carrd for the Building a Ship of 74 Guns by voluntary Subscriptions, wch was immediately set on Foot by some Noblemen & Gentn. I din'd on my return Home at Mr Grigby's. Met Lord Cornwallis, Sr Charles Davers, Mr Trotman, Mr Kedington, Mr Rogers & Mr Case.

Wednesday Aug 7 Hall calld by the Alderman for filling up. Not Membership enough of the Lower House [20] to make a Hall.

---

[19] The French had just captured St Kitts and were planning a massed attack on Jamaica having 14 Spanish ships and 8,000 soldiers at Cape François waiting to be joined by the Comte de Grasse with 35 ships of the line and 5,000 soldiers from Martinique. Rodney, with 36 ships of the line, had taken up a position in St Lucia to await de Grasse. A partial action took place on 8 April in the lee of Dominica and the French were finally forced into action and defeated on 12 April. The fact that they were in the lee of the Island and that the wind was very variable told against them. In spite of the victory there was much criticism of Rodney who, it was felt, should have pursued and captured at least 20 more French ships instead of sticking with Admiral de Grass's wounded flag ship. However the victory did restore English prestige after the surrender of Cornwallis and the Government was able to negotiate on more favourable terms.

[20] The Corporation consisted of 24 Common Councilmen, elected from among the townsmen by the whole Corporation, and 12 Capital Burgesses elected from among the Common Councilmen by the whole Corporation.

Thursday [August 8] At Home. Mr Chambers set out upon his Yorkshire Journey.

Saturday August 10 Mr Heigham, Mr Wright & Self began the Subscriptions for the Borough for the Ship. Met at the Guild Hall in the Evening & elected Mr Mathew, Mr Mats Wright & Mr Martin Cocksedge into the Upper House;[21] Mr Jno Garnham, Mr Jno Fairfax, Mr Hubbard, Mr Henry Bullen & Mr Tho Rutter, Burgesses of Common Council.

Wednesday Augt 14 . . . School Hall Meeting. NB Part of Saturday, all Monday, all Tuesday & Part of Wednesday I was abt Town with Mess Heigham, Wright, the Aldermn, Mr Robinson in collecting Subscriptions for the 74 Gun Ship intended to be built by the County. This Day Mr R.Adamson returnd Home after an Absence of 4 mo[nth]s to London, Bath, Oakley &ca.[22]

Saturday Augst 24 I went to meet Maria at Scole Inn on her return from Yarmouth, very ill . . .

Monday Augt 26 Mr Rd Adamson & Self went in his Chaise to dine at Revd Mr Patteson at Weston (Mrs O did not go Maria not being well). Met Mrs Patteson from Norwich, Mr & Mrs Thurston, Mr Stanniforth & Mr Humfrey. Return'd Home to supper.

Thursday Aug 29 Bottl'd off a Pipe of Red Port of Mr Spink at Mr Mathew's Cellar.

Wednesday Sept 11 Company at Home on Venison Dinner: Mrs Patteson, Mrs Durrent, Mr Stanniforth, Mr H.Patteson, Mr Josling, Mr Kedington, Mr Rd Adamson & Mr Humfrey. Mr Humfrey, Mr Kedington & M[r] RA stay'd at supper with Us.

Saturday the 21 Began Stocktaking on the Tuesday & ended on Saturday being the whole 5 Days. Left all the Livery & Locks unweighed.

Saturday Sept 28 Mrs O & Self dind at Lord Bristol's . . . returnd to sup at Mr Adamson's.

Saturday Nov 23rd At Home the whole Day except[in]g the Ladys went to see a Farce acted by some of the Grammar [School] Boys at Mrs Boldero's.

[During December the Newmans stayed with the Oakeses but had to rush back to Fenchurch Street because Mr Newman's brother-in law and business partner, Monkhouse Davison, was ill. Capt. and Mrs Whaley stayed on their way from Yarmouth to Chelmsford, the second subscription ball was a moderate success, Miss Adamson returned to Wareham after a two month visit and James Oakes officiated at the distribution of Alderman Johnson's Charity.[23] Christmas fol-

---

[21] That is to say they were elected Captial Burgesses.
[22] Oakley was Benjamin Adamson's seat in Wiltshire.
[23] Under his will, dated 5 May 1708, Alderman Jacob Johnson left three houses in Looms Lane to house three poor widows, two from St James's Parish and one from St Mary's. A fourth house was let to provide the income to keep the others in good repair. The women were to be over 60, of good character and not in receipt of poor relief.

lowed its usual pattern with the Oakes family spending the day with Mrs Oakes senior while their servants, workers and pensioners had their own party at Home. Orbell and James stayed four days with their friend, Master Derisly, from December 24 until December 28.]

Monday Janry 6 Boys went to Wearham. Charlotte being taken ill detain'd us a Day.

Tuesday Janry 14 At Home & in the Evening a Dance for our Young Ones, about 7 couple. They had a Cold Supper.

Friday Janry 24***** News of a General Peace came to Bury this Evening, arriv'd in London the preced[in]g Eveng.[24] At Home alone.

Fri April 25 At Home alone. 3 of my sorters quitted my /works/. Sat April 26

Tuesday April 29 1783 Mr Adamson, Mrs O & Self all went to make Mr & Mrs Patteson of Norwich a visit. Mr Adamson took my Wife in his Chaise & I went on Horseback. We got there abt 7 O'Clock in the Evening. Din'd on Wednesday at Mr P & all went to the Play that Eveng – the Roman Father,[25] for the Benefit of Mrs Sharp.

Saturday May 3d We return'd Home between 6 & 7 O'Clock in the Eveng to Tea.

Monday May 5 Mr & Mrs Baker /& Bessy/ came to Bury. We drank Tea & suppd at my Mother's.

Tuesday May 20 . . . <u>William Coachman died.</u>

Wednesday May 21 . . . William buried.

Friday June 6 My Mother & Mrs Harrison & Mr Adamson all din'd with Us on a Turbot: [a] pres[en]t from Mr Spink. We drank Tea & spent the Evening at Mr Leheup's. Met Mrs & Miss Heigham, Dr Mills, Mr & Mrs Palmer, Mr Adamson & Mr Goddard.

Tuesday June 10 Mrs EO & Self drank Tea & spent the Evening at Dr Norford's . . . The Little Boys dind with Us.[26]

[24] Peace between Britain and the newly independent American Colonies, France and Spain which was ratified in the Treaty of Versailles.
[25] *The Roman Father* was a tragedy by W. Whitehead first produced at Drury Lane in February 1749/50.
[26] Dr Norford was rumoured to have fathered 26 children including seven sons by his second wife.

Wednesday June 11   Messrs Pemberton & Partridge from School Hall din'd with Us & drank Tea.[27]

Sunday June 22d   We all din'd at Mr Adamson's. After Church in the Afternoon went and Drank Tea at Mr Simpson's of Flempton. This Evening Mr Adamson receiv'd the melancholy Acct of Mr Benj Adamson's Death of Bath He died at Bristol on Thursday Morning June 19 at 1/2 past 8 O'Clock in the Morning.

Tuesday June 24   We had engagd ourselves to spend the Evening at Lady Cullum's but, on Acct of the Death of Mr B.Adamson, were oblig'd to decline going.

Wednesday July 2   I went with my Sons in a Chaise & met the Funeral of Mr B. Adamson from Bath at Brandon. Mr Rd Adamson went in his Chaise. We all took the mourning Coach at Brandon & followd the Corps to the Bull at Stoke where the Herse dress'd & we went in procession to Wearham Church where the Corps was interr'd abt 4 O'Clock in the Afternoon. We all dind at my Father Adamson's.

Friday the 18th . . . I this Eveng sold the Boys' Poney to Mr George Boldero of Ampton for Three Guineas.

Monday July 21   I went to meet Mr Revett at Stowmarkett abt the Melton House Spinning.[28] Din'd with Him at the White Horse & returnd to sup. Mr Adamson & Mr Humfrey went into Norfolk to old Mr Humfrey for a few Days.

Fridy July 25   Family at Home alone. Maria rode her Uncle's Horse in the Evening [for the] first Time.

Thursday Aug 7   I rode over to Depden[29] to meet the Gentlemen appointed to value Jno Ambrose's Crops in order for Thos Green to take the same & become my Tenant. Mr Canham on my Behalf, Mr Lancaster for John & Mr Pawsey as Umpire between Them. We all dind at the Publick House at Wickhambrook. Bot my new little mare for Daughter & sons of Mr Mills of Hundon.

Wednesday Aug 13   Maria & Miss Norford went to dine & spend the Day at Chadacre.[30] Return'd Home to sup [and] Brot Home Miss Plampin. /(Bot the new Grey Packing mare of Mr Sier at the Horsemarket, Stanton.)/

Sunday Augst 17 1783 . . . NB This Day sent my Horse for a month's keeping into Sir Charles Davers's Park.

---

[27] Messrs Pemberton and Partridge were at Bury School with James Oakes junior and were sons of the Rev Jeremiah Pemberton of Trumpington and Henry Partridge of King's Lynn, both family friends.

[28] Spinning done in the Union Workhouse at Melton near Woodbridge in East Suffolk. See Chapter II.

[29] The farm originally obtained by James Oakes's father from his first wife, Mary Godfrey.

[30] Chadacre Hall was the Plampin family home.

23. Dr William Norford (1715–93), surgeon and physician, of Guildhall Street.

Monday Augst 18 ...A Hall calld by the Alderman to fill up 3 vacancys in the Common Council. Mr Bran[white] Green, Mr Buchanan & Mr Michael Apsey elected. The Corporation now complete.

Friday Aug 22 Mr Reed of Leeds dind with Us ...

Tuesdy Septr 2 ... (Old Jockey Horse died.)

[The Oakeses visited Mrs Oakes's father at Wereham for three days and found her brother, James Adamson, dying. He died the day after they had returned to Bury. James Oakes promptly returned to Wereham and organized the funeral and burial in Scottow Church.]

Thursdy Sept 25 I went wth Mr Cumberland & Mr Mathew to Sturbitch Fair & returnd [the] same Night.

Tuesdy Sept 30 Bottled off a pipe of Red Port between Mr RA & myself. I went to dine at Mr Cowper's. Met Sir Walter & Lady Rawlinson, Mr & Mrs Maynard, Mrs Halsey, Mr Horrex. Mrs O & Maria were invited but could not go.

Fri Oct 3 Bottled off a pipe [of] Old Beer. At Home alone.

[Mr Edge, James Oakes's cousin, his friend Mr Hillersdon, Mr Maltby from Norwich, the Staniforths from Norton and the Pattesons from Norwich and Coney Weston were entertained by the Oakeses for part of the Fair.]

Thursdy Oct 16 Mr Hillersden & Mr Edge went to Mr H.Patteson for a Day's shooting to return on [the] next Day to Dinner. We went to Lady Bristol's Play in the Evening.

Fri Octr 17 The Gentlemen returnd to dine with Us. Mr Cullum & Mr Davers also dind with Us [and] all went to the Children's Ball in the Evening.

Fri Oct 24 JO to Woodbridge to see Amb Taylor [who is] very ill.

Saturday Oc 25 JO returnd Home. Bot a new sorrell Horse for [the] coach & cost £24.

Thursday Nov 27 I accompanied Mr Symonds & Mr Jermyn Symonds to Euston & din'd & spent the Evening with the Duke & Dutchess of Grafton & Lord Charles. Return'd Home next Day after Breakfast.

Tuesday Dec 9 1st County meetg of yarn Makers at [the] King's Head, Stowmarket. [There were] between 50 & 60 prest. [It was] unanimously resolvd to petition parliament for legal Authority to appoint general Inspectors of the Spinning for an Act founded [on] the York, Lancaster & Chester in 1776 &ca, & get Home 9 O'Clock.[31]

Sat Decr 13 A few of the School Boys perform'd a Play (The Revenge)[32] in my Keeping Parlour – 30 Gentm, Ladys & young Folk present. After the Play a Farce calld (Who's the Dupe).[33] My Mother, Mr Adamson, Mr Blachley, Mr Haggett, Mr & Mrs Heigham all suppd with Us.

Tuesdy Decr 16 I dind at the Wool-Pack, 1st Committee Meeting to be preparing for a Bill in Parliament to appoint Inspectors. We all drank Tea & suppd at my Mother's [with] Lady Cullum, Mrs Vernon, Mr & Mrs Palmer, Mr Johnson, Mr Adamson, Mr Haggitt.

Fri Decr 19 Orbell came Home . . .

Thursdy Decr 25 Xmas Day. We all din'd at my Mother's. Met Mr Adamson, Mr Creed, Mr Haggett & all drank Tea & spent the Evening there. Servants, Wool Sorters &ca at Home:

---

[31] Worsted Acts 1777: 17 Geo III c1; 17 Geo III c16.
[32] *The Revenge* a tragedy by Edward Young, first produced in c1721.
[33] *Who's the Dupe?* a farce by Mrs Hannah Cowley, first produced at Drury Lane in 1779.

```
 2  Own Man Servants
 4  2  Maid D[itt]o
 1  Wm Hill Junr
21  Wool sorters, Warehouse Men & Includ[in]g
        Amb. Taylor, Benj. Knop.
___
28
```

```
      3 Dinners sent out to Poor Familys.
      A Sir Loyn Beef        37 ld ½
      Legg Mutton             9 ld
                             _____
                             46½
```

8 Plumb Puddings
28 minc'd Pyes, 14 Bottles Beer.

Supper

```
      7 own Servants
      9 others
      _____
      16 in all
```

Cold Beef, 2 large apple Pyes, 1 Bottle Rum, 1 pint Brandy, 4 Bottles Old Beer.

Mondy Decr 29 I spent the Eveng at the Wool-Pack wh Mr Rogers & pd my Bottle on receipt of my /Money/ from the Corporation. Mr Cocksedge, Mr Mathew & abt ½ Dozen of Us.

Wednesday Decr 31 Our young Ones had a little Ball at my House, abt 1/2 Dozen young Ladys & 1/2 Dozen young Gentlemen. They all supp'd & parted abt 12 O'Clock.

[Vol. I]   [1784]

Friday Janry 23rd A Ball at Mr R.Adamson for our young Ones . . . All danc'd makg up abt 8 or 9 Couple. A very elegant supper; 4 Dances after & got Home soon after 2 O'Clock.

Wednesday Janry 28 I din'd at the Wool-pack with the Committee of yarnmakers. Evening at Home.

Friday Janry 30 I din'd at Mr Kedington's, Rougham . . . I walk'd there & back again.

Tuesday Febry 3 At Home all Day. Mrs O & Maria in the Evening to see Mimickry at the Assembly House . . .

Fridy Febry 6 At Mr Symonds['s] to drink Tea & pass the Evening. A remarkable deep Snow insomuch as it was with the greatest Difficulty we got up. Met

Mr & Mrs Heigham & the young Ladys, Miss Moyle & the French Gentlemen.[34]
Mr Charles Cook died.

/Wednesday/ Febry 11 Company at Home at Tea & Supper. The two Miss Heighams, Monsieur Lazoosky & his two young Friends, Mr Laurents, Mr Adamson, Mr Creed, Mr Haggett.

Tuesdy Febry 24 1784 Mrs EO, Self, Maria, Charlotte & Servt Maid all went to London to Mr Heaton's by Angel Post Coach. All at Mr Heaton's that whole week, Dinner & Evening. NB I was attending Parliament on our Bill to appoint Inspectors for preventing Frauds.

Thursday March 4 We all went to the Play at Drury Lane this Evening, The Reparation, a new Play, & Harlequin Junior, the Entertainment.[35]

Sunday March 7 Charlotte this day deliverd at Campden House.[36]

[The Oakeses returned to Bury and the Spring Assizes opened. Parliament was dissolved on March 24 and one of the sitting Members, General Conway, came to Bury to canvass support.]

Fridy March 26 General Conway went to Newmarket upon finding he was not likely to be well receiv'd. Jury discharg'd at Noon. Company din'd & supp'd with Us . . . An air Balloon let off at Noon.[37] A concert at Noon – very thin, a Dance after.

[34] The French gentlemen were François de La Rochefoucauld, his younger brother Alexandre, and their tutor, Maximilien de Lazowski. Their father, the duc de Liancourt, was Grand Master of the Wardrobe to Louis XVI, and had himself, as his son Gaétan wrote, travelled 'usefully, to learn' in England when he was 21, in 1768. In 1780, he established the first of the famous écoles des Arts et Métiers at Liancourt, followed by one that is still very flourishing in Châlons-sur-Marne. In 1781–83, François, Alexandre and Lazowski travelled observantly round France (Jean Marchand, ed., Voyages en France de François de La Rochefoucauld, 2 vols, 1933 and 1939). At Christmas 1983 they came to England, intending to go to Bristol to learn the language, but persuaded by Horace Walpole's cousin to go to Bury or Norwich, as that was where it rained least and where English was spoken best – whereas many people in Bristol spoke French. They arrived at the Angel early on 9 January, 1784, with letters of introduction, and Dr John Symonds took the lead in finding them accommodation. See A Frenchman's Year in Suffolk, 1784: François de La Rochefoucauld, edited and translated by Norman Scarfe, S.R.S. XXX, 1988, Introduction and p. 16. 'The remarkable deep Snow' was part of more than a year of bad weather in England endured by the French visitors.
[35] Eighteenth century theatre performances usually consisted of a full length play which was followed by an entertainment or burletta which included songs and recitations, or one of the many Harlequin stories. A farce was sometimes performed after the entertainment or instead of it.
  The Reparation a sentimental comedy by Miles Peter Andrews first performed at Drury Lane in 1784. It was written for Mrs Siddons but was rejected by Covent Garden.
[36] Charlotte Oakes's school in London.
[37] Following the flights of both hot air and hydrogen balloons in France from June 1783 onwards many miniature (unmanned) ballons were sent up in England. The first successful untethered manned flight in a balloon in England was by Vincenzo Lunardi in a hydrogen

Saturdy March 27 1784 I went to Newmarkett, saw the Duke of Grafton [and] Genl Fitzroy. Din'd at the ramm & return'd Home to dinner.

Thursdy April 1st Sr Chas Davers, Captn Geo Fitzroy, Lord Charles Fitzroy, Mr Symonds, Mr J. Symonds, the 3 French Gentlemen, Mr & Mrs Cullum, Miss Moyle &ca all din'd with [us] & stayd till ten O'Clock.

Fridy April 2d General Election for the Burgh. Captain Geo Ferdinand Fitzroy & Sr Chas Davers unanimously elected, Lord Hervey having the preceding Day withdrawn Himself. Abt 54 din'd with the Members at the Angel & at Night at a general Ball at the Assembly House. Reckon abt 250 present at the Ball.

Tuesdy April 6 The Nomination Day for [the] County Members at Stow[marke]tt. Candidates   Sr John Rous
           Mr Grigby
           Sr Charles Bunbury.
The Show of Hats declar'd in the Favour of the two former – Sr Charles Bunbury determin'd to stand the Poll. The Poll commenc'd at Ipswich April 7, Wednesday, & that Night Close of Poll Sr CB was upwds of 500 Behind & early the next morning determin'd to decline.

Thursdy April 8 JO set out wth an Intention to go to Ipswich wh Dr Wollaston & was met upon the Road with the acct of Sr CB having given up, upon which, we return'd Home.

Fridy April 9h Good Friday, at Home alone.

Wednesday April 28 At Home alone. The Boys at the Grammar School rebelld Locking their Master out of the School & afterwards left their Master's House in Triumph. NB This was done entirely by the master's Boarders, abt 45 in Number. Only 4 remain'd in the School, the rest all dispersd to their own Homes or Relations. The Town Boys had no concern in this Rebellion.[38]

Thursdy April 29 ... NB the Governors met this morning at [the] School Hall Chamber at 11 O'Clock, heard the Master's Complaint, examin'd 4 Boys & dismiss'd Geo Plampin & [blank] Sparrow.*

Fridy April 30 At Home alone. NB School opend again & all promisd to go on orderly.

[During April and May the Oakeses had visits from various friends including Miss Routh, the girls' old governess. In June Charlotte returned home from school and the coachman sold the little grey mare in Newmarket for £7.]

Thursday June 17 I set off to London with Mr Buck to attend Parliament in order to get our Bill thro the House appointg Inspectors for the regulation of the Suffolk yarn. I lodg'd at Houghton's. We attended Mr Coldham['s] agents, Messrs Lyons, on Friday & Saturday, in preparing the Bill & on the Monday appeard before the Committee of the House of Commons at the 3d & last reading of sd

---

balloon which flew from the Artillery Ground in London to Standon in Hertfordshire on 15 September 1784.

38 That is to say boys from Bury itself. James Oakes Junior was a 'Town Boy'.

Bill. On the Tuesday & Wednesday attended to my own Business in Spittalfields &ca & return'd Home on the Thursday with an Intention of going again next week to attend the Commttee of the House of Lords.

Mondy June 28 I went up to London again in order to answer Interrogations before a Committee of the Lords which expected would have come on immediately. We were not sworn before the Lords till Thursday. I was obligd to attend &, not being able to take a place Home for 2 or 3 Days, I waited in Town the whole time . . . Our Business came on before the Lords on Monday abt 4 O'Clock.[39] Our Bill pass'd[40] & I took the Night Coach & got Home Tuesday morning 5 O'Clock. Miss Newman to continue with Us till after the Assizes.

Saturday July 10 I din'd at the Angel with Sr Charles Bunbury's Friends on a Turtle sent by Him. Abt 40 Gentlemen – 2/6 ordinary & 1/6 extra – Wines pd for by the partys as calld for. NB The Ladys at Tea with Mrs Holworthy.

Tuesdy July 13 Mr Shepherd came to spend the Day with Us. We all went up to St Edmund's Hill to drink Tea.[41] Suppd at Home: Mrs Norford & Mr Haggett. Mr Shepherd [went] by coach to Town at Night.

Tuesdy July 20 . . . Charlotte return'd to Town accompanied by Mr Adair.

Tuesday July 27 Went to Mr Symonds['s]: Bishop of Landaff (Dr Watson), his Lady & sister, Mrs Halsey, Mr, Mrs & Mr T.Senior, Mr & Mrs Leheup, Mr Young &ca, the French Noblemen.

Thursdy July 29** The General Thanksgiving Day for the Peace. Shops all shut up, not any of my Journeymen or Combers came to work till the Afternoon. Not any Illuminations or Fire works.

Tuesdy Aug 10 Our first County Meeting at Stowmarkett agreeable to our new Act of Parliament to choose a committee for carrying sd Act into Execution.[42] 36 Yarn Makers present, Mr Buck in the Chair, Mr Collett[43] attended. Return'd Home to sup. The Ladys went to Mr Symonds['s]. A very wet Day, very little Company. Mrs Bridge went with the Ladys.

Thursdy Septr 23 The first Quarterly Meeting of the Yarn Committee.[44] The 14 out of the 15 of the committee present & din'd at the Wool-Pack Inn. Elected 4

---

[39] During the second reading on 1 July 1784 the bill was committed to a committee made up of five peers and three bishops who were to meet the following Monday at ten in the morning in the Prince's Lodgings at Westminster. No record of this meeting survives. *Journal of the House of Lords (1783–87)*, XXXVII, p. 103.

[40] 24 Geo III c3 An Act for More Effectually Preventing Frauds and Abuses Committed by Persons Employed in the Manufactures of Combing Wool, Worsted, Yarn and Goods made from Worsted in the County of Suffolk.

[41] Dr Symonds's house, now Moreton Hall Preparatory School. It was designed by Robert Adam.

[42] Under the 1784 Act the committee were to choose two men, to be licensed by the Justices at Quarter Sessions as inspectors, & a clerk. The inspectors had wide ranging powers to search out abuses and to bring prosecutions.

[43] Clerk of the Peace for the County. He came from Westerfield, near Ipswich.

[44] Under the 1784 Act the Yarn Committee was to meet quarterly at Bury on the

Inspectors to be licens'd by the Justices at the ensuing Michlemas Sessions, viz: Benj Downs [The next two lines are left balnk.] We drank Tea & spent the Evening there.

Wednesday Sept 29   Fair proclaimd . . .

Fridy Oct 8   I bottled off my Butt of sherry . . .

Tues Octr 19   We were at the Play being Mr Barrett's Benefit. A little Disturbance owing to Mr Murray.

Friday Oct 29   I din'd at Sr Chas Bunbury's. Met Mr Symonds & Monr Rochfaucauld, drank Tea & return'd Home to sup.

Saturday Novr 13   We had a Ball & Supper at our own House: Mr Symonds & the French Gentlemen, Mrs, Mr & Miss Heigham & Harry D[itt]o, Miss Moyle, Dr & Mrs Norford, Mr & Mrs Probys, Mr Jas Norford – 9 Couple of Dancers. All left us between one & two O'Clock.

Mondy Novr 151784   I passd the whole Day at [the] Wool-Pack attending [the] Yarn Committee both din'd & suppd there. Did not get Home till one O'Clock this morning. Mrs O–, Maria & [the] Boys drank Tea & passd the Eveng at Mr Adamson. Met Mrs Heigham's Family.

Mondy Decr 20   We drank Tea & suppd at my Mother's . . . Dispos'd of Badby's Gift at [the] Guild Hall. Bot Mr Cullum's Corporation Note £25 for £20.

Tuesdy Decr 21st   Charlotte came Home.

[Christmas followed its usual pattern and the year ended with visits to the Grammar School boys' plays and another prolongued quarterly meeting of yarn makers for James Oakes.]

Fridy Janry 14   We gave a Ball at the Guild Hall: 13 dancing Ladys & 15 D[itt]o Gentm, in the whole abt 36 or 38. Supp'd in the Council Chamber [and] departed between 2 & 3 o'Clock. Sr Patrick & Miss Blake, Mr J.Plampin & 2 other Gentm from Langham, Mr Heigham, Miss Cullum, Mrs Vernon, Miss Moyle, Miss Symonds &ca &ca.

	£	[s.	d.]
The Amot of all Charges	9	18	
2 Violins & Tabor	1	—	–6
19 Bott Wine	1	9	9
16 D[itt]o Hock Wine			
12 Bottle[s] Beer		6	—

Thursday before midsummer, the Thursday before Michaelmas, the Thursday before Epiphany and the Thursday before Easter at eleven in the morning.

Wednesdy Febry 2 I went to London with Charlotte, del'd her to Mr Davison's. I slept at Houghton's Bull Inn.

Fridy Febry 4 . . . went to the Play in the Evening, Drury Lane, & saw Mrs Sydons in Lady Macbeth.[45]

Saturday Febry 5 I drank Tea at Mr Davison's escorted the Miss Newmans & Charlotte to the Play at Covent Garden House 'The Follies of a Day'[46] & Rosina.[47] /Return'd Home & supp'd with Them./

Sundy Feb 6 I din'd at Mr Davison's & immediately after Dinner Carryd Charlotte Home to Campden House. Return'd to Tea at Mr Heaton's, supp'd at Mrs Grenside's.

Mondy Febry 7 . . . returnd Home by the Night Coach wch set out /for/ Yarmouth at six o'Clock & got Home at 6 o'Clock next morning.

Wednesdy Febry 9 . . . Lord Charles Fitzroy in Town & visited many Gentlemen of the Corporation. At Home alone.

Thursdy March 3 Several of [the] principal Inhabitants met at the Guildhall & a Committee appointed (one of wch I was) to see Mr Palmer in the Eveng at Mr Maulkin's & hear his plan for the Mail Coach. 5 or 6 of the Committee at 6 o'Clock at Mr Maulkin's & was informd no Alteration could be made in the plan that at pres[en]t the Mail Coach could come no nearer than Newmarkett & we should have a By-post for our Bagg from thence. We reported the same next Day at Guildhall. The Family Drank Tea & suppd this Evening [at] Mr Adamson's . . .

Saturday March 5 . . . Mrs O & Maria went to tea & pass the Evening at Mrs Heigham's quite in a Family way. NB In this week 21 Chald[ro]n of Coals were del[ivere]d out at the Guild Hall to [blank] Familys, some 1, some 2 & a few 3 Bush[els] each being a free Gift of the young Gentn of the Grammar School, the net profit aris[in]g from their Plays at Xmas.[48]

/Wednesday/ March 23 I was upon the Grand Jury, 23 prisoners. Not any Assembly being Passion Week. I din'd with the Judge.

Thursdy April 14 I rode over to Depden with Mr Thompson the Carpenter & plannd an Alteration in the House and determind to new roof the Head House with Tile. I return'd Home to Dinner. Mrs O & Family drank Tea & Supp'd at Mr Adamson's. I drank Tea with my Mother & followed Them to Mr A to sup.

Fridy April 22 At Home alone. Bottled a Pipe of Red Port.

---

[45] Eighteenth century productions of Shakespeare's plays were often severely adapted or re-written.

[46] *The Follies of a Day* or *The Marriage of Figaro* a comedy derived from de Beaumarchais first produced at Covent Garden in 1784.

[47] *Rosina* a comic opera first produced at Covent Garden in 1782.

[48] A note at the beginning of the entries for 1784 suggests that the boys took a total of £61 and, after expenses had been paid, made a profit of £35.

Mondy April 25 I din'd at the Angel by Invitation of Mr Heigham & Mr Creed being the Determination of a Wager. Present Mr Heigham, Mr Creed, Mr Adamson, Mr Patteson, Mr Dive, Mr Haggett & myself. <u>A great deal of wine drank in a little Time – the Consequence of which is very well known.</u>

Saturday the 30 At Home alone. NB The Grammar School Boys Complain'd to the Governors of ill Treatment receiv'd from Mr Laurents. It did not appear to the Governors as coming under their Cognizance.

Monday May 2d The Governors met at [the] School Hall Chamber [and] examin'd the Boys who complaind of their Master's unmerited severe Discipline. It appeard the Boys were innocent. The Master was accordingly admonish'd not to be guilty in future of such improper Treatment.

Thursday May 5 Mr Chambers & my Son return'd Home off their Journey.[49] They were absent just 19 Days & ½. Amo[un]t of Expences Includg Horse Hird for Mr C – Chaise £2 17 – & their Expences of Coach from Manchester to Liverpool & return 36/–, just abt £19 16 –.

Tue May 17 I went to Newmarkett wh Son James being Horse Fair Day. Breakfasted at the Ram & returnd Home to Dinner. Bot a brown little Horse for Daughter & Sons near 14 Hands high.

Thursday May 26 . . . Bot a Bay-mare of Mr Woodward £18 18 –. Prov'd Lame & returnd her.

Tuesday June 7 At Home alone. The only Evening I attended Mr Arden's Lectures. James Coachman left my Service <u>yesterday.</u>

Wednesday June 8 I went to Norwich in the Tunns Coach, slept at Mr Patteson's, return'd Home on Thursday. Came as far as Scole Inn in the Mail Coach & by Post Chaise from thence to Bury. Trade exceedingly bad in Norwich.

Saturday June 11 At Home. Henry Montague, who came on Tuesday on liking, I dischargd as unsuitable. Mr Adamson return'd Home.

Tuesday June 28 I set off for London with Charlotte & James. We left Charlotte that Evening at Mr Davison's. I & James had our Lodging at Houghton's Black Bull Leadenhall Street & were very comfortably accommodated.

Wednesday June 29 We saw the Balloon ascend with a Lady & Mr Biggin in the Rotunda in St George's Fields. Din'd at the Black Bull, drank Tea & took a ride wh Miss Jane Newman in the Evening.

Thursday June 30 1785 Breakfasted at Mr Davison's. Saw the Tower with James & Charlotte, attended Business, returnd & din'd at Houghton's. Went to Asshleys Amphitheatre in the Evening.[50]

---

[49] They had left for Yorkshire and Lancashire on 16 April 1785.

[50] In the eighteenth century, as today, the Tower of London was one of the sights of London. It housed the Mint, the armoury and a zoo which, by this time, contained lions, leopards, tigers, wolves, hyenas, bears, monkies and eagles. Astleys 'hippodramas' were the precursor of the circus; next to the site of the present Saint Thomas's Hospital.

Friday July 1 Breakfasted & din'd at Mr Davison's. James & I went to the Theatre in the Hay-Market in the Evening [and] saw the Separate Maintenance & the Son in Law.[51]

Saturday July 2d Breakfasted with Mr Edge, went to Westminster Abbey &ca &ca, din'd at St Clement's Coffee House, drank Tea at Mr Davison & accompanied Miss Jane Newman & Charlotte to Vauxhall.[52]

Sundy July 3 I carried Charlotte to Campden House. James & I returnd to dine at Mr Ainge's & drank Tea there. Supp'd at the Black Bull.

Monday July 4 Breakfasted at Mr Davison's, attended Business, din'd at the Black Bull. Took the Yarmouth Coach at 6 this Evening & got Home abt 6 O'Clock in the Evening.[53] James had a Tooth extracted at 3 O'Clock by Mr Beardmore just before we left London.

Tuesday July 19 I rode over in the morning to Depden. A most remarkable Thunder Storm abt 2 O'Clock & a heavy fall of Hail-Stones in & about Bury. Many that measurd one Inch & ½ in Circumference. Cart Loads were to be seen in Shaker Lane . . . some days after. At Home alone.

Tuesday Augst 9 1785 Mrs O –, Daughter, Self & Maid Servt all set out in my own Coach for Liverpool. Mr RA['s] Horses drew us to Kennet Bell, my Horses to Cambridge & wh a p[ai]r of Leaders to Huntingdon. From thence we took 4 Post Horses & reachd Kettering that Night. The next Night we slept at Leek & got to Bror Bridge's abt ½ hour after 6 O'Clock Thursday Evening. We could only get one Stage done /by/ a p[ai]r of Hack Horses – 4 Horses Cost 1/9 p[er] mile — Turnpikes, Postillions & Expences for 4 upon the road from 7d. to 9[d.] p[er] mile viz: from 2/4 to 2/6 p[er] mile. We continued at Liverpool from the Thursday Eveng augst 11 to Saturday Morng Sept 2d, just 23 Days & passd our Time very happily havg continual Engagements with Company at Home & Abroad.

Its computed there are upwards of 50,000 Inhabitants at Liverpool. It has been a wonderful, flourishing & encreasing place, tho not by any means reckon'd so opulent as [a?] place as Manchester.

We left Liverpool Saturday morng Sept 3d & got that Evening to Mr Thos Edge's, King Street, Manchester, where we continued till Wednesday morning followg, Sept, 7 & pass'd our time very agreably amongst our Relations. On Wednesday Night Sept 7 we slept at Derby, Thursday Night at Huntingdon & arriv'd safe & well at Home Friday at 3 O'Clock to Dinner. My own Horses drew us from Cambridge to Kennet Bell & Mr Adamson's from thence to Bury. From Liverpool to Manchester we p[ai]d 36 Miles, from Manchester to Cambridge we p[ai]d for 155 Miles, from D[itt]o to Bury 26 – in all 181 Miles from Man[cheste]r to Bury.

Building goes forward at an amazing Rate at Manchester. There is a Street or

---

[51] *The Son-in-Law*, a comic opera in three acts by John O'Keefe (1747–1833).
[52] Vauxhall Gardens were London's oldest pleasure grounds. They occupied 12 acres of land opposite Westminster Abbey, on the other side of the river, and were open to all for one shilling or a silver guinea season ticket.
[53] Oakes must mean *morning* here.

two new building wherein some Houses will lay the Occupiers in from 3 to 400 Rent annually.

			[£	s.	d.]
We pd Post Horses 4	360 miles	[at] 2/4	42		
Includg all Expences	67	[at] 1/0	3	7	
Own Horses & Mr A['s horses]					
	427 miles		£ 45	7	——
Sundry Other Expences, say 15			15		

Orbell & James liv'd with their Grandmother during our Absence.

Wed Sept 14
Thurs Sept 15   At Home alone high busy these 4 Days in taking Acc[oun]t of
Fri Sept 16   Stock.
Sept 17 Saturday Mr Poole suppd with Us this Eveng & my Sorters had their Frolick with [the] Servants &ca. 1pt Rum, 1 Bottle of Brandy & 18 Bottles of Old Beer, a Tongue, piece of Beef roast & left cold with Apple Pyes for Supper.

Thursday Oct 6 1785 I took my Place as Chief Magistrate.[54] My Dinner was at the Guild Hall. Abt 100 Gentn & Tradesmen dind with Me, amongst whom were the Duke of Grafton, Sr Charles Davers &ca.

Port drank	9 Doz		3 Bottles
Sherry	2		4 D[itto]
Lisbon	2		1
Clarett			4
Hock			7
Madiera	1		
Rumm			1
Brandy			1
Amo[unt]	15		9
Old Beer D[itto]	10		11 Bot

Abt 50 supp'd & all departed at 12 O'Clock.

Saturday Oct 15 1785 The Town remarkably full. Mr Poole ascended exactly at two O'Clock in his Balloon and was up in the air One hour & 20 minutes descending at Monk Soham abt 27 miles from hence. He return'd to Bury at 12 at Night & was three times drawn round the Cross by the populace.

We all dind at Mr Adamson's. Met Mr & Mrs Creed, Mrs Herring, Mr Robt Herring, Miss Herring & my Mother. The Ladys & most of the Gentlemen to the Play – most astonishingly full this Eveng.
NB Mr Poole imagines he might be abt 2 miles ¾ in Height. [See book jacket and plate 19.]

---

54 That is to say the Alderman or Mayor of Bury.

Saturday Oct 22 The Alderman & Corporation Play – we bespoke the new Comedy of 'Ill tell you what'.[55] The Box's in general very full, a thin Pitt. The Play universally admird. /Bottld off pipe/ of old Beer. The Poor Soldier[56] for the Entertainment.

Sunday Octr 23 1785 We all din'd at Mr Adamson's, drank Tea & supp'd with Him. My Mother not being well I pass'd an hour or two with her in the Evening & drank my Tea.

Wednesday Oct 26 The Ladys at the Play, a Benefit for the last Night of Performing in Town. (Mrs L– left Mr L–).

[The Oakeses' Fair guests left and during the next two months James Oakes went on business to Norwich and London, paid a visit to Wereham with his wife and elder daughter, dined with Sir Charles Bunbury and the Duke of Grafton amongst others, attended a yarn makers' committee meeting and the first sub-scription ball notable for having 'London musick' costing seven guineas. Several dinner parties were held at Guildhall Street.]

[January opened unusually quietly with very few social engagements apart from the third subscription ball, the Guildhall Feoffment annual dinner and the yarn makers' quarterly meeting. James and Orbell spent three days at Wereham with their Grandfather and Aunt.]

Tuesday Janry 24th The 1st meeting at [the] Guildhall to promote Sunday Schools not above 14 or 15 Inhabitants present. Adjournd to this Day fortnight. I this Day invited the Clergy & Justices to dine with me in order to make the Catalogue,[57] present: Sr Charles Davers, Mr Godbold, Mr Mathew, Dr Mills, Mr Sharp, Mr Craske, Mr Adamson, Mr Wennerquist, Mr Haggett, Miss Moyle staid till 9 O'Clock.

Thursday Febry 16 Miss Symonds['s] Ball. Abt 43 Ladys & Gentlemen, 16 couple of Dancers, only one card Table. The Ladys all set down first at Supper at ½ hour /after 11/, hot Soups, Turkey & Chickens, everything besides cold. The Gentlemen suppd after the Ladys at one O'Clock. Dancd again & continued till 3 when all the Company broke up.

---

[55] I'll Tell You What, a comedy in five acts by Mrs Elizabeth Simpson Inchbald (1753–1831).
[56] The Poor Soldier, a comic opera in two acts by George Colman the younger (1762–1836).
[57] The list of those to give the weekly lecture at the two Bury Churches.

Wednesday   1st March At Home alone.
               2
               3
               4   The weather provd very severe [and we] were obligd
to go to Woodbridge wth 4 Horses.

Thursday March 23 Attended the Judge to Church & to [the] Shire-Hall to
answer to my Name as Alderman. [I was] not upon the Jury. I din'd at Mr
Adamson's to meet Messrs Everards from Lynn & Mr Houchen. We all went to
the Assembly in the Evening – abt 80 Ladys & Gentlemen – abt 15 Couple of
Dancers, 5 Card Tables. [There was] a great want of Ladys, scarce 30 Ladys in the
room & could hardly make 15 dancing Ladys.

Mondy April 10 (Passion Week) Messers Troughton, Webb & Jno Taylor,
Delegates from the Norwich Combers, came here in their way from Norwich to
London in order to attend a general Meeting of the Woolen Manufacturers at
the Crown & Anchor Tavern in the Strand, Mr Anstie in the Chair. I din'd with
them at the Wool–Pack wh 5 of our Yarn Committee, pass'd an hour wh them &
they set off on their way. They wrote our Committee & wish'd to have a
Deputation from hence in order to assist in forming an Act to prevent [the] illicit
Exportation of wool. We excusd Ourselves for the pres[en]t, intendg to call a
general meeting of the Trade as soon as their Resolution appears.

Mondy April 17 I din'd with the Leet at the Bell, 22 at Dinner. Attended the
Vestry meeting for electing Church Wardens. Return'd Home to Tea.

Saturday April 22 At Home alone. Receiv'd a special Message from Wereham
abt 6 O'Clock advising that my Father Adamson was exceedingly bad & that it
was apprehended he could not continue long.

Sundy April 23rd Mrs EO, Self & Maria set out early this morning for Wereham. Got to Brand[on] by Breakfast & to Wereham by one O'Clock [and] found
/my Father/ Adamson extremely bad. Upon my seeing him I said I came just time
enough to see him in his last Moments.*** He expir'd exactly at ¼ hour after 9
O'Clock this Evening.***

Mondy April 24 1786 We gave [the] necessary orders & returnd home this
Evening.

[James Oakes organized the funeral which took place at Wereham on 1 May with
James Oakes, Richard Adamson, Orbell Oakes, James Oakes junior and Mr
Heaton as mourners.]

On Saturday April 8h 1786 Mr Chambers & my Son Orbell set out in a one
Horse Chaise on their Journey thro' part of Yorkshire, Lancashire from thence to
Kiddr[minster] in Worcestershire & Home thro' Coventry. They completed their
Journey in 19 Days & I observe their Expences p[er] Day abt 17/–, vizt: 7/– for
each of themselves & 3/– their Horse.

Thursday May 25 I went up to London, lodg'd at the Black Bull.

Fridy May 26 1786 Attended the Wool Delegates at the Crown & Anchor
Tavern, din'd with Them, to prevent the illicit Exportation of wool.

Mondy May 29 Attended the Wool Meeting again. Went at 11 O'Clock at Night to Ranelagh,[58] return'd to sup at Mr Davison's.

Tuesday May 30 Finish'd my Business in Town in attending a third Meeting of the Delegates.

Wednesday May 31 Return'd to Bury with Charlotte. Mr Thoytes took a part of a Post Chaise with Us to Sudbury. [We] set out from Town at ½ hour after 11 O'Clock & got home by ¼ after nine at Night.

Mondy June 5 Licencing Day at the Angel,[59] very few at Dinner. [The] Town Clerk could not attend being confind wh the Gout. The Rose & the White Hart were refused their Licences.

The King's Birth Day kept. We summonsd the Corporation to drink his Majesty's Health but not ½ Doz of the Corporation attended.

[James Oakes went to Wereham twice in June to supervise the auction of his father-in-law's property, to Norwich on business and to inspect his mother's property at Depden. Miss Routh, Maria's governess, came to stay.]

Fridy June 23 1786 I had dinner Company, nine Gentlemen of the Corporation din'd with me: Mr Cocksedge, Mr Spink, Mr Johnson, Mr Mills, Mr Maulkin, Mr Hustler, Mr Garnham, Mr Barwick, Mr Buchanan. Mr Hustler & Mr Haggett drank Tea & all left us between 8 & 9 O'Clock.

Sundy June 25 We all din'd and drank Tea & supp'd at Mr Adamson's. Mr Haggit taken with a violent fit of coughing at Mr Adamson's between 7 & 8 O'Clock in the Eveng & supposd to have burst a small blood vessell.

Monday July 3 1786 At Home alone. Mr Geo Haggit returnd to Cambridge, Mr TH[60] continud mend[in]g. Miss Newman & Mr Caswell to S——d.[61]

Wednesday July 12 Mr Walker's 2d Lecture, Mrs O & Self attended. I went to the Wool-Pack Inn & passd the Eveng, 7 of us there [at the] Yarn Committee Club.

Monday July 17 At Home alone. I suppd & spent the Evening at the Wool Packet with the Corporation.

Tuesday July 18 We all went to Mr Symonds['s] to Tea, abt 23 Ladys & Gentlemen. Orbell to Yarmouth.

Saturdy July 22 1786 . . . at 6 O'Clock I attended the Hall summonsd by me to fill up the Corporation. Mr Jno Garnham elected into the upper House, Messrs Jno Cooke, Jacob Kendall, Reuben Sturgeon & Jas Hailstone Burgesses of the Common Council & all this Business done in less than 2 Hours without one

---

[58] Ranelagh Pleasure Gardens were in Chelsea and were considered more grand than those at Vauxhall.
[59] The day on which the inns of Bury were licensed.
[60] Thomas Haggitt.
[61] Scotland?

24. *Memorial to Christopher and Elizabeth Adamson, James Oakes's parents-in-law, in Wereham Church.*

dissenting voice. I adjournd to the Wool Pack with about 19 others were [where?] we pass'd a very pleasant Evening.

Monday July 31   I went to Norwich in [by?] Coach at Night. Trade extreme bad.

[The Summer Assizes began on 4 August and Oakes was on the Grand Jury. He and his wife went to the Assize Assembly.]

Tuesday Aug 15   The General Meeting of the Manufacturers & Dealers in Wool at [the] King's Head, Stowmarket, to take into Consideration the Bill pend[in]g in Parliament for the prohibiting the smuggling of wool, false wind[in]g &ca. 24 Traders present. Approvd sd Bill & commencd a Subscription, return'd Home at 11 O'Clock at Night.

Wednesday Augst 23rd   I went at Noon to Campden House to see Charlotte Dance. From thence took her to dine at Mr & Mrs Caswell's, little Chelsea. Returnd home with her after Tea and repair'd to the Black Bull to sup.

Thursdy Augst 24   I din'd at Mr Davison's, drank Tea & supp'd at Mr Wm Haggitt's, West Ham, & return'd Home by Norwich Coach that Night.

Friday Septr 29 1786   At Home at Dinner. A meeting of the Corporation; an address unanimously resolvd to congratulate his Majesty on his providential Escape from an attempt made on his Life by an Insane woman, Nicholson.[62] The Alderman desird to affix the Corporation Seal & Deliver sd address to the Representatives of the Borough & request their presentment of the same to his Majesty the next Levee Day. Other business done. The Fair proclaim'd. NB Not any Address from this Corporation since the Year 1762 on the Birth of the Prince of Wales.

[Sir Charles Davers presented the address and received the official thanks of the Corporation from Oakes. Alderman Garnham took his place, followed by three weeks of the Fair, with the usual round of assemblies, plays, dinner and supper parties. At the end of October James Oakes went to London on business combining it with a visit to Charlotte.]

Fridy Novr 3   At Home Alone. Mr Haggett elected Town Clerk &ca unanimously.

Saturdy Nov 14th   At Home alone. Mr Haggett receiv'd a Letter from the Duke of Grafton appointg Him Clerk to the General & Subdivision Meeting of Militia.*

Sundy Novr 5 1786   Mr Adamson & Mr Wennerquist din'd with Us & Mr Haggitt. We drank Tea at my Mother's, She being Confin'd to the House with Gout. Suppd at Home.

Mondy Nov 27   I went with my two Sons to Cambridge in order to admit Son James at Trinity College. We set up at the Bear [and] Messrs H.Heigham, G.Mathew, R,Spurgeon & J.Borton all din'd with Us. We spent the Evening at Dr Symonds['s] Rooms. Mr Humphry met us.

Tuesday Novr 28 1786   We breakfasted at Mr Henry Heigham's Rooms. Son James was examin'd by Mr Collier, his intended Tutor, the Dean &ca & was admitted with the usual Form at Trinity. We return'd home to tea this Afternoon.

---

[62]   The King was attacked as he stepped from his carriage in Saint James's by a domestic servant, Margaret Nicholson, who attempted to knife him. She was later found to be mad.

Fridy Decr 15 1786 Mrs Oakes, Maria, Mr Haggett & Self all went to Mr Collett's of Westerfield. Only stoppd for a quarter of an Hour at the King's Head, Stow[marke]tt & went forward & got to Mr Collett rather before 4 O'Clock.

Saturdy Decr 16 I attended a Deputy Lieutenants' Meeting at Ipswich with Mr Collett & Mr Haggett. . .

Sundy Decr 17 I rode over to Woodbridge to have some talk with Thos Scot, went to Church & returnd to Mr Collett's to dinner. (Miss Ray died.)

Mondy Decr 18 1786 We all went to Ipswich & made some visits, return'd to Mr Collett's to dinner.

Tuesdy Decr 19 We all return'd Home, Mr Adamson's Horses met us & we got home by 4 O'Clock Dinner – all well. (Miss Heigham married Geo. Haggitt.)

Mon Janry 1 1787 I went wth Mr Haggitt to Euston & din'd at the Duke of Grafton's. Met [the] Bishop of Peterborough & Miss Hinchcliffe, Mr Symonds &ca &ca.

Fridy Janry 5 I accompanied Mr Haggett to a general Meeting of Deputy Lieutenants at the King's Head Stow[marke]tt. Met Mr Brook, Mr Stisted, Mr Grigby, Mr Revett, Mr Godbold. Enterd into certain Resolutions respecting the new Militia Act & return'd home to sup.

Tuesdy Janry 16 Accompanied Mr Symonds to Euston, dind & slept at the Duke of Grafton's & returnd home on Wednesday morng.

Wednesday Janry 17 Tea & Supper Company at home. . . Thursdy Janry 18 I dind at the Angel with the Corporation at spending the Forfeitures, only 19 prest.[63] First acct of Fenn's Illness.**

Fridy Janry 19 Lord Charles Fitzroy waited upon all the Corporation requesting their Votes in Case Captn Fitzroy should vacate his [seat] in Parliament. We drank Tea & pass'd the Evening at Mrs Heigham's. Met Mr & Mrs Leheup, Mr Adamson. Our young People were all there.

Mondy Janry 22 I rode over to see Sr Charles Davers. At Home alone.

Wednesday 24th At Home alone. School Hall Meeting [to] choose a new Comptroller & 6 new Governors: Sir Thos Cullum, Mr Godbold, Dr Norford, Mr Spink, Mr Hasted, Mr Mathew. New writ movd for in Parliament for a Member for the Borough in Lieu of Captn Fitzroy.

---

63 Forfeits paid by members of the Corporation who refused office.

Sundy Janry 28 . . . we all dind at Mr Adamson's, at Home Tea & Evening. I attended the Sunday Schools this Day.

Mondy Janry 29 <u>Writ came down to the Alderman.</u> At Home alone. Mr Chambers returnd from Norwich.

Sundy Febry 4 Lord Charles Fitzroy, Sr Thos Cullum, Mr Adamson, Mr Wennerquist & Mr Haggitt all dind & suppd with Us after Church in the Afternoon.

Mondy Febry 5 Day of Election of Lord Charles Fitzroy in the stead of Captn Geo. Ferdinand Fitzroy who accepted the Chiltern Hundds. This Election was unanimous his Lordship was Chair'd [and] afterwards gave a genteel Entertainment to the Corporation & other Gentlemen to the Number of abt 60 at the Angel. In the Evening a genteel Ball at the Assembly House at which were present abt 250 Ladys & Gentlemen, a[bou]t 50 Couple of Dancers. The Ball broke up abt 3 or 4 O'Clock. His Lordship distributed to the Amot of £50 Favours, 6 H[ogs]h[ead]s of Beer to the Populace – 5 guineas in Silver to them out of the Angel windows & abt 3 Guineas & 1/2 to the Prisoners at the Gaol.

Wednesday Febry 7 Land Tax Meeting at the Angel – <u>acct rec[eiveld of the Death of Mr Fenn Receiver General of the Land Tax for the Western</u> Division – <u>he died Tuesday Eveng ten O'Clock.</u>* I rode over to Euston & return'd home by 5 O'Clock.

Friday Febry 16 <u>Recvd from the Duke of Grafton Mr Pitt's Letter of my appointment to the General Receivership of the Western Division.</u>*

Saturdy Febry 17 I breakfasted at Euston, returnd home between 11 & 12 O'Clock. Mrs Haggitt came to Bury.

Saturdy Febry 24 At Home alone. The Scheme fixd for Mr Haggitt's going to Bristol.[64]

Mondy Febry 26 I went to London in a Post Chaise with Mr Garnham. It cost us £2 6 8d. each. I passd the Evening at Mr Davison's.

[James Oakes visited Abraham Newman's son-in-law, Mr Caswall, and his wife's cousin, Mr Heaton, before returning to Bury.]

Mondy March 5 Mr Haggitt & his Mother set off at ten O'Clock for Mr Wm Haggitt's at Westham on their way to Bristol.* At Home alone.

Wednesdy March 7 1787 Self & Son Orbell went to Norwich on Horseback, dind at the Maid's Head, supp'd at Mr Patteson's.

Fridy March 9 Breakfasted at Mr Rd Gurney, din'd at Attleburgh in our way Home – suppd at Home.

Mondy March 12 Mr Bailey came as my clerk.* At Home alone.

---

[64] He was going to take the waters.

Tuesday March 27 1787 At Home.* Bror & Sister Bridge & Family came to Bury. The two eldest Daughters made our House their Home.[65] We suppd at my Mother's. Mrs O, Maria, Charlotte & Miss Scholey all drank Tea at Mr Kedington's of Rougham.

Fridy April 13 Company at Tea & Supper at Home. . . 19 of us all together.

Saturdy April 14 At Home alone. My Pallisades before my House completed.

Mondy April 16 The first Day of my Receipt at Sudbury. Bror Bridge accompanied me. We all return'd Home at Night.*

Wednesdy April 18h My 2d Day's Receipt at Home.

Fridy April 20th My 3d Day's Receipt at Clare. Home at 7 O'Clock in the Evening.

Mondy April 23 My 4th Day's Receipt at [the] White Lyon Eye. Got home abt 8 O'Clock in the Evening. Mr Haggit died this Evening at Bristol just abt 5 O'Clock.

Wednesday April 25h Militia Meeting – At Home alone.

Thursdy April 26h My 5th Day's Receipt at Stowmarkett. Home at 7 O'Clock.

Mondy April 30 I was confin'd with an Erysypilas.

Wednesday May 2 Mr Chambers went to Norwich. Sister Baker came to my Mother's from Cawston.

Tuesdy May 8 At Home alone. Mr Jenkins elected Town Clerk in the stead of Mr Haggitt.

Wednesdy May 9 Militia Meeting, swore on abt 70 & ballotted for 260.

Thursdy May 17 Yarn Committee Meetg. Mr & Mrs Stanniforth from Norton din'd with Us. Mr Reuben Sturgeon & Miss Perkins married.*

Fridy May 18 1787 Militia Meeting, swore on abt 200. Dind at the Angel with the Major, Adjutant & Captn Bird.

Saturdy May 19 Militia Meeting, ballotted for 100. At Home alone.

Mondy May 28 . . . Militia meetg. Mr Collett came & supp'd with us. Bror Baker came from Cawston.

Tuesdy May 29 At Home alone. the Militia embodied.

Fridy June 1 The Family all din'd, drank Tea & suppd with Us, 19 in Number.

[The Bakers returned to Cawston on 2 June and the Bridges to Liverpool the following week.]

Thursday June 14 Bottled off a Pipe [of] Red Port. . .

---

[65] The rest of the Bridge Family were staying with Mrs Oakes senior.

Fridy June 15 Bottled off a Pipe [of] Old Beer. I dind at Mr Adamson's. Met the Militia Officers, Mr Blachley, Mr Blomfield, Mr Bird & Mr Bloom. I left abt 6 O'Clock & went to Tea & Supper at Mrs Denton's with my Family. . .

Thursdy June 21 The Quarterly Yarn Committee Meeting, 7 of us. Returnd home to Tea.

Fridy June 23 I had the Officers of the Militia to dine with Me: Lord Euston, Coll Shutz, Coll Moyle, Mr Adamson. All staid till 8 O'Clock.

Sundy June 24 My Day of attendance on the Sunday Schools. My Mother din'd wth Us. Mr Adamson had the Officers of Militia dind wth Him. I went to Them at 6 O'Clock.

Mondy June 25 1787 . . .Militia disembodied.

Wednesday June 27 . . .Maine the Clerk died.

Mondy July 30 At Home alone. Mr Wm Haggitt came here to settle his Brother's Affairs. NB Mr Chinery went to Ipswich for me & pd Mr Canning £2,200 for [the] Harkstead Living.[66]

Monday Augt 6 Meeting in the Morning at the Angel relating to the intended Turnpike meeting from Brand[on] to Bury. In the Afternoon a Corporation meeting to fill up the Vacancy in the lower House.[67] Mr Wm Mathew nominated by Alderman Garnham & seconded by Mr Spink; Mr Thos Singleton nominated by Mr Jos. Maulkin and seconded by Mr Bullen. On the Pole Mr Singleton had a Majority in the lower House & a Majority at length. Mr Wm Mathew had a Majority only in the upper House. The Alderman by the advice of the Recorder declard it to be a void Election & thus the Business terminated.

Thursday Aug 9h Yarn Committee adjournd meeting,[68] 6 of us present. Finishd Business by Tea. This Evening [there was] a very sever Tempest wch lasted from 10 O'Clock to 3 next morng with incessent Lightning. A good deal of Damage done but not within 14 miles of Us.

[James returned from a stay in Liverpool with his Aunts and Orbell from a month in Yarmouth. The Caswalls came to stay.]

Saturdy Sept 15 At Home alone. Mr Caswall & Orbell went to Depden for a days shootg.

Saturdy Sept 22 We finishd Stocking this Day by Dinner. . . This Evening the Men had their Hawkey and havg 3 Servt more in [the] Family[69] I allowd them 20 Bottles of Old Beer, one Quart Brandy & one pint of Rum, a large pi[e]ce of cold roast Beef, a p[i]ec[e] of boild Beef and Apple Pyes. . .

---

[66] The Rev. Richard Canning was the incumbent of Harkstead.
[67] The Common Council.
[68] The committee held on 11 July 1787 had been without a quorum because only four members were present.
[69] The Caswalls and the Greens brought their own servants with them.

Mondy Sept 24 At Home alone. Sister Green & Daughter left Bury on their return to Liverpool. They went in a post Chaise as far as Cambridge with Miss Apsey this Evening.

Tuesdy Sept 25 I went to Sturbitch.[70] Mr & Mrs Caswall, my Daughter Maria & two Sons all accompanied me [in] a Post Chaise & my Phaeton. We all return'd home in the Evening, Breakfasting as we went at the Ram, Newmarkett, din'd at the Rose, Cambridge, drank Tea at the Ram & suppd at home.

Wednesdy Sept 26 We all din'd at Sir Walter Rawlinson's, drank Tea & returnd home to sup. Met Mr & Mrs Orbell Ray.

Mondy Oct 1st I drove Mr & Mrs Caswall to Newmarket in my Phaeton. Son James went with us. We saw 9 Races, much Sport & a good deal of Company. We all dind at Potters at the Ram at 5 O'Clock, Captn Wathes & Captn Dive with Us, & returnd home to sup abt ½ hour after 9 O'Clock. Mrs Barnard died this Day.*

[The Caswalls stayed on for the Fair and were joined by Mrs Caswall's sister, Miss Newman, and the Harveys from Norwich. The Michaelmas Receipt coincided with the last nine days of the Fair.]

Mondy Oct 29 I went to Cambridge with my Son James where he was to reside as a Student in Trinity College. Not being able to procure Rooms in the College he took up wh Lodgings at Mr Sharp's in Greek St. I procurd & pd for what furniture he was in immediate want of on Tuesday morng & returnd Home the same Afternoon. (Mr & Mrs Baker brot Betsy.)[71]

Thursdy Novr 15 Yarn Committee Meeting, 7 of us present. Much Business detaind [us] from 11 till 9 in the Evening. Commencd a second Subscription to prevent the illicit Exportation of wool.

Sundy Dec 23 Mr Adamson & my Mother din'd with us. This Day a Sermon was preachd by Dr Knowles in Behalf of the Sunday Schools to raise a fund for rewarding the Children wh some necessary p[ai]rs of cloathing.

At St Mary's in the morng	13	14	–
At St James's in the Afternoon	16	13	6
	30	7	6

Mr Le G[ri]ce preachd at St James in the morng in Opposition.*

Mondy the 24 At Home alone. A Corporation [meeting?] for the disposing of Badby's Gift. A vote of Thanks to Dr Knowles for his Sermon & a request to publish the same.

Tuesdy the 25 Xmas Day The Corporation went to St Mary in the Morng & St James's in the Afternoon to hear Dr Knowles. We all dind & drank Tea & suppd at my Mother's wh Mr Adamson. My Sorters & Workmen as usual dind at my House.

---

70 Stourbridge Fair.
71 James Oakes's neice, Elizabeth Baker, from Cawston.

Dinner	Supper
4 Maid Servt	7 own Family
2 Men	3 Mr Smith Family
3 Warehousemen	2 Wm Hill & Wife
7 Sorters	2 Jas Hill & Wife
3 Women	2 Amb Taylor & Wife
Mrs Smith Mrs Allin Mrs Seal	1 Thos Scot's Wife
Thos Scot's Wife Himself at	1 Bailey
Woodb[ridge]	

16

David Shadow
Baileys
3 Mr & Mrs Smith & Son
26 Should have been Wm Wright

For Dinner
A Sr Loin Beef	26 ld
Legg of mutton	11 ld
Plumb Puddings	8
Mincd Pyes	30
Old Beer	14 [bottles?]

Supper
Cold Beef
two large Apple Pyes
4 Bottles Old Beer
1 d[itt]o Brandy
1 Pint Rum

A very sever[e] heavey fall of snow.

Wednesdy Decr 26 1787 A continued fall of Snow. Horse sent to Ipswich to meet the Cart. At home alone.

Thursdy Decr 27 At home alone. Weather continued bad, Roads unpassable. The second Subscription Ball at the Angel: no Country Company could come to the Town. Abt 45 Ladys & Gentlemen, only 9 couple of Dancers.

Thursdy Janry 3d I attended the Yarn Committee Quarterly Meeting, 8 of us prest. I was Chairman. The Factors' Treat of Supper & Wine. I passd the Evening there: ½ dozen of us.

Fridy Janry 4 Mr Beecher elected Head Master of the Grammar School unanimously. Mr Pratt from Norwich stood as a Candidate but not one vote. . .

Tuesdy 8   Went from Eye to Stowmarkett & receiv'd there and return'd home to Tea. Mr Priest resignd the Undermastership of the School. Dance at Mrs Hasted's.

Thursdy Janry 10   I receiv'd at the White Horse Wickhambrook,[for?] the first [time the receipt?] being now removd from Clare. Return'd Home to Tea.

Sundy Janry 20   Robt Adamson & my Mother din'd with Us. Mr Charles Harvey came likewise to the Sessions & din'd with Us. I went to Euston wth Son James & din'd at the Duke of Grafton's, Sr Thos & Lady Cullum from Bury. Met Mr, Mrs Adean, Mr Greaves. In the Family Lord & Lady Euston, Lord Charles, Lord Henry & Lord Frederick, Coll White, Captn Fitzroy &ca. Returnd home to sup abt 10 O'Clock.

Mondy Janry 21st   Mr Adamson's Ball. . . a very Handsome Supper. We all got home abt one O'Clock.

Saturdy Janry 26   . . . son James got a Fall hunting.

Mondy Janry 28   Lord Charles Fitzroy waited on the Corporation, din'd & drank Tea with Me, also Sr Thomas Cullum.

Tuesdy Febry 2   I went to London with Maria & Maid Servt in [a] post Chaise, own Chaise carrd us to Sudbury, cost us [blank]. We arriv'd at Mr Caswall's (4 miles on the Stones) ¼ before 6 O'Clock. I drank Tea & suppd & left Maria there. Returnd myself to the Bull Inn Leadenhall Street.

Wednesdy Febry 13   Attended the Wool Delegates at the Crown & Anchor Tavern, Strand: between 30 & 40 Delegates from the different manufacturing Countys. Returnd to [the] Bull Inn at 10 O'Clock at Night.

Thursday Febry 14, 15, 16   Attended all these Days the same as Wednesday. On Saturday the 16 I attended Mr Hosier the Auditor wth Mr Addison to state our Acc[oun]ts.[72] We left Them & were desird to attend again on Tuesday. This Evening I went to the Opera in the Gallery with Mr Harvey, Mr Patteson & Mr Partridge. Got to the Bull Inn abt one O'Clock.

Wednesdy Febry 20   Return'd Home by the Bury Fly.

Thursdy Febry 21   Waited on Sr Charles Davers. . .

Tuesdy Febry 26   Orbell went to Cambridge to make his Bror a visit.

Fridy March 8   We were at Tea & Cards at Mr Hasted's. . . Home at Supper. Mr Chambers returnd from Norwich. By This morning's Post a Letter from Mr Anstie requiring my Attendance on the Wool-Bill in London.

Sundy Mar 9 1788   I set off for London abt 12 O'Clock in a post Chaise with Sir Charles Davers from Rushbrook. We got to Ingatestone, without baiting, where we Slept.

Tuesdy Mar 11   I went round to all the Suffolk Members informing Them the Report setting forth the Extent of the illicit Exportation of wool made before a

---

[72] James Oakes's accounts as the Receiver General for the Western Division of Suffolk.

Committee of the House would be deliverd in at the House of Commons as [on?] Friday next. I din'd, drank Tea at Mr Caswall's, returnd to Mr Davison's to sup & slept at Houghton's. [He returned to Bury next day with Maria & her maid who had been staying with the Caswalls.]

Saturdy March 22 1788   At Home alone. Attended a County Meeting calld by the Sheriff in order to petition Parliamt that the Slave Trade migh[t] be taken into the most serious Consideration. It was voted unanimously.

Sundy March 23 Easter Day   We all din'd at Mr Adamson's after Church in the Afternoon. Mr Partridge, Mr Jodderell & Mr Adair of the Party. We drank Tea & suppd wh him.

Thursdy May 8 1788   The Adjournd Meeting of the Yarn Committee at the Wool Packett. I staid with them till one O'Clock when I was oblig'd to leave Them being engagd at dinner. We all went & din'd with Mr & Mrs Patteson at Weston. Met Mr, Mrs & Miss Thurston. Got home by ten O'Clock.

Fridy May 9   We drank Tea with Mr & Mrs Gage at the Priory. Returnd Home to sup.

Sundy May 11   Whit Sunday. . . Mr Collett came to Us from Ipswich.

Mondy May 12 1788   The Militia were embodied here to be traind & exercizd for 28 Days. I din'd at the Angel with Lord Euston & the rest of the Officers & Mr Collett. Mr Collett suppd with Us.

Mondy May 20   I waited on his Grace of Grafton respecting the Wool Bill now passd the House of Commons & expected to be opposd in the House of Lords. I went to Westminster Hall to Mr Hasting's Tryal with Lord Chedworth's Tic-ketts.[73] Drank Tea & suppd with Miss Hovil, Queen's Square.

Wednesdy May 21   Attended the Wool Committee at the Crown & Anchor the whole Day. Suppd by myself at Houghton's Black Bull.

Thursdy May 22 1788   I went on my Business into Spitalfields the whole Day, din'd at Mr Davison, drank Tea at Mr Grenside's, suppd at Mr Davison's. This Day Mr Thoyts was married to Miss Jane Newman at 11 O'Clock & set off immediately for Brook House.[74]

Fridy May 23d   I attended the Duke of Grafton's again on the wool Business, also Lord Chedworth. Finishd my Business in Town & returnd Home by the Yarmouth Coach settg out at 6 O'Clock in the Evening & got home by six O'Clock next morng.

Tuesdy May 27   Bottled off a pipe of Red Port & took home a Pipe into my vault.

---

[73] Warren Hastings (1732–1818) first Governor General of India, was impeached in 1787 by the House of Commons for corruption as a result of political intrigue by the opposition to embarrass Pitt. The trial began on 13 February 1788 and lasted 145 days spread over seven years. Hastings was acquitted in April 1795.

[74] Brook House in Mount Bures, near Sudbury, was the Newmans' country house.

Wednesdy May 28 Mr Houchen at Bury at Mr Adamson's. I bot a mare of Mr Simpson, Wickhambrook, at £18 18 –.

Fridy June 6 Mr Collett came to Bury to settle the Militia acc[oun]ts, din'd with Us. Tea & Supper Company at Home: Dr & Mrs White, Mr & Mrs Jenkins, Mr & Mrs & Master Hasted.

Saturdy June 7 Mr Chambers & Mr Bailey set out on [their] Yorkshire Journey. Mr Collett Breakfasted with Us. [The] Militia disembodied. Sons at Mr Beecher's Tea & supper.

[On 16 June the Oakes family and Richard Adamson all went to Norwich for four days. They stayed with the Partridges and saw John Patteson take his place as mayor.]

Sundy June 22 My Mother dind with Us. Dr & Mrs White, Miss Moyle & my Mother all drank Tea with Us in the Tent in Cobs Orchard.

Wednesday July 9 A meeting of the Governors at the Grammar School to order the necessary Repairs. My Mother taken in a Fit ½ hour after 12 O'Clock in which she continued without Senses for nearly 3 hours & being in strong Convulsions was deprivd of the use of one Side. She began to recover abt 3 & in the course of a Day or two was perfectly restord.

Saturdy July 19 The Combers rode in Procession by way of rejoicing on the passing [of] the Bill for the more effectual preventing the smuggling of wool.[75] Mr Corsbie's & my Men were not of the Number we objecting to it on acc[oun]t of the melancholy & oppressd State of the Trade at this time. Maria, Charlotte and James all drank Tea at Dr Preston's, Rougham.

Sun July 20 We all dind at Mr Adamson's. Drank Tea at my Mother's. (Mr Legrice suspended.)[76]

Saturdy July 26 At Home alone. Bottled off a Pipe [of] Sherry at Captn Symons's [and] took Home my ¼ share.

Mondy Aug 4h Dr Baker canvassd many of the Corporation for their Votes[77] for the Lectureship of St James in the Place of Mr Le Grice who, being elected in the stead of Dr Wollaston who never gave up his Licence, & Mr Le Grice had never taken out a Licence, the Bishop thought proper to suspend him. This made a Re-election necessary. I accompanied Dr Baker. We soon found that many Gentlemen of the Corporation had previously engagd themselves to Mr Le Grice. This determin'd Dr Baker immediately to give up all Thoughts of it. We dind & supp'd at home.

Fridy Augt 8 Mrs O, Self, Maria, Charlotte & James all set out for Yarmouth taken [taking?] with Us one Maid Servt, Coachman & Footman with Coach & Horses & 3 saddle Horses. We set out at 7 in the Morng & got to Mr Spurgeon's

75 28 Geo III c38.
76 The incumbent of St James's Church in Bury.
77 The Corporation held the advowsons of both Churches in Bury and, therefore, appointed the incumbents.

at 8 O'Clock in the Evening. NB On Saturday Augt 9 came on at Bury the Election of a Lecturer for St James's when Dr Mills was unanimously appointed in the stead of Mr LeGrice.[78]

[The family staid in Yarmouth for twelve days being well entertained with plays, assemblies, calls and dinner parties.]

Wednesday Aug 20 We all din'd at Mr Adamson's on a Turbott I bro from Yarmouth. Met Mr & Mrs Creed, Mr Wm & Mr Jas Norford, returnd home to sup.

Thursdy Aug 21 1788 The Day of electing an Alderman for the ensuing year.* Several Gentlemen were of [the] Opinion Mr Norman ought to be elected & fin'd if he did not accept. However, it was at length over ruled & Mr Hasted unanimously elected. A large Dinner provided & very few to partake of it. Only Sr Charles Davers prest of the Assistant Justices of the Body. The Recorder at Cambridge & Mr Spink from home. I stai'd till Supper.

Sundy Aug 24 My Mother & Mr Adamson din'd with Us. I was very unwell with a complaint in my Bowells. Did not stir out the whole Day.

Mondy Augt 25 (Election of Guardians) I was better tho yet unwell. . .

Mondy Sept 1 I attended the Governors' meeting at the Hospital. Son Orbell shooting at Depden, son James at Mr Tyrrell's. Brot Home a Leash [of] Partridges. At Home alone.

Tuesdy Sept 2 1788 I went to Norwich with Son Orbell. . .

Wednesdy Sept 3d We breakfasted at Mr Smith's, din'd with Mr & Mrs Lacon at [the] Maid's Head, drank Tea at Mr Smith's. Orbell & Self at the Play, Venice Preservd[79] to see Mrs Siddons in the Character of Belvidera. House remarkably full. Suppd with Mr & Mrs Lacon at the Maid's Head. No possibility of doing any Business at Norwich.

Fridy Sept 5 1788 At Home alone. I was very ill wh a feverish Disorder.

Fridy Sept 12 Tea & Supper Company at Home. . . My Mother very indifferent all this week her Dropsical Complaint encreasing.

Saturdy Sept 13 Dinner Company at Home, the second Haunch of Venison of the Duke of G[rafton]. . . (Mr Hasted not well enough). All went away 9 O'Clock. Mr Jas Edge came to us this Eveng by coach.

Mondy Sept 15 I consulted wh Mr Spink respectg my enterg into the Banking Business.* At Home alone.

---

[78] The Rev. Charles Le Grice, Lecturer of Saint James's Church since 1778, was reported to Dr Bagot, Bishop of Norwich, for not having been licensed by him to preach. The Bishop refused to rectify the omission on the grounds that Le Grice was already Rector of Thwaite and of Wickhampton (Norfolk) and should live in his parish. He was removed from the Lectureship and the Rev. Edward Mills elected in his place.

[79] *Venice Preserv'd or A Plot Discover'd* by Thomas Otway (1652–85).

25. *John Spink (1728/9–94), by G. Ralph.*

Tuesdy Sept 16 Woolpit Horse Fair Day. I rode over in the morng & advisd with Mr Ray & Mr Moseley as to Mr Walpole's offer. Returnd Home to Dinner in the Eveng. Mrs O, Son James & Orbell went to St Edmund's Hill & drank Tea with Mr Symonds. No other Company. Returnd home to sup.

Sundy Sept 28 1788 We all dind at Mr Adamson's after Church in the Afternoon. Returnd home to sup. My Mother confind to her dining Room.

Mondy Sept 29 We went to Newmarkett with Mr Edge, Mr & Mrs Creed, George Green [in] my Coach & Post Chaise [for] the 1st Day of hos Races. We all din'd at the Ram ab 4 O'Clock. Returnd home soon after 8 O'Clock. All Expences together Cost £4– nine of Us divided into 4 Parts ea[ch] 20/–.

Thursday Oct 2 ***** My Mother a very restless Night but would rise & be dressd in the morning & laid on her Couch. Her Senses varied much all the morng & on Dressing her Leggs the Mortification appeard to have made a very rapid Progress. Between one & two O'Clock She appeard to be quite composd & from that time never spoke or scarcely mov'd till abt ½ hour after 9 O'Clock when she expird but so perfectly easy & composd that it was with the utmost Difficulty to ascertain when She breathd her last. During the whole of this Day she appeard not to suffer the least pain.*****

Fridy Oct 10 1788 We buried my Mother at 4 O'Clock in the Afternoon. Mr Adamson din'd wh Us at 2 O'Clock in the Afternoon [and] we all went to my Mother's House at 4 in the Afternoon. Sister Baker & Self, Dr Baker & Daughter Charlotte, Mr Adamson & Son Orbell, Son James & Nephew G.Green attended as 4 Couple of Mourners in one Mourning Coach & my own Coach. Mrs Harrington & my Mother's Head-maid, Molly, followd in Mr Adamson's Chaise. The Revd Mr Sharp attended & performd the Service. My Mother was interrd in the Family vault in St James's Church. On opening this Vault, wch had not been opend since my Father's Buriel in Augt 1759, on his left hand laid his first Wife, Mary, & on his left his Uncle Woods & his Wife & over Them my Father's 2 Children by his first Wife. I had some brick work carried ou[t] each side of my Father's Coffin & Irons laid across upon wch an oak plank was laid as a resceptacle for my Mother's Coffin, wch was accordingly put on. It appears to one that good room is left for 3 other Coffins**. . .

Saturdy Oct 11 1788 At home alone. Began taking an Inventory of my Mother's Plate, Household Furniture & lotted the Plate into 4 Divisions. Dr & Mrs Baker assisted.

[The Oakeses joined in the rest of the Fair, their sons going to the Assembly and various friends drinking tea and supping with them. The Michaelmas Receipt was without incident.]

Mondy Oct 27 *I went to London with Son Orbell & Nephew George Green in a Post Chaise carr[in]g Bills & Cash after my Michs Quarters Receipt. Got to Town by 2 O'Clock & del[ivere]d my charge. Suppd that Evening at the Bull.

Thursdy Oct 30 Breakfasted at Mr Davison's. We din'd at the Bull. George set out for Liverpool at 5 O'Clock in the Post Coach and I & Orbell suppd at Mr Davison's.

Tuesdy Novr 4 My Mother's Auction concluded. I dind with Orbell at Mr Adamson's... A great dinner at the Greyhound to commorate the Centenary of the Glorious Revolution. Abt 60 Gentn dind there, Sr Charles Bunbury presided.

Thursdy Novr 6 At Home alone. *The King so exceedingly bad as to be given over by his Physicians.[80]

Fridy Nov 7 1788 At Home alone. Miss Adamson came to Us on a visit & her maid Servt.

Mondy Nov 17 I dind at Sr Charles Bunbury's. Met Sir Patrick Blake, Mr Robinson, Capt William, Mr Sparke &ca. Staid till 9 O'Clock & returnd home. The Ladys all at Colling's Evening Brush.

Saturdy Nov 22 . . . ***The King continued very bad all this Week, rather worse than better —— little Expectation of a return of his Intellects. Parliament met on Thursdy Nov 20 & adjournd for 14 Days.

Saturdy Nov 29 * Mr Soane came to us at Breakfast in order to look over the House I intend to Repair. Mr Plaistow likewise came to us from Ipswich after my Harkstead Living. They both din'd. Mr Soane returnd that Eveng in his way to London. Mr Plaistow staid & suppd with Us.

[A week later Soane's clerk, Sanders, came to draw up plans of the premises.]

Fri Decr 12 Mr Plaistow from Ipswich respecting [my] Harkstead Living & further proposals made. Thos Green came to pay his year's Rent. We all went to Tea & sup at Mrs Buxton's. . .

Saturdy Decr 13 Mr Plaistow returnd to Ipswich wh proposals for Mr Berners.

Thursdy Dec 18 . . . Dinner Company at Home: all the Family of Symonds, the 2 French Gentlemen, viz. Marquis de Tourpin,* Chevalier de Roult, Captain William, Mr Adamson. All staid till ten O'Clock.

Saturdy Decr 20 At home alone. The Frost continued all this Week remarkably intence. Coals to the Poor, ea[ch] of [the] Trustees 18 Bushells.

Saturdy Dec 27 At Home alone. At [a] meeting in the Evening at the Bell of some Gentn respect[ing] a new intended Canal from Bishop Storforth to Brand[on] & so to Bury.

Wednesdy Dec 31 1788 . . . a good deal more Snow.

[80] George III's first bout of madness began in November 1788 and lasted until February 1789.

* Presumably the father-in-law of the celebrated Marquise de La Tour du Pin, whose journal covered much the same period as these diaries. He was the last War Minister of Louis XVI, and was guillotined 28 April 1794.

[Vol.II]   [1789]

[The weather continued to be very cold. A charity concert and ball raised £36 for the relief of the poor and the Alderman opened a subscription.]

Mondy Janry 5   I began my Xmas third Quarter['s] Receipt for 1788 at Eye —— the Roads so remarkably bad from the fall of Snow I was obligd to take 4 Horses to my Chaise. Slept at Eye that Night & returnd home next Morning. This Morning intensly cold.

Tuesdy Janry 6   . . . Mr Rout receivd for me this Day at Stow[marke]tt.

Saturdy Janry 10h   Mr Cartwright of Oxford dind with Us. This week the Weather continued remarkably cold, the frost very intense. There is a prospect this Evening of milder Weather. **Mr Canning died this Day & I came into Possession of the Purchase money for the Living sold to Mr Berners.[81]

Mondy Jan 19   (County Sessions.) Corporation Meeting at [the] Guildhall to take under Consideration Mr Le Grice's Requisition to take some Extracts from the Charters & Books respecting the lectureship —— there was a Hall —— Granted —— a Committee appointed: The Alderman, Recorder, Self, Mr M. Wright, Mr Bullen, Mr Sturgeon & Town Clerk, or any Three, to meet at 11 O'Clock next morng. We set on Tuesday till 8 that Evening. Met again Wednesday & set till 11 O'Clock at Night & finishd. In Behalf of the Rev. Mr Le Grrice his Bro John & 2 Clerks attended.[82]

Thursdy Janry 22   At home alone. Bot 1,250 Tod Fleece Wool of Bean.

Mondy Febry 2   At home alone. James went to shoot with Mr Ord. Mr Mills receiv'd [a] Copy from Mr Le Grice of a Rule granted by the Court of King's Bench to the Bishop to shew cause why a Mandamus should not be issued for him to licence Mr Le Grice to our Lectureship. Mr Mills went up to Londn to consult with the Bishop.

Fridy Febry 6   Mr Adamson dind wh Us. Our Ball in the Eveng at the Guild Hall. We had abt 53 Ladys & Gentlemen. . . All staid supper except Mrs Halsey, Mrs Vernon, Mr & Mrs Jenkins. We drank Tea at 7 O'Clock, dancing began ½ hour after 7, suppd at eleven O'Clock & broke up at ½ hour after 2 O'Clock.

[Mr and Mrs Oakes with Maria and Charlotte went to London to stay with Mr Harvey for thirteen days and returned via Cambridge to visit James.]

Saturdy Febry 28h   I reckon includ[in]g every Expence attend[in]g this Journey (not includ[in]g sundry Articles bot) the Sum Total might be fairly estimated at £30 —— 53 post miles from Bourn Bridge to London with 4 Horses, Turnpikes, Postillion &ca cost abt £6 10 –.

---

[81] The incumbent of Harkstead near Ipswich, Richard Canning, succeeded his father as rector in 1769. His father was the reviser of *The Suffolk Traveller* (1764).
[82] The Rev. Charles Le Grice, having been removed from the Lectureship of Saint James's Church, brought an action against the Bishop of Norwich.

Tuesdy March 10 Illuminations in London on his Majesty's Recovery. Mr Houchin call'd on me & settled acc[oun]ts. My Son James new Farm house at Shouldham cost £510.[83] Mr Houchin left Mr Adamson's.

Thursday March 19 1789 This Day was observ'd as a Day of general Rejoicing for his Majesty's happy Recovery. The Corporation assembled, voted an Address to his & her Majesty, went in Procession & drank his Majesty's Health, also the Queen's, being kept as her Birth Day. A publick Dinner at the Angell & very superb Illuminations in the Eveng: a great Number of Transparancies & Devices. The Day pass'd thro' wh every Demonstration of Joy, Festivity & Harmony. The Members gave 12 H[ogs]h[ea]ds of Beer to the Populace and everything was conducted wh the utmost Decency & Regularity.

Wednesdy Mar 25 Mr Soane came to breakfast & settle the Plan of my House. Judge Gross came in to the Town to hold the Lent Assizes.

Thursdy March 26 1789 Mr Soane continued with me & finish'd the intended Plan of my House. Mr Walpole & Mr Adamson dind with Us. I serv'd on the Grand Jury, Sr Charles Davers Foreman, Sir Patrick Blake &ca. We were all at the Assembly at Night. 24 couple of Dancers, 120 Ladys & Gentlemen present.

Mondy Mar 30 The Corporation met to let the Farms in Mr Roger's Corporation [occupation?] but could not make a Hall. . .[84]

Thursday April 23 The general Thanksgiving Day for his Majesty's Recovery. The Shops all shut up, divine Service attended in the Morning, publick Dinner at the Bell, 96 Gentn, Tradesmen & Farmers dind together. . .

Fridy April 24 . . . The Corporation met this Afternoon & let Almoner's Barn & Farm, late in Mr Roger's Occupation, to Mr Gooday at 100 p[er] ann.

[James Oakes went to London for four days probably to take up the Receipt and to consult Mr Soane.]

Thursday May 7 . . . The Corporation allowd Mr Le Grice an authenticated Copy of his Appointment to the Lectureship.

Fridy /May 8/ At Home alone. The Bishop of Norwich declind licensg the Rev Mr Le Grice.

Saturdy May 16 *****. . . Lord Bishop of Norwich licens'd the Rev Mr leGrice.*****

Thursdy May 21 At home alone. Mr Chambers returnd Home out of Yorkshire.

Fridy 22 Licensing Day at the Bell. The Recorder, Alderman, Mr Mills, Mr Wright, Mr Barwick & Self all dind wh the Town Clerk & at six O'Clock repaird to [the] Guild Hall at a Summons from the Alderman respecting the Lectureship of St James on acc[oun]t of Mr Le Grice's being licensd by the Bishop. A Committee of three, The Alderman, Mr Wright & Self appointed to meet 3 of

---

[83] Left him by his grandfather, Christopher Adamson. Mr Houchin was a Wereham estate agent who looked after the Adamson family property there.
[84] There were insufficient members to form a quorum.

Mr LeGrice's Friends in order to settle some matters & a further Hall appointed on Thursday next when the same is to be reported.[85]

Thursdy June 11 **Son Orbell's <u>Birth Day</u> /he came of Age/. Mr Adamson, Mr H. & Mr Geo. Heigham, Mr Wollaston, Mr Jermyn & Miss Symonds, Miss Moyle, Mr White, Mr Hasted [all dined with us?]

Wednesdy July 1 Mr Chambers to Norwich. At home alone.

Thursdy July 2d Jno Crick examin'd as to the Robbery of Gold & Silver, my Cash entrusted wh Isaac Smith on the 15h of May. It appeard clear beyond all doubt that He & him only had committed sd Robbery but being only Cash it was impossible to convict him & therefore [he] was dischargd.

Tuesdy July 21 I din'd at Rushbrook at Sr Chas Davers's. Met 6 or 8 Corporation Gentlemen, drank Tea, returnd home.

Thursdy July 23 Son Orbell to Londn with Remittance to Messrs Ladbrooks.[86] We had Tea & Supper Company at home. . .

Fridy July 31 I attended on the Grand Jury /13 of us/. The Ball at the Guild Hall (the New Assembly Room building) 13 couple of Dancers, abt 54 Ladys & Gentn present. I could not be there Mr Soane coming this Eveing to Bury to superintend my Building.

Tues Aug 11 Jno Waller into Kent by coach to London and next day by D[itt]o to Mr Baxter at Ashford. At home alone.

Thursdy Augt 13 Yarn Committee Meetg at the Wool Pack Inn, my Turn to take the Chair, 7 prest. Tea & Supper Company. . .

Saturdy Augt 15 At home alone. Jno Waller return'd out of Kent.

Wednesdy Augt 26 Mr Soane came to us by Coach from Londn in the Eveng. At home alone.

Thursday Augt 27 I rode over to Mr Henry Patteson's with Mr Soane, left Him there to dine. I returnd home to Dinner. Mr Soane came to Us ab 7 O'Clock wh Mr Adamson in his Chaise.

Fridy Aug 28 Mr Soane left Us abt 11 O'Clock. Sent him in one horse Chaise as far as Melford. . .

Fridy Sept 11 Finishd Stocking by Breakfast, weighd up 500 Tod fleece wool, have not had one Tod in the House of six[?] weeks. The men had their Hawkey

---

[85] The case came to court and it was ruled that the power of choosing clergy in Bury rested entirely with the Corporation and the Bishop of Norwich was forced to license the Rev. Charles Le Grice to preach. Several men had felt that Le Grice had been unfairly treated and published a pamphlet to that effect, among them the Rev. Orbell Ray, James Oakes's cousin, the Rev. Robert Garnham and Robert Walpole, who formed the committee referred to, to negotiate on Le Grices's behalf with the Corporation. Le Grice was reinstated as Lecturer.

[86] Messrs Ladbroke and Company of 10, Lombard Street, who were James Oakes and Son's London correspondents at the time. See page 84.

this Eveng: a large piece Roast Beef, apple Pyes, 18 Bottles Old Beer, one Bottle Brandy & one pint Rum. Ask'd Benjn Knop, Amb. Taylor & Natl Miller extra wh Wilm Wright & his Son.

Thursdy Sept 24 I breakfasted wh Sr Charles Davers & rode with Him to Stowmarkett to attend a Meeting to be held there as a Deputation from Bury wh Mr Ely /Mr Maulkin/ Mr Sharp, Mr Braddock & others, in order to prepare an Itnry with the promoters of a Navigation from Ipswich to Stowmarkett wch it was our Wish should be extended to Bury. But it was not assented to on their part. We dind by Ourselves & returnd home.[87]

Thursdy Oct 1 1789 Sir Thos Cullum took his Place as Alderman the 2d time of his servg the Office. About 60 Gentn dind wth him at the Hall: The Duke of Grafton, Lord Charles Fitzroy & Sr Charles Davers were prest. I left the Hall between 9 & 10. The Company all broke up abt 2 O'Clock.

Fridy Oct 2d Sons shooting at Mr Tyrrell's. At home alone.

Sundy Oct 4 89 Mr Adamson din'd wth Us. My Turn for attend[in]g [the] Sundy Schools.

Fridy Oct 9 At home alone. A meeting at the Angel of the Navigation Committee.

Sundy Oct 11 We all dind at Mr Adamson. Mr & Mrs Harvey & Daughter came to Us at Tea & stay during the Fair. P[ai]d a visit to Mr Smith & Mr Leheup.

Saturdy Oct 17 1789 Dinner Company at Home: Captn & Mrs Symonds, Mr Jermyn & Miss E. Symonds (The Recorder engagd), Captn Onslow, Mr Adamson. All left us soon after 9 O'Clock.
  45 Clo. more Kent wool from Ipswich.

Mondy Oct 19 My Receipt at Sudbury, returnd home by six O'Clock. 1st Assembly for the Great Week of the Fair. Mr Harvey, Orbell & James went; the Ladies & Self staid at home. There was an exceedingly thin appearance, not more than 1/2 Doz couple of Dancers & two Card Tables. 1st Night opening the New Assembly Room wch was one Reason the Ladys being Apprehensive of the Damp.

Wednesday Oct 21 1789 My Receipt Day at Bury; engagd there from 9 O'Clock in the morng till between 7 & 8 in the Eveng. I took in £7,500 at the Wool Pack. The 2d Assembly: my whole Family was there. A very genteel Appearance, full as much Company as could be expected. Suppos'd to be between 2 & 300 Ladys & Gentn, 60 Couple of Dancers, very few Minuets.

Fridy Oct 23 Mr Harvey, Self & Sons all dind wh Mr Adamson. Met Mr Jno & Mr Henry Patteson. Returnd home to Tea. We all went to the Assembly wch was most exceedingly full & brilliant. Suppos'd to be nearly, if not altogether, 400 Ladys & Gentlemen, 80 couple [of] Dancers.

---

[87] See page 65.

Mondy Oct 27 We all went to Newmarke[t] wh Mr & Mrs Harvey. A most remarkable Pleas[an]t fine Day, great Sport & never more Company. Captn Watham performd at [the] Theatre.

Tuesdy Nov 3 I went up to Londn with my Michlemas charg[e], say ab £4,500 [in] Gold & abt £4,000 [in] Bills. Mr Jos Grigby & Mr Walpole accompanyd me in a Post Chaise from Sudbury. We got to Londn by 5 O'Clock.

Saturdy Decr 12 At home alone these 4 Days. Mem[orandu]m: In the year 1771 the Guildhall Feoffment was filld up by 36 new Trustees, only 3 old then Living, and it is very remarkable that there have been 27 Deaths out of sd 39 (now only surviving 12) in 18 years.*

Thursdy Janry 7 Receipt at Wickhambrook. I went with Bailey [and] returnd home between 4 & 5 O'Clock. I was taken very ill at Night.

Fridy Janry 8 I was better. This should have been my Receipt Day at Mildenhall but by mistake of Johnson, the Clerk, it was obligd to be postponed to this Day sen[ni]g[ht].[88] We had Tea & Supper Company at home: Mrs Vernon, Mr & Mrs Valpy, Miss Pocock, Mr Adamson &ca. I left the Company at nine O'Clock.

Mondy Janry 11 My Receipt Day at Sudbury. Went in [a] Chaise [and] got home by 5 O'Clock Mr Addison[89] took the whole Amo[un]t of my Receipt.

Saturdy Janry 16 At home alone. Sr Chas Davers [and] Mr Metcalf canvass for Sr Charles Bunbury.

Thursdy Febry 11 The Borough Sessions: very little Business, 15 at Dinner. In the Evening auditing Mr Palmer's acc[oun]t for 3 years Grammar School. 8 of us at Supper. Mr Godbold succeed Mr Palmer[90] & requested of me keeping the Acct...

Saturdy Febry 13 ... One of the finest Days ever rememberd for the time of year.

Tuesdy Febry 23 ***** I attended the Meeting at Stowmarkett calld by Advertize[men]t of several Gentlemen to think the most effectual Measures to preserve the Establishd Religion in Opposition to the Meeting held some few Weeks since by the Dissenters.[91] A very numerous & respectable Meeting attended & certain

---

[88] That is to say for a week.
[89] The Sudbury banker, who had been in partnership with the previous Receiver General, Thomas Fenn.
[90] As Comptroller of the Grammar School.
[91] A meeting of protestant dissenters was held on 1 December 1789 calling for the repeal of the Test and Corporation Acts.

Resolutions agreed & signd by upwds of 200 Gentn then pres[en]t. There were not above 1/2 Dozn dissenting Voices. On my return from Stow[marke]tt I dind at Mr Moseley's wth Sr Gilb[ert] Afflick, Mr Godbold, Mr Adamson, Mr Moseley & Mr Steckuls. I got home abt 9 O'Clock.

Fridy Febry 26   At home alone. I was ill these 2 Days with a Disorder
Saturday Febry 27   in my Bowells.

Thursdy Mar 4   We all went to Cambridge. Mr Tyrrell & Miss Tyrrell of the Party. We set off ab[ou]t one O'Clock & arriv'd at Cambridge [at] 5 O'Clock. We drank Tea & went to hear Son James declaim in English at Trinity Chapple. We set up at the White Bear. Mr Geo. Mathew & Mr Little Hales & Mr Miller spent the Eveng with Us. (Mr Heaton to Mr Adamson's.)

[The family remained in Cambridge for four days entertained by young James Oakes and his friends. The Lent Assizes began nine days later.]

Friday Mar 19   Our Jury dischargd before Dinner. Miss Nesfield returnd home [and] Son James & Mr Corey to Cambridge before Dinner. I din'd with the Gentle[me]n, 31 in Number — the Dep[ut]y Sherriff below with the 3 Candidates[92] & abt ½ Sco[re] other Gentlemen — abt 7 in the Evening Sr Charles Bunbury & Sr Jno Rous came up to Us & we all drank their Health & Success. It appeard the unanimous /wish/ of their Friends there should be an union of Interests between Them. Sir CB, from the Engagem[en]t he had made, could not agree to a Juncti'on himself, but, 'If the Friends of ea[ch] Party thought proper to canvass jointly, it must be as they please. He could not have any Objecti'ons to his Friends giving their second Voices to Sr John['], & it was accordingly agreed upon by all present that that Mode should be adopted.

Saturday Mar 27   Mr Saunders from Mr Soane's to measure over the New Building & plan what we were first to proceed upon. Son James & Mr Miller from Cambridge, Daughter Charlotte & Miss Houghton from Norton.

Thursday April 1st   Speaches at [the] Grammar School, Ladys as well as Gentn were present for the first time. Yarn Committee Meeting, 7 of us prest. I dind & staid till five O'Clock. Miss Moyle dind & drank Tea with my Family.

Friday April 2   Good-Friday. At home alone.

Saturday April 3   At home. Miss Lamb drank Tea & suppd. Pipe of Red port from Mr Strothoft's this Day laid into my Cellar.

Monday April 5   Mrs O & Family all din'd at Mr Tyrrell's & staid till 9 O'Clock. I stai'd at home expecting Mr Soane. *** Got into [my] new Banking Rooms.

Tuesdy April 6   Son Orbell appointed Constable by the Leet, was summonsd to appear & be sworn on. He declin'd the office offering a substitute. The Justices were doubtfull as to the Propriety of accepting a Substitute & defferrd the Business to Thursday. At home alone.

---

92 The candidates were Sir John Rous, Sir Charles Bunbury and Sir Gerard Vanneck. See 29 June for the election.

Thursday April 8   Son Orbell attended the Justices but no Determination came to respecting his Substitute for a Constable — but to wait the Opinion of the Recorder. At home alone.

Fridy April 9   We all din'd at the Revd Mr Patteson's at [Coney] Weston: The Christening of their Son John. Mr John Patteson & Self Proxys. I was Proxy for Mr Bracey. We all drank Tea & got home by 9 O'Clock. Mrs Staniforth & Miss Houghton and Mr Adamson were all of the Party at Dinner.

Sunday April 11   Mr Soane came this Morng at 7 o'Clock by Mail. I attended Mr S all this Day. He left Bury Monday morng 3 o'Clock by Yarmouth Coach. Mr Adamson & Mr H.Hasted din'd with Us, they drank Tea & left us.

Thursdy April 15   3d Receipt Day at Wickhambrook — the most Snow & the most winterly Day we had the whole winter. I dind with Son Orbell at Mr Nesfield's. Met Mr & Mrs Carter, returnd home before 7 o'clock.

Sundy April 18   We all dind at Mr Adamson's at one O'Clock (For the 1st time. . . so early this Spring). After Church in the Afternoon p[ai]d a visit at Mr Cowper's, Barton, & drank Tea.

Mondy April 19   Receipt Day at Sudbury, got home soon after 7 O'Clock. Mess Fenn & Addison only took their own Notes.

Wednesdy April 21   My last Receipt Day at Bury, amo[un]t rec[eive]d abt £7,600 – –. Mr /Thos/ Kerrich, Mr Simpson of Nowton & Mr Simpson of Flempling, the 2 collectors & Rodwell din'd with me. We settled our Accts & got home abt 9 O'Clock.

Saturday April 24   At Home Alone. ** Son James['s] Letter to Thurston.[93]

Mondy April 26   I went to Londn by Bury coach carrying up my Receipt. Got to Town at 7 O'Clock & del[ivere]d my Charge. Lodgd at Houghton's Black-Bull.

Tuesdy April 27   Breakfasted at Mr Davison's, din'd at Dr Smith's wh Sr Thos Cullum, suppd at [the] Bull Inn. *** Bo[ugh]t into the Stocks. ***

Mondy May 3   Mr Chambers set out into Yorkshire. At home alone.

Wednesday May 5   Son Orbell to Norwich. At home alone.

Thursday May 6   *** Yesterday in London a general Press took place and at many sea Ports on acct of Spain havg captured 3 or 4 of our Fir[st] Ships.[94] Stocks fell 5 p[er] c[ent]. We drank tea & passd the Eveng at Mrs Heigham's. . .

Tuesday May 11   Son Orbell to Cambridge to meet his Aunt Bridge. At Home alone.

Wednesday May 12   Sister Bridge, Miss B & Susan all came to Us by 4 o'clock Dinner.

---

[93] The home of the Rev. Charles Tyrell.
[94] Spain claimed control of all the territory washed by the Pacific as far north as sixty degrees latitude and took possession of Nootka Sound, a small natural harbour on Vancouver Island, where there had been an English trading settlement.

[During the next fortnight James Oakes went to a Deputy Lieutenants' meeting in Ipswich, the Licensing Day dinner at the Bell Inn and went to Norwich on business. Sister Baker and her daughter Eliza came to stay.]

Friday June 11 Mr Adamson dind with Us [on] a Turbot, [a] pres[en]t from Mr Tilbrook. Family all drank Tea & suppd at Mrs Vernon's. **** Lord Charles Fitzroy arrivd to canvass the Corporation.* Parliament Prorogued.

Saturday June 12 Parliament Dissol'd. ** Lord Charles Fitzroy & Sr Charles Davers din'd with me & drank Tea. They canvassd the Corporation. Captn Hervey applied to some of the Corporation for their Votes for his Brother Lord Hervey or Himself. This Opposition lasted but a few Hours [and] was given up at Night.

Sundy June 13 I rode over to Euston and breakfasted with Lord Charles. We all dind at Mr Adamson's after Church in the Afternoon, drank Tea & suppd with him.

Thursday June 17 At home alone. Sons, R[ichar]d Baker & Ja[mes] Bridge all din'd at Mr Adamson's. I dind at the Wool Pack: Yarn Committee. Election for [the] University of Cambridge:

Mr Pitt	502
Lord Euston	478
Mr Dundas	227
	1,207

Fridy June 18 Election for the Borough of Bury St Edmunds —— no Opposition. Rt Honble Lord Charles Fitzroy [and] Sir Charles Davers unanimously elected.[95] The members gave an Handsome Dinner /at the Angel/ to the Corporation & many Gentlemen [and the] Duke of Grafton din'd with Us & abt 24 other Gentlemen, in all abt 50. In the Evening a very full Ball at the New Assembly House —— abt 70 couple of Dancers —— the Number pres[en]t abt 400. We got home at two o'clock.

Tuesdy June 22d The most remarkable hot Day that has been rememberd for many years. Thermometer up to 90. At home alone. Sister Baker, Richard & Susan return'd home.

Monday June 28 At home alone. Mr Adamson & Son Orbell set out for Ipswich for the Election.

Tuesday June 29 ***** The general Election for County Members commencd at Ipswich: Candidates — Sr Charles Bunbury, Sr John Rous, Sr Gerard Vanneck. On this Day, being the first, Sr Charles Bunbury polld 93 single votes, Sr Jno Rous 176 & Sr G.Vanneck 923, and the second Day polld 276 makg in the whole for Sr Gerard 1,199 single Votes. The Number of Freeholders who voted at this Election is 4,816. At the Strong contested Election for the County in Augst 1727 there were 5,231 Freeholders voted — Sr Jerm[y]n Davers had 3,079, Sr Wm Barker 2,963, Mr Holt 2,365 — the latter of whom had 1,944

---

[95] Only the 37 members of the Corporation elected the Members of Parliament for the Borough.

Plumpers. At the Election in Oct 1710 Sr Thos Hanmer had 3,436, Sr Rob Davers 3,233 & Sr P.Parker 2,034.The Poll closd at 5 O'Clock on the Wednesday, Sr Gerard Vanneck declin[in]g to contest the Matter any longer when the Nos were declard as follows:-

Sr Charles Bunbury	3,049
Sr Jno Rous	2,761
Sr G.Vanneck	2,080

when of Course the 2 former were declard by the Sheriff duly elected.******** We had Tea & supper Company at Home. . .

Wednesdy June 30 At home alone. ***** Poll Closd. Mr Adamson & Son Orbell returnd from Ipswich to dine wth Us.[96]

Thursday July 1 Sister Bridge & Miss B & Susan left us at 6 o'clock in the morng to return home intend[in]g to sleep this Night a[t] Market-Harborough:

	81 miles
Friday Eveng at Stone meeting Mr Bridge on his return from Bristol	80
Saturday at Home	60
	———
miles	221

Tuesdy July 20 Mr Chambers went to London [and] carrd up my first Quarter's Receipt to [our] Bankers. [He] took up wh him Nephew Jas Bridge who set out for Liverpool Wednesday the 21st at 5 O'Clock in the Afternoon. At home alone.

[James Oakes was on the Grand Jury for the Summer Assize and at the end of July the whole family went to visit Mrs Oakes's sister, Sarah Adamson, in King's Lynn.]

Fr[iday] July 30 . . . This Journey cost us exact £10 18 –, 40/6 of wch was for Post Horses.** We were gone four Days from Tuesday Morng to Friday Night.

Sunday Augst 1 Mr Adamson dind with Us. I was not well — we staid at home alone all the Afternoon & Evening. Mr Chambers to Ipswich & was to return by way of Norwich.

Monday Augst 2 At home alone. I was but very indiff[eren]t.

Thursday Augt 5 Yarn Committee. I attended [blank] Gentn prest. I got home to Tea [and] was much better today.

Friday Augst 6 /Mr Chambers from Norwich./ At home alone. ***** Extraordinary Gazette arrivd containing professions of Peace signd by the Spanish Minister & accepted by Mr Fitzherbert on the part of England.[97]

Sunday Aug 15 Mr Adamson [and] Mr Gould dind with Us after Eveng Service, drank Tea & left Us. Daughter Maria not well.

Tuesday Augst 17 . . . Mrs O & Maria at home better than she was. Mr Chambers set off for Halifax.

---

[96] James Oakes could not vote because he held Government office as Receiver General.
[97] The British had appealed to their new allies in the Triple Alliance and Spain, unable to secure support of the French revolutionary government, was forced to withdraw.

Friday Sept 10 3rd D[itt]o [Day of Stocktaking] Finishd [the] Wool Chamber by 4 O'Clock in the Afternoon. The Men had their Hawkey this Eveng. Benj Knop, Amb. Taylor, Nat. Miller, Jos. Bailey all came & spent the Evening with the Men and Wm Wright. [They had] Cold roast Beef, Apple Pyes, 18 Bottles old Beer, one Bottle Brandy, 1 Pint Rum. We all went to dinner at Mr Adamson's. . . Mrs Adamson came to us abt 5 O'Clock from Lynn.

Saturday Sept 11 The Sorters finishd [the] Barn & Noyle Room [and] were pd 3/4 Day. . .

Thursday Sept 30 Mr Spink the Alderman elect took his place. The grandest Dinner given by Him ever rememberd, full 300 Gentlemen were invited — supposd 250 pres[ent including the] Duke of Grafton, Lord Charles Fitzroy & Sr Charles Davers, Sr Charles Bunbury &ca. Two Turtles & 3 Bucks. The Dinner was in the New Assembly Room & Card Room was likewise filld. Self & Sons not there. I dind wh Orbell at Sr Walter Rawlison.

Fridy Oct 1 Son Orbell & Mr Edge went to shoot at Thurston Park. We all went to Tea & Supper at Dr White's. . .

Monday Oct 4 Mr Chambers to Norwich. At home alone.

Tuesday Oct 5 Mr Edge, Self & Son to Newmarket Races, din'd at the Ram, at home by 8 O'Clock.

Friday Octr 8 Tea & Supper Company at home: Mrs Denton & eleven other Ladys & Gentn from her House. . . & Mr Adamson.

Saturday Octr 9 Mr Edge & Son James went shooting at Beyton & dind at Mr Walpole's. Family at home alone.

Friday Oct 15 Second Fair Assembly and remarkably full & very genteel supposd abt 300 Ladys & Gentlemen prest — Duke of Norfolk, Dutchess of Chandos, Lord Petre &ca &ca, two Dancing Rows, say abt 80 couple — only 4 Minuets. Mr Edge left us this Morning by Coach.

Wednesday Oct 20 My last Receipt Day at Home, receivd ab[ou]t £7,700 – – got home abt 7 O'Clock.

Monday Oct 25 We dind at home [and] after Dinner I set out in a chaise for Newmarket wth my Son James, from whence I took the mail for London leaving my Son to go on to Cambridge. I arrivd in London at 7 O'Clock /Tuesdy morng/, Breakfasted at Mr Davison's & went & deposited my Cash &ca at Messr Ladbroke & Co.[98]

Wednesday Oct 27 Breakfasted with Mr Davison <<dind>> attended the Auditor & settled my Balance for 1789, din'd at Monday's Coffee House with Mr Edge & Mr Walpole [and] suppd at [the] Bull Inn.

---

[98] Messrs Ladbroke and Company of 10, Lombard Street, London. Sir Walter Rawlinson, of Devonshire Place and of Stowlangtoft Hall, Suffolk, was a partner in the firm. He was a distant cousin of James Oakes through his mother Dorothea Ray of Haughley.

Thursday Oct 28 I attended before a Master in Chancery [and] sworn [swore?] to my Acct [for] 1788, din'd at the Bull Inn & suppd at Mr Davison's. The same Uncertainty between Peace & War in London.

Tuesday Nov 2d . . . Letter from Son James.

Wednesday Nov 3 Mr Chambers to Norwich. At home alone.

Thursday Novr 4 Son Orbell dind at Mr Adamson at his Club. In the Evening we were at home alone. Miss Moyle supp'd wth Us. ****Messenger arriv'd in London from the Court of Spain wth the News that Articles of Peace were agreed upon & were to be signd on the 27h ult — Stocks rose 4 & 5 P[er] C[ent].

Saturday Nov 6 At home alone. Advice of the sale of my Stock from Mr Lambert.[99]

Tuesday Nov 15 [16] * I din'd at the Ixworth Club for the first Time since my being [a] member. 15 Gentlemen prest.[100] I went in Mr Adamson's Chaise. We got home by 9 O'Clock. Mr Folk of Weston was in the Chair for Mr Henry Patteson. Daugh[te]r Maria taken ill wh [a] Soar Throat.

Wednesday Nov 17 Family went to the School Hall to see a Play perform'd by the Young Gentlemen: [Blank] & Who's the Dupe.[101]

Friday Nov 19 We all went to Tea & Cards at Mr Pickup's, returnd home to sup. Maria got down stairs.

Sunday Nov 28 I pd a Morng visit at Mr Tyrell's ***** We all din'd & drank Tea & suppd at Mr Adamson's. Mr Gould met us.

Thursday Dec 2d . . . Sister Adamson left Bury.

Wednesday Dec 8 Deputy Lieutenant's meeting for swearing in the Constables with their Lists.[102]

Thursday Decr 16 Borough Sessions. Son Orbell appeard to shew cause before the Bench why he hopd the Justices would accept <word deleted> [a] Substitute in Lieu of Himself. Mr Chinery as his Advocate brot forward several Precedents & Cases and the Bench, consisting of the Recorder (Coroner Sir Thomas Cullum) Captn Symonds, Mr Pretyman, Mr Hasted, Mr Mathew & Mr Wright (The Alderman, Mr Spink, ill). All the above Justices were unanimous in Opinion that the Reasons allegd were sufficient (Mr Wright excepted, who chose to decline giving any opinion) & accordingly made an Order of Session for his Substitute Jno Gallant who was allowd to be an unexcepti'onable man . . . & accordingly in the Afternoon after the Business of the Session sd Substitute was sworn in. I din'd at the Angel wh the Justices & left Between 9 & 10 O'Clock.

---

[99] Of Lambert and Cotton, James Oakes's London broker.
[100] The Ixworth Book Club usually met once a month at the Pickerell Inn, Ixworth, although the 1790 annual meeting was held at Stowmarket.
[101] Who's the Dupe? a farce by Mrs Hannah Cowley first produced at Drury Lane in 1779.
[102] See note 2 above.

Friday Dec 17 Own Family dind at Mr Tyrrell's (except[in]g Son Orbell at Home). Meant this as a Family visit [and so] did not meet any Company. Staid till 9 O'Clock & came home to sup.

Mondy Decr 20 . . . **Mr Jno Bridge died.

Tuesdy Dec 21 Ixworth Club. I went with Mr Adamson — a very wet Day — only 9 Members pres[en]t. Got home by 1/2 hour after 9 O'Clock.

Monday Decr 27 We all went to pass the Day at Sr Thos Gage's at Coldham. . . We staid with Them till one O'Clock in the morning and were particularly merry.

Fridy Dec 31 At home alone.

[Vol. III]   [1791]

Monday Janry 3d 1st Receipt for Xmas Quarter at Eye — went to Hoxne & din'd & slept at Mrs Gould's. Mr Brook din'd with Us. Mr & Mrs Mynard came to Bury. Son Orbell at Home.

Tuesdy Janry 4h Return'd to Eye to Breakfast & from thence to Stowmarket, 2d Day's Receipt, din'd at Stowm[arke]tt & got home by Tea.

Wednesday Janry 5h ***** At home alone. Mr G[ould].[103]

Sunday Janry 16h Mr Adamson din'd with Us. Son Orbell din'd with Day at Whepstead [and] returnd home to sup.
Mr Gould at T[ea] & S[upper].

Mondy Janry 17 County Sessions. Mrs O, Charlotte & Orbell went to Mr le Blanc's Ball at Cavenham. Maria & Self at Home alone. They returnd home at 4 O'Clock in the morng. Miss Nessfield came to dinner & to the Ball.

Mondy Janry18 I accompanied Mr Adamson to the Ixworth Club. <word deleted> I was President, Mr Burroughs vice, 13 of us present — a very pleasant Day — returnd by 9 O'Clock.

Satdy Janry 22 At home alone. The Town Meeting for the Navigation from Bury to Mistley. [There were] abt 50 Gentn Prest at the Guild Hall, Sr Chas Davers in the Chair. Sundry Resolutions movd & unanimously agreed. Miss Nessfield returnd home.

Mon Janry 24 Son Orbell, Mr Ray & his two sons went to London by Coach. Mrs O, Self & Daughter went to Dinner at Sr Patrick Blake's . . . we were 23 in Number. We suppd & staid till 1/2 hour after 3 O'Clock. Got home at 5 O'Clock.

103 Written in red ink.

Fridy Janry 27 Son James from Cambridge having taken his Degree that Day Sennight, vizt the 13th Senior Optime. There were 120 Gentn took their Degrees, viz. 18 Wranglers, 17 Senior Optimes & 13 D[itt]o Juniors. Son James cleard every Acc[oun]t & left the University free of every debt. We all went to Tea & pass the Evening at Mrs Lemon's. . . [Both James Oakes and Peter Chambers made separate business trips to Norwich in February and March, while his sons went to 'Lynn Marts' for four days at the end of February. Oakes also attended the yarn committee, the Ixworth Club and four subscription balls as well as the usual round of social engagements. Mr Adamson was 'confind with gout' for part of the time.]

Wednesday Mar 16 . . .**Mr Gould din'd & suppd with Us.****

Friday March 18 We all din'd at Mr Adamson's. Met Mr & Mrs Tyrrell, Mr & Mrs Mills, Mr Heaton & Mr Wennerquist who came this Day to Mr A. We Drank Tea & suppd with Him. **Maria not well enough to go.**

Saturday April 2d At home alone. A Letter from Mrs Bell acquainting Us Sister Adamson was extremely ill.****

Sunday April 3 A[n] Express arriv'd this Morning at 1/2 hour after 5 O'Clock that Miss Adamson was dangerously ill of an inflamatory Fever & desiring we would come over immediately. Self, Wife & Daughter Charlotte set out for Lynn at 9 O'Clock Sunday morning & arrivd at Lynn at 3 O'Clock. The melancholy Event of [our] Sister's Death had taken place. ***She died at 1/2 hour after 10 O'Clock in the Morning.

Ap[ril] 4 We slept at the Duke's Head, Breakfasted next Morning, set out for Home abt 12 O'Clock & got to Bury at seven to Tea.

Saturday April 9 I went to Wereham wh Son Orbell & Daughter Maria to meet the Funeral. We got there abt 11 O'Clock & went to Mr Houchin's. The Corpse did not arrive till past one – Mr Bell with the Dr & Apothecary – Mrs Maitland – Molly the Maid Serv & Undertakers came in a mourning Coach – Mr Bell read Mrs A[damson's] Will & gave me a Copy. Mr B[ell] left sole Executor. She considerd all her Relations. Mr B &ca returnd to Lynn to Dinner. We din'd at Mr Houchin's & returnd home between 9 & 10 O'Clock.

Tuesdy April 26 I went to London to carry up my 4th Q[uarte]r's Receipt. Mr Gould accompanied me in the Stage Coach. We arrivd in Town rather before six O'Clock. I lodg'd at the Bull Inn, Mr Gould at [the] Turk's Head Coffee House in the Strand. I spent this Eveng at the Inn.

Thursday April 28 I Breakfasted at Mr Davison's, went wth Mr Gould intending to dine at Mr Geo. Lee's, No 25 Hatton Garden. *****Mr G taken ill just at dinner time***** obligd to go with Mr G to his Lodgings. I afterwards suppd at Mr Caswall's.

Friday April 29 I breakfasted & dind at Mr Davison's, suppd at the Bull Inn wh Mr Gould, who lodgd there in order to return home with me next day. *Mr Chinery married Wid Sturgeon.

26. *Wereham Church, Norfolk.*

Saturday April 20 [30th] I returnd home with Mr Gould as far as Sudbury by Sudbury Coach, din'd at the Swann & took a Post Chaise from thence. Got home by 7 O'Clock.

Sundy May 1 We all din'd at Mr Adamson's [at] one o'clock <u>with Mr Gould,</u> drank Tea & supp'd at Home.

Wednesday May 4 Mr Gould returnd home. **I acquaintd Daughter M[aria].** At home alone.

Tuesday May 24 Self, Wife, Son James & both Daughters with Maid & Man Servants all set out for London in [the] Bury Coach. We arriv'd at our Lodgings, No 5, Norfolk Street, Strand, abt 1/2 hour after 7 O'Clock.

Friday May 27 Breakfasted, din'd & suppd at our Lodgings. Friday Evening [we] all went to Ranelagh [at] 11 o'clock & return'd home at 3.[104] [On] Friday [I] had some Conversation wh Mr Pater respect[in]g our Banking Business.

Sunday May 29 I went to [the] Foundling Chapel in the morng, a Charity Sermon preachd by Dr Gregory. Afterwards we all went to Hyde Park & Self & Son into Kensington Gardens. We all din'd & drank Tea this Day at Mr Caswell's, returnd home to sup.

Monday May 30 I went into Spittalfields in the Morng. We all din'd & drank Tea at Mr Ainge[r]'s.

[104] See note 58 above.

Tuesday May 31   I was with Mr Bloxham in the Borough[105] & all if Us din'd this Day at Mr Harvey's [and] met Mr & Mrs Bullock, Mr & Mrs Whaley, Mr & Mrs Twining, Miss Hayes, Mr Hayes, Mr Boycott, Mr Squires &ca, staid [and] drank Tea & suppd.

Wednesday June 1   Maria, Self & Son James all went to the Abbey to hear the Messiah. Remarkably full this Day. The King, Queen & 6 of the Princesses – a full Court, 12 Bishops &ca. The Permorfance began soon after 12 & lasted 4 Hours. We returnd to Dinner at Mr Harvey's & met Mrs O & Charlotte. Drank Tea & suppd with Them.

Friday June 3   We returnd Home the Epping Road in 2 Post Chaises. Servant Man by Night Coach. My own Coach met us at Newmarkett with Mr A[dam-son's] Chariot. We set out abt 1/4 before ten O'Clock & arriv'd at my own House exact at Ten. We were 9 Days in London besides one Day going & one Day returning. Includg all Expences on the Road, Lodgings in London 6 Guineas, Glass Coach [£]44 2 9½, includg Amusements &ca. What Cloaths &ca we bot was an extra but had our own Coach &ca not met us instead of 2 Guineas would have been £3 10 –.

Saturday June 4   At home alone. <u>Militia disbanded.</u>

Monday June 6   At home, drank Tea at Mrs Haggett's to meet Mr & Mrs Collett [and] settled the Militia Acc[oun]ts with Mr Collett.

Thursday June 9   This Evening the Man playd on the Harp at the Assembly Room.

Saturday June 11   Son Orbell's Birth Day = 23 **his Apprenticeship expir'd. On this Acc[ou]nt [I] gave the Sorters & Combers a Treat at Natl Miller's:

	[£	s.	d.]
say warehousemen & sorters 12 /at 2/–/	1	4	–
50 Combers at Green Dragon 1/–	2	10	–
	3	14	–

Mr Adamson & Charlotte din'd at Mr Tyrrell's.

Wednesday June 15   At home alone. Miss Tyrrel came to stay a Day or Two. Family at [the] Assembly Rooms to hear Mr Adams [Evans] on the Pedal harp & Mr Evans afterwards came & suppd wth Us & brot his Harp & playd till 12 O'Clock.

Tuesday June 21   At home alone. Washing day.

Wednesday June 22   Son Orbell into Norfolk. At home alone.

[105] Possibly a partner in the bank of Bloxham and Company started by Sir James Sanderson of Sanderson, Roxby and Company hop merchants of 3, London Bridge Road, Southwark. The bank provided services for many country banks, especially those involved in the hop or leather trades.

Thursday June 23   We all drank Tea & suppd at Mr Symonds's . . . 1st Remitt[an]ce to Sr Jas Sanderson /& C[ompany]/.[106]

Tuesday June 28   Borough Sessions. I was bound over for my Son's Appearance to answer the Indictment for not taking upon Himself the Office of Constable.[107] At home alone.

[James Oakes was much occupied with the Quarter's Receipt in early July and did not have time to go to the Ixworth Club. Peter Chambers went to Norwich.]

Thursdy July 14   Annual Clergy Meeting. I din'd at the Angel, abt 45 Gentn pres[en]t: Sr Chas Bunbury & only 3 or 4 other Lay Gentn. [I] got home by Tea. Son James din'd at Thurston.
****************Anniversary of [the] French Revolution.
****************Riots commencd at Birmingham.[108]

Friday July 15   Son Orbell to Norwich wth 1st Quart[er]'s Receipt to be deposited in Mess Gurneys' Hands.[109] He was to go from thence to Cawston & then to Yarmouth for Sea Bathing for the Recovery of his Health. . .

Tuesday Aug 16   My Wife, Self, Maria & Charlotte with their Maid Serv[an]ts set out at 4 O'Clock for Yarmouth in [my] own Coach. I went on Horseback with [my] Man Serv[an]t. We all slept this Evening at [the] Scole Inn.

Wednesday Augst 17h   We set out between 6 & 7 O'Clock & went to breakfast at Bungay were we staid till 12 O'Clock & went to Dinner at Hadscot. [We] staid till 5 O'Clock & slept this Evening at our Lodgings, Mr Pettinger's on the Quay, next door to Mr Spurgeon's. [Hadscot is Haddiscoe.]

Thursday Augt 18   I drank the Sea Water, din'd & supp'd at our Lodgings.

Friday Augst 19   I bath'd in Allin's Bath.[110] I din'd at the Angel at the Free & Easy Society. The Mayor, Dr Cooper, Mr Spurgeon & abt 15 Gentn pres[en]t. [I] returnd to my Lodgings at 7 O'Clock & accompanied Mrs O & Charlotte to the Assembly – a genteel Meeting, not full, abt 15 Couple of dancers. Returnd Home abt 12 O'Clock.

---

[106] The bank of Sir James Sanderson and Company was founded in 1791 by Sir James Sanderson and Mr Brenchley. The bank was was in Mansion House Street and provided City of London banking services for the Southwark bank of Bloxham and Company until 1793. It stopped trading in 1866.
[107] See Chapter IV.
[108] Popular revulsion from radicalism erupted in a series of 'Church and King' riots in Birmingham, during which dissenting chapels were wrecked and the house and laboratory belonging to Dr Priestley were destroyed. Dr Priestly was a radical scientist and theologian who ran a dissenting academy in Birmingham. The La Rochefoucauld boys were deeply impressed on their visit to him in 1785.
[109] The Norwich bank founded in 1775 in St Augustine's by the Quaker merchants John and Henry Gurney.
[110] A bath house was built in Yarmouth in 1759 on a piece of waste ground near the jetty containing two large plunge baths for ladies and gentlemen, each surrounded by dressing rooms. In 1800 the baths were filled up and a number of smaller baths made for hot and cold water. See C. J. Palmer, *Perlustration of Yarmouth* (Gt Yarmouth, 1875), 3 vols.

Saturday Augst 20 Mr & Mrs Mills call'd upon us at our Lodgings. Abt 12 O'Clock we all rode to the Baths & from thence to the Fort. They din'd with Us at our Lodgings [and] we went to Allin's new Room to Tea.[111] Mr & Mrs M went to the Bear Inn to sup.

Sunday Augst 21 I bathd. Two Charity Sermons preachd at Yarmouth. I accompanied Mr & Mrs Mills to both. We din'd with Mr & Mrs M at the Bear [and] we all went together to Allin's new Room to Tea. Mr & Mrs M supp'd with Us at our Lodgings.

Wednesday Augst 24 I bathd; din'd & drank Tea at our Lodgings. Ball at the Hall for Allin's Benefit [to which] we all went. [There were] abt 180 Ladys & Gentn prest, 24 Couple of Dancers & 7 Card Tables. [We] staid till one O'Clock.

Friday Aug 26 I bathd. We din'd & drank Tea at our Lodgings. Ball at the Hall for Smith's Benefit – abt 150 Ladys & Gentn prest – 2 rows of Dancers, say 30 Couple – 6 card Tables. We stai'd till one O'Clock.

Saturday Augst 27 We all din'd at Mr Spurgeon's. Met Mr & Mrs Jno Grove Spurgeon, Mr CS & the Miss Bakers. [We] went to the Play in the Evening, very full, return'd to our Lodgings to supper.

Sunday Augst 28 I bath'd, went twice to Church. We din'd at our Lodgings & all went to Allin's new Room to Tea, remarkably full. Returnd to our Lodgings to sup.

[The Oakeses left Yarmouth the next day and returned home via Cawston and Norwich.]

Tuesday Sept 6 I accompanied Mr Adamson to the Ixworth Club – Sr Walter Rawlinson pres[iden]t, Mr Adamson vice D[itt]o, 16 Gentn prest, 1/2 Clergy & 1/2 Lay. Returnd home by 1/2 hour after 8 O'Clock.

Friday Sept 9 Sons din'd at Mr Tyrrell, a shooting Party. At home alone.

Thursday Sept 22 Yarn Committee Meeting. I dind at the Wool Pack, 5/6. I was in the chair, only 5 Present.

Friday Sept 23 Mrs & Miss White, Mrs & Mr H. Hasted, Mrs Smith Tea & Cards – left us at 9 O'Clock.

Saturday Sept 24 At home alone. Son Orbell from Wickhambrook after 3 Day's shooting.

Saturday Oct 1 At home alone. Mr Chambers to Ipswich & Norwich.

Monday Oct 3 At home alone. Son Orbell to Newmarkett Races.

Friday Oct 14 Mr Adair came to dinner, Mrs Adair left ill. Coll Goat with Us – A very brilliant & full Assembly. Supposd ab[out] 300 Ladys & Gentn prest, reckond 80 Couple of Dancers – every Body of Rank & Fashion around Us

---

[111] In 1788 a ball room was added to the north end of the original bath house. In 1791, during gales, a heavy sea broke against the bath house and it was in danger of collapse. By the end of the nineteenth century it was used as a billiard room.

except the Dutchess of Grafton [who was] unwell. We returnd home soon after 2 O'Clock. Only 5 Minuets dancd.

Wednesday Oct 26   My last Receipt Day for [the] Second Quarter at Bury. [The] first time of Receiv[in]g at my Banking Office.[112] Mr Ray & Mr Pawsey din'd with Us at 2 O'Clock in the little back Room. Finishd by 5 O'Clock. Miss Tyrrell came for a couple of Days. Waddy's Benefit at the Theatre. All my Family went except Self & Orbell.

Thursday Oct 27   At home alone. (Mr Trudgett the Pastry-Cook dropp'd down in a Fit & expir'd.)* All my family except Orbell went to the Play this Eveng to see Brunton in King Lear.

Monday Oct 31, Tuesday 1, Wednesday 2d   I went to Norwich by Maulkin's Coach, got there by 3 O'Clock & deliverd my Charge,[113] dind at the Angel, drank Tea at Mr Patteson's, suppd at [the] Maidshead.

Monday Nov 7   At home alone. Miss Cocksedge came to Us. I rode over to Mr Symonds['s] & Mr Ray in the morng. My Birth Day 50.

Thursday Nov 10   Yarn Committee Meeting, 8 Gentlemen prest, Mr Burkett in the Chair. I staid till 6 O'Clock. Our first Sub[scriptio]n Ball, 66 Ladys & Gentlemen pres. The greatest want of Gentn Dancers ever rememberd, began with 5 couple & at most could not make more than 11 couple. Mr Howard & Mr Sullyard stewards. Son Orbell to [the] Ipswich Ball. Old T. Scot buried.

Thursday Nov 17   At home alone. *****Mr Grigby's Bank opend.**[114]

Monday Nov 21   At home alone. I was ill with a Cold & pain of my Face.

Tuesday Nov 22   At home alone. I was better.

Wednesday Nov 23   [I] receivd an Acc[oun]t from Liverpool of Bro. Bridges being in a very precarious State of Health. At home alone.

Thursday Nov 24   <Two words illegible> At home alone at Dinner. Drank Tea in the Eveng at Mr Garnham's. . . *****Late this Night or early Friday Morning one of my Comb Shops, No 16, was broke into & robbd of 5 Dozen of Rough wool.

Friday Dec 2   We all din'd & drank Tea & suppd at Mr le Blancs's, Cavenham. Son James went from thence to Barton Mills where he slept in order to take the Mail for Norwich to be examin'd by the Bishop's Chaplain for orders.

Sunday Dec 11   ***Son James Ordaind at Bugden by [the] Bishop of Lincoln.** Mr Adamson dind wh Us, Mr Creed & Mr Spark drank Tea & left Us. Charles Tyrrell not well. [Buckden, Hunts., was the Bishop of Lincolns' palace on Ermine Street.]

---

[112] This was the upper, or north, of the two wings designed by Sir John Soane for James Oakes. Until now Oakes had collected taxes for the Bury area at the *Wool Pack*.
[113] Oakes was taking the quarter's tax collection to Messrs Gurneys, the Norwich bankers.
[114] Joshua Grigby IV was in partnership with Samuel Cork and his sons, Benjamin and Thomas, who were Quaker leather cutters in Abbeygate Street.

Thursday Dec 15 ***At home alone. <u>At 4 O'Clock this morning died Bror Bridge.</u>****

Thursday Decr 22 Miss Routh came to Us from Norwich. At home alone. ****<u>Bror Bridge was buried this Day at Liverpool.</u>

Friday Dec 23 At home alone. A fine Thaw.

Saturday Dec 24 At home alone. A severe Frost.

Wednesday Dec 28 (<u>Bailey left me</u>)[115] . . .

Thursday Decr 29 We all drank Tea & spent the Eveng at Dr White's. Met Sr Thomas & Lady Gage, Mr Day [and] Dr Temple din'd with Us.

Friday Dec 30 ***Son James read Prayers at St Mary's Church for the first time of officiating at Bury. Miss Norgate drank Tea & suppd with Us. Daught[er] Maria went to Mr Whaley's, Colchester.

Tuesday Janry 3 My Receipt Day at Stowmarkett. I went with Son Orbell & Coachman. Finish'd my Business between one & two & I returnd to my Club at Ixworth to Dinner. Mr Burroughs in the Chair – 14 Gentlemen pres[en]t – Sr Charles Bunbury of the Number. We accompanied Mr Adamson home in his Chaise.

Friday Janry 6 My 4th Receipt Day at Mildenhall. [I] went with Son Orbell & Coachman, returnd home to Dinner, 4 O'Clock. Mrs Ray & Master Gery Cullum din'd with Us. Mr Ray's Rent Day for his Tenants at the Bell. Mr Chambers from Norwich.

Sunday Janry 8 We all din'd & drank Tea at Mr Tyrrell's, Thurston. We first went to hear Son James read Prayers & preach at Thurston Church. Mr Adamson was not well enough to accompany us. We returnd home between 9 & 10 O'Clock in the Evening.

Wednesday Jan 11 My last Day's Receipt at Bury for [the] 3d Qtr. Mr Simpson & Mr Pawsey din'd with Us. The Collectors did not begin to come in till near 12 O'Clock. We finishd abt 5 O'Clock & balancd exactly abt 8 O'Clock.

[January ended with a Militia meeting, the County Quarter Sessions, a Sunday School meeting for James Oakes and two private balls for the children. Sister Bridge and her daughter, Susan, came from Liverpool and her son, James, from Birmingham. This was their first visit since Mr Bridge's death.]

[115] Joseph Bailey had been Oakes's clerk since 12 March 1787.

Thurs Febry 9 Miss Tyrrell & Son James from Thurston. All the Family /except myself/ went to the 4th & last Subscription Ball [which was] an exceeding good one, the best of the 4. 20 couple [of] Dancers, full 80 Ladys & Gentlemen. Mr Adamson & Mr Henry Patteson dind with Us. Mr HP went to the Ball & took a Bed with Us. I staid at home with Sister Bridge, Susan & James Bridge. They got Home abt 2 o'clock. *Mr Creed's youngest Daughter died.*

Monday Febry 13 A Corporation Dinner at Sr Chas Davers['s] nine others of the Corporation there – ten in all. I got home by 9 O'Clock – most others staid till 12 O'Clock. Most surprising fine, warm weather.

Friday, Febry 17 At home. Mr Bridge, Mrs O & Self din'd alone. All the young Folks din'd & suppd at Mr Creed's.

Monday Febry 20 At home. Son James from Thurston to dinner. Mr Miller from Cambridge on [a] visit to Son James. Intense cold Weather & remarkable heavy fall of snow.

Monday Febry 27 Sunday School Meeting. At home alone.

Tuesday Febry 28 At home alone. Charity School Meeting.

[James Oakes went to Norwich on business for three days and brought his sister Baker and her daughter Susan back to Bury with him.]

Sunday Mar 5 [4th?] 1792 I attended the Sunday Schools in my usual Cours. Staid at the Sacrament. Mr Adamson dind with us & staid till 8 o'clock. Rd Baker continued with Us.

Monday March 5 Rd Baker returnd to Cambridge to Breakfast. We all dind at Mr Moseley's, Drinkstone & staid till between 9 & 10 in the Evening. [We] met Mr & Mrs Ray [and] bo[ugh]t of Mr Ray 6 q[uarte]r shares of Lottery Tickets. Daughter Charlotte, Niece Baker & Son Orbell staid at home. Son James from Thurston.

Wednesday March 7 At home alone. Militia meeting. Mr Heigham & Self attend[ed], swore in abt 20 & ballotted abt 70.

Thursday March 15 Son Orbell to Diss for Cash. Son James & J.O. Bridge dind at Mr Adamson's . . .

Saturday Mar 24 I attended Court to hear Bensted's Tryal – the Father found Guilty, the Son acquitted.[116] At home alone. Mr Joddrell suppd with Us.

Monday Mar 26 Roger Bensted was hangd at the North Gate exact 9 o'clock, carried off to Lakenheath to be Gibetted. Rd Baker returnd to Cambridge at 6 O'Clock.

Tuesday Mar 27 Dr Baker, Sister & Susan set out for Home after 7 O'Clock this morning.

---

[116] Roger Bensted, his son and a boy servant were accused at the last Assizes of murdering a man named Briggs. The boy was found guilty and the Bensteds remanded in custody until the next Assizes to stand trial.

[At the end of March James Oakes and his son James went to Wereham to look over the house and land that his son was to occupy.]

Tuesday April 3 I accompanied Mr Adamson to [the] Ixworth Club, only 9 Gentlemen present, Dr Preston, President. I was Vice pres[iden]t. Returnd home by 8 O'Clock. ****Mrs Leheup died this Day abt Noon. . .

Monday April 9h My first Receipt Day at Eye, got home by 1/4 after 7 O'Clock – Self & Son Orbell. ***Mr Leheup died this morning.

Wednesday April 11 Mrs O, Sister Bridge, Miss B, Daughters Maria & Charlotte, Son James & Nephew James all went to Newmarkett to the Races [and] returnd home to Dinner at 1/2 hour after 6 O'Clock. The Dutchess of York [was] present & the greatest Number of Ladys & Gentn ever rememberd & remarkably fine, warm Weather. I was attendg a Militia meeting from 10 till 6 O'Clock wth Mr Blachley.

Tuesday April 17 A Militia Meeting for ballotting. Mrs O, Self, Charlotte & Orbell all attended a Ball given by Mrs Bennett for her son's coming to Age at the Angel. Between 50 & 60 Ladys & Gentlemen pres[en]t, from 10 to 16 couple of Ladys drew for Places, Gentn for Partners. We went at 8 O'Clock, Tea was brot in soon after – suppd at 1/2 after 12 O'Clock, staid till 4 O'Clock. [The] Company all broke up abt an hour after.

Wednesday April 18 My last Receipt Day at Bury for [the] 4th Qr 1791. I took in upw[ar]ds of 100 Parish[es], say abt £8,300 – –.

Saturday April 21 At home alone. ****Mr A———r threw Himself out of a 2 p[ai]r stairs window.[117]

Tuesday April 24 At home alone. ****Mr G——d[118] came to Bury & calld here.****

Wednesday April 25 Nephew James Bridge sett off for Liverpool. Militia Meeting at the Angel, Mr Blachley & Self attended. We din'd there, a very handsome Dinner, & staid till 9 O'Clock. Only 1/2 Dozen of Us.

Sunday April 29 We dind at Mr Adamson at one o'clock for [the] 1st Time this Summer. . .

Monday April 30 At Home Alone – a remarkably Hot Day.

Tuesday May 1 A very Cold Day – Club at Ixworth which I did not attend. Mr Vincent came to Us from Wereham in time for Dinner – slept with us.

Thursday May 3 Mr Vincent made his further propositions respect[ing] Wereham House & premises to which I was to reply in 3 or 4 Days at farthest. Mr Vincent left Us this Day abt Noon. Miss Bridge & Charlotte accompanied Mr Adamson to dine at Weston. . .

Friday May 4 Mr Le Grice buried at his parish Church at Thwaite. . .

---

[117] From a second floor window.
[118] William Gould.

27. *Sir Thomas Cullum's house in Northgate Street.*

Saturday May 5 *****Mr Mills unanimously elected Preacher of St Mary's in the room of Mr Le Grice.[119] I breakfasted with Mr Adamson convers[in]g abt Mr Robt An.[120]

[James Oakes went to London for five days in early May and the Militia was embodied on his return.]

Thursday May 17 Yarn Committee Day, Mr Buck in the Chair, 6 Gentlemen present. I did not stay Dinner. We all din'd at Mr Creed's. Met Mr Adamson, Mr & Mrs Herring. Staid Tea & Supper.

Sunday May 20 Mr Cotman dind wth us at 1/2 hour after 1 O'Clock. Mr Adamson dind wh Mr & Mrs Herring at his own House. Mr Rose of Boxford read prayers at St James as a Candidate for the Readership. Mr Haggitt, Mr Godfrey & Mr Wm Norford [are the] other Candidates.[121]

Saturday May 26 At home alone. [I] made an Estimate of new Paving Guildhall St. The Cost, wh all materials & Work, £100 to £120.

Sunday June 3 We all dind & drank Tea at Mr Adamson's. I walkd up to Mr Symonds's & pd a visit after Tea. Suppd at Home.

---

119 See note 85 above.
120 Probably Robert Adamson, only son of Mr Adamson's brother, Benjamin.
121 The Corporation held the advowsons of both the parish churches in Bury and appointed clergy to them. These were elected by a ballot of the whole Corporation which were often preceded by auditions as here.

28. *Sir Thomas Gery Cullum (1741–1831)*.

Thursday June 7 All the Militia Officers din'd with me: Lord Euston & 7 other[s], Mr Hervey, Mr Mumbee, Mr Mills (Mr Moor's Friend) 2 Sons & Self – we set down 14 at Table. The Gentlemen staid till after 9 O'Clock. Mrs O, Sister & Daughters all din'd at Mr Adamson's, suppd alone at home.

Saturday June 9 The Militia disbanded. [I] Settled with Mr Collett & paid all the Militia Balances. Mr Collett din'd, drank Tea & suppd with Us.

Thursday June 14 . . . I went abt thro' this end of Guildhall Street to collect 1/2 the sums due from Owners of Houses for new paving the Street. Mr Wm Mathew

29. *Lady Cullum (1745–1830)*.

accompanied me & took what money we receivd. [I] think the Compistation amo[un]td to £118. My share for all my Houses £36.

Sunday June 17   We all din'd at Mr Adamson's [and] drank Tea at Home. Took a ride in my new Chaise after church in the Afternoon.

Monday June 18   I rode to Norwich with Servt for the Guild-Day. Daughter Maria was to have accompanied me but very ill with a swelld Face. I was at Mr Patteson's.

Tuesday June 19   Mr John Harvey's Guild-Day. I accompanied Mrs Patteson &

Miss Newman to the Dinner at St Andrew's Hall. It was supposd there wer[e] at least 450 Ladys and Gentlemen pres[en]t, the Number of Ladys smaller than usual & more Gentlmn. We dind abt 5 o'clock & left the Hall abt 8 D[itt]o, returnd to Mrs Patteson to Tea & then attended the Assembly wch was very full & splendid. [We] got to Mrs Patteson again abt twelve. Mr Patteson [is] on a Tour into Germany & Holland.

Wednesday June 20 I visited the Manufacturers [and] found them not inclind to buy yarns. Returnd Home in the Afternoon.

Saturday June 23 Lady Cullum, Son Palmer & Daughter all dind with Us, and Miss Moyle, and drank Tea. Daughter Maria confind very indiff[eren]t all the week.

Tuesday June 26 Company at Home, Tea and Cards. . .

Friday June 29 We all drank Tea & suppd at Lady Cullum's, only Ourselves.

Tuesday July 3 (Receipt Day at Stowmarkett[)] I din'd with the Gentlemen of the Navigation[122] at the other House.[123] Home soon after 7 O'Clock.

Saturday July 7 *First meeting of the Commissioners to put in Execution the Act for [a] new Turnpike from Bury to Thetford & from Thetford to Cranwich. Sr Charles Davers, Mr Buxton & Mr Burk, Mr Symonds, The Alderman of Bury (Mr Mathew) & sundry others, abt 22 or 23 Gentn. Most of us dind at the George. I carried Mr Ord in my new one Horse Chaise. Got Home abt 8 O'Clock. The Business of the Day was carryd thro with much Cordiality.*

Wednesday July 11 My Receipt Day at Bury, took in abt 94 Parishes, say ab[out] £3,800. Mr Simpson, Mr Pawsey & Mr Lawrence dind with Me & Mrs Simpson wh [the] Family in the Parlor. Finishd my Receipt by Tea.

Friday July 13 We all dind at Mr Tyrrell's . . . went in the Coach, return'd Home by 11 O'Clock.

Monday July 16 This Morning at 6 O'Clock Sister Bridge, Susan with my Son Orbell set off for Liverpool. . .

Thursday July 19 I made purchase this Morning for Sr Thomas Cullum of Coe's premises for 800 G[uinea]s to be enterd up at Xmas.[124] Master Mills & his sister Sophia dind with Us.

Sunday July 22 We dind at home at one O'Clock. 7th & last Sunday of Son James preaching for Dr Knowles. We rode over to Norton after Church in the Afternoon & drank Tea at Mrs Staniforth wh Mr & Mrs Patteson &ca &. This Morning Mr Vivian, in his way to Wereham, sent for me to breakfast with Him at the Bell wch prevented my going to Church.

Monday July 23 An Assembly calld of the Gentlemen, Clergy & Inhabitants of the Town of Bury. Calld by the Alderman for the purpose of addressing his

---

[122] The Stowmarket Navigation Trust.
[123] There were two large inns in Stowmarket: the White Hart and the King's Head.
[124] In Northgate Street.

Majesty on his proclamation at the Guild Hall — the Gentlemen met abt 11 or 12 O'clock, in Number abt 40.[125] The Alderman announcd the Business, Mr Pretyman movd an Address wch was seconded with a Speach by Mr Bullen — (the only speaker on the Occasion) not one dissenti'ent Voice [and] of course carr'd unanimously, reservd to be presented by the Borough Members. Mrs Patteson & 4 of her sons dind with Us & drank Tea & returnd to Norton. Mr Ray & his Son Walter drank Tea with Us – Mr Ray brot his Son as Clerk to Mr Spink.[126]

Tuesday July 24 Mr Patteson /& his eldest son/ breakfasted with us. He came to have some Conversation with me respect[in]g the Norwich Brewery. He returnd to Norton to dinner. I rode with him to Thurston & paid a Visit at Mr Tyrrell's. . .

[The Summer Assizes were unusually quiet and the Assize Assembly very successful.]

Saturday July 28 The Grandjury dischargd abt 12 O'Clock. [I] Attended a meeting calld by the High Sheriff for the purpose of addressing his Majesty wch was very numerously & most respectably attended. Suppose [there] might be 200 in the Room & most of the first Familys in the County. The Sheriff opend the Business, Mr Freer movd the Address, seconded by Councellor Mingay. The Address was read & generally approvd but Mr Lofts movd two Amendments. He was requested to stand on the Table & deliver his Reasons [and] was heard for some time.[127] His 1st Amendment was seconded but upon a shew of hands only 4 or 5 appeard. His second Amendmt was not seconded. Councellor Mingay spoke & was much applauded also Mr Freer, Mr Golding, Mr Brook. In short, it might almost be said, the Address was carried unanimously there not being more than 3 or 4 who appeard dissenting. I dind with the Sheriff at the Angel at 4 O'Clock. One of the fullest Meetings ever known, suppose abt 60 Gentlemen at Dinner. I returnd home at 7 O'Clock, Mr Harvey & Mr Joddrell suppd with Us. Serjt Le Blanc pd us a visit.

Monday Augst 6 2d Turnpike meeting at Thetford. Mr Dalton rode with Me – Mr Pretymen & Mr Sturgeon were there from Bury. Abt 10 Trustees present. We got Home by 9 O'Clock. Mrs O drank Tea at Mr Tyrrell's & Daughters.

Tuesday Augst 7 . . . Maria & I took an outing in the Chaise.

Thursday Augst 9 Yarn Committee meetg, 6 of us attended. I dind with Them at the Wool Pack, got Home by 5 O'Clock. Fleece-wool got up to 26/– a Tod.

Wednesday Augst 15 Mr Ray breakfasted with Us. News of the French King being deposd. . . This Day Mr Young convened the Growers of wool, Buyers & vendors of wool to meet at the Angel & agree in appointing an annual Fair on the 30th of July at Thetford in every year & the Growers to unite in determining

125 The King's Proclamation against seditious practices.
126 John Spink was the leading Bury banker at this time. Walter and one of his brothers were at the same school as Orbell Oakes: Shepherd's Acadamy, Clapton.
127 Capel Lofft was not very tall and had a rather high-pitched voice which was not easy to hear.

not to sell any wool previous to their Meeting. There might be abt 24 Gentn met, principally Growers, & the string of Resolutions proposd by Mr Young (in the Chair) agreed to.

Thursday Augst 16 . . . Mr Greaves, Mr Patteson's Porter Brewer, came to Breakfast with me from Norwich. He /breakfasted/, dind & drank Tea with Us. We lookd over Buckley's new Brewery Office.[128] He likewise inspected Mr Wright's.[129]

Friday Augst 17 . . . We all went to Tea at Mrs Waith's. . . Son Orbell returnd Home out of Lancaster. Mr Adamson to Norwich.

[James Oakes, his wife, daughters and a servant went to Yarmouth for seventeen days staying at the Star Inn on the Quay. They returned home via Harleston.]

Friday Sept 7 . . . We were absent abt 18 Days [and] 1/2.

		[£	s.	d.]
Lodgings / 5 18 –/	ab[ou]t	13	03	0¼
Board	D[itt]o			
Amusements		4	15	2
Travelling Expences		7	3	8½
Horses & Horstler		6	12	6
Sundries		1	8	11½
		£33	3	4¼

Wednesday Sept 12 . . . *****I dind at Mr Tyrell with Son James to meet Mr Brown to settle [the] marriage Articles.

Friday Sept 14 We finishd wei[ghin]g over Sorts. The heaviest fall of Rain all this Day & succeeding Night have known for many years.

Saturday Sept 15 The Sorters'[?][130] Hawkey includ[in]g 8 of our Servt, say 28 in all: Benj. Knopp, Nat. Miller, Mrs Scott, Wm Wright. . .
   A Tongue piece of Beef roasted weighd 18 ld
   3 large Apple Pies
   18 Bottles of Old Beer
   1 Bottle Brandy
   1 pint Rum

[128] Messrs Buckley and Garniss, Ale and Porter Brewers of the Capital Brewery, St Andrew's Street, Bury.
[129] The Westgate Brewery in Westgate Street owned by Mathias Wright. Between 1805 and 1806 it was sold to Benjamin Greene and William Buck and was the forerunner of the present Greene King Brewery. See R. G. Wilson, Greene King: A Business and Family History (1983).
[130] This word is unclear in the text. It could be 'shiftiers'. No such word can be found although Haliwell gives 'shifter' which can mean superintendent in the North of England. It is most likely that Oakes means 'Sorters' as on previous similar occasions he used that word.

Tuesday Sept 18 Second meeting at the Wool Pack for Buckley's Comm[issio]n.[131] I din'd with the Commissner. Assignees chosen:

> Mr Kitson
> Mr Hustler
> Mr Lyon

Mr Spink Treasurer. Ab[ou]t £3,000 Debts provd [and] expected [there will be] from £1,000 – £1,500 – – more.

Friday Sept 21 At home alone. Bottled off a Pipe of Red-Port – & H[ogs]h[ea]d of Sherry, see Acc[oun]t Book.

Wednesday Sept 26 <<At home alone>> We dind at Mr Cowper's, Mrs EO, Self, Daughter Maria & Son James. We met Sr Walter & Lady Rawlinson, Mr & Mrs Rd Moseley & Mr Bunbury Jnr. Got home before ten O'Clock. Brewd.

Thursday Oct 4 Alderman Wright was sworn into his Office & gave an elegant Dinner at the Assembly House — abt 130 Gentn at dinner: Turtle, Venison &ca. The Duke of Grafton not prest being in Northamptonshire. Duke De Leincour, Lord Charles Fitzroy, Sr Chas Davers, Sr Thos Gage &c. The Recorder not returnd off his Tour. I went to the Hall to the Swearing <word deleted> in the Alderman, also to Church & Dinner.

   Mr Jno Mills died this Even[in]g, Oct 4th 7 o'Clock. He was /in/ the 80th Year of his Age & stood Senr on the Corporation Books. I now walk seven.

Tuesday Oct 9 <<10>> We had dinner Company: Mr & Mrs Mich. Leheup, Mr Alderson, Mr Holworthy, Mr Pawlett, Mr Adamson. No one suppd but Mr Holworthy.

Friday Oct 12 Mr & Mrs Harvey dind with Us [and we] all went to the Assembly at Night. A most grand Ball, supposd prest Lady[s] & Gentlemen abt 350, 80 couple [of] Country Dancers. Dutchess of Grafton, Lady Charlotte & Lady Eliz &. Mrs O not well [so I] returnd home with her abt 12 O'Clock. Not one Minuet dancd.

Tuesday Oct 16 ***
Son James married to Miss Tyrrell. My Family & Mr Adamson went to breakfast at Mr Tyrrell's. Revd Mr Ray performd the ceremony. Directly after Breakfast we repaird to the Church & as soon as the Ceremony was over the new married couple immediately set off for Lowestoft. [My] Family returnd Home [and] I went forward with Son Orbell to Stowmarkett.[132] We returnd Home to Dinner at 1/2 hour after 3 O'Clock. Mr Adamson dind with Us [and] went home after Tea. They got to Lowestoft by 1/2 hour after /4 o'clock/.
****

Monday Oct 22 <<Mr Thos Singleton died>> My Receipt at Sudbury. I went with Son Orbell, Lease & Servant [in] my one Horse Chaise. We got home before 6 O'Clock. Immediately on my return Home [I] was taken ill with [a] Complaint in my Bowells. . .

---

131 Messrs Buckley and Garniss were bankrupted within three months of opening.
132 Oakes was going to receive taxes there.

Tuesday Oct 23 At Home alone. I continued very Indiff[eren]t all the Day.

Wednesday Oct 24 My Receipt Day at Home. I was much better tho' still continued very <word deleted> unwell. We took in 97 Parishes amo[untin]g to £7,185 &ca & agreed to a farthing & finishd abt 8 o'clock.

Monday Nov 12 At home alone. Son Orbell coursing wh Mr Hockley.

<<Tuesday Nov 13. . .>> A meeting by Call of the Alderman of the Inhabitants for suppressing the barbarous Custom of Bull Baiting, abt 50 prest the Alderman in the Chair. The Resolution discounting the practice signd by all prest & carried round the Town for signing then advertizd.

Thursday Novr 15 Yarn Committee meeting, 7 Gentn prest. As soon as the Curr[en]t Business was settled we took under Consideration the Incroachment made on our Spinning in high Suffolk by the Norwich Weavers & Combers & came to the Resolution of advancing 2d p[er] ld in the Super & fine Oyld on the Eastern side of the County. I could not dine wth the Gent being engagd <<with>> at Mr Adamson's. . . we staid till 9 O'Clock.

Saturday Nov 17 . . . *** Mr John Gurney of Norwich died. ***

Tuesday Novr 20 I went to Wereham with Son James and Mr Bullen to Settle with Mr Vincent abt the Fixtures, value all the Liquors &ca &ca. We dind with Mr Houchin, suppd and slept at Mr Cutles at the Crown & breakfasted next Morng.

Wednesday Novr 21 We went again to Wereham from Stoke to meet Noah Baker as Mr Vincent's appraiser. He did not come till near one o'clock when Son James & I set out for home. Left Mr Bullen to finish with Noah Baker & follow after. We dind at Brand[on] & got home soon after 6 o'clock. Mr Bullen slept at Thetford & got home by Breakfast.

Saturday Decr 1 At home alone. Dinner, Tea & Supper Company At Home: Mrs Knowles (Dr Knowles not well), Mrs James Cullum, Lady Cullum (Sr Thomas in London), Sr Thomas Durrent, Mrs Godfrey, Charles Tyrrel.
**Mr Wright died, Guildhall Street. **
****Combers in the Town petitiond an advancd of 1d. p[er] ld. in the Super wages. *****

Sunday Dec 2 Mr Adamson & Charles Tyrrell dind with Us. The Rays not well were to have dind with Us. . .
*****By Post 3 Proclamations from the King: meeting of Parliament, Embodying the Militia &ca. *****

Tuesday Decr 4 Son James wh Mr Houchin to Wereham, his Wife to Thurston. I accompanied Mr Buck to attend a Justice meeting at Ixworth, Mr Loft, Mr Patteson & Mr Stone, as a Deputation from [the] Yarn Committee.[133] We returnd Home to Dinner. The Lord Lieutenant, Lord Euston, came to Bury to issue Precepts for Bodying the Militia.

---

[133] They were probably discussing the combers' wage demand.

Wednesday Dec 5 I attended a Militia meetg for swearing the Constables on Delivering the Lists. Mr Heigham, Mr Blachley & Self prest. Saw Lord Euston. Mr Collett returnd Home with me to Dinner, staid Tea & supper.

Thursday Decr 6 Attended Lord Euston at the Angel. Lord Euston left Bury at 4 O'Clock, Mr Collett returnd Home. We were at Home alone. My wedding Day, we had this Day been married 28 years.
******I had this Day a meeting wh all the Combers [and] they were perfectly well satisfied wth the old wages.

Monday Dec 10 I dind at the Bell with the Capital Burgesses to dispose of Alderman Jacob Johnson's annual Benefaction:[134] prest Mr Pretyman, Treasure[r], the Alderman, Recorder, Coroner, Sr Thos Cullum, Mr Spink, Mr Cocksedge & Self. The Alderman at this Meeting proposd summons[in]g the Gentn, Clergy & Inhabitants to meet at Guildhall next Saturday the 15 to agree on a Declaration to support the King [and] Constitution at the Pres[en]t critical Crisis. It was highly approvd by all pres[en]t & an Advertizement in Consequence drawn up. I left the Company at 7 O'Clock.

[Mr and Mrs Oakes and their daughters went to Norwich to stay with the Pattesons for four days at a cost of £5 15s. 0d.. The Rev. James Oakes and his wife went to live in the Adamson family home in Wereham.]

Wednesday Decr 19 A meeting of the Eau Brink /Navigation/ at the Bell to oppose it.[135] The brewery, late Buckley & Garnish, sold this Day by Auction at the Bell to a Morris of Ampthill for his Nephew, Mr Clark, at £2,500. It is supposd full £500 under its real Value. He likewise bo[ugh]t the Two Brewers at £500 – – & the Unicorn at [£]420 –.[136] We were at Home alone.

Thursday Dec 20 I rode to Brandon to settle Acct with Mr Vincent who was confind to his bed with the Gout.

	[£	s.	d.]
He chargd me with ab[ou]t for Repairs	6	4	–
Garden work	8	10	–
Tax	3	10	–
	18	4	–

---

[134] See note 23 above.
[135] The Eau Brink Cut was made across the bend in the river above King's Lynn. There was much opposition to the proposal and the Eau Brink Act was not passed until 1795. Years of pamphlet warfare followed before the Cut was opened in 1821. It was opposed by navigation interests, who feared increased tolls would damage trade, and by the citizens of King's Lynn, who feared increased silting of the harbour would result. It was promoted by the Bedford Level Coporation. In the event trade increased and benefited those who most opposed the scheme. The Alderman and Capital Burgesses of Bury St Edmunds were Commissioners of the Bedford Level. See John Boyes and Ronald Russell, *The Canals of Eastern England* (1977), pp.145–48.
[136] Inns belonging to Buckley and Garniss's Brewery: the Two Brewers in Westgate Street and the Unicorn in Eastgate Street.

that I had only between 6 & £7 to take for my Balance of 3/4 yrs Rent. [I] have paid him includ[in]g:

Fine	200
Fixtures	
Furniture for Son	
Liquors for Son	————
	————

& we parted on fair Terms. We all dind at Mr Leheup's . . . staid till 9 O'Clock.

Sunday Dec 30   Mr Adamson, Mr Munbee, Philip & Walter Ray all dind with Us, the two latter suppd. I staid again at the Sacrament wth a view of qualifying at the County Sessions, the 21st Janry, for Deputy Lieutenant.[137]

Monday Dec 31   I went to Eye with my Sons: 1st Day's Receipt at Xmas, the 3d Qr Land Tax. Returnd home before 6 O'Clock. Mr Gould came to Us on a visit.

Saturday Janry 12   At home alone. Richd & James Baker to stay with Us a few Days. ***Letter from Sister Bridge.****

Monday Janry 14   Richard Baker to Cambridge.** Meeting of the Guildhall Feoffm[en]t & Coporation wh [the] Church Wardens to view the Ground opposite Mr Singleton's. At home alone.

Tuesday Janry 15   At home alone. Mr Gould came to Us.

Wednesday Janry 16   Meeting of the Yarn Makers: a <u>Considerable</u> Reduction in the Spinning Wages agreed on. I dind at Mr Mills['s]. Met Coll Bunbury, Mr Adamson, Mr Smith, Mr Hockley, staid till near 10 O'Clock. Marching Orders for the Militia came down.

Friday Janry 18   First Division of Militia marchd to Newmarkett on their Rout to Portsmouth to guard the dock Yard, Lord Euston & Major Bunbury at their Head. I din'd this Day wth Son Orbell at Mr Adamson's. Met Coll Bunbury, Mr Mills, Mr Hockley, Mr Leheup. Staid till 9 O'Clock. Mr Gould left Us.

Sunday Janry 20   Mrs O & Family dind at Mr Adamson's. I accompanied Sr Thomas Cullum to dine at Euston at [the] Duke of Grafton's — Lord Charles & Lord Henry, Mr Vary, Mr Symonds, Mr Smith & a young Clergyman. We left Euston ab 1/4 before 9 O'Clock. Home ab 10 O'Clock.

[137] Under the Test and Corporation Acts 1673 no-one could hold either civil or military office under the Crown without taking the Sacrament according to the rites of the Church of England within three months of their appointment. If they failed to do so they were liable to prosecution. The Acts did not apply to the offices of church warden and constable.

Monday Janry 21 County Sessions: Sr Thos Cullum qualifyd for a County Justice. Mr Leheup & Self qualifyd for Deputy Lieutenant. Mr Harvey & Mr H.Patteson suppd with us.
****

<u>This Day at 20 minutes after ten o'clock the French King was beheaded in Conformity to the Sentence of the Conventions by which He was doomd to this Death on Sunday morning, 2 O'Clock, wch was to have been executed in 24 Hours.</u>
****

Thursday Jnry 24 Our third Subn Ball, 73 Ladys & Gentn prest, 20 couple of Dancers. Capt Symons prest for Himself, I officiated for Sr Thos Gage. Mr Wm Woodley & Mr Acton were drank to as Stewards for the Balls next Winter. We got home abt 1/2 hour after one O'Clock.

Wednesday Jan 30 At home alone. School Hall meeting. Message to Mr /W/ Wright to know whether He accepted the Exhibition.[138] Son Orbell dind at Mr Adamson's.

Friday Febry 1 At home alone.
*************War declard by France against England.******************

Monday Feby 4 ... Son Orbell to Norwich.

Tuesday Feby 5 ... *****1st Meeting of [the] New Pub[lic] Library, Mr Acton in the Chair, 24 G[entlemen].[139]

Friday Febry 8 I accompanied Mr Jenkins in a chaise to Newmarkett to meet the Cambridge Merets[?] respecting the Eau Brink Navigation. The Alderman & Mr Cook from Bury besides Mr Everard & Mr Bagy from Lynn.

Saturday Febry 16 Orbell returnd from Wereham. Mr Chambers to Ipswich. At Home alone. The Lincoln Militia marchd into Bury.

Thursday Febry 21 Mr Patteson came to Us from London to Dinner, Mr Adamson met Him. At 7 O'Clock Mr Buck & Mr Umfreville came to talk over wh Mr Patteson the propriety of petitioning his Majesty not to prosecute the war being so particularly injurious to the Manufact[uring] & trading Interests of the Kingdom.

Our 4th & last Subn Ball, abt 46 Ladys & Gentn prest, 13 couple of Dancers, reckond very thin but upon the whole as well as might be expected.

---

[138] Under the will of Edward Hewer, citizen of London, in 1569 property in the City was left to the governors of the King Edward VI School in Bury to provide an annual grant of £6 13s. 6d. which would fund four boys of the school at either Oxford or Cambridge for four years. Waller Wright was a future Recorder of Bury.

[139] The Suffolk Public Library had been started in Bury in 1790 and by 1793 was in the hands of political and religious radicals. This, together with widespread anxiety caused by events in France and radicalism at home, provoked the establishment of the New Public Library which was moderately Tory. For further information see G.V. Heap, 'Subscription Libraries in Bury Saint Edmunds', typescript in SROB. Heap puts the opening date of the New Public Library two years later, in 1795.

Monday Mar 4 At home alone. Read Mr Young's Pamphlett.[140]

Wednesday Mar 6 I rode to Norwich, took my Servt Charles. Din'd this day at the Maid's Head & slept there.

Thursday Mar 7 Breakfasted at Mr Herring's, dind at Mr Patteson's. Old Mrs P there at Dinner. [I] went with Mr P to Pockthorp in the Afternoon & look[ed] over the Brewery. Mr Greaves return'd with Us. [We] had much Conversation respecting his proposals of quitting his Share. Mr Greaves supp'd with Us at Mr P. [We] could come to no Settlement this Eveng.

Friday Mar 8 I breakfasted at Mr Smith. The Trade of the City in the most distressd State I ever remember to have seen it . What Yarns the necesitous Makers war selling were sold considerably under prime Cost. There appeard a general Stagnation and what was most to be apprehended was the Mortality among the sheep by which the Growth of the pres[en]t year was likely to be lessened at least 1/3. This was likely to keep up the price of Wool from 24/– to 28/– wch the Trade was by no means likely to support. The Consequence may probably be the turn[in]g out of most of the Hands generally employd. I could not sell a Skein of Yarn except best soft Bom[ba]zeen.

On my return to Mr Patteson [I] met Mr Grieve again & we partly agreed to his proposals for the Brewery. I set off for Home abt one O'Clock, dind at Attleburgh and got to Bury at 7 O'Clock. Son James, his Wife & Charlotte came from Wereham. They went to Thurston, Charlotte came Home.[141]

Sunday Mar 10 We din'd at Mr Adamson's, Miss Moyle met us at Tea, Mr & Mrs Mills drank Tea with Us. Returnd home by 1/2 hour after 7 O'Clock. ****Mr Jno Cumberland died abt 4 o'clock in this Afternoon. 68 yrs old.****

****

Wednesday Mar 13 At home alone. Meeting of the Yarn Makers on acct of the depressd State of the Trade & the continued high price of wool. Wages reducd to 11 for 18, 7 for 14, 6 for 12, 16 for 2/– clean & 15 for 2/– Oyld 72 –.[142]

****

Friday Mar 15 Tea & Supper Company at Home. . . Mr Cumberland Buried.

Saturday Mar 16 At home alone. ****Great Stop in London of Gregory & Forbe's House for £170,000 – –.*****

Saturday Mar 23 At home alone. Sons dind at Mr Bennet's. *****In the course of the last 10 Days many Failures in London & several other Place[s] wch has causd great Consternation in the Commercial World. One or two Londn Banks & several Country Banks have stoppd paym[en]t. Particular distressing Times at

---

[140] Arthur Young, *The Example of France, a Warning to Britain* (Bury Saint Edmunds, 1793).

[141] She had been staying with the Rev. James Oakes and his wife at Wereham.

[142] The calculation of spinners' wages was very complicated. They were calculated according to the size of reel on which the yarn was wound and the fineness of the yarn. These reels were named after a price, hence the 2/– reel, although the price actually paid for spinning a reel of a particular size varied according to the market.

Liverpool &ca. **
* (Dr Wollaston's friend Huntingdon came to settle as a Physcian.)

[The Lent Assizes were uneventful and there was no Assembly being Passion week. Sister Bridge and her daughter Susan arrived from Liverpool on 12 April and the Receipt was successfully completed on 17 April.]

Friday April 19   The General Fast very solemnly attended. At Home alone. Sr Thos Cullum & Lady returnd from London.

Saturday April 20   . . . ****Mr Geo Mathew unanimously elected Reader of St James. ****

Monday April 22   I went to London in a Post Chaise with Mrs Jenkins & Mr Chinery. Cost us all three together £4 12 6, Postchaises, Postillions, Turnpikes & Expences each £1 10 10. We set out at 20 Minutes after six & got to Town 20 minutes after 4 O'Clock. [I] drank Tea at Mr Davison's (found him very much on the Decline), suppd at Houghton's Bull Inn.

Tuesday April 23   Attended [the] Sale in Bermondsey Street [of] Wool by Auction. Dind at Mr Harvey's & drank Tea, pd [a] visit at Mrs Buggen's, Mr Powell's & Mr Hovell's. Returnd to [the] Bull Inn to sup.

Wednesday April 24   /Went into Spittalfields/. Attended [the] Wool sale by auction in Bermondsey Street. Mr Buck & Self bo[ugh]t one Lott, ab 140 Tod Northamptonshire Fleece & 4 Clos Super Cast. It was supposd that a great deal was brot in, but at [the] same time many hundreds [of] Packs sold from £4 to £5 per P[ack] under prime cost. Dind this Day at Mr Davison's, went on [the] Change &. . . suppd at [the] Bull Inn.

Thursday April 25   Attended Spittalfields, from Thence to the Tax Office & Auditor's Office to Mr Robt Adamson's. Din'd at a Coffee House, calld on Mrs Vernon, took part of a play in the Hay Markett[143] & returnd to [the] Bull Inn to sup. Mr Gould from Londn to Bury by coach.

Friday April 26   Attended again in Spittal-Fields &ca, went again to [the] Auditor's Office, Old Palace Yard & Mr Horner not within but attended one of his Clerks into the Court of Exchequer & swore to my Acc[oun]ts. Calld again at Mrs Vernon's, returnd into the City, dind at Houghton's at the Bull [and] went on [the] Change. [I] drank Tea at Mr Davison's with Him, Mr Newman & Mr Caswell & then went to Tea & Cards at Mrs Hovell's to meet Mr Ainger's Family & other Company. [Oakes returned to Bury next day.]

Thursday May 2   I accompanied my Wife & Maria in my Coach to pay a visit to Mrs Gould, Hoxne. Miss Gould, Miss Ann, Eliza & Mary all four at Home. We set off at 11 O'Clock & got there by 4 to Dinner. I was taken ill with [a] Cold & feverish Disorder in [my] head & Feet.

Friday May 3   We breakfasted and left Mrs Gould's soon after ten O'Clock. My Face much swelld & I was in much pain. Mr Gould returnd home with Us. We

---

[143] In the eighteenth century it was common to go to a play half way through for half price.

got home abt 1/2 hour after 3 O'Clock. I was extremely ill all the way & remainder of the Day.

Saturday May 4   I continued very ill the whole of this Day. . .

Sunday May 5   I continued mend[in]g tho very slowly. At home alone.

Thursday May 9   At Home at dinner. Mrs O, Sister & Daughters at Tea & Cards at Mr Garnham's. I was a good deal better.

Friday May 10   I had this Morning my Tooth drawn by Mr Creed & was much better. Tea & Supper Company at Home. . .

Saturday May 11   At Home alone. A Militia Meeting at my own House. Mr Symonds attended. [I am] nearly well. *****Mr Isham Dalton died, the Registra, this Day at 11 o'clock. ******

Sunday May 12   We din'd at Home <word deleted> after Evening Service. The Recorder dind & drank Tea with Us. Miss Moyle at supper. *************Mr Davison died, 80 yrs of Age, in Fenchurch Street. ******************

Monday May 13   Attended a Parish Meeting calld abt consecrating a piece of Ground for a Buriel Place where the old Alms House stood. Sr Thos Cullum & Self were deputed to wait on the Bishop next Day to put off the Consecration till his Lordship's visitation next Year. At Home alone.

Thursday May 16   At home alone. It was discoverd by Dr Wollaston Mr Adamson had lost the Sight of his right Eye. **********

Friday May 17   The Bishop came to Bury & Confirmd for the Town only. His Lordship went to the Grammar School to hear 3 Latten Speaches from three of the Head Boys at 4 O'Clock when He set off for Norwich. We all went to Tea & Cards at Mr Pretyman's. . . ******NB Summons read for filling up the Corporation.*******

Saturday May 18   At home alone. In the Evening I attended a general Invitation by the Alderman of the Corporation calld with a view of friendly agreeing on proper Persons to fill up the Body. 8 of the Upper House attended & 10 of the Lower. I staid till 1/2 hour after Ten. Several were mentiond & there appeard but few objections.

Monday May 20   A Meeting of the County Justices to take in Consideration the State of the Gaol wh had been presented by [the] Grand Jury as unhealthy & unsafe. They determind on Building a new Gaol & Consult[in]g the Corporation upon the Lease remain[in]g of 76 yrs of the Old Gaol on Wednesday 5th. The Borough Licencing Day – Town Clerk's Dinner at the Bell. . .[144]

Tuesday May 21   I rode out with Mr Adamson in his Chaise & he came Home & dind with Us. *********This Afternoon we met at the Guild-hall by Summons from the Alderman to fill up 4 vacancies in the Capital Burgesses & 5

---

[144] The day on which the inns and public houses of Bury received their licenses. It was customary for the Town Clerk to provide dinner for the Justices at one of the inns on this occasion.

Burgesses in the Common Council. Mr Barwick, Mr Jos. Maulkin, Mr Chambers & Mr Fairfax were uanaimously elected from the Lower House to fill the Upper and Mr Thos Maulkin /Grocer/, Mr Browne (Surgeon), Mr Dickinson (Attorney), Mr Lawrence (Grocer), Mr Smith (surgeon), were all unanimously elected out of the Inhabitants of the Town to fill the Burgesses of Common Council, excepting 4 vacancys made this Day by Those taken into the upper House wch still remain to be filld up. The whole of the Business of the Day went thro without any Desent excepting in the Last Instance for the 5th person. Mr Abm Jenkins was put up by Self & it being doubtful how far the Town Clerkship was compatible with being a Burgess of Common Council Mr Jenkins was withdrawn & an Opinion ordered to be taken & Mr Smith, Surgeon, unanimously elected. The Business was all finished by abt 1/2 after 7 O'Clock.

Sunday May 26   Mr Adamson din'd with Us at one O'Clock (the first Sunday of dining between Church & Church). Mr Adamson drank Tea with Us.

Tuesday June 4   I bottled off a Pipe of Red Port at Mr Leheup's & took home my half share. Provd very fine & good and afforded a fair Length. Committee Meeting of the Corporation to consider of the proposals to settle with the County Justices abt the Gaol. The Corporation, wh the Gentlemen of the Town, walkd in procession to the Angel & drank the King's Health. The Excellent Volleys fird by [the] Huntingdonshire Militia. We all drank Tea & passd the Evening at Mr Mills['s]. . .

Wednesday June 5   Militia meeting, pres[en]t: ***Sr Charles Davers*** Mr Symons & self. Afterwards the Corporation Committee met Sr Chas Davers & Mr Metcalf to consider & hear the proposals abt their giving up the Lease of the Gaol for the remain[in]g Term of 78 years. Forming any Resolutions postpond to [the] next County Sessions. Mrs Stanniforth of Norton, Mr & Mrs Henry Patteson & Harry & Mr Adamson all dind & drank Tea wh Us. Suppd alone.

Thursday June 6   I set off for Norwich with Sister Baker & her Daughter Mary. We arriv'd a little before 2 O'Clock. We dind together at [the] Maid's Head & Sister Baker & Daughter set off for Causton abt 5 O'Clock. I went to Mr Patteson's & accompanied Him to Coney in his Whiskey. [I] Returnd with Mr P on Friday Morning to Norwich to breakfast, dind wh Mr P, accompanied Him to the Pockthorpe Brewery in the Afternoon & to Coney in the Evening to Tea.

Saturday morng, June 8   From Coney to Norwich wh Mr P to breakfast. Mr Greaves met us. I declind having any Connection in the Pockthorp concern with Mr G. I dind at the Maid's-Head & returnd to Thetford by Mail from 1/2 hour after 4 O'Clock to 1/2. . . hour after 8 O'Clock. Took a Post Chaise & got Home 1/4 before Ten O'Clock. ********************************** ********** I never met with a more depressd Markett, never Sold one Bundle of Yarn not withstanding every possible Endeavor. This is the 4th Month of attending at Norwich without being able to make any Sales. The Manufacturers can get no Remittances owing to the Difference of Exchange & have nothing to do except a few E[ast] I[ndia] orders wch came in yesterday.**************************

Wednesday June 12   At home alone. Sister Bridge drank Tea at Mrs Leman's. This Day I bot 1,000 Tods of Long Fleece Wool, 1/3 Hogg of Mr Broughton at

Mr Green's Hall at 19/– good wool toddy 3s. NB this is a fall of 9/– a Tod some wool havg been sold at 28/– only 2 or 3 months since.

Tuesday June 18   I went to [the] Ixworth Club wh Mr Adamson & Mr Hockley. Only 7 members pres[en]t. A very great Dinner 4 Turbotts.

Thursday June 20   Yarn Committee. I dind at the Wool Packett. I was in the Chair, only 6 Gentn pres[en]t at Dinner. Spinning Wages settled. Own Family all went to Tea & supper at Mrs Vernon's. Met Sr Thos & Lady Cullum.

Saturday June 29   At home alone. Orbell went this Day to Mr Cooper's Decoy at Hockesould and fishd wth Mr Cooper. [He] brot Home 4 Pike & several brace of Perch &ca. They weighd 30 ld together.

Wednesday July 10   My Receipt Day at Bury, took in abt 90 Parishes, finishg ab 7 O'Clock. Mr Pawsey & Mr Lawrence, Mr Smith & Lease all dind with me.

Thursday July 11   Mr Chambers to Norwich to up my Receipt. ********This is the 4th or 5th month have been at Norwich & returnd without selling a Bundle of Yarn.*** I dind at the Annual Clergy Meeting at the Angel, abt 20 Clergy & 5 Lay Men. Mr Moseley in the Chair. Dr Ord returnd home & drank Tea with Me.

[The Summer Assizes opened on 18 July with James Oakes on the Grand Jury. He was in the chair for the Ixworth Club meeting at the end of July and at the beginning of August the whole family, except Orbell but including Sister Bridge and her daughter, spent three days at Wereham with the Rev. James Oakes and his wife. On his return James Oakes was at a Deputy Lieutenants' meeting, a yarn committee meeting, a Thetford Turnpike meeting and another Ixworth Club meeting.]

Wednesday Augst 21   ******A Militia meeting in the Morning. In the Evening Sr T[homas] C[ullum] & I Ballotted for the Ald-man/ship/. It was decided for Sir TC. The Day for electing [the] Alderman. Sir TC unanimously elected. Sr Chas Davers, Mr Leheup, JO, J[ohn] S[ymonds], G[odbol]d & H[urst] B[arwick] Assistant Justices. A Conference between the Corporation & a Committee of the County Justices respecting giving up the Lease of the Gaol wch was assented to by the Corporation having the like priviledges in the new Gaol. A very grand Dinner given by the Alderman Wright at the great Room at the Angel. There were upwards of 70 Gentn including the Coporation at Dinner. The Room much too full. I left the Angel before ten.

Thursday Augst 23   Bo[ugh]t abt 800 Tods of wool at Mr Mathew's at 15/– to be parted between Mr Buck & Self.

Thursday Augst 29   Tea & Supper Company at Home: Mr Edgar & Miss Plampin (Mrs Halsey not well enough[)], Mrs Leman, Mrs Mason & Mrs Salmon, Mr & Mrs Toosey Jnr.

[James Oakes went to Norwich at the beginning of September where he found the trade '. . . in the most depressd State imaginable'. He began Stock-taking on his return and the men had their usual Hawkey.]

Saturday Sept 14   At home alone. daughter Charlotte & Niece Susan drank Tea & [at?] Mr Adamson's. ***********Finishd taking Stock & balancing my Books, /tres Mal/.****************

Wednesday Sept 18   At home alone. Mr Chambers went into Cambridgeshire to examine J.Hill's Stocks. ******Nephew James arrivd from Liverpool.*****

Saturday Septembr 21   At home. Mr Norford din'd & passd the Day wth Us. ************Mr Chambers returnd from Cambridgeshire & found J.Hill's cash very deficient, no less than £53 – 6 chargd to Putters-out beyond what they really stand —— bad indeed. ******************

Wednesday Sept 25   Self & Son Orbell to Sturbitch. [We] took my Horse & 1/3 of a Chaise. The Party from Bury breakfasted, dind and drank Tea together as usual. We got home 1/4 before 11 O'Clock. A remarkably fine Day, a large Meeting.

Thursday Octr 3   This Day Sr Thos Cullum took his place as Alderman & chief Magistrate. He gave an elegant Dinner at the Assembly Room ordered of Mr Anderson & agreed at 4/– a head for Eating & 6d fruit besides sending a large Turtle, Venison & Game. (NB This is the first Time of . . . mak[in]g Terms wh Anderson at so much a Head.)[145] About 80 at Dinner. The Duke of Grafton, Lord Charles, Mr Symonds, Mr Spink & Myself not prest. Abt 28 of the Corporation there, 24 Gentn out of the Country, 12 Gentn of the Town & 16 Tradesmen. I was not well enough to attend any Part of the Day. Mrs O & Sist B at Tea at Mrs Buggin's.

Saturday Oct 5   Attended [a] Special Sessions at [the] Guild Hall. At home alone. Mr Wennerquist came to Mr Adamson's.

Sunday Oct 19   Mr Gould arrivd ab 12 O'Clock. Licence procurd. I was bond with Mr G. The Registrar sd the Cost [£]1 11 6. Mr Gould presented him with Two Guineas. At home alone.

Monday Oct 21   **
My Daughter was marr[ie]d to Mr Gould by Mr Sams at St Mary's Church at 1/2 hour after 8 O'Clock. Present: Self, Sister Bridge, Niece Bridge & Charlotte. Returnd Home to Breakfast [and] Mr Adamson & Mr Wennerquist came to us. The Bride & Bridegroom set off in Mr Adamson's Chaise soon after 10 O'Clock for Hoxne. **
My 5th Receipt Day at Sudbury. Son & Lease went off in a Post Chaise early in the morng. I set off soon after 9 O'Clock on Horseback as soon as the Wedding was over. Got home 6 O'Clock, brot Bessy.

Wednesday 23 Octr   My last Receipt Day at Home, took in full £8,000 – – & agreed to one half penny. Finishd between 8 & 9 O'Clock. Mr & Mrs Gould returnd to us from Hoxne to Tea.

---

[145] George Anderson was the proprietor of the Angel Inn from 1780 to 1799 and of the Assembly Rooms from 1777 to 1801.

Thursday Oct 24   At home alone. Morning Visits to Mr & Mrs G. We had Dinner Company At Home. . . all staid till between 9 & 10 O'Clock.

Wednesday Oct 30   Sister Bridge, Susan & James left us this morning at 1/2 hour past 6 O'Clock for Liverpool. *************************************** Son Orbell set off for Wereham to pass 2 or 3 Days with his Brother.

Friday Novr 1   Mr & Mrs Gould & Mrs O return'd visits. I went to pass an hour with Mr Symonds at the Hill. Returnd Home to Dinner.

[James Oakes, his wife, Charlotte and the Goulds set off for London in two post chaises on 5 November.]

Wednesday Novr 6   We breakfasted together. I went upon my Business, returnd to Bates Hotell to Dinner at 5 O'Clock wth Mr Edge. Alone at Supper. Miss Leadbeater dind & drank Tea with Us.

Thursday Novr 7   *******My Birth Day, now 52 years of Age. ************* Mr & Mrs Gould & Servt left us at 9 O'Clock on their way to Barnstable, the Head Quarters of the North Gloucester Militia. Mrs O, Self & Charlotte dind, drank Tea & suppd at Mr Harvey's. Met Mr [&] Mrs Jodderell & Mr Preston. Returnd to the Hotell to sleep.
*****************My Birth Day, 52 years old. ***********************

Friday Novr 8   We left the Hotell & went to stay at Mr Harvey's, dind wth Them alone abt 5 O'Clock.

Saturday Novr 9   Attend[in]g my Business: got Abel Adams Note pd, balancd my Acc[oun]t wth Messr Ladbrokes &ca &ca. Returnd to Mr Harvey's to Dinner at 1/2 hour after 4 O'Clock, dind & passd the Evening alone.

Sunday Novr 10   I went to the middle Temple Church wh Mr & Mrs Harvey, paid several Visits with Mr Harvey, got home to Dinner at 1/2 hour after 4 O'Clock. Passd the Afternoon wth Mr & Mrs H alone. We calld on Mr Robt Adamson & He calld on Us.

Monday Novr 11   We set off from Mr Harvey's for Home at 1/2 hour after 7 O'Clock. Got home by 7 O'Clock & found all well at Tea.
********************* Expences of this Journy ***********************
**** £16 17 6

	[£	s.	d.]
Tra[velling to London?]	2	10	–
R[eturn Journey?]	2	10	–
House [Bates Hotel]	11	17	6

Tuesday Novr 12   I dind this Day at the Angel [at] 5 O'Clock by Invitation of the Officers of the West Kent [Militia] on [a] Turtle presented Them by Mr Spink. 10 Officers & 9 other Gentn. I returnd home before 9 O'Clock.

Thursday Novr 14   I dind at our Yarn Committee meeting. 1/2 a Dozen of us pres[en]t, Mr Maling in the Chair. The 1st Subscription Ball, Mr Acton, Mr John Moseley stewards. A most brilliant Appearance, abt 90 Ladys & Gentlemen, 26 couple of Dancers. We got home abt 3 O'Clock.

Thursday Decr 5 Dinner Company at Home: The Duke De Rouchefocaul,[146] Mr & Mrs Moreland, Mr & Mrs Blachley, Mr Heigham, Mr Geo. Heigham, Mr Adamson & Mr Wennerquist, Mr Campbell staid till ten O'Clock.

Friday Decr 6 At home alone. Our Wedding Day. Married 29 yrs.***********

Sunday Decr 15 Mr Adamson & Mr Wennerquist din'd & drank Tea wth Us, staid till 8 O'Clock.
****
This Evening at 9 O'Clock Son James's Wife was safely deliver'd of a Girl at Wereham. Acc[oun]t receivd by his Man Monday morng, 9 O'Clock.
****

Monday Decr 30 My first Receipt Day at Eye. Self, Son Orbell & Coachman went. The Cross Road very bad, returnd by Turnpike – 2 miles longer way. At home by 1/2 after 5 O'Clock.

[Vol. IV]   [1794]

[In spite of the War Bury society followed its usual hectic course in January with a card assembly, the third subscription ball and the Guildhall Feoffment Annual Meeting and Dinner. James Oakes completed the Receipt, Peter Chambers went to York on business and Miss Routh, Charlotte's old governess, came to stay for a week.]

Tuesday Janry 21 Meeting of Parliament. A very great Majority for continuing the War in both Houses. At home alone.

Monday Janury 27 A vast deal of Snow fell this Morning; a terrible bad Day. This evening, just before 7 O'Clock, came Son James, his Wife & little Girl. They had a most fatiguing, bad Day, 5 Hours coming from Brand[on] in Mr Adamson's Chaise & from the great fall of Snow & the Depth were obligd to get out of the Chaise 5 times. Very happily they caught no Cold.

Thursday Janry 30 Sons Orbell & James wth Charles Tyrrell all din'd at Mr Adamson's. The Second Card Assembly & private Dance. Abt 64 Ladies & Gentlemen present, Mr Geo Grigby & son Orbell Stewards, 18 couple of Dancers. The Company met abt 7, drank Tea soon after 9 O'Clock, left dancing punctually at 12 O'Clock.
********This day appointed by the Alderman, Sr Thos Cullum, for the meeting of the Inhabitants to raise a Subscription for the Relief of the Poor on acc[oun]t of the severe weather, the Scarcity of Work & the extreme Low Wages to be earn'd by Spinning. The meeting was very respectable — abt 60 G[uinea]s was

[146] François de La Rochefoucauld's father, who had escaped to England and lived in a house in Whiting Street for a time. He was Duc de La Rochefoucauld-Liancour since his cousin was stoned to death by the mob in 1792.

immediately subscribed by the Gentn prest. The Day following was approved to meet again. Each of the Borough members sent 50£ & the Amo[un]t, includg sd £100, was ab £270. Expected when completed might amot to £300. It was resolvd to distribute the same in B[r]e[a]d & expected that abt 3,600 Poor would receive the same that every one should receive 4d of Bread each week, say at twice each 2d, this would be abt 560 each week & would hold 5 or 6 Weeks.

Monday Febry 3   Mr & Mrs Gould came to Us /from Barnstable/ abt 6 O'Clock this Evening. At home alone.

Friday Febry 14   Son Orbell went into Norfolk to attend the Meeting at Should-ham for the intended Inclosure.[147] We all drank Tea & Cards at Mr Garnham's.

Saturday Febry 15   My Grandaughter's Christening at Thurston (Mary Anne). Mrs Tyrrell, Mrs Oakes & Mr Adamson were Sponsors. We all din'd at Mr Tyrrell's at 4 O'Clock, met Mr Walpole, staid till 1/2 hour after 9 O'Clock.

Monday Mar 3   Mr Adamson & Mr Creed din'd with Us. Mr Creed came to Tea & Supper. Mr A not well, went Home to sup. I rode up to Hardwick & made /a Merry visit/.[148]

Tuesday Mar 4   At home alone. ******Marquis Cornwallis to Culford after [an] Absence of 6 years. *******

Wednesday Mar 5   Mr Gould left us this Morng by London Coach. . .

Thursday Mar 6   Mrs Oakes very unwell with [a] cold & feverish Disorder. Mrs Gould, Self & Son Orbell to Dinner at Mrs Bennett's. Staid Tea & return'd Home to sup.

[Orbell and Charlotte went to Wereham to stay with their brother James for the Stoke Ball. James Oakes was unable to go because his wife was ill. Mr Adamson was also 'very unwell' so that neither he nor James Oakes went to the Ixworth Club. The Lent Assizes opened on 19 March.]

Friday Mar 21   Continued attendg the Grand-Jury. . . A subscription opened on a Motion made by Sir Charles Bunbury by Desire of the Lord Lieutenant for an Augmentation of the Militia & full £1,300 signd by [the] Gentlemen prest. I put my Name down for £20. Mr Le Blanc & I return[ed] Home to Sup.

Saturday Mar 22d   Mr Le Blanc & Self continue attending the Grand Jury. The only Bill coming before Us was the Nichols Father & Son for the murder of the Daughter. There were 37 witnesses at the Back for Examination & took us 7 Hours. Found a True Bill. . .

Sunday Mar 23   Orbell to Wareham for his Sister Charlotte. Mr Adamson din'd with Us, returnd home at 7 O'Clock. Mr H.Patteson came & took a Bed with Us.

---

[147] The intended enclosure of property inherited by James Oakes's children from their maternal grandfather, Christopher Adamson. The Bill began its course through Parliament in May 1794. The House of Commons Journal 49 (1794).
[148] Hardwick Hall was the country seat of Sir Thomas Gery Cullum.

Monday Mar 24 The Nichols try'd & both found Guilty. The Tryal lasted abt 6 or 7 Hours. Mr H.Patteson returned Home immediately after. Orbell returned home with his Sister Charlotte from Wareham abt 6 O'Clock. At home alone. Miss Gould came to us.

Tuesday Mar 25 Hammond try'd for the Murder of the woman and aquitted. Tryal lasted 5 Hours. Miss Gould continued with Us.

Wednesday Mar 26 Daughter Gould, Miss Gould & Orbell all set out for London in a Chaise on her Journey to [blank][Barnstable?]. At home alone. Miss Staniforth & Miss Horton din'd with Us.

Wednesday April 2 Mr Chambers to Norwich. Militia meeting. At home alone. *******Mrs Rainbird call'd in her Money. *******£8,600 ***

[James Oakes and Mr Mills went to a County meeting at Stowmarket called by the Lord Lieutenant to raise further funds to augment the Militia.]

Friday April 4 Miss Wish dind with Us. At home alone. Mr Chambers returnd from Norwich. [He had] made a few more sales than for some Months back. Mr Chinery very bad, thought to be in great danger.

Saturday April 5 ******I bo[ugh]t of Mr Mathew abt 700 Tods [of] Fleece Wool, not having left in the House of every kind & sort 10 Po[unds?] of Wool – nor bot any Fleece since last August. Weighd up all the said Wool, price from 15/6 to 16/6. Very good Wool. Miss Staniforth din'd wth Us & carried Miss Houghton to Norton. Mr Chinery worse; not likely to live.
*********Mr C[hambers] first mentioned his thoughts of withdrawing at Mich[aelma]s 1795.*********

Friday April 11 4th Day's Receipt at Mildenhall. Self & Son returnd home by 1/2 hour after 5 O'Clock. Tea Company at Home. . . Son Orbell to London /this Eveng by Norwich Coach/ to settle Mrs Rainbird's money with Mr Lambert in the Stocks.

Thursday April 17 Self & Son Orbell to Stowmarket to an open Committee Meeting for raising a Subscription for Cavalry & volunteer Companys &ca &.

Friday April 18 (Good Friday) at Home alone. Mr Wennerquist returnd from London.

Saturday April 19 Son Orbell to Norwich wth [the] remainder of [the] Receipt, Notes &ca. At home alone. Mr Cocksedge drank Tea with Us. Mr Chambers to Ipswich.

Saturday April 26 I breakfasted at Sr Chas Davers['s]. At home alone. Son Orbell had his Tooth drawn.

******Mr C[hambers] gave me to understand he had fully made up his mind to withdraw Mich[aelma]s 1795. **

Sunday April 27 We all din'd at Mr Adamson's at one O'Clock, the first of Summer early dining. Went again at 6 O'Clock to Tea & to the Parade. Home to supper.

Monday April 28   . . . Niece Baker came to Us by Norwich Coach at 9 O'Clock in the Evening.

Thursday <<April>> May 1   I went wth Son Orbell to Stowmarkett to attend [a] Committee meeting. Mr Maynard, vice Sheriff, was in the Chair. Mr Broke, Mr Acton, Mr Golding, Sir Jno Blois & Sundry other Gentlemen between 30 & 40. The Subscription amounted to £5,230. . . Ordered 4 Troops of Fencible Cavalry ea 50 Men – £200 allow /for/   £2,080

Encrease of the Militia of 7 to every Company of the Regiments   800
56 to each, say 112 Men allowd £6,166 each=£400 to ea Regiment
2 Companys of Infantry for the Coast, ea 60 Men   624
Extra for Equipment of 200 Cavalry 5 each men   1,000
Extra for Batterys   500
Extra for Incidental Expences   500
                                                                      ————
                                                                     £5,504

Ordered Subdivision Meetings thro' the County on Wednesday the 14th May for taking the Names of those that offer for the Cavalry and on the 21st at Bury for receivg the Muster Rolls. About 1/2 Dozen of Us din'd together and Self & Son Orbell drank tea at Mr Ray's of Haughley on [our] return. Home abt 1/2 hour after 8 O'Clock. . . .

Monday May 5   The Borough Sessions. Cadney & his Wife found Guilty, both sentenced to stand in the Pillory & to Imprisonment. We Din'd & drank Tea at the Angel, returnd Home to sup.

Monday May 12   We rode over to Drinkstone in the Morng to Mr Moseley & returnd home to dinner. West Kent Militia began marching out on their way to Camp between Yarmo[uth] & Lowestoft.
*********Mr Ray of Tostock[149] brot me a Message from Mr Spink this morning.
*********Rd Baker left us.

Wednesday May 14   The first Subdivision meeting for Thedwastre & Thingoe Hundred for establishing 2 Troops of Cavalry, abt 12 or 14 Gentn prest: not either of the Members or principal Land owners. Sir Tho Cullum in the Chair. Came to some Resolutions & adjournd for the Muster Roll to Monday. Mr Davis, Mr Tyrrell &ca din'd, drank Tea & suppd wth Us.
******************First Acct from London of some Discovrys of Seditious Packets. *************************[150]
I was indisposd this week with a Rheumatic disorder in my Head & Face.

[149] One of his sons was a clerk in Messrs Spink and Carss's Bank.
[150] Following the break-up of the British Convention in Edinburgh the London Corresponding Society held an open air meeting at Chalk Farm in April 1794 at which government policy was roundly denounced. Meanwhile the Society for Constitutional Information held their annual dinner in early May at which revolutionary toasts were drunk. The government reacted by seizing the correspondence of the Societies in May and June and by arresting Thomas Hardy, John Horne Tooke and eleven other leading members of the Societies, on charges of High Treason. Horne Tooke and Hardy were subsequently discharged and the charges against the others were dropped.

Friday June 6 At home alone. Son & Daughter Gould got to Us between 8 & 9 O'Clock.

Tuesday June 10 Accompanied Mr Adamson & Mr Gould to the Club at Ixworth. Ten Gentlemen prest. Returnd Home by 1/2 hour after 8 O'Clock.

Wednesday June 11 ************Militia Meeting also Meeting of Yarn Makers. *********** At home alone. ************News arrivd of Lord Howe's Victory over the French Fleet. 6 ships taken & one sunk /June 1st/.[151]

Thursday June 12 Self & Son Orbell in the Whiskey to [the] County Meeting at Stow[marke]tt. 40 Gentlemen prest: Mr Acton, Mr Goulding, Mr Berners, his 3 sons &ca &ca. Mr Broke in the Chair. Officers all recommended. Business finishd abt 4 O'Clock, abt 18 Gentn staid Dinner. [We] left Stow[market] abt 8 O'Clock. Home at 1/2 after ten.
***************Great Rejoicings at Stowmarkett********************
The Bishop came to Mr Mills being his primary visitation.

Monday June 16 At home alone.
****
We this Day heard of the Death of Mr George Heigham who was killd on Board the Royal George <<last>> Sunday June 1st in the Engagement between the English & French Fleet — 6 French Ships of the Line taken & 4 Sunk.
****

Wednesday June 18 At home alone. ********This evening very unexpectedly the town was illuminated on acc[oun]t of the Victory gaind over the French Fleet the 1st June never hav[in]g had any Rejoycing in the Town on the Acc[oun]t. It was pretty general considering the short Notice — Ringing of Bells — fir[in]g of Guns &ca. All was not over before 2 O'Clock in the Morning.*********

Thursday June 26 Purchasd the Grey Poney of Mr Beeton at £12 – –.******
We all dind at Mr Adamson's. . . all staid till 9 O'Clock.

Tuesday July 1t At home alone. Mr Chambers returnd from Norwich, brot a very bad acc[oun]t of Trade — the E[ast] I[ndia] orders arrivd the fore part of the preceding week but not 1/3 what wer[e] expected.

Friday July 4 Mr Adamson din'd and drank Tea with Us — no other Company. He was not mighty well.

Tuesday July 8 2d Receipt Day at Stowmarkett, Son Orbell & Robt. Mr George Mathew dind with Us to meet Mr Miller. ****************First Conversation wth Mr Spink on opening my Bank. ****************

Monday July 14 My Receipt Day at Sudbury, Self, Son Orbell, Lease & Coachman. Got Home at 1/2 hour after 7 O'Clock.

---

[151] Howe defeated a squadron of the French Navy and captured about a third of the French ships of the line engaged.

30. *A Visit to the Camp, by Henry Bunbury.*

****
This Day at one O'Clock my Daughter Gould was safely deliverd of a Boy.
****

Thursday July 17 . . . I had some Conversation with Mr Carss[152] informing him I had fully determin[ed] on opening my Bank.***

[James Oakes took the receipt up to London on 21 July, Charlotte and Mr Adamson went to stay with James at Wereham for two weeks and Peter Chambers went to Yorkshire to sell yarn for the second time that year.]

Friday Augst 1 At home alone. A Dish of fish [a] pres[en]t from Mr Shreeve[?].

Tuesday Augt 19 My Daughter Gould set out for her Journey for Totness in Devonshire. Sent her in my Coach to New[marke]tt. From thence in Chaises to Epping Place where she slept, took up Mr Chinery in London who accompanied her to Exeter. At home alone.

Wednesday August 20 At home alone.
****
On this Day Daughter Gould robb'd on Bagshot Heath on her way into Devonshire wh Mr Chinery. /[She] lost ab £3 – –, Mr Chinery £30 – –./
****

[152] Robert Carss was John Spink's partner.

[James Oakes, his wife, daughter Charlotte and a maid went to Yarmouth on 22 August.]

Thursday Aug 28 . . . I was extremely ill with a Disorder in my Bowels.

Friday Augt 29 I was much better. Mr Willm Taylor elected Mayor for the year ensuing. /Drank tea at Sr/ Edmnd Lacen's. Rooms at Night.

Monday Sept 1 Mrs O taken very ill. We were all to have din'd at Mr Spurgeon's. I only went. Mr Adamson to Mr Herring's, Norwich.

Wednesday Sept 3d I dind at the East Suffolk Camp [with] Coll Goat, Liut Coll Stisted, Major White, The General Garth & his aid De Camp & several Yarm[out]h Gentlemen, at least 28 or 30 of Us. I returnd Home before 8 O'Clock & we all went to the Rooms — at Cards &ca &.

Friday Sept 5 Morning very wett. I dind at Hopton Camp with the West Kent. The Duke of Dorset prest, no other Company. I returnd to Yarmouth before 9 O'Clock.

Sat morng Sept 6 9 O'Clock we all left Yarmouth with own Coach & Horses, baited at Acle & got to [the] Maid's Head, Norwich, by 3 O'Clock. Dind there & set off for Cawston at 4 in the Afternoon. [We] reach[ed] Dr Baker's by Tea, rested there all Sunday. Monday morning Sept 8 I left for Norwich very early, got here soon after 7 O'Clock. The Day most exceedingly wet & Bad. [I] found the Trade of the City in the most desponding State imaginable — did scarcely any Business. Mrs O & Charlotte left Dr Baker's after Dinner & got to [the] Maid's Head to Tea in the pouring Rain almost the whole of the Way. I completed the little Business I could do in Norwich before 12 O'Clock. Sent my own Horses before to Long Stratton, took a p[ai]r of Hacks so far & came on from Thence to dine at Scole Inn abt 4. Took own Horses on to Stanton where Mr A['s] Horses met Us. We reachd Home before 9 O'Clock & found all well.

This Excursion in which [we] had promised Ourselves much pleasure was a good deal allayed by none of Us having been well and the Weather proving remarkably wet and Unpleasant. Neither did we find the Company we Expected & further the Lodgings at the Star by no means so comfortable. We were absent 19 Days going out on the 22 Augs & returng Sept 9h. Expences as follows:-

	£	[s.	d.]
On the Road	6	3	5
3 Horses at Yarmouth	4	10	6
Diversions Rooms &ca	1	10	6
Living at Yarmouth includ[ing] Lodgings 3–13–6	13	1	3½
	25	05	8½

besides what I charged [the] House for [the] Apothicary &ca — Trade for Norwich journey[153] —— the whole came very little short of £28.

---

[153] The cost of going to Norwich was a business expense unlike the apothecary which was a domestic or 'House' expense.

Saturday Sept 13 The sorters had their Hawkey. The same asked as usual & same Allowances.

Tuesday Sept 16 At home. This Evening Mr Booth came from Norwich to talk abt the Woodbridge Spinning Division. Drank Tea & suppd with Us.

Wednesday Sept 17 Mr Booth breakfasted & dind with us & after Dinner set off for Norw[ic]h. We enterd into an Agreement for Him to take the Woodbridge Spinning Division wch was signd by each respectively. At home alone.

Saturday Sept 20 . . . ****I have been particularly engagd for abt ten Days in taking Stock & settling all my Books & Accts. Altho much better than the last, yet taken the 2 years together, am a Loser of between 16 & 1,700 & no prospect of much better Times.

****Mr Hasted died this evening abt 6 o'clock aged 72. The report of the Town is that He left a considerable part of what He died possessd to his Nephew, Mr Reuben Sturgeon, away from his wife & son wch has causd a general clamer against Him. **

Monday Sept 22 I attended the Assesment at the Vestry & din'd wth [the] Church wardens at the 6 Bells, abt 20 of the Parishioners, Mr Wright, Self &ca.[154] We drank Tea at Mrs Alexander's. Met Sir Thos & Lady Gage, Miss Aflick, Dr Wollaston & Mrs Goddard. We staid & suppd without formal Invitation in a friendly way.

Monday Sept 29 Proclaimd the Fair the first time at 12 O'Clock at Noon. We all drank Tea at Mr Garnham's. . . staid till 9 O'Clock & from there I went to the Angel & passd an hour or two wth abt 10 of the Corporation.
************************Opened my Bank. ************************

[George Green, James Oakes's nephew from Liverpool, and James Edge his cousin, came for the Fair.]

Tuesday Octr 7 Ixworth Club Anniversary. Mr Edge accompanied Mr Adamson & Self. Returnd Home before 9 O'Clock.

Wednesday Oct 8 First Fair Assembly, abt 30 couple Dancers, 150 Ladys & Gentlemen & a very genteel Appearance, but not full. The Marquis of Cornwallis honourd the Assembly with his presence. We got Home abt 2 O'Clock.
******************** Cash notes first issued.************************

Friday Oct 10 Second Fair Assembly. Alowed to be remarkably full & very Splendid. 2 setts of Dancers, suppose abt 50 Couple of Dancers & thought to be very near 400 Ladys & Gentn in the Room: Duchess of Grafton & her 3 Lady Daughters, Duchess of Chandos, Marquis Cornwallis &ca &ca &ca. We staid till near 3 O'Clock. Generally allowd to be as good a Ball as has been known for several years.*************Mr & Mrs Sturgeon prest. ********************
Much more Company in Town than was expected. 2d Play Night, not £5 in the House.

---

[154] This was the quarterly parish poor rate asesment.

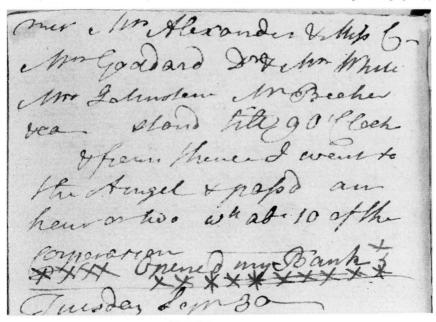

31. *Diary entry for 29 September 1794.*

Wednesday Oct 22 Last Receipt Day. At Home in [the] Bank office Self, Son, Mr Smith & Lease. Only Mr Pawsey Junr din'd wth Us. Took in 119 Parishes, abt £8,800. We finishd before 8 O'Clock & agreed to a farthing. Son & Daughter James Oakes, Charlotte & Geo. Green all din'd at Mr Symonds['s] to meet Coll & Mrs Ashley, Mr Godbold & Mrs Symonds & Capt Whitaker.

*************************** Mr Spink died this Afternoon at 1/2 hour after 4 O'Clock. Left Dr Wollaston, Mr Geo. Wollaston, Mr Mathew & Mr Carss executors. 200£ Legacy to [the] Dispensary. *****************************

Saturday Oct 25 At home alone. Mrs O continued all this Week quite In-diff[eren]t with a rheumatick Fever. Call'd in Dr White yesterday.

Tuesday Oct 28 **************** Mr Spink's Funeral ****************
An Hearse & 4 & Coa[c]h & 4 Horses. Exact at 9 O'Clock in the Morning the Funeral came round by the Guild Hall when the Corporation in their Robes preceded the Funeral and the 3 Clubs, to wch he had left £50 each, followd & after Them the Sunday School Children & then the Charity School Children making a grand Procession. The whole concluded by 1/2 after ten O'Clock.
****
We were all at home alone.

Wednesday Oct 29 A Militia Meeting at the Angel. This evening my Daughter Gould came from the Camp in Devonshire to Bury abt 7 O'Clock.

Thursday Oct 30 At home. Son & Daughter & G[eorge] G[reen] all went to

Mrs Creed's Christening. Son Orbell stood Godfather. The Boy's Names: Jno Adey. They came home 12 O'Clock at Night.

Saturday Nov 8h I went to Dinner at Mr Keddington's, Rougham. Met Sir Charles Bunbury, Mr Moseley, Mr Macklin, Mr Young, Captn Powell, Capt Armstrong, Mr Cowper, Mr Geo. Grigby, Mr Allen. Returnd Home by 10 O'Clock.

Wednesday Nov 12 This & the preceding Day we brew'd. Nephew Geo. Green left Us for London. At home alone.

Monday Novr 17 Mrs O, Self, Charlotte all din'd & drank tea at Mr Leheup's. Staid till 1/2 hour after 9 O'Clock. . . ********** Began raising the Bank Chimney. *****************

Fri Novr 21 Son Orbell din'd at Mr Macklin's, Bradfield. Staid till 11 O'Clock. At home alone. I had a complaint in my Head & Face.

Sat Nov 22 At home alone. Finish'd raising my Banking Room chimney. Raised it 35 course, cost me £5 11 –. *****

Mon Novr 24 Mr Adamson dind with Us alone. Mrs O & Charlotte Tea at Mrs Creed's. Mr Adamson & Mr Gould, Orbell & Self a party a Casano.

Saturday Nov 29 **
I breakfasted at Bradfield at Mr Macklin's.
****
We all went to Tea & Supper at Mr Adamson's (except Orbell). . .

Friday Decr 5 We all went to Dinner at Mr Macklin's, Bradfield, (5). Met Mr & Mrs Rebow, Mr Gerard, Mr Young &ca. Mrs O & Maria returnd Home ab 1/2 after 6 O'Clock & all the remainder of the Company set off for [the] Melford 2nd Subn Ball. Miss Plampin, Mr Young, Self & Orbell in the Coach. We got Home ab 1/2 hour after 4 O'Clock.

Saturday Decr 6 At home alone. Orbell to Dine at Mr Young's at Bradfield. ***************Our wedding Day. We have this Day been married 30 years. ****************

[James Oakes went to Norwich on Monday 8 December.]

Wednesday Decr 10 I breakfasted at <u>Mr Herring's.</u> Trade universally dull & bad in Norwich. Sold only 1 Parcell, abt 3 pls [pounds?] of yarn. Left Norwich soon after 12 O'Clock Noon, din'd at Scole Inn & reachd Home before 7.

Thursday Decr 11 Attended Mr Maynard at Mrs Halsey's, executed [the] parchase Agreem[en]t for Mrs H–. Taken ill this eveng with a bad swell'd Face.

Fri Decr 12 Tea & Supper Company at Home. . . My face continued very indifft.

Sat Decr 13 Son Orbell dind at Mr Godbold's wth [the] Bradfield Family.[155] My Face rather worse.

---

[155] Mrs Macklin's sister, Elizabeth Plampin, was to be Orbell Oakes's wife.

Monday Decr 15   At home alone. Orbell dind wth Company at Mr Adamson's. I was better.
***********Granddaughter Mary Ann's Birth Day: one year.**************

Thurs Decr 18   Dinner Company at Home: Mr & Mrs Macklin, Miss Plampin, Mr Young, Mr Adamson, Coll James, Mr Cobb, Mr Sackville. All staid till past 7 O'Clock when the whole Company, exceptg Coll James, attended the Card Assembly. Present abt 60 Gentn & Ladys.
*********** Mr Adamson dancd wth Miss Plampin one Dance. ***********
We left the Room at 12 O'Clock.

Sunday Dec 21   We all dind at Mr Adamson's. I rode over to Bradfield & paid a Morning visit to Miss P[lampin] ********* Son Orbell dind at Bradfield. . .

Tues Dec 23   Orbell at Bradfield. At home alone. Little Edward taken ill wh [a] Convulsion Fitt.

Thurs Decr 25   Xmas Day. We all din'd at Mr Adamson's. Met only Miss Bridge.
******* Orbell not in Spirits. *********

Our Xmas Dinner at Home as usual:
```
            10 Serv[ants]
             5 Sorters
             7 others
            ─────
            22
```

	lb
Sr Loin of Beef	33
Legg of mutton	81/2
Plum Puddings	8

sent 8 Dinners out to poor Family[s].
            14 Bottles beer at Dinner
Supper Party:
```
            10 House Serv[an]t
             8 others
            Apple Pyes — cold Beef
             4 Bottles Beef [Bear?]
            one Quart Brandy
```
*************** Wrote Letter to Miss P[lampin]. *********************

Friday Dec 26   At home alone. Orbell at Bradfield.

Mond Decr 29   I went to the Duke of Grafton's to dinner & slept. Sr T.G. Cullum was to have accompanied but not well enough & Mrs Symonds there & Mr Vernon.
     NB Miss Plampin & Mrs Macklin came to look over Mrs Buggen's House.[156]

---

[156] This house was next door but one to that of James Oakes in Guildhall Street and was owned by him. It was between that of Dr Robert White and John Creed, also owned by Oakes, and forms what is now part of the house belonging to Greene and Greene.

Tues Decr 30 I had some Conversation with the Duke, left Euston with Mr Symonds abt 11 O'Clock, got home before one. Orbell to Bradfield.

Janry 1 Thursday   I went with Daughter Charlotte to dine at Mr Mills['s] (Mrs O should have gone but not quite well enough). . . In the Evening a private Ball being the Anniversary of Mr & Mrs Mills['s] Wedding Day wh they always keep. Abt 9 couple of Dancers. I came away before 10, the Dancers staid till after 12 o'clock. Mr Gould came to Us at 10 o'clock at Night.

Monday Janry 12   Sudbury Receipt Day. Self, Mr Gould, Lease & Servt — Post Chaise. Mr Addison dind with Us. We got Home by 6 o'clock.
    This day the Inhabitants convened by the Alderman to raise a Subn for the Poore — a very respectable appearance.

The 2 Members ea[ch]	£50	[£]100
More then subscribd, say ab		[£] 60

The total of Subscription say ab 2d a Head due in a week £300 — Bread.

Tues Janry 13   Mr & Mrs Gould came to Us to Dinner on a visit. I accompanied Mr Clerk 5 streets collecting Subs for the Poor.

Fri Janry 16   I walkd over to Culford with Son Orbell & Mr Gould & paid Lord Cornwallis & Lord Brome a morng visit. Returned at 12 o'clock.
**************The Christeng of my Grandson E.M.Gould.**************

	[£	s.	d.]
I stood Godfather for Self	1	1	—
Son Orbell for Mr Maynard	2	2	—
Miss Gould for Mrs Gould	3	3	—

Six Guinies for Nurses & Servt.
Mr Goddard, Mr & Mrs Mills, Mr Adamson, Mr Sams & Mr Hasted all dind, the Ladys suppd with Us & Mr A.

Sun Feb 8   Mr Adamson & Mr Hasted dind & drank Tea with Us. The <u>Thaw commencd</u> after <u>8</u> weeks /most severe/ Frost, Snow & causd the greatest Flood that has been <u>rememberd by the</u> oldest Man living in these parts. The Thaw continued. . . *****

****

Wed Febry 11   The Day of Lord Brome's appointm[en]t for meetg the yeoman at Dinner at the Angel who meant to serve in his Lordship's Troop. It happened so remarkably unfortunately that his Lordship was taken ill in London wth a Cold & Fever & could not attend. Mr Fowke [for] his Lordship presided at the head of the Table & my Son Orbell as Cornett at the Bottom. Sr Charles Davers, Mr Pooly, Self & Mr Rodwell with the yeoman were at Table. The 15 with Lieut & Corntt all signd a Paper to serve under his Lordship's Command. 21 at Table.

The Day pass'd off Exceedingly well, his Lordship's Absence much regrettd. Mr Fowke & 6 or 7 others staid till 3 O'Clock in the Morng. The Dinner Wine &ca cost [blank] & was defrayed by [blank]. The guests & yeoman <u>did not</u> pay anything.
****

Thursday Febry 12 The Charitable Ball at the Angel. The Members, Sr Chas Davers & Lord Charles Fitzroy, subscribd 5 Gs each includg their subn. 371 Tickets were deliverd at 5/– each, all clear for the Poor disignd to be deliv'd in bread. The Sum cleard £99 15 – Tickets. Expences amo[un]ted to £7 14 for Fires & Wax Candles, printing Cards, Advertizm[ent]s, Musick 31/6, Liquer for [the] Band 15/–, £5 was pd by the Subn Ball Fund & £2 14 – by the extra Money arisg from the odd 1/– & –/6d pd by those who pd 10/6 for 2 Tickets & 21/– for 4 Tickets.

	Persons
There were in the Room	205
Tickets not come in	166
(60 couple Dancers)	———
	371

The Evening passd off extremely pleasantly & gave general Satisfaction. Those who call'd for Tea / 6d. a H[ea]d/ [and] Neagus pd for watever was orderd, also Cards, but believe only one Card Table. Mr Mills & Self acted as Stewards.***

Tuesday Febry 17 I rode over this Morng & paid a Visit to old Mr Plampin of Chadacre. Passd an hour with him & returnd Home to dinner. Mr P gave Me his most faithfull of his Intentions & Determination of doing the same by Miss P as his other Daughters. At Home alone.

Thursday Febry 19 Guildhall Meeting. Mr & Mrs Hd. School Hall Meeting at one O'Clock afterwards adjournd to the Angel to Dinner 3 O'Clock. After Dinner auditd Sir Thos Cullum's acct [for] 2 yrs [as] Comptroller & directed 400 £3 Consols to be bot. Afterwards held a Meeting for Sutton's Charity & elected Bath & Robison.[157] At 8 O'Clock I went to meet my Family at the Card Assembly Dance, ab 10 or 12 Couple [of] Dancers, abt 43 ladys & Gentn present. ******************Servant Withers returnd again. ******************

Tuesday Mar 3d I accompanied Mr Adamson to [the] Ixworth Club. 9 Gentn prest, Mr Pell Pres[iden]t Rich[?] 5/–, I likewise paid Forfeits 8/–.[158]
Began pulling down the small House at [the] end of Mr Buggen's.

---

[157] The two men were to benefit from the charity. Under his will, dated 1696, John Sutton left land and money to provide six poor men with a annual allowance of four pounds paid quarterly and a dark grey cloth gown each. The provision was later extended to include eight poor men plus two from Brockley. In addition thirty pounds a year was to keep six poor boys at the Free School, although one pound of that sum was to go to the minister of St Mary's Church to pay for a sermon to be preached in Easter week. A further four pounds a year were to go to the school master and one pound to the writing master. The charity was administered by 13 trustees.
[158] Forfeits paid for meetings missed.

Wed Mar 4   ***
This morng at 5 O'Clock died my Grandson /7 months old/ Edwd Gould. He went off very suddenly, supposd a stricture on his Breath. He was always a weakly Child & latterly rather warted. He was by other People not thought a living Child.*********

****I rode over to see Mr Geo Plampin at Long Melford [and] found him very ill, supposd declin[in]g. I went most particularly on acc[oun]t of Mrs M[acklin] & Miss P[lampin] — They being very desirous of calling on Him. NB He thought proper to decline their visiting Him. ****

Saturday March 7   At 8 O'Clock /this morng/ we buried our Grandson. He was carried to Church in my Coach with Nurse & Maid Servant & interrd in the Garnham Family vault at [the] South sid[e] [of] St James['s] Church. Mr Sams['s] Fees 6/8 pd[?] Him 10/6. No Hatband or Gloves. At home alone. Saturday Mar 14   I rode over wh Mr Chinery to see Mr Geo. Plampin. He executed the Conveyance of [the] next Turn of Depden to Me for £1,045.[159] We then balancd our Cash Acct & I had an Order to pay Mr Chinery & settle his Acct. I returned Home to Dinner at 1/2 past 8 O'Clock. Orbell dind at Mr Godbold's wh Miss P.

Thursday Mar 19   Old Mr Plampin made me a Morning Visit. I din'd with Son Orbell at Mr Adamson's. Met 7 of the West Kent Officers, viz: Capt Lambert, Capt Benjafield, Mr Campbell, Mr Coast, Mr Masters, Mr Davis & Mr Ryder, Major Hockley, Mr Macklin & Self [and] Son Orbell. We Staid till 8 O'Clock & went to the Card Assembly. Very thinly attended, only 9 Ladys & 9 Gentn prest. Dancd till one o'clock.

Wednesday March 25   I met Mr Jno Plampin at Mr Mills['s] & conversd with Him on Family Matters for near an Hour. Baron Perryn came into Town to hold the Lent Assize. Mr Whitbread of London High Sheriff. At home alone.
*************Lady Louisa Harvey married in London to Mr Jenkinson[160] son of Lord Hawkesbury by special licence.***********************************

Friday April 3   (Good Friday) ************** I went to Melford with Son Orbell & met at Mr Geo. Plampin, Mr Plampin from Chadacre & Revd Jno Plampin. On certain Conditions I resigned my purchase of [the] next presentation of Depden, see my Memorandum Book where the Particulars of this Meeting were enterd. Returnd Home to dinner at 4 O'Clock.

******************** Walter Ray left Mr Carss. ********************[161]

[James Oakes went to Norwich on business and returned with his nieces Mary and Judith Baker.]

---

[159] Oakes had bought the next presentation to the living at Depden.
[160] Robert Banks Jenkinson (1770–1828), later Lord Liverpool, Prime Minister 1812–27. Neither set of parents approved of the match, which lasted happily until her death in 1821.
[161] Robert Carss became sole proprietor of the bank on John Spink's death.

Friday April 10th ... I found Norwich in the dullest State as to Trade imaginable. Did not get the offer for a B[und]le of yarn nor could make any Sales at any price. Norwich Cambletts short yarn sold currently at 11/– a Gross.

Monday April 13   1st Receipt Day at Eye. Self & Lease in a Post Chaise got home before 7 O'Clock. Son James, his Wife & Daughter came to Mr Adamson's on a visit for a Week.

******* A rumour of an intended Riot in our markett as next Wednesday.*****

Tuesday April 21   I went with Sons Orbell & James to Bradfield to Execute the writings. ***

Wednesday April 22   My last Receipt Day at Home. Mr Chambers, Mr Simpson of Nowton, Mr Pawsey & Mr Lawrence wth Mr Smith & Lease all din'd with Me. Son Orbell went to Bradfield to dine & sleep. We took abt 100 Parishes & to the Amot of £8,000. Finishd at 10 O'Clock.

Thursday April 23rd   **
My Sons Orbell's Wedding Day
We all went to Bradfield arriving there by 8 O'Clock. Mr Adamson, Judith Baker, Self & Son James. We first alighted at Mr Macklin's, staid 1/2 of an hour. Mr Macklin taken exceedingly ill in the Night could not perform the Ceremony. Son James supplied his Place. Mr Plampin gave his Daughter away. All attended the Church except Mr Macklin & myself, & returned to Mr M's where a most elegant Breakfast was prepard. The new married Couple set off for Londn abt 1/4 before 10 O'Clock & we all retured Home wth Master & Miss Macklin. Mr & Mrs Tyrrell, Son & Daughter Jas Oakes, Mr Adamson, Lady Cullum & Mrs George Mathew all din'd with Us & staid till 9 O'Clock. We heard the Bride & Bridegroom arriv'd at their Lodgings, No 4, Princes Street, Hanover Square (Merlin's) before 8 O'Clock.
****

Friday April 24   At home alone. *************************************
First meeting of Lord Brome's Cavalry. Lord Brome attended himself & mounted abt 20. There are abt 5 or 6 that could not possibly attend. They paraded the streets & formed twice on the Angel Hill afterwards dismounted & dind wh his Lordship at the Angel. Only Myself & Son James prest besides the Cavalry Themselves. We all parted by abt 8 O'Clock.*****************************
******Mr Macklin continued very ill.

Wednesday April 29   **
This Morning abt 10 O'Clock [a] Disturbance began in our Markett the Populace seizing the Butchers' Meat & obliging Them to sell off at their prizes. Some Meat was taken away without anything being paid for it — much Confusion ensued. The Justices & Gentn of the Town all met at the Guild Hall & swore in abt 40 additional Constables then on foot went & made a proclamation for the protection of all who brot to our Markett, their Persons & properties, & recommedn[in]g good & peaceable Order. At 3 O'Clock abt 50 Gentn paraded on Horseback till 4 & return'd to their respective Quarters.
At 7 in the Eveng the Gentn, Farmers &ca to the Number of 150 or 200

mounted their Horses & rode thro many Streets in the Town till full 8 O'Clock. Many Stones at length being thrown & Mr Smith wounded by one we quitted our Horses & returnd to the Guild Hall. The Major of the West Kent came & informd the Alderman & Justices that his Magazine where all his Powder & Ball were lodgd were threatened to be taken possession. If & as he apprehend'd Danger should mount a Pickett Guard of 50 men. At ten O'Clock the people not all dispersing the Riot Act was read <word illegible> after they retird to their own Homes. All remaind Quiet for the rest part of the Night. 50 West Kent & 20 West Norfolk Militia continud at the Guild Hall the whole of the Night.
****

Saturday May 2 At home alone. The Market this Day very thinly supply'd — however all remain'd quiet.

Wednesday May 6 The Town perfectly peaceable.

Thursday May 14 Dinner Company at Home. . . all staid till 9 O'Clock. This Evening the young Ladys' Ball by Mr Harrington.[162] A very splendid Appearance & it was generally allow'd they excelld dancing. The Room was remarkably full of the first Company. We staid till 12 O'Clock. Private dancing afterwards till 4 O'Clock.

Thursday May 21 Daughter Gould left us this Morng for Weymouth at 7 O'Clock in a Post Chaise intendg to sleep at Mr Harvey's, Barwell Court, this Night & set off early next Morng. . .

Saturday May 23 At home alone. Sent Servt to Elden[163] wh Son James. Cook to meet there.

Sat the 30 *******Combers petition'd for [an] Advance of 1d a ld for combing Super Work. *********************

Sunday May 31 Mr Adamson din'd wh Us. The first time this Summer at one O'Clock. We all staid the Sacrament. Rode over to Bradfield & drank Tea with Son Orbell & his Wife.

Monday June 1 We drank Tea at Mr Dallas's.

************This Day it was resolvd by the Master Yarn–makers to advance the Combing of the Super Wool one penny a ld from 4d to 5d. *************

Thursday June 4th ************King's Birth Day********************* Lord Brome's Troop of Yeomanry Cavalry exerciz'd & came into Bury in parade to drink his Majesty's Health. A Publick Dinner at the Angel abt 40 Gents includg abt 14 or 15 of the Yeomanry. Lieut Fowk in [the] Chair at the First Table & Cornett O.Oakes at [the] 2d Table. Anderson charg'd the ordinary: 4/6

Beer & Bread 6d, Fruit 6d, Serv[ants]   1/6

———

6/–

Thought much too extravagant.

---

[162] A ball given by the dancing master for his pupils.
[163] Elvedon.

A Ball at the Guildhall was intended & abt 1/2 a score Ladys assembld at my House but could not muster sufficient Number of Young men who were in [a] proper State for dancing, therefore necessarily perspond. Miss Cocksedges came to Us.

Monday June 8 . . . **********Bricklayers & Labourers all turnd out for [an] Advance of wages deman[din]g 4[d.] more a Head a Day. **********

Tuesday June 9 At home alone. Capt Rose with Us at Tea & brot the acct of Captn St Jno, alias H. Jessop, decamping having been here under a feignd Name borrowg Mony &ca.

Sunday June 14 Mr Adamson dind with Us at one O'Clock. After Church in the Afternoon Mrs O, Self, Charlotte & Miss Bakers all went in the Coach to pay Mr & Mrs Ray a visit at Tostock. Mess P & W Ray were there. Returnd Home to sup. Captn Ross supp'd with Us.

*********** Between the Hours of 12 & one O'Clock Sunday Night & Monday morng my Son James's Wife was safely deliverd of a Girl – the second. Both Mother & Child finely. A very favourable time.*****************

Monday June 15 Sister Baker & her son Richard to Dinner. Tea & Supper Company in the Eveng. . . After supper had a little Dance to the Harpsicord & singing. Company left us soon after one O'Clock.

Tuesday June 16 ********Sister Green & her Daughter came to us from Liverpool. . .

Saturday June 20 Sister Baker, her two Daughters Mary & Judith, & Rd Baker all left Us at 7 O'Clock to return to Cawston– my Horses to Thetford.

*********This Day came Home by Londn Waggon my Coach bot for me by Mr Chas Harvey in London of a Gentleman who had ruirsd [?] [164] it a couple of years – quite new wheels & lately fresh painted. Cost £84 – – & allowd by our coachman to be remarkably good & well worth the money.
****

Captn Ross at Tea & supper.

Sunday June 21 We all dind at Mr Adamson's. Met Mrs Campbell, drank tea with him & went to Bradfield for a Ride.

Monday June 22 Miss Cocksedges came to Us to dinner. In the Evening had a Ball at the Guild Hall intended to have been on the 4th June.
Prest:Ladys

Mrs Macklin	Revd Mr Macklin
Mrs /Hen/ Heigham	Rev Mr H.Heigham
Mrs G.Green	Rev Mr Hasted
Mrs Oakes	Rev Mr J.Fiske
Mrs O.Oakes	Mr Cullum
Miss Grigby	Mr Oakes

[164] This is very unclear in the text. *Used* would fit the sense but does not seem to be what is written.

		[£	s.	d.]
Miss Symonds	Captn Corry			
Miss Spratt	2 Mr Rays			
2 Miss Fiske	Capt Ross			
2 Miss Cocksedge	Mr O.Oakes			
Miss Green				
Miss Oakes				
14	11=25			

	[£	s.	d.]
Mr Yardly found Tea at 1/–	1	5	–
Wax Candles	1	3	–
[word illegible]		1	–
Cards		4	–
Musick		15	6
D[itt]o Wine		3	–
Hall Keeper		7	6
Yardly's Waiters		2	6
Carpenters bring[in]g & returning Chandilier		2	6
	4	4	–
25 Ladys & Gents at 2/6 =	3	2	6
collected for Musick of 10 Gent		10	6
	3	12	6
JO extra to pay		11	6 4 4 –

The Company all left the Room a little before 2 O'Clock.

Saturday June 27 At home alone. ******* Parliament progued. A General Talk of Dissolution but did not take place. **********

Monday June 29 I rode over to Sr Charles Davers's & from thence to Mr Tyrrell's were I breakfasted. Calld at Mr Symonds['s] & from thence Home by 12 O'Clock.

Sunday July 5 We all dind at one O'Clock at Mr Adamson. ******** Son James preachd at St Mary's in the Morning & set off after dinner at 3 O'Clock for Cambridge to take his Master of Arts degree. ****** Mrs O & Family to tea at Mr Tyrrell's. I drank Tea at Sr Thos Cullum.

Thursday July 9 Receipt Day at Wickhambrook, Self & Servt. I went over The Green Farm, also my new Purchases. T.Woolard, Tenant.

[A public meeting was held at the Guildhall to consider the scarcity of wheat flour and bread and to begin a subscription to raise money to buy bread for the poor.]

Thursday July 16 We all dind at Mr Ray's, Tostock. Met Mr Kedington, Son Orbell & his Wife. Got Home at 10 O'Clock. ************* I was sent for by Special Messenger on acco[u]nt of a Riot at Bury but, by the time we got Home, all was perfectly quiet & no sort of Mischief had been done.*************

[James Oakes went to London with the second quarter's receipt and swore his accounts before a Baron of the Exchequer. Maria arrived from Weymouth on 10 August.]

Thursday Augt 13 Mr Young, Orbell & Betsy din'd with Us & staid till 8 O'Clock.

Sunday Aug 16 . . . The 1st Sunday of the Cavalry exercizing on the Heath, neither Lord Brome or Lieut Fowke prest. Son Orbell commanded. . .

Thursday Aug 20 <<19>> ********* I breakfasted at Son Orbell's, Bradfield. *******

The Day of the Election of an Alderman. Mr Jos. Maulkin unanimously elected. Sr Chas Davers, Sr Thos Cullum, Mr Leheup, Mr Oakes, Mr Wright & Mr Chambers Assistant Justices. We all dind at the Angel abt 56 Gentn pres. I returnd Home before 7 O'Clock. I bot [a] Pipe of Lisbon of M Brook at £50 pipe, 140 gall[o]n.

Friday Aug 21 Self, Wife, Daughter Gould, Sister Green & Maid Servt all set out for Wereham abt 1/2 hour after 9 O'Clock. Sent my Horses to Elden & took the Cart Horses so far. Took a Sandwitch[165] at Brandon & got to Wereham at 1/2 hour after 3 O'Clock.

Monday Augst 24 Son James & Self to Lynn, returnd to Wereham 4 O'Clock Dinner. Look'd over Daughter Maria's Estate at Sadlebow.[166]

Tuesday Aug 25 Mr Houchen from Wereham. We christend Son James['s] youngest Daughter.* Sister Green, Daughter Gould & Self Sponsors. We made up £2 2 – for the /nurse &/ Servt on the Ocassion. *Louisa.

Wednesday Augst 26 We returnd Home leaving Wereham at 1/2 hour after 2 O'Clock first dining.Came to Brandon to Tea & arriv'd at 9 O'Clock. Cart Horses met us at Elden.

************** Mr Bullen died early this Morng. **********************

[Sister Green returned to Liverpool on 4 September.]

Sunday Septr 6 Mr Derrisley, Mr Adamson & Mr W.Ray all of the Yeomanry Cavalry din'd with Us then all went upon the Heath to see the Yeomanry exercize. Son Orbell returnd to Tea & then went to Bradfield.

Tuesday Septr 8 We bottled off a Pipe of Red Port & D[itt]o Sherry. The former wholly to myself, the latter divided between myself & Orbell. Did not finish till 7 O'Clock.

Wednesday Septr 9 At home alone. My mare lam'd by a Slip in the Pasture.

Thursday Sept 10 We all drank Tea at Lady Cullum's. Met Mr & Mrs Belgrave. *****Son Orbell's Horse came down wh him. *****

---

165 Sandwitch (sandwich) – supposed to have been named after John Montagu, 4th Earl of Sandwich (1718–92), who in 1763 spent twenty four hours at the gaming table without any food other than beef sandwiches.
166 Property that she had inherited from her Aunt, Sarah Adamson.

Friday Sept 11 At home alone. Settl'd with Jermyn Brand. . .

Thursday Sept 17 We had Dinner Company at home: Mr & Mrs /Rd/ Moseley, Mr & Mrs Leheup, Mr & Mrs Thompson wh Son & Daughter O. Oakes, Mr Young. All staid till 9 O'Clock. We had [a] Haunch of Venison & Venison Pasties. I sent the Neck to Mr Adamson at Mr Herr[in]g, Norw[ic]h.

Thursday Sept 24 Yarn Committee Meeting, 5 of Us. *****I attended & resign'd as quitting the Manufacturing at Michlmas.

Friday Sept 25 *********** Mrs Buggen's Auction began. *************** ***Wool-Fair Day at Sturbich. The first of a great many Years that I omitted attending. *******

[Daughter Gould left for Weymouth on 1 October.]

Monday Oct 5 ********Mr H.White & Miss Man to Gretna Green. ******** *******Son Orbell & his Wife came to their House in Bury. *********** We were at home alone.

Wednesday Oct 7 ****Mr H.White & Miss Man married at Gretna Green. Mrs O pd a visit at Ickworth. . . 1st Fair Assembly, not any one of my House went. Allowd to be a good Ball for the first — say 30 couple of Dancers. Mr Berners & Mr Jno Moseley Stewards.

Friday Oct 9 Mr & Mrs Moseley, Mr & Mrs Tyrrell, Miss Quail all took beds with Us. Philip Ray din'd wth Us. 2nd Assembly: Dutchess of Chandos prest & a great Show of Beauty & Elegance tho not so full as I have seen it. Suppose to be at 200 – & 50 Couple of Dancers. All our Party left the Assembly House ab 1/2 hour after one [o'] Clo[ck], suppd at my House & all left us <<abt No>> before [blank].

Friday Octr 16 My Receipt Day at Mildenhall, Self & only Coachman. Get home 1/2 before 4 O'Clock. Mr Ray din'd with Us. Lord Brome's & Yeomanry bespoken Play – the Battle of Hexham[167] & Spriggs of Laurel.[168] The House completely f[i]lld & many disappointed of [a] Place. Mrs Ray /& Mr Walter Ray/ slept here. Mr Ray not well & could not come. All the Family went to the Play except Mrs Bridge & Miss B.

Monday Oct 19 My Receipt at Sudbury. Self, Mr Smith & Lease in a Post Chaise. Returnd by 1/2 hour after 6 O'Clock. NB In future if Mess F[enn] & A[ddison] take Cash or Bank besides their Notes to pay at one day due. *****

Wednesday Oct 21 My Receipt Day at Bury. Took in upwds of £8,300, finishd abt 8 O'Clock. Short 20/–.

Monday Oct 26 Mrs O & Self dind at Mr Young's, Bradfield. Met Mr & Mrs Macklin & Mr & Mrs Plampin, Captn Stopford & Mr Floud. Staid till 1/2 hour after 9 O'Clock. *********** Son James & Family from Wereham to Thurston.

---

[167] *The Battle of Hexham*, a comedy in three acts by George Colman the younger (1762–1836).

[168] *Sprigs of Laurel*, a musical farce by John O'Keefe (1747–1833).

Tuesday Oct 27 I went to [the] Ixworth Club wh Mr Adamson, ten of Us present: the Anniversary Meeting.Son James visited Us.
   Young Lady wh Lord Brome at the Play.

Thursday Oct 29 First Subn Ball. Stewards Lord Brome & Son Orbell, 107 Ladys & Gentn present. . . Lady Hervey & Miss Hervey, Mr Fred Hervey &ca &ca. ********** Parliament met. [The] King insulted in going to the House & [his] Coach broke. ************************[169]

Friday Oct 30 **
Lord Brome's Colours for the 4th Troop of Yeomanry Cavalry consecrated. The 3 Officers & 36 privates present. Son James, Chaplain, preachd the Sermon. Lady Mary Singleton presented the colers to Lord Brome & his Lordship to the Chaplin. From thence to St James['s] Church. The Corporation attended in the Procession, [the] Church extremely full. After the Service Lord Brome desird th Corporation to attend him to the Angel to drink his Majesty's Health. The Troop then paraded on Horseback & went into the Field to Exercize. [They] returnd at 3 O'Clock & at half after 4 O'Clock assembled to dine wh his Lordship. Ab 34 [of] the Gentn, say abt 74 at Dinner in the Assembly Room: Mr Howard, Sir Thos. Cullum, Mr Hayward etc etc. A most elegant Dinner was servd up & many loyal Toasts drank with several Songs well adapted to the Day. **

Mrs Jas Oakes, Miss Aldrich,[170] 2 Miss Goulds & Mrs Cock all dind wh Mrs O.

Sunday Novr 1 We all dind at Mr Adamson's. . . home at supper.
***************Amb Taylor died this Eveng ab 8 O'Clock**************

Thursday Nov 5 Yeomanry Cavalry exercized by Lord Brome apprehend[in]g some tumultuous proceedings in the Town & no Bull Baitd. *******All perfectly quiet. Most remarkable, high wind Friday near 3 O'Clock. A very great deal [of] damage done. I sufferd at Bury £20. ******************************

Friday Novr 6 Sister Bridge & her Daughter Susan went home to Cawston on a visit to Dr & Mr[s] Baker. At home alone. Lease left Me very ill.

Saturday Novr 7 At home alone. Bottled off Rasin Wine.
************** My Birth Day, 54 yrs of Age. ************************
*************Edwd Brand left me & went to his Father for [the] Remainder of his Apprenticeship.

Tuesday Nov 10 Son James Oakes, his Wife, 2 Children & 3 Servt came to Us from Wereham to pass a week or 10 Days. Mr Hasted drank Tea & suppd with Us.

Sunday Novr 15 . . . Mr Hasted & Son James changd their Churches.

---

[169] While riding in state to open Parliament George III's carriage was mobbed by crowds demanding bread and an end to the war. A stone, at one time thought to have been a bullet, was thrown through the carriage window. On returning, the royal carriage was chased into St James's Park where a door was pulled off.
[170] Miss Aldrich was probably the Rev. James Oakes's childrens' governess.

Thursday Nov 19 Tea & Supper Company at home: Sr Th & Lady Cullum, Mr & Mrs Allen, Mrs Bennett, Son Orbell & his Wife. . . Address by [the] Corporate Assembly voted to his Majesty.

Monday Nov 23 Mrs O, Sister Bridge & Family to Miss Goddard's, Tea & Cards. I could not go. Son Orbell & his Wife to [the] Melford Ball.
****
<two words deleted> Signd A Petition to the House of Commons against the Bills pendg in Parliament to prevent seditious Meeting & the better preservg his Majesty's Person against the Attack of ill desposd people. <u>Signd principally by the Dissenting Party</u>.[171]
****

Tuesday Nov 24 At home alone. Ixworth Club Day but [I] did not go. Mr Baker from Norwich offering himself as Clerk but did not suit.
*************My Nephew Geo. Green of Age, 21 years. *****************

Monday Nov 30 We all dind at Drinkstone. Met Mr Kedington & Son James from Thurston. Got Home at 11 O'Clock. The County meeting at Stow[marke]tt calld by 1/2 Dozen Gentn (4 of wch Clergy) to petition Parlaiment against the Bills pendg in Parliament to prevent seditious Meetings etc etc. It is said about 600 prest. Mr Grigby in the Chair.

Friday Decr 4 Tea & Evening at Mrs Rose's. . . Closd my annual Receipt for 1794.

Saturday Decr 5 All at home. Son & Daughter Gould came to Us from Pool. Arriv'd at 9 O'Clock, own Horses wth Mr A Chaise from Sudbury. . .

Sunday Decr 6 . . .*********Our wedding Day, married 31 years.***********

Monday Dec 7 We kept our Wedding Day. Dinner & Supper Company at home: quite a Family Party excepting Mr & Mrs Belgrave from Cockfield, Son Orbell & his Wife, Son James & his Wife, Son Gould & his Wife, Mr Adamson, Sister Bridge & her two daughters. We set down 15 at Dinner. Mr Denbeigh /Pay Master/ of the Kent Romney Fencibles & Mr P.Ray came to Tea & Supper.
    My new Clerk, Rd Biggs enterd on his Service.

Thursday Dec 10 At home. Mrs O, Self, Miss Bridge & Daughter Charlotte all went to the Card Assembly wch was extremely full: a great deal of the best Company, suppose not less than from 50 to 66 Ladys & Gent but a great want of Gent. We came home at 1/2 hour after 11 o'clock. Mrs Bridge, her Daughter Susan, Mr & Mrs Gould staid at Home: Mrs G not well.

********The Justices met at the Hall to consider what steps to take on acct of the high price of Wheat. The averidge Price on a fresh assize of this Day set at

---

[171] The Government reacted to the attack on the King by a proclamation against seditious assemblies and the Treasonable Practices Act which made it a treasonable offence to incite people to hatred of the King, Government or Constitution either verbally or in writing. Subsequently the Seditious Meetings Act restricted all public meetings to under 50 people unless a magistrate was asked to attend. The magistrate had the power to close the meeting if he felt that seditious language was being used.

46/– per Comb. [It was] determind to call a Meeting of the Inhabitants.*********

********This Day came an Acct of his Majesty's message [to] the House signif[yin]g his Desire of treating for Peace.********

Friday Dec 11 (Yeomanry Exercize.) Mr Gould & Son Orbell dind at Mr Adamson's. (Sister B answ[ere]d Dr Baker.) We all drank Tea & suppd at Sr Tho. Cullum – first set Company in their new Rooms. . . abt 23 in all.

This Eveng abt 7 O'Clock came /from Liverpool/ Nephew James Bridge /to Bury/ to accompany home his Mother & 2 Sisters.

Saturday Decr 12 At home alone. Further Acct of the victory gaind over the French by the Austrian Troops.********* Every Appearance of an approaching Peace[172] – Stocks advanced 3 per C[en]t. The Contracters for the new Loans gaind 10 & 1/2 per Cent, £18,000,000.*********

Monday Decr 14 Son & Daughter Gould went to Hoxne for a Week. At home alone. *********A Meeting of the Inhabitants to consider what Method is best to be adopted on acct of the great Scarcity & high Price of Wheat wch a Committee of the House of Commons had been debating upon & recommended 3 or 4 different Measures. That is to say:
1st That every Family should abate 1/3 of their usual Consumption
2nd Or that a certain Proportion of Barley or other Grain should be mixd
3 Or that only 5ld per Bushel should be taken from the Wheat & that the whole besides should be consumd together fine & course wch is only taken out the bread Bran & would make a considerable Saving.
This last Mode adopted as the most likely to be generally adheard to and accordingly enterd into Certain Resolutions to be as generally signd by [as many of?] the Inhabitants as possible at [the] same time recommending as little use of fine [flour] for Puddings & Pastry as possible.

Very few Gentn attended. The Recorder, Mr Ranby, Mr Paston, Dr White, abt 30 or 40 others of the Trading part of the Town. Dr White very much question whether a Mixture of Barley would be wholesome without the same proportion of Rye to counteract & qualify it – and Rye was as difficult to be procurd as Wheat.

The pres[en]t price of Wheat from 46/– – to 50/– per comb & the Results of the Committee Enquiry was a real apprehension without the greatest economy it could not possibly hold out. Barley at this time   17/6

Oats from	13/– to 14/6
Butchers' Meat from	5d to 7d per ld
Bacon	10d & almost every< word

illegible> other sort of the necessarys of Life in Proportion.
****

Tuesday Dec 15 Paid a morng Visit at Thurston, Ladys & Self. Grandaughter Mary Ann['s] Birthday: 2 yrs old. At home alone.

---

172 The Austrians were Britain's only Continental allies at this time.

Wednesday Dec 16 Ladys pd a morng visit at Hengrave to the Nunns.[173] ***General meeting of Militia, Deputy Lieutenants for returng the Lists. Mr Leheup, Mr Heigham & Self prest.

Wheat continue rising. Sold this Day in the Markett from 52/– to 54/–. A very few Samples offerd apparently not any Quantity to be procurd at any price. The greatest Apprenhensions are entertain'd of not being able to procure /Wheat/ Meal for the out Poor. . . **************************************

Friday Dec 18 We had a very large Party at Tea & a Sandwich Supper. . . NB Several other Officers & Ladys were to have been of the party but happend to be engagd. With 7 of our own Family we set down 23 to supper. Mr & Mrs Gosling did not stay. Nephew Bridge, Son Orbell & Son James dind at Mr Adamson & staid till 9 O'Clock.

Thursday Decr 24 Xmas Eve Son James, his Wife & 2 Children, 2 Maid Servt &ca came from Thurston [and] calld here on their way to Wereham after 9 Week's visit: a Fortnight with Us & 7 weeks Thurston. This Evening Self & Daughter Charlotte went to Mr Symonds's Rout at St Edmund's Hill to Tea & cold Supper. There were 17 Ladys & 18 Gentlemen many of which were Officers [of the] Kent Romney Fencibles & East Kent /Militia/ marching thro the Town. Got Home soon after 11 O'Clock.

**********(Mr & Mrs Eldred came to Me & set [a] price on their Nowton Estate.)*************

Friday Decr 25 Xmas Day Attended Alderman Maulkin to Church Morning & Evening Service. After Evening Service dind at my Son Orbell's, Mrs O & Self, Son & Daughter Gould, Daughter Charlotte, Mr Adamson, Mr Young & Mr Debeigh. Staid till between 11 & 12 o'clock. **********The Weather remarkably mild all this month of December have not rememberd a finer & milder Xmas Day of many years.**********

William /Coachman/, Wife & Children, Widw Sleet, Betsy Hogg dind with my Servants. Sent Wid Tayler her Dinner & several other Dinners to poor Peop[le]. NB None suppd her[e] exceptg Will Coachman [and his?] Wife. Allowd Them 1/2 Doz Bottles Old Beer & promisd a pint of Rum wch was forgot.*

Sunday Decr 27 Self, Mrs O, Mr & Mrs Gould & Charlotte all dind at Mr Adamson's. Met Mr Arthur Young. *******Son Orbell & his Wife dind at [the] Marquis Cornwallis, Culford.

Monday Decr 28 . . . ********I rode over this Day to Nowton & had some Conversation wth Mr & Mrs Eldred respectg the Purchase of their Farm. Offerd them £4,500 & to accept all the stock at a fair valuation & enter upon it next May Day. They agreed to consider of my proposal & let me know.*********

---

[173] An order of Nuns had lived at Hengrave Hall under the auspices of Mrs Moore since they were driven out of Flanders during the early years of the French Revolution. They were the object of much curiosity in the neighbourhood and the *Bury and Norwich Post* reported that 'The Courtesy, Politeness and attention of these sequestered females will long be respectfully remembered by their numerous visitors' when they returned to Bruges in the Autumn of 1802. BNP 25 August 1802.

Janry 7 Thursday   3rd Day's Receipt at Wickhambrook, Self, Biggs & Coachman [took in] abt 12 Parishes, nearly £700. Got home by 1/2 hour after 5 O'Clock. The 3rd Card Assembly: Mrs O, Self, Daughter Gould & Charlotte [went]. A very genteel appearance, extremely full of Ladys, scarcity of Gentlemen who came very late. 15 couple of Dancers, 2 Card Tables, in all abt 50 Ladys & Gent. Came home exact at 12 O'Clock.

Janry 8 Friday   4th Day's Receipt, Mildenhall, Self & Willm Coachman. Only took in 7 Parishes, ab £300. At home by 5 O'Clock. Lady Cullum's Ball this Eveng: Daughter Charlotte from our House, Son Orbell & his Wife, 15 couple of Dancers & abt 40 Ladys & Gentlemen. Mrs O, Self & Daughter Gould at home.

Janry 10 Sunday   We all dind at Mr Adamson's. . . staid till 8 O'Clock. . . New Coachman, George.

Janry 11 Monday   5th Day's Receipt, Self, Biggs & Willm Coachman on Horseback, hird 2 Horses. Took in abt 30 Parishes: £1,710 7 10½. Mr Fenn & co took only their own Notes for wch they were to order Paymt at their own Bankers in London. We got home at 1/2 after 5 O'Clock. Mr Jno Plampin at Tea & Supper with Us.

**Mr Corsbie buried.[174]

Janry 12 Tuesday   At home. Lord Charles Fitzroy did me the honour of a morng visit. Mr & Mrs Eldred were with me to settle abt the /Sale/ of their Estate at Nowton. We had Mr Chinery with Us & he had Instructions for drawg up an Article of Agreement to be mutually signd. Daughter Gould & Charlotte at Tea with Miss Moyle.

Janry 13 Wednesday   My last Day's Receipt at Bury, Self, Son, Mr Smith & Biggs. We took in 109 Parishes, £4,322 5 1¾. Finishd by abt 6 O'Clock but, havg Notes to send off & willing likewise to balance, we made it near 9 O'Clock. Only Mr H.Twight, Mr Smith & Biggs din'd with Self & Son Orbell.

Janry 16 Saturday   . . . ******The Weather continued this Week most remarkably soft & mild. So fine & mild a Winter <<weather>> was scarcely ever remember'd.

Janry 18 Monday   Queen's Birth Day kept. At home: Mr Adamson dind with Us alone & staid till between 7 & 8 O'Clock.

**********This Morning I provd the Boy Wm Pentuney guilty of stealing several Shillings. I had some time suspected him of these petty Thefts & by markg Money, wch being missd & found upon him, brot the fact clearly to his Charge. I immediately sent for his Mother & his Uncle Prigg and instead of presenting him mean, if possible, send[in]g him to Sea.********************* County Sessions this Day.

[174] Oakes reported John Corsbie's death on 5 January 1796.

Janry 19 Tuesday   Annual Settlement of Dr Battley's Acct.[175] Present Self, Mr Cook, Mr Pawsey, Mr Barwick & the Receiver, Mr Dickenson. The 3 Trustees Absent Mr Wright, Mr Carss & Mr Sharp. We agreed in future that the absentees should always allow 2/6 for their Dinner &, indeed the same was now p[ai]d for those absent. The annual Rent of [the] Estate £31 10 –, the Balance left in [the] Receiver's Hands ab £24 – –, wch may be thought abt, or nearly, a clear year's Rent. However, considering the dearness of every Article of life, we orderd each of the Objects, Bidwell & Plumpton, 2 Gns a year extra & agreed to continue their Quarterly payment of 50/– = £10 a year each. We all drank & went home. Mrs O & Daughters at home alone.
************Mr Dallas said to be gone to America.*********************

Janry 20 Wednesday   At home alone.********************************
For the last Market Days Grain has been dropping. Wheat now from 63/– to 50/–, Barley from 19/– to 16/6, Oats from 15/– to 14/– & expected to be <u>considerably lower.</u> This Day had some Conversation with my Tenant Thos Green. I expressd my Desire of selling but as He could not purchase, rather than turn him out, I agreed to accept £130 – – a year Rent but not 1/– less on any acct.

NB He paid before	£104	5	–
this is a rise of	£ 25	15	–
	130	—	–

but observable there has not [been] 20/– advance on this Estate of 50 years. S[ai]d advancd Rent to be paid next Micklmas that is to say <u>Mick 1796.</u>

NB	acr[es] Plough			pasture		
of Cobnals Farm say	72	–	–	53	–	–
Sinall Farm	36	–	–	3	2	–
	108	–	–	pas[tu]r[e]	56	2	–
				pl[oug]h	108	–	–
					164	2	–

64 acres at 16/– an acre R[ent] = £131 4 –, so that I now let it at base 16/– an acre, say Gross R[en]t 130£ an year. 27 years Purchase would am[oun]t [to] £3,500 – –.
****

Janry 21 Thursday . . . In the Evening to the 4th Sub[scriptio]n Ball, very full & splendid. . . 3 Card Tables & 27 couple of Dancers all the Officers & their Ladys of the Romney Fencibles. Mrs O, Self & Daughter Charlotte from my House & Mr C. Tyrrell, who took a Bed with Us. We left the Ball Room 1/2 hour after 2 O'Clock.

---

[175] Under his will, dated 14 October 1708, Dr John Battley left an estate in Chevington the rents from which were to provide for the maintenance of two poor men, provided that they were members of the Church of England, led a good life and were of 'honest fame'. He also left one pound a year to be spent on a dinner for the Trustees, receiver of the rents and the two objects of the charity.

32. *Front View of Ickworth Park* (1818) by *William Henry Brooks: see p.* 326.

Self & Orbell made a rough Settlement of [the] Bank Acct for the Year 1795.
**************Miss Buck married.***************

[James Oakes took his daughter Maria and her maid to London to join the Mail
to Pool. He cleared his Receiver's accounts for 1794 at the Auditor's Office and
made visits to friends, the theatre and coffee houses before returning home by
stage coach.]

Wednesday Febry 3 At home till Eveng at Mrs Ranby's Rout. Pres[en]t abt 50
Ladys & Gent, 7 Card Tables.

**********************This Day Thos Green & his Son call'd on me and
agreed to accept the Terms offerd for my Farm that is to say 130£ a year from
Michs 1795. . . Thos Green sign'd & his Son witnessd the same.

Mr Ranson came to my Son to say he had lookd over his Farm at Thorp & desird
another week to consider of it.*************176

Febry 5 Friday Company Tea & Cards at Home. . . The Day for Lord Brome's
Troop exercizing but so wet could not do anything in the Field.

Febry 6 Saturday Sent in a Letter of Resignation to the Ixworth Club by Mr
Adamson to Mr Boldero who was to deliver the same next Club Day. . .

Febry 12 Friday . . .*****Acct arriv'd pf Lord Hervey's Death. Leaving no Son
his brother Mr Frederick takes the Title Lord Hervey.*******177

Febry 13 . . . This Day an acct from London of some Expectations of Peace thr'
the Emperor & Stocks rose 3 per ct, that is to say Consols 3 p ct 67½ to 70½.

Febry 14th Sunday **********After Church in the Morng I rode over to Sr
Charles Davers & deliverd him a Sheet of paper fill'd wh Remarks on the Danger
of our cross post from hence to Newmarket & requesting Sr C.Bunbury & his
renew[in]g their requests at the Post Office for a Mail as he was going up to
Town.********** From thence I rode & pd a Morng Visit at Mr Tyrrell's. Mr
Adamson not well enough to dine with Us. . .

Febry 15 Monday ******I rode with Mr Godbold & viewd the Land of Mr
Wright's intended to be chang[in]g in the Feoffment,178 then call'd to see Banks
of Whepstead who, apparently, was in a very declining State. Mrs O, Self &
Daughter Charlotte at Tea & supper at Dr & Mrs Wollaston's. . .

Febry 16 Tuesday At home. Mr Adamson dind with Us also Son & Daughter
OO. All drank Tea &, except Mr A, suppd with Us. (Mr A indifferent & very
low in Spirits.)

Febry 21 Sunday *****Son Orbell to Wereham to pay his bro a visit & particularly to see Mr Houchin with a view of informing him his Inten[tio]n to sell the
Thorp Estates etc, Mr R A[damson] quite approving it. . .

176 The farm was inherited from his maternal grandfather, Christopher Adamson.
177 The 4th Earl of Bristol had two sons: Lord Augustus John and Frederick William who
succeeded his father as 5th Earl of Bristol in 1803.
178 An intended exchange of land between the Guildhall Feoffment Trust and Mr Wright.
This exchange was questioned in 1831.

33. Rotunda at Ickworth in the Course of Building by William Henry Brooks: see p. 326.

Febry 22 Monday Son Orbell from Wereham /to Dinner/. Mr Houchin much approve of Son's selling his Thorp Estate, expect it will fetch at least £4,000 & to sell all the Tenements separately afterwards. At home. Son Orbell & his wife at Tea & Supper.

Febry 23 Tuesday Tea & Cards at Dr Knowles's. . .
****

This Morning a Meeting was held at the Angel calld by a hand Bill to prepare a petition to the Post Masters General for the Norwich Mail to come from Nor' wich thro' Bury to Thetford & Norwich. There were abt 30 or 35 Gentn prest: Sir Tho Cullum, Dr Ord, Mr Loyd & the rest principally in Trade. Sir Tho Cullum was voted in the Chair. A petition was produc'd & carr'd and signd by all prest /& orderd to be carrd thro' the Town to be signd/. It was the Opinion of those who calld the Meeting, wh[o] believe were Mr Carss, Mr Gedge, Mr Clarke & another or two, that it should <u>not</u> be deliverd by either Borough or County Member, they not having succeeded in their several Attempts before, but sd Gentn who introducd it would see it was properly deliverd.
****

Febry 25 Thursday   The 5th Subn Ball, one extra this Year being to be afforded they having flourishd this Winter more than ever before rememberd.
> Abt   <u>84 Ladys</u> & Gentn
> 18 <u>Couple</u> of Dancers

much fuller than might be expected considering the chief of the country Com-pany being now in London. 3 Card Tables. Continued till 3 O'Clock. Mrs O, Self & Daughter only from our House.
**********Nephew Rd Baker's Wedding Day to Miss Martin. Advisd by Bro the 26th.*****

Sunday Febry 28   I walkd to Ickworth Lodge wh Miss Shutz, Captn Symonds & Son Orbell to see the Modell of the Earl of Bristol's new House. . .[179] Some Snow & very cold.

[On 3 March James Oakes, his wife and daughter Charlotte went to Norwich to stay with the Pattesons. They should have gone on the 1 March but were prevented by bad weather.]

Friday Mar 11   I breakfasted at Mr Bartlett Gurney's & this Day I also dind at Mr Jno Gurney's, Earlham. Returnd home to Tea to meet a very large Party for the Evening at Mr Patteson's: Mr & Mrs Harvey, Mr & Mrs Thos Harvey, Miss Harvey, Mr & Mrs Pocklington, Mrs Chas Harvey, Mr & Mrs Hudson, Col

---

[179] The highly eccentric 4th Earl of Bristol, the Earl Bishop, was immensely wealthy and had a consuming interest in the arts and architecture. He built splendid and unusual houses at his see in Ireland and on his estates in England but had a very cavalier attitude towards architects whom he took up on a whim and dropped as quickly. The rebuilding of Ickworth had been planned by his grandfather the first Earl, and from 1779 the 3rd Earl had commissioned many plans for the house but had given them up. Work finally began on the house in 1795 under the supervision of the architect, Francis Sandys and his brother Joseph, who had worked for the Earl in Ireland. It was almost certainly designed by Mario Asprucci. The neo-classical house with its central rotunda and curved wings was intended to display the Earl's art collection. Most of this was confiscated and never recovered when the French invaded Italy in 1798. The building was unfinished at the Earl's death in 1803 and work was not resumed by his son until 1824. See Gervase Jackson-Stops, Ickworth (The National Trust, 1987); William S. Childe-Pemberton, The Life of Frederick Hervey of Ickworth, Bishop of Derry, Earl of Bristol, 2 vols (1924); Dorothy Stroud, The Architecture of Sir John Soane (1961).

Hatton, Capt Benjafield, Captn Cobb, Captn Beevor &ca. We set down at supper 23 of Us.

Saturday Mar 12   We left Mr P– at abt 1/2 hour after 10 O'Clock. Took a p[ai]r Norwich Post Horses to Titshall Ram & after a pr from thence to Bottesdale where we din'd & my own Horses met Us. We got home abt 1/2 hour after 6 O'Clock & found all well.

	[£	s.	d.]
Post Horses in all cost Us	3	11	–
Keep[in]g own Horse at Swann, 1/6 a day & Night Hay, 1/0 Corn	1	2	6
Mr P Servts	1	2	6
Sundries, Expences on Road to & from &ca	3	5	5½
	9	1	5½

Monday Mar 21   At home alone. 1st Brew[in]g in this year. *****Sr Thos Gage died this Day at 3 O'Clock [this] afternoon.

Friday Mar 25Good Friday   This Fast observd remarkably Strict in & thro out the Town. No Shops opend or Business done by any but Dissenters. Churches very full. At home alone.

Sunday Mar 27 Easter Day   Mrs O, Self & Daughter staid the Sacrament. We all dind & drank Tea at Mr Adamson's. Met Miss Moyle, Mr Young, Captn Otley, Son & Daughter OO. Mr Ray supp'd with Us. Cold wh little Snow & sleet.

Thursday Mar 31   Son Orbell to Stowmarkett to attend the County meeting for Cavalry. *****Lord Hervey came to canvass the Corporation against the next General Election. . .

Sunday April 3   At home. . . Wm Doe came this Evening into my Service as Head Footman.

Tuesday April 5   /1st Day of [the] Star newspaper.[180] We had the Sun[181] likewise for [the] last Day/. . . *****Sir Thos Gage buried. Kept above ground 15 Days.

Thursday April 7   . . . *Mr Houchen came to Bury & settled with my Son respectg the advertizing the sale of his Norfolk Estates by auction. Mr Adamson dining at Bradfield & Mr H din'd with Us & drank Tea. Mention[in]g the Sale of Daughter Gould's Estate he thought it might fetch from £1,000 to £1,200.

Wednesday April 13   Tea & Sandwich Party at Home. . . staid till 1/2 past eleven O'Clock.

Friday April 15   4th Day's Receipt, Mildenhall. Self, Biggs & Coachman took in 12 Parishes, abt £980 – –. Great Misunderstandings between the Grand Dupli-

---

180 *The Star* was a London evening paper at this time. It had been a paper extensively used for booksellers' advertisements but, by 1798, was described as a tepid opposition paper supportive of the Prince of Wales but neutral in elections.
181 *The Sun* was a London paper which, by 1793, was one of nine daily papers controlled by the Treasury in an attempt to regulate public opinion at a time of revolutionary ideas.

cate & [the] Collectors' acct owing to the total Neglect of the Clerk (Mr Isaacson Jnr) in makg the first 1/2 year's copy. Got home before 7 O'Clock. At tea & Supper at Son OO...

Monday April 18   5th Day's Receipt at Sudbury. Self, Mr Smith & Biggs in my son's Chaise & my Coachman & Horses. We get Home 1/2 after 7 O'Clock. Took in 36 Parishes, abt £3,500 – –. NB Mr Haycroft's Charge for my Dinner, Fruit, Servt &ca very Extra[vagen]t, considering what we had. Mr Adamson & Mr Fenton din'd with Us.

Tuesday April 19 . . . *Mr A[damson] gave Daughter OO [a] Purse [of] 50 G[uineas].

Wednesday April 20   6th Day's Receipt at Home. Self, Son, Mr Smith & Clerk. We took in 113 Parishes, £8,500. Mr Smith, Mr Goer, Mr Bushell (all three Collectors) Mr Canham, Mr Brook /Jn, Horringer/, Mr Henry Twights & Mr Chambers all dind with me. Did not finish till just upon 10 O'Clock.

Friday April 29   At home alone. Lord Brome's Troop exercized. *****Lease died this Night.*****

Monday May 2   At home alone. *****Took out the old <<Grate>> Stove from the Keeping Parlor & put a Register Stove & intend cleaning the room.

*****Coll Shutz married his Cousin Miss Shutz.

[The Rev. James Oakes and his family came to Bury and the Goulds arrived from Pool.]

Tuesday May 10 . . . Son James agreed wh Mr Creed for the Innoculation of his two little ones at Thurston: £5 5 –; 2 Servt £1 1 –. ***Began putt[in]g in the new Sash Frames to Son Orbell's House.[182]

Wednesday May 11   *Son James & 2 Daughters innoculated by Mr Creed at Thurston. . .

Monday May 16   *********Lord Charles Fitzroy came to canvass the Corporation for the ensuing General Election expect[in]g the Parliam[en]t will be dissolvd next Friday the 20 Jne. His Lordship Breakfasted, dind & drank Tea with me. . .

Tuesday May 17   At home alone. Sr C.Davers canvassd the Corporation.

Wednesday May 18   Sr CD again with the Corporation.

Thursday May 19   Lady Cullum, her Son & Daughter & Master Martin dind, drank Tea & suppd with Us. Lord Hervey came to canvass the Corporation. Son James & his Wife drank Tea with Us.

Parliament prorogued.

Friday May 20 . . . **Parliament dissolvd.***** Orbell & his Wife slept at my House.

---

[182] Orbell Oakes's new house in Guildhall St, now Messrs Greene and Greene, solicitors.

Sunday May 22 Mrs O, Self & Daughter were at the Sacrament. . . *****The Alderman (Mr Maulkin) receivd this eveng at 9 O'Clock the Writ from the County Sheriff for electing 2 members to serve in Parliament.*****

Monday May 23 Family at home. Licensing Day – the Town Clerk's Dinner at the Greyhound. Pres[en]t: the Ald[erma]n, Mr Leheup, Mr Pretyman, Mr Barwick, Mr Fairfax, Mr Chambers & Self. Staid till 7 O'Clock. Lord Charles & Lord Hervey both in Bury canvassing.

This Day Son Orbell's Estates /at Thorpe/ Norfolk were put up for Sale by auction at [the] /Crown/ Stoke Ferry but, on acct of the Uncertainty of the Allotments of land from the Enclosure before the sale began, there was little probablity of its being sold. There were no real Bidders besides those who were appointed on Behalf of my Son & solely for the above reason and, as the Tenant, Hegbin, is desirous of staying another year, it may be all for the best. Before which time it is to be hopd the Quantity of Common Land will be allotted & the Farm wholly laid together. . . Mr Houchen thinks it will make very near, if not altogether, £5,000 – –.

Tuesday May 24th Son Orbell & James returnd from Wereham at 3 O'Clock. Family at Tea & Cards at Mr Palmer's. I could not go. Lord Charles Fitzroy drank Coffee with me & Son Orbell & returnd to Euston. Mr Symonds from Cambridge.

Thursday May 26 I rode over & pd [the] Marquis Cornwallis a morng visit at Culford and returnd home to breakfast. Lord Charles Fitzroy, Sir Tho Cullum & Mr Symonds din'd with me & staid till 9 o'clock.

Friday May 27 General Election for Members

Lord C. Fitzroy	Lord Hervey	Sir Chas Davers
	Smith	Smith
Lawrence		Lawrence
Browne		
	Dickonson	Dickonson
Maulkin, Rob		Maulkin, Rob.
	Hailstone	Hailstone
Sturgeon		Sturgeon
	Cooke	Cooke
	Apsey	Apsey
Buchanan		Buchanan
Green		Green
Rutter		Rutter
Hubbard	Hubbard	
	Hustler	Hustler
Oliver		Oliver
	Carss	Carss
	Hawes	Hawes
	Hill	Hill
	Ward	Ward
9	11	17

		Fairfax	Fairfax
Chambers			Chambers
		Wright	Wright
		Mathew	Mathew
Cullum			
Pretyman		Pretyman	
		Norman	Norman
Barwick		Barwick	
Maulkin, Ald.			Maulkin, Ald.
9			

28	14	17	23

Jas. Oakes Receiver General did not vote. 29 in all on [the] Corporation, 28 voters, upper House 4 v[a]c[ancie]s

Lower House 5 Vcs

The Names of the Corporation calld over at 12 O'Clock & the Business over abt 1/2 hour after one. Every Gentn on the Body prest. The Bribery Oath movd by Mr Sturgeon & seconded by Sir Thos Cullum. Lord Charles nominated by Sir Tho.Cullum & seconded by Mr Buchanan. Lord Hervey nominated by Mr Wright & seconded by [blank], Sr C.Davers nominated by Mr Ward & secondd by [blank].

The 3 Candidates ea[ch] orderd 25£ Ribbands: Lord Charles Orange & Blue, Lord Hervey plain Green & Sr Cha Davers plain pink & this Expence they were each to pay successful or not. All other. . . Expences – Dinner, Ball & Fees of every kind to be equally divided between the successfull Candidates. Lord Hervey & Sr Charles were both chaird. The Town was exceedingly full but no sort of Irregularity or Mischief ensued, not a paine of Glass broke. Beer, as usual, was given away in different parts of the Town and the new elected /Members/ just before Dinner from the windows of the Angel threw amon[gs]t the Populace ea[ch] ten Guineas in sixpences.

At Dinner there were only the 2 Members, Assistant Justices & Corporation and their friends /say abt 50/. Altho Cards of Invitation were sent to more than 20 Gentn, scarce one appeard. The Cards were not sent till after the Election wch made it so late they had not time to prepare. In future it would be better to send out Cards early in the <u>Morng</u> in the <u>Name of the Candidates</u>. The Ball was very full from the highest to the lowest not less than 400 appeard. It was supposd not well regulated as all Descriptions came, even the footmen of the Town in Livery set down at Table. This was not over till 4 O'Clock. I went to the Ball for 1/2 hour, but none other of my Family.

Tuesday May 31 ***
Nomination Day for County Members at Stowmarkett. Self & Son went together in Son Orbell's Chaise being a Wet Day. Breakfasted at Mr Tyrrell's & took Mr Tyrrell with us. Get to Stow[marke]tt by 1/2 hour after 10 O'Clock. Business began att eleven. Sir Charles Davers nominated Sr Charles Bunbury and Mr Brook nominated Lord Brome. No other Gentn was nominated as such, the Sheriff declard for Sr Chas Bunbury & Lord Brome. There was a misunder-standing abt the place, whether the Church or Markett Place. The Church was

34. *A View Near Bury, Suffolk: Capel Lofft published by*
S. Knight.

nearly filld & the Gentn got into Waggons opposite the White Hart & many
were disappointed and displeasd. Mr Capel Loft was there & on that Acct was
depriv'd of makg his Speach. We returnd & dind at Mr Tyrell's & got home to
Tea. Own Family at home alone.

Began painting inside of my House.

Thursday June 2d . . . a rumour prevaild this Day of an Opposition for the
Suffolk [Election].

***This Day the Election for the County of Norfolk. Mr Coke & Sir John
Woo[d]house returnd as Opposition to Mr Coke was some days in agitation but
at last given up. ***

Friday June 3 <u>General Election</u> for [the] County [of] Suffolk. I went wth Son Orbell in Mr A[damson's] Chaise sending our own Horses forward early in the Morng. We got to the White Hart, Stow[marke]tt by 8 O'Clock. Met Sr Chas Bunbury, Sr Tho Cullum & many Gentn. We all breakfasted & intended riding on Horseback from thence but, proving so heavy a Rain, I got into a Chaise wth Mr Guilts.

The Business was open'd abt 11 O'Clock when Mr Lofts made a long Speech importing much blame to those who had the Direction of the Business at the Nomination at Stow[marke]tt. . . he was followd by Mr Ranby [and] by /him/ given to understand theire was nothing unfair in the proceedings of that Day & that he had time and Opportunity, & all others who choosd, to have nominated any other Candidate. No other Gentn being nominated or now offerd, Sr Chas Bunbury & Lord Brome were declard duly elected by the Sheriff without further Opposition or harranging. The two Members were chair'd at one O'Clock. Our party return'd to dine at Stowmarkett.

Sir Charles gave no Ribbands, Lord Brome a profuse Quantity all blue and treeted all the common Free Holders with Dinner. The Town was thought to be pretty full but on acct of the heavy Rain, wch continued without Intermission the whole Day, no doubt numbers were deprivd of the Opportunity of coming & made it very unfavourable to the show. We got home by 7 O'Clock.
****

[James Oakes attended a Yeomanry Cavalry meeting and went to Norwich to sell yarn. He staid with Charles Harvey and was a guest at William Herring's Guild Day.]

Thursday June 23d   **
This Morning abt 1/2 hour after ten O'Clock my Daughter Orbell Oakes was safely deliver'd of a Son. Her Sister, Mrs Macklin, attended her from 4 O'Clock Wednesday Morng. . . *****Revd Mr Maurice Moseley taken very bad with a Paralittick Stroke, left side. ******

Sunday June 26 Mr Biggs din'd with Us at 1/2 hour after one O'Clock also Son Orbell & Miss Cocksedges & Charlotte. After Evening Service Self, Mrs O & Miss Cocksedge & Charlotte all went & drank Tea at Thurston. Mr Biggs & Son Orbell suppd wth Us.

Monday June 27 **********This Morng 3 O'Clock died the Revd Maurice Moseley of Tostock, the next turn of wch Living I bot in March 1793 of Jno Moseley Esq for my Son James.

The Gross Rent was then estimated at	£140	–	–
Curacy Land-Tax, first Fruits & Repairs estimated at	40	–	–
Net income	100	–	–

The sd Rector's age at this time 49 yrs. [It] was at the Midsum[mer] valuation of Mr Morgan set at £528 4 6. **********

Tuesday June 28 I rode over to Tostock & breakfasted at Mr Tyrrell's.

Friday July 1 **********I rode over to Ousden & din'd wth Mr John Moseley & Miss Cocksedges. I gave up to Mr J.Moseley my purchase Deed of [the]

Tostock Living, the next presentation, & Mr M– signd a presentation for my Son. I returnd home abt 10 O'Clock. **********

Thursday July 7   3rd Day's Receipt at Wickhambrook. I went early in the Morng and breakfasted at Thos Green's, Depden. Walkd over all his Farm. Crops extraordinary fine & good. /Set out ab 10 o'clock./ My clerk went forward direct to Wickhambrook. I got to him soon after 12 O'Clock, we returnd home soon after six O'Clock.

Sunday July 10   Mr Adamson dind with Us at one O'Clock, not at Tea. In the Evening Mrs O, Self & Charlotte went to Drinkstone & paid a visit to Mr & Mrs Moseley. Met Mr & Mrs /Henry/ Heigham. NB I talk'd wth Mr Moseley on my Son James's Business of [the] Tostock Living on the Death of Mr Maurice Moseley. We return'd home by 9 O'Clock.

Monday July 11   5th Day's Receipt at Sudbury. Self, Clerk & Coachman took in as usual ab 35 Parishes = £1,900 – –. Left the whole with Mess's Fenn & Addisons for [a] Bill at one month & 5 p[er] cent Int[erest]. Rode home by way of Stansted, Boxted, Hartest & Brockley, get home before 8 O'Clock. P[ai]d a visit at Mr Harrington's: not at Home.

Wednesday July 13   6th Day's Receipt at Home, took in abt 95 Parishes £3,781 11 – or thereabouts. Finishd abt 7 O'Clock. Self, Son, Mr Smith & Biggs, Mr Chambers, Mr Bran Green, young Mr Brook of Herringsfleet, Mr Pawsey, Mr Smith, Biggs, Son Orbell, Mrs O, Self & Daughter all dind together.

Monday July 25   I breakfasted at Mr Tyrrell's & rode over to Tostock Parsonage wth him to meet Mr Westrop & Mr Ray in order to look over the premises. Deferrd coming to any conclusions abt Delapidations or accepting any Fixtures till my son comes over next week.[183] Returnd to Dinner at home alone.

Wednesday July 27   First Intimation by Mr Ray of Tostock Estate being to be sold. ********** ...

Friday July 29   I rode to Sudbury to enquire after the Sale of [the] Estate at Tostock adjoining to my Son's Parsonage of Messr Wm Oliver & Son, Auctioneers, & spoke with Mess Fenn & Addison on [the] same Subject. Returnd by Thurston wh Thos Grey [Green?] & Son, lookd over the wood & then attended Mr Oliver's to view the Moat Farm wh he offerd me to sale say £55 Acres let only at £42 on a Lease 7 years, of which are unexpird by Mr Oliver's acct. Considerably under let, say worth £50 – –. Mr O askg £1,800 – – all freehold with only ab 10/– or 12/– Quit Rent. The Farm House in bad Repair. I calld & passd 1/2 hour wh Mr Oliver at his House at Hawkedon & got Home to 4 O'Clock Dinner. ***********

  Son James & his Wife & Daughter Mary Ann came from Wereham to dine wh Us, drank Tea & then went to Thurston. . .

---

[183] The Rev. James Oakes was away being instituted to the living by the Chancellor of the Diocese.

Sunday July 31 I rode over & breakfasted with Mr & Mrs Tyrrell & from thence went with my Son to /the/ Parish Church at Tostock & heard him read himself in. After Service went & paid a visit at Mr Ray's & from thence at Mr Moseley's, Drinkstone, & returnd home to dinner. Mr & Mrs Charles Harvey & [their] little Boy came to Us from Norwich to Dinner to stay 2 or 3 Days.

Tuesday Augt 2 I rode over to Tostock with Mr Harvey to meet Mr Tyrrell, my Son & **Mr Braddock** at the Parsonage. [It was] his Opinion nothing to be done effectually under £800. Resolvd to wait the Sale of the Estate. Mr & Mrs Harvey, Mrs O, Self & Daughter all went to Tea at Mr Gosling's, returnd home to sup.

Wednesday Augt 3 Dinner Company at Home. . .

Monday Augst 8 We din'd at home alone. Mrs O, Self & Daughter all drank Tea at Mr Tyrrell's, Thurston. I attended this Afternoon at my Son's Parsonage, Tostock, to meet Mr Westrop & Mr Ray & the Farmers who had valued the Tythes. They brot in the total sum of the Crops on abt 134 Acres Land £90 1 3, reckon[in]g one piece[?] Wheat at 8 Combs an acre, 1 D[itt]o 5 Combs, the Barley at 10 Combs, the Oats at 13 Combs, priz[e]s 30/–, 13/– & 10/–. We all returnd home to sup.
****

Tuesday Augt 16 At home alone. This Day the Hall-Summons was held pursuant to the Notices sent by the Alderman to the respective members of the Corporation for fill[in]g up the 5 Vacancies in the Common Council. (NB the three Vacancies in the upper House were not included in the Summons.) There were at this time 10 Gentn in the upper House & 19 D[itt]o in the lower. There were 6 of the former attended & only 8 of the latter therefore not a Majority in the Common Council & consequently no Business could be done. NB The Party in the Interest of the Hervey Family almost to a man away. ********
********************************* . . .

Friday Augst 19 Dinner Company at Home to partake of a Haunch of vennison from the Duke of Grafton. . . all staid till near 10 O'Clock.

Wednesday Augst 24 At home.*************************************
Tostock Estate this Day sold by Auction at the Bell. I purchas'd it for my Son James at Two Thousand & ten Pounds & p[ai]d Down £201 —— deposit Money, also £14 13 10½ the Auction Duty. To pay the Remainder at Xmas next & take possession <<this Michaelmas>> next Xmas, 2/5 to remain on the Estate for the minors, one wanting a year & 1/2 & the other abt 2 yrs 1/2 being of Age. Mr Canham bid for me & was the last Bidder. . . ****************

Friday August 26 ****Mr Dugmore came to survey my Son James's Living of Tostock. We din'd together at my House & set off directly. Went over all Mr Ray's Occupation, drank Tea at Mr Ray's. I return'd home & Mr Dugmore to lodge at Woolpit. *Mr D did not expect to finish till Monday.

**********This morning [at] 5 O'Clock died Mr Jno Patteson's 2nd Son, William, of a /Scarlet Fever./**********

Saturday Augt 27 At home alone. I rode this Morng to Norton[184] to announce the Death of Master Wm Patteson, then to Tostock & had some Conversation with Mr Dugmore, who was continu[in]g his Valuation of Tostock Parish, returng home by Dinner.

**********This Afternoon, between 4 & 5 O'Clock, died Master Henry Patteson 3rd Son, of [the same Disorder as /his Bro[the]r/.**********

[James Oakes, his wife and daughter went to Wereham for three days at the end of August.]

Monday Augt 29 We rode round to Shouldham Thorp & Crimplesham, got home to Dinner & passd the Day among ourselves.

**********This morning at 2 O'Clock died Master Edward Patteson, 5th Son of Mr Patteson, of Scarlett Fever, [the same Distemper as his two Brothers.********

Monday Sept 5 . . . *****Revd J[ohn] P[lampin] went to my Son's at 6 O'Clock forward in Liquor under [the] pretence of seeing his Sister & behavd to Her & my Son as if he come with a view of insulting both. **********************

Tuesday Septr 6 At home alone.** The /Revd/ Mr Mills [and] The Revd Mr J– P– came & made such an apology for his Behaviour /to me/ that I was inducd to accept tho' my Friends thought [it] by no means equal to the Offence he had given. My Son & Daughter OO could not think of accept[in]g any other than an Acknowledgement of his having behavd very ill in their House & promising not to do the like again, wch He could not be persuaded to make. Therefore they did not meet.**********

Wednesday Sept 7 At home alone. Son & Daughter Orbell suppd with Us. Hospital meet[in]g.[185] Mr Symonds, Mr Godbold & Self present, passd the year's acct, elected Sr Chas Davers pres[iden]t for [the] year ensuing.

Gross Income as near as may be	£426	–	–
Averidge of annual outgoings	480	–	–
Averidge of Expenditure more than Income	54	–	–

Thursday Sept 8 . . . Dinner at my Son's being the Christening of his little Boy, Henry James. Mrs Macklin, Godmother, Mr Robinson & Self, Godfathers. Neither Mr R or Self got there in time. Mr Adamson & Son Orbell stood as Proxys. We all get to Dinner, 14 set down to Table includ[in]g the above also old Mr Plampin, Mr Macklin, Mr & Mrs Pooley, Mr Debbing, Mr Robbinson's Son.

---

[184] Little Haugh, Norton was inherited by Mrs John Patteson from her father Robert Staniforth.

[185] Under his will, dated 10 October 1730, Poley Clopton MD left land in Essex and Suffolk the rents from which were to provide not more than £300 to be spent on building a house for six poor men and six poor women, half from St Mary's Parish and half from St James's Parish. They were to be over 60 years of age, to have lived for at least one year in Bury and were not to be in receipt of poor relief. The charity was administered by 13 trustees. The Hospital building, in the Churchyard, is now the Provost's house.

Mr Macklin's Son & Daughter came after Dinner. Most of us staid till near one O'Clock in the Morning.*****

	[£	s.	d.]
Coll Robinson left	5	5	–
Mrs Macklin	2	2	–
JO	2	2	–
	9	9	–

****

Monday Sept 12 Mrs O, Self & Daughter all drank Tea at Mrs Palmer's. . . I rode over this Morning & breakfasted with Mr Tyrell & from thence attended the workmen in Tostock Parsonage.

Tuesday Sept 13 The Review of the new Romney Fencibles by General Toning from 11 till one O'Clock. The officers afterwards gave a Dinner to all the Military in the Town and, in the Evening, a very handsome Ball & Supper, abt 120 Ladys & Gentlemen. The Rule of Invitation: to all who had notic'd the Corps since its being quarter'd in Bury. Everything conducted with much Elegance & a most pleasant Evening.

Wednesday Sept 14 At home alone. Concert by [the] Leader of [the] New Romney Fencible Band at the Theatre. Daughter Charlotte of my Family only there.

Thursday Sept 15 At home alone. Bottled off a Pipe [of] Red port between Self & Son Orbell. Drawn into Bottles it ran 56 Doz clear & 1/2 Dozen Filt & promises to be very good.

Monday Sept 26 **********I rode over to Depden & breakfasted at Thos Green's, took an acct of all the Workman's Bills for Materials & work to repair of Wollard's House, Barns & Stables, in all amo[un]t[in]g to abt £150 ——. I also took the plan of Depden Estate out with me & made the Alterations according as the piece now lay & also how & in what manner the pieces had been croppd for 4 yrs past. Returnd home at 1/2 hour after 3 O'Clock.*******

Family all dind on part of an Haunch of venison at Sr Thos Cullum's. . . staid till near 10 O'Clock.

Tuesday Sept 27 I rode over to Tostock Parsonage, returnd & breakfasted at Mr Tyrrell's. Met Mr Towgood abt my Wereham House.[186] Get home before 11 O'Clock. Guild Hall Feoff[men]t meeting, Charity School Meeting & Dispensary D[itt]o all this Morng.

New Parlaiment assembled.

Thursday Sept 29 At home. This Eveng a Corporation Meetg /at the Angel/, being the Day of proclaiming the Fair, to take into Consideration the mode of filling up the vacancy in the Body. All but Mr Norman, Mr Ward, Mr Hustler & Mr Hailstone, Mr Hawes & Robt Maulkin & Mr Brown appeard, say 9 in the Upper House, 12 in [the] Lower House. Mr Carss, Mr Sturgeon & Mr Cook

---

[186] The old Adamson family home at Wereham which the Rev. James Oakes and his wife were about to leave.

proposd for the 3 vacancys in the upper House & 9 Gentn named for [the] Lower House. There will be 9 vacanceys when the upper House is completed but nothing absolutely determind on.

Tuesday Oct 4 At home with Family & no Company. Day of Election in pursuance of a Summons issued last Saturday by Ald[erma]n Maulkin for electing 3 Capital Burgesses & 5 Common Council. Mr Robt Carss, Mr Jno Cook, Mr Reuben Sturgeon Elected unanimously Capital Burgesses. Mr Abram Jenkins, Mr O.R.Oakes, Mr Blomfield, Mr Thompson elected unanimously burgesses of the Common Council. Mr Jno Pate, Attorney, & Mr Jno Gooday, Carpenter, the former proposd by Mr Reuben Sturgeon & the latter by Mr Wharton Barwick & here began the Contest. The Corporation voted as follows:

Mr Pate		Mr Gooday	
Oakes		Thompson	
Jenkins		Blomfield	
Brown		*Smith	
R.Maulkin		*Lawrence	
Mr Pate		Mr Gooday	
Buchanan		Dickonson	
Green		Hailstone	
Rutter		<<Cook>>	
Oliver		Apsey	
Hawes		**Hubbard	
		Hustler	
—————	9 Ward	—————	9
Sturgeon		Cook	
Chambers		Carss	
Wright		Fairfax	
Cullum		Mathew	
Oakes		*Pretyman	
The Alderman		Norman	
		*Barwick	
15		16	

***Mr Jno Gooday came to demand being sworn in wch was declind. See Thursday.

Thursday Oct 6 Alderman Chambers took his Place but previously Mr Jno Gooday came to demand his being sworn into the Office of /Common/ Council-man. Alderman Maulkin, by the advice of the Recorder, declind it for the pres[en]t there being some doubts as to the Legality of the Election He havg only an even Number of votes of the Lower House (not a majority) —— He havg, as is supposd, not receivd the Sacrament within the last 12 months,[187] also a further Query respectg the validity of Norman's vote. Alderman C had his Dinner at the Angel. In the large Room might be abt 66 & in the opposite Room abt 1/2 a score. The Representatives attendg Parliament were both Absent, Duke of Grafton & Lord Charles not present & indeed no Gentlemen that were not of the

[187] It was necessary to have received Holy Communion within three months of taking office under the Test and Corporation Acts. See note 137 above.

Body except Mr Leheup & Mr Adamson. Mr C made a point of asking all who bore office in the Town at this time as Court of Guardians & [blank]. I left the Room soon after 9 O'Clock.

Saturday Oct 8h I rode to Brandon on Horseback, from thence took Post Chaise to Stoke where I met Mr Greenwood & let him my House & Fixtures with yardes, Gardens, Pightles & Offices, also 2 acres of 1/2 year Land, all together at 35 Guineas per acre to be enterd upon Oct 20 on a Term Certain of 7 years. We signd a written agreement for each of [us?] witnessd by Mr Helsham. I rode wh Mr G & lookd over the House & premises, orderd the Pump to be repaird & the Kitchen new laid. Returnd to Brandon & get a Cutlet & took my Horse from thence home by abt 7 O'Clock. Mr Houchen not at Home. Mrs Greenwood & Children at Stoke.

Wednesday Nov 2d Mr Patteson left us at 9 O'Clock for Norwich. His Son continued with Us. Son Orbell & his Wife to Colchester. Pipe of Sherry from London deposited in my Cellar. . .

Sunday Novr 6 We all din'd at Mr Adamson's. . . ten of Us, all staid Tea & Supper. *****At 1/2 hour after Ten O'Clock I went with Master Patteson to Mr Hasted's & deliverd him there. ********** Son Orbell & his Wife returnd from Colchester at 8 O'Clock.

Thursday Novr 10 Son Orbell to meet Mr Houchen['s] Clerk at Brandon to execute the W[r]itings for the Sale of Stadsett to Miss Baggle, that is to say Purchase Sum £450 – –, Timber £210 = £660. He returnd home by 2 O'Clock. We were at Tea 7 Cards at Mr Garnham's. . .

Thursday Novr 17 Lieutenancy meeting the 1st on the new Acts of Parliament Supplementary Militia & /Provisional/ Cavalry.[188] Prest Lord Euston, Sr Charles Bunbury, Sr T.G.Cullum, Mr Symonds, Mr Heigham, Mr Blachley & Self from 11 till 3 O'Clock.******************************** At Night first Sub[scriptio]n Ball. Prest abt 65 Ladys & Gentn, 20 couple of dancers. Daughter Charlotte returnd from Mr Macklin.

Monday Novr 21 My Niece Bakers /left us &/ returnd home to Cawston by Norwich Coach after a visit of 6 weeks. They came Oct 7.********** My Daughter Gould left us returning to Ashford. Mr A's Chaise to Sudbury. A visit of 3 weeks, came with me from London Oct 29. At home alone.

Tuesday Nov 22 At home alone. Mrs Moseley a morng visit & I appointed to take upon myself the Receipt of the Cocksedge's Rents.

Saturday Nov 26 At home alone. *****Acc[oun]t in the News Papers of the Death of Captn Jermyn Symonds by the Loss of the Helena Sloop of War. Everyone /perishd/.*****

---

[188] The Supplementary Militia Act 1796, 37 Geo III c3, empowered the raising of 60,000 men by ballot and 20,000 provisional cavalry raised by levy of one horse and a trooper for every ten horses, subject to the new horse tax, and 7,000 marksmen raised by requiring all employers of game keepers to provide one man. There was such opposition to the last provision that it was withdrawn.

Tuesday Nov 29 At home alone. A Morng visit at Mr Symonds['s] on supposd Death of his Nephew.

Thursday Decr 1 *****Miss Symonds was married this morng at 8 O'Clock to Captn Benjafield of the West Kent Militia & set off after Breakfast on their way to Bath. I attended 3 hours this morng on the Cavalry Bill at the Angel. At home alone. The 1st Card Assembly not any of us there. The weather continued very sharp. Beast Fair Day.

Friday Dec 2 **
Third Meeting of Cavalry – Prest: Sr T.G.Cullum, Mr Leheup, Self & Dr Ord. The Act appearing so imperfect could not proceed upon it but stated many Instances & desird the Clerk to lay them before the Lord Lieut. ************ Son James came accidently to Bury & took a piece of Dinner with Us. We drank Tea & spent the Eveng with Miss Norgate. . . Weather continues very severe.

Sat Night Decr 3 At home alone. Weather continues very severe. Not 200 Chald[ron] Coals left in the yards, River Frozen up. *****Mr Maulkin & Mr Leach went to Thetford & Bot 200 Chaldron to supply the Town & the Poor. 36/– at Thetford, 7/6 carr[iage] & Port[era]ge, 2/6 waste & Delivery – cost 45/–.***

Tuesday Decr 6 **********Anniversary of our Wedding Day. Married in 1764, 32 years. *** At home alone. Jno Patteson din'd with Us. . .

Wednesday De 7 **********Militia Meeting, Old & New. Sr T.G.Cullum, Mr Heigham, Mr Leheup & Self. Lists for [the] Old & New [Militia Acts] returnd by [the] Constables of all Divisions. Parishes took us full 10 Hours without any recess. Got thro' the whole. We then din'd with Mr Jenkins & the chief Constables at ½ hour after 8 O'Clock and got home ½ hour after 10 O'Clock . . .

Tuesday Decr 13 Meeting at St Mary's Vestry for findg 7 Men for [the] Navy. Guildhall Feoff[men]t for shirts, shifts, shoes & stockings. Meeting [of] Sutton's Charity,[189] Thos Bennett electd. In the Eveng at Mrs Gosling's Rout, Tea & Cards & 7 Card Tables, abt 34 Ladys & Gents. . . 7 Days alone 3ld Candles.[190]

Wednesday Dec 21 ** (Frosty) Balloting at the Angel for abt 735 Supplimentary Militia. Pres[en]t: Sir Thos Cullum, Sr Cha Davers, Mr Heigham, Mr Moseley, Self, Dr Ord. 4 of us staid & din'd wh Mr Jenkins & p[ai]d the Dinner /7/–/ ea[ch]. . . ***

Saturday Dec 24 At home alone. The Frost continued very sharp the last Night, thought to be the severest of any hitherto this Winter. Finishd deliver[in]g out my Blankets.

Sunday Dec 25 Xmas Day. Attended Alderman Chambers morng & Eveng Service, St Mary's. We din'd at Home this Day /4 O'Clock/, Mr Adamson, Mr

---

[189] See note 157 above.
[190] Duty was payable on candles so Oakes was probably trying to keep a firm track of how many were used in order to curb household expenses.

Hasted, Son & Daughter OO. We cooked a large Legg of Beef on the Friday & made the small Copper full of Broath wch [we] deliverd out to 5 or 6 poor Familys on the Saturday. Sunday between 12 & one O'Clock we had 3 large Plumb Puddings wch we distributed to 7 or 8 Familys.Not havg any hot meat /at Noon/ could not send any. Sent Widw Tayler her Dinner at Noon. Wm Hill dind with Us & sent his wife some Pudding meat & minc'd Pye. 4 Bottles Old Beer to [the] Family.[191] The Last Night very severe Frost continued intense all the Day. For Dinner Gravy Soup, a large joint Rump of Beef & large Turkey 12ld,[192] plumb Puddings & mincd Pyes.

Monday Decr 26 At home alone. A meeting of the Corporation at 6 this Eveng to dispose of Badby's Gift.[193] 5 more of the 25£ were orderd to be pd off. Sir Thos Cullum's one of them wch I had bo[ught] many years ago.[194] The weather continued very severe, no Snow at prest. Mr Biggs at his Father's, Mildenhall. Son Orbell & his Wife to Bradfield.

Saturday Janry 7   . . . Lord Charles Fitzroy call'd on me. This week continued dry & mild. ***Sir C.Davers [had a] fall from his Horse & broke his Collar Bone.

Sunday Janry 8 Mr Adamson din'd wth Mrs O, Self & Charlotte. No one else. Staid till 8 O'Clock. I pd a Morng visit at the Recorder's & talkd over [the] R[eceiv]ership.

Thursday Janry 12 3lb Candles. 2nd Supplimentary Militia meetg for swearing in the Ixworth Division, abt 130. I attended at the Angel the whole Day from 10 in the Morng till 8 at Night. Captn Heigham, /Mr Leheup, Sr Thos Cullum/ & sundry other Dep[uty] Lieut[enan]ts wth Dr Ord. . . The 3d Ball Night abt 95 Ladys & Gentlemen & 35 couple of Dancers. . . Staid till 2 O'Clock. /A consid-erable/ fall of Snow in [the] course of [the] Day & a pretty sharp frost at Night.

---

[191] That is to say the servants dining in the kitchen.
[192] It was common in the eighteenth century for guinea fowl to be confused with turkeys. The information given by Oakes does not make clear which he meant as it would be possible for the bird to have been either a hen Turkey or large guinea fowl at that weight. The fact that he says the bird was large suggests that it was a guinea fowl.
[193] See note 15 above.
[194] In February 1780 it was decided that each member of the Corporation would lend £25 for which a bond would be given to help pay outstanding bills and to cover the cost of 'repairing and ornamenting' the Market Cross. The bonds did not bear interest and were to be discharged when a member died, otherwise only when the Corporation debts were paid off. They were then to be paid out of savings made from Corporation rents and members were to draw lots to determine the order in which they would be repaid. New members were required to loan £25 on election. SROB D4/1/4.

Wednesday Janry 18 . . . ***** Mr Chandler, Corn-factor of Stowmarkett, stoppd Paym[en]t afterwards a Bankrupt.*****

Thursday Janry 26 Mr P. Ray & Mr Norford din'd & drank Tea with Us. In the Eveng we all went to the Card Assembly at the new Assembly Room. Abt 58 or 60 Ladys & Gentlemen. We came home soon after 12 O'Clock. Mr P. Ray slept here. *****This morning died Amb Taylor's Widw. An annuity from £10 to 12£ a year.*****

Monday Janry 30 Anniversary of King Charles's Martyrdom. At home alone. Mr O. Ray & Mr P. Ray left Us for London this morng by Coach. /Br[e]w[in]g/; Candles 3ld.

Tuesday Janry 31 At home alone till Tea & Eveng at Mr Squire's. . . This evening the Grand Ball at Mr Howard's, Fornham. Son Orbell & his Wife were there. Abt 70 or 80 Ladys & Gentlemen met abt 9 O'Clock & staid till 4 in the morng. Everything extraordinary Handsome. From 20 to 22 Couple of Dancers.

Friday Febry 3 Blaze.[195] [The] Trustees of Dr Battley's Charity met, 5, that is to say: Mr Wright, Mr Cooke, Mr Barwick, Mr Pawsey Jnr & Self. We dind at the Angel & staid till 7 O'Clock & passd the year's accts. Allow the Objects one Guinea ea[ch] over their annual Stipend of £10 – –. Afterwards attended the Meetg of the Coal Merch[an]ts at the 6 Bells & settled the Loss on the Coals bot in Partnership from Thetford wch, to 7 of us, was £3 12 – each. The Gentn gave up all Thoughts of purchasg the River & Estate of Mr Palmer at £8,500 now would not think of it at £8,00 or in shop at any money in its prest state. Mr Cook, Mr Ridley & Mr [blank] were appointed a Committee to wait on Mrs Palmer & state the absolute Necessity for an Engineer to be appointed to examine & advise what was to be done. I got home to sup. Family alone.

Sunday Febry 5 I rode over to Culford & left my Card at [the] Marquis of Cornwallis. Mr Adamson, Captn Otley & Mr Sams dind & drank Tea with Us.

******I this Day commencd drink[in]g the pipe of wine bottled Sept 18th 1795 bo[ught] of Mr Strothoss, Bin No 2.

**************News arrivd of [the] total Defeat of the Austrians by the French in Italy.***

Friday Febry 10 At home till Eveng. Mr Jno Moseley came to converse with me respect[in]g the advowson of Tostock Living & took some Days to consider whether He should sell it to me or not. At Tea & Eveng at Mrs Molineux's. . . staid till 1/2 hour after 11 O'Clock.

Saturday Febry 11 At home alone. I had [an] Invitation from the Officers to Dinner but declind it. . . *****Plannd my new Study & gave orders for its being done without Delay.

Wednesday Febry 15 **********A general Day held by the Depty Lieutenants & Justices to the Lists wch had been exhibited to the Publick for those liable to

---

[195] The feast day of Saint Blasius or Bishop Blaze, the mythical patron saint of wool combers, was on 3 February.

be classed in the new Cavalry Bill to find one man & one Horse for every ten Horses. A very great Number claimd Exemption. [The meeting lasted] from 10 O'Clock in the Morng till 5 at Night. We likewise held a Meeting for the Supplimentary Militia.********* Son Orbell came over from Mr Falk for the Business of the Day & returnd to Dinner. Mrs O & Daughter Charlotte at Mrs Gosling's Card party.
************Mrs Patteson brot to Bed this morning of a Daughter.**********

Wednesday Febry 22 Mr Adamson & Son James dind with Us & drank Tea. Son Orbell & his Wife at Tea. A further Day of Appeal for Cavalry: Sir Thos Cullum, Mr Leheup & Self & Dr Ord. I heard that Mess Watson & Wilcocks had stoppd Payment. Our Debt £494 9 6.

Friday Febry 24 At home alone. Cold & Cough continued very indiff[eren]t. Son James & his Wife from Tostock to dine with Us. Staid till 1/2 after 4 O'Clock.

**********Mr Jno Moseley gave in his Answer by Mr Chinery that he would not part with the advoswon of Tostock for less than £1,000. I had no Thoughts of giving more than £600 so that all idea of purchas[in]g that is now at an end.

**********This Day began my Alteration for my New Room to be added to [the] Bank.

Saturday Febry 25 At home alone. The weather all this week remarkably fine, scarce a cloud to be seen. Nights Frosty, Days quite dry & warm. Said to be rather sickly, many Colds & Coughs. Mine Continues [at] best Indiff[eren]t. Specie continues to grow more & more scarce. A most distressing time in money Matters & likely to be more so.

Sunday Febry 26 Mr Symonds & Mr Adamson & young Martin all dind with us. At Tea & Supper Son & Daughter OO & young Martin.

Monday Febry 27 At home alone.************************************** By order of Council the Bank issued a publick Notice that to guard against <u>a want of Specie all Dividends & Bank Stock</u> would be paid in Bank Paper & not in Guinies.[196] ************************** <u>This Day all the 5 Norwich Banks suspended transacting any more Business until it could be known what Parliament would do in Consequence of the order.</u>***

Wednesday March 1st <u>Ash Wednesday</u>******************************** The three Banks in Bury, JO & Son, Spink & Carss & B & T Cork thought it expedient to follow the Example of the Norwich Bankers & suspend all their Transactions in their Business for the present waiting the Event of Parliament. A general Meeting of the Inhabitants was calld by the Alderman & many attended with the principal Merchants, Farmers & Others & an Agreement was signd by upwards of 100 to support the Credit of [the] said Banks & Town by receiving their Cash Notes as usual.***

[196] See page 77 for a discussion of the suspension of cash payments and its effect on trade in Bury.

Thursday March 2 The Suspension of Business continued by the Bankers, excepting in trifling matters for mere accommodation. The Gentlemen, Traders
&ca all in general very well satisfied.*********************************
Family at alone. *****The Cavalry ballotted for 193 Men & Horses to be
enrolled March 15.

Saturday March 4 **
The Bankers commencd transacting Business as usual excepting that they paid
only in Bank of England Notes & no specie excepting the fractional parts as not
a Guinea could be procurd from Town. The Bankers accepted the Notes of other
banking Houses usually in Circulation in payment on acc[oun]t but did not give
Bank[197] for these if Payment was requird then by Dr[af]t on a month on Town.
(Weather continud dry wh Cold South East winds.) Family at home alone.

Coroner's Inquest sat on the Body of Sparham supposd to have died by taking
some poisonous potion. The Juley's [jurey's?] verdict cleard the Person suspected.
****
We this Day receivd by post the joyful News that John Jervis's Fleet consisting of
only 15 sail of the Line had defeated the Spanish Fleet of 27 sail of the Line [and]
had capturd 2 of 112, 1 of 80 & 1 of 74 Guns = 4 Ships. At this Critical Juncture
perhaps the most providential & happiest Event that could have happend to this
Kingdom & considering the wonderful superiority of Numbers & weight of metal
one of the most glorious victories ever obtaind.[198]**************************

Sunday March 5 We din'd at Mr Adamson's, drank Tea & staid till 8 O'Clock.
No other Company. **********My Son Orbell went to London by this Evening's Mail to bring home some of the new small Bank 20/- & 40[/-], also, if
possible, some specie & Dollars and to bring home our own Cash Notes.[199]
****

Monday March 6 *****Some of Mr Cork's Notes returnd from London pro-
tested but paid in Bury.*********** Mr Adamson, Son Orbell & Lou[is]a
Macklin dind with Us. At Tea & Supper we went to Mr Mills's. . . my Cold &
Cough returnd.

Tuesday March 7 Market Day on acct of the Fast on the Morrow. A great
number of applications for Cash. We paid [our] own Notes with Bank £5, £10 &
had abt £50 of 20/- & 40/- to distribute but soon gone. We parted with as little
Cash as possible & upon the whole rather encreasd our Specie. The Day passd off
upon the whole very pleasantly every Body seemd disposd to make the best shift
that was possible hoping a few weeks might remedy the prest Inconveniencys. I
continued very unwell.

Wednesday March 8 The General Fast wch was duly observd thro out the
Town. Son Orbell returnd home this Morng by the Mail from London. Not any

[197] Bank of England notes.
[198] The Battle of Cape St Vincent in which Admiral Sir John Jervis with 15 ships defeated
a Spanich Fleet of 27.
[199] To relieve the acute shortage of specie in Britain, Spanish dollars were used, stamped
with the King's head.

small Bank 20/- & 40/- to be procurd at prest of any Consequence. We are deliberating abt the issue of our own small Notes of 20/-, 15/- & 5/-. At Home alone. Jno Patteson dind with Us.

Thursday March 9   The 5th Subn Ball (one Extra). My Cold & Cough continuing so very indiff[eren]t & Daughter Charlotte far from well, not any of us went from my House. At home alone the whole Day.

Friday March 10   At home till Evening. Tea & Supper at Mr Allen's. . . disappointed of many of their expected Company. My Cold & Cough but very indiff[eren]t.

Monday March 13   Mrs O, Self & Daughter Charlotte to dine at Mr Poley's, Boxted, from thence we accompanied Mr & Mrs P & Miss Whaley to [the] Melford Assembly; abt 50 Ladys & Gentn & 18 couple of Dancers. We returnd to sleep at Mr Poley's.

Monday Morng*****************Mess B & T Cork stopp'd payment at their Bank.******************** Monday Eveng a fire broke out in the Risby Gate Street at the Hare & Hounds stable & burnt down a Stable. No further accident, a very providential Escape for the Town.*****************

Wednesday Mar 15   Enrolling Day for Cavalry at the Angel.
****

This Day abt 12 O'Clock Mess Spink & Carss's Bank stoppd Payment. The Consternation & Confusion occasiond in the Town by this Event passes Description. Son Orbell to Norwich in a Post Chaise abt one O'Clock.
****

Thursday Mar 16   *****Bury continued in much Confusion on acct [of] Mess Spink & Carss Stopping. A Dockett is said to be struck by Mr Leech. Very few of our own Cash Notes continue coming in. Several applications from most respectable People as Customers to our Bank & every attention shown us.***** Family at home alone.

Friday Mar 17   **
From the Reports of the Day Mr Carss's Affairs are in an very perplexd State & apparently a large Number of Creditors. It is said that £6,000 remains unp[ai]d by Mr Spink['s] Executers to the Exchequer.[200] Our Banking Concerns continue to go on very smoothly — no Quantity of our Notes brot in for payment.*********
Family at home alone.

Saturday Mar 18   *****This being our Second Market Day did expect [we] might have been more hurried in Business but all seemd to pass on very quietly. Few, very few, of our Notes brot in & we continue to restrain them from going out as much as possible.**********Family at Tea & Supper this Eveng at Dr [and] Mrs Wollaston's. I went to them at 1/2 hour after ten o'clock. I took Lease's Son in to assist.

---

[200] John Spink, the Bury banker who had died in 1794, had been Receiver General for the Eastern Division of Suffolk.

Sunday Mar 19 I rode over & call'd on Sr C.Davers at Rushbrook, a morng visit. We dind at Mr Adamson's, no other Company. Home at 8 o'clock. Mr Norford suppd with us.

Monday Mar 20 ****************The Disrtess of the Publick in general & Individuals in particular seem daily encreasing on acct of S——k & C—— stopping. The Commission was seald on Friday the 17 but not at present proceeded upon nor any acct that can be relied upon how their Affairs are likely to turn out. It is rumourd today that the Widw Bullen, Mr Apsey & Mr Hailstone cannot keep thir Heads above water, also that Messr Dalton & Squire are to open a Bank.[201] They have been riding abt the Country among the principal Farmers to engage wh Them. We have had Hints from our Friends that a run is intended on our Bank. . . next Wednesday. Son Orbell to London by Norwich Coach this Eveng to return with a further Supply of Bank against Wednesday.[202]**********. . .

Tuesday Mar 21 At home alone.************************************** The rumour continued to prevail that we should certainly have a sharp run upon my House <<this day>> as to Morrow but have no question shall be most amply provided being determind to carry it thro' with Spirit. Thank God, situated as we are, [we] have nothing to fear. All continued this Day very pleasant our Business encreasing from all Quarters.***************************************

March 22 Wednesday *** This Day passd off with us most pleasantly. So far from any run upon Us the No of Notes came in were very inconsiderable. The Town extremely full & our Bank was /resorted to/ from Morng till Night by the most respectable Merch[ant]s, Farmers &c &c. It is impossible the prospect can be more flattering to Us. Son Orbell returnd by Norwich Coach this Morng very amply supplyd with Bank &ca. Family at home. Judges of Assize came into Town. We have nearly enough in Bank & Specie brot to Us to discharge every Cash Note of our own now in Circulation.
****

Thursday Mar 23 Assizes commencd. I did not [sit?] at the Jury. The first time I have omitted for many years. Business continues to increase & multiply upon Us & every thing goes on as we could wish. Nothing fresh has transpird respect[ing] S & C Affairs. Do not yet hear the Commiss[io]n is proceeded upon. The Town seems very full & have the satisfaction of findg the greatest Confidence is reposd in our House.
  Mr Houchen came this Morng to Mr Adamson's. I dind with him at Mr A. Son & Daughter JO came from Tostock & dind with Mrs O.

*****Spink & Carss's Comm[issio]n opened by Mr Lofts, Mr Case & Mr Jenkins this Eveng.

---

[201] Their plan probably came to nothing as there is no mention of Squire's bank in any directory until 1811 and Oakes makes it plain that his was the only bank in Bury between 1797 and 1802 when the Essex and Suffolk Bank opened.
[202] Bank of England notes.

Friday Mar 23[24] Nothing particular occurrd in[the] course of the Day. Many fresh Applications for openg Acc[oun]t[s] from respectable Persons & every full & satisfactory Confidence p[ai]d to our House wch is highly flattering to Us. Jno Patteson dind wh us. Daughter Charlotte dind at son OO. Settled Acct with Mr Houchen this Eveng for Self, Son O, Mr Gould & son James.

*****Acc[oun]t of Harley Cammeron & Co, large Bank[in]g House in London, stopping.[203]*******

Monday Mar 27 *****Son Orbell wth yeomanry Troop, Lord Brome, Mr Fowke pre[sen]t. At home alone. *****Mr Brewster brot wth him Mr Wm Scales from Pakefield & recommended him as a Clerk. He is a Man who has been unsuccessful in Life — a widower, abt 33 yrs of age, 2 Children who are taken off his Hands. We agreed for one month on Tryal &, if each party approved, to allow him 50£ the first year. To board himself.******

Tuesday Mar 28 Corporate meeting on Acct of Bonds at Comms /advancd to 5 per C[en]t/ to take into Consideration the state of the Income & Expenditure of the Corporation. I calld upon Mr Carss & set an hour with him. Nothing particularly occurrd in [the] course of this Day. Began drawing one pound Cash Notes payable here only, dated March 25, & intend beginning to issue them to Morrow. Mr Wm Scales came to Us on liking for a month this Day. Daughter Charlotte with her Uncle at Son James's to dinner. Son Orbell & his Wife drank Tea & suppd with Us.

Wednesday Mar 29 We were extremely full of Business, many principal Merchts & Farmers came to Us. We would not issue our Notes for Dr[af]ts with any Time upon Them without full Disc[ount] of 9/- in the £100 & they readily submitted. The Day passd off very pleasantly, nothing particulary new occurrd. Family at home alone. *Issued our own £1 Notes.

Thursday Mar 30 Nothing particularly fresh. Business went on as usual. Mr Scales, who came on liking as Clerk from Pakefield, not being likely to suit, deficient in Book keeping & Figures, I gave him a Guinea & discharg'd him. Mrs O, Self & Daughter dind & drank Tea with Mr Adamson. . .

Friday Mar 31 Family at home alone. Son Orbell & his Wife to dine & sleep at Mr Fowke's, Weston. H.W.Pizey of Lavenham stoppd.[204] We are in £67. Mr Hines, Cork's late Clerk, offerd himself to Us but could not get speedily releasd.

Sunday April 2 We din'd & drank Tea at Mr Adamson's, suppd at home alone. *****This Eveng I sent off my Letter to Messrs R B & J Gurney[205] Signifying my Intention of leavg them & establishing a London House.*****

Monday April 3 Family at home alone. Not anything particularly new. *****Mr Hines (Messr Cork's clerk) & as he could not be immediately dischargd from Mess C—— we thus far agreed he should come some hours in a Morng &

---

[203] Messrs Harley Cameron and Company of George Street, Mansion House, London. Hilton Price claims that it became 'extinct' in 1789.

[204] Henry William Pizey of Lavenham, baker, corn merchant, tea dealer and chapman.

[205] Richard and John Gurney the Norwich bankers.

some in an Eveng until he could wholly attend & that we would give him £60 the first year & put [him] on exact same footing with Mr Biggs.**********

Tuesday April 4 Family at home alone. Nothing particular in [the] course of the Day. **********A very handsome reply from Mess[er]s Gurneys that we part on the Pleasantest Terms.

Wednesday April 5 Very full of Business. Mr Henry Patteson & Mr Jno Sparke of Walsham din'd with me. Mr HP took a bed. Nothing particularly new.

Thursday April 6 Dinner Company at home. . . all staid till between 9 & 10 O'clock. . .*****Mr Gedge married to Miss Johnson.*****

Tuesday April 18 Easter. I rode out to Newmarkett & visited the Duke of Grafton. Self with George Coachman. Return'd home by 1/2 hour after one o'clock. . .

Wednesday April 19 My last Home Day's Receipt. Self & Biggs in [the] Bank Parler, Son Orbell, Mr Smith, Hines & Boy Lease in the Bank taking in the Collecters. The most parishes came in this Day ever rememberd to the Amot & when the 2 Parishes of St Mary & St James are pd will be full £9,500 – –, & at the Close of this Day both acct agreed exactly.

Thursday April 20 . . .*****Lord E[uston] wh me & gave full Instructions.

Saturday April 22 . . .1st Comm[issio]n Meeting of Carss Bank-ruptsey at the Angel. *****Son & Daughter Gould came to us from Ashford. Nothing remarkable.

Tuesday April 25 I went to London in the Stage from the Angel taking up with me upw[ar]ds of £10,000 – –, all in Bank Notes. Deliverd the same that Eveng at Messr Ayton Brassey Lees & Co.[206] Lodgd at Allen's at the Bull Inn, Bishopsgate.

Monday May 1 ***
County Sessions at which I was appointed County Treasurer & was sent for [by] the Justicess at the Angel. . . Salary 20£ a year &, in Case at any time being in advance, a power of charg[ing] 5 per C[en]t int[eres]t. . . ***************

Thursday May 4 . . . *Wm Adkin at [the] Green Dragon, my Tenant, died.[207]

Friday May 5 Family at home. Mr Gould returnd from Dedham.[208] *****This was the Day advertizd for choosing assignees to Mr Carss's Bankruptcy. I was unanimously appointed Treasurer to the Bank-ruptcy & Sr Charles Davers, Mr Thomas Cocksedge, Mr Jno Green & Mr John Cook assignees without one dissenting Voice. Family at Home, Son Orbell & his Wife drank Tea with Us.

Sunday May 7 At home alone. Mr Adamson could not dine wth Us being confind with a slight touch of the Gout. We din'd after Eveng Service. *****Son Orbell & his Wife to London by [the] New[marke]tt Road. *****I receivd this

---

[206] Oakes's new London corresponding bank Messrs Ayton, Brassey, Lees and Satterthwaite of 71, Lombard Street.
[207] *The Green Dragon* was next to Oakes's house in Guildhall Street.
[208] William Gould's widowed mother had moved to Dedham, Essex.

Morng a Letter from Mr Rose to Lord Euston advis[in]g my Son's appointment as Receiver in my stead was full noticed at the Tax Office.

Monday May 8 /(See forward to this Day sennight & read the Minutes of the 15th with this.)/. . . **********Committee of [the] Corporation to inspect the Income & Expenditure of the Corporation met at my House at 1/2 hour after 7 O'Clock. That is to say: The Aldn Mr Chambers, Mr Maulkin Cor[onor], Mr Oakes, Mr Buchanan, Mr Dickenson, Mr Blomfield, all of which attended & in addition to the Number I asked Mr Fairfax & Mr Cook as succeeding next to the Chair. We took a view of the income, that is to say:

		[£	s.	d.]	
Rentall Gross		389	7	–	
Tythes Net		217	16	4½	
	Total	607	3	4½	
Expenditure					
Clergy Charity	128				
	4	132			
Alderman's allowance		20			
Taxes on Rentall exclusive of Tythes		71	8	—	
3 Sessions Dinners		7	—	—	
King's Birth Day & proclaiming musick		4	4	—	
Catechism Bread		11	—	—	
Fee Farm Rents & crownd [word illegible]		46	15	7	
Hall Keeper & small wage		8	8	—	
Badby's Gift		6	—	—	
Annual Repairs		60	—	—	
Calthorpe's Charity		3	—	—	528 14 7
Town Clerk & Receiver		4	—	—	
Sundry small Rents uncollected annually		7	10	—	
Surveyor's Rate		5	—	—	
Insurance		4	4	—	
Sundry small Bills		5	5	—	
Int[erest] on 25 Bonds, ea[ch] 100£, 5 per ct		125	—	—	
	Annual savings	78	8	9½	

It appeard we could in no manner lessen the Expenditure more than 6 or 8£ by having done with the Musick & less Expend on the Births, so that no way whatever could we see a probability of attaining an annual saving of more than £84 or 85£. It appeard there were still outstanding 8 of the twenty five pounds lent by Corporation [members] not pd off.[209] It was proposd & generally approvd by all that in future every one who should come upon the Corporation in the future should lend £25, free of any Int[erest] for the certain term of 7 years, & so it was hopd & expected that in a very few years we might pay off 150£ a year of our Debt & once it could be made £200 a year we might be soon out of Debt.

[209] See note 194 above.

The party all suppd together at my House & abt 11 O'Clock the State of the Corporation became the Topick & the particular unpleasant Situation of Mr Gooding who stood in a very aukard prediclament not havg the Majority of both upper & Lower Houses that there were, with his, now 5 Vacancies. After many Alter[c?]ations abt filling up, it was at length generally settled & agreed by all present (after the Alderman, Mr Chambers, & Mr Buchanan had quitted the Company) 7 of us remaining, that Mr Pate should be given up, that Mr Gooding should be unanimously elected, Mr Otley the 2d & Mr Complin 3d, Mr Jas Mathew 4th, Mr Foster 5th, wch would completely fill up the Body. It was further agreed that the next two Persons coming on the Corporation should be Mr Kitson the first & whoever We should think proper to nominate & that the 7 Gents prest pledgd to vote for Mr K as also for that Person Mr Maulkin or Mr Oakes should wish to Nominate. . .

*****An express arrivd with Us at 4 O'Clock this morng for Mr Gould to join his Regt at Portsmouth with all possible Dispatch.*****

Tuesday May 9   Meeting of the Commissn, Mr Carss's Bankruptsy. ******Very bad News by the Post from the Fleets at Plymouth & Portsmouth. A renew'd Mutiny among the Sailors & some Lives lost between the Officers & Sailors.[210] Son Gould set off to join his Regt at Portsmouth by the Mail. Family at Home alone.******************************

*****We have our Apprehensions that from this Mutiny of the Sailors may be dated the Commencement of a Revolution in this Kingdom.****************

Wednesday May 10   Family at home alone. **********News from the Fleet at Portsmouth continue to be most unfavourable. The Mutineers apparently havg the Command of the Fleet & sendg all the principall Officers ashore.********

Thursday May 11   Family at home alone. *****We hope may have reason to flatter Ourselves the Disturbances among the Sailors at Portsmouth & Plymouth may be in a Train of being settled from the acct recd by Post this Morning.**************

Friday May 12   Family at home alone. A much more favourable Acct from the Fleet at Portsmouth. Admiral Colpoys releasd & the mutineers all seemingly returng to a sense of their Duty. Sent up my 4th Q[uarte]r's Statements to the Commiss[ioner] of Taxes for 1796.

---

210 In April 1797 seamen in the fleet at Spithead refused to obey orders after their representations to the Government in March concerning pay and conditions had been ignored. The Admiralty agreed to most of their demands but the men, fearing that the Government would not honour the Admiralty's undertaking, refused to obey orders again on 7 May 1797. To calm the situation the Government pushed through a supplementary estimate to provide for the promised pay increases and the Channel Fleet set sail on 17 May. Meanwhile, on 12 May 1797, a mutiny broke out in the fleet at the Nore, ignoring the Spithead agreement. Seamen demanded the right to dismiss their officers and crews blocked the Thames to commercial traffic. Government and public suspected treason and links with radical societies, although this was never proved. On 6 June they were proclaimed rebels, their supplies cut off and offers of pardon made to those who surrendered, except the leaders. The Mutinies were over by the end of June.

Monday May 15 Family at home alone. *****This Day the Corporation was filld up by a Hall call'd for that purpose by the Alderman. . .

The 1st	Mr John Gooday
2	Maths Ostley [Otley?]
3	Saml Miles Complin
4	Jas Mathew
5	Thos Foster

These Gentn were all unanimously elected & were present & accepted the Office being each duly sworn in. There was not a single word of Dispute or anything upleasant. The Alderman (Mr Chambers) opened the Business of the Day by stating the Report of the Committee for inspecting the Income & Expenditure of the Corporation & it was agreed that all the Savings that could be thought of should be made. Now indeed appeard possible best in abolish[in]g the Musick £4 4 –, & abt 4 or 5 in the Expenditure on the King's Birth Day & proclaim[in]g the Fair, 40/– for each only being hence-forth allowd. It was likewise generally agreed, previous to commencing this election, that every Gentleman chosen should lend £25 for 7 years certain to the Corporation without Int[erest] & by this means hopd we should soon be enabled to pay off one hund[re]d pound annually. Once we should get to £150 a year there would be a fair appearance of liquidating our Debt. No other Business done this Day at the Hall. In the Evening abt 23 or 24 Gentn of the Corporation met at the Six Bells Inn to sup & passd an agreeable Eveng. . .*****************************

Wednesday May 17 Miss Moyle din'd & passd the Day with Us. Mr Gould return'd to Us from Portsmouth —— all points settled with the Sailors by Lord Howe, but He was obligd to accede to all their Propositions & admit of their turning out 10 or 15 Commis[sione]d Officers who are all superceded. It is generally allowd this Business to be miserably settled for the Nation & yet there was no Alternative. Mr G left the Fleet preparing for Sea but a vast Number of Sailors drunk on shore.***

*****Pipe of Red Port from London by water to Ipswich deposited in my cellar.*****

Thursday May 18 Family at home alone. Nothing particular in [the] course of this day. Cavalry for [the] Division of Bury musterd.

Friday May 19 Mr Gould dind at Mr Adamson's. Family at home alone. Yeomanry Cavalry, Lord Brome's Troop, exercizd. Cavalry Division of Ixworth muster'd.

Wednesday May 24 This Morng ab 2 O'Clock my Daughter Gould was safely deliverd of a Girl. . .

Monday May 29 *Mr Gould left us this Morng by Coach to join his Regiment at Winchester. Family at home. ****Mr Robt Adamson came this Morng from London by the Mail to consult his Uncle abt his acceptence of the Consulship to Naples, to clear £600 a year. His pres[ent] [word illegible] £300.*****

Thursday June 1 *Bottled off [a] Pipe of Sherry. Mr Hill of Buxhall 1/3 share. Mr H breakfasted & din'd with Us. ****Continued bad acct from Sheerness, Plymouth &ca of Mutinous Behaviour of the Seamen.*****

Friday June 2 Family at home. ****Executed a Bond wth Mr Geo Chinery & Son Orbell in the penal Sum of £500 to answer for my appointment to the Treasurership of the County & sent to Mr Notcutt, Dep[uty] C[ler]k [of the] Pe[a]ce on the 3d Ins. Rather more favourable accts from the Navy.

Sunday June 4 Mrs O, Self & Charlotte din'd at Mr Adamson's. . . *****Still a worse acct from the Navy at Sheerness: more mutinous than ever. Every lenient Measure havg been tryd with Them to no purpose, [the] Government seem determin'd to adopt the most coercive [measures] to bring them to a sense of their Duty.***

Thursday June 8 Mr Vernon's Birth Day —— kept at his House at Orwell Park.[211] Daughter Charlotte went with Miss Rose on Wednesday & returnd Sat Eveng. The House very full of Company: all the Cullum Family[212] except Mrs Palmer & Mr Cullum, <<full>> 20 to 23 Ladys & Gent in the House, on the Ball Night only 12 Couple —— but one Officer from Ipswich.
    I rode over to Thurston this Morng & breakfasted with Mr & Mrs Tyrrel. Son James & his Wife met me to talk over their Income & Expenditure & see what was best to be done respecting a House for Them, they having given up the House they had hird in Bury. I made it appear to Them they had a clear annual Income of £555, even now whilst they were at near £50 a year decrease by the purchase of their Tostock Estate, that, considering the great & voluntary Things I had done for Them, it was impossible for me to do more. I thought they could afford to lay out 6 or even £800 wch would make their own House comfortable &, with respect to the advowson of the Living, if it could be purchasd for £600 was there any possibility I would advance the Money & they must be chargd Int[eres]t at their coming into possession of [the] Rattlesden Living & thus the matter ended. Family at home alone.

*****No better acct from the Sailors at Sheerness. They continue in the same mutinous state.

Saturday June 10 . . .If anything a better acct from the Mutineers at the Nore —— there is a Hope of returnng to their Obedience without proceed[in]g to Extremitys. The weather this week very cold & some Quantity of wet.

Sunday June 11 I rode to Tostock & breakfasted with Son James & went to Tostock Church. Afterwards went to & pd Mr Ray a Morng visit & had a good deal of Conversation with him /respecting Son James/. . .***** Mr Adamson & Mr Martin dind with Us & spent the Day.

*******Son Orbell's Birth Day   29 yrs
         Mr Gould's —— Day   29 yrs[213]

---

[211] Orwell Park is on the north bank of the Orwell, at Nacton, near Ipswich.
[212] John Vernon's mother was Jane Cullum, daughter of Sir John Cullum, 5th Baronet, who had married Henry Vernon of Great Thurlow. John Vernon inherited Orwell Park from his uncle, Frances Vernon, 1st Earl Shipbrook.
[213] William Gould's birthday was on the same day as that of Orbell Oakes but they were not the same age. Gould was born in 1759. SROI J426/46.

Monday June 12 . . .*****An acct of a total Suppression of the Mutineers at the Nore. . .[214]

Friday June 16 Family at home alone. Lord Brome's Troop exercized. *****This morng we had an acct by Post of the complete Suppression of <u>all</u> the mutinous Ships at the Nore & Sheerness. Every Ship is come in & surrenderd. Parker, the President, & Davis, Vice Presd, & 20 men of the Delegates were deliverd up [by] the Ship's crew in Irons.*****

Monday June 19 Family at home. *Began mowing Cob's Orchard.[215]

Friday June 23 Family at home. Son Orbell din'd wth Us. **Grandson Henry's Birth Day: one year old.

Monday June 26 Daughter Maria left Us for Winchester. She intended sleeping this Evening at Brentwood & reaching there to Morrow Eveng. Our Grandaughter Maria remaing with Us. Mr Symonds drank tea with Us. . .

Wednesday June 28 Miss Norford & Mastr Rd Cocksedge dind with Us. Family at home.

****************The valuation of [the] advowson of Tostock by Mr Chinery

	[£	s.	d.]
by Direction of Mr Jno Moseley of Mr Morgan	927	–	–
By Direction of Me of Mr Brand	678	14	–
Net annual value of £140 Incumbant 27 yrs old	1,605	14	–
I offerd	802	17	–

It is extraordinary these 2 great men in so small a Matter, word for word the Case put to them, should vary £248 6 –.

[James Oakes, his wife and Charlotte went to Norwich and stayed with the Pattesons in Surrey Street. The journey was undertaken 'more particularly for the Advice of Dr Lubbock for my Daughter'.]

Saturday July 1 I breakfasted at Mr Henry Patteson's. **Dr Lubbock visited my Daughter. . .

******NB I had abt 47 Pack [of] yarn to sell but the E[ast] India Orders were not arriv'd & there was a general Expectation of Peace —— wools advancing & Spinning going off —— under all these Considerations I did not think it advisable to call upon any of the Manufacturers or offer my Yarns to sale to anyone. I took an opportunity of calling at the several Banking Houses, wishing to consult with Them on some new System of Banking as little else but Bank of England Notes were likely to circulate of some time. That is to say: to charge 1/4 per C[en]t Comm[issio]n over & above Int[eres]t &ca &ca & further shewing Them Messr Alexanders & Co propositions.[216]

---

[214] See note 210 above.
[215] Cobbs Orchard was a piece of land in Saint Andrew's Street opposite the back gate of Oakes's house.
[216] The Alexanders were bankers in Needham Market and Ipswich.

Sunday July 2   Mrs O, Self returnd home leav[in]g Daughter Charlotte at Mr Patteson's for 8 or 10 Days longer for the Advice of Dr Lubbock. We got home 1/2 hour after 6 O'Clock.

Monday July 3   1st Day's Receipt for the year 1797. I went with Hines in a post Chaise being very wet. Got home at 7 O'Clock, took in 25 Parishes, ab £1,017 – –.
****

My Son's Appointment to the Receivership came down on Saturday, July 1 1797 in lieu of Me. JO appointed in Febry 1787 & collected last Quarter of 1786 & ten following years. . .**

Tuesday July 4   Self & Coachman to Stowmarkett, 2nd Day's Receipt, took in all but 2 Parishes. Home by 4 O'Clock Dinner.

*****Son Orbell with his Wife to dine at Chadacre —— a general Family meet[in]g includ[in]g Revd Jno Plampin, his Wife, Mr & Mrs Macklin, Mr /& Mrs/ Harrington &ca,[217] Captn Robt Plampin &ca. An accommodation took place thro out the Family with every promising appearance of restoring Unanimity & Harmony to this, for some years back, much divided Family.*****

Thursday July 6   My 3d Day's Receipt at Wickhambrook, only Self & Coachman took in only 8 Parishes, abt £320, not worth going this Quarter. Got home by 1/2 hour after /6 o'clock./ Mrs O din'd at Son Orbell's.

Friday July 7   My 4th Day's Receipt, Self wth Coachman to Mildenhall. The Commission had their first Meeting this very day for appointing Collectors so that no one of them came prepard to pay their 1st Q[uarte]r Land [Tax]. There ever was & am afraid will continue to be great irregularity in this Hundred whilst the pres[en]t clerk, Mr Isaacson Jnr, is continued & there being only 3 acting Commissioners is against it. I returnd Home by 2 O'Clock. Son & Daughter Orbell suppd with Us.

Sunday July 9   . . . *****I rode over & made a Morng visit at Mr Symonds & also Sr Charles Davers thank[in]g Sr Charles for his hav[in]g been one of my Securities, thou[gh?] now my Son being appointed Receiver I should be my Son's Security & would no longer trouble Sr Charles.***** Mr & Mrs Jno Plampin came to Son Orbell's.

Tuesday July 11   . . . *****Son Orbell had Mr Plampin, Mr & Mrs Jno P, Mr Robt Plampin, Mr & Mrs Macklin, Mr Harrington &ca &ca all dind, being the Reconciliation Family meeting at their House.*****

Thursday July 13   . . . ***Miss Patty Young died of a Consumption at Bristol.[218]

---

[217] Mrs Macklin and Mrs Harrington were Betsy Oakes's sisters.
[218] This probably refers to Arthur Young's much loved daughter, Bobbin, who died on about 14 July 1797, in Boston, Lincolnshire and not in Bristol. Oakes liked to fill in this kind of information on the appropriate day and not the one on which he received the news. See John Gerow Gazley, *The Life of Arthur Young 1741–1820*, Memoirs of the American Philosophical Society, 97 (Phildelphia, Pa, 1973), p. 372.

Friday July 14 Troop reviewd by his Royal Highness Prince William & he was pleasd to say they performd infinitely beyond his Expectations. Lord Brome gave a Dinner servd from the half Moon /at the Guild hall/. Lieut Folkes, Cornett Oakes & 48 of the Troop, Son James as Chaplain & 3 or 4 others din'd with him. Troop parted at ten O'Clock. We had Dinner Company at home: /Daughter OO/ Mrs & Miss Fowke, Mr & Mrs Macklin, Mr & Mrs John Plampin, Captn /Jno/Plampin,[219] Mr Harrington & 4 young Ones, 16 in all of us set down to Dinner. Son & Daughter OO, Captn Robt, Mr Harrington all at Supper.

Sunday July 16 Mr Adamson dind with Us & drank Tea. Son Orbell & his Wife at Supper. Son set out for London at 11 O'Clock this Eveng by Yarmouth Coach carr[yin]g up £3,900 Bank [of England Notes] to Lambert & Cotton,[220] 2,700 Gs in Gold, 48 Gs Silver, sundry Bills to Ayton & Co.[221]*****

Monday July 17 . . . *County Sessions. I attended & deliverd in <<my>> the Balance for my first Quarter's acct as County Treasurer.

Friday July 21 At home without company. Son Orbell & his Wife at Mr Fowke's. **The advowson of Tostock: agreed the Purchase wh Mr Jno Moseley, £800.***

Sunday July 30 Family at home. Rode after Morng Service to Mr Sandys's, Ickworth Park, & saw the Plans & Build[in]g for Lord Bristol's new House wth Mr Collett & Mr Reed.[222] Mr & Mrs Collett, Mr & Mrs Reed & Miss Clerk, their Relation, also Mr & Mrs Wise, their Bro & Sistr all din'd with Us at 3 O'Clock, also Mr Adamson staid Tea. Mr & Mrs Collett & their Friends went on stage towards Home. . .

Friday Augst 4 Bottled [a] Pipe of Red Port equally divided between Son Orbell & Self, see particulars in Wine Cellar Book. Mrs O & Self din'd with Sir Tho & Lady Cullum on [a] Haunch of Venison. Met Sr Chas Davers, Admiral Symonds, Mr & Mrs Mills, staid till 9 O'Clock. Daughter Charlotte at Home.

Friday Augt the 11th I attended the [Grand] Jury till one O'Clock when we got dischargd. I presented a Memorial to the Grand Jury stating the Danger the property of [the] Publick was in from the unguarded manner our Mail was sent on Horseback to New[marke]tt wch was signd by all the Grand Jury, 20 Names requir[in]g either a Mail [by] the middle Road thro Braintree [and] Sudbury to Bury, or that our prest Post to New[marke]tt might be guarded. Sr Charles [Davers], Foreman, was requird to deliver the same to the Post Master General.**
I dind this Day at Mr Adamson's. . . My Son's man & Daughter's Servt set out in the Cartes on their way to Yarmouth.

[219] This should be Captn Robert Plampin.
[220] Messrs Lambert and Cotton of 25 Cornhill, London, were Oakes's stockbrokers from November 1790 until 1808.
[221] Messrs Ayton, Brassey, Lees and Satterthwaite of 71 Lombard Street, Oakes's London bankers.
[222] See note 142 above.

35. *Orbell Oakes's house in Guildhall Street.*

***Business at [the] Crown Bank ended this Day.[223]**

[Orbell Oakes accompanied his wife Betsy, his son Henry and his sister Charlotte to Yarmouth. The Rev. James Oakes's wife gave birth to a third daughter at her parents' house in Thurston.]

Sunday Augt 13   After morng Service Mrs O & Self rode over to Congratulate the Family on the safe Delivery of Eliza. . .

Tuesday Augt 15   . . . before Breakfast this Morng I rode to Tostock to see my son's new Building.

Wednesday Augt 16   Miss Moyle din'd & drank Tea with Us. We began paying Messrs Corks'[224] 1st Div[iden]d of 10/– in the £ wch will amot to from £1,800 to £2,000. Made out & gave Lord Brome [a] statm[en]t of our acct for. . . his Lordship's Troop.

Saturday Augt 26   . . .*Got home by Coach £5 new copper coinage, carr[ia]ge 7/2.[225]

---

[223] The Crown Bank was often a name given to a bank which organized the receipt of taxes. According to a list of country bankers of 1797 Messrs Harvey and Company of Norwich were known as the Crown Bank although they were not the Receivers for Norfolk until 1808. This entry probably means that they syspended payments temporarily.
[224] Messrs Corks of Abbeygate Street were bankrupted in the March crisis.
[225] Between 1797 and 1799 Matthew Bolton was contracted to make regal copper coins and forgers were threatened with prosecution. One thousand tons of two penny pieces,

Sunday Augt 27 Son Orbell & I rode over to Thurston & Tostock this Morning after Service. Mr Symonds, Dr White, Mr Jenkins & Mr Adamson wh Son Orbell & Miss Macklin all dind with us & staid till 8 o'clock. NB A Turbot bo[ugh]tt from Yarmouth.

[James Oakes and his wife went to Yarmouth on 31 August to join Charlotte, Betsy and Henry.]

Yarmouth Journey continued: Minutes.

This Journey was originally undertaken for the Benefit of Daughter Charlotte who had been in very ill Health & by the advice of Dr Lubbock. Son Orbell, his Wife & their Son went with her on Saturday Aug 12. Son Orbell staid till Tuesday Augst 22 & Mrs O & Self went Augt 31. I promised to be at the whole of the Expence. My Daughter Charlotte not being at all benefited whilst at Yarmouth we returnd home by way of Norwich for Dr Lubbock's further Advice. . .

Wednesday Sept 20 . . . *****Acct arrivd of Lord Malmsbury's Return from Lisle. No Peace.[226]*****

Tuesday Oct 3 Mr Patteson & Mr Crackenthorp from Norwich dind & drank Tea & suppd with Us. We walkd to Ickworth between Dinner & Tea. They slept at the Angel & set off by Coach in the Morng to Braintree Hop Fair.

Friday Oct 6 Family at home alone. Son & daughter OO suppd with [Us]. The first Day of Lord Brome's 4th Troop exercizing since the Review. *The privates of the Troop gave an handsome Dinner to their Officers. Marquis of Cornwallis honourd them wth his Company, abt 60 din'd at [the] Guildhall. Dinner servd by Mrs Beatniff at the Greyhound. Mr Chambers to London.

Sunday Oct 8 We dind at Mr Adamson's. . . I rode after Morng Service & pd a Visit at Mr Tyrrell, Thurston & from thence to see Building at Tostock. NB This morng Mr Chambers returnd from London with £11,000 to pay Mr Carss Div[iden]d.[227]

Monday Oct 9 . . . This Day commencd payg Mr Carss first Divd of 6/8 in the £. Amt of Debts provd was upwds of £59,000 & 800 separate Claimants includ[in]g the Notes.

Wednesday Octr 11 First great Fair Day. We were remarkably full in the Bank the whole day. The Town scarce ever rememberd more crowded. . .
****
This day from 11 to 3 O'Clock was fought the great Battle at Sea between the English & Dutch Fleets in which Admiral Duncan gaind a complete victory.

known as cartwheels and weighing two ounces each, were made, together with one penny, half penny and farthing pieces. This coin drove out most of the tokens in circulation.
[226] Lord Malmesbury was sent by the Government to meet the French plenipotentiaries at Lille in an attempt at peace negotiations.
[227] To pay the creditors of Messrs Spink and Carss's Bank which had failed in March.

Capt[ure]d 10 Ships of the Line & 12 [of] the line & one Frigate. The force nearly equal both sides, say 16 Line of Battle ships & a few frigates. The Dutch had great weight of metal & fought well. At Camperdown within 8 miles of the Texall.***

[The Receipt went well apart from the discovery at Stowmarket that there was a 20% error in all their statements for the year.]

Wednesday Oct 25 My last Day's Receipt at Home. Son Orbell, Mr Smith, Hines & the Boy attendant on the Receipt. Self & Biggs on the Bank. Took in abt 120 Parishes, say full £11,000, & agreed in the Business of the whole Day, both Receipt & Bank, to an sixpence. I did not ask any Body to dine but those who were assisting being so very full [we] had only 1/4 of an hour. Shut the Door soon after 6 & quite finishd balancing by 9 O'Clock.

Saturday Oct 28 Family at home. Mr & Mrs Gould at the Play, the last Night. [I] gave the Clerks, all 3, a Play each this eveng.

Wednesday Novr 1 *****I went up to London accompanied by Mr H.Jodrell & Mr Patteson. I carried up 2,400 G[uinea]s Specie & Bank [of England Notes] & ca[sh] mak[in]g up together full £14,000. We went up in Post Chaises. My 1/3 cost me 32/–. We get up exact in 10 Hours, sett[in]g out 1/2 hour after 6 & reach[in]g Town at 1/2 hour after 4 O'Clock. I deliverd my Charge at Mess Aytons & Co & went & dind at the City Coffee House with Mr J & Mr P. The same Eveng to the Play wth Mr P. Slept at the Bull Inn.

Thursday Nov 16 Family at home alone. Only Mrs O, Self & Daughter Maria. *****Daughter Charlotte & her Maid to Dedham /to Mrs Gould's/.

Friday Nov 17 Family at home alone. *****Son Orbell fortunately escapd injury himself by taking a wrong dose of Physic.

Thursday Nov 23 *Receivd a Letter from Daughter Charlotte /Dedham/ intimating a Wish of going to Bristol wch we estemd a great point gaind.*** Tea & Supper Company at home. . . Very cold.

Saturday Nov 25 Miss Cocksedge & her 3 Brothers din'd, drank Tea & suppd with Us.

**********Mrs O, Self, Daughter G, Son & Daughter OO had a Meeting. Very cold.

Sunday Nov 26 . . . Wonderfully warm wth a good deal of Rain. Everything running down with water in the House, so very moist.

Monday Novr 27 Family at home alone. Nephew Bridge dind & spent the Day at Mr Adamson's. *****Daughter Charlotte returnd from Dedham apparently mended for her Excursion.

Tuesday Novr 28 Family at home alone. Nephew James passd the Eveng at Son Orbell's. ****This Morng at 8 O'Clock died my poor old Dogg, Tartar.

Tuesday Dec 5 We all set out /abt 9 o'clock/ on our Journey for Bristol thro London in our own Coach. Mrs O, Self, Daughter Charlotte, Daughter Gould &

Servt Maid Sier.[228] Took our own /Coach & as far as <u>Bourn Bridge</u>, our own Horses wh Mr Adamson's Leader. Man Servant on a temporary seat in the place of [the] Coach Box.

	M[i]l[e]s
Tuesday Night–Hockerel	44
Wednesday–London Baliso	36
Thursday–Reading	43
Friday–Devizes	50
Saturday–Bath	19
Sunday–Bristol Hot Wells	16
miles	298

We drove to Barten's Gloucester House Hotel on the Hot Wells, passd all Monday there engaging Lodgings at Mrs Bonett's near St Vincent's Parade. Slept again at Barten's. Monday Eveng the 11th Dec, Tues /Dec 12/ Daughter Maria left us in a Post Chaise for Weymouth. This Day we got into our Lodgings. My Daughter Charlotte attended by Dr Nott & Mr Barry. After a few Days Nephew George Green came to visit us. He slept at Bristol & boarded with Us. He continued wh Us abt 10 Days. We boarded Ourselves, Mrs Bonnett finding us with all Necessarys, use of Furniture & ca.

For the first 10 or 12 Days Daughter Charlotte continued tolerable, drinking the Water at the Pump, riding on a double Horse & taking moderate Exercize as prescribd by her Physicians. She then apparently alter'd much for the worse & appeard rapidly declining in so much that the Family apprehending we might find Difficulty in getting her home if we delayd it too long. On Thursday Janry 4th we <<set>> left the Wells & set out in her own coach for Home. . . My Daughter [was] exceedingly indiff[eren]t all the way in so much as we much apprehended several times on the road whether we should have been able to proceed. . . We were 36 Nights from Home, slept 10 Nights on the Road going & returng. . . We travell'd 416 miles.

	[£	s.	d.]
416 miles, 4 Horses, Postillions & Turnpikes, 2/4½	46	19	3
Expences 12 Days on the Road, 6 going & 5 returng <u>per mile</u> 1/2½	24	8	–
Lodgings, Board, Firing, Furniture & 24	25	15	5
Days Physicians & Apothocary	13	13	–
Use of Harpsicord, Library, hird Horses there, Coach standg, cleaning, greas[in]g & repairing	3	11	6½
	£114	7	2½
I think it probable my Daughter might pay for Sundries extra not coming to my Knowledge ab[out]	2	12	9½
See full particulars in Bristol Book	£117		

---

[228] Sier was Charlotte Oakes's maid.

[1798]

Wednesday Janry 10 to Tuesday Janry 16   Mrs O & Self attending Our Daughter
Charlotte. Extremely bad, apparently drawing near her end.   [page 2]

Tuesday Janry 16   ***
At 1/2 hour after 11 O'Clock at night our dear Charlotte died without a groan
or even a sigh in the 27th year of her Age, universally esteemd —— a good
Christian, a dutiful Daughter, loving Sister, sincere Friend & most benevolent
Disposition.**

Tuesday 16 – Tuesday 23 Janry

Mrs O & Self entirely alone on the Day we buried our dear Charlotte, that is to
say 23rd Janry at 4 O'Clock in the Afternoon. I did not suffer her to be movd
from the hour of her Death until an inside Coffern was prepard & then wrappd
round in the sheet she died upon with her Head-dress just as she died put into
her Coffern & afterwards, when an evident Change had taken place, the Shell
put into an outside lead Coffern & solderd down.   [page 4]

Tuesday Janry23   At 4 o'clock [in the] Afternoon a walking procession from my
own Door to the Church —— not any upper bearers & only followd by myself, Mr
Adamson & my 2 Sons with the House Servants —— the Parish Minister only
preceding.
    Mr Adamson /& Son James/ afterwds dind at Son Orbell's. My Wife & Self
retir'd to our Meditations havg din'd at one o'Clock. At 7 my two   [page 5]
Sons & Mr Adamsons came to Tea with Us. Mr A retird before 9, my Sons &
Betsy suppd & passd the Evening. I took this Opportunity of informing them it
was my Intention to divide their late Sister's Property equally between the 3
Survivors. Her Fortune consisted of Eighteen hundred pounds 3 per Ct Consols
& it was my Wish, for the sake of preserving the Memory of the dear deceasd,
they should suffer the Stock to remain as it now & ever has   [page 6]
stood since the purchase in my Name & that the Interest, amotg to 54£ a year,
should be paid to each, that is to say £18, by me. They neither of them, if they
wanted 2 or 3 hundred Pounds but could have it paying legal Int[erest] &, at my
Decease, I should take the necessary care that the 1/3, that is to say six hundred
pounds 3 per Ct Consol Stock, should come to each Family for the joint Lives of
Husband & Wife, then to the elder of their Children who shall attain the Age of
21 years. In the failure   [page 7]
of Issue to go & be equally divided between the Survivors & their Children. This
Proposal [was] with no other view than keeping up the Memory of their belov'd
Sister.

[Detailed accounts of Charlotte's funeral expenses and outstanding personal
debts follow this entry.]

Funeral Mem[orandu]m Continued: [page 9]

The Vault sunk in St Mary's Church is in the middle Aisle at the Entrance into
the Chancel & this, on several Tryals, was the only vacant place we could find.

A huge Stone was taken up of immense thickness & astonishg Weight, sd to be between 2 & 3 Ton. This, on further proof, was found to be Marble & was allowd me by the Church Wardens to be laid down again. I spard no Expence in polishing & squaring it, in doing which full 4 In[ches] in thickness were taken off. Nearly £7 expended in Polishing   [page 10]
& Preparing this Stone. When finishd it was of a beautiful ash Color &, tho a good deal reducd in weight & somewhat in Size by squar[in]g, yet contin[ue]d very thick & immense weight for the size. As there would be no Occasion ever to have it again removd on any future Interment I had it laid down in the hand-somest Manner, surrounded by a border of black Marble a foot wide, 28 feet, wch added to the Cost £8 7 –, the stone Cutter's Bill amo[un]t[ing] to in all £23 8 10½. . . The vault was sunk by Mr Elsgood, his Bill £20 19 –, large enough to contain at least 15 Cofferns. The Inscription   [page 11]
for my Daughter was put as high up on the Slab as possible being the first <u>3 Lines</u>, but, whoever has the ordering of the 2d or any future, is to understand only <u>2 Lines</u> can be allowd.

Dimensions of the vault: Length from Mouth to further end   7 feet 6 In[ches]
                                                         Width   8 feet
                              Height from Floor to Crown of Arch   7 feet 9 In[ches]
Interrd my Son Orbell['s] Infant Child Charles Adamson Oakes, 9 weeks old —
— 2 Cofferns.[229]

Monday Febry 5 **Miss Gould came from Dedham & brot to us our little Grandaughter Maria Gould after havg been on a visit to her Grandmother 9 weeks. They arriv'd rather before 4 O'Clock.************

Monday Febry 19 . . .*****A meeting at the Guildhall call'd by the Alderman of the Inhabitants in general for the purpose of open[ing] a Voluntary Subscrip-tion for [the] Government as most likely to defeat the designs of the Enemy & preserve Publick Credit. About 30 or 40 Gentn pre[sent]. The Alderman opened the Business & desiring to withdraw from the Chair, Mr Ranby was requested to take it. Certain Resolutions were enter'd into & Subscriptions immediately commenced.

	£
Mr Ranby	25 – –
Dr Wollaston	25 – –
Mr Oakes	50 – –
Mr O.Oakes	25 – –
Mr Squire	25 – –
Mr Buchanan	20 – –

Sundries other amotg to ab £250 – –. The Sub Books desir'd to be lay open at Messrs Oakes & Son till Thursday March 1st to receive Subn, when the Inhabi-tants are to meet again to direct the Amt to be paid at the Bank.****

Saturday Febry 24 *****A Corporate Assembly calld by the Alderman (Mr Fairfax) for the purpose of look[in]g into the Corporation Income & Expenditure & seeing in what manner most fitting the Body could come forwd at this

---

[229] This sentence was added later.

momentous Juncture by a voluntary Contribution to express their Loyalty for their King & Country, it being now in agitation thro'out the Kingdom. On calling over the Names their appear'd a Majority of both Houses prest.

	[£	s.	d.]
The Amt of our Income	607	3	4½
Annual Outgoings	528	14	7
Annual Savings	78	9	9½
Our Debts carrying Int 25 Bonds,ea[ch] £100 in Circulation at 5 p[er] Ct	2,500	–	–
4 of the old £25 to Members without Int to be pd off in next 2 yr	100	–	–
8 of new £25 to fresh members not to be pd off nor to commencement of 6 /year/ without Int	200	–	–
Total amt of Debt	2,800	–	–

As it was the wish of the Gentn prest to preserve the Credit of the Corporation they by no means thought it advisable to encrease the Expenditure by borrowing Money at Int[erest]. A proposal was made & come into by several Members to lend certain Sums each to be pd off after the first 4 of £25 were dischargd, say to commence payin[g] off Xmas 1800, makg no doubt that, at most, they might have ea[ch] 5/- Div[iden]d, that thru succeed[in]g years previous to the new 25£ carr[in]g incomes for payment. Accordingly it was Voted that the sum of 200 Gs should be thus rais'd for the Service of Government & it was accordingly sub-scribd as follows:

	£
The Alderman Mr Fairfax	10
Mr Oakes	25
Mr Maulkin	25
Mr Wright	10
Mr Mathew	10
Mr Cook	10
Sr Thos Cullum	10
Mr Sturgeon	10
Mr Barwick	10
Mr R.Maulkin	15
Mr Hawes	10
Mr Green	10
Mr Jenkins	10
Mr Smith	5
Mr Blomfield	5
Mr Thompson	5
Mr Otley	5
Mr O. Oakes	25
	210

This Business concluded much to the Satisfaction of the Gentlemen pre[sen]t.

Wednesday 28   Drank Tea & suppd at my Son Orbell —— a Musick party: Dr Winthorpe, Son James & his Wife, Mr Frank Sandys, Mr [blank], Mr Harrington & his Son. Staid till 1/2 hour after 12 o'Clock.

Wednesday Mar 7   *****General Fast on acct of the War. After Morng Service the Dep[ut]y Lieutenants held a Meetg at the Angel to ballot for 1/2 the Supplimentary [Militia].

The No ought to have been prest		735
Absent not to be accountd for	20	
Inlisted into the 9th	17	
At Sea	3	
At a Distance	3	
Sick	4	
Dead	4	
		49
Appeard		686
We ballotted for		350
of wch No the 9th to enlist men		100
		250

ought to be sent to join the West Suffk Regiment. The 1/2 upon whom the Lot did not fall were sent home. The Ballotted Men likewise allowd to go home to prepare Themselves to return on the 10th to Bury, remain here till 18th & then join the Regiment.**
At Home. John Patteson dind & spent the day with Us.

Wednesday Mar 14   At home Lord Euston came & held a Deputy Lieuts Meeting. Pipe of Red Port from Mess Watson & Son taken into my Cellar.

Tuesday Mar 20   Guildhall Feoffm[en]t Quarterly meet: Disposal of Shirts & Shifts. Tea & Supper at Mrs Rose's. . . **********First Evening spent out in Company since [the] Death of our Daughter Charlotte, <u>10 Weeks</u>.

Saturday Mar 31   At home. The weather this week very cold but chiefly dry, north easterly winds, a little fall of Sleet now & then.

Monday April 2   Passion Week at Home.

Sunday April 8   Easter Day. I had intended being at Church & attendg the Sacrament but my face continued so much swelld dare not venture. We dind at Mr Adamson's. . .

Monday April 9   *Meetg /at the Angel/ of abt 50 of the Inhabitants desirous of forming Themselves into a Company of Infantry for [the] Defence of the Country. Sr Charles Davers prest who was voted in the Chair. Certain Resolutions enterd into to be printed in the Wednesday's Paper. My Face continued swelld. Family at home.

***********Miss Molineux & Mr Frank Sandys married this Day.***********

Thursday April 12 At home alone. 2d Meeting this Morning of the intended Association for a Company of Foot to be calld the Bury Loyal Volunteers.

Monday April 16 1st Day's Receipt for the Lady Day Quarter at Eye. I went with Mr Steel & Biggs in a Post Chaise. Got there by 9 o'Clock & returnd home by 1/2 after 7 o'Clock. We took in 26 Parishes, [£]2,734 12 7½, first of the additional Levys on assessd Taxes.[230] NB Sister Baker & her Daughter Mary came to us from Causton.

Tuesday April 24 At home. 6th Day Receipt. We this year began receiv[in]g the Hund[re]ds of Thedwastre & Thingoe on this Day & took in abt 2/3 Parishes, say abt £3,000, apprehend[in]g the Business would be too much on the Wednesday considering the new assessd Taxes entirely by Mr Steel.

Thursday April 26 At home. Miss Cocksedge & master Spurgeon dind with Us, drank Tea & suppd. A Meeting this Eveng at the Angel, abt 12 or 14 Gentn, with a view of forming a Civil Association for assisting the Majistrates of the Town.[231] Signd a Requisition to the Alderman for calling a meeting of the Inhabitants.

Monday April 30 Son Orbell at London. A Meeting call'd by the Alderman of the Inhabitants & a Civil Association formd to assist the Majistrates in keep[in]g peace & good Government in the Town. Signd by [blank] Names includg the most respectable House-keepers, to be under the Chief Majistrate /as their Chief/ &, at any time, to assemble when he shall think proper to call &, upon Necessity, to be sworn in additional Constables according to Resolutions publishd. Also a Depty Lieuts Meeting at the Angel held for the Division of Thedwastre & Thingoe to receive the returns from the Constables for Sr Chas Davers, Sr T. G. Cullum, Dr Ord, Mr Grigby, Self & Mr Jenkins. Dind at the Angel, got home at 7 o'Clock.

Mrs O & Mrs Baker & her Daughter drank tea at Mr Johnstone's. *******Mr Grigby Junr calld at our Bank & refusd B[an]k of England [Notes] for our Cash Notes & insisted on Specie.*******

Wednesday May 2 Family at home. Mr Chambers din'd wth me. Mrs O, Sister Baker & her Daughter in [the] Eveng to Mr Harrington's Concert. *****Mr Grigby made his second Demand at our Bank for Cash.*****

Monday May 7 I attended the Muster & embodying of the Provisional Cavalry at Stow[marke]tt. Sr Wm Ranby, Coll & 8 or 10 other Officers, Coll Bacon. Mr Mileson Edgar as Depty Lieut from [the] Eastern Division, Mr Cartwright [and] Self for [the Western Division. We <two words illegible> musterd on Thorny Green 416 Men & Horses. Did not return to Stow[marke]tt till just 10 o'clock. We got a snap & it was near one o'Clock /in the Morn/ when we got home. . .

---

[230] 38 Geo III c16 trebled the last year's assessment of Assessed Taxes and in some cases raised taxes by up to five times.
[231] An association to assist in the prosecution of felons.

Sunday May 13 Mr Symonds, Mr Adamson, J & H.Patteson dind wth Us. At tea & supper Son & Daughter OO. *****Son James & Family left Mr Tyrrell's & get into their new House, Tostock.

Friday May 18 Review Day: Lord Brome's 4th Troop Cavalry by Lieut General Manners. They musterd abt 50 includg Officers & much approvd. Mr Henry Patteson, his Son & Jno Patteson, Mr Adamson & 2 Miss Cocksedges dind with Us.

Tuesday May 22 We all went to Tostock to tea with Son James & his Wife. Got home between 9 & 10 o'Clock.

Wednesday May 23 Mr Ray breakfasted with us. Family at home. *****Acct arrivd of 1,300 of our army being taken Prisoners on the Expedition against Ostend.

Thursday May 24 . . .*Grandaughter Maria's Birth Day: one year old. Son & Daughter OO to Mr Jno Plampin /Whatfield/.

Saturday May 26 Sister Baker returnd to Cawston in Mr Adamson's Chaise to Attleburgh.

Monday May 28 Family at home. *I pd a morning visit to Mr Plampin of Chadacre.

Thursday May 31 Mr Godbold's House & the Church yard sold under an Extent[232] at the Angel by Mr Spink's Ex[ecu]tors. Mr Benjafield purchas'd Mr Godbold's House & Pightle at £260. I purchasd the Church yard at £330 with a view of reserving it for the Corporation, hoping they will be in a very few years Capable of repay[in]g me the purchase money & all Expences. We were at Mr Denton's at tea & cards. . .

Friday June 1st Family at home. Mr Plampin from Chadacre came to Son Orbell's to dinner & settle an Acct.*

Monday June 4 <u>King's Birth Day</u>***
The Corporation wth the Clergy & other Gentlemen met at the Guildhall & walkd in procession to the Angel at 12 o'Clock to drink his Majesty's Health. Lord Brome's Troop was drawn up &, to the left, Lord Hervey's Bury Volunteer Company in front of the Angel & together made a most respectable Appearance. Lord Brome's Troop fird 3 excellent volleys in honour of the Day. Lord Hervey, major Commandr, Sr Thos Gage, Captn & the Company of Volunteers consisting of abt 76 all dind together at the Assembly rooms. Mr Robt Davers, Mr

---

[232] Extents in aid were legal devices for recovering Crown debts but could be extended to the recovery of private debts if it could be proved that without payment of a private debt a crown creditor could not repay a crown debt. Extents were much abused as they gave precedence over all other creditors in bankruptcy proceedings, often forced men into bankruptcy unnecessarily and meant that other creditors got less than their due. By 1815 country bankers felt it vital to hold some Government account in order to be eligible for extents as a form of insurance against bad debts. In 1817 an Act, 57 Geo III c35, regulated their issue and they were finally abolished in 1838 in 1 and 2 Victoria c110. As Spink died heavily indebted to the Exchequer an Extent was probably fully justified. See L. S. Pressnell, *Country Banking in the Industrial Revolution* (Oxford, 1956), particularly Appendix 29.

36. Tostock Rectory the Rev. James Oakes's house.

Cartwright & myself had Invitations & dind wth them. Sat down to dinner abt 80. Lord Brome's Troop had a Dinner at the Guild hall (Lord Brome in Lond) Lieut Fowke & my Son. They were near 50 at Dinner. There was likewise a third Dinner at the Angel: The Alderman, Mr Mills, Mr Becher, th Town Clerk, Mr Cook, Mr Blomfield &ca, ab 16 Gent of the Association for the Defence of the Town. The Day passd off very pleasantly in all Company many loyal Tosts & constitutional Songs.

Saturday June 16 Family at home **********Corporation Meeting agreed to accept the Purchase I made of the Church yard at £330. A Committee appointed to take the Direction & Management of the same, that is to say the Alderman for the time being, Self, Mr Cook, Mr Maulkin & Mr Otley, to grant 7 Bonds, ea[ch] £50, to pay for the same allow[in]g 20£ for Expences.****************

Saturday June 23 Grandson Henry's Birth Day, 2 years old. . . *****This Eving Biggs, our Clerk, went to London by Norwich Coach, carrying wh him abt 3,00£ small Bank [Notes] &ca.

Friday June 29 Dinner Company at home: the Officers of [the] Northamptonshire Supplementary or 2d Regiment. . .

Tuesday July 10 Family at home. *This Eveng abt 1/2 hour after 7 o'Clock came Son & Daughter Gould from Portsmouth.

Wednesday July 11 Last Receipt at Bury, took in ab 100 Parishes, say ab 4,850£. Son Orbell, Biggs & Mrs Steel with the Boy taking Receipt, Self & Hines at the Bank in my Study. Finishd ab 7 & prepard to send up what we could by Son

Gould to Morrow. They all dind with me & Mr Shillito. Son James & his wife came to call on Mr & Mrs Gould & drank tea with us.

Friday July 20 I went to Colchester to see Lord Euston on Acct of a Letter I receivd from his Lordship respectg an Appointm/t/ to a Central Commisary for the County of Suffolk.[233] Mr Jenkins accompanied me by Coach to Sudbury where a Deputy Lieuts meetg was held & took a post Chaise from thence to Colchester. Din'd at the 3 Cups, returnd in [a] Chaise to Melford Bull where my own Horses met me in Mr A['s] chaise & got home abt 11 o'Clock at Night.

Sunday July 22 I rode over to Tostock & Breakfasted with Son James to meet Mr Patteson, then pd a Morning visit at Mr Ray's, calld at Mr Tyrrell's on my return. My mare Lam'd. Wrote an answer to Lord Euston in favour of Mr C. Mr Adamson, Son & Daughter OO din'd with Us.

Tuesday July 24 Daughter Gould & her Daughter Maria wh Nurse to Dedham on a visit to her Grandmama. Family at home.

Tuesday Augst 7 I rode over to Mr Chambers, Stanton, wth his Appointm[en]t of /central/ Commissary from Lord Euston.*******************************
Family at home.

Monday Augst 20 5th Day's Receipt, Self & Mr Steel to Sudbury. Mr Sparke attended to settle Isaacson's Mortgage. I receivd 1,200£ principal & 3 years & 1/2 Int[eres]t. We did not get home till past 8 o'Clock.

Tuesday Aug 21 Dinner Company at home. . . Haunch of Vennison from [the] Duke of Grafton. *****Mr Chambers['s] appointment came down for the central Commissariship datd Aug 15th at 15/– per Day from that date, licensd by [the] Earl of Euston.*****

Monday August 27 Family at home.*****NB This Day Mr Carss['s] assignes began paying 2d Div[iden]d of 5/– in the £ requir[in]g abt 15,000£ better than 800 Claimants, abt 60,000, every 1/– in [the] £ requires £3,000 – –. Biggs from Lond by Yarm[outh] Coach wh Bank [Notes] &ca to pay Carss 2d Div[iden].*****

Wednesday Augt 29 Son Orbell & his Wife went off on a visit to their Bror John's at Aldborough. Family at home.

Sunday Sept 2 Our Sunday for Dinner, Mr Vernon, Dr Wintrop, Mr Adamson, Mr Cullum, Mr Dalton, Mr Jno Patteson & Mr Rogers. Girling at [the] Hospital[234] droppd down dead.

Tuesday Sept 4 Family at home. Son & Daughter JO din'd with Us. **********About 4 o'Clock this Afternoon part of the West Suffolk Regt, abt 600 /men/, Lord Euston at the Head, passd thro Bury in Waggons, Carts & Chaises on their way to Nantwich, supposd inten/d/ to be shippd off for Ireland

---

[233] Each camp had a Commissary from the Treasury assisted by an officer to see to supplies from contractors. I can find no reference to a Central Commissary. Possibly he was concerned with supplying all the camps in an area.
[234] See note 185 above.

37. A View of the Church Yard at St Edmunds Bury published by J. Kendall, painted by F. Jukes: see p. 364.

there havg been a recent descent made at Hillara by abt 1,500 of the French & some of the Irish Regiments had behav'd very ill. In consequence a large force was intended to be sent /to Ireland/.

Wednesday Sept 5   Family at home. P[ar]t of [the] South Lincoln marchd thro Bury into Chester supposd for Ireland.

Thursday Sept 13   ******************Acct arrivd that the French Invaders in Ireland, abt 800 strong, had surrenderd at Discretion to General Lake.[235]

*****I set out on Horseback with George, my Coachman, abt 12 o'Clock on my Journey to Yarmouth to <word illegible> /get/ some Information respect[in]g Mr Patteson's Brewery there. I got to Scole Inn by Dinner 3 o'Clock, met Mr & Mrs Moseley & Mr Cowper. From thence went to Beccles & slept at the Crown. Friday Morning I got to Yarmouth by Breakfast, went to the Angel in the Market Place, calld upon Mr Watson, Atterney, Mr Spurgeon &ca of whom made some Enquirys. Din'd at the Angel where I saw Mr Iselin from Norwich[236] to whom I related my particular Business & who gave me a satisfactory Acct as far as he knew. We passd a hour or two convers[in]g on the Subject. I suppd alone at the Angel. Breakfasted Saturday Morng at the Wrestlers wh Mr Iselin who promisd to gain every further Information possible & write me in [the] course of a Week or ten Days. I din'd at the ordinary on Saturday at the Angel & left Yarmouth abt 4 o'Clock, got to Bungay before 7, drank tea & spent the Eveng at Mr [and] Mr[s?] Routh's, slept at the Tunn's. Left Bungay on 6 o'clock Sunday Morning, breakfasted at Scole Inn & got home by one o'clock.***************

Wednesday Sept 19   Messr Alexanders from Ipswich & Needham din'd with me. Family at home.

Tuesday Sept 25   Bottled of Pipe Red-Port divided between Self & son. . . I attended, with Steel, the Justices meeting to have the Treasurer's acct better understood respectg Pay of Militia. Family at home.

Thursday Septr 27   **************Self with Son Gould to Norwich in [a] Chaise, Mrs Ann Wright accompanied Us. We got to Mr Patteson not till 1/2 hour after 5 o'clock (havg had bad Horses from Scole Inn). We din'd & slept at Mr Patteson's. Our Journey thither was with a view of fixing the intended Partnerships between Mr Patteson & Mr Gould in the Yarmouth Brewery, Mr P havg offer'd the one half Share of the Yarmouth Concern to Mr Gould. For Particulars of their Negotiations see Stock Book.**************

Friday Sept 28   Mr P, Self &c Mr Gould went in [a] Chaise to Yarmouth & lookd over the Premises. Mr Sinclair (Mr Patteson's Clerk) was acquainted wh what was going forward & din'd with Us at the Wrestlers. We left Yarmo before 4 & returnd to Norwich that Evening by 7 o'Clock. Passd all the Saturday the 29th

---

[235] A small detachment of French, including Irish levies, under General Humbert reached Killala in Western Ireland at the end of August 1798. This was defeated by a force consisting of about 1,000 veterans from campaigns in Italy and the Rhinland under General Lake, at Ballinamuck on 8 September.

[236] Iselin was John Patteson's business partner.

with Mr Patteson consulting on the Terms of the intended Partnership as minuted in [the] Stock Book.**********

Monday Oct 1 *****Son Gould commencd Partner[ship] wth Mr Patteson in [the] Yarmouth Brewery.*****

Tuesday Oct 2 *****First Authentick acct re[ceive]d of Admiral Nelson's Vis-tory over [the] French Fleet. . .*****[237] Mr Harrington's Ball for his Scholars. Mrs O, Self & Miss Baker went for 2 or 3 hours.

Friday Oct 5 Family at home. A general Illumination took place thro' the Town on acct of the glorious victory by Admiral Nelson over the French Fleet. The Evening remarkably mild & very dark; the Town look uncommonly well.

Saturday Octr 6 Family at home. *****The Members for the Borough, Lord Hervey & Sir Charles Davers, gave to the Populace 12 H[ogs]h[ea]ds of beer (provided by Mr Wright) in order that they might drink the Alderman's Health & partake of the general Joy.***** Mr Charles Harvey suppd wth Us.

Sunday Oct 7 Mr Charles Harvey, myself & Mr Gould walkd to Ickworth after Morng Service to view Lord Bristol's Building. We dind at Mr Adamson's. Met Mr Sandys & Mr Mills.

Tuesday Oct 16 2nd Day's Receipt. Self & Mr Steel to Stow[marke]tt took in 11 Parishes, say abt £1,100. Home by Dinner. I breakfasted at Son James. I settled with my Tenant, Saml Kent /Stow[marke]tt/, rec[eive]d his 1/2 year's Rent & gave him Notice I intended selling the House. Offerd to give him the preference at £120 & allow him 2 or 3 weeks to consider it. Mrs O, Mrs Gould & Miss Baker with Dr Wintrop & his Bro[the]r pd a Morning visit at my Son James, Tostock.

Friday Oct 19 . . . Dinner Comapany. . . all went to the Play bespoke by the Military associations. **The Pitt entirely fill'd by Lord Brome's Troop, Lord Hervey's Ickworth Troop, Lord Hervey's Bury Volunteers & Dr Ord's Village Association, abt 180 in the Pitt besides. The 2 upper Forms taken off for the female part of their Familys. The House never known so full, should imagine nearly 70£ House. Mr & Mrs Poley took a Bed with us, also Son James.

Tuesday Oct 23 6 Day's Receipt at <<Bury>> Home: Thedwastre & Thingoe Hund[re]d, took in ab 24 Parishes includg Bury, say abt £4,000. Family at home.

*****News confirmd of Sr Borlace Warren having taken La Hoeke of 80 Guns & 4 French Frigates off Ireland (3 Frigates escapd). These were a Squadron from Brest wth 4,000 Men for invadg Ireland.[238]

---

[237] The battle actually took place on 1 August 1798 when Nelson finally found the French Fleet anchored in Aboukir Bay and destroyed it ending French naval control of the Mediterranean and isolating their bases in Egypt, Malta and the Dodecanese.

[238] A small French invading force was sent to Ireland but by that time all hope of Irish support had been crushed. The exiled Theobald Wolfe Tone was taken prisoner with seven out of nine ships and 2,500 soldiers, including Tone's United Irishmen. Tone cut his throat rather than be executed and the Irish rebellion was over.

A great Ball this Day at Sr Thos Cullum on his son's coming of age. Not one from my House invitd but heard there were upwards of 40 Ladys & Gentn...

Wednesday Oct 24   7th & last Day's Receipt at Home. *Took in ab 98 Parishes, say upwds of 10,000£, for 2 Days together £14,500 – – the largest ever rememberd. Self & Hines in [the] Bank, very full. *The Clerks & Mr Smith din'd with me & drank Tea. Suppd wth my Son. We finishd every thing abt 9 o'Clock & balancd in both rooms in less than 6d.

Monday Oct 29   I went to London in the Bury Coach carrying up with me abt £14,00 – – to Mess Lambert & Cotton & abt 4,000 to Mess Lees & Satterthwaite. We got to Town abt 7 o'Clock. I went & deposited my Charge at Mess Lees, suppd this Eveng at Mr Newman's, slepd at the Bull Inn, Bishopsgate.

Thursday Novr 1   I returnd by Bury coach, got home ab 1/2 hour after 6 o'Clock bringing with me ab £8,000 of [our] own Notes.

**********A grand Ball & supper at the Assembly House to commemorate the late, glorious naval Victorys. Every Gentn within ten miles of Bury to be a Subscriber, other Gentlemen within that Distance, unless single & not Housekeepers, could not be admitted. Gentlemen residing beyond 10 miles or single Gentlemen 1/2 a Guinea each. There were 12 or 14 principal Gentlemen who were originally appointed Managers, only 3 however appeard to be acting Manager: Coll Pettywood, Captn Plampin & Captn Benjafield. There were present 223 <<nearly 250>> Ladys & Gent of the first Fashion and Distinction, a most splendid appearance as was ever rememberd upon any occassion <<and>> Supper &ca in the handsomest Stile, supposd to be at least 60 couple of Dancers & was kept up till between 4 & 5 o'Clock.

				[£	s.	d.]
Subscrib[in]g Gentn	67	£1 4 6	=	82	16	
Non Subg D[itto]	51	10/6	=	26	15	–
	118			109	16	6
Ladys	105					
	223					
Supper Tea Wine Musick as by Bill				82	2	–
Whitmore paint[in]g				5	17	–
Lyon				3	–	–
Buss – Candles Oil				6	3	–
Rackham printg				1	15	2
Sundries				10	16	6
				109	16	6

Tuesday Novr 13   Son & Daughter Gould left us in [a] Chaise this Morng abt 11 o'Clock on their way to Yarmouth (with Miss Gould) where they are now going to settle (at prest they have taken Lodgings) in Partnership with Mr Patteson in the Brewery. Their Dear little Maria they have left with us for the present.

This Eveng a 2d Ball for the Inhabitants at large in honour of the late naval

Victories with a view of paying only the Comm[o]n Expences & all that could possibly be savd intended for the Subscription in London for the Widows & Orphans of the Sailors who fell in the several Engagements. The Number of Ladys & Gentn prest, includg the Chief of the trading part of the Town, say abt 250. The Surplus, or saving, amots to £38 left at our Bank to be remitted to Lloyds.

Wednesday Nov 14 I din'd at Sr Charles Bunbury's. Carr[ie]d in my Coach Sr Tho Cullum, Mr Symonds & Dr Wintrop. . . sat down at Dinner ten. We staid till 1/2 hour after ten o'Clock.

Friday Novr 16 Family at home. *Corporation met & voted on [an] address to his Majesty on the late Naval Victories. It was drawn by the Recorder orderd to be Ingrossd & presented to his Majesty by the Members.

Thursday Nov 29 General Thanksgiving Day for our glorious Naval Victories, more particularly that obtaind by Admiral Nelson by Destroying the French Fleet at Alexandrea, the Nile. Shops shut up the whole day. Bury Volunteers accompanied the Alderman & Corporation to Church. In the Eveng we had Tea & supper Company at home. . . in all of Us ab 18.

Monday Decr 3 Family at home. ****C. F. Lease, under Clerk in my Bank, dischargd for having taken small Sums away dishonestly.

Wednesday Decr 12 Family at home. ***Spoke with Mr Henry Patteson. ***Grandaughter Maria Gould innoculated.** *Extreme cold, easterly wind & Frost.* ****Saml Steel came into my Service as Clerk in [the] Bank.

Friday Decr 14 Miss Baker left us at 4 this morng by Norwich Coach on return home after a visit of full 8 months. Mr Gould dind at Mr Adamson's.[239] Family at home. Extreme Cold wth Wind & Frost.

Monday Decr 17 Self & Mr Steel to Sudbury, 5th Day's Receipt, in Mr Adamson's Chaise & own new Horses —— performd their Journey very well. Took in abt 18 Parishes, £985. Got home 1/4 before 6 o'Clock. Nephew Richd Baker came to Bury to Dinner to enquire of me abt the Reader's Place [at] St James, wch was likely to be vacated by Mr Geo Mathew. Warm & thick Fogg.

Tuesday Decr 18 Guildhall Feoff[men]t meetg. Anderson gave Notice to quit the Angel.[240] I dind with the Feoffees of Dean Sudbury's Charity at the Angel. Warm & foggy.

Thursday Dec 27 Family at home. *****The last Night supposd to be the Coldest has been rememberd these 7 years. Thermometer down to <<8>> 0°, 32 degrees under freezing point.

****Old Mr Grigby of Drinkstone died this Morng.

[239] The Goulds had returned to Bury for their daughter's innoculation.
[240] The Guildhall Feoffment Trust owned the Angel Inn. George Anderson had been their tenant since 1780.

Friday Decr 29 Family at home. Some little Snow & wind got Southerly wh a prospect of a favourable change of Weather. The Feoffm[en]t gave away 6 Chald[ro]n [of] Coals to the Poor.

Monday Dec 31 Family at home. Weather continue thick & hazy & not so very cold. Wind vearing ab[ou]t. Sent my Coach up to London to Hopkinson's.

Wednesday Janry 2d Family at home. Wind in the East, Thermometer ab 4 Degrees under freezg point.

Tuesday Janry 15 *****We this Day Christened our Grand Daughter Maria Catherine Gould now full 1 yr & 1/2 old. She had been privately /baptizd/ when very young. The Sponsors were Mr Henry Collett of Westerfield, Old Mrs Gould, her Grandmother, & Miss Moyle for Miss Barry. I stood for Mr C, Mrs O for Mrs G & Miss Moyle for Miss Barry. We had to dine with Us Dr & Mrs White & Miss White, Mr, Miss & young Mr Mills, Mr Sams, Mrs Goddard, Miss Moyle & Son Orbell. Miss Cocksedge at tea. The whole Company, except Mrs Sams, staid supper. The Weather fine & mild, the Thaw complete. Mr Adamson finely but did not think himself well enough to be with Us.

Monday Janry 21 Son & Daughter Gould left us for Yarmouth early this Morning to reside. Left their dear Maria with Us. Mr Charles Harvey came & suppd with Us & /we/ perfectly agreed as to the Articles of Partnership between Mr P & Mr G. 1st Day County Sessions. I had an extremely bad cold in my Head.

Thursday Febry 7 Charity Concert & Ball at the Assembly-room for the Relief of the Poor this inclement Season. Set on foot originally by [the] Church Wardens of both Parishes. I was prest. Mrs O dare not venture on acct of the Severity of the Weather.

	£
Sum collected by Tickets from 5/– to 2/6	109
Expence for Candles, Fire, Musick, & Assistants	10
Net Amot for the Poor	99

A Committee appointed of the Alderman, Justices, Governors & Dep[u]ty Governs.

Numbers who applied for Bread in St Mary's Parish of Necessitous Poor	1,640
St James['s] D[itto]	1,560
	2,200

orderd 2 penny worth of Standard wheaten Bread p[er] Head be deliverd to every person twice a Week.

Saturday Febry 9 Tea & Supper Company at home. . . Weather for ten days past has been <u>very cold</u> with a <u>considerable Quantity of drifted Snow</u>, inasmuch that the roads in many parts have been renderd quite impassible. This day there appears a prospect of favourable Change & a general Thaw taking place.

Monday Febry 11   1st Day's Receipt on 6th Instalment at Eye. Son, Mr Steel & Servt on Horseback. Very bad travelling, home abt 7 o'Clock. This Eveng the wind turnd North East & more Snow fell with a good deal of wind.

Monday Febry 25   *****Mrs O, Self, Grand daughter Maria & her Nurse set out for Yarmouth ab one o'Clock in my own Chaise, Son Orbell['s] Horses to Stanton & from thence wh my own Horses to the Swan at Harleston.

Tuesday Feby 26   After breakfast went to Beccles, stoppd an hour & 1/2 from thence to Lowestoft, stoppd an hour & got to my Son & Daughter Gould's at 4 o'Clock. . . **On the road to Yarmouth I rode my horse the whole way & the Footman in the Chaise wh [the] Coachman. On my return rode the whole way in [the] Chaise with Mrs O.

Mr Patteson & his Son came to us on Sunday Noon at Yarmouth, Mar 3d. The next Morng Mr P & Mr Gould executed the Articles of Partnership, also the Security from Mr P to Mr G for 5/m,[241] being one half Mr G['s] Advance on the real Estates & everything appeard to be settled to the mutual Satisfaction of all Partys. ***Mr P & his Son left Yarm on Monday Noon. He sent Me the Bond drawn by his Attourny for Mr G to execute for the 10/m advancd by me to him, also /Mr P/ sent me [a] Dr[af]t for £336 12 4 to balance all our Acct at 2 mo[nths] wh was disco[un]td at his charge by Mr Sinclair.

   *During our stay at Yarm we passd our time very happily with Mr & Mrs G & only once din'd out wch was at Sr Edm[un]d Lacon's, that is to say Wednesday Mar 6, where we met Admiral Dixon, his Sister & Niece, Captn & Mrs Morss & staid till 11 o'Clock.

Expences attendg Journey as follows	[£	s.	d.]
On the Road to & from Yarmo, sleeping one Night on the way there	3	18	8
*Horses hire one Stage 21 Mile	1	3	6
Swan Man & Horses	3	9	
Bill at the Bear & for 3 Horses 10 Days & 9 Nights & 2/6 Chaise	2	17	—
Standg & Horstler 5/3 Servant at Mr Gould's 3		15	—
Mr Smith		2	6
Bievers		5	—
Sundries		4	4½
	9	9	9½

**************Friday March 8 1799 died in London at one O'Clock Mr Ab[raha]m Newman my very old Friend & Aquaintance.******************
NB My new Horses performd admirably well.

---

[241] £5,000.

Friday Mar 22   *****Mr Houchen with me his morning & settled the last year's Acct & pd me the Balance & this Eveng same with my Son Orbell. I attended the Grand-jury from 12 to 3 & we were then dischargd. From 10 to 12 in the morng & from 3 to 1/2 hour after 4 o'clock I attend the Grandjury for [the] appointment of Commercial Commissioners wch appointment was not fill'd up when I left the Angel.[242] Mrs O & Self dind at home alone & I was at home the whole of the remain[in]g day.

Monday April 1   At home. Nephew Rd Baker came to us by Dinner in order to propose himself for the Readership of St James, likely to be vacated by Revd Mr Geo Mathew.

[James Oakes went to London to see his bankers and brokers and to swear to his tax accounts for 1796.]

Tuesday April 9   . . . Nephew Rd Baker returnd home havg once again gone round to all the Corporation to say, if he should be approv'd as a Reader, he should esteem their preference at the ensuing Election.[243] Son Gould to Dedham this Morng on a visit to his Mother. We drank Tea & suppd this Eveng (Mrs O & Self) at Major Webb's. . .

Wednesday April 10   First meetg of the Commissner for the Income Act, Mr Ranby, Mr Leheup & Self qualifyed as Commiss[io]ner of Appeal.[244]

Tuesday April 16   Family at home. 2d Day's Receipt at Stow[marke]t, Mr Steel & Biggs took in all the Parishes, an £1,500. Self not well, confind wh a swelld face.

NB The Town has been remarkably distressd for Coals for 6 weeks or 2 months back; most of the Inhabitants oblig'd to burn nothing but wood & Turf. This, added to the uncommonly cold Season, has made it most distressing.[245]

Friday April 26   **********This Morng abt 9 o'clock died my Tenant, Thos Green of Depden, aged [blank]. He had been dropsied a year back & his breath

---

[242] In 1799 the Triple Assessments Act was repealed and Income Tax introduced, 39 Geo III c13, levied at the rate of two shillings in the pound for incomes above £200 and with exemptions below £60. The machinery for collecting the tax was built on existing tax legislation. Commissioners for the House Tax made lists of all persons named in the Land Tax account and sent the lists to the Commissioners of the Affairs of the Taxes at the Tax Office and a duplicate to the local Grand Jury. The Grand Jury for each county division chose from between two and five names from the list to be General Commissioners, four men to fill up any vacancies when necessary and 13 Commissioners of Appeal to hear complaints against tax assessments. The function of the General Commissioners was to appoint and supervise Income Assessors and Collectors in each parish. Commercial Commissioners were specifically chosen to deal with commercial incomes. Their establishment was not a success because, unlike the General Commissioners, they lacked the support of qualified officials. For further details see Arthur Hope-Jones, *Income Tax in the Napoleonic Wars* (Cambridge, 1939).
[243] See note 121 above.
[244] See note 242 above.
[245] These lines were written in red ink across and down the side of the entries for the 18, 19, 20 April.

bad. He was, however, better this Morng, had breakfasted, shavd himself & was coming to Bury, but set himself down in his chair & died without a sigh. . .

Saturday April 27 Family at home. Most uncommonly cold & wet all this week, such weather as was scarcely ever rememberd so late in the Spring & the distress for coals has been what was never be[fore?] rememberd, wch had added much to the Distress of the Inhabitants & this want of Coals have been universal thro out this part of the Kingdom. Coals are now becoming more plentiful but at enor-mous prizes — the Freights are from 16/– to 17/– per Chald[ron], 51/– per Chal[dro]n at the River, 1/5½ per Bushel includg carr[iag]e sold per Bushel in the Town 1/8. NB My Head & Face much mended but yet not well.

Monday April 29 Son Orbell & his Wife set out for London. He took with him abt [£]8,000 for Mess Lees & ab £2,000 for Mess Lambert & Co. Went in their own chaise & took their own Horses to Sudbury. . .

Thursday May 2 *****Mr Ranby, Mr Leheup & Self met as Commissners of Appeal at Mr Dalton's & opened the returns of Income from the general Com-miss[io]n & opened the next meetg next Thursday May 9th at same place. . . Summonse servd on the Act[in]g Commn of Land Tax <u>Yesterday</u>, Mr Swale & others for not issuing their precepts in Lackford Hundred for [the] 7th Instalment due Apr 5.

Friday May 3 Mr Gould din'd at Mr Adamson's. Family at home. *****Auction for Mr Carss['s] great House[246] & other Estates. Not one Lot sold by Publick Auction.

Monday May 6 Mr Gould to Norwich after Breakfast. This day I sent my Chaise to Tostock for Son & Daughter JO & their Children to drive & pass the Day with Us. The Family returnd soon after 7. Son JO took a bed with Us.

Saturday May 11 Family at home. The last 3 or 4 Days have been remarkably fine growg, soft Weather & Vegetation has got on rapidly.

Wednesday May 15 Family at home. Nephew Rd Baker came this Day to dinner. Mrs Oakes get a fall & hert her Face very /much[?]/.***

Thursday May 16 Family at home. This Eveng the Corporation were summoned by the Alderman to meet at 6 o'Clock to elect a Reader for the Parish of St James in the lieu of Mr Geo Mathew who had resignd. The Candidates were: Revd Richd Baker, Revd Wm Norford, Revd Caleb Rose. I nominated my Nephew, Mr R.Baker, seconded by Mr Wright. Mr Pretyman nominated Mr Wm Norford, seconded by Mr Dickenson. Mr Hailstone nominated Mr Caleb Rose, seconded by Mr Thompson. Out of the 37 of the Corporation Gentn 31 attended. . .

Mr Norman		
Mr Brown		
Mr Ward	4 out of Town	
Mr Apsey		
Rev Robt Carss		6 Alderman
Sr Thos Cullum	In Town	

246 Now a branch of Lloyd's bank, Buttermarket, Bury.

voted for Mr Baker	Mr W. Norford	Mr C. Rose
Mr Foster	J. Mathew	Thompson
Complin	Jenkins	Hailstone
Otley	Dickenson	
Gooday	Hubbard	
Blumfield	Pretyman	
O. Oakes		
Smith		
Lawrence		
R. Maulkin		
Green		
Rutter		
Oliver		
Hustler		
Buchanan		
Hawes		

_____ 247

Sturgeon
Barwick
Chambers
Maulkin
Wright
Mathew
Oakes
Fairfax Cor[one]r
Cook Ald[erman]

Revd R. Baker		24
Revd W. Norford		5
Rev. C. Rose		2
		___
		31

Revd R. Baker of course returnd by [the] Alderman duly elected.

Saturday May 18 Mr Gould & Mr Baker din'd at Mr Mills's. This Eveng my Nephew Richd Baker gave a Supper to the Clergy & Corporation at the Six Bells on Acct of his being elected to the Readership of St James. The Alderman, Recorder & Coroner were prest, abt 5 of the Town Clergy & 18 or 19 of the Corporation. Say 28 at 6/– ab £8 8 –. Being Saturday Eveng every Gentleman left the room when the Clock struck 12.

Thursday May 30 Mr Tyrrell, Mr Adamson, Son Orbell & Wife, Son James & his Wife, Miss Cocksedge all din'd , with 5 in own Family, makg up a Dozen, on a fine piece of Salmon sent as a prest from Mr Jno Moseley. . .

Monday June 3 Nephew Rd Baker returnd home by Norwich Coach. I went this Day to Depden to look over my Farm wh Robt Green who was to take Possession of the same in room of his late Father. From thence to Thurston Park to measure

---

247 The line divides the Common Council from the Capital Burgesses.

timber, see particulars in Mem[orandum] Book. Got to Depden by Breakfast & home by 4 o'Clock Dinner. Some fine Rains much wanted.

Thursday June 13   2d Day's Receipt of Income [Tax]. Son Orbell & Mr Steel to Wickhambrook. No Duplicates from the Clerk. Took in abt 17 Parishes, just when the Collectors thought proper to leave, say [£]312 1 9½. Son Orbell returnd to Dinner.

Dinner Company at home. . . with ourselves 14 at Dinner. All the Ladys, except Wife & Mrs Gould, wh the Gentn, except Mr Symons, Mr Kedington, Mr Adamson, Mr F. Sandys & Self went to Mr Walker's Lecture /at the Theatre/. I made them a present of 6 Ticketts, ea[ch] 3/- ——— 18/-. My Chaise went for Son James & his wife to Tostock & carried them home. Horses & Carriage returnd next morng.

Wednesday June 19   Family at home. Home Receipt for 1st Instalm[en]t of Income [tax], took in abt 70 Parishes, [£]1,830 – –. *Finishd cutting my Grass in Cobb's Orchard, the largest crop & Best Quality have had for many years expect upw[ar]ds [of] 4 ton.

Saturday June 22   Family at home. **********This Morning at half hour after 10 o'Clock my Daughter Gould was safely deliverd of a Boy. Nephew Rd Baker came to us at nearly 11 o'Clock this Eveng.

This may be said to be almost the first Day of Summer. Hot sun in [the] middle of the day.

Monday June 24   . . .***finishd gettg in my Hay, say 5 Ton.

Sunday July 7   Mr Adamson, Mr & Mrs Richd Baker dind & drank tea with Us. Mrs Gould din'd below [for the] first time [since] being confin'd.

Monday July 8   . . . I attended this Morng a Turnpike Meeting at Alpheton Red Lyon to agree wth the Surveyor for undertakg the Road for [the] next 3 years from Bury to Sudbury. Returnd home to dinner. . .

Thursday Augt 1   Bottled off [a] Pipe of Old Beer, see <u>Book</u> for Contents. Began a double brew[in]g of Table Beer. . .

Saturday Augt 3   Family at home. Sister Bridge & Miss Routh drank tea with Mr Adamson. Sister Baker came to us very unexpectedly this Eveng from Cawston. Her son brot her in the Market Cart.

Wednesday Aug 14   Family at home. Dinner, Tea & Supper at Son Orbell's. . . ***The Alderman (Mr Cook) died at 12 o'Clock at Night.***[248]

Saturday Aug 17   Family at home. Son James, his Wife & Child contin[uin]g wth Us. Miss Routh left us at 3 o'Clock return[in]g by Coach wch was going to Yarmo[uth] for Mr Symonds.

Monday Augst 19   5th Day's receipt. Son Orbell, Mr Steel & Servt took in abt 30 Parishes, say abt £2,000. **********Assembly of the Corporation: summons from the Coroner for electing an Alderman for the remainder of the year of Mr

---

[248] He had had a stroke on 10 August 1799.

Cook, deceasd, that is to say from prest Day to Oct 3d. <u>I was unanimously chosen</u> & accepted the same & immediately after orderd summonses to be issued for electg 2 Capital Burgesses.[249] Orderd likewise that the Corporation attend the Funeral of the deceasd Alderman to Morrow Eveng, 5 o'Clock.

Tuesday Augst 20 . . .***The Funeral of [the] late Alderman Cook this Afternoon at 6 o'Clock. All the Corporation attended. I went as now prest Alderman with the Mace coverd wth Crape & also Staves carrd by the Beadles. We assembled at Mr Maulkin's in St Mary's Square at 1/2 hour after 5. We preceded the Hearse, the junior going first and the Town Clergy followd me as Alderman next the Hearse. Every Gentn was in mourning & went in their Robes, but no Hatbands, Gloves &ca allowd to be given by the Friends of the deceasd, it being taken up wth a view of paying every Respect due to the Chief Magistrate dying in his Office without putt[in]g the Family to any sort [of] Expence whatever. He died in the 52d year of his age.

Thursday Aug 22 Family at home. ***Hall day calld by myself for filling up 2 vacancies in the Capital Burgesses by the Resignation of Mr Carss & Death of Mr Cooke. *Mr O.R.Oakes & Mr Bran Green unanimously elected. After Church, being the annual Day for electing a Chief Magistrate for the year ensuing, at my & my Son's particular Request, Mr B.Green accepted the office, being unanimously chosen. <Two words illegible> (Mr Reuben Sturgeon who stood /Snr/ in rotation havg been chosen & refusd accept[in]g the Office, was find £50).

*****I gave the Dinner to the Corporation as Alderman at the Angel inviting solely the Corporation, Town Clergy, Governors & Deputy Governors of [the] Workhouse, Assistant justices, Mr Adamson & Son James. We were 41 at Table. 2 Bucks given by the Members. Agreed wh Geo. Anderson at 2/6 per head, 15/- Beer & Fruit, 8d per head Tea, Coffee for the full no 41, tho not more than 32 prest. Port 2 Doz Bottles, Sherry 6 D[itto].

Particulars of our Yarmouth Journey:

Monday Augt 26 We set out soon after 2 o'Clock, Mrs O, Mrs Bridge & Mrs Baker in my Chariot, Miss Bridge in a one Horse Chair drove by Mr Rd Baker. Sent own Horses forwd early in the Morng to Wattisfield Swan. Took Son Orbell's Horses so far & went forward, without baiting, to Harleston Swan where we slept & breakfasted. Next Morng Mr R. Baker returnd to Bury in the Chair & Mrs Bridge & Mrs Baker hird a Chaise thro to Yarmo. Mrs O & Susan went forward in own Chariot. We baited at Hadsco & arrivd at Yarmouth very soon after 3 o'Clock, finding Mr & Mrs Gould & Family all well. Mrs Baker went to Mrs Judith Baker's. . .

[Mr Gould's Mother died on 29 August and he went to Dedham for the funeral.]

On Friday Sept 6th I went on board the Ganges Man of War, laying in [the] Yarmouth Roads, with Niece Susan Bridge by Invitation from Admiral Dixon.

---

[249] A meeting had been called for this purpose on 12 August but was unable to proceed because of the Alderman's absence.

Three Boats went 3 times carrying every time abt 10 Ladys & Gentlemen besides the Boat crew, say abt 90. We all got on Board abt one o'Clock, were receivd by the mareenss under Arms & the Band playing. Soon after we were on Board the Russian Admiral (Tate) with his Suit came on Board and the Bishop of Norwich, his Lady & Company. Dancing began abt 1/2 hour after one, say 20 Couples in 2 rows on the Quarter decks. At 3 Dinner, or rather Breakfast, for such was the Invitation, was announced & we all went up the Poop wch, as well as the Quarter Deck, was coverd with an handsome Awning. There were 2 tables elegantly coverd for 52 each. Every thing that could be procurd, Beef, Ham, Chicken, Lamb, &ca & with all kinds of Fruit: Prunes, Pines, Melons, Grapes, &ca &ca, also choice of Wines as Claret, Port, Madiera, Sherry &ca &ca. We sat in all abt an hour & half & retird to [the] Quarter Deck when Dancing continued till 6 o'Clock & the Company went off in Boats as they came, highly gratify[d] with their elegant Entertainment.

Saturday Sept 14   We all left Yarmouth abt 1/4 after 9 in the Morng. Being a wet Day Sister Bridge & her Daughter, Mrs O & Self all get into the Chariot. We sent our own Horses forward <<the>> Friday Afternoon to Bungay, hird Horses from Yarmouth to Bungay, but own Horses brot us from thence to Stanton. Stopt an hour & 1/2 at Scole to dine. At Stanton Son Orbell's Horses met us & we all got safe & well Home between 7 & 8 o'Clock. We were out 19 Nights & 19 Days & 1/2.

	[£	s.	d.]
3 Horses for 17 Nights at the Bear cost us	5	15	9
Horstler		10	6
Servt Son Gould's	1	2	6
Expences on Road to & from	3	11	9
Yarmouth Horses to Bungay 21 Miles 1/2 &			
Post H[orses]	1	7	6
Sundries	3		9
	15	8	9
Sundry Expence extras	4	11	3
Say ab[out]	20		

Saturday Sept 7   *****Daughter James Oakes driving Miss Aldrich[250] in her Chaise, the Horse fell down & Daughter fell out upon the Horse but, providentially, receivd no harm whatever.

Saturday Sept 28   Tea & supper at Mr Allen's. . . Very much rain. ***Run a rusty Nail into my foot this Morning & found my foot very painfull at Night.

Monday Sept 30   Son James & his Wife came to dine & take a bed with us — Mr F. Sandys['s] Musick Evening. Obligd to lay my foot up all the day & was at times in a good deal of pain.

---

250 See note 170 above.

Thursday Oct 3 Alderman Bran[white] Green took his place as chief Magistrate. I was well enough to attend the Business of the day. A very handsome Dinner was provided by Sol[oma]n Maulkin at the Guildhall. From 120 to 140 Gentn were present, includ[in]g the Corporation. Not any of the trading part of the Town were invited. The Invitations were principally to Gentlemen in the Town & Gentlemen in the Neighbourhood. The Members for [the] Boro were both prest (Sr Charles Davers & Lord Hervey) Lord Charles Fitzroy also attended, Sir Patrick Blake, the Officers of the two Troop of the Lothians & 12 or 15 Officers of the Warwickshire Militia. I left the room ab 8 o'Clock.

Thursday Oct 15 2d Day's Receipt at Stow[marke]tt, Mr Steel & Biggs took in 12 Parishes, £1,453 17 8¾. Home by 6 o'Clock. Part of [the] Family at the Play this Eveng, Mr & Mrs Gould, Miss Cocksedge & Miss Bridge.

**********Very bad news arrivd by Post this Morning from Holland. All our Forces oblig'd to retire with considerable Loss to the Naval head Quarters at Helden.[251]

Monday Oct 21 5th Receipt Day at Sudbury. Self, Mr Steel & Biggs in a Post Chaise with own Servt on my Mare. Rain'd for 8 hours incessantly causing a general flood. Only 30 Parishes came in, say abt £5,000. We got home by 1/4 after 6 o'Clock. Miss Cocksedge of Ingham returnd home.

Wednesday Oct 23 Last Receipt Day at home. Self & Hines in the Bank Business, Son, Biggs and Steel on the Receipt. They took in abt 108 Parishes 2d Quartrs Land, 1/2 year assessd Taxes, 3d Income & Cavalry, £9,685 15 4¼ <u>without</u> Bury St Mary & St James. Very full Day in the Bank. They agreed exactly in the Receipt Balance, we wanted 20/- in the Bank Balance. Did not finish till after 10 o'Clock. The Clerks getting only a scrambling dinner they all <word illegible> had a hot supper with me.

Saturday Oct 26 Family at home. The Alderman's Play,[252] <u>Pizarro</u>.[253] Son Orbell went /for an hour/ & I sent my Nephew Bridge for me. Being Saturday Night & prepar[in]g for my Son's Journey to London I could not possibly go. A very full House. A fine Day.

Monday Oct 28 Son Orbell to London, took with him abt 12 thousand pounds /in Notes, Bills &ca/ only 400 G[uinea]s in 7/- pieces, no other Specie. Mr Chambers wanting to go to London accompanied him. Mrs Gould & Nephew

---

[251] A British force, including many hastily enlisted Militia men, landed in the summer at Helder and captured the port, naval base and the Dutch battle fleet. The plan was to join with a Russian contingent and to advance on South Holland hoping to trigger off a revolt against the French and to penetrate French territory as part of a joint offensive in the north and south. In the event the forces mobilized were inadequate, as was the naval and military intelligence available. The hoped-for Dutch revolt never materialized, the strength of the French in the Low Countries was underestimated and the weather so bad that it was decided to withdraw.

[252] The play was chosen by the Alderman, who would have been expected to buy a large number of tickets in return.

[253] A comedy in five acts by Richard Brinsley Sheridan.

Bridge dind at Mr Adamson. We all went to the Play /in the Evening/ except Sister Bridge.

Wednesday Nov 6   Mr Geo Rogers, Mr Walpole, Mr Adamson & Mr Sams dind with us. *This day was fixd upon some weeks since by my old Friend Geo Rogers between *his Birth day, now 58 yrs old, & within one day of mine. We took the prest Opportunity of havg our Grandson Christend as Mr & Mrs Gould were with us. Mrs Stephens had offerd & sent 5 Guineas & Mr Patteson was so obliging to stand with myself. He had been named Willm / Oborne/ before & now the Service of Christeng completed at St James Church by Mr Sams. . .

*Sponsors   [£   s.   d.]
  Mrs Stephens   5   5   –
  Mr Jno Patteson   2   2   –
  Jas Oakes   1   1   –

William Oborne Gould Born June 22. We passd a very agreable day.**********

Monday Nov 11   Assembly of the Corporation for letting the Theatre. It had been proposd to [the] late Tenant, Mr Brunton & Mr Wilkin the late Contractor for [the] Norwich Theatre, that whichever should send in the highest Proposals should have a Lease for 7 years. Mr Brunton had originally intended bidding for it & had left proposals, offering 50£ Advance, say from £80 to £130, accepting a Lease for 7 years but, previous to this Day's meetg of the Corporation, he withdrew them & entirely gave up all thoughts of hiring the Theatre at any price.

 When the Hall was call'd consequently only Mr Wilkin's proposals could be presented &, on opening them, he had not mentiond any specifick Sum but offerd 15 Gs a year more than Mr Brunton's Bid let it be what it would. However, it was afterwards agreed Mr Wilkins should have the Theatre on a 7 year's Lease at 50£ a year adv[an]ce, say at £130 a year clear Rent (Land Tax only exempted) from 1s of Nov Inst to be performd in only by his own Company & that not exceeding 6 weeks in the year. NB In case such an offer as above stated /<<from Mr Wilkins>>/ could not have been recd by the Corpor[atio]n from Mr Wilkins, he had in reserve another Letting offering £40 advance, say £120. However, this was not attended to but fully settled, Mr Wilkins being present as above, to the Satisfaction of both Partys.
****
Family at home. **(Mrs B[ridge?] & Self had much Conversation with Mr B.) Mr B went to Tostock, dind & slept.

Thursday Nov 14   Family at home exceptg Mr Gould & Mr Bridge who dind & drank tea at Mr Adamson's. This Evening the 1st Winter Ball. Not any from my Family there except[in]g Nephew Bridge. Abt 24 couple of Dancers & Ladys & Gents. Captn Benjafield & Captn Symons stewards.

 Meeting of Justices this Day to take into Consideration the State of the Poor now generally distressd from the excessive high price of Wheat. A fresh Assize made at 12/– per Bushel
  1/6 baking
  ———
  13/6

wch brings the Standard Wheaten Bread to full 3d p[er] ld. It being so early in the Season & the Weather fine & open it was /not/ thought expedient to attempt a Subscription & the only adviseable mode to administer Relief was by recommend[in]g it to the Guardians to encrease the Weekly Alowance to the Poor & for some sort of Government. It was stated that the Averidge price of Secon[d?] Flower, wch was the sort generally consumd by the Poor, might be fixd at 2/- a Stone, the present price 3/10. Then, supposing it might be possible that the Poor could have struggled thro & made Shift had the price not exceeded 2/10 or 3/-, then the extra Rise of 1/- per Stone ought in some measure to be made to those who took Collection.

It was thought that on the averidge of Familys every one individually con-sumd 1 ld flower a Day = 7 ld per week. This 7 ld being 1/2 a stone wch, at 1/- extra price a Stone, causd 6d extraordinary to be expended in the Maintenance of every one in [the] Family & might need in some particular Instances to be allowd in Addition to the weekly Stipends. Then it was conjecturd that to the Amo[un]t of 3,000 in this Town took Collection & supposing only 2/3 of 6d[254] might be done with on the Averdige than there would be 3,000 four-pences = 1,000 shi[llin]g =50£ weekly requird in addition to the Rates. This in 13 weeks would amt to £650, fully equal to an extra rate of 1/6 reckoning that a 3/- rate raises £1,200 thro the Town = £200 for every 6 penny rate in both Parishes.

The Governor, Mr John Green, was prest at this Meetg & agreed, takin[g] all Circumstances into Consideration, this would be the most advisable plan to pursue for the pre[sen]t.

Thursday Nov 28 Mrs O & Self went to the Fortnight Ball at the Angel wch was particularly well attended, ab 18 couple of Dancers & between 70 & 80 Ladys & Gentn. We staid till 12 o'Clock. Remarkably fine & dry. **Grandson Oborne /Wm/ Gould innoculated by Mr Penrice at Yarmouth.

Friday Nov 29 Meeting at the Guildhall of a Committee of Gentlemen, 14 Gentn prest, to take into Consideration the prest scarcity & high Prize of Wheat Flower &ca with a view of endeavoring to lessen the Consumption. The Prizes of Wheat last Markett Day:[255]

say highest price	52/6
second D[itto]	50/-
third D[itto]	48/-
avaridge Price	52/-
finest Flower	4/5
second	4/3
third	4/1

A Resolution was formd & seconded and signd by many of the Committee that nothing but Strippd Meal should be usd in all Familys for one month from Decr 8 and that no Puddings or Pastry should be made & every Endeavor us'd to less[e]n Consumption.

---

[254] That is to say two thirds of six pence which is four pence.
[255] Prices given per comb.

Tuesday Dec 3   Mrs O & Self at home. Mr Squires & Self round a part of the Town to induce the Inhabitants to consume only Stripp'd meal & use no Flour for Puddings or Pastry.

Wednesday Dec 4   Mrs O & Self at tea & supper at Mrs Rose's. . . I attended at the Angel this day to receive the Militia Lists from the Hands of the Constables, swearing them. Mr Acton & self went thro this Business taking up full 3 Hours. At 4 o'Clock I attended the Alderman & Mr Wright to a general Meeting of the Millers & Bakers in order to prepare for a Supply of the Town of strippd meal. . .

Friday Dec 6   *****Our Wedding Day. We have be[en] married** 35 years.***
Mr Adamson dind wth us only. . .

Thursday Decr 12   ***
This morning died /1/2 past 5 o'Clock at Yarmouth/ our Grandson Willm Oborne Gould of the small Pox by innoculation. He was born June 22, innoculated at Yarmouth Nov 28, publicly baptizd Novr 6 at Bury. 5 months 20 days old.
     Mrs O & Self at home. 2d Subn Ball. 3d Day's Receipt. Mr Steel alone to Wickhambrook, took in 10 parishes, [£]271 13 11½. Home before 5 o'Clock.

<<Thursday>>Friday Dec 13   Mrs O & Self set out at 1/2 past 7 this Morning for Yarmouth. Owing to all impossibility of getting Horses we were obligd to sleep at Beccles this Night. 4th Day's Receipt, Mr Steel alone at Mildenhall, took in 1/2 doz parishes, [£]228 14 0½.

Saturday Decr 14   We left Beccles early this Morng & reachd Yarmouth by Breakfast. Did not know of our dear little Grandson's Death till we arriv'd & a most aflicting meetg it was. The dear Infant was buried in the Chancel of Yarmouth Church this day at 3 o'Clock.

Sunday Dec 15   We passd this whole day with our Son & Daughter Gould indeavor[in]g to comfort them as much as possible. Weather very cold but continues dry.

Monday Dec 16   We left Yarm at 1/2 hour after [blank] & got home by 6 o'Clock. The parting with the distressd parents was truly melancholy, nothing but a true thought & relyance on Providence and time can console them.
     This Journy cost abt £7 10 –
     This Morng died Admiral Symons after a few hours illness. Cold, dry, Easterly wind.–

Tuesday Dec 17   Mrs O & Self at home. We were engagd to tea & cards at Mr Wright's but sent our Excuse.

Monday Dec 23   General Meeting of the Inhabitants for opening a Subn to provide Soup for the poor to be sold at a modest Price. The Alderman in the Chair, Mr Ranby, Dr Wollaston, Mr Allen, Dr Wintrop & ab 35 Gent prest. Ab[ou]t 70 G[uinea]s was sub[scribe]d & pd at the Hall & a Committee appointed to prepare Coppers & provide plans. . . *********************

Saturday Decr 28   Mrs O & Self at Home. First Day of deliver[in]g out Soup to the Poor at ½[d.] per Pint, abt 125 Gall ea[ch] Parish, all taken off. The Frost continue Sharp with Snow remain[in]g on the ground. Biggs to Londn by Norwich Coach with between 6 & 7,000£.

Tuesday Dec 31 Mrs O & Self at home. 2d Day of deliverg Soup to the Poor.
*The Frost this last Night more severe than any have had this year. In an open, exposd situation the Thermometer 2 degrees below 0.

[Vol. VI]   [1800]

Wednesday Janry 1st Mrs O & Self at home. Our Clerk Biggs returnd from London this Morng bring[in]g upwds of £7,000 of our Cash Notes. Frost not so severe, Symptoms of a Thaw.
***Mr Tho. Wilson (late steward to Mr Palmer) died this morng at one o'Clock.
***Mr Charles Russel died this Morning.

Wednesday Janry 8 Mrs O & Self with Son & Daughter JO at home. A remarkably full Day of Business at the Bank.

**********This day I contracted with Mr Lancaster of Nowton (in the presence of Mr Edwards) for the Purchase of his Estate at Nowton & Little Whelnetham, abt 150 Acres, at a Price to be valued by Messr Jno Ward & Jno /Canham/. They to fix on an Umpire before Valuation & their Decision to be binding under a Penalty on either Side of £500. JO drew up an Agreement, signd by the Partys prest, wch was afterwd put into the Hands of Mr Chinery to be sent up to Town to be stampd.

Thursday Janry 9 Dinner Company. . . in all 15. The Company all staid tea 9 o'Clock & then most went to the 3d Subn Ball wch was not large but very genteel, say abt 20 couple of Dancers & ab 85 Ladys & Gentm in all. We got home by 2 o'Clock.

Saturday Janry 18 . . . I have had a troublesome cough & cold for 2 or 3 days. Weather mild but with a good deal of wet chief p[ar]t of this week.

Sunday Janry 19 Mr Adamson, Mr Hine & his Wife wth Mr Biggs dind wth us to day & staid till 8 o'Clock. My Cold somewhat better. Some little Snow fell.

Thursday Janry 30 *I rode to Euston to dine with the Duke of Grafton. Slept there. . . took my Servt, went on Horseback.

Thursday Febry 6 Family at home.
**********Mr Adamson taken very ill yesterday wh cold, shivering fit & confind to his Bed all this Day. Dr Wintrop call'd in. This Eveng the 4 Sub Ball, but on acct of Mr Adamson's Indisposition we none of us went. I should have gone to have met Mr Mills at Lavenham with his Hadleigh Bank Notes[256] &

---

[256] Messrs Mills and Bawtree, bankers of Colchester, had a branch at Hadleigh.

38. Richard Adamson's memorial in Wereham Church.

Mess Marrolds but sent my Coachman, George, not caring to be from Home on Acct of Mr Adamson.

Friday Febry 7   Borough Sessions held now, so much sooner on Acct of the great scarcity of bread Corn & to put in force the sole use of standard Wheaten Bread as the Act directs. No other business. We dind at the Angel, the Alderman, Recorder, Mr Leheup & self with 3 or 4 more. I left the Angel abt 6 o'Clock.

Mr & Mrs Gould went to dine with Son James at Tostock. I should have gone, but on Acct of Mr Adamson's Illness. They returnd soon after 9 o'Clock. *Mr Adamson quite confind to his Bed, apparently declin[in]g very fast. Little hopes of his ever getting up again.
****

Sunday Febry 9   At home, not any of the Family went to Church Mr Adamson laying so very bad. All this day he continued insensible, apparently, at times, in much pain but still shewd signs of inward Strength. Son Orbell, his Wife & Boy dind with Us. Son James came to tea. I rode for an hour in the morning & calld upon Mr Tyrrell, Thurston.

Monday Febry 10   Family at home. Mr Adamson continuing very rapidly declin[in]g, totally insensible & thought scarcely possible to continue 24 hours longer.**********
1st Day's Receipt at 3d Q[ua]tre Land & 5 Income [tax]. Son Orbell & Mr Steel in Post Chaise & came round home next Day & took in Stow[marke]tt, together nearly £2,000.

Tuesday Febry 11 Family at home. *****Son James came to dinner & slept here. Mr Adamson very bad all the Day wh repeated returns of Convulsions almost every 2 hours. Thought hardly possible he should exist till Morng.

These 2 Days hard Frost.

Wednesday Febry 12** Mr Robt Adamson[257] came from London by Mail & arrivd here 1/2 hour after 8 o'Clock in the Morng. This Morning at 20 Minutes after ten o'Clock died our Uncle, Mr Richd Adamson, after a confinement to his Bed of one Week. He was born in the year 1717=83 yrs of age. He appointed me Sole Executor to his will.[258]

Saturday Febry 15 Family at home. Son James left us before Breakfast. This week has continud dry & frosty, rather sever[e]. *My Coal Heap robbd this eveng by Wm Wright.

Sunday Febry 16 Not any of the Family went to Church on acct of Mr Adamson laying by the Wall. . .

Monday Febry 17 Family at home. 5th Day's Receipt. Son Orbell with Mr Steel & Servt took in 33 Parishes £2,459 4 2. Home at 7 o'Clock. Full meetg this Morng of [the] Soup Committee agreed to buy a large Quantity of Potatoes & sell to those who buy soup at a reducd Price.

Thursday Febry 20 Mr Adamson's remains were removd from his House to the Family Vault at Wereham for Interm[en]t in Norfolk. . .

Friday Febry 28 ****I rode over to Thurston this Morng by Appointment to meet my Son James at Mr & Mrs Tyrrell's in order to talk over & consider whether he had better continue at Tostock or remove to Bury into [the] late Mr Adamson's House. It was clearly determin'd in favour of his remaing where he was on his Living. See my memorandum Papers. Son Orbell & his Wife suppd with us.

Sunday Mar 9h Mrs O & Self after morng service pd a visit to Lord & Lady Charles Fitzroy at Ampton, returnd home to dinner. . .

Monday Mar 10 Mrs O dind at Son Orbell's. I dind today at Mr Ranby's to meet Mr Symonds & Captn Benjafield to talk over the plan of establishing a Publick Mill & bak[in]g Office for the Use of the Town. I staid till 9 o'Clock. Mrs Bunbury drank tea there, Mrs Ranby not well.

Friday Mar 14 At home. Tea & Supper Company. . . with our 2 Selves 16 at Supper.

Saturday Mar 15 At home. Weather much milder these last 3 or 4 days, some wet. Just now a very favourable season for sowing soft Corn & [blank]. Mr Heigham resignd all thoughts of hiring Mr A['s] House.

Wednesday Mar 19 At home alone. *****Particularly full of Business [in the bank]. Mr Lanchester, Mr Canham & Mr Ward met at my House & by Lot chose

---

[257] Robert Adamson was Richard Adamson's nephew, the son of his brother Benjamin.
[258] Richard Adamson's will can be found at PROB 11/1344 fol. 500.

39. Richard Adamson's house on Angel Hill now the Clock Museum.

an Umpire to decide any differences of Opinion in Mess Ward's & Canham's Valuation of Mr Lanchester's Estate at Nowton &ca. Mr Canham mentiond Mr Widge, Mr Ward D[itt]o Mr Catling. The Lott fell on Mr Catling.

Tuesday Mar 20 At home. This Day agreed with Mr Wm Smith to let him my house, late Mr Adamson, for 7 years from Michs next a[t]

	[£] 45
Fixtures	20
	65

I to pay Landlord's Taxes & Mr Sm[ith] to pay Window Lights & all Tenant's Taxes & Town dues.

Judge Gross came late this Evening into Bury to hold [the] Lent Assizes. In the whole County 42 Prisoners to take their Tryals & [blank] Causes. We had Tea & Supper Company this Eveng. . . 2 only staid Cards. We had 18 at Supper.

Saturday Mar 22 The Grandjury met 1/2 hour after 10 0'Clock, did not finish our Business till 1/2 hour after 4 0'Clock when we were dischargd. A remarkable Bill for willfully firing a House at Hadleigh[259] & another D[itt]o for rape on a Girl under 10 years of age. Son James dind wth Us.

Tuesday Mar 25 I attended Wright's Tryal [at the] Shire Hall for Stealing Coals out of Coalyards. Found Guilty.

*******I went to Mr Adamson's, packd up 18 Doz of Red Port in 6 Hampers, ea[ch] 3 Doz, to send to Mr Gould; also 18 Doz in 3 Doz Hampers for Son James

[259] Details of this case can be found in SROB 317/1 pp. 42, 305.

& also told 18 Doz more into a Bin for Son Orbell, but this was a pipe of Mr Squir[e]'s Wine wch Mr A bot of him & bottled abt 4 months ago. I understood there ought to have been 54 Doz & we made out not altogether 50 Doz, an apparent Deficiency of abt 4 doz. The Bottles were certainly very irregular & som[e] very [much?] larger. We loaded Mr Gooday's Waggon wh sd 18 Dz Port, some Linen, China, Plate & Bedding & other Furniture of Mr Adamson for Daughter Gould. The Waggon was to leave Bury tomorrow, Wednesday Morng 3 o'Clock, & expectd to arrive at Yarmouth on Thursday afternoon ab 3 o'Clock. I also told over the 1/2 Pipe of Red Port in [the] Larder Cellar bo[ugh]t & bottled wth Mr Leheup in April 1783, expectg to find at least 25 Doz, & could make out only 19 Doz put into 2 Bins from right hand. I have great reason to mistrust that I have been defrauded of 5 or 6 Dozn of this wine &, if so, that my late man Servt, Doe, must have been a party concernd.

   Mrs O & Self drank Tea & suppd this Eveng at Dr Wintrop's. . . Assizes not finishd.

Monday Mar 31   Mrs O & Self at Tea & Cards at Mr Wright's. . . I this Day removd the Wine from Mr Adamson's wch I meant for myself:

	Doz	[Bottles]
Oldest O Hock	1	9
Newest D[itto]	2	11
oldest Red Port, Lond[on?]	10	1
New D[itto], Mr Squire	19	1
Large Bottle		8
Son Orbell Mar 24	18	–
Son James D[itto]	18	–
Son Gould D[itto]	18	–
Doz	88	6

As the Bottles were som[e] extraordinary large say, in all, 1 Pipe 3 Qrs.
****

April 1 Tuesday   Killd a Hogg of our own Fatting, N[et] W[eight] 7 ston 8 lb. Mrs O & Self at home. Son Orbell removg into Mr Adamson's House.[260]

Friday April 4 . . . Began moving Mr Adamson's Table Beer in Pipes & H[ogs]h[ea]ds to the Am[oun]t of 13 Hhds. Left one Hhd for Son Orbell, then left 4 Pipes & 5 Hhds, 2 other empty Pipes & 2 other empty Hhds. 2 [of] Mr Thacker's Men & his Apparatus, Horse &ca, David Shadow & George Coachman. Finishd Saturday morng.

Saturday April 5 . . . ***Account arrivd of the Queen Charlotte blowing up at Lea Mar[ch] 18 & 750 Souls perishd.

Wednesday April 9 . . . very full of business all this day. ******Respite for th[e] woman in Gaol who robbd her Mistress at Hadleigh & fird the House for <u>one</u>

---

[260] He stayed in the house until 11 June 1800, presumably to look after it until William Smith took possession.

<u>Fortnight</u>. Done by the Under Sheriff at the Instigation of Dr Drummond & Mr Loft. She was to have suffered this Day.******[261]

Monday April 14 Began pulling down the old back part of my House in order to make [a] new Wash House, Brew House, Scullery & Offices. Employd Melsom as my super intendent.[262] Mrs O & Self at home. *First Day's Receipt on 4th Q[uarter]'s Land & 2d 1/2 yrs assessd Taxes & 6h Income. Son Orbell wth Mr Steel in Chaise (they took Miss Walker with them) 28 Parishes came in, abt £2,400. Home before 8 o'Clock.

Wednesday April 23 Last Day's Receipt at home. Son Orbell, Steel & Biggs receivg Taxes, Self & Hines at the Bank Business. On Taxes took in 75 Parishes, £6,624 14 1, left only 14 in Arrears. . . The Clerks all dind & drank tea with us. Agreement between Mr Lanchester & Self respect[ing] his Nowton Estate this day cancelld & given up.
    *Sarah Loyd executed after much fruitless Endeavor by Mr Loft to get her reprievd. /A long speech from the/ Cart by Mr Loft.

Friday April 25 . . . *Sarah Loyd buried today. Mr <u>Lofts</u> & a vast concourse of canting People attended her Funera[l].

Monday April 28 *Mr Steel set out this Morng by Coach from [the] Angel for London wh [£]10,828 1 1 for Lees in Bills, Cash Notes & Specie & 4,920£ in Cash Notes for Mess Lambert & c[ompany]. County Sessions attended at the Angel & had my year's acct signd.[263] Mrs O & Self at home. I did not dine with the Justices at the Angel. *Son Orbell had intended to go to London but thought him self not quite well enough to undertake the Journey.

Thursday May 1 Mrs O & Self at home. Lent our Chariot to Mrs Ranby to go to Newmarkett [with] her own Man & Horses. Suffolk Militia marchd into Bury for the first time since the commencement of the war.[264]

[Mr and Mrs Oakes and Miss Latitia Cocksedge went to Yarmouth to stay with the Goulds from the 4 May until 15 May.]

Wednesday 4th June ***
King's Birth Day. Intended to be observd (if possible) with more general Demonstrations of Joy than ever on acct of his Escape from the late Assassination of <u>Hadfield</u>, who shot at him at the Theatre on [blank].[265] Unfortunately the day provd very wet, much rain fell from Monday till Evening & prevented much of the general parade thro' the Kingdom that was intended, more particularly in the City of London. I gave a Dinner to the Officers of the West Suffolk Regiment &

---

[261] See note 259 above.
[262] James Oakes's housekeeper.
[263] As County Treasurer for West Suffolk.
[264] Militias did not usually serve in their own locallity to deter men from absconding.
[265] On 15 May 1800 the King was shot at as he stood in the royal box at Drury Lane Theatre acknowledging the crowd. His attacker, James Hadfield, was subsequently found to be insane. Anxieties were heightened because that morning the King had been nearby when someone was shot accidentally during the Grenadier Guards' grand field day in Hyde Park. Sheridan was inspired by these events to add a verse to *God Save the King*.

some other Gentn. Pres[en]t, Lord Charles Fitzroy, Gen[era]l of this part of the District, his two Aid De Camp, Major Fitzroy & Captn Mundy, Major Parker & 10 other West Suffolk Officers, Coll Hockley, Suffk Fencibles, Lieutt Rives of the 22d, Mr Powell, Mr Benjafield. My Son James assisted me & sat at the Lower end of the Table. We set down 19 or 20. I was obligd to have fish from London, a fine Turbott & Lobsters, a fine Salmon Trout procurd by Captn Blachley & Captn Blachley sent me a remarkably fine Quartre of House Lamb as a pre[sen]t. We passd the Day very pleasantl[y] & all departed abt 10 o'Clock. Did not dine till 5. Wine drank: 8 Bottles Hock

> 6 D[itto] Sherry
>
> 15 D[itto] Port

. . . I presented the Privates of the West Suffolks in my own Name & Son Orbell's with ten Guineas to drink his Majesty's Health. This I was most particularly inducd to do from an Intention I had of rais[in]g a Subscription for them on their volunteerg for Ireland at the time they passd thro' Bury. This I could not succeed in at the time & therefore had ever since waited some favourable Opportunity of doing what I had then intend[e]d & could not possibly think a more favourable Opportunity than the prest.****

Friday June 6 Mrs O & Self at home. This Evening came to us Son & Daughter Gould with their Daughter. Sent my Chaise & Horses to Bottesdale to meet them. Maria bro[ught] for [a] Change of Air with the Whooping Cough.

Saturday June 7 . . .***********This Evening at 6 o'Clock discoverd the Fraud in our Notes. Several five Guineas made ten Guineas of say abt 24 of them.********************

Thursday June 20 Family at home. **********This [day?] finishd getting in my Hay. Got in abt 2 tons & stacked abt 4 Tons includ[in]g Son Orbell's small piece. Never remember to have had so large a crop & never better made, not a drop of rain since cutt[in]g. In all full 6 Tons.**********

Monday June 23 ***Grandson Henry's Birth Day, 4 years old. . .

Sunday July 6 Mrs O & Self, Mr & Mrs Gould all drank tea at Mr Walpole's. I attended Church twice & staid the Sacrament.
************************This Afternoon at 1/2 past 5 o'Clock my Daughter Orbell was safely deliverd of a Boy. Now they have two Boys & a Girl.*******

Tuesday July 8 Sudbury Turnpike meetg at Alpheton Lyon to determine on a petition for extendg the Act for 21 year[s]. The Act was granted 1762 for 42 years, sd Act expir[in]g 1804. From Bury Sr Thos Cullum, Mr Mills, Self & Mr Otley, from Sudbury Mr Fenn, Mr Addison, Mr Finch, Mr Daking &ca. It was resolvd upon accordingly. I accompanied Sr Thos Cullum in his 4 Wheel Chaise. We dind there & returnd home to tea. . .

Wednesday Augt 20 *Son Orbell & his wife returnd home with Mr Gould to dinner from Yarmouth by way of Norwich. . . [Orbell] was absent 23 days for the Benefit of his Health at Mr Gould's. . . ***A Thunder Storm this Eveng with a great deal of Rain after a very long Drought & uncommon hot Weather. Had not any Rain, except a little one Day the middle of June, since the King's Birth Day nearly 11 Weeks.*

Thursday Augt 21 Day of electing a chief Magistrate for [the] year ensuing. B.Green Esq., prest Alderman. Son ORO unanimously elected. He appointed assistant Justices: Sir Charles Davers Bart
      Michl Leheup Esq.
declind acting* Jno Ranby Esq.
      Sr Thos Gerry Cullum Bart
      Jas Oakes Esq.
      & Matt Wright

We all dind at the Angel abt 60 Gentn at Dinner, say ab 30 of the Corporation, 4 Town Clergy & abt 20 other select Friends of the Alderman who he had invited. Also Sir Charles Davers & Lord Charles Fitzroy. Lord Hervey not in the Country. Self & Son returnd to sup at my House.

[James Oakes, his wife and her maid set out for Yarmouth once again to stay with the Goulds.]

*Friday Sept 5 We set out for Home at 1/2 before 9 in the morng, hird Horses to Gillingham, havg sent our own Horses so far the preced[in]g Eveng. Son Orbell's Horses met us at Bottisdale & we got home 1/2 hour after 7 o'Clock find[in]g all well. But a most uncommon Wet Day, more rain fell in the Causes of 18 hours than had been known for many months. We were 2 Days on the road & 12 Days at Mr Gould's.

*Expences as follows:	[£	s.	d.]
Post Horses & Postilion 24 /miles/ going 7 returng	1	14	6
Horses at Yarmouth 12 Days 12 Nights &			
2 Nights on the road, Oats 6d.	5	18	6
Horstler		7	6
Mr Gould's Servt 20/–, Mrs Smith 2/6	1	2	6
Son Orbell's Coachman		5	–
Men at Brewery		5	–
Expences on road going & returng	3	4	1
Pres[en]t to Son & Daughter Gould['s?] Child	1	5	1
Plays & Assembly		12	–
Bath		8	–
Barber		5	–
Cards		7	–
Carrge & Portridge		3	10
	15	18	—

Wednesday Sept 17 Receipt at home 1st Qr Land. Finishd 96 Parishes, £2,616 16 6½. Son Orbell, Mr Steel & Son & Biggs in [the] Bank room for [the] Receipt. Self & Hine in my Room for the Bank Business. Finishd by 7 o'Clock. The 4 Clerks dind & drank tea with me. Mrs O & Self at home.

Sunday Sept 21 Family at home. Son Orbell's 2 Children dind with us, also master Anniss. Wet Day.

Monday Sept 22   Mrs O & Self at home. Son James came to dine wh us & slept here being his Musick Night.

Tuesday Sept 23   Mrs O & Self at home. Mr Patteson dind with Us.

*****A meeting this Eveng of the Justices at Guildhall to take into Consideration his majesty's gracious Proclamation to prevent riots & discords. Orderd a hand bill to be printed wh a resolution formd thereupon &, there having been several inflamatory Letters droppd & some posted up, the Militia & Volunteers was requested to be ready to render their Assistance in case of any riotous Assemblys of the People.********************************

**Son Orbell & his Wife returnd from London, brot home all our Cash, Notes &ca.
*****All was peaceable & quiet in the Town this Night.*****

Wednesday Sept 24   Mrs O & Self at home. *****Markett Day. Butter continued at 14d, Wheat from 50/– to 55/– a Comb. The drop on Wheat not more than 5/–, allowd to be vastly too high.*****

Friday Sep 26   Bottled off [a] Pipe of Lond[on] Red Port divided between Self & Son, see Cellar Book. Sent a Statm[en]t of first Quarter's Receipt for Land [Tax] to the Board for 1800. Son Orbell & his wife suppd with us.

Thursday Oct 2   ***************Miss Symons was married to Captain Rose.

******Son Orbell took his place as Alderman & Chief Magistrate of the Town with a very full Appearance of the Body Corporate. He entertaind the Corporation with tea & coffee at his own House when the old Alderman calld upon him to go to the Hall. After being sworn in to his office he addressd the Corporation in a short but appropriate Speech on the present critical Times from the exorbitant Prizes of every Necessary of Life &ca. Afterwards went to Church & heard an excellent Discourse from Dr Knowles. On [our] return from <<the>> Church, the West Suffolk Band attendg, the Corporation were again led to his own House & entertaind with a cold Collation. His Dinner was prepard by Boldero of the Angel Inn at the Assembly Room. Two long Tables were laid & most completely filld, abt 83 Gents at each, in all 166 & 4 Gent at a side Table.

My Son made a point of asking almost every Gentleman & Tradesman thro'out the Town & none but the County & Borough Members out of the Town, exceptg his Relations &, here & there, a Gentleman who came accidentally into the Town. Neither of the County members prest & only Sr Charles Davers of the Borough. Lord Charles Fitzroy was present, all the Officers of the West Suffolk & every officer of the several other Corps who happened to be in Bury. The day passd off exceedingly well & a very general Satisfaction pervaded the whole Company. Tea and Coffee were brot in abt 1/2 hour after 7 o'Clock. There were 5 or 6 Card Tables for a couple of Hours. At 1/2 after 10 o'Clock supper was servd up with the Cold Relicts of the Dinner. Abt 66 Gentn set down to supper. I left the room with my Son James at 1/2 hour after 12 o'Clock. I set at the bottom of the second Table, opposite the Coroner at Dinner & at the bottom at Supper.***

Friday Oct 3   Mrs O & Self at home. This Evening abt 7 o'Clock Daughter & Mr Gould with their little Girl came to us from Yarmouth. I sent my own Chaise to meet them at Bottesdale.

Friday Oct 10   Family at home till Eveng when Mrs O, Self & Mr Gould went to the Assembly which was very brilliant. The Dutchess of Grafton & her three Ladys, the Dutchess of Rutland & a Number of other Familys of the first Distinction. It was supposd full 300 Ladys & Gentn were present, two rows of Dancers, together full 50 Couples. Mr Gould left the Rooms soon after 11 o'Clock. Mrs O & Self at one o'Clock.

Saturday Oct 25   Family at home. This Eveng we sent up Mr Steel to London with a large Amt of Bank Cash Notes & Bills by Norwich Coach, say full [£]23,000 for Lees /& co/ & Lambert & Co. Particularly full of Business at [the] Bank all this day. *****A fortnight of remarkably fine, dry weather. The finest seed Time ever known.

Tuesday Oct 28   ****This Morng at 4 o'Clock my Daughter Gould was safely del[ivere]d of a Boy. . . Mr Gould to dine wh Mr Patteson at Norton. By return of Yarmouth Coach this [evening?] Mr Steel came home with £8,893 5 – of our Notes.

Sunday Nov 2   Family at home. I attended Church twice ******also, in the Eveng, was upon a Coroner's Inquest on the Death of Mrs Mary Burroughs whose Death appeard to have been hastend by some laudenum having been given her thro a mistake instead of an Emetick.*****

Tuesday Nov 4   . . .********A meeting of the Inhabitants (paying to the /Poor/ Rates) convened by the Alderman in Consequence of a Requisition signd by ab 30 of the Occupiers for the Purpose of taking the Sense of the Town respectg the measure of Badging the Poor. (It is to be understood this had been before the Court of Guardians who had, in a majority, wishd the measure to be postpond considering there were many who, at this particular Instance from the enormous prizes of every necessary of Life, were under an obligation of crav[in]g some temporary Assistance who it might be a very great hardship to badge. There were abt 140 of the Inhabitants who assembled in this Occasion most, say 9 out of 10, small Traders who were no doubt much aggrievd. The Measure was carried by a great Majority wch was to be expected & two Resolutions voted desir[in]g the Governor might be requested to call another Meeting of the Court of Guardians to reconsider the Measure.*******266

Thursday Nov6****   At home till Eveng. 1st Subn Ball. Mrs O & Self went to it. (Mrs O carried Mrs Squire & Miss Cocksedge). Uncommonly thinly attended, not more than abt 66 Ladys & Gentn & 16 couple of Dancers. Sr Partrick Blake

---

266 Under an Act of 8 and 9 William III paupers could be made to wear a letter P on their right shoulders so that they could be distinguished. James Oakes was the only Guardian who voted against this proposal when it was reconsidered at their next meeting. SROB N5/1/2, 8 November 1800.

& Captn Blachley Stewards. New Rules adopted that is to say: Drawing Nos for Places in the Dance, Keeping their Places & not sitting down. The Stewards contracted with Mr Anderson to allow him £32 for 80 in Number & up to 90 the same. He was to have this Sum if ever so few & to be pd for all above 90 [at] 5/– a Head includg Rooms, wax Candles, Fires, Musick, Tea, Cards, Supper, Wines &ca &ca. Mr Patteson calld this Eveng in his way to Londn & passd [the] Eveng wh Mr Gould.**

Friday Nov 7 ****My Birth Day 59 Years Old.***** I carried Mr Gould to dine at Mr Shillito's at Ickworth, took Mr Dalton in my Chaise. . . sat down 13 at Table. We staid till 9 o'Clock. Son Orbell & his Wife came to supper wh us & drunk my Health.

Tuesday Nov 11 Family at home. ******1st Brewing in my new office—— 4 Comb ea[ch] Day. . .

Friday Nov 14** Family at home. Son & Daughter innoculated their little Boy Richard with the Cow Pox by Mr Creed from master Heigham.*******

Saturday Nov 15 . . .******************The poor in the Workhouse conducted themselves riotously & broke out of the House.[267]

Wednesday Nov 19 Family at home. *****Much Conversation in the Markett respecting our Cash Notes. A malicious Report had been propagated but some evil minded Person that our Bank had stoppd Payment & without any sort of Foundation whatever —— Our House standing at this very time in the highest State of Character & Credit. We were first appriz'd by a Letter. . . from Mess Alexander of Ipswich on Saturday. Nothing could astonish us more. It appeard to have been carr'd from thence last Thursday Morng by [the] Yarmouth Coachman. On endeavoring to investigate the Business it seem[s] this Man & another drunken Man had been in Conversation the Eveng before, had understood that there was to be a 7/– /Poor/ rate in order to pay the Oakeses off a Debt wch was owing to the Parish, they havg been in the habit of lendg Money to the Guardians & without Int[eres]t. The Debt was at this time £800, altho never so much as desird /on our Part/. On the Contrary, the Guardians had full Liberty of keeping the money as long as was convenient to themselves & payg it off by Instalments. However, some of the Guardians said they did not like to be beholden to the Oakeses. Then it was Construed by these 2 drunken Men that the Oakes could not pay their Notes without this Money wch was circulated by [the] Yarmouth Coachman and the next additional report was that the House stopp'd Payment & this spread all over the eastern Quarters of the County & into Norfolk.

This malignant Report causd much uneasiness among some small Holders & their Notes were actually refusd by many for a Day or two but several of respectable Gentlemen immediately interposd & quieted the minds of most People. We

---

[267] As a result seven people were committed to the House of Correction. SROB N5/1/2 20 November 1800.

could not but suppose all this might have causd a run upon our House but, most Extra-ordinary, it has been scarcely perceivd with Us at Bury, nor can we at present learn that other country Bankers have had any extra quantity of our Notes pourd in upon theirs'. All Principal Men skouted the Possibility of any such event happening, know[in]g that there scarcely was a more solid Foundation, It ever havg been, & most assuredly ever will be, a Maxim of this House never to issue more Notes than we are prepard to turn into Cash in 24 Hour[s]. It has, however, determind us not to issue any more <u>One Pound</u> Notes, for these never having been made payable at London (tho' always paid by our Bankers if presented to them) they have not been so negotiable. It indeed was the Design of them more for the Use of Bury for change & among the Military, & by no means the Circulation should be extended to any Distance. May hope that Possibly Gold will be more plentifull &, if at any rate, [we] can get on without them so much the better. The Stamp must be doubled <word illegible> is 4d in the room of 2d if made payable at more than one place & this extra Expence, with Paper, printg & uncommon wear, they could not be made to answer.**************

Wednesday Nov 26 Family at home. Mrs O & Mr & Mrs Gould all made a morng visit at Son James['s], Mr Ray's &c. *****************This morng 11 o'Clock died my old Servt Will Hill.*******************

Monday Decr 1 Fair Day. Very full of Business [in the bank]. Family at home. The Town uncommonly full of Cattle & the greatest Number of Farmers that have been known of many years.

Wednesday Dec 3 Family at home. Mr Gould to Norwich. His Wife & Children were to have gone but, on acct of the small Pox being so bad at Yarmo, they remaind to innoculate the Boy again wh the Cow Pox. . .

Sunday Decr 14 Attended Church twice. Master Jas Cocksedge din'd with Us. Mast[er] Amys was to have dind but was ill. Proclamation read in the Church to reduce the ordinary consumption of Wheat Corn & to limit Familys to the Quartern Loaf p[er] Head round, that is to say 4 ld 61/2oz, not on any acct to exceed more.

Tuesday Decr 16 2d Receipt Day at Stow[marke]tt. Mr Steel from Eye, Son Orbell went from hence & carrd Mess Alexanders' Notes & brot home ours with Mr Steel who took in all but one parish, say £220 13 9. They get home by 5 o'Clock.

Wednesday Dec 17 This morng at 9 o'Clock Son & Daughter Gould, wh their 2 Children, set off for Mr Patteson, Nor[wic]h in their way to Yarmouth. Very full of Business in the Bank all the Day. Mr Chambers dind with Us. In the Eveng Tea & Sandwich Party at Mr Ranby's. . .

Wednesday Dec 24 Last Day's Receipt of 4th Instalm[en]t of Income [Tax]. Son & Steel in my room on receipt, Self wh the 2 Clerks in the Bank Room on the Bank Business. They took in 89 Parishes, say £2,905 12 5¾, & we were extremely full the whole day of Bank Business. An unusal Quantity of Business done.

*********My man, Mark Sheperd, left my Service as head Footman this Day in a very disgraceful Manner for himself.*****************

Tuesday Decr 30   Tea & Supper Company at home. . . NB first company since finish[in]g our antiroom & stair case. Son Orbell's Christing of his youngest Son, Orbell. Lord Broom [blank] sponsors. Snow & Frost continued.

Wednesday Dec 31   Full of Business at the Bank. Tea & Supper Company at home. . .

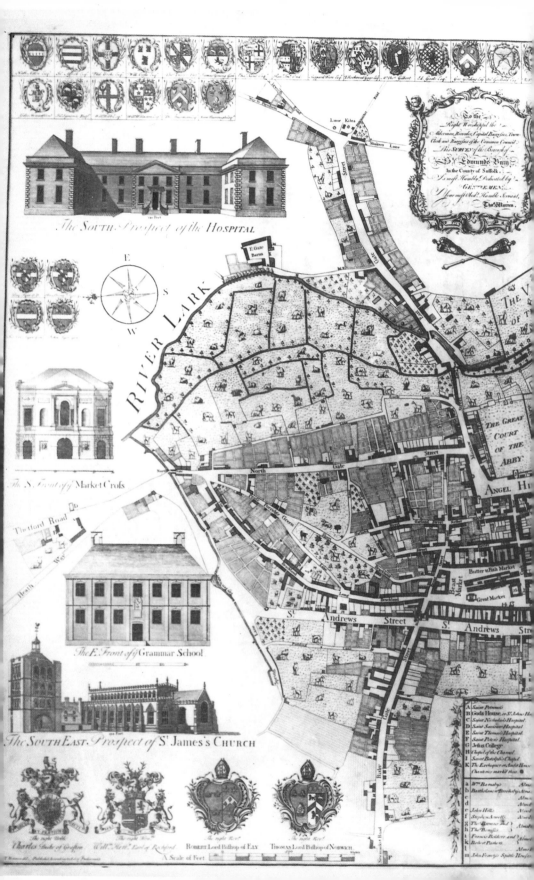